The Limits of Human Rights

University of Sunderland
University Library Services

Renew and manage your account online
library.sunderland.ac.uk
Tel: (0191) 5153691
Facebook/UniOfSunLib
Twitter/UniOfSunLib

FOUR WEEK LOAN
St. Peter's Library

Please return on or before the date shown below.
Fines will be charged for all late returns.

The Limits
of Human Rights

Edited by
BARDO FASSBENDER
KNUT TRAISBACH

OXFORD
UNIVERSITY PRESS

OXFORD
UNIVERSITY PRESS

Great Clarendon Street, Oxford, OX2 6DP,
United Kingdom

Oxford University Press is a department of the University of Oxford.
It furthers the University's objective of excellence in research, scholarship,
and education by publishing worldwide. Oxford is a registered trade mark of
Oxford University Press in the UK and in certain other countries

© The Several Contributors 2019

The moral rights of the authors have been asserted

First Edition published in 2019

Impression: 1

All rights reserved. No part of this publication may be reproduced, stored in
a retrieval system, or transmitted, in any form or by any means, without the
prior permission in writing of Oxford University Press, or as expressly permitted
by law, by licence or under terms agreed with the appropriate reprographics
rights organization. Enquiries concerning reproduction outside the scope of the
above should be sent to the Rights Department, Oxford University Press, at the
address above

You must not circulate this work in any other form
and you must impose this same condition on any acquirer

Crown copyright material is reproduced under Class Licence
Number C01P0000148 with the permission of OPSI
and the Queen's Printer for Scotland

Published in the United States of America by Oxford University Press
198 Madison Avenue, New York, NY 10016, United States of America

British Library Cataloguing in Publication Data
Data available

Library of Congress Control Number: 2019946461

ISBN 978-0-19-882476-3 (pbk.)
ISBN 978-0-19-882475-6 (hbk.)

Printed and bound by
CPI Group (UK) Ltd, Croydon, CR0 4YY

Links to third party websites are provided by Oxford in good faith and
for information only. Oxford disclaims any responsibility for the materials
contained in any third party website referenced in this work.

Contents

Notes on Contributors	xiii
Introduction: A Ride on the Human Rights Bus	1
Bardo Fassbender and Knut Traisbach	
I. The Journey Begins	6
II. After the Journey	10
III. Before the Next Journey Begins	18
Prologue: Limits and their Varieties	23
Henry J. Steiner	
I. Introduction	23
II. Limits Distinguishing Human Rights from other Fields of International Law	24
III. Legislatures and Courts: Economic and Social Rights and Political Democracy	29
IV. Conclusion: Majestic Ideals, Limited Means	35

PART I. LIMITS OF IDEAS, LIMITS OF COMMUNITIES: PARADIGMS AND BIASES

1. Humanity and the Claim to Self-Evidence	39
Lynn Hunt	
I. 1776 and 1789	39
II. The Cultural Learning Implied by Self-Evident Universal Human Rights	43
III. Limitations	48
2. The Self-Evidence of Human Rights: Origins and Limits of an Idea	55
Bardo Fassbender	
I. The Origins of Self-Evidence	56
II. 'All Men'? The Limits of Self-Evidence	63
III. The Shattered Belief in the Self-Evidence of Human Rights	65

3. Human Rights, Global Justice, and the Limits of Law 69
   Kate Nash
   I. Human Rights are Globalizing … 69
   II. … through States 71
   III. Two Sovereignties 74
   IV. The Citizen/Human Paradox 75
   V. Human Rights are Political 79

4. Human Rights beyond the Double Bind of Sovereignty: A Response to Kate Nash 81
   Mark Goodale

5. Emergencies and Human Rights: A Hobbesian Analysis 89
   David Dyzenhaus
   I. Legitimacy, Justification, and Human Rights 93
   II. Hobbes and the Basic Legitimation Demand 96
   III. Constitutionalism versus Reason of State 101

6. Reason, Faith, and Feelings: A Response to David Dyzenhaus 109
   Conor Gearty
   I. The Flight from Reason 109
   II. Land 112
   III. Community 114
   IV. Justification by Faith 116

PART II. LIMITS OF FUNCTIONS, LIMITS OF USES: ACTORS AND PRACTICES

7. Being a Realist about Human Rights 121
   Christian Reus-Smit
   I. Realist Scepticism 122
   II. Power and Agency Reconceived 124
   III. Orders, Rights, and Uncertainty 126
   IV. The New Scepticism 128
   V. To Cut a Long Story Short 130
   VI. Conclusion 133

8. Political Limits of International Human Rights: A Response (or a Rejoinder) to Christian Reus-Smit 137
   Başak Çalı
   I. Realism about International Human Rights: A Simple Story Line 139
   II. Modern versus Contemporary International Human Rights: An Even More Complex Story on Political Limits 141

III.	Political Limits of Contemporary International Human Rights	142
IV.	Conclusion	144

9. Human Rights Bodies and the Structure of
   Institutional Obligation ... 147
   Jan Klabbers
   I. Introduction ... 147
   II. Human Rights Institutions ... 150
   III. Institutionalization ... 153
   IV. Three Illustrations ... 157
   V. To Conclude ... 162

10. Dissecting the Institution: A Response to Jan Klabbers ... 167
    Rosa Freedman and Ruth Houghton
    I. Individuals and the Institution ... 169
    II. Institutionalism: The Structure and Function of
        an Institution ... 171

11. Differentiating Fundamental Rights and Economic Goals ... 175
    Aryeh Neier
    I. Economic Goals ... 176
    II. Upholding the Rights of the Unpopular ... 178
    III. Conflicts between Economic Goals ... 179

12. Advocating for Social and Economic Rights—Critical
    Perspectives: A Response to Aryeh Neier ... 185
    Jeremy Perelman
    I. Conceptual and Pragmatic Considerations:
       SER as Rights and as Political Strategies ... 186
       A. SER as Rights ... 186
       B. SER as Political Strategies ... 188
    II. SER as Rights and Political Strategies: Responses from
        the Fields ... 190
        A. The Positivist Answer: SER as International Law ... 190
        B. Theoretical Rejoinders ... 191
        C. Doctrinal Rejoinders: The Structure of Rights and
           the Respect, Protect, and Fulfil Trilogy ... 193
    III. Revisiting and Transcending Critique: The Limits of the Human
         Rights Framework and Beyond ... 195
    IV. Conclusion ... 198

PART III. LIMITS OF SCOPE, LIMITS OF RECOGNITION: THE CASE OF WOMEN'S RIGHTS

13. Between the Margins and the Mainstream: The Case of Women's Rights — 205
Hilary Charlesworth and Christine Chinkin
    I. Introduction — 205
    II. The Human Rights Field — 205
    III. Women, Peace, and Security — 213
    IV. Conclusion — 219

14. Women's Rights are Human Rights: A Response to Hilary Charlesworth and Christine Chinkin from a Chinese Perspective — 223
Bai Guimei
    I. Introduction — 223
    II. The Margin and Mainstream Discourse — 224
    III. The Specialist and Generalist Approaches — 225
    IV. The Family Values Debate — 225
    V. Women in Armed Conflicts: The Security Council Resolution 1325 — 227
    VI. Article 5 of CEDAW and its Implementation — 228
    VII. Concluding Remarks — 229

15. Women's Progress and Women's Human Rights — 231
Martha C. Nussbaum
    I. Women's Progress: What Does International Law Have to Do with It? — 232
    II. Does Law Deter Crimes against Women? — 236
    III. 'Already a Form of Improvement in Itself' — 238
    IV. CEDAW as a Victory and Midpoint — 241
    V. CEDAW, the CEDAW Committee, the Protocol, the Recommendations — 244
    VI. The Limits of International Human Rights Law for Women's Human Rights — 246
    VII. CEDAW's Modest Contributions — 251

16. The Limits of Law: A Response to Martha C. Nussbaum — 267
Fareda Banda
    I. On Seeing the Unseen: CEDAW and Intersectionality — 268
    II. Reproductive Rights — 270
    III. Beyond CEDAW — 274
    IV. On the Challenge of Measuring Progress — 276
    V. Conclusion — 278

PART IV. LIMITS OF PRAGMATISM, LIMITS OF COMPROMISE: THE CASE OF ARMED CONFLICT

17. The Limits of the Laws of War 283
    Frédéric Mégret
    I. Contingent Limits 284
        A. Lag behind the Reality of War 284
        B. Lack of Enforcement 285
        C. The Interstate Character of the Regulation of War 286
    II. Inherent Limits 288
        A. The Limits of Legalism 288
        B. The Limits of Compromise 290
        C. The Limits of Pragmatism 292
    III. Conclusion 294

18. The Banality of Humanity (as an Absolute): A Response to Frédéric Mégret 297
    Knut Traisbach
    I. The Limits of Law 298
    II. Inherent Limits 299
    III. Conclusions 303

19. The Limits of Human Rights in Times of Armed Conflict and Other Situations of Armed Violence 305
    Andrew Clapham
    I. Introduction 305
    II. Human Rights in Armed Conflict 305
        A. A Limited Role for Human Rights in Targeting Decisions? 305
        B. A Limited Role for Human Rights in Challenging Internship and Detention? 310
    III. Human Rights in Other Situations of Armed Violence 312
        A. Human Rights Law for Those Subjected to Targeted Killings by Drones 312
        B. Human Rights for Those under the Control of Armed Groups 314

20. The End of the War/Peace Limit on the Application of International Human Rights Law: A Response to Andrew Clapham 319
    Yuval Shany
    I. Substantive Expansion 320
    II. Institutional Concerns 324
    III. Fear of Backlash 326

PART V. LIMITS OF PROSPECTS, LIMITS OF MEANS: AN OUTLOOK

21. The Limits of Human Rights in a Moving World—Elements of a Dynamic Approach — 331
    Mireille Delmas-Marty
    I. Introduction: Limits, Crossing Limits, and Refusing any Limit — 331
    II. The Limits of 'Reason of State' in Light of the Humanist and Universalist Ideal of Human Rights — 334
        A. Human Rights *or* Raison d'État — 334
        B. Human Rights *and* Raison d'État: Towards a Common Standard — 336
    III. The 'Reason of Planet' and Risk Anticipation as Overcoming the Limits of Time — 338
        A. 'Reason of Planet' as a Limit of Human Rights: The Precautionary Principle — 338
        B. From Zero Risk to Acceptable Risk: Limiting Limits — 340
    IV. Does 'Techno-Scientific Reason' Lead to the Refusal of any Limit? — 341
        A. The Ambivalence of New Technologies — 341
        B. The Contours of the 'Irreducible Human Core' — 342
    V. Conclusion — 343

22. Where are the Limits of Human Rights? Four Schools, Four Complementary Visions: A Response to Mireille Delmas-Marty — 345
    Marie-Bénédicte Dembour
    I. The Four-School Human Rights Model — 347
    II. The Limits of Human Rights According to the Four Schools: Inherent Defects, Limited Results, Specific Domain, Unfortunate 'Mishaps' — 350
    III. The History of Human Rights as Viewed by the Different Schools — 352
    IV. Conclusion — 354

23. Strategizing for Human Rights: From Ideals to Practice — 357
    Douglas A. Johnson and Kathryn Sikkink
    I. Context and Background — 359
    II. What Does It Mean to Strategize? — 360
    III. Is There a Downside to a More Strategic and Outcome Oriented Human Rights Practice? — 360

IV.	How to Strategize for a More Effective and Outcome Oriented Human Rights Practice	362
	A. Using Tools and Exercises for Strategic Training	365
	B. Using Historical and Social Science Research for Training	369
V.	Conclusions	372

24. Historical Strategies for Human Rights: A Response to Douglas A. Johnson and Kathryn Sikkink 375
    Micheline Ishay
    I. Mapping the Terrain of Human Rights 376
    II. Sustaining the Capacity for Change 376
    III. Mass Dispersal versus Mass Concentration 377
    IV. The Importance of a 'Spectrum of Allies' 377
    V. Human Rights Ideology and Strategic Thinking 378
    VI. Are Non-Violence Tactics more Likely to Lead to Successful Strategies? 378
    VII. When Can We Declare 'Success'? 380
    VIII. Conclusion 381

Index 383

Notes on Contributors

Bai Guimei is Professor of International Law and Executive Director of the Research Centre for Human Rights and Humanitarian Law at Peking University Law School. Her main research interests are in theories of international law and international human rights law, particularly human rights protection mechanisms, women's rights and rights of the child. Her books in Chinese include *International Law* (3rd edn., Peking University Press 2015), *Human Rights Law* (2nd edn., Peking University Press 2015), and *Self-Determination in International Law* (China Overseas Chinese Press 1999). She was editor-in-chief of the Chinese Yearbook of International Law and has published numerous papers on international law and human rights law in major Chinese law journals.

Fareda Banda is a Professor of Law at the University of London, School of Oriental and African Studies. Her areas of interest include the human rights of women, law and society in Africa, alternative dispute resolution and family law. She holds a DPhil from the University of Oxford and BL Hons, LLB from the University of Zimbabwe. She was a Hauser Global Visiting Professor at NYU in 2009 and 2014. Her publications include a book entitled *Women, Law and Human Rights: An African Perspective* (Hart Publishing 2005). She also authored reports on *Laws that Discriminate against Women* (Office of the UN High Commissioner for Human Rights 2008) and on *Gender, Minorities and Indigenous Peoples* (co-authored with Christine Chinkin, Minority Rights Group International 2004).

Başak Çalı is Professor of International Law at Hertie School, Berlin and its Centre for Fundamental Rights. Her research spans general international law, international human rights law and European human rights law. She is the editor of *International Law for International Relations* (Oxford University Press 2010) and the author of *Authority of International Law: Obedience, Respect and Rebuttal* (Oxford University Press 2015). Her research has been published in peer reviewed journals, including the European Journal of International Law, Human Rights Quarterly, Human Rights Law Review, Law and Social Inquiry and the International Journal of Constitutional Law. She is the editor in chief of Oxford University Press United Nations Human Rights Law Reports. She has been a Council of Europe expert on the European Convention on Human Rights since 2002.

Hilary Charlesworth is a Melbourne Laureate Professor at Melbourne Law School. She is also a Distinguished Professor at the Australian National University. She received the American Society of International Law's award for creative legal scholarship for her book, co-authored with Christine Chinkin, *The Boundaries of International Law: a Feminist Analysis* (Manchester University Press 2000). She was also awarded, with Christine Chinkin, the American Society of International Law's Goler T. Butcher award for 'outstanding contributions to the development or effective realization of international human rights law'. Hilary has held both an Australian Research Council Federation Fellowship (2005–10) and an ARC Laureate Fellowship (2010–15). She is an associate member of the Institut de Droit International and served as judge ad hoc in the International Court of Justice in the *Whaling in the Antarctic Case* (2011–14).

Christine Mary Chinkin, FBA, CMG, is a Professorial Research Fellow and former Director of the Centre for Women, Peace and Security at the London School of Economics, a William W. Cook Global Law Professor at the University of Michigan and a member of the Bar of England and Wales and Matrix Chambers. She was previously Professor of International Law at the LSE. She is the author of many articles on international law and human rights law, in particular on the human rights of women. She is co-author of *The Boundaries of International Law: a Feminist Analysis* (with Hilary Charlesworth, Manchester University Press 2000), *The Making of International Law* (with Alan Boyle, Oxford University Press 2007) and of *International Law and New Wars* (with Mary Kaldor, Cambridge University Press 2017).

Andrew Clapham is Professor of International Law at the Graduate Institute of International and Development Studies, which he joined in 1997. He was the first Director of the Geneva Academy of International Humanitarian Law and Human Rights (2006–14). Andrew Clapham teaches international law, human rights law, and the laws of war. His current research focuses on war. He is an Associate Member of Matrix Chambers in London. In 2014, he was nominated by Switzerland as an Arbitrator under the UN Law of the Sea Convention. He has been a member of the UN Commission on Human Rights in South Sudan since October 2017. He has produced a 7th edition of *Brierly's Law of Nations* (Oxford University Press 2012). He is the co-editor with Paola Gaeta of the *Oxford Handbook of International Law in Armed Conflict* (Oxford University Press 2014) and co-editor with Paola Gaeta and Marco Sassòli of *The 1949 Geneva Conventions: A Commentary* (Oxford University Press 2015).

Mireille Delmas-Marty is Honorary Professor at the Collège de France in Paris, France, where she occupied the Chair on Comparative Legal Studies and Internationalization of Law. In 2007, she was elected member of the *Académie des Sciences Morales et Politiques*. Her teaching career has led her to teach at the Universities of Lille-II (1970–77), Paris-XI (1977–90) and Paris-I (1990–2002). Mireille Delmas-Marty created the *Unité Mixte de Recherche de droit comparé de Paris* (University of Paris-I/CNRS) that she directed from 1997 to 2002. She has been awarded doctorates *honoris causa* from Universities of Liege (1992), Urbino (1994), Uppsala (1995) Beijing (1996), Louvain (2003), Montreal (2003) and Ferrara (2004). She is Honorary Fellow of the Society for Advanced Legal Studies, London (1998) and was elected member of American Law Institute (2012).

Marie-Bénédicte Dembour is Professor of Law and Anthropology at the Human Rights Centre, Ghent University. She studied law at the Free University of Brussels (ULB) and Social Anthropology at the University of Oxford. Her numerous publications include the seminal collection *Culture and Rights: Anthropological Perspectives* (co-edited with Jane K. Cowan and Richard A. Wilson, Cambridge University Press 2001), the monograph *Who Believes in Human Rights? Reflections on the European Convention* (Cambridge University Press 2006) and the award-winning *When Humans Become Migrants: Study of the European Court of Human Rights with an Inter-American Counterpoint* (Oxford University Press 2015). Her presentation of her human rights four-school model in *Human Rights Quarterly* 32 (2010) immediately became, and remains, one of this journal's most downloaded articles. In 2019, she was awarded an Advanced Grant by the European Research Council (ERC) to lead a five-year research project entitled 'DISSECT: Evidence in International Human Rights Adjudication'. An engaged and engaging scholar, she has been invited to teach and speak all over the world.

David Dyzenhaus is a Professor of Law and Philosophy at the University of Toronto, and a Fellow of the Royal Society of Canada. He holds the Alfred Abel Chair of Law and was appointed in 2015 to the rank of University Professor. In 2014–15, he was the Arthur Goodhart Visiting Professor in Legal Science in Cambridge. In 2016–17, he was a Fellow of the Wissenschaftskolleg zu Berlin. His books include *Hard Cases in Wicked Legal Systems: Pathologies of Legality* (2nd edn, Oxford University Press 2010), *The Constitution of Law: Legality in a Time of Emergency* (Cambridge University Press 2006), and *Legality and Legitimacy: Carl Schmitt, Hans Kelsen, and Hermann Heller in Weimar* (Oxford University Press 1997).

Bardo Fassbender is Professor of International Law, European Law, and Public Law at the University of St. Gallen in Switzerland. He studied law, history, and political science at the University of Bonn (Germany) and holds an LLM from Yale Law School and a Doctor iuris from the Humboldt University in Berlin, where he also completed his Habilitation and became Privatdozent. He was a Ford Foundation Senior Fellow in Public International Law at Yale University and a Jean Monnet Fellow at the European University Institute in Florence. Before joining the University of St. Gallen, he held the chair in international law and human rights law at the Bundeswehr University in Munich. His books include *UN Security Council and the Right of Veto: A Constitutional Perspective* (Kluwer Law International 1998), *Der offene Bundesstaat* [Foreign Relations Powers and the International Legal Personality of States Members of Federal States in Europe] (Mohr Siebeck 2007), and *The United Nations Charter as the Constitution of the International Community* (Martinus Nijhoff 2009).

Rosa Freedman is the inaugural Professor of Law, Conflict and Global Development at the University of Reading. She received her LLB, LLM and PhD from the University of London and is a member of Gray's Inn. Freedman's research focuses on the UN and human rights, and she works closely with the UN, State governments, and civil society. She has published extensively on UN human rights bodies and systems, and on UN peacekeeping and accountability for human rights abuses committed during such operations. Her published work includes two monographs, two co-edited collections, and articles in the American Journal of International Law, European Journal of International Law, Leiden Journal of International Law and Human Rights Quarterly, amongst others. Freedman is a member of the UN Secretary-General's Civil Society Advisory Board on prevention of sexual exploitation and abuse, is a Specialist Adviser on Safeguarding to the UK government International Development Committee, and sits on the UK FCO Women, Peace and Security Steering Group.

Conor Gearty is Professor of Human Rights Law at the London School of Economics and Political Science where he has recently been Director of its Institute of Public Affairs and, before that, Director of its Centre for the Study of Human Rights (2002–09). He has published widely on terrorism, civil liberties, and human rights. Conor is also a barrister and was a founder member of Matrix chambers from where he continues to practise. He has been a visiting professor at Boston University, the University of Richmond, the University of New South Wales, and the University of Sydney. Conor is a Fellow of the British Academy, a Member of the Royal Irish Academy, a Bencher of Middle Temple and has honorary doctorates from Sacred Heart University in the United States, University College Dublin in Ireland, and Brunel and Roehampton universities in the UK. His books include *Can Human Rights Survive?* (Cambridge University Press 2006), *The Cambridge Companion to Human Rights Law* (co-edited with Costas Douzinas, Cambridge University Press 2012), *Liberty and Security* (Polity Press 2013), *The Meanings of Rights: The Philosophy and Social Theory of Human Rights* (co-edited with Costas Douzinas, Cambridge University Press 2014), and *On Fantasy Island: Britain, Europe and Human Rights* (Oxford University Press 2016).

Mark Goodale is Professor of Cultural and Social Anthropology at the University of Lausanne. He is the founding series editor of Stanford Studies in Human Rights and the author or editor of a number of books, including *A Revolution in Fragments: Traversing Scales of Justice, Ideology, and Practice in Bolivia* (Duke University Press 2019), *Letters to the Contrary: A Curated History of the UNESCO Human Rights Survey* (edited, Stanford University Press 2018), *Anthropology and Law: A Critical Introduction* (New York University Press 2017), and *Human Rights at the Crossroads* (edited, Oxford University Press 2013). The winner of the 2017 International Geneva Award, he is currently developing a new project on the future of human rights.

Ruth Houghton joined Newcastle Law School as a Lecturer in Law in September 2017. Previously, she was a Research Assistant for the European Research Council funded project 'Neo-Federalism', which was led by Professor Robert Schütze at Durham Law School and she worked at Durham Law School as a Graduate Teaching

Assistant from 2013 to 2016. Ruth's research focuses on global constitutionalization and democracy. She has published on democracy and international organisations, as well as the United Nations Human Rights Council. She also works with Aoife O'Donoghue on feminist utopias and global constitutionalism.

Lynn Hunt is Distinguished Research Professor at the University of California, Los Angeles. Her abiding focus has been the French Revolution. She has also been concerned with historical method, human rights, and epistemology. Her books include *History: Why It Matters* (Polity Press 2018), *The French Revolution and Napoleon: Crucible of the Modern World* (co-authored with Jack R Censer, Bloomsbury Academic 2017), *Writing History in the Global Era* (WW Norton & Co 2014), and *Inventing Human Rights: A History* (WW Norton & Co 2007).

Micheline Ishay is Professor of International Studies and Human Rights at the Josef Korbel School of International Studies at the University of Denver; she is University of Denver Distinguished Scholar, and Director of the International Human Rights Program. She is author and editor of numerous books, including *The Levant Express: The Arab Uprisings and the Future of the Middle East* (Yale University Press 2019), *The History of Human Rights: From Ancient Times to the Globalization Era* (2nd edn, University of California Press 2008), *The Human Rights Reader: Major Political Essays, Speeches and Documents from Ancient Times to the Present* (2nd edn, Routledge 2007), and *Internationalism and Its Betrayal* (University of Minnesota Press 1995).

Douglas A. Johnson is a Lecturer in Public Policy and the former Director of the Carr Center for Human Rights Policy at the Harvard Kennedy School. Until 2012, he was Executive Director of the Minnesota-based Center for the Victims of Torture, a preeminent treatment facility in the US. He has been a committed advocate of human rights since the 1970s with ample experience in practical human rights campaigns, consultancy and organizational leadership. Another of Johnson's major initiatives was the New Tactics in Human Rights Project to broaden tactical knowledge and improve strategic thinking amongst human rights NGOs. The NGO that emerged from this project—New Tactics—continues to be a source of innovation and inspiration to human rights defenders around the world.

Jan Klabbers is Professor of International Law at the University of Helsinki. He holds degrees in international law and political science as well as a doctorate in law from the University of Amsterdam, where he taught international law and EU law in the early 1990s before moving to Helsinki in 1996. His main publications include *The Concept of Treaty in International Law* (Kluwer 1996), *An Introduction to International Organizations Law* (3rd edn, Cambridge University Press 2015), *International Law* (2nd edn, Cambridge University Press 2017), *Treaty Conflict and the European Union* (Cambridge University Press 2008), *The Challenge of Inter-legality* (co-edited with Gianluigi Palombella, Cambridge University Press 2019) and, as co-author, *The Constitutionalization of International Law* (Oxford University Press 2009). His areas of interest include the law of international organisations and the law of treaties, and he has held visiting positions at, amongst others, New York University, the Graduate Institute in Geneva, and Sorbonne.

Frédéric Mégret is a full-Professor and Dawson Scholar at the Faculty of Law, McGill University. From 2006 to 2016, he held the Canada Research Chair on the Law of Human Rights and Legal Pluralism. Before coming to McGill, he was an Assistant Professor at the University of Toronto, a research associate at the European University Institute, and an attaché at the International Committee of the Red Cross. He is the editor, with Philip Alston, of the forthcoming second edition of *The United Nations and Human Rights: A Critical Appraisal* (Oxford University Press 2019) and the co-editor of the *Oxford Handbook of International Criminal Law* (Oxford University Press *forthcoming*). His research interests are in general international law, the laws of war, human rights and international criminal justice.

Kate Nash is Professor of Sociology at Goldsmiths, University of London, where she is Co-Director for the Centre for the Study of Global Media and Democracy, and Faculty Fellow at the Center for Cultural Sociology, Yale University. She has written and published widely on political sociology and on the sociology of human rights, including *The Political Sociology of Human Rights* (Cambridge University Press 2015), and *The Cultural Politics of Human Rights: Comparing the US and UK* (Cambridge University Press 2009). She is currently researching human rights films, and published 'Film that brings human rights to life' in Public Culture 30 (2018).

Aryeh Neier is president emeritus of the Open Society Foundations where he was president from 1993 to 2012. Before that, he served for 12 years as executive director of Human Rights Watch, of which he was a founder in 1978. He worked 15 years at the American Civil Liberties Union, including eight years as national executive director. He served as an adjunct professor of law at New York University for more than a dozen years, and has also taught at Georgetown University Law School and the University of Siena, Italy. Between 2012 and 2017, he served as Distinguished Visiting Professor at the Paris School of International Affairs of Sciences Po. Neier is a frequent contributor of op-ed articles and book reviews to leading international newspapers and periodicals, and he also wrote a column on human rights for The Nation for a dozen years. He is author of seven books, including his most recent, *The International Human Rights Movement: A History* (Princeton University Press 2012).

Martha C. Nussbaum is currently the Ernst Freund Distinguished Service Professor of Law and Ethics, appointed in the Department of Philosophy and the Law School of the University of Chicago. She is an Associate in the Classics Department, the Divinity School, and the Political Science Department and a Member of the Committee on Southern Asian Studies. Professor Nussbaum is internationally renowned for her work in Ancient Greek and Roman philosophy, feminist philosophy, political philosophy, and philosophy and the arts and is actively engaged in teaching and advising students in these subjects. She has received numerous honorary degrees and awards, including the Kyoto Prize in Arts and Philosophy (2016), the Don M. Randel Prize for Achievement in the Humanities from the American Academy of Arts and Sciences (2018), and the Berggruen Prize for Philosophy and Culture (2018). Her publications include *Women and Human Development: The Capabilities Approach* (Cambridge University Press 2000), *Frontiers of Justice: Disability, Nationality, Species Membership* (Belknap Press 2006), *From Disgust to Humanity: Sexual Orientation and Constitutional Law* (Oxford University Press 2010), *Creating Capabilities: The Human Development Approach* (Belknap Press 2011), *The Monarchy of Fear: A Philosopher Looks at Our Political Crisis* (Simon & Schuster 2018), and *The Cosmopolitan Tradition: A Noble but Flawed Ideal* (The Belknap Press of Harvard University Press 2019).

Jeremy Perelman is Associate Professor at the Sciences Po Law School in Paris, where he also serves as the founding Director of the Sciences Po Law School Clinic, a pluridisciplinary experiential learning and applied research public interest program. He is the co-editor of *Stones of Hope: How African Activists Reclaim Human rights to Challenge Global Poverty* (co-edited with Lucie E White, Stanford University Press 2010), a volume co-authored by African human rights advocates and social justice scholars. He was invited to teach as a Lecturer-in-Law at Columbia Law School, and as a Visiting Professor at the University of Connecticut School of Law and the Buchmann Faculty of Law at Tel Aviv University. Perelman holds Masters Degrees from Stanford Law School and the Fletcher School at Tufts University, as well as a Doctorate (SJD) from Harvard Law School. He sits on the Editorial Committee of the European Journal of Human Rights.

Christian Reus-Smit is Professor of International Relations at the University of Queensland and a Fellow of the Academy of the Social Sciences in Australia. Among his many books, he is author of *On Cultural Diversity: International Theory in a World of Difference* (Cambridge University Press 2018), *The Globalization of International Society* (co-edited with Tim Dunne, Oxford University Press 2017), *Individual Rights and the Making of the International System* (Cambridge University Press 2013), *American Power and World Order* (Polity Press 2004), and *The Moral Purpose of the State: Culture, Social Identity, and Institutional Rationality in International Relations* (Princeton University Press 1999). His work has been awarded the Northedge Prize (1992), the BISA Prize (2002), and the Susan Strange Prize (2014). He is co-editor of the *Cambridge Studies in International Relations* book series, a General Editor of the *Oxford Handbooks of International Relations*, and a former editor of the leading journal *International Theory*.

Yuval Shany is the Hersch Lauterpacht Chair in International Law and former Dean of the Law Faculty of the Hebrew University of Jerusalem. He also currently serves as the Vice Chair of the UN Human Rights Committee, the Academic Chair of the Minerva Center for Human Rights at the Hebrew University, and a Vice President for Research at the Israel Democracy Institute. Since 2016, Professor Shany also coordinates the work of the Cyber-Law programme in the International

Cyber-Security Research Center at the Hebrew University. Professor Shany received his LLB cum laude from the Hebrew University, LLM from New York University and PhD in international law from the University of London.

Kathryn Sikkink is the Ryan Family Professor of Human Rights Policy at the Harvard Kennedy School and the Carol K Pforzheimer Professor at the Radcliffe Institute for Advanced Study. She works on international norms and institutions, transnational advocacy networks, the impact of human rights law and policies, and transitional justice. Her publications include *Evidence for Hope: Making Human Rights Work in the 21st Century* (Princeton University Press 2017), *The Justice Cascade: How Human Rights Prosecutions are Changing World Politics* (WW Norton & Co 2011), *Activists Beyond Borders: Advocacy Networks in International Politics* (co-authored with Margaret E Keck, Cornell University Press 1998), and *The Persistent Power of Human Rights: From Commitment to Compliance* (co-edited with Thomas Risse and Stephen C Ropp, Cambridge University Press 2013). She holds a PhD in political science from Columbia University. Sikkink has been a Fulbright Scholar in Argentina and a Guggenheim fellow.

Henry J. Steiner is Jeremiah Smith, Jr. Professor of Law, Emeritus at Harvard University where he also gained his B.A., LL.M. and LL.B. degrees. He served as law clerk to Justice John M. Harlan of the US Supreme Court and practiced law for several years before becoming a faculty member at Harvard Law School in 1962. His teaching and writing over several decades were primarily in the fields of international and transnational law. In 1984 Steiner founded the Harvard Law School Human Rights Program, which he directed until 2005 when he became professor emeritus. His lectures, courses, investigations, and consulting, mostly concerning international human rights, covered over 40 countries. Steiner's legal-political writings were published as several books, articles in law and political journals, and chapters in edited books. His most recent publication of a book in 2016, *Eyeing the World*, displayed a selection of his photographs taken over half a century.

Knut Traisbach is Associate Professor (Adjunct) of International Law at the University of Barcelona and tutor for three international postgraduate programmes in International Affairs and Diplomacy organized by UNITAR and UOC. He also teaches human rights at ESADE Law School in Barcelona. He holds degrees from Humboldt University Berlin, the European University Institute and was a visiting researcher at Yale Law School. He has held positions as lecturer, programme director, researcher and course convenor in the areas of international law, human rights and international relations at various higher education and research institutions in Berlin, Florence, Venice and Barcelona. His main research interests include meaningful interdisciplinary and critical approaches to international law, human rights and international relations theory.

Introduction
A Ride on the Human Rights Bus

Bardo Fassbender and Knut Traisbach

The purpose of this volume is to engage frankly with the question of what 'limits of human rights' are and what these limits can 'mean'. We start out from the assumption that human rights do have certain (albeit very different) limits, and that human rights discourses have their own pathologies and dilemmas. We believe that it is only by acknowledging these limits that we can understand the substance of human rights. We also believe that an open and constructive discourse about these limits will prove more valuable to the protection of human rights than a tactical marginalization or even negation of limits in the name of a self-defined progress. Accordingly, we do not equate limits with weaknesses or gaps that need to be 'cured' or 'closed', respectively.

Publishing a book about the limits of human rights seems to imply a particularly sceptical approach to human rights. However, we have not chosen a specific *Vorverständnis* of human rights (in general or in international affairs) or a particular method of analysis.[1] We neither aim at expounding an alternative theory of human rights or international law. Rather, the authors of the chapters and comments in this volume seek to identify and to conceptualize limits of human rights, using different disciplinary understandings from anthropology, history, international relations theory, law, legal and political theory, philosophy, and (political) sociology, as well as different professional perspectives from advocacy and legal practice. Much to our benefit, we are confronted with different 'versions' of human rights and their limits. To learn from these different perspectives requires a flexible mindset on all sides of disciplinary divides because the vocabulary and the reasoning do differ.[2]

---

[1] If the title of this volume bears resemblance to that of Jack Goldsmith and Eric Posner, *The Limits of International Law* (Oxford University Press 2005), this does not imply a similar approach, form, or content. Our understanding of 'limits' is closer to that of the following authors: Anne Orford, 'A Jurisprudence of the Limit' in Anne Orford (ed.), *International Law and its Others* (Cambridge University Press 2006) 1; Amartya Sen, 'Human Rights and the Limits of Law' (2006) 27 Cardozo Law Review 2913; and Wiktor Osiatynski, *Human Rights and their Limits* (Cambridge University Press 2009).

[2] For a cautionary warning in this regard, see Jan Klabbers, 'Counter-Disciplinarity' (2010) 4 International Political Sociology 308.

Bardo Fassbender and Knut Traisbach, *Introduction: A Ride on the Human Rights Bus* In: *The Limits of Human Rights*. Edited by: Bardo Fassbender and Knut Traisbach, Oxford University Press 2019. © The Several Contributors.
DOI: 10.1093/oso/9780198824756.003.0001

When considering the role human rights have played over the last seven decades, it is easy to portray these rights as a form of panacea or, conversely, as a pandemic. The continuous expansion and refinement of normative human rights regimes together with domestic, regional, and international protection mechanisms may appear positive and limitless but can also be viewed as doomed and counterproductive. But both views are extremes that distort realities.

Human rights have taken a prominent place in law, politics, philosophy, and other social sciences, but also in everyday life and in professional settings.[3] During the second half of the last century they have become a dominant vocabulary meant to foster domestic and supranational change. What has been dubbed the 'humanisation' of international law[4] describes an expanding, and by tendency all-inclusive, effect of human rights considerations throughout international law, with a special focus on, but by no means limited to, humanitarian, international criminal, and international economic law.[5] The transforming effect of human rights law has arguably changed our very conceptions of the state, the rule of law, and individual and political responsibilities. The conditionality of state sovereignty, the transformation of the fundamental principle that the will of states is the sole source of international legal validity, the idea of an international community that is based on shared interests and values, the concepts of peremptory norms and obligations *erga omnes*, the idea of a 'responsibility to protect', processes of supranational constitutionalization, and a renewed concern for the unity of the international legal order—all this would not have such a prominent place in recent discourses without the influence of human rights as a recognized central pillar of international law.

At the same time, we need to remember that the conceptualization and defence of human rights in the name of humanity or an international community does not mean that the entire international legal order has moved from bilateralism to community interests, or from co-ordination to co-operation. Although these conceptual shifts can be powerful social forces, we must not forget that sovereignty, the nation state and hard power persist.[6] What lies behind much of the co-operation

---

[3] See, e.g., Henry Steiner, 'Human Rights: The Deepening Footprint' (2007) 20 Harvard Human Rights Journal 7; Mark Goodale, *Surrendering to Utopia: An Anthropology of Human Rights* (Stanford University Press 2009); Jeremy Perelman and Katharine G Young, 'Rights as Footprints: A New Metaphor for Contemporary Human Rights Practice' (2010) 9 Northwestern Journal of International Human Rights 27; Kate Nash, *The Political Sociology of Human Rights* (Cambridge University Press 2015).

[4] See Theodor Meron, *The Humanisation of International Law* (Martinus Nijhoff 2006).

[5] See, e.g., Saladin Meckled-García and Başak Çalı, 'Lost in Translation: The Human Rights Ideal and International Human Rights Law' in Saladin Meckled-García and Başak Çalı (eds), *The Legalization of Human Rights: Multidisciplinary Perspectives on Human Rights and Human Rights Law* (Routledge 2006) 10; Knut Traisbach, 'International Law' in Stephen McGlinchey (ed.), *International Relations* (E-International Relations 2017) 57, 65–7; Andrew Clapham, 'Human Rights in Armed Conflict: Metaphors, Maxims, and the Move to Interoperationality' (2018) 12 Human Rights and International Legal Discourse 9.

[6] See Bardo Fassbender, 'The State's Unabandoned Claim to be the Center of the Legal Universe' (2018) 16 International Journal of Constitutional Law 1207.

of states and the rationale of community interests is not a harmonious solidarity but struggles about influence and contentious processes of supervision, evaluation, demands for change, and substitution. Numerous supranational bodies engage in activities of supervision and evaluation of national performances. In case of non-compliance with international standards they demand change, and some international bodies may, under certain conditions, even substitute national decisions with their own. These processes of evaluation and substitution are processes of socialization and entail difficult struggles about competencies and hierarchies. They raise important questions of legitimization, representation, and autonomy.

It is thus not astonishing that the ubiquitous presence of human rights has also provoked criticism.[7] Concerns have been voiced, for instance, about the long marginalization of women, about the proliferation of rights through the establishment of special protection regimes, about the role of 'human rightism' and 'humanitarians', the continued presence of a 'civilising mission' of 'the North' and 'the West', and a human rights activism going (occasionally) wrong and being 'a part of the problem'.[8] Doubts persist about the political relevance of human rights, their effectiveness, the sometimes questionable roles of bureaucracies and technocrats, the self-righteousness of activists, and the false promise of samaritanism. Critics continue to question the trans-civilizational universality of human rights and their use for politicized purposes.[9] For some observers

---

[7] See Chris Brown, 'Universal Human Rights: A Critique' (1997) 1 The International Journal of Human Rights 41; Frédéric Mégret, 'Where Does the Critique of International Human Rights Stand? An Exploration in 18 Vignettes' in José María Beneyto and David Kennedy (eds), *New Approaches to International Law: The European and the American Experiences* (TMC Asser Press 2012) 3; Malcolm Langford, 'Critiques of Human Rights' (2018) 14 Annual Review of Law and Social Science 69.

[8] See, e.g., Abdullahi Ahmed An-Na'im, 'Problems of Universal Cultural Legitimacy for Human Rights' in Abdullahi Ahmed An-Na'im and Francis M Deng (eds), *Human Rights in Africa: Cross-Cultural Perspectives* (Brookings Institution Press 1990) 331; Hilary Charlesworth and Christine Chinkin, *The Boundaries of International Law: A Feminist Analysis* (Manchester University Press 2000); Makau Mutua, *Human Rights: A Political and Cultural Critique* (University of Pennsylvania Press 2002); Onora O'Neill, 'The Dark Side of Human Rights' (2005) 81 International Affairs 427; David Kennedy, *The Dark Sides of Virtue: Reassessing International Humanitarianism* (Princeton University Press 2004); Fareda Banda, *Women, Law and Human Rights: An African Perspective* (Hart Publishing 2005); see also the contributions in Jose-Manuel Barreto (ed.), *Human Rights from a Third World Perspective: Critique, History and International Law* (Cambridge Scholars Publishing 2013) and in Mark Toufayan, Emmanuelle Tourme-Jouannet, and Hélène Ruiz-Fabri (eds), *Droit international et nouvelles approches sur le Tiers Monde: entre répétition et renouveau / International Law and New Approaches to the Third World: Between Repetition and Renewal* (Société de législation comparée 2013).

[9] See Marie-Bénédicte Dembour, *Who Believes in Human Rights? Reflections on the European Convention* (Cambridge University Press 2006); Boaventura de Sousa Santos, 'Toward a Multicultural Conception of Human Rights' in Felipe Gómez Isa and Koen de Feyter (eds), *International Human Rights Law in a Global Context* (University of Deusto Press 2009) 97; Onuma Yasuaki, *A Transcivilizational Perspective on International Law* (Brill 2010); Rosa Freedman and Ruth Houghton, 'Two Steps Forward, One Step Back: Politicisation of the Human Rights Council' (2017) 17 Human Rights Law Review 753; Yuval Shany, *The Universality of Human Rights: Pragmatism Meets Idealism* (The Jacob Blaustein Institute for the Advancement of Human Rights 2018) <https://www.jbi-humanrights.org/BlausteinLecture2.Online.24July18.pdf> accessed 31 January 2019; on the possibility of a non-hegemonic approach to human rights, see Han Sang-Jin, Bai Guimei, and Tang Lei, 'A Universal but "Nonhegemonic" Approach to Human Rights in International Politics: A Cosmopolitan Exploration

the post-Second World War 'success story' of human rights has ended, if it ever existed.[10]

This volume, however, is not intended to be a stock-taking exercise trying to answer the question of whether all that criticism is justified, or to determine where the human rights project is standing right now. The book is neither meant to deny the importance of human rights nor to discredit them. None of the authors contributing to this volume believes or argues that human rights do not matter or that they have failed. Of course, 'they' can fail (if a right can fail by itself), but there never is only one single human rights project, or one single history, or one grand failure or success. The starting point of this volume is rather the observation that the existence of human rights in domestic and international law is not self-evident. Instead, human rights result from hard social and political struggles, and human rights violations—horrendous or small—are not a matter of a distant past but a reality of today.

Professor Tony Judt wrote that, at the beginning of the twenty-first century, we (in the Occident) live in an 'age of forgetting' by which he meant 'the difficulty we seem to experience in making sense of the turbulent century that has just ended and in learning from it'. 'With too much confidence and too little reflection', he continued, 'we put the twentieth century behind us and strode boldly into its successor swaddled in self-serving half-truths: the triumph of the West, the end of History, the unipolar American moment, the ineluctable march of globalization and the free market.'[11] The current rise of so-called 'populist' parties and governments is a stark reminder that the recent past is nothing that can be left behind or be put into simple 'lessons' that just need to be 'learned'.

Given the current political landscape and the frequent critique of human rights, it is no surprise that both the history[12] and the

for China' in Michael Kuhn and Yazawa Shujiro (eds), *Theories About and Strategies Against Hegemonic Social Sciences* (ibidem Press 2015) 299.

[10] See, e.g., Stephen Hopgood, *The Endtimes of Human Rights* (Cornell University Press 2013); Eric Posner, *The Twilight of Human Rights Law* (Oxford University Press 2014).

[11] Tony Judt, 'Introduction: The World We Have Lost' in Tony Judt (ed.), *Reappraisals: Reflections on the Forgotten Twentieth Century* (William Heinemann 2008) 1–2 (hereafter Judt, 'The World We Have Lost'). He further wrote: '[W]e should not be surprised to see the revival of pressure groups, political parties, and political programs based upon fear: fear of foreigners; fear of change; fear of open frontiers and open communications; fear of the free exchange of unwelcome opinions', ibid, 20.

[12] One can gather at least two insights from the works mentioned in this and the following footnote: first, at the turn of the century, a profound political, legal, social, and economic disquietude induced a renewed interest in the histories, meanings, and purposes of human rights, and, secondly, both the historiography and the 're-thinking' of human rights still originate predominantly from North America and Europe. On the history of human rights, see, e.g., Micheline Ishay, *The History of Human Rights: From Ancient Times to the Globalization Era* (University of California Press 2004); Yves Dezalay and Bryant Garth, 'From the Cold War to Kosovo: The Rise and Renewal of the Field of International Human Rights' (2006) 2 Annual Review of Law and Social Science 231; Lynn Hunt, *Inventing Human Rights: A History* (WW Norton & Co 2007); Samuel Moyn, *The Last Utopia: Human Rights in History* (Harvard University Press 2010); Aryeh Neier, *The International Human Rights Movement: A History* (Princeton University Press 2013); Christian Reus-Smit, *Individual Rights and the Making of the*

future[13] of human rights attract considerable attention in contemporary academic writing. And so do the foundations and functions of these rights.[14] Human rights, we are told, need to be rethought, reinvigorated, and defended against populist backlashes and the erosion of the rule of law, and also the shrinking (or already vanished) space of civil society needs to be re-established.[15] Of course, there is no agreement on either the diagnosis or the cure. But what these discussions demonstrate is that 'cascades of progress' do not only develop in one direction but can also turn 'backwards'. A more uncomfortable proposition would be that the progress has never really materialized to the degree that has been postulated by many writers.

The discussions also demonstrate that the constant use, appropriation, critique, and rethinking of human rights forms an intrinsic part of their history and nature. In this regard, Professor Judt warned us against too much confidence and too little reflection. One can have an 'ideological tunnel vision'[16] in both directions: by focusing too much on achievements or on failures; by overemphasizing particularities or universalities; by spinning an over-generalized progress narrative through history or by insisting that modern human rights have nothing (or very little) to do with earlier rights claims.

International System (Cambridge University Press 2013); Jan Eckel, *The Ambivalence of Good: Human Rights in International Politics since the 1940s* (Oxford University Press 2019).

[13] On present and future challenges to human rights see, e.g., Conor Gearty, *Can Human Rights Survive?* (Cambridge University Press 2006); Upendra Baxi, *The Future of Human Rights* (3rd edn, Oxford University Press 2012); Joe Hoover, *Reconstructing Human Rights: A Pragmatist and Pluralist Inquiry into Global Ethics* (Oxford University Press 2016); Kathryn Sikkink, *Evidence for Hope: Making Human Rights Work in the 21st Century* (Princeton University Press 2017); Stephen Hopgood, Jack Snyder, and Leslie Vinjamuri (eds), *Human Rights Futures* (Cambridge University Press 2017); Alison Brysk, *The Future of Human Rights* (Cambridge University Press 2018); Mireille Delmas-Marty, *Sortir du pot au noir: L'humanisme juridique comme boussole* (Buchet-Chastel 2019); Dapo Akande, Jaakko Kuosmanen, Helen McDermott, and Dominic Roser (eds), *Human Rights and 21st Century Challenges: Poverty, Conflict, and the Environment* (Oxford University Press 2020).

[14] See, e.g., Costas Douzinas, *The End of Human Rights: Critical Thought at the Turn of the Century* (Hart Publishing 2000); Michael Ignatieff, 'Human Rights as Politics and Idolatry' in Amy Gutmann (ed.), *Human Rights as Politics and Idolatry* (Princeton University Press 2001) 1; Jack Mahoney, *The Challenge of Human Rights: Origin, Development and Significance* (Blackwell Publishing 2007); James Nickel, *Making Sense of Human Rights* (Blackwell Publishing 2007); James Griffin, *On Human Rights* (Oxford University Press 2008); Charles R Beitz, *The Idea of Human Rights* (Oxford University Press 2009); Martha C Nussbaum, 'Capabilities, Entitlements, Rights: Supplementation and Critique' (2011) 12 Journal of Human Development and Capabilities 23; John Tasioulas, 'Towards a Philosophy of Human Rights' (2012) 65 Current Legal Problems 1; Allen Buchanan, *The Heart of Human Rights* (Oxford University Press 2017); Gráinne de Búrca, 'Human Rights Experimentalism' (2017) 111 American Journal of International Law 277; see also the contributions in Adam Etinson (ed.), *Human Rights: Moral or Political?* (Oxford University Press 2018).

[15] Susan Marks, 'Backlash: The Undeclared War against Human Rights' [2014] European Human Rights Law Review 319; Hurst Hannum, 'Reinvigorating Human Rights for the Twenty-First Century' (2016) 16 Human Rights Law Review 409; Philip Alston, 'The Populist Challenge to Human Rights' (2017) 9 Journal of Human Rights Practice 1.

[16] Judt, 'The World We Have Lost' (n. 11) 19.

The contributions to the present volume do not primarily focus on particular 'issues' or 'issue areas' with respect to a perceived limitation of the reach of human rights. They rather discuss limits that are functional, pragmatic, systemic, ideological, or epistemic in nature. The discussions show how our very understanding of human rights depends to a large extent on the meaning(s) of these limits, and how we think and act in light of their existence. The two areas with a stronger focus, namely women's rights and humanitarian law, we have chosen for several reasons. Women's rights have been one of the earliest and most successful critiques that made limits and their effects visible that were so inherent that the dominant 'culture' was (and unfortunately often still is) not even aware of their existence. Women's rights are also connected to wider social movements which address systemic biases in the public and private sphere in order to instigate social change. Naturally, these movements have also established their own new limits and have struggled with critiques from within. The humanitarian field, on the other hand, exhibits more pragmatic limits of human rights. It is an area where different, and at times contrary, functional interests need to be balanced. The interaction that has developed between rules of international humanitarian law, international criminal law, and human rights uncovers deep contestations of the limits of human rights but also manifests the constitutive force of these limits.

All limits are contentious, and their meaning depends in part on the respective personal outlook on (international) society. This situation motivated us to combine each contribution with a comment by another author who often comes from a different discipline. This, we hope, will not only provide a wider spectrum of viewpoints but also be the start of conversations between authors and readers who draw inspiration from the different expositions. However, in one regard we, the editors, did not succeed: The volume is dominated by northern-occidental voices although we did invite scholars and practitioners from other regions of the world to contribute chapters and comments. Some of them kindly confirmed their participation but later, and for various reasons, were unable to complete their work. We hope that others will continue the efforts made in this volume and further expand the range of voices.

I. THE JOURNEY BEGINS

We would like to further introduce the subject of the present volume with a thought experiment inspired by the famous 'A ride on the bus' presented by Joel Feinberg in his analysis of offensive nuisances.[17] The advantage of this kind of experiment is that it grounds abstract reasoning in concrete examples. It obliges us

---

[17] Joel Feinberg, *The Moral Limits of the Criminal Law*, vol. 2 *Offense to Others* (Oxford University Press 1988) 10.

to put ourselves in specific situations and *experience*—at least to some degree—the complexities and ambiguousness of the situation. You, as the reader, are invited to project yourself into these situations as they unfold and determine as best as you can how you would evaluate the situation from a human rights perspective. What do these stories tell you about human rights, the relevant actors, and their limits? Much in the same way as in Feinberg's original version, you are not a captive on the bus. You could leave (or quickly move on to the next story) but doing so would be avoiding the dilemma. You are invited to face (and think through) the situations as they present themselves to you.

Story 1. Imagine yourself entering a small public bus on your way to work. You take a free seat next to a young woman who has a folder on her lap and taps nervously on it. You strike up a conversation with her and eventually she confides in you that she is a PhD researcher and has recently discovered a hitherto unknown correspondence between Thomas Jefferson and a British citizen who signed his letters only with J.B. The correspondence shows that Jefferson considered a radically different formulation for the opening paragraph of the Declaration of Independence:

> We solemnly declare and claim these rights as our law, for they are not self-evident truths but need to be accomplished, that all civilised men are created equal, that they are endowed by Constitution with certain Rights, that among these are Life, Liberty, Property and the pursuit of economic Happiness. — That to balance these rights, Governments are instituted among Citizens, deriving their just powers from the consent of the governed right-bearers only. — That at times when a Form of Government becomes destructive of these ends, it can be the Right of a People to alter and abolish it, and to institute new Government, laying its foundation on such principles and organizing its powers in such form, as the principles of the Law of Nations require.

Story 2. On the other side of the aisle sits a man reading a current global bestseller about a Muslim family and its plight of living under an extremist regime and military occupation in a war-torn country. While reading one particular section, tears run down his face. All of a sudden, repeated message notifications interrupt his reading. Parents in his children's school group complain that a new maths teacher wears a headscarf during classes. Some parents compare it to a veil. The man is appalled. He closes the book and types an answer comparing the situation to a recent case of a judge who wanted to wear her headscarf during court sessions.

Story 3. Much like story 2 except that this time the judge wants to wear a court dress with a cross embroidered on it.

Story 4. This time a Christian teacher is on exchange in a country where it is obligatory for all women to wear a headscarf in public. She wears the headscarf outside her home but does not want to wear it during classes. The regional human rights court eventually confirms that the obligation to wear the headscarf in all public places, including schools, is necessary in a democratic society to avoid biased religious statements by public officials.

Story 5. Close by on the bus sits a judge of another regional human rights court. She looks tired and mentions that yesterday they reviewed more than sixty cases of individual complaints during a three-hour meeting. 'By the time I had put my papers on the table,' she says, 'we were already discussing the third case.'

Story 6. On the other side of the aisle sits the Secretary-General of an international organization which receives the largest part of its funding from only eight major economies around the world. She explains that she had several meetings yesterday: first came a delegation from the 'Global South' promoting a treaty for the progressive realization of economic and social equality of nations. The draft treaty stipulates that a certain percentage of national expenditure shall go to an international redistribution fund. Then came a delegation of non-governmental organization (NGO) representatives and victim associations who claimed compensation for instances of child trafficking that occurred during a recent international support mission led by the organization. Finally, she met with representatives of the two economically strongest member states who intimated that their governments would cut funding if the proposed treaty on equality received the organization's support, or if the conduct of their soldiers who participated in the mission was investigated.

Story 7. In the next row of the bus sits a young woman who fled from a war-torn country and barely survived the long journey to Europe. In a reception centre, she explains, she was handed an information leaflet that 'specifies' her human right to asylum and describes the necessary criteria and procedural steps until asylum is granted or denied. The first question she had to answer was whether she had already requested asylum in another Schengen country.

Story 8. The woman continues to narrate how a local NGO recently approached her and asked her to participate in a campaign about women's rights in the refugee crisis. The project is part of a major funding campaign in which the NGO secured a special grant from a philanthropic foundation. She explains how members of the NGO worked with her on how to tell her 'story' most effectively. At public campaign meetings and media presentations, she was alternately presented as a victim, a witness, or a survivor.

Story 9. The woman also confides to you that she had been tortured and abused by fundamentalist fighters at home and that she recognized one of these men in the asylum reception centre. Upon her complaint to the police, he was arrested, and investigations revealed that he was only sixteen years old. In one of her meetings with the NGO she overheard a declaration of a global human rights expert demanding that children should not be deprived of their liberty. He apologized to children for what had happened to them. 'Whatever they have done,' he said, 'children should not be detained.'

Story 10. Next to her sits a well-dressed lady, clearly not used to commuting to work by bus. She talks on her mobile phone and informs a friend that her car broke down and that she had to take an overcrowded and smelly bus. At work, she explains, she recently found out that a female colleague with comparable experience and responsibilities is paid a considerably higher salary. She does not know what to do without endangering her position and future career in the company. She also doubts whether the law can help her.

Story 11. In a variant of story 10, the higher compensated colleague with comparable experience and responsibilities is male. In this case, she feels more confident about her prospects in a court of law.

Story 12. The phone conversation continues: She complains to her friend about her housekeeper who has asked her for a pay rise from 7 to 8 dollars per hour. Her domestic worker comes from an Asian country and tries to send 80 per cent of her salary home to her children whom she has not seen for the last six years.

Story 13. In the next row sits a man with scars on his face and arms. He fled from a country with a long history of ethnic-based violence between the two major ethnicities living there. Over the last one hundred years, there have been multiple instances of large-scale killing campaigns, civil wars, and violent clashes between the ethnic groups. After the end of one particularly horrendous genocide, the international community established an international criminal tribunal. This particular genocide is now engrained in the international public memory and has become a watershed moment in the development of international criminal justice. Today, one ethnicity is generally regarded as the perpetrators and the other as victims or survivors.

Story 14. Incidentally, the president of the aforementioned country sits also on the bus. He belongs to the minority ethnicity of the 'survivors' and has ruled the country for the last eighteen years. He was elected three times with more than 90 per cent of the votes and a voter turnout of over 95 per cent. The international community is largely content with the reforms undertaken by the president, and with the fact that no major clashes have occurred between the two ethnic groups since he took office. However, recently, his military is allegedly involved in systematic killings of members of the majority ethnicity living in one of the neighbouring countries. Amused, he tells you about the growing international concern about these activities and rumours that the UN Security Council might refer the situation to the International Criminal Court. The president adds: 'Can you imagine that the Council will give another case from my continent to the court? And what do they think will happen again in my country and the region if I was indicted or even sentenced?'

Story 15. Next to the president sits a military lawyer. She is a specialist in international humanitarian law and advises special operation units before and during their employment. 'This morning was tough,' she says. 'I can't give you details but one of our units caught enemy fire. Air support wanted to drop a RBL or CBU—sorry, I mean a cluster bomb. We considered alternatives in order to achieve the same effect: sending in more troops would have taken too long and was too dangerous; we would have needed ten times more conventional non-cluster weapons to achieve the same effect, and it would also have taken too much time. Dropping one of our RBLs takes only thirty seconds. We estimated that 94 per cent of enemy targets would be wounded or killed. We estimated that there was a 12 per cent chance that a close-by school building would receive some shrapnel and of course there is always a 1 to 5 per cent possibility that some bomblets fail—on average.' After a short pause she mumbles: 'What we do must be proportionate.'

Story 16. In the first row of the bus sits an accomplished human rights scholar. Confidently, he has taken a seat in the front row and has asked the bus driver for a microphone to comment on the journey for the passengers. He enjoys telling success stories about human rights and indeed there are many. The assertions that human rights are only idealist talk, or that their post-Cold War rise has ended (and with it his own) upset him. In his long speech to the passengers, he underlines that in the absence of an 'alternative language' human rights are the best possible foundation of international peace and security, and that there is no need for a further proliferation of rights because new rights are already 'present' in already existing provisions. He ends by stating once more that human rights, when 'properly' defined, reflect a global consensus in all regions of the world regarding their core content.

II. AFTER THE JOURNEY

The stories above highlight some of the complexities that we often overlook or choose to marginalize. Some of the stories may make us wonder how easy it is for rights holders to disregard or infringe the rights of others. Other stories point to the importance of context, to systemic biases in our actions, and to the 'darker sides' and unintended consequences of well-meant human rights work. A number of stories address the particular roles of the state, supranational institutions, NGOs, and other actors in the definition and 'realization' of human rights. More stories could be added of course, and we hope the readers will do exactly that—add their own stories.

Already a cursory reading of the stories above shows that human rights mean very different things to different people. In fact, when you discuss some of the stories you may come to the conclusion that a human rights-based argument alone cannot provide a satisfying answer or 'solution' to the dilemma, especially if you consider different understandings of human rights. This is perhaps one of the most fundamental limits of human rights as we understand them: they do not provide answers; they can only provide reasons.

***

In this volume, Professor Henry Steiner opens the floor with a fine illustration of how limits function in human rights law. In law—and elsewhere—human rights have never been limitless. As he explains, international human rights law stands in a complex relationship with general international law. It may seem that human rights law is only supposed to limit state prerogatives, but in many ways these rights depend on and remain intrinsically connected to the state. As Professor Steiner explains, any reformatory aspirations that are expressed through human rights always encounter numerous obstacles that are rooted in local particularities but also in the 'indelible language' of human rights itself (compare stories 2–4).

Some of these limits of human rights lie already in the foundational claim to self-evidence while actually the political and legal relevance of human rights is not self-evident at all. Professors Lynn Hunt and Bardo Fassbender discuss the historical origins and the political realities of this claim in the founding period of the United States and in revolutionary France (cf story 1). Professor Hunt tries to answer the question how human rights could resonate with a broader public across social status. Beyond the rights declarations of the eighteenth century, she looks at more subtle changes in society, such as new ways of conducting one's life, the wide success of novels, or the attentive care for one's own body. She also admits that empathy and a common humanity felt from a distance in the warmth of an armchair and in the security of a privileged life remain a shaky ground for global human rights (cf story 2). Bardo Fassbender investigates further the origins of the formulation of self-evident truths in the Declaration of Independence. He also emphasizes that the universal aspiration of rights declarations was inherently limited because these acts of liberation were also exclusionary and required further acts of emancipation and actualization.

The following six contributions explore in different ways the complex relation of human rights with the state and the need for a political housing in the sense of institutionalization.[18] Professors Kate Nash and Mark Goodale highlight the tensions that exist between the universal category of being human and the political category of citizenship (cf story 7). The state structure and the 'general will' remain both a constitutive precondition and a limit for the enjoyment of human rights. As Professor Goodale points out, from the very beginning in the eighteenth century citizen rights were both anti-individualist and anti-universalist. These tensions make human rights 'necessarily political', as Professor Nash explains—a position that resonates with the political philosophy of Hannah Arendt. This politicization, Professor Goodale remarks, also means that human rights norms 'must be vernacularized in terms that are immediately recognisable and woven into relevant histories' (cf stories 13 and 16).

---

[18] On the importance of institutional housing, see Jeremy Waldron, *Political Political Theory: Essays on Institutions* (Harvard University Press 2016) 6.

The intrinsic connection between human rights and the state is further explored by Professors David Dyzenhaus and Conor Gearty. Professor Dyzenhaus reconfigures the limits of human rights that traditionally were thought to become visible during a state of emergency when considerations about the safety or welfare of the people prevail. He relocates this question to the context of the constitutional state and the rule of law. In this context, he argues, human rights and the welfare of the people are not juridical opposites, not even during emergencies. Rather, even in such exceptional times human rights shall shape how states may respond to this situation by establishing a requirement of justification in terms of these rights. Professor Dyzenhaus is of course aware of the fact that human rights were used, and continue to be used, as a justification for various purposes, and not always the most virtuous ones. There is no legal or political language that is immune to 'abuse' even within institutional frameworks of the rule of law and the constitutional tradition. Ultimately, it is a risk that we must accept, he writes, but one that is countervailed by the opportunities and benefits of rule of law institutions. Professor Gearty is more wary about this, especially in the current 'climate of post-rational politics' in which actors try to change these constitutional set-ups and institutional safeguards. He emphasizes that rational justification can differ profoundly when feelings of patriotism and national anxieties dominate, even if the language of emergency is not employed. Thus also the vernacularization of reason and justification reflects the deeper political preferences of a community, and not only do these preferences change but, as Professor Gearty writes, they are not immune to momentous passions (cf stories 2–4 and 7–8).

How interest and power constitute limits of human rights, and how on the other hand these rights constitute limits of power, is further investigated by Professors Christian Reus-Smit and Başak Çalı. Professor Reus-Smit questions the orthodox realist view of power and agency in international relations that is so connected to a particular conception of the nation state and international society. He stresses instead the complex institutional settings and the dynamics of how actors use rights claims 'in the cracks and contradictions of [these] complex institutional environments' (cf stories 6, 8, and 14). It is this form of flexible power that he identifies as 'protean power'. If human rights are conceived in light of that power, that is, as tools of innovation under conditions of uncertainty, this does not only permit a reassessment of the limits of human rights but also facilitates a better understanding of the potential role of human rights in sustaining or subverting the legitimacy of political orders. Professor Çalı establishes an important link between the vernacular and the protean power of human rights by placing them in the context of the 'public authority' of multiple supranational human rights institutions, including regional and local courts, supervisory bodies, and civil society. These actors can contribute to 'a multi-authored concept of international human rights practice' and to a more effective implementation of these rights. She highlights that protean claims, too, need to be translated into more binding public power. At the same time, she and

Professor Gearty point to the danger of backlashes against human rights that she regards as a reassertion of a normative democratic identity rather than an endorsement of realist power. But these backlashes can also employ protean power to promote their agendas. To stay within the same metaphor, a further aspect needs consideration: Proteus was not only known for his extraordinary capabilities (he could foretell the future and change his shape), but used his versatile and mutable form to escape and to avoid having to give a concrete answer (he foretold the future only if compelled to do so). Thus it is worth remembering that flexibility and elusiveness never stand far apart.

This also holds true for human rights institutions. Professors Jan Klabbers and Rosa Freedman together with Dr Ruth Houghton discuss the limits (and promises) of institutionalization. Professor Klabbers shows that as soon as an activity becomes institutionalized there is a risk of tension between the substantive interests behind a given activity and the interests of the institution. Ideally these interests coincide but they can also diverge, and then the question arises which interest shall take precedence (cf stories 5–6, 8–9, and 14–15). As he observes, when an institution enters the equation the situational ethics can also change. Jan Klabbers dissects the structural bias of institutional functionalism (and functional aspirations) and provides several examples of how institutional interest can prevail over better practices. In the opinion of Professor Freedman and Dr Houghton, these examples are somewhat too crude. They call for a finer distinction that acknowledges the multiple interests and actors within an institution and also takes into consideration different types of institutions. The authors emphasize in particular the role played by individuals working for (or acting in the name of) an institution (cf stories 8–9 and 15–16), and also describe how the functional interests of alliances between actors can determine opportunities. Professor Klabbers probably agrees with the need for further differentiation, but the question remains who ultimately determines the institutional interest and the limits of engagement in a particular situation. In addition, it remains important to investigate the 'institutional field' in order to understand how functional limits of different institutions interact. We also need to remember that these functional opportunities and limits do not arise in a space void of politics (cf story 14).

Activist organizations are institutions with a very specific functional agenda. They seek to shape the interests and behaviour of other institutions and actors. Aryeh Neier's essay about human rights activism exemplifies how certain limits get established, and how they are sustained from within a movement. He sees a clear division between activism for civil and political rights on the one hand, and for economic and social benefits on the other hand (he refrains from calling the latter 'rights' in his chapter). Many human rights lawyers and activists (passionately) disagree with many of his arguments: that economic benefits or goals are matters of public policy rather than of human rights and litigation; that civil and political rights do not involve conflicts that require balancing; or that advocacy for the two categories of rights takes place in different venues, by different means, and according to different criteria. Professor Jeremy Perelman raises many of these objections in his response. More importantly, he takes us beyond the well-known debates by accentuating other profound arguments about the potential and the pitfalls of the human rights discourse in achieving social justice by challenging structural features of globalization, in much the same way as Professor Henry Steiner does (cf stories 6 and 12). Professor Perelman also hints at a more pragmatic way forward that combines established practices and critiques with new strategies—an approach that resonates with the discussion in the last two chapters of this volume.

Professors Hilary Charlesworth and Christine Chinkin then lead us into the discussion of women's rights as one of the most profound critiques of rights discourses. By charting the complex geography of actors, sites, and mechanisms, the authors discuss several structural limits of human rights (cf stories 6 and 10–12). Going beyond the often mentioned limits of commitment and compliance, they shine a critical light on limits of location and scope when they describe how international treaties dealing with specific issues of women's rights at the margin allowed the mainstream to proceed undisturbedly. Limits of terminology and compromise come into focus when Professors Charlesworth and Chinkin recount how conflicting interests and agendas resulted in broad definitions of a general prohibition of sex discrimination that favoured compromise over more specific issues. Institutional limits become visible when they describe how the existence of the Convention on the Elimination of All Forms of Discrimination Against Women (CEDAW) may have initially reduced the willingness of other United Nations (UN) bodies to deal with sex-based discrimination. Also limits of inclusion and exclusion persist in this context, as their discussion of violence against men and boys and the relational aspect of gender shows. Limits established through particular definitions, structural assumptions of vulnerability, or specific choices of references (e.g. male lives or the family) thus play a crucial role. Moreover, the authors expose how many different actors, fora, and mechanisms were needed, and how they eventually interacted with each other and contributed over time to the 'to and fro' of women's rights. Professor Bai Guimei adds valuable insight from the People's Republic of China and describes the difficulty in using transnational legal frameworks to overcome strong locally ingrained stereotypes which persist in society. She emphasizes, for example, that the choice of terminology ('women's rights' instead of 'human rights') has tactical advantages in China. Context matters, Professor Bai seems to say, including cultural and social particularities beyond a global consensus (cf stories 2–4 and 16). She also stresses that it is important to look beyond the legal and political framework for other forms of regulation and influence, including education and the media.

This leads us to the role of social movements which campaign not only for normative change but also for a deeper social change and internalization of these norms. Professors Martha C Nussbaum and Fareda Banda discuss the relationship between law and a wider social movement in the context of women's rights. For Professor Nussbaum, an important aspect of treaties like CEDAW and other legal documents dealing with women's rights is that they establish a common language and thus make a transnational communication possible which promotes the formation of political and social movements and interest groups. This, she argues, is a crucial effect of international law beyond actual compliance with legal norms which may remain weak and vague, especially when the norms have to reach into socially engrained limits in society (cf stories 10–12). Professor Banda agrees with much of her colleague's argument but assesses the relevance of CEDAW more positively. She provides many examples of how institutionalized normative mechanisms have contributed to expanding established limits of meaning and scope of women's rights. In particular, she underlines that CEDAW is a common language not only of social movements but also of numerous other bodies and actors *within* the UN system, and of regional human rights institutions.

Professor Frédéric Mégret leads us into the area of armed conflict. In his critical study of the humanitarian tradition, he identifies a number of contingent (characteristic but not defining) and inherent (deeper rooted) limits of the laws of war. He links these limits to the underlying normative choices, priorities, and dominant mindsets that construct the (changing) meanings and functions of these limits within the field. Besides the more practice-dependent limits (such as the changing nature of armed conflict and of belligerents, the complexity of compliance and enforcement, or the dependence on state preferences), he also discusses conceptual and systemic limits of legalism, of proportional assessments and humanitarian policies (cf stories 13 and 15). Professor Mégret questions the potential of normative regulations and also asks which other approaches to mitigate the effects of war might be possible, including approaches originating outside 'the Occident'. A deeper concern of his is the constitutive effects of laws of war: laws do not only prohibit certain actions and protect individuals but also constitute a 'legalized' way of conducting war, thus ultimately legitimizing particular forms of warfare. Knut Traisbach adds in his comment a critical view on the alleged oscillation between limits and opposing interests. He argues that these interests usually function as absolutes which distort our vision for the space 'in-between'. It is in this space, he argues, where a politically more relevant conception of humanitarian law exists. This conception does not focus on an understanding of limits as demarcating the width of an oscillation between opposing interests. Rather, the discourses about these limits create a space which makes it possible to acknowledge the need to take sides and which enables us to act (cf stories 13 and 14).

Professors Andrew Clapham and Yuval Shany discuss more specific limits of international humanitarian law and international human rights law. They reflect on how and why the limits between humanitarian and human rights law have been established, defended, moved, or functionally changed due to the complex interactions between these two legal regimes. Professor Clapham distinguishes situations of armed conflict from other situations of armed violence. He describes how human rights considerations have influenced targeting decisions and situations of detention, and questions their applicability to extraterritorial situations and to armed groups. He carefully identifies the multiple actors and their differing interests in shaping these discussions. It becomes evident how the limits of applicability and scope do not only relate to the strategic interests of actors but are structurally engrained in the specific 'rationales' of the legal regimes themselves and in the functional aspirations of the institutions, as Professor Klabbers also explains. Professor Shany speaks in this regard of the 'normative assumptions', 'functional limits', and also policy concerns that shape the conceptualization of these limits. In particular, he highlights how 'new realities' of conflict can influence established functional limits and enable new normative constructions (of jurisdiction, for example) which in turn provoke reactions in defence of hitherto established meanings.

The last four contributions to this volume discuss possible outlooks for human rights in light of their limits. Professor Mireille Delmas-Marty contrasts the 'reason of state' (*raison d'État*) with the humanist and universalist ideal of human rights, and adds to this 'type' of reason two novel ones: 'reason of planet' (or planetary reason) and 'reason of technology and science' (or techno-scientific reason). Arguments about human rights and their limits change categorically depending on which type of 'reason' takes precedence (cf stories 2–3, 7, 10–11, and 13–16). Similar to Professor Dyzenhaus, Professor Delmas-Marty regards human rights as a means to conceive the 'reason of state' not as standing in opposition to those rights but in a symbiosis in accordance with the rule of law. But this is 'not enough', she seems to say, when it comes to environmental considerations and the protection of future generations in light of the ambivalence of scientific and technological progress. It is here that her elaboration of, and hopes for, a 'truly common law' become most evident. In her comment, Professor Marie-Bénédicte Dembour places Professor Delmas-Marty's argument within her own model of four human rights schools. She proposes an understanding of her colleague's conception of human rights as 'limiting' particular 'reasons' in the light of the natural school of her quadripartite model. For Professor Dembour, this means that Professor Delmas-Marty leaves the orthodox conception of human rights intact which regards human rights mainly as limits of prerogatives. She shows how our understanding of human rights and their limits depends on latent assumptions. The discussion provokes deeper questions about the importance of constituency—whose rights and whose limits are we talking about? And who is human?[19]

---

[19] On the latter question, see, e.g., Joel Feinberg, 'The Rights of Animals and Unborn Generations' in William T Blackstone (ed.), *Philosophy and Environmental Crisis* (The University of Georgia Press 1974) 43; Sue Donaldson and Will Kymlicka, *Zoopolis: A Political Theory of Animal Rights* (Oxford University Press 2011).

Douglas A Johnson and Professor Kathryn Sikkink propose a more strategic and outcome oriented approach to human rights that employs new tactics beyond law and beyond the established strategies of human rights bodies, such as 'naming and shaming'. They propose strategic thinking as a new mindset which questions what works and looks for new tactics to achieve specific objectives. The authors urge increased innovation instead of sticking to an excessive legal focus of human rights that can result in a counterproductive inflexibility and inertia. In order to be able to innovate, activists need better criteria for assessing success and failure and a better understanding of targets, tactics, and timing (cf stories 6, 8, and 14). The authors explain how specific tools and capabilities can help in these strategic processes, such as mapping the terrain of relevant actors and their relationships (as adversaries or allies, but also between the strategic actors themselves), the creation of new opportunities for participation and learning, a better understanding of complex processes of change, and the employment of multifaceted and flexible tools. In her comment, Professor Micheline Ishay adds a number of critical points to this kind of 'effectiveness politics'. One of her biggest concerns is a sensibility for particularities and a need for greater differentiation regarding the social and economic contexts. This requires a more flexible heuristic which acknowledges the need for adaptation of tactics, and also for compromise, in order to secure long-term results. The cost-benefit assessment varies and needs to be adapted, Professor Ishay emphasizes, depending on contexts, preferences, and unexpected developments. She lays emphasis not only on the challenge of deciding which objectives to pursue and which tactics to employ but also on the difficulty of how to measure success (cf stories 5, 9, 14, and 16).[20] The discussion points to a more pragmatic approach that starts in the midst of things and acknowledges that we often must choose between non-ideal alternatives and without knowing what will happen in order to be able to 'go on'.[21] Similar to renewed warnings not to construct history in light of 'results' that we know only today, one of the biggest challenges for tactical thinking is then how to assess options and strategies without being influenced by our preferences.

***

These discussions show that when we consider the limits of human rights we need to understand that these limits are actor- and context-dependent and historically contingent, and that they are not normatively universal and neutral. We

---

[20] See Thomas B Jabine and Richard P Claude (eds), *Human Rights and Statistics: Getting the Record Straight* (University of Pennsylvania Press 1992); Todd Landman and Edzia Carvalho, *Measuring Human Rights* (Routledge 2009); Malcolm Langford and Sakiko Fukuda-Parr (eds), 'Special Issue: Quantifying Human Rights' (2012) 30 Nordic Journal of Human Rights 222; Francisco López-Bermúdez, 'Creating and Applying Human Rights Indicators' in Dinah Shelton (ed.), *The Oxford Handbook of International Human Rights Law* (Oxford University Press 2013) 873.
[21] Friedrich Kratochwil, *The Status of Law in World Society: Meditations on the Role and Rule of Law* (Cambridge University Press 2014) 284–91.

should always consider how these limits are defined, by whom, for what purposes, and with which effects. These effects are particularly important because limits are always both restricting and enabling, displacing and constituting, excluding and conflating, as well as separating and connecting.

We mentioned at the beginning that there is not one single human rights project, or one single history of human rights, or one grand failure or success of those rights. Neither has there ever been a single human rights movement, a sole historical source of human rights, or a unique meaning of these rights. Of course, there are dominant histories, meanings, and practices but human rights have never been universal panacea or universal pandemic. We are drawn too easily towards binary oppositions such as perpetrator–victim, compliance–violation, morality–politics, centre–periphery, particular–universal, or (nation) state–humanity. Too easily are we presented with the shallow diagnosis that human rights are justifications of particular projects, and that they can mean anything to anyone. We believe too easily the promise of emancipation and liberation without noticing exclusions. Too easily we condemn or praise. We therefore hope that the reflections on the limits of human rights presented in this volume will at least yield a more differentiated sensibility and also a certain modesty that eschews conventional or fashionable arguments.

An essential limit of human rights is that they do not proclaim an objective and universal truth of 'the good' or 'the right'. To invoke human rights always means to make a claim, and this claim in its legal, political, or moral realization is (and must be) contested, defended, and reformulated. Human rights always entail both an objective record of experience and a subjective view. A meaningful conception of human rights also needs to embrace the necessity for political materialization which encompasses the reality of both claiming and contestation, because the 'balancing' of rights ultimately always means taking sides, with all the subjectivities and possible injustices this involves.

III. BEFORE THE NEXT JOURNEY BEGINS

Before we continue our journey, we would like to sincerely thank every contributor to this volume for her or his dedication and patience. It is the authors who have made this work possible. We very much appreciate that they devoted a substantial part of their limited time to this volume, and we hope that they too find that the volume as a whole is more than a sum of its individual parts. At Oxford University Press, Ms Merel Alstein, Ms Nicole Leyland, Ms Emma Endean-Mills, Ms Natasha Flemming, Mr James Baird, and in the final stage of the project, especially Mr Jack McNichol provided their invaluable assistance. Also the excellent team of copy editors has our gratitude and appreciation.

Ms Eman Nawaya, a Syrian figurative painter, gave us permission to use one of her paintings, which is untitled, for the book cover for which we are very grateful.

Writing and editing are processes that require dedication and patience not only of the authors but also of those closest to them—families and friends. This volume would not have been possible without their support. Clara Marsan Raventós made so much possible, and little Ona and Kai Traisbach Marsan showed more patience than one could have reasonably expected from them. Both will hopefully continue to challenge limits and also establish new ones of their own.

Bibliography

Akande D, Kuosmanen J, McDermott H, and Roser D (eds), *Human Rights and 21st Century Challenges: Poverty, Conflict, and the Environment* (Oxford University Press 2020)

Alston P, 'The Populist Challenge to Human Rights' (2017) 9 Journal of Human Rights Practice 1

An-Na'im AA, 'Problems of Universal Cultural Legitimacy for Human Rights' in An-Na'im AA and Deng FM (eds), *Human Rights in Africa: Cross-Cultural Perspectives* (Brookings Institution Press 1990) 331

Banda F, *Women, Law and Human Rights: An African Perspective* (Hart Publishing 2005)

Barreto J-M (ed.), *Human Rights from a Third World Perspective: Critique, History and International Law* (Cambridge Scholars Publishing 2013)

Baxi U, *The Future of Human Rights* (3rd edn, Oxford University Press 2012)

Beitz CR, *The Idea of Human Rights* (Oxford University Press 2009)

Brown C, 'Universal Human Rights: A Critique' (1997) 1 The International Journal of Human Rights 41

Brysk A, *The Future of Human Rights* (Cambridge University Press 2018)

Buchanan A, *The Heart of Human Rights* (Oxford University Press 2017)

de Búrca G, 'Human Rights Experimentalism' (2017) 111 American Journal of International Law 277

Charlesworth H and Chinkin C, *The Boundaries of International Law: A Feminist Analysis* (Manchester University Press 2000)

Clapham A, 'Human Rights in Armed Conflict: Metaphors, Maxims, and the Move to Interoperationality' (2018) 12 Human Rights and International Legal Discourse 9

Craven Nussbaum M, 'Capabilities, Entitlements, Rights: Supplementation and Critique' (2011) 12 Journal of Human Development and Capabilities 23

Delmas-Marty M, *Sortir du pot au noir: L'humanisme juridique comme boussole* (Buchet-Chastel 2019)

Dembour M-B, *Who Believes in Human Rights? Reflections on the European Convention* (Cambridge University Press 2006)

Dezalay Y and Garth B, 'From the Cold War to Kosovo: The Rise and Renewal of the Field of International Human Rights' (2006) 2 Annual Review of Law and Social Science 231

Donaldson S and Kymlicka W, *Zoopolis: A Political Theory of Animal Rights* (Oxford University Press 2011)

Douzinas C, *The End of Human Rights: Critical Thought at the Turn of the Century* (Hart Publishing 2000)

Eckel J, *The Ambivalence of Good: Human Rights in International Politics since the 1940s* (Oxford University Press 2019)

Etinson A (ed.), *Human Rights: Moral or Political?* (Oxford University Press 2018)

Fassbender B, 'The State's Unabandoned Claim to be the Center of the Legal Universe' (2018) 16 International Journal of Constitutional Law 1207

Feinberg J, 'The Rights of Animals and Unborn Generations' in Blackstone WT (ed.), *Philosophy and Environmental Crisis* (The University of Georgia Press 1974) 43

Feinberg J, *The Moral Limits of the Criminal Law*, vol. 2 *Offense to Others* (Oxford University Press 1988)

Freedman R and Houghton R, 'Two Steps Forward, One Step Back: Politicisation of the Human Rights Council' (2017) 17 Human Rights Law Review 753

Gearty C, *Can Human Rights Survive?* (Cambridge University Press 2006)

Goldsmith J and Posner E, *The Limits of International Law* (Oxford University Press 2005)

Goodale M, *Surrendering to Utopia: An Anthropology of Human Rights* (Stanford University Press 2009)

Griffin J, *On Human Rights* (Oxford University Press 2008)

Han S-J, Bai G, and Tang L, 'A Universal but "Nonhegemonic" Approach to Human Rights in International Politics: A Cosmopolitan Exploration for China' in Kuhn M and Yazawa S (eds), *Theories About and Strategies Against Hegemonic Social Sciences* (ibidem Press 2015) 299

Hannum H, 'Reinvigorating Human Rights for the Twenty-First Century' (2016) 16 Human Rights Law Review 409

Hoover J, *Reconstructing Human Rights: A Pragmatist and Pluralist Inquiry into Global Ethics* (Oxford University Press 2016)

Hopgood S, *The Endtimes of Human Rights* (Cornell University Press 2013)

Hopgood S, Snyder J, and Vinjamuri L (eds), *Human Rights Futures* (Cambridge University Press 2017)

Hunt L, *Inventing Human Rights: A History* (WW Norton & Co 2007)

Ignatieff M, 'Human Rights as Politics and Idolatry' in Gutmann A (ed.), *Human Rights as Politics and Idolatry* (Princeton University Press 2001) 1

Ishay M, *The History of Human Rights: From Ancient Times to the Globalization Era* (University of California Press 2004)

Jabine TB and Claude RP (eds), *Human Rights and Statistics: Getting the Record Straight* (University of Pennsylvania Press 1992)

Judt T, 'Introduction: The World We Have Lost' in Judt T (ed.), *Reappraisals: Reflections on the Forgotten Twentieth Century* (William Heinemann 2008) 1

Kennedy D, *The Dark Sides of Virtue: Reassessing International Humanitarianism* (Princeton University Press 2004)

Klabbers J, 'Counter-Disciplinarity' (2010) 4 International Political Sociology 308

Kratochwil F, *The Status of Law in World Society: Meditations on the Role and Rule of Law* (Cambridge University Press 2014)

Landman T and Carvalho E, *Measuring Human Rights* (Routledge 2009)

Langford M and Fukuda-Parr S (eds), 'Special Issue: Quantifying Human Rights' (2012) 30 Nordic Journal of Human Rights 222

Langford M, 'Critiques of Human Rights' (2018) 14 Annual Review of Law and Social Science 69

López-Bermúdez F, 'Creating and Applying Human Rights Indicators' in Shelton D (ed.), *The Oxford Handbook of International Human Rights Law* (Oxford University Press 2013) 873

Mahoney J, *The Challenge of Human Rights: Origin, Development and Significance* (Blackwell Publishing 2007)

Marks S, 'Backlash: The Undeclared War against Human Rights' [2014] European Human Rights Law Review 319

Meckled-García S and Çalı B, 'Lost in Translation: The Human Rights Ideal and International Human Rights Law' in Meckled-García S and Çalı B (eds), *The Legalization of Human Rights: Multidisciplinary Perspectives on Human Rights and Human Rights Law* (Routledge 2006) 10

Mégret F, 'Where Does the Critique of International Human Rights Stand? An Exploration in 18 Vignettes' in Beneyto JM and Kennedy D (eds), *New Approaches to International Law: The European and the American Experiences* (TMC Asser Press 2012) 3

Meron T, *The Humanisation of International Law* (Martinus Nijhoff 2006)

Moyn S, *The Last Utopia: Human Rights in History* (Harvard University Press 2010)

Mutua M, *Human Rights: A Political and Cultural Critique* (University of Pennsylvania Press 2002)

Nash K, *The Political Sociology of Human Rights* (Cambridge University Press 2015)

Neier A, *The International Human Rights Movement: A History* (Princeton University Press 2013)

Nickel J, *Making Sense of Human Rights* (Blackwell Publishing 2007)

O'Neill O, 'The Dark Side of Human Rights' (2005) 81 International Affairs 427

Onuma Y, *A Transcivilizational Perspective on International Law* (Brill 2010)

Orford A, 'A Jurisprudence of the Limit' in Orford A (ed.), *International Law and its Others* (Cambridge University Press 2006)

Osiatynski W, *Human Rights and their Limits* (Cambridge University Press 2009)

Perelman J and Young KG, 'Rights as Footprints: A New Metaphor for Contemporary Human Rights Practice' (2010) 9 Northwestern Journal of International Human Rights 27

Posner E, *The Twilight of Human Rights Law* (Oxford University Press 2014)

Reus-Smit C, *Individual Rights and the Making of the International System* (Cambridge University Press 2013)

Sen A, 'Human Rights and the Limits of Law' (2006) 27 Cardozo Law Review 2913

Shany Y, *The Universality of Human Rights: Pragmatism Meets Idealism* (The Jacob Blaustein Institute for the Advancement of Human Rights 2018)

Sikkink K, *Evidence for Hope: Making Human Rights Work in the 21st Century* (Princeton University Press 2017)

de Sousa Santos, B, 'Toward a Multicultural Conception of Human Rights' in Gómez Isa F and de Feyter K (eds), *International Human Rights Law in a Global Context* (University of Deusto Press 2009) 97

Steiner H, 'Human Rights: The Deepening Footprint' (2007) 20 Harvard Human Rights Journal 7

Tasioulas J, 'Towards a Philosophy of Human Rights' (2012) 65 Current Legal Problems 1

Toufayan M, Tourme-Jouannet E, and Ruiz-Fabri H (eds), *Droit international et nouvelles approches sur le Tiers Monde: entre répétition et renouveau / International Law and New Approaches to the Third World: Between Repetition and Renewal* (Société de législation comparée 2013)

Traisbach K, 'International Law' in McGlinchey S (ed.), *International Relations* (E-International Relations 2017) 57

Waldron J, *Political Political Theory: Essays on Institutions* (Harvard University Press 2016)

Prologue

Limits and their Varieties

Henry J. Steiner

I. INTRODUCTION

Limits are, well, limitless, given their varied and nuanced meanings. We talk of a limited imagination, resources, person, effort, life, perspective, patience, and chances. We may refer to something precise and even statistical, like a limited budget. We may refer to something more abstract and conceptual, like limits to individual freedom or to popular democratic participation.

This prologue focuses on some kinds of limits that we encounter in the field of international human rights. Its topics underscore their variety—what they limit, how they limit, why they limit—within that ample field. The goal is not to build a unifying structure of powers and limits covering the entire field, but to illustrate some commonplace and some distinctive ways in which limits do their job. The limits described are those attaching principally to the definition, implementation, and protection of rights. This introduction sets forth some commonplace examples.

Whether explicitly or by necessary implication, the human rights treaties limit the reach of some of the rights they declare. Consider the threshold limitation that lies at the core of the International Covenant on Economic, Social and Cultural Rights (ICESCR) of 1966. A state party to that Covenant agrees to take steps 'to the maximum of its available resources with a view to achieving progressively' the full realization of the included rights. Such qualifications to the obligations imposed by the Covenant must be taken into account before it can be determined whether a state has complied with or violated the treaty. The two limits to a state party's obligations—the 'available resources' that vary so greatly among states, and 'progressive' steps towards compliance rather than instant compliance—might appear to impose a sharp distinction between this Covenant and the International Covenant on Civil and Political Rights (ICCPR) of 1966, which includes no such provision. But in important respects noted below, that distinction is anything but clear; the two Covenants have much here in common.

A different type of limitation operates more narrowly as it traces the boundaries of a number of rights. The European Convention for the Protection of Human Rights and Fundamental Freedoms (ECHR or European Convention) of 1950 offers a typical example in its Article 11, defining the freedoms of assembly and

Henry J. Steiner, *Prologue: Limits and their Varieties* In: *The Limits of Human Rights*. Edited by: Bardo Fassbender and Knut Traisbach, Oxford University Press 2019. © The Several Contributors.
DOI: 10.1093/oso/9780198824756.003.0002

association. It prohibits restrictions on such rights except for those 'necessary in a democratic society' in the interests of national security, public safety, preventing crime, or protecting health, morals, or rights of others.

A similar type of internal limitation may simply surround a right with others that inevitably limit the reach of the first. The definition of speech-related rights in Article 19 of the ICCPR has a similar structure to the provision above of the European Convention. Both prohibitions and rights set forth in other articles of that Covenant may effectively limit the reach of the provision for free speech, such as Article 20 prohibiting hate speech and Article 17 protecting a right to privacy.

The remaining sections of this prologue examine limits of a more diffuse character that lack textual bases within the relevant documents.

II. LIMITS DISTINGUISHING HUMAN RIGHTS FROM OTHER FIELDS OF INTERNATIONAL LAW

It may seem odd to talk of the field of international human rights from the perspective of its limits in comparison with other bodies of international law. After all, that field opens so much of great importance to international inquiry, criticism, and remedies by giving prominence to the universal rights of the individual and thereby necessarily curtailing the effects and significance of state sovereignty. From that perspective, it would appear that international human rights should be understood as a liberating body of norms and processes, no longer limited in its reach and power by the concept and doctrine of state sovereignty.

Notwithstanding the field's bold departure from traditional international law, this section examines aspects of international human rights that can indeed be understood as limitations on the field's effectiveness. Four illustrations follow. They address distinctive characteristics of human rights treaties and of the violations that their state parties commit.

(A) The delinquent state may violate rights of only its own citizens by conduct taking place entirely within its borders. No other state is directly affected. Such familiar circumstances affect the strategies open to such other states that seek to criticize and act against the violator. (B) The violations of citizens' human rights by a delinquent state can reach deeply into that state's governing structure, social institutions, and culture, unlike violations of more familiar treaties. Those violations may be essential to maintain in power a dictatorial and abusive government. (C) Efforts in such circumstances to prevent violations and their recurrence will often require substantially more time, more energy, and more significant internal changes in the delinquent state than do efforts to halt violations of more familiar types of treaties. (D) Consequently the route towards eliminating violations may be far more complex and demanding than when more conventional issues and treaties are at issue.

A. Human Rights Violations Can Affect Only a Single State

In many types of treaties, a violation by a state party or the related injury or both will involve more than one state and thus have an international character. Enacting tariffs that violate a trade treaty may cause harm to foreign exporting countries that are parties to the treaty. Denying an alien a licence to do business in violation of a commerce treaty with the alien's state, or taxing an alien in a way forbidden by a tax treaty with that state, may provoke reactions from its government.

The situation often differs when international human rights are at issue. The 'international' element may stem simply from the fact that an act by a delinquent state has violated a multilateral (human rights) treaty. Assume that all relevant conduct, as well as the harm stemming from that conduct, takes place or harms people in only the delinquent state. Denial of free speech to its citizens in violation of the norms of a multilateral treaty may harm only *its* press, education system, elections, and population. Denial of procedural due process may harm only its citizens. (Nonetheless, other states may feel the consequences of the delinquent state's conduct through the refugee flows to which it may lead.)

In such circumstances, other state parties to the treaty may be unlikely to protest, or to take action against the delinquent state through any of a range of sanctions. Their interests—for example, narrowly conceived material interests—have not been harmed by the delinquent state. Nor would the classical self-help remedies or countermeasures allowed by customary or treaty law make sense. Other states do not respond to the delinquent state's maltreatment of its citizens by in turn maltreating their own.

To be sure, there are circumstances in which this distinction has no consequence. Multilateral human rights treaties' own organs may be empowered to act in response to the delinquent state's conduct. At the least, such treaties frequently impose on state parties an obligation to submit to a designated treaty organ periodic reports about their own human rights related conduct, and to respond to questioning and recommendations bearing on violations. In extreme situations, such as commission of a genocide within the delinquent state, other states come under obligations to act in specified ways.

Other states can always apply direct pressure against a delinquent state by threatening to break important bilateral relations with it, such as diplomatic relations, or by directing its own commercial sanctions against it. Moreover, human rights organizations act in some respects through the votes of representatives of their member states, thereby offering a route for advocacy within an organization by those state parties which are distressed by the violations at issue but unwilling to engage bilaterally with the delinquent state.

The sources of pressure against a delinquent state reach beyond other states and treaty organs. Non-governmental human rights organizations bring human rights violations to light and bring their own criticism to bear while lobbying in other states or in international organizations for action against the delinquent state. They remain indispensable to the human rights movement as a whole.

B. Human Rights Violations Have a Systemic Character

A second feature that limits the capacity of other states and international organs to protest violations and prevent their recurrence stems from a distinctive characteristic of many human rights violations. Consider typical violations in treaties that, for example, protect the environment or natural resources, regulate the terms of trade and impediments such as tariffs or import bans, or determine the degree to which diplomatic officials like ambassadors and consuls are subject to the civil and criminal laws of the foreign country in which they serve. Generally disputes involving such treaties concentrate on specific violations that do not seriously impair the interests of the delinquent state. Settlement of a dispute one way or the other, however reached, is not likely to threaten the viability of the treaty as a whole, or cause damage to the basic policies or structure of the delinquent state. (Certain categories of treaties outside the field of human rights would not be covered by these observation but would have their own distinctive problems—peace treaties and military alliances, for example.)

Human rights disputes may differ. Particularly when authoritarian states are involved, an alleged violation like torture or denial of equal protection to a member of a particular racial, religious, ethnic, or gender group rarely stands alone. The particular case is more likely to form part of systemic violations affecting all or most members of any such groups; such conduct may be instrumental to the state's success in subduing critics and opponents of its abusive rule. For example, were the state's prohibition of many forms of political association to be terminated because of outside pressures, the entire authoritarian regime may be shaken to its roots and no longer be viable. The task for the outsider, whether a state or international organization, seeking to overthrow that regime becomes more complex, for it must take into account the consequences to which that overthrow may lead. It becomes important not simply to marshal a strategy responding to a particular violation, but a strategy that uproots the systemic practice behind it and considers how to substitute a different practice in its place.

C. Time Framework for Terminating Violation

A third problem addresses the time frame within which violations should be terminated through corrective action by the delinquent state. The prompter the deadline for compliance, the stricter the system of enforcement. The ICESCR gives state parties some leeway to achieve compliance with it by explicitly providing that states violating the Covenant are to take steps to achieve compliance 'progressively'. The comments below in this subsection, however, address only the ICCPR, which has no similar provision. Nonetheless, significant leeway may be allowed the delinquent state to determine how and in what time frame to overcome serious violations and achieve compliance.

Many of the civil-political rights that protect individuals against abusive action by the government involve matters of high constitutional significance, including freedom of speech and its associated rights protecting other forms of expression, freedom of religion, voting rights and fair elections, equal protection of the laws, due process of law, and independence of the judiciary. Violations of these rights cannot be as promptly and definitively settled as commonplace disputes arising in recurrent encounters and transactions between the government and citizens. No threat emerges from these disputes to the continuity of the state's current regime. Elections are not fought over them.

But human rights instruments declare ideals meant to determine, within broad boundaries, how the state should be governed and how government-citizen relationships should be understood. As the Universal Declaration of Human Rights (UDHR) explains, these rights are meant to represent 'a common standard of achievement' towards which state parties should move. The distance that state parties must move to achieve compliance of course varies with the nature of their government. That distance grows for an authoritarian state, whatever its precise character: theocratic; ruled by a military junta, hereditary monarchy, or an ideologically committed group; effectively controlled by an economic elite or a dominant racial, ethnic, or religious group. Reforms to protect the rights noted above could lead to substantial shifts in status, wealth, power, and opportunity among different groups and economic classes. They could have strong redistributive consequences.

The achievement of such reforms is not overnight work. Other states do not expect it to be. Suppose that China ratifies the ICCPR and indicates that its first step towards compliance will relax the prohibitions against public political speech. Of course the country would remain in violation of many vital rights declared in that Covenant, at the extreme the right to political participation through genuine elections at the national level to choose political leaders. Nonetheless, in all likelihood the first step taken by China would be supported and praised by liberal democracies and international human rights organizations with the hope that similar bold steps would follow. For a time, the praise would exceed criticism of the many remaining violations. The notion of instant compliance with the entire Covenant would appear to be an absurdity, whatever the occasion for or methods of reform-oriented change.

Abundant illustrations make a similar point. Torture is sharply reduced within an authoritarian regime, but imprisonment of adversaries may remain an important element in that regime's control of political life. Even a decline in the use of torture to investigate the commission of a crime and secure a confession, or to terrorize the population into obedience, cannot occur in a moment by simply ratifying a treaty on torture or issuing a decree. The process of transforming a culture that had long condoned abusive treatment, and of educating law enforcers to adhere to the new policy, lies ahead. Note that Article 40(1) of the ICCPR requires a state to submit periodic reports to the treaty's Committee indicating 'the progress made in enjoyment' of rights.

D. Cultural Obstacles to Reform

The fourth feature suggests a further complexity in displacing traditions and practices of a delinquent state. Our learning over these decades of the human rights movement has made more evident how the roots of major rights violations reach to cultural obstacles of a deep and tenacious character: foundational myths, traditional practices, religious tenets, political ideology. The human rights treaties give little recognition to cultural foundations of societies and their modes of governance. The language of the ICCPR, for example, requires states to respect and ensure the treaty rights, to provide an effective remedy for violations, and to enforce those remedies. The image is that of instructing violators to restore the rule of law.

Rarely does a treaty suggest how to get 'from here to there', from the existing state of things to greater observance of human rights norms within a democratic polity. Even more rarely do we find recognition of issues stemming from cultural relativism or diversity that so encumber the task of identifying universal norms. The goal of universality in observance of human rights seems to thwart such explicit recognition. Only a few treaties show an awareness of the challenges of overcoming tradition and culture, as revealed by their suggestions about steps to be taken to achieve a rights-observing society.

Perhaps the most striking treaty in this regard is the 1979 Convention on the Elimination of All Forms of Discrimination against Women (CEDAW). It is explicitly concerned with the difficulties of disentangling a country from cultural understandings that have dominated its past. What is rooted must be uprooted. The Convention offers numerous illustrations, like eliminating stereotyped images of roles of men and women in textbooks or in teaching methods, or highlighting the denial to women of access to credit and loans. Culture must be understood as plastic, made and remade over the course of history, not essentialist and unshakable in character but in important respects contingent on circumstances and open to purposeful changes through human agency informed by human rights ideals. Among the requirements for achieving one or another degree of cultural transformation is sufficient time for retraining and reeducation. Here again we find limits to any rapid let alone automatic sequence of violation–enforcement–compliance with human rights.

III. LEGISLATURES AND COURTS: ECONOMIC AND SOCIAL RIGHTS AND POLITICAL DEMOCRACY

This final illustration of limits to implementation and development of human rights moves to a more abstract level. Its concern is the relationship between two large systems of thought and practice: human rights and democracy. Both concern the modern state, particularly its structure, fundamental norms, and mode of governance. In particular, this section examines an aspect of the relationship between them to inquire whether adherence to democratic government sets any limits on methods or processes for developing and resolving conflicts about economic-social rights in the courts.

The discussion thus concerns a relatively weak and less well established member of the human rights family. It is not that economic-social rights have lagged far behind civil-political rights in the postwar human rights movement. To the contrary, both were prominent in the threshold UDHR, and the two principal human rights treaties—the ICCPR and ICESCR—both became effective in 1976. Nonetheless civil-political rights have enjoyed a greater prominence and exercised a deeper influence on law and politics over the last seventy years. State constitutions, to offer one illustration, have historically given more attention to them, though some newer constitutions, particularly in developing countries, now include both categories.

The last two decades have seen a resurgence of interest in the economic-social side of rights coupled with some evolving strategies for developing and enforcing them.[1] The obvious approach to strengthening such rights, at least in democracies, would feature lobbying, demonstrations and related activity, campaigns, and elections. Such an approach, all within the ambit of popular political participation,

---

[1] The following contemporary books provided the author with background for this section on economic and social rights: Helena Alviar García, Karl Klare, and Lucy A William (eds), *Social and Economic Rights in Theory and Practice: Critical Inquiries* (Routledge 2015); Doutje Lettinga and Lars van Troost (eds), *Can Human Rights Bring Social Justice: Twelve Essays* (Amnesty International Netherlands 2015) <https://www.amnesty.nl/content/uploads/2015/10/can_human_rights_bring_social_justice.pdf> accessed 31 January 2019; Samuel Moyn, *Not Enough: Human Rights in an Unequal World* (Harvard University Press 2018); Alicia Ely Yamin, *Power, Suffering and the Struggle for Dignity: Human Rights Frameworks for Health and Why They Matter* (University of Pennsylvania Press 2015); Catherine G Young, *Constituting Economic and Social Rights* (Oxford University Press 2012).

would seek to persuade state and federal legislatures to enact or amend regulatory statutes in fields like health, education, housing, social security, and environmental matters, while adjusting taxation schemes as necessary. But the times may not be friendly to such efforts. Over the last decade the governments in power in a growing number of democracies pursue a policy of austerity, or at least one of limiting spending on welfare.

Perhaps in these less-than-happy circumstances, advocates of welfare rights can turn to other governmental bodies—courts, for example. Such has been the aspiration of a number of advocates and scholars. Within ten or so countries, courts have made some imprint after assuming more responsibility in this field. In different ways depending on the country, such an expansion brings to courts cases involving the rights declared in the ICESCR, or the comparable rights incorporated (through identical or similarly worded provisions or through fresher and more inventive drafting) in state constitutions and legislation. As a result, a relatively small number of judicial decisions around the world has launched a major discussion in legal, political, and academic circles about the potential contributions of courts to the development of basic economic-social rights like health, education, and housing. The decisions spurring this discussion came out of countries that differ among themselves in their modes of government and stages of development.

The two following opinions of the Constitutional Court of South Africa suggest the kinds of issues that these decisions present. The earlier of the two decisions, *Soobramoney v. Minister of Health* (1997), involved the interpretation of constitutional provisions on economic-social rights. These rights were relevant to a case where a seriously ill appellant sought expensive treatment from a state hospital whose resources were so slender that the hospital could not provide it to all needy patients. The treatment would be lifelong; it would extend life, but would not cure the appellant's serious health problem.

Examining the constitutional provisions on health and other rights and the hospital's guidelines for such cases, and bearing in mind the lack of adequate resources, the Court upheld the hospital's decision to deny treatment. It found the guidelines and their application to be reasonable, and to be fairly and rationally reached. 'A court will be slow to interfere with rational decisions taken in good faith by the political organs and medical authorities whose responsibility it is to deal with such matters.' Thus the case involved a relatively conventional application of a familiar judicial power to review action taken by a government agency regulating a particular economic-social right.

Treatment Action Campaign v. Minister of Health (2002) addressed an HIV/AIDS epidemic in South Africa, particularly a common method of transmission of HIV from mother to child at childbirth. The drug Nevirapine reduced the risk of transmission. Manufacturers of Nevirapine offered to provide the drug to the government free of charge for five years. The government decided to make the drug available for doctors and patients in public sector hospitals and clinics, but only at a limited number of pilot sites with facilities for research and training. As a consequence, doctors working in the public sector but not at such sites were unable to prescribe the drug for their patients.

The Court examined a number of constitutional and regulatory issues related to provision of health care before finding the government's restrictions on providing Nevirapine outside the selected pilot projects to be unreasonable. It ordered the government to take reasonable measures to extend the use of Nevirapine to the entire public health sector. Moreover, it required the government to provide related services that further increased the government's costs. The opinion considered, under the principle of separation of powers, the possible limits to judicial power in relation to powers of a legislature (including power to give injunctive relief), but found that no such limits were breached here.

Similar adjudications of cases involving economic-social rights have become frequent. A controversy between citizens and government might involve constitutionally or legislatively based housing rights or a right to social security. Perhaps the claimants argue that they were denied equal protection because of alleged racial or gender discrimination by a government agency in selecting recipients of government-subsidized housing, or because of discrimination in termination of social security payments. Perhaps the courts strike down government action on the ground that it lacked a rational basis and hence appeared arbitrary. Or the courts might conclude that the agency had incorrectly reached its decision because of its misunderstanding/misinterpretation of a regulatory statute's provisions. In all these circumstances, judicial decisions in favour of welfare claimants protesting governmental denial of welfare (that would increase the cost of welfare schemes) would not constitute a radical change in relationships or serious shift of power between courts and the legislature.

Compared with *Soobramoney*, the *Treatment Action Campaign* opinion opened the door to more significant judicial participation in monitoring or revising public welfare programmes. Courts examining economic-social issues have become more willing to challenge conservative decisions by the legislative or executive branches of government. In more innovative countries, a number of recent decisions have reached boldly to augment their power to check and, to some extent, supplant or reverse legislative and executive planning on economic-social policy issues. The consequence of some decisions has been to revise government welfare policy and increase in one or another way the government's costs. The two judicial decisions described above have turned out to serve as forerunners to more daring judgements.

Economic-social rights are much disputed economically and politically even in the world of democratic countries, despite the ratifications of the Covenant by a large majority of states. They are at the core of major political battles during electoral campaigns. In the United States, which is not a party to this Covenant and whose Constitution gives no explicit attention to these rights, elections may direct most attention to perhaps health care—for example, political campaigns fought over the Affordable Care Act ('Obamacare') or over two pillars of the US health system, Medicare and Medicaid. In European democracies that are parties to the Covenant, political parties and successive governments may take radically different positions on welfare issues—for example, expand welfare coverage and increase payments, or pursue a policy of austerity that trims financial support.

In such circumstances, what do we make of the potential growth in the role of courts in ongoing struggles over economic-social rights? Does an increased competence of courts to deal with these matters challenge an important aspect of political democracy?

Such questions lie at the core of contemporary debate among judges, scholars, political actors in state or international contexts, non-governmental organizations (NGOs), and citizen groups. Some view the project to endow courts with greater powers in the field as chimerical. Economic-social rights are radically different from the civil-political rights that courts have long been familiar with, they argue. These rights raise vexing questions requiring choices that lie beyond the capacity of courts to make. Such choices may involve issues like deciding about resource allocation in a situation of scarce resources, or resolving disputes about budgetary and fiscal issues.

Others advocate that courts figure more prominently in ongoing debates about economic-social rights in order to respond more effectively to society's growing needs, particularly as inequality in income and wealth escalates. Within this context, an empowered judiciary can bypass to some extent political and legislative stalemates over these rights. Avenues surely are open. Like other components of government, courts are not frozen in time. They have evolved in structure and functions. Today's sharp debates over welfare rights may provide an impetus for further innovations.

Injunctions and declaratory judgments of far greater complexity and broader reach are no longer unusual. They stretch over time and organizations. Institutional options, like appointment of a Special Master in US courts, vastly expand the choices about how litigation can proceed. The Master appointed by a judge may, for example, be charged in cases of unusual complexity with helping to run school districts and oversee prison systems that were found to have violated the law. Contemporary judicial innovations in some countries facilitate bringing together a diverse group of stakeholders, including parties and outsiders, for purposes like collectively discussing an issue, collecting statistical and other information relevant to the conflict, and monitoring the implementation of complex judicial decrees. These activities generally culminate in reports to the judge.

Such phenomena enable judges to manage litigation involving economic-social rights more effectively. Cases like *Soobramoney* and *Treatment Action Campaign* lie at the easy end. At the complex end, the strategies and processes noted could free the judicial process from being dominated in traditional ways by the parties to the litigation and the supervising judge. The consequence could be to generate proceedings (to use terms employed by scholars and participants) of a more 'dialogic' and 'deliberative' (and also collective) character. Those proceedings might bring more exploratory and provocative proposals to the table for consideration by the legislative and executive branches of government. Decisions of the Constitutional Court of Colombia, particularly its Judgment T-760 of 2008 on the right to health, are at the forefront of innovation in several of these respects.

Consider the range of possibilities open to courts in the increasing flow of cases involving welfare rights. Do the decrees amount to judicial suggestions, or judicial directions to 'consider' certain proposals, or judicial orders to make specified changes? Would a judge authorize assembling discussants from relevant social, professional, and other groups who would submit a summary of their discussions to the court for possible further transmission to members of the legislative and executive branches, for whatever purpose it might serve? Would a court order significant changes in a regulatory scheme administering health care that would update benefits and broaden the scheme to cover a larger percentage of the population? Judgment T-760 moved in such directions.

Consider examples of more politically charged and deeper issues than those just noted—basic policy choices that could underlie litigation about economic-social rights. Should a health plan rely on a blend of public institutions and private ones (perhaps insurers), or create a single payer system? Should such a plan aim at maximum possible coverage of the relevant population and limit expensive treatment, or limit coverage and thereby permit more advanced treatment? Should the plan cover contraception and abortion? Should a housing plan subsidize rental of privately owned facilities or increase construction of government-owned housing? If increased tax revenues appear essential to create or improve a welfare system, what type of tax should be imposed and how should its burden be distributed among taxpayers? If expansion of one welfare system appears to require contraction or stasis in another, will it be necessary to devise general priorities among welfare systems serving different purposes and constituencies? If not, what criteria will be applied to reach a decision?

Were courts to become explicitly involved in developing answers to questions of similar complexity, depth, and political significance insofar as they were relevant to a case, the argument would strengthen that the judiciary (assuming that no constitutional issues were under consideration within the courts' power of judicial review) had exceeded its proper powers within a democratic state. Such matters are likely to require fundamental political choices on which elections and even a country's reputation may turn, such as a choice between market fundamentalism and a goal of social justice, or between nationalism or internationalism in the conduct of foreign affairs. In democratic countries today the resolution of such profound issues is likely to fall within the realm of political life, interest groups, collective pressures exerted on the legislative or executive branch through a variety of strategies, election campaigns featuring the views of the opposing political parties, and the vote.

These comments are not meant to suggest that courts are to be understood as polar to elected political institutions like legislatures, and therefore divorced from issues of policy. Many would understand the judiciary in broader terms, as an actor that participates in the larger processes that determine the course and character of the country. It does so in its distinctive and far more bounded ways, within its distinctive ethical constraints and modes of argument, and with the distinctive purposes of adjudication and dispute resolution in mind. Its work does engage with issues of basic policies, but in radically different ways than the political branches.

How then does one approach the question whether judicial reforms of the types indicated, together with growing judicial willingness to consider economic-social rights more broadly and deeply, are open to criticism as contrary to the spirit of political democracy? We have no universal multilateral treaty about the necessary and sufficient elements of democracy. We have no authoritative legal text as a starting point, but basic human rights instruments do include one essential ingredient of a democratic state.

Similar provisions about voting and elections appear in Article 21 of the UDHR and Article 25 of the ICCPR. Both guarantee the right to vote by universal and equal suffrage and by secret ballot at genuine periodic elections. Both explain the foundation or postulate for such a provision. The UDHR states that 'the will of the people shall be the basis of the authority of government', and that will is expressed in elections. The ICCPR seeks to guarantee 'the free expression of the will of the electors'. The spirit of these phrases is well captured by contemporary popular slogans about democracy, like 'Here the people rule'. Numerous United Nations (UN) documents extol democratic societies, including General Assembly Resolution No. 55/96 of 2001 entitled 'Promoting and Consolidating Democracy', and recognizing the 'indissoluble link between human rights ... and the foundation of any democratic society'.

It is fascinating to imagine what a multilateral treaty on democracy would say. Some serious conflicts among countries or regions, or indeed among factions within one country, would emerge in the course of a global conference charged with drafting such a treaty. There can be no doubt about the necessity of the right to vote in political elections, as well as the need to act consistently with related ideas about separation of powers. How else can we determine the 'will of the people?' It remains democracy's most distinctive and important characteristic, an essential element.

Nonetheless, voting in elections is not by itself sufficient. General understandings of what democracy requires of the modern state have changed substantially since the Second World War. Rights play a much larger role. Probably most people today would understand observance of civil and political rights to be vital for a democracy, surely including rights to free speech (with its several surrounding rights) and religion, equal protection of the laws, due process, and judicial independence. Some would insist that democratic states must accept the full body of civil-political rights declared in the treaties. Probably there would be more disagreement about the degree to which certain economic-social rights would figure among democracy's essential components. Compound nouns come to our rescue as we point to different emphases and configurations of modern democratic states: *liberal* democracy, *social* democracy, *welfare-state* democracy.

It is in the sense of these last paragraphs that democracy can be understood as a restraint or limit on what courts, with expanded facilities and functions, can achieve in the world of economic and social rights. The deep and unresolved issues that these rights pose at this stage of their development call for consulting the will of the people, for political contestation through the elected branches of government rather than through reliance on decision-making by a judiciary that has not been elected by popular vote.

IV. CONCLUSION: MAJESTIC IDEALS, LIMITED MEANS

A first impression of the norms of international human rights might fasten on their majesty and the breadth of their ambition. How high they reach in imposing obligations on states to respect and protect individual rights! How boldly they rethink long-standing conceptions of state sovereignty. Perhaps most striking, how deeply many states would be transformed by their observance of such obligations, given that the human rights movement's goals tower above the historical ways in which states have treated, and maltreated, their populations.

Such an impression suggests that these rights may never completely shed their ideal and aspirational character. The modern movement's threshold instrument, the UDHR, made that aspirational element explicit. It lingers to this day, despite the degree to which rights are now embedded in treaties and international bodies, and in many states' constitutions, legislation, and executive agencies. Numerous specialized institutions in both international and national contexts perform human rights functions including monitoring, exploring, resolving disputes, protecting, and sanctioning. Indeed, if we look at the achievements since the Second World War from an optimistic perspective, human rights might seem to have embarked on a long voyage from the hortatory to the mandatory. Surely that voyage remains distant from its final goal, but surely this vastly ambitious undertaking is at least en route.

In one of its grandest successes since the Second World War, the human rights movement has developed and universally spread an indelible language permeating law, morals, economy, diplomacy, philosophy, public advocacy, and more generally politics. This now familiar discourse, together with its institutional grounding throughout the world, have given hope to many repressed and abused populations—hope that stems largely from what has developed beyond their states' borders. The rhetoric of human rights is not readily blocked by borders. Rights-endowed constitutions have spread widely. These and other foundational instruments are now well known, and inform such mainstays of society as the educational systems that carry the message of human rights to the new generation. So rooted and widely known a discourse would now be difficult to uproot.

We must place the movement's successes side by side with the relative paucity of effective protection, prevention, or punishment of systemic mass violations reaching to genocide. The very immensity of the ideal and aspirational elements of human rights has led the states creating the treaty bodies to be cautious about the power and efficacy of the machinery of enforcement. The entire movement is at once so promising and threatening, daring and cautious, venturesome and hesitant. Each state supporting efforts towards a more effectual movement must recognize that its decision may heighten its own vulnerability to foreign influences and the related threat to its own sovereignty. No wonder that the significant limits upon powers of international organizations or states to prevent, protect against, and sanction violations of human rights have contributed to many states' willingness to join the human rights movement at all.

PART I
LIMITS OF IDEAS, LIMITS OF COMMUNITIES: PARADIGMS AND BIASES

1
Humanity and the Claim to Self-Evidence

Lynn Hunt

Human rights depend on universal claims made at a particular place and moment in time. The most crucial and vulnerable of these claims is the assertion of the self-evidence of the rights of all humans. The claim to the self-evidence of the rights of 'all men' or 'man' was established in the eighteenth century for distinct historical reasons; some of these still have resonance today and others do not. A consideration of this founding moment of self-evidence can provide a critical perspective on discussions of human rights today by drawing attention both to its power and its limitations.[1]

I. 1776 AND 1789

Although the origins of human rights can be traced backwards in time to many different places and eras, the Declaration of Independence of the British North American colonies and the French Declaration of the Rights of Man and Citizen galvanized attention in new ways because they explicitly linked the affirmation of rights to demands for popular sovereignty. Those who cite the Declaration of Independence often leave out the second part of the key paragraph:

> We hold these truths to be self-evident, that all men are created equal, that they are endowed by their Creator with certain unalienable Rights, that among these are Life, Liberty and the pursuit of Happiness. — That to secure these rights, Governments are instituted among Men, deriving their just powers from the consent of the governed, — That whenever any Form of Government becomes destructive of these ends, it is the Right of the People to alter or to abolish it, and to institute new Government.

---

[1] I broached these issues in Lynn Hunt, *Inventing Human Rights: A History* (Norton 2007) (hereafter Hunt, *Inventing Human Rights*). A large number of new works on the history of human rights have appeared since 2007. This is not the place to repeat my argument or to review the literature that has appeared since then. In this essay I try to develop some new evidence to expand the argument about self-evidence and its limitations.

Lynn Hunt, *Humanity and the Claim to Self-Evidence* In: *The Limits of Human Rights*. Edited by: Bardo Fassbender and Knut Traisbach, Oxford University Press 2019. © The Several Contributors.
DOI: 10.1093/oso/9780198824756.003.0003

Thomas Jefferson and his fellow committee members did not list the rights, other than the rather general life, liberty, and the pursuit of happiness, but they did clearly argue that the legitimacy of any government rests on its ability to guarantee those rights; if a government fails to uphold those rights, then the people have the right to institute a new government. Rights precede and therefore can supersede government.

Similarly, the French Declaration of the Rights of Man (*droits de l'homme*) and Citizen of 1789 repeatedly makes the connection between rights and representative government. Article 2 asserts: 'The purpose of all political association is the preservation of the natural and imprescriptible rights of man. These rights are liberty, property, security and resistance to oppression.' Article 3 makes obvious the link to representative government: 'The principle of all sovereignty rests essentially in the nation. No body and no individual may exercise authority which does not emanate expressly from the nation.' The French Declaration implied self-evidence, without using the term. The preamble begins: 'The representatives of the French people, constituted as a National Assembly, and considering that ignorance, neglect or contempt of the rights of man are the sole causes of public misfortunes and governmental corruption, have resolved to set forth in a solemn declaration the natural, inalienable and sacred rights of man.' In other words, the rights of man need no prior justification; they simply exist, even if some are ignorant of them.

In both Declarations rights were conceived as universal: 'all men are created equal' and 'endowed with certain unalienable rights' in the American Declaration; 'Men are born and remain free and equal in rights', in the French one. Since the basis for the universality of rights was taken to be self-evident, it needed no explanation and rarely got one. As Voltaire wrote in 1765 in his *Questions sur les miracles*, 'Qu'est-ce en effet que d'être libres? C'est raisonner juste, c'est connaître les droits de l'homme; & quand on les connaît bien, on les défend de même.'[2] How it is one knew them is never specified by Voltaire beyond the cryptic reference to just reasoning.

Voltaire was not thinking of the transformation of government when he wrote those words in 1765, but the Americans of 1776 and the French of 1789 were. Their Declarations therefore included three claims of self-evidence: the self-evidence of rights, the self-evidence of their universality, and the self-evidence of their foundational political status. These three assertions were inextricably intertwined in the thinking of the men who wrote the Declarations because they had distinct political purposes in mind: to justify rebellion against the British king and parliament in the American case and to legitimize a constitutional revolution in the French case. The universality and foundational nature of rights provided the rationale for changing the basis of governmental legitimacy. The frequent appeals by the colonists to their historic rights as British subjects could not validate a complete rupture from

---

[2] Voltaire, *Oeuvres completes de Voltaire*, vol. 46 (la Société littéraire-typographique 1784–89) 453.

Britain; they needed something more sweeping to accomplish that end. Not surprisingly, then, they increasingly utilized the language of natural rights between 1772 and 1776.[3] Similarly, the deputies to the National Assembly in France could not explain their institution of a constitutional monarchy by reference to the traditional rights of French subjects, since French tradition included no right of the nation to institute anything on its own. The expanding use of the language of *les droits de l'homme* from the 1760s onwards and especially in the 1780s gave the deputies of 1789 an effective platform to claim the right of institution.

Something less palpable but at least as momentous was also at stake: a shift away from a religious framework towards a secular one. The specific references to 'their Creator' in 1776 and to 'the presence' and 'auspices of the Supreme Being' in 1789 actually confirm this transformation rather than contradicting it. According to the American Declaration, the Creator endowed humans with certain rights but those rights are discoverable by humans and not revealed by a Judeo-Christian God. Religion has no required role. The French Declaration is made 'in the presence and under the auspices of the Supreme Being', but the Supreme Being is not cited as the fount of rights and the Catholic Church is not mentioned in the Declaration. The notion of self-evidence is so crucial because it enables the displacement away from the divine toward the human. Self-evidence is the human replacement for God-given truths; it could operate even without a God. One of the earliest French translations of the American Declaration rendered self-evident truths as 'des vérités évidentes par elle-mêmes'.[4] They were truths that required no transcendental support. Self-evidence is the secular grounding for the equality of rights of all humans.

This notion of self-evidence can be traced back to John Locke. In his widely influential *Essay Concerning Human Understanding* (1690) Locke argued vociferously against innate ideas while readily admitting the existence of self-evident truths. He explained:

This cannot be deny'd [sic], that Men grow first acquainted with many of these Self evident Truths, upon their being proposed: But it is clear, that whosoever does so, finds in himself, That he then begins to know a Proposition, which he knew not before; and which from thenceforth he never questions; not because it was Innate; but because the consideration of the Nature of the things contained in those Words, would not suffer him to think otherwise, how, or whensoever, he is brought to reflect on them.[5]

Locke insists that people find in themselves the truth of these propositions and that these truths are available to any reasoning being. Even though Locke had

---

[3] Richard D Brown, *Self-Evident Truths: Contesting Equal Rights from the Revolution to the Civil War* (Yale University Press 2017) especially 3.
[4] *Affaires de l'Angleterre et de l'Amerique*, vol. II (np 1776) 89.
[5] John Locke, *An Essay Concerning Human Understanding*, vol. I (7th edn, J Churchill 1715–16) 23.

rather narrow propositions in mind (of the variety 2 + 2 = 4), he made it possible for eighteenth-century philosophers and political writers to push the notion of self-evidence further.[6] Voltaire, for example, linked 'raisonner juste' to knowing the rights of man.

Although many critics of such views feared their potential for godlessness, it is clear from the Declarations that atheism is not at issue. God exists, the Creator may even have played a vital role, and human rights simply operate in a separate realm. In one of many eighteenth-century educational tracts influenced either directly or indirectly by Locke, the French lawyer Guillaume Grivel made the connection to rights of man in 1775: 'Tels sont les premiers droits de l'homme, institués par l'Être suprême et consignés dans le grand livre de la Nature, auquel il faut toujours avoir recours pour trouver les principes de toute loi et de toute justice.'[7] The Supreme Being institutes, but people must continually refer to the book of nature in order to grasp the principles that arise from those rights. Grivel himself took these principles very much to heart; he tried to present himself as a candidate for deputy from Paris to the Legislative Assembly in 1791, but he was not selected.[8]

Locke was one of Jefferson's favourite philosophical sources but Jefferson was not the author of the key phrase about self-evidence in the Declaration of Independence; Benjamin Franklin took Jefferson's draft with its reference to 'sacred and undeniable' truths and changed it to 'self-evident'.[9] Since neither Franklin nor Jefferson wrote down exactly what they had in mind at this time, it is impossible to be certain whether Locke, David Hume, Thomas Reid, or someone else had the most influence on those who framed the American Declaration. The men who drafted the French Declaration were even less forthcoming since it was the product of sub-committees and committees and extensive deliberations over the wording of many clauses. Even if it were possible to pin down the origin of the wording, it would still prove next to impossible to trace the precise philosophical influences being expressed. In the end, however, the more pertinent question is why the notion of self-evident universal rights with foundational political status was persuasive to people at the time. We can be fairly certain that conviction did not follow automatically because the notion of universal rights had a Lockean, Humean, Voltairian, or Rousseauian pedigree.[10]

---

[6] The literature on Locke and eighteenth-century philosophical influences on the American and French founding fathers is much too immense to treat here. See, e.g., Robert Curry, *Common Sense Nation: Unlocking the Forgotten Power of the American Idea* (Encounter Books 2015).
[7] M [Guillaume] Grivel, *Théorie de L'Education* (chez Moutard 1775) 43. Grivel cites Locke eight times.
[8] Étienne Charavay (ed.), *Assemblée électorale de Paris, 26 août 1791–12 août 1792* (Cerf 1894) 140.
[9] Walter Isaacson, *Benjamin Franklin: An American Life* (Simon and Schuster 2003) 338.
[10] Rousseau used the term *droits de l'homme* once in *The Social Contract* (first published 1762) but never showed much interest in developing it.

II. THE CULTURAL LEARNING IMPLIED BY SELF-EVIDENT UNIVERSAL HUMAN RIGHTS

In *Inventing Human Rights* (2007), I argued that human rights rely on more than legal, philosophical, or political articulation, as important as these may be. Universal human rights have to resonate with a broader public. How could peasants—or slaves—be imagined as equal to aristocrats, so evidently different in social status? Crucial to this imagined equality was the emergence of new behaviours in the second half of the eighteenth century that established the potential psychic likeness of autonomous individuals. The counterintuitive belief in human equality was made possible by a wide range of intellectual, cultural, and social developments: changing family practices (growing emphasis on individual choice in marriage), the individuation of domestic and public space (bedrooms, sleeping in bed alone, listening to music in silence), writings about the education of children that underlined their potential for good, the loosening of the bonds of deference, the growing importance of portraiture, and the newly popular genre of novels that taught readers to empathize across social class barriers. Eighteenth-century people began to view individuals, even those very different from themselves, as potentially autonomous and as psychologically similar in their aspirations. The learning process did not touch everyone, not even all readers of novels or viewers of portraits, but the new perspective on personhood helped to inspire the imagination of equality.[11]

Some of these practices had longer-term histories; others had shorter-term ones. The novel, for instance, took off as a cultural form after 1740 and especially in the last decades of the eighteenth century in both the Anglophone and Francophone worlds. One hundred novels appeared in English in 1799, as compared to one in 1701.[12] The numbers are very similar for France.[13] The language of human rights took shape at about the same time. With the literary databases available at the time, I traced the emergence of the French term *droits de l'homme* to the early 1760s. Further developments in digitizing texts in just the last few years have made a more complete picture available. In French *droits naturels* was used more frequently until the mid-1780s when *droits de l'homme* overtook it (see Figure 1.1). *Droits humains* had virtually no currency.[14]

---

[11] Hunt, *Inventing Human Rights* (n 1).
[12] J Alan Downie (ed.), *The Oxford Handbook of the Eighteenth-Century Novel* (Oxford University Press 2016) xvii–xviii.
[13] Lynn Hunt, *Family Romance of the French Revolution* (University of California Press 1992) 22.
[14] For a different approach see Peter de Bolla, *The Architecture of Concepts: The Historical Formation of Human Rights* (Fordham University Press 2013). De Bolla only discusses the Anglophone side of this question and does not use n-grams (not that n-grams are immune from criticism, but they at least provide frequencies rather than just raw data).

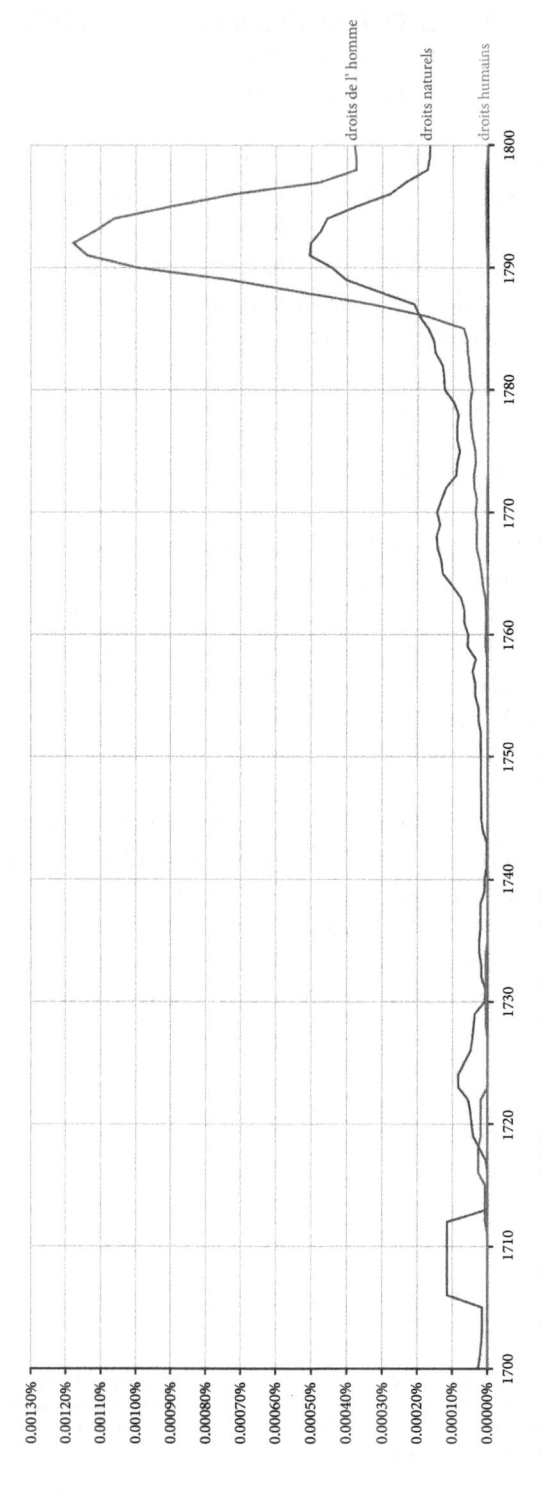

Figure 1.1 Google n-gram of *droits naturels*, *droits de l'homme*, and *droits humains* in French, 1700–1800.
Source: <http://books.google.com/ngrams> accessed 31 January 2019.

The evolution in English is not exactly the same since 'natural rights' had a longer history in English of use in political settings (see Figure 1.2). 'Natural rights' was the preferred term in English until the French Revolution when 'rights of man' overtook it, even though the phrase rights of man was a direct translation from the French. 'Human rights' barely makes a mark.

My aim is not to suggest some kind of direct correlation between the number of novels and the language of human rights, even though at least one contemporary French commentator attributed the rise of the language of *droits de l'homme* directly to Rousseau, who was the best-selling French novelist of the eighteenth century and also one of the first to use the term *droits de l'homme* (in 1762 in his *Social Contract*).[15] Novels, because they are more readily quantifiable than most cultural practices, stand in for a variety of interconnected cultural changes that promoted a sense of the individuation of bodies and psychic similarity of minds. These transformations provided a receptive matrix for the germination of notions of human rights but they cannot account for the stunning rise of *droits de l'homme* in the late 1780s. Only constitutional crisis can account for that.

Droits de l'homme began increasing in usage after 1785 and soon outdistanced both *droits naturels* and *droits de l'humanité* (Figure 1.3).

It is impossible to say with certainty why these choices were made. A closer study of the texts using these terms suggests that *droits naturels* could be used in a religious context; they were contrasted to divine rights, they could be possessed by towns, and in an anti-deist tract, they were attributed to divine revelation.[16] *Droits naturels* therefore had too much religious baggage in French; moreover, as much as natural rights language might have influenced the British North American colonists, the term 'natural rights' does not appear as such in the Declaration of Independence, the US Constitution, the Bill of Rights, or the Virginia Declaration of Rights of 1776, so the French translations of these documents would not have circulated *droits naturels* in a more explicitly secular and political context.

Droits de l'humanité seems to have been quite promising as an alternative but closer attention to specific uses indicates that it lacked the political punch of *droits de l'homme*. When arguing for the rights of Protestants in 1784, for example, the Calvinist minister and future deputy Jean-Paul Rabaut Saint-Étienne affirmed that 'les droits de l'humanité sont respectables, même dans les Cannibales', but he distinguished between these more general rights to humane treatment and the rights

---

[15] In discussing a recent play on stage in 1763, an underground newsletter opined, 'Il y a un rôle de sauvage qui pourrait être très beau: il débite en vers tout ce que nous avons lu épars sur les rois, sur la liberté, sur les droits de l'homme, dans le *Discours sur l'Inégalité des conditions*, dans *Émile*, dans le *Contrat social*.' In PL Jacob [pseud.] (ed.), *Mémoires secrets de Bachaumont* (Adolphe Delahays 1869) 76.

[16] See, e.g., Abbé Regnaud, *Traité de la foi des simples: dans lequel on fait une analyse de cette foi …* (np 1770) 80, who introduces one chapter in these terms: 'La révélation présente un corps de lumière qui met l'homme en possession de ses droits naturels & primitifs. On explique à cette occasion le mot naturel, & l'abus qu'en font les Déistes.'

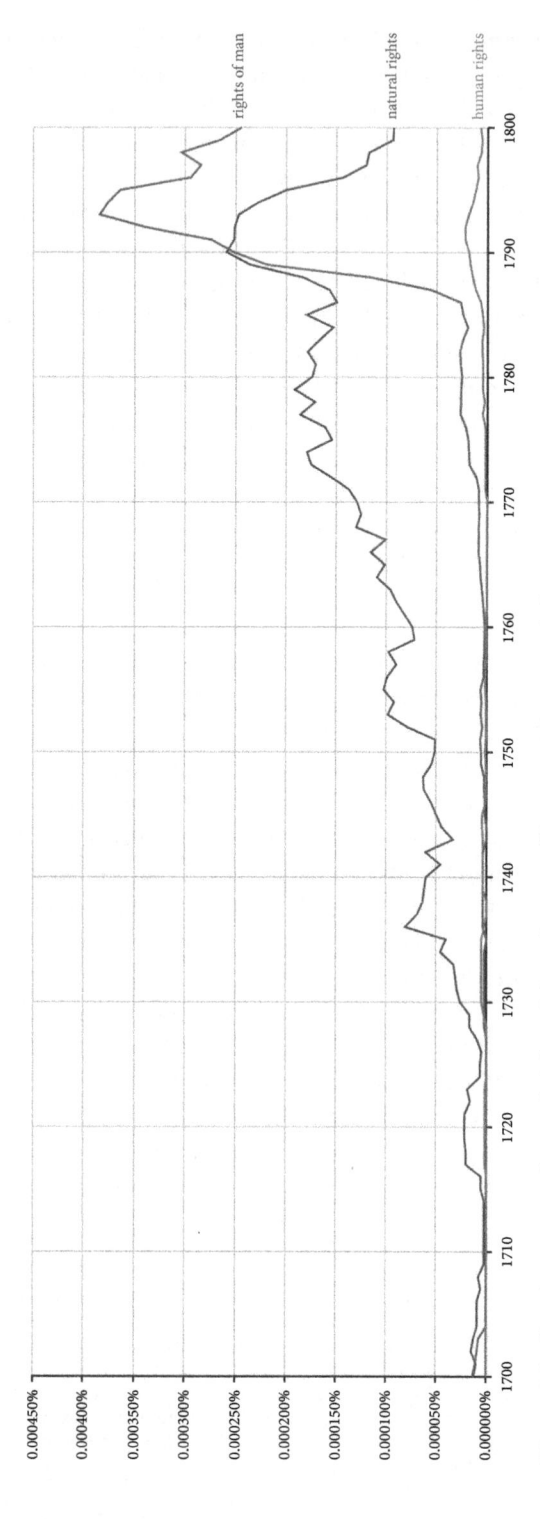

Figure 1.2 Google n-gram of natural rights, rights of man, and human rights in English, 1700–1800.
Source: <http://books.google.com/ngrams> accessed 31 January 2019.

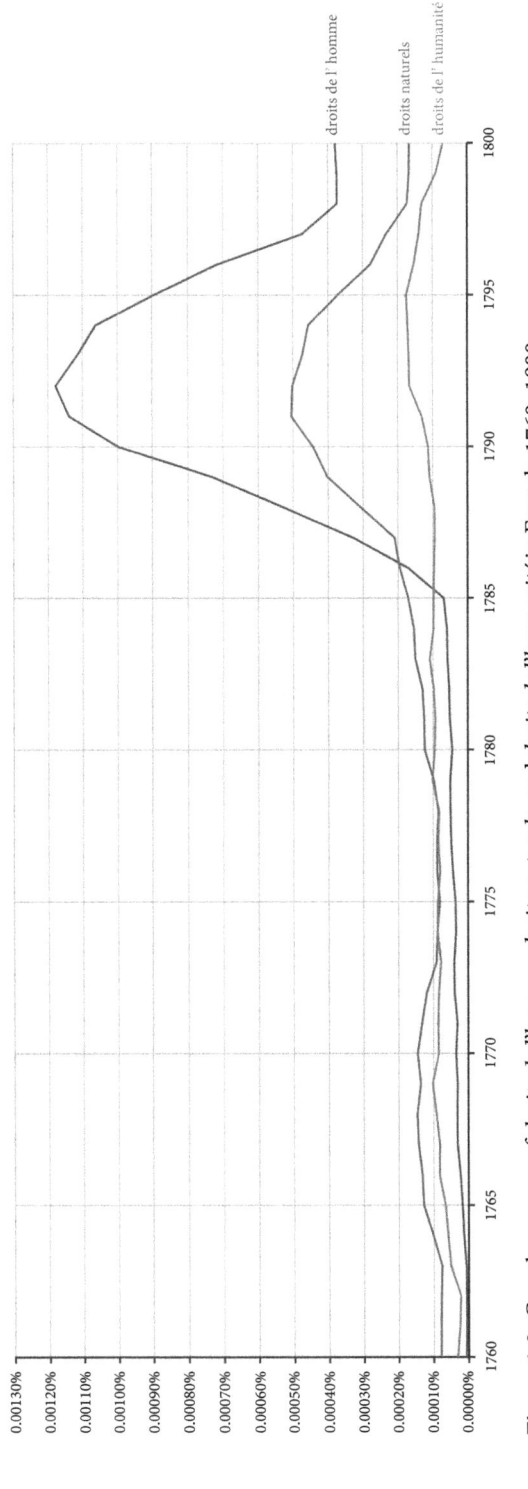

Figure 1.3 Google n-gram of *droits de l'homme*, *droits naturels*, and *droits de l'humanité* in French, 1760–1800.

Source: <http://books.google.com/ngrams> accessed 31 January 2019.

of citizens.[17] The grievance lists submitted to the Estates General in 1789 included more than twice as many references to *droits de l'homme* as *droits de l'humanité*, and as far as I can determine, hardly anyone ever referred to a declaration of the *droits de l'humanité*.[18] When Robespierre used the phrase in his newspaper in autumn of 1792, he was arguing against going too far too fast in opposing the Catholic Church: 'si la déclaration des droits de l'humanité était déchirée par la tyrannie, nous la retrouverions encore dans ce code religieux que le despotisme sacerdotal présentait à notre vénération'.[19] Even for Robespierre, the *droits de l'humanité* could be found in Catholic doctrine. This is not to deny, however, that 'les droits les plus sacrés de l'humanité' could serve on occasion, for Robespierre and for others, as a synonym for 'les droits de l'homme' along with 'les droits des hommes', 'le droit de l'homme', etc.[20] The Declaration itself crystallized the utilization of 'les droits de l'homme' for future generations.

As these brief chronologies of the terms show, political and constitutional crisis played a critical role in galvanizing interest in declarations of universal rights and precipitating out a language for their expression. The limitations implicit in the notions of an autonomous individual and psychic equality, and therefore in the universalism of eighteenth-century articulations of human rights declarations, only became apparent over time. The political debate provoked by the process of writing constitutions and defining the rules of citizenship brought some of them into view relatively quickly. Yet others became more evident during the security crises prompted by civil and foreign wars in the 1790s.

III. LIMITATIONS

The most obvious practical limitations followed from the notion of autonomy. 'All men are created equal' meant that all humans are born with the capacity for reason and therefore independent decision-making. Yet no one in the eighteenth century (or now) concluded that everyone enjoyed equal powers of independent decision-making: children below the age of majority, virtually all women, slaves, and servants were generally viewed, and not just by men, as lacking in such capacities.

---

[17] Jean-Paul Rabaut Saint-Étienne, *Le Roi doit modifier les loix portées contre les protestants: Démonstration* (np 1784) 25.

[18] I base this on results available from searches at the French Revolution Digital Archive <https://frda.stanford.edu/en> accessed 31 January 2019.

[19] As quoted in Philippe-Joseph-Benjamin Buchez and Pierre-Célestin Roux-Lavergne, *Histoire parlementaire de la Révolution française, ou Journal des assemblées nationales depuis 1789 jusqu'en 1815: contenant la narration des événements ... précédée d'une introduction sur l'histoire de France jusqu'à la convocation des États-Généraux*, vol. 20 (Paulin 1834–38) 452.

[20] See, e.g., Robespierre's speech of 10 May 1791 in Jérôme Madival, Émile Laurent et al. (eds), *Archives parlementaires de 1789 à 1860: recueil complet des débats législatifs & politiques des Chambres françaises*, vol. 25 (Librairie administrative de P Dupont 1862) 692 (hereafter Madival and Laurent, *Archives parlementaires*).

The debates about the political rights of men without property, the rights of slaves, the age of majority, and even the rights of women show that the boundaries of autonomy were (and are) susceptible to change. John Adams explained his defence of property requirements in a letter to James Sullivan written in May 1776:

> Depend upon it, Sir, it is dangerous to open so fruitful a source of controversy and altercation; as would be opened by attempting to alter the qualifications of voters. There will be no end of it. New claims will arise. Women will demand a vote. Lads from 12 to 21 will think their rights not enough attended to, and every man, who has not a farthing, will demand an equal voice with any other in all acts of state. It tends to confound and destroy all distinctions, and prostrate all ranks to one common level.[21]

Adams clearly grasped the potential link between political rights and equality, and wanted to hold the line, but he also understood the workings of the logic of autonomy, especially as it pertained to women and children:

> The same reasoning which will induce you to admit all men who have no property, to vote, with those who have, for those laws which affect the person, will prove that you ought to admit women and children; for generally speaking, women and children have as good judgements, and as independent minds, as those men who are wholly destitute of property; these last being to all intents and purposes as much dependent upon others, who will please to feed, clothe, and employ them, as women are upon their husbands, or children on their parents.[22]

In other words, eighteenth-century men had to work very hard at simultaneously demanding rights and universal equality while also maintaining insurmountable barriers that could keep out children, women, slaves, servants, and men without property. Most of those impediments have crumbled over the succeeding centuries, but children are still excluded, even though the boundary between childhood and voting age has shifted. In the United States the age of voting was lowered from twenty-one to eighteen years old by the 26th amendment to the US Constitution ratified in 1971. All but two US states prohibit felons from voting while they are in prison; the boundaries of citizenship are therefore still in question.

The most difficult dilemmas created by the universalizing move concerned citizenship, which is always linked to a particular state entity. Here the French case is especially pertinent because the rights of political participation were defined by the national government; in the United States they were and remain the province

---

[21] John Adams and Charles Francis Adams, *The Works of John Adams, Second President of the United States: With a Life of the Author, Notes and Illustrations*, vol. IX (Little, Brown 1850–56) 378.
[22] Ibid, 377.

of the state governments and consequently can vary greatly. The title of the French Declaration of the Rights of Man and Citizen makes clear that the rights of man are not exactly the same as those of the citizen but also suggests that they are related. A fundamental ambiguity therefore runs through the French Declaration; sometimes 'citizens' refers to both men and women but other times it clearly refers to just men. For example, Article 6 affirms, 'Tous les Citoyens étant égaux à ses yeux [la loi] sont également admissibles à toutes dignités, places et emplois publics, selon leur capacité, et sans autre distinction que celle de leurs vertus et de leurs talents.' The deputies seem to have intended that women be citizens in the sense of being covered and protected by the law but they clearly did not intend for them to hold public office, no matter their talents. Still, when Article 7 proclaims, 'Nul homme ne peut être accusé, arrêté ni détenu que dans les cas déterminés par la Loi, et selon les formes qu'elle a prescrites', women seem to be included under the rubric 'nul homme'; similarly, under Article 9, 'Tout homme étant présumé innocent jusqu'à ce qu'il ait été déclaré coupable', 'tout homme' seems to include women as well. But the Declaration says nothing specifically about women or any other specific category. It aims for the most consistently universal formulations.

The deputies consequently chose to remain silent on the question of the citizenship of religious minorities, affirming only in Article 10 that 'Nul ne doit être inquiété pour ses opinions, même religieuses, pourvu que leur manifestation ne trouble pas l'ordre public établi par la Loi'. Once again the universalizing negative—in this case 'nul ne' [nobody]—seemed to exclude no one, and Protestants and Jews immediately seized upon the article to insist upon their rights to full participation. Those who argued against citizenship for the Jews produced an argument that would weigh heavily in the future; abbé Jean Maury insisted on 23 December 1789 that 'le mot juif n'est pas le nom d'une secte, mais d'une nation qui a des lois, qui les a toujours suivies et qui veut encore les suivre. Appeler les juifs des citoyens, ce serait comme si l'on disait que, sans lettres de naturalisation et sans cesser d'être Anglais et Danois, les Anglais et les Danois pourraient devenir Français'.[23] In this view, the Jews constituted a separate nation and therefore could not be considered French.

Even those in favour of Jewish emancipation emphasized that the Jews must give up their status as a separate nation and become citizens as individuals, not members of a distinct community. In September 1791, the deputies finally granted citizenship to the Jews on the condition that each individual swear the civic oath, 'qui sera regardé comme une renonciation à tous privilèges & exceptions introduits précédemment en leur faveur'.[24] Rights governed the individual's relationship

---

[23] Madival and Laurent, *Archives parlementaires* (n. 20) vol. 10, 756–7.

[24] Décret qui révoque tous ajournemens, réserves & exceptions insérés dans les Décrets, relativement aux individus Juifs qui prêteront le serment civique [27 September 1791] Collection générale des décrets rendus par l'Assemblée Nationale <http://artflsrv02.uchicago.edu/cgi-bin/philologic/getobject.pl?c.18:117.baudouin0314> accessed 31 January 2019.

with the state; citizenship could not include an intermediary community identity because it would stand in the way of the individual's bond with the nation. The autonomous individual had to remain autonomous and not connected to a community that would stand between him/her and the state. The current French debates over the Muslim headscarf are still working for and against this same understanding of the individual's relationship to the nation.

Universalism thus worked, ironically, to strengthen national feeling. The individual could only enjoy his or her supposedly universal rights by becoming unambiguously French. With the advent of nearly constant war after 1792, the potentially nefarious underside of universalism became all the more apparent. The revolutionaries believed they could bring the gospel of liberty and equality to all peoples but they were not very impressed with the readiness of others to embrace the message. The Prussian nobleman, Anacharsis Cloots, who styled himself 'l'orateur du genre humain', gave voice to the universalist message four months before war was even declared. On 1 January 1792, speaking to the Jacobin Club in Paris, he intoned,

> Or, maintenant que la france [sic] possède la plus belle constitution de l'univers, il ne reste aux peoples opprimés & ignorants, qu'à secouer brusquement le joug pour s'assurer un Bonheur durable, sous la direction des législateurs français. Depuis qu'une vaste & puissante monarchie est libre, il ne faut qu'un Spartacus, un Ziska, un Muncer, un Horia, un Pugats-chef, pour délivrer à jamais l'Italie, la Bohême, l'Allemagne, la Hongrie, la Moscovie.[25]

All of Europe could now become free but only if it followed the French lead. The ensuing wars, even under Napoleon, would continue to be justified, at least in part, by this messianic conviction. When he invaded Egypt in 1798, Bonaparte issued a proclamation that was meant to be mollifying: 'Peuple de l'Egypte, on dira que je viens pour détruire votre religion; ne le croyez pas! répondez que je viens vous restituer vos droits, punir les usurpateurs, et que je respecte, plus que les Mamelucks, Dieu, son prophête et l'Alcoran. Dites-leur que tous les hommes sont égaux devant Dieu.'[26] Thus began the long and very vexed history of Western liberators promising to restore rights to peoples oppressed by their rulers. From the beginning of the declaration of war in 1792, the revolutionary deputies had promised 'guerre aux tyrans; paix aux peuples' [war on tyrants; peace for the people], but they came to view those who opposed them as the 'vile henchmen of despotism', 'liberticidal heads', 'oppressors of liberty', 'enemies of equality', 'anarchists', 'fanatics', or finally, 'this horde of slaves', as they were described in the Marseillaise.

---

[25] The speech was reproduced in *Courier français*, no. 18 (18 January 1792) 8.
[26] Louis Antoine Fauvelet de Bourrienne, *Mémoires de M. de Bourrienne sur Napoléon, le directoire, le consulat, l'empire et la restauration*, vol. II (Hoffmann 1829) 39.

This lack of fellow feeling was not reserved exclusively for foreigners fighting against France; those who opposed the French republic at home, especially in the Vendée rebellion of Western France, were similarly vilified and considered deserving of extermination. On 1 August 1793, the spokesman for the Committee of Public Safety, Bertrand Barère, laid out the thinking in no uncertain terms: 'le comité [de salut public], d'après votre autorisation, a préparé des mesures qui tendent à exterminer cette race rebelle, à faire disparaître leurs repaires, à incendier leurs forêts, à couper leurs récoltes'.[27] Psychic likeness lost its power to promote empathy when survival was thought to be at issue; then opponents became utterly unrecognizable, lacking all kinship, and in the end, less than human (as the reference to 'dens' suggested).

In this way, universalism could divide the world into us and them, those who supported liberty and equality (as defined by the French or other Western imperial powers thereafter), and those who refused to embrace them. The deep connection established in the late eighteenth century between the rights of man, political participation, and individual autonomy had long-lasting and not always positive consequences. On the one hand, that connection facilitated the breakthrough to representative, and even to increasingly democratic, government as well as to an ever-widening domain of personal freedoms; as the men without property, servants, slaves, and women began to insist on their capacity for autonomy, they won the right to participate directly in politics through voting and holding office. On the other hand, the secularism that made the connection so powerful—that rights were to be justified by the nature of the autonomous individual rather than by a transcendental framework—set the stage for the conflicts over state authority, community identities, and religion that have hardly diminished over time. Human rights as formulated in the late eighteenth century may not be identical to those in debate today, but the history of their articulation helps us understand the potential pitfalls that lay before us still.

Bibliography

Abbé Regnaud, *Traité de la foi des simples: dans lequel on fait une analyse de cette foi ...* (np 1770)

Adams J and Adams CF, *The Works of John Adams, Second President of the United States: With a Life of the Author, Notes and Illustrations*, vol. IX (Little, Brown 1850–56)

de Bolla P, *The Architecture of Concepts: The Historical Formation of Human Rights* (Fordham University Press 2013)

Brown RD, *Self-Evident Truths: Contesting Equal Rights from the Revolution to the Civil War* (Yale University Press 2017)

---

[27] Madival and Laurent, *Archives parlementaires* (n. 20) vol. 70, 101.

Buchez PJB and Roux-Lavergne PC, *Histoire parlementaire de la Révolution française, ou Journal des assemblées nationales depuis 1789 jusqu'en 1815: contenant la narration des événements ... précédée d'une introduction sur l'histoire de France jusqu'à la convocation des États-Généraux*, vol. 20 (Paulin 1834–38)

Charavay E (ed.), *Assemblée électorale de Paris, 26 août 1791–12 août 1792* (Cerf 1894)

Curry R, *Common Sense Nation: Unlocking the Forgotten Power of the American Idea* (Encounter Books 2015)

Downie JA (ed.), *The Oxford Handbook of the Eighteenth-Century Novel* (Oxford University Press 2016)

Fauvelet de Bourrienne LA, *Mémoires de M. de Bourrienne sur Napoléon, le directoire, le consulat, l'empire et la restauration*, vol. II (Hoffmann 1829)

Grivel MG, *Théorie de L'Education* (chez Moutard 1775)

Hunt L, *Family Romance of the French Revolution* (University of California Press 1992)

Hunt L, *Inventing Human Rights: A History* (Norton 2007)

Isaacson W, *Benjamin Franklin: An American Life* (Simon and Schuster 2004)

Jacob PL [pseud.] (ed.), *Mémoires secrets de Bachaumont* (Adolphe Delahays 1869)

Locke J, *An Essay Concerning Human Understanding*, vol. I (7th edn, J Churchill 1715–16)

Madival J, Laurent É, et al. (eds), *Archives parlementaires de 1789 à 1860: recueil complet des débats législatifs & politiques des Chambres françaises*, vol. 25 (Librairie administrative de P Dupont 1862)

Rabaut Saint-Étienne JP, *Le Roi doit modifier les loix portées contre les protestants: Démonstration* (np 1784)

Voltaire, *Oeuvres completes de Voltaire*, vol. 46 (la Société littéraire-typographique 1784–89)

2
The Self-Evidence of Human Rights
Origins and Limits of an Idea

Bardo Fassbender

We hold these truths to be self-evident, that all men are created equal, that they are endowed by their Creator with certain unalienable Rights, that among these are Life, Liberty and the pursuit of Happiness.
The Declaration of Independence, 4 July 1776

all eyes are opened, or opening to the rights of man.
Thomas Jefferson, 24 June 1826[1]

It is a pleasure to comment on Lynn Hunt's vivid reconsideration of a truly crucial moment in the history of human rights when in North America and in France for the first time a 'self-evidence' of certain rights of 'all men' was claimed in constitutional discourse and documents, and a fundamental shift occurred in the explanation of human rights 'from a religious framework toward a secular one': 'Self-evidence is the human replacement for God-given truths.'[2]

Drawing on her widely acclaimed and influential book *Inventing Human Rights*, of 2007,[3] and using new data gathered by n-gram analysis, Professor Hunt first leads us back to the British colonies in North America on the verge of their separation from Great Britain, to revolutionary France, and to the writings of John Locke in which the notion of 'self evident truths' played an important role. She next puts the question 'why the notion of self-evident universal rights with foundational political status was persuasive to people at the time',[4] finding some of the answers in the language of human rights as it appeared in eighteenth-century novels and newspapers in the Anglophone and Francophone worlds. In the last section of her

---

[1] Thomas Jefferson, Letter to the Mayor of Washington, D.C., Roger C. Weightman, 24 June 1826, in *The Papers of Thomas Jefferson* <http://founders.archives.gov/documents/Jefferson/98-01-02-6179> accessed 31 January 2019. Jefferson died on 4 July 1826.
[2] See Lynn Hunt, 'Humanity and the Claim to Self-Evidence', ch. 1 in this volume, 41 (hereafter Hunt, 'Self-Evidence').
[3] See Lynn Hunt, *Inventing Human Rights: A History* (WW Norton & Co. 2007) (hereafter Hunt, *Inventing Human Rights*). A paperback edition was published in 2008.
[4] See Hunt, 'Self-Evidence' (n. 2) 42.

Bardo Fassbender, *The Self-Evidence of Human Rights* In: *The Limits of Human Rights*. Edited by: Bardo Fassbender and Knut Traisbach, Oxford University Press 2019. © The Several Contributors.
DOI: 10.1093/oso/9780198824756.003.0004

chapter, Lynn Hunt addresses the limitations of the enjoyment of civil and political rights in the colonies and the independent United States as well as in post-revolutionary France—limitations which often amounted to a complete exclusion of rights, and which applied to a majority of the population: 'Eighteenth-century men had to work very hard at simultaneously demanding rights and universal equality while also maintaining insurmountable barriers that could keep out children, women, slaves, servants, and men without property.'[5]

Having read Lynn Hunt's fascinating account of the events and debates in North America and France, I wanted to know more about how exactly the notion of 'self-evident truths', so central to Professor Hunt's line of reasoning, found its way into the Declaration of Independence of 1776. Was it Benjamin Franklin's idea,[6] or rather introduced by Jefferson himself in the course of drafting the Declaration? What does it mean, and why does it matter, that Jefferson's original expression 'sacred & undeniable' was replaced with 'self-evident'? Accordingly, the first part of my present comments (which focus on North America) is devoted to the Declaration's drafting history and to the meaning and importance of the claim to 'self-evidence' in the Declaration of Independence. In a much briefer second part, I then return to Lynn Hunt's analysis of the 'limitations' of the actual enjoyment of rights in eighteenth-century North America and France, adding a few remarks regarding the treatment of the 'Indians' and of the slave trade in the Declaration. The third and last part of my comments deals with the importance, or rather unimportance, of the notion of the self-evidence of human rights in the present age. I argue that, against the expectations of his time, Jefferson's idea of self-evidence failed to find general recognition, so that we must search for a new credible foundation of universal human rights.

I. THE ORIGINS OF SELF-EVIDENCE

On 7 June 1776, Richard Henry Lee, in accordance with instructions from the Virginia Convention, proposed to the Continental Congress in Philadelphia to adopt a resolution 'That these United Colonies are, and of right ought to be, free and independent States, that they are absolved from all allegiance to the British Crown, and that all political connection between them and the State of Great Britain is, and ought to be, totally dissolved.'[7] On 11 June, consideration of the Lee Resolution was postponed, and Congress recessed for three weeks. Before receding, and expecting

---

[5] Ibid, 49.

[6] Ibid, 42 (referring to Walter Isaacson, see n. 22).

[7] For this and the following, see 'The Declaration of Independence: A History' (no author given) <http://www.archives.gov/founding-docs/declaration-history> accessed 31 January 2019. See also Julian P Boyd, *The Declaration of Independence: The Evolution of the Text as Shown in Facsimiles of Various Drafts by its Author, Thomas Jefferson* (Princeton University Press 1945) 7–16 (hereafter Boyd, *Declaration*); Pauline Maier, *American Scripture: Making the Declaration of Independence* (Alfred A Knopf 1997), ch. III: Mr. Jefferson and His Editors, 97–153 (hereafter Maier, *American Scripture*); Gerard W Gawalt, 'Drafting the Declaration' in Scott Douglas Gerber (ed.), *The Declaration of Independence: Origins and Impact* (CQ Press 2002) 1.

an adoption of the resolution after the break, Congress appointed a Committee of Five to draft a statement that would present to the world the colonies' case for independence. The committee consisted of John Adams, Roger Sherman, Benjamin Franklin, Robert R Livingston, and Thomas Jefferson. In 1823, Jefferson remembered that the other members of the committee 'unanimously pressed on myself alone to undertake the draught. I consented; I drew it; but before I reported it to the committee I communicated it separately to Dr. Franklin and Mr. Adams requesting their corrections.... I then wrote a fair copy, reported it to the committee, and from them, unaltered to the Congress.' Jefferson's account reflects three stages in the making of the Declaration: the original document written by Jefferson; the changes made to that document by Franklin and Adams, resulting in the version submitted by the Committee of Five to the Congress on 28 June; and the version that was eventually adopted by Congress on 4 July 1776.

The Declaration consists of five distinct parts: an introduction; a preamble; a body, which can be divided into two sections (the indictment of King George III, and the denunciation of the British people); and a conclusion. The statement we are concerned with here opens the preamble which 'outlines a general philosophy of government that makes revolution justifiable, even meritorious'.[8]

When drafting the Declaration's preamble, Thomas Jefferson very likely was aware of two very recent documents, namely George Mason's draft of the Virginia Bill of Rights (of ca. 20–26 May 1776, published on 6 June 1776), and the Virginia Declaration of Rights, adopted on 12 June 1776. The pertinent part of Mason's draft reads as follows:

> A Declaration of Rights, made by the Representatives of the good People of Virginia, assembled in full Convention; and recommended to Posterity as the Basis and Foundation of their Government
>
> That all men are born equally free and independent, and have certain inherent natural Rights, of which they can not, by any compact, deprive or divest their Posterity; among which are the Enjoyment of Life and Liberty, with the Means of acquiring and possessing Property, and pursuing and obtaining Happiness and Safety.
>
> That Power is, by God and Nature, vested in, and consequently derived from the People, that Magistrates are their Trustees and Servants, and at all times amenable to them.[9]

With few changes, that draft was adopted on 12 June 1776 by the fifth Virginia Convention at Williamsburg as the Virginia Declaration of Rights, the title and first two sections of which have the following wording:

---

[8] See Stephen E Lucas, 'The Stylistic Artistry of the Declaration of Independence' <http://www.archives.gov/founding-docs/stylistic-artistry-of-the-declaration> accessed 31 January 2019 (hereafter Lucas, 'Stylistic Artistry').

[9] Boyd, *Declaration* (n. 7) Doc. I (facsimile), also available at <http://www.gunstonhall.org/georgemason/human_rights/vdr_first_draft.html> accessed 31 January 2019.

A DECLARATION OF RIGHTS made by the Representatives of the good people of VIRGINIA, assembled in full and free Convention; which rights do pertain to them and their posterity, as the basis and foundation of Government.

1. That all men are by nature equally free and independent, and have certain inherent rights, of which, when they enter into a state of society, they cannot, by any compact, deprive or divest their posterity; namely, the enjoyment of life and liberty, with the means of acquiring and possessing property, and pursuing and obtaining happiness and safety.
2. That all power is vested in, and consequently derived from, the people; that magistrates are their trustees and servants, and at all times amenable to them.[10]

Neither text contains a reference to 'self-evident truths', and instead of the later Declaration's phrase 'certain unalienable Rights', use the expressions 'certain inherent natural Rights' and 'certain inherent rights', respectively. According to Julian Boyd, the similarity of the texts is a similarity of ideas: 'Jefferson and Mason were both dealing with the concept of natural, inherent rights and on this subject both appealed, as all men of the day did, to Locke and other exponents of the idea of the social compact, the inviolability of rights, the trusteeship nature of government, and the right of revolution.'[11] Jefferson himself later emphasized that it was the object of the Declaration '[n]ot to find out new principles, or new arguments never before thought of ... but to place before mankind the common sense of the subject, in terms so plain and firm as to command their assent'.[12]

Jefferson's so-called 'Rough Draft' of the Declaration, which has survived in his Papers in the Library of Congress, represents the text as Jefferson submitted it to the other members of the Committee of Five, together with all corrections, additions, and deletions made by the Committee, and by the Congress,[13] that way serving Jefferson as a complete record of the drafting process. Very likely, the 'Rough Draft' was preceded by earlier compositions.[14]

According to the 'Rough Draft', Jefferson first wrote: 'We hold these truths to be sacred & undeniable.' In the draft, the words 'sacred & undeniable' are crossed out, and 'self-evident' is written in above the line:

> We hold these truths to be sacred & undeniable; self-evident; that all men are created equal & independant; that from that equal creation they derive rights some-

---

[10] For the full text, see <http://www.gunstonhall.org/georgemason/human_rights/vdr_final.html> accessed 31 January 2019; see also James Madison, 'Notes of the Virginia Convention, May–June, 1776' in Library of Congress, *James Madison Papers* <https://www.loc.gov/exhibits/creating-the-united-states/battle-joined.html#obj15> accessed 31 January 2019.
[11] Boyd, *Declaration* (n. 7) 15.
[12] Thomas Jefferson, Letter to Henry Lee, 8 May 1825, quoted in David Armitage, *The Declaration of Independence: A Global History* (Harvard University Press 2007) 21 (hereafter Armitage, *Declaration*).
[13] Boyd, *Declaration* (n. 7) 40.
[14] Ibid, 25–7.

of which are they are endowed by their creator with certain [inherent &] inalienable rights; that among which these are the preservation of life, & liberty, & the pursuit of happiness; that to secure these ends rights, governments are instituted among men, deriving their just powers from the consent of the governed; that whenever any form of government shall becomes destructive of these ends, it is the right of the people to alter or to abolish it, & to institute new government, laying it's foundation on such principles & organising it's powers in such form, as to them shall seem most likely to effect their safety & happiness.[15]

In his seminal book about the Declaration of Independence, the historian Carl Becker asked: 'Was this correction [the replacement of 'sacred & undeniable' with 'self-evident'] made by Jefferson in process of composition? Or by the Committee of Five? Or by Congress? There is nothing in the Rough Draft itself to tell us.'[16]

In Boyd's reconstruction, the 'original rough draft', as he called it, had approximately the following wording when it was submitted by Jefferson to Franklin and Adams:

We hold these truths to be sacred & undeniable; that all men are created equal & independant, that from that equal creation they derive rights inherent & inalienable, among which are the preservation of life, & liberty, & the pursuit of happiness; that to secure these ends, governments are instituted among men, deriving their just powers from the consent of the governed; that whenever any form of government shall become destructive of these ends, it is the right of the people to alter or to abolish it, & to institute new government, laying it's foundation on such principles & organizing it's power in such form, as to them shall seem most likely to effect their safety & happiness.[17]

In an early copy of the draft, made by John Adams sometime between 11 and 21 June 1776,[18] the expression 'self evident' is already there:

We hold these Truths to be self evident; that all Men are created equal and independent; that from that equal Creation they derive Rights inherent and unalienable; among which are the Preservation of Life, and Liberty, and the Pursuit of Happiness; ...[19]

---

[15] Ibid, Doc. V (facsimile of the original kept in the Library of Congress).
[16] Carl Becker, *The Declaration of Independence: A Study in the History of Political Ideas* (2nd edn, Alfred A Knopf 1942) 140 (hereafter Becker, *Declaration*).
[17] See Boyd, *Declaration* (n. 7) 19; Julian P Boyd (ed.), *The Papers of Thomas Jefferson*, vol. 1, 1760–76 (Princeton University Press 1950) 423–8 <https://founders.archives.gov> accessed 31 January 2019. See also Becker, *Declaration* (n. 16) 141, 142: 'The Rough Draft, as it probably read when Jefferson first submitted it to Franklin'.
[18] See Boyd, *Declaration* (n. 7) 40.
[19] Ibid, Doc. IV (facsimile).

Boyd wrote about the replacement of 'sacred & undeniable' with 'self-evident': 'This famous and altogether felicitous change has been attributed both to Franklin and to Jefferson. Such feeling as it exhibits for precisely the right word is quite Franklinian in character, but the handwriting in the phrase 'self-evident' bears the appearance of being equally Jeffersonian.... If my interpretation of these alterations is correct, ... then it appears that Franklin had made no changes in the text when Adams made his copy of the Rough Draft'—so that Jefferson, rather than Franklin, is responsible for introducing the term 'self-evident'.[20] As we shall see,[21] the omission of the word 'sacred' gave the entire preamble of the Declaration a secular character, basing the proclaimed rights entirely on reason instead of religion or (a Christian) God's will. The remaining 'undeniable' could easily be replaced with the stronger expression 'self-evident' which was equally familiar to contemporary readers. These arguments support Jefferson's authorship of 'self-evident', which is also assumed by the more recent literature on the Declaration.[22]

Further changes were made before the Committee approved the Declaration and reported it to Congress. By using certain copies made by Jefferson (for Richard Henry Lee, for Madison, and for George Wythe) 'in comparison with the Rough Draft as it stood after Adams had made his copy, it is possible to arrive at the number of changes made before the Declaration went to Congress'.[23] In that stage, the phrase 'from that equal creation they derive rights' was changed to 'they are endowed by their creator with', while the phrase 'equal rights some of which are' was struck out in the process of making the correction, and the words 'rights; that' were inserted between the lines of writing after 'inalienable'.[24]

Finally, Congress, discussing the draft of the Declaration on 3 and 4 July, changed 'inherent &' to 'certain', and 'inalienable' to 'unalienable'.[25] Accordingly, the text in

---

[20] Ibid, 22 and 24. Becker, too, attributes the change to Jefferson; see Becker, *Declaration* (n. 16) 198.
[21] See text accompanying n. 29.
[22] See Michael P Zuckert, 'Self-Evident Truth and the Declaration of Independence' (1987) 49 Review of Politics 319, 328 (hereafter Zuckert, 'Self-Evident Truth'); Allen Jayne, *Jefferson's Declaration of Independence: Origins, Philosophy and Theology* (University Press of Kentucky 1998) 110 (hereafter Jayne, *Jefferson's Declaration*); Maier, *American Scripture* (n. 7) 133, 136 left the question undecided, while Isaacson in his biography of Franklin claimed the latter's authorship: 'He [Franklin] crossed out, using the heavy backslashes that he often employed, the last three words of Jefferson's phrase "We hold these truths to be sacred and undeniable" and changed them to the words now enshrined in history: "We hold these truths to be self-evident".'. See Walter Isaacson, *Benjamin Franklin: An American Life* (Simon & Schuster 2003) 312. However, the same kind of backslashes was used by Jefferson in his copy of *A Summary View of the Rights of British America* (see n. 34) on pp. 7, 8, 12, and 17, so that it cannot be seen as Franklin's peculiarity. In fn. 34 (on p. 547 of his book), meant to verify his quoted statement, Isaacson confuses the 'original rough draft' as reconstructed by Boyd with Jefferson's 'rough draft' preserved in the Library of Congress.
[23] Boyd, *Declaration* (n. 7) 28.
[24] Ibid, 29. See also Becker, *Declaration* (n. 16) 161: 'The Rough Draft as it probably read when Jefferson made the "fair copy" which was presented to Congress as the report of the Committee of Five.'
[25] Boyd, *Declaration* (n. 7) 32. According to Boyd, ibid, the latter change 'may possibly have been made by the printer rather than at the suggestion of Congress.... Both forms were apparently current in the eighteenth century.'

the copy of the adopted Declaration made by Jefferson for Richard Henry Lee (between 4 and 10 July 1776), reads as follows:

> We hold these truths to be self-evident; that all men are created equal; that they are endowed by their Creator with <u>inherent and inalienable</u> rights [on the left margin: certain unalienable rights]; that among these are life, liberty, and the pursuit of happiness; that to secure these rights, governments are instituted among men, deriving their just powers from the consent of the governed; that whenever any form of government becomes destructive of these ends, it is the right of the people to alter or to abolish it, and to institute new government, laying it's foundation on such principles and organising it's powers in such form, as to them shall seem most likely to effect their safety and happiness.[26]

The method of underlining certain words and of placing others in the margin was explained by Jefferson at the beginning of his copy of the Declaration made for James Madison: 'as the sentiments of men are known not only by what they receive, but what they reject also, I will state the form of the declaration as originally reported [by the Committee of Five to Congress]. the parts struck out by Congress shall be distinguished by a black line drawn under them, & those inserted by them shall be placed in the margin or in a concurrent column.'[27]

According to Stephen Lucas, the first half sentence of the Declaration's preamble ('We hold these truths to be self-evident') is the opening sequence of five propositions that build upon one another:

Proposition 1: All men are created equal.
Proposition 2: They (all men) are endowed by their creator with certain unalienable rights.
Proposition 3: Among these rights are life, liberty, and the pursuit of happiness.
Proposition 4: To secure these rights, governments are instituted among men.
Proposition 5: Whenever a form of government becomes destructive of this end (securing man's unalienable rights), it is the right of the people to alter or abolish it.[28]

But is, for that sequence of arguments, the phrase 'We hold these truths to be self-evident' really necessary? Does it add something to the set of propositions? Would

---

[26] Ibid, Doc. VI (facsimile). See also Becker, *Declaration* (n. 16) 174–5, and the copy made by Jefferson for James Madison (sent to Madison on 1 June 1783; Boyd, *Declaration* (n. 7) Doc. VIII [facsimile]): 'We hold these truths to be selfevident [sic]; that all men are created equal; that they are endowed by their Creator with (<u>inherent &</u>) inalienable rights [on the left margin: certain]; that among these are life, liberty, & the pursuit of happiness; ...'.
[27] Boyd, *Declaration* (n. 7) Doc. VIII, 2.
[28] Lucas, 'Stylistic Artistry' (n. 8).

the Declaration's preamble have a different meaning if the phrase was missing, and the preamble would only say, in the style of the Virginia Declaration of Rights:[29] 'All men are created equal, they are endowed by their Creator with certain unalienable Rights' (and so forth)?

Indeed, the 'added value' of the phrase lies in what Lynn Hunt concisely calls the 'claim to self-evidence' of fundamental human rights. 'Self-evident' means 'evident by itself; requiring no proof or explanation; obvious, axiomatic'.[30] The concept of self-evidence allowed the authors of the Declaration to introduce the rights to life, liberty, and the pursuit of happiness as a given, as something which does not need to be explained or deduced from something else, and which does not need a foundation in the form of a specific religious or philosophical belief system.[31] That idea of the indisputable existence of certain human rights would not have been conveyed by Jefferson's original expression 'We hold these truths to be sacred & undeniable',[32] the adjective 'sacred' being too strongly associated with (Christian) religion (as in 'sacred book', 'sacred blood', 'sacred heart', or 'sacred music'). (In the Declaration's introduction, it is true, Jefferson also referred to 'the Laws of Nature and of Nature's God' as providing a right to a 'separate and equal station' of the American people, but that reasoning is not used in the following paragraph as an explanation of the existence of 'certain unalienable Rights'.[33])

Jefferson's secularism—new in comparison with his earlier writings[34]—was nevertheless to some extent diluted by the Committee of Five which introduced the word 'Creator' into the Declaration's preamble, and by Congress which added

---

[29] See text accompanying n. 10.
[30] See *The Oxford English Dictionary* (3rd edn, Oxford University Press 2018).
[31] There is a rich literature on the philosophical meaning and background of the term 'self-evident' which I can only mention here. The debate mainly concerns, in the words of Sanford Levinson, 'Self-Evident Truths in the Declaration of Independence' (1979) 57 Texas Law Review 847, 851: 'the relative importance of John Locke and several Scottish philosophers, particularly Francis Hutcheson, David Hume, and Thomas Reid, upon the Jefferson of 1776'. See, in particular, Morton White, *The Philosophy of the American Revolution* (Oxford University Press 1978); Garry Wills, *Inventing America: Jefferson's Declaration of Independence* (Doubleday & Co. 1978) 181–92; Zuckert, 'Self-Evident Truth' (n. 22); Jayne, *Jefferson's Declaration* (n. 22) particularly ch. 6; Owen Anderson, *The Declaration of Independence and God: Self-Evident Truths in American Law* (Cambridge University Press 2015).
[32] See text accompanying n. 17.
[33] That difference was disregarded by Bentham in his critique of the Declaration of 1776: 'In this preamble however it is, that they attempt to establish a theory of Government; a theory, as absurd and visionary, as the system of conduct in defence of which it is established, is nefarious.... They are about "to assume", as they tell us, "among the powers of the earth, that equal and separate station to which"—they have lately discovered—"the laws of Nature, and of Nature's God entitle them".... If to what they now demand they were entitled by any law of God, they had only to produce that law, all controversy was at an end. Instead of this, what do they produce? What they call self-evident truths.' Jeremy Bentham, *An Answer to the Declaration of the American Congress* (London 1776), reproduced in Armitage, *Declaration* (n. 12) 173–4.
[34] In his 1774 essay *A Summary View of the Rights of British America*, Jefferson had still referred to 'those rights which God and the laws have given equally and independently to all', and had closed his resolutions by saying: 'The God who gave us life gave us liberty at the same time; the hand of force may destroy, but cannot disjoin them.' See Thomas Jefferson, *A Summary View of the Rights of British America. Set Forth in Some Resolutions Intended for the Inspection of the Present Delegates of the People of*

references to 'the Supreme Judge of the world' and 'divine Providence' to the text of the conclusion.[35]

However, the Declaration does *not* say: 'These truths are self-evident, that all men are created equal, that they are endowed by their Creator with certain unalienable Rights ... '. Instead, it says 'We hold these truths to be self-evident ...'. Emphasizing the first word ('*We* hold'), one can see that phrase as modifying the following propositions: The propositions are subjectivized, and thereby their qualification as 'truths' is relativized. '*We* hold' implies that not necessarily everybody else holds, or must hold, the same opinion. And who is 'we'? It is, as stated in the very first words of the Declaration, 'the thirteen united States of America' and, more exactly, as it is said in the Declaration's last paragraph, 'we, the Representatives of the United States of America, in General Congress, Assembled'. *To us*, the authors of the Declaration seem to say, the following propositions are self-evident truths, and we hope to convince a 'candid world' to share this view.[36]

II. 'ALL MEN'? THE LIMITS OF SELF-EVIDENCE

There is, as Lynn Hunt convincingly explains in her chapter's section entitled 'Limitations', a contradiction between the Declaration's claim to a self-evidence of universal human rights ('*all men* are created equal', '*they* are endowed ... with certain unalienable Rights')[37] and the exclusion, in the law not only of the American colonies but also of the independent United States, of women, children, slaves, and servants from most civil and political rights (and of slaves even from the emphatically proclaimed rights to life, liberty, and the pursuit of happiness). In the Declaration, the political philosophy of universal rights was used to justify the separation of the colonies from Great Britain but, it seems, otherwise not taken seriously.[38]

Virginia now in Convention. By a Native, and Member of the House of Burgesses (Clementina Rind 1774) 5 and 23, respectively <https://www.wdl.org/en/item/117/> (facsimile) and <https://founders.archives.gov/documents/Jefferson/01-01-02-0090> accessed 31 January 2019 (hereafter Jefferson, *Rights of British America*).

---

[35] See Boyd, *Declaration* (n. 7) 29 and 34.
[36] See also Zuckert, 'Self-Evident Truth' (n. 22) 322 and 329: '[T]he "we hold" emphasizes the premises of the argument as particularly the property of the Americans, and not necessarily shared in the opinions of the rest of mankind.... [T]he truths announced in the Declaration are not in fact self-evident, nor are they pronounced to be. They are rather *to be held as if self-evident* within the political community dedicated to making them effective. The truths must serve as the bedrock or first principles of all political reasoning in that regime.' (Emphasis added).
[37] Emphasis added.
[38] But see Abraham Lincoln, speaking in 1857: 'They [the authors of the Declaration] meant to set up a standard maxim for free society, which should be familiar to all, and revered by all; constantly looked to, constantly labored for, and even though never perfectly attained, constantly approximated .... The assertion that "all men are created equal" was of no practical use in effecting our separation from Great

One group of people which in the Declaration itself is clearly excluded from the rights attributed to 'all men' is 'the merciless Indian Savages'. In the last paragraph of the indictment of George III, it is said: 'He [the King] has excited domestic insurrections amongst us, and has endeavoured to bring on the inhabitants of our frontiers, *the merciless Indian Savages*, whose known rule of warfare, is an undistinguished destruction of all ages, sexes and conditions.'[39] An accusation with an almost identical wording was already included in Jefferson's 'First Ideas' on the Virginia Constitution.[40] Jefferson clearly made an effort to justify that exclusion of the Native Americans from 'all men', in the first place by calling them 'savages', and further by emphasizing their allegedly cruel, that is, inhuman, warfare against the settlers, by which they have separated themselves from humanity.

On the other hand, Jefferson's draft included an indictment of the King because of the slave trade, calling that trade a 'cruel war against human nature itself, violating it's most sacred rights of life & liberty in the persons of a distant people', namely the Africans:

[H]e has waged cruel war against human nature itself, violating it's most sacred rights of life & liberty in the persons of a distant people, who never offended him, captivating and carrying them into slavery in another hemisphere, or to incur miserable death in their transportation thither. This piratical warfare, the opprobrium of *infidel* powers, is the warfare of the *Christian* king of Great Britain, determined to keep open a market where M E N should be bought & sold; he has prostituted his negative for suppressing every legislative attempt to prohibit or to restrain this execrable commerce, and that this assemblage of horrors might want no fact of distinguished die, he is now exciting those very people to rise in arms among us, and to purchase that liberty of which *he* has deprived them, by murdering the people upon whom *he* also obtruded them: thus paying off former crimes committed against the *liberties* of one people, with crimes which he urges them to commit against the *lives* of another.[41]

That paragraph of the draft was only deleted by Congress,[42] in deference to the Southern colonies[43] but also because the delegates realized that they could hardly

---

Britain; and it was placed in the Declaration, not for that, but for future use.' Speech on the Dred Scott Decision at Springfield, Illinois, 26 June 1857, in Abraham Lincoln, *Speeches and Writings 1832–1858* (Don E Fehrenbacher, ed., The Library of America 1989) 390, 398–9.

[39] Emphasis added.
[40] See 'First Draft by Jefferson' (of the Virginia Constitution), before 13 June 1776, in Julian P Boyd (ed.), *The Papers of Thomas Jefferson*, vol. 1, 1760–76 (Princeton University Press 1950) 337 et seq, also available at <http://founders.archives.gov> accessed 31 January 2019.
[41] See Copy made by Jefferson for Richard Henry Lee; Boyd, *Declaration* (n. 7) Doc. VI (facsimile).
[42] See Boyd, *Declaration* (n. 7) 31, 33.
[43] Jefferson recorded in his 'Notes' that the clause 'reprobating the enslaving the inhabitants of Africa, was struck out in complaisance to S. Carolina & Georgia, who had never attempted to restrain the importation of slaves & who on the contrary still wished to continue it. Our northern brethren

convincingly charge the King alone with a slave trade in which the colonists actively participated and from which they benefitted.[44] Jefferson had already formulated a similar charge against the King in a set of instructions for the Virginia delegates to the first Continental Congress, published in July 1774 as *A Summary View of the Rights of British America*.[45]

III. THE SHATTERED BELIEF IN THE SELF-EVIDENCE OF HUMAN RIGHTS

The 'we' of Jefferson's 'we hold these truths' could rightfully claim to stand not only for the representatives of the thirteen United States but for a broad majority of educated people in Europe and North America in the second half of the eighteenth century. As Pauline Maier wrote in her book about the Declaration, 'the sentiments Jefferson eloquently expressed were ... absolutely conventional among Americans of his time'[46]—and also in that sense 'self-evident'. In other words, the 'we' was conceived of as being in harmony with the spirit of the age, with the thinking of all righteous, honest, and virtuous men and women; and reason would sooner or later enlighten those who had not yet discovered the truth.

However, in the meantime, and in particular in the course of the twentieth century, that Enlightenment belief in the self-evidence of human rights has been shattered. War, genocide, and systematic violations of human rights make it impossible still to assert that the existence of fundamental human rights is obvious to all people endowed with reason. The 'we' of the Declaration of 1776 has not become universal. In 1948, the member states of the United Nations deemed it necessary to adopt the

---

also, I believe, felt a little tender under those censures; for tho' their people have very few slaves themselves, yet they had been pretty considerable carriers of them to others'. See Becker, *Declaration* (n. 16) 171–2; Boyd, *Declaration* (n. 7) 37. For the entire text, see Barry Alan Shain (ed.), *The Declaration of Independence in Historical Context* (Liberty Fund 2014) 501–2.

---

[44] See also Maier, *American Scripture* (n. 7) 146–7: 'Some people recognized the contradiction and were ready to move toward greater consistency between principle and practice, but so monumental a change as the abolition of slavery could not be accomplished in a moment. For the time being, it was wise at least not to call attention to the persistence of the slave trade and to the anomaly of American slavery.'

[45] See Jefferson, *Rights of British America* (n. 34) 16 et seq: 'The abolition of domestic slavery is the great object of desire in those colonies, where it was unhappily introduced in their infant state. But previous to the enfranchisement of the slaves we have, it is necessary to exclude all further importations from Africa; yet our repeated attempts to effect this by prohibitions, and by imposing duties which might amount to a prohibition, have been hitherto defeated by his majesty's negative: Thus preferring the immediate advantages of a few African corsairs to the lasting interests of the American states, and to the rights of human nature, deeply wounded by this infamous practice.' In his personal copy, preserved in the Library of Congress, Jefferson replaced the word 'African' in 'African corsairs' with 'British'. See the facsimile of the copy <https://www.wdl.org/en/item/117/> accessed 31 January 2019.

[46] See Maier, *American Scripture* (n. 7) 135.

Convention on the Prevention and Punishment of the Crime of Genocide.[47] In the preamble of the Convention, it was rightly said that 'at all periods of history genocide has inflicted great losses on humanity', including, unfortunately, the periods following the proclamation of the Declaration of Independence.

Fifty years after the adoption of the Convention against Genocide, states agreed on the Rome Statute of the International Criminal Court,[48] establishing a permanent court with 'jurisdiction over persons for the most serious crimes of international concern' (Article 1 of the Statute), namely the crime of genocide, crimes against humanity, war crimes, and the crime of aggression (Article 5 of the Statute). It is undeniably true what the states parties to the Statute declared in the Statute's preamble: 'during this century millions of children, women and men have been victims of unimaginable atrocities that deeply shock the conscience of humanity'.

In that situation, it is impossible to content ourselves with the fact of the discovery of a 'self-evident truth' in the eighteenth century. One could also say that Jefferson's idea of self-evidence turned out to be an illusion. The existence of fundamental human rights may be a truth, but that truth is *not* evident to everybody. The importance of fundamental human rights is not self-evident. Instead, such rights need to be understood, learned, accepted, and respected in order to become real. It is not enough to throw the spotlight of reason on such rights to make them work. Instead, human rights need a solid foundation.

In the world of today, such a foundation must be of a truly universal character. If there is a universal right to life, liberty, and the pursuit of happiness, we need to find forms of acceptance of such a right and of the underlying ideas and concepts in all parts and all cultures of the world. A serious effort to arrive at such a 'common understanding' of human rights was made early in the history of the United Nations when the Human Rights Commission drafted the Universal Declaration of Human Rights (UDHR).[49] Eleanor Roosevelt, the chairperson of the Commission, spoke of a 'flow backwards and forwards of ideas and understanding'.[50] Unfortunately, the

---

[47] Convention on the Prevention and Punishment of the Crime of Genocide (adopted 9 December 1948, entered into force 12 January 1951) 78 UNTS 277. In Article II of the Convention, genocide is defined as 'any of the following acts committed with intent to destroy, in whole or in part, a national, ethnical, racial or religious group, as such: (a) killing members of the group; (b) causing serious bodily or mental harm to members of the group; (c) deliberately inflicting on the group conditions of life calculated to bring about its physical destruction in whole or in part; (d) imposing measures intended to prevent births within the group; (e) forcibly transferring children of the group to another group'. Of the vast literature on the Convention's genesis, I only mention the recent study by Douglas Irvin-Erickson, *Raphaël Lemkin and the Concept of Genocide* (University of Pennsylvania Press 2017) 152–96.

[48] Rome Statute of the International Criminal Court (adopted 17 July 1998, entered into force 1 July 2002) 2187 UNTS 3.

[49] GA Res. 217 A (III), 10 December 1948; (1948–9) UN Yearbook 535–7. The last paragraph of the preamble of the Declaration reads: 'Whereas a common understanding of these rights and freedoms is of the greatest importance for the full realization of this pledge [to achieve the promotion of universal respect for and observance of human rights and fundamental freedoms].'

[50] See Eleanor Roosevelt, 'Writing the Universal Declaration of Human Rights' in Bardo Fassbender (ed.), *Menschenrechteerklärung—Universal Declaration of Human Rights* (Sellier European Law Publishers 2009) 31, 41.

later universal human rights treaties reflected political compromise reached by the Western and the communist states rather than universal perceptions and concepts.

Today, new efforts to build and sustain a universal foundation of fundamental human rights are necessary, not only and not even primarily by states but rather by civil society, so that these rights, in the words of Lynn Hunt, continue 'to resonate with a broader public'[51]—and this time not just in France and North America. One example of a civil society initiative working in that direction is the *Projekt Weltethos* (Global Ethic Project) initiated by the Swiss theologian and philosopher Hans Küng[52] that tries to identify and to strengthen, across cultures and religions, 'a fundamental consensus on binding values, irrevocable standards, and personal attitudes'.[53] In that sense, the Project's 1993 'Declaration Toward a Global Ethic' said: 'We are convinced of the fundamental unity of the human family on Earth. We recall the 1948 Universal Declaration of Human Rights of the United Nations. What it formally proclaimed on the level of *rights* we wish to confirm and deepen here from the perspective of an *ethic*: The full realization of the intrinsic dignity of the human person, the inalienable freedom and equality in principle of all humans, and the necessary solidarity and interdependence of all humans with each other.'[54] And yet it will be impossible to recover the self-assurance with which in the summer of 1776 Thomas Jefferson and his fellows placed their trust in the self-evidence of rights of all men.

Bibliography

Anderson O, *The Declaration of Independence and God: Self-Evident Truths in American Law* (Cambridge University Press 2015)
Armitage D, *The Declaration of Independence: A Global History* (Harvard University Press 2007)
Becker C, *The Declaration of Independence: A Study in the History of Political Ideas* (2nd edn, Alfred A Knopf 1942)
Bentham J, *An Answer to the Declaration of the American Congress* (London 1776), reproduced in Armitage D (ed.), *The Declaration of Independence: A Global History* (Harvard University Press 2007) 173
Boyd JP, *The Declaration of Independence: The Evolution of the Text as Shown in Facsimiles of Various Drafts by its Author, Thomas Jefferson* (Princeton University Press 1945)
Boyd JP (ed.), *The Papers of Thomas Jefferson*, vol. 1, 1760–1776 (Princeton University Press 1950)

---

[51] Hunt, 'Self-Evidence' (n. 2) 43.
[52] See Hans Küng, *Global Responsibility: In Search of a New World Ethic* (Wipf & Stock 2004).
[53] Declaration Toward a Global Ethic (adopted 4 September 1993), part I, last para. <https://www.weltethos.org> accessed 31 January 2019. For a discussion of Küng's work in the wider context of the global ethics literature, see Kimberly Hutchings, *Global Ethics: An Introduction* (Polity Press 2010) 11–19.
[54] Declaration Toward a Global Ethic, part I, para. 4 (emphasis in the original).

Gawalt GW, 'Drafting the Declaration' in Gerber SD (ed.), *The Declaration of Independence: Origins and Impact* (CQ Press 2002) 1

Hunt L, *Inventing Human Rights: A History* (WW Norton & Co. 2007)

Hunt L, 'Humanity and the Claim to Self-Evidence' in Fassbender B and Traisbach K (eds), *The Limits of Human Rights* (Oxford University Press 2019) 39

Hutchings K, *Global Ethics: An Introduction* (Polity Press 2010)

Irvin-Erickson D, *Raphaël Lemkin and the Concept of Genocide* (University of Pennsylvania Press 2017)

Isaacson W, *Benjamin Franklin: An American Life* (Simon & Schuster 2003)

Jayne A, *Jefferson's Declaration of Independence: Origins, Philosophy and Theology* (University Press of Kentucky 1998)

Jefferson T, *A Summary View of the Rights of British America. Set Forth in Some Resolutions Intended for the Inspection of the Present Delegates of the People of Virginia now in Convention. By a Native, and Member of the House of Burgesses* (Clementina Rind 1774) <https://www.wdl.org/en/item/117/> (facsimile) and <https://founders.archives.gov/documents/Jefferson/01-01-02-0090> accessed 31 January 2019

Jefferson T, 'Letter to the Mayor of Washington, DC, Roger C Weightman', 24 June 1826, in The Papers of Thomas Jefferson <http://founders.archives.gov/documents/Jefferson/98-01-02-6179> accessed 31 January 2019

Küng H, *Global Responsibility: In Search of a New World Ethic* (Wipf & Stock 2004)

Levinson S, 'Self-Evident Truths in the Declaration of Independence' (1979) 57 Texas Law Review 847

Lincoln A, *Speeches and Writings 1832–1858* (Don E Fehrenbacher, ed., The Library of America 1989)

Lucas SE, 'The Stylistic Artistry of the Declaration of Independence' <http://www.archives.gov/founding-docs/stylistic-artistry-of-the-declaration> accessed 31 January 2019

Madison J, 'Notes of the Virginia Convention, May–June, 1776' in Library of Congress, *James Madison Papers* <https://www.loc.gov/exhibits/creating-the-united-states/battle-joined.html#obj15> accessed 31 January 2019

Maier P, *American Scripture: Making the Declaration of Independence* (Alfred A. Knopf 1997)

Roosevelt E, 'Writing the Universal Declaration of Human Rights' in Fassbender B (ed.), *Menschenrechteerklärung—Universal Declaration of Human Rights* (Sellier European Law Publishers 2009) 31

Shain BA (ed.), *The Declaration of Independence in Historical Context* (Liberty Fund 2014)

White M, *The Philosophy of the American Revolution* (Oxford University Press 1978)

Wills G, *Inventing America: Jefferson's Declaration of Independence* (Doubleday & Co. 1978)

Zuckert MP, 'Self-Evident Truth and the Declaration of Independence' (1987) 49 Review of Politics 319

3
Human Rights, Global Justice, and the Limits of Law

Kate Nash*

I. HUMAN RIGHTS ARE GLOBALIZING...

Men are born and remain free and equal in rights....
...
The principle of all sovereignty resides essentially in the Nation.
The French Declaration of the Rights
of Man and of the Citizen 1789

The paradoxical principles expressed in the French Declaration of Rights subsequently became so taken-for-granted as to be invisible: humans have rights as such, and what counts as justice is a matter for the democratic decision-making of citizens of the nation state.[1] In Europe and North America in recent times, it is as an accompaniment to the rhetoric and practices of globalization that questions are being raised concerning justice beyond the national frame. Human rights defenders and lawyers have contributed to raising questions about the *scale* of justice that have, at the same time, been raised by activists against neo-liberalizing policies of global elites. Following the end of the Cold War, especially in the 1990s, 'global justice' became a rallying cry for activists and a topic of debate for political theorists.[2]

---

* I would like to thank Knut Traisbach for suggestions on this chapter which I think have much improved it, and also participants in the conference on 'International Human Rights and Freedom' organized by the Centre for Law and Society at Queen Mary, London, in 2017.

[1] As post-colonial sociologists have pointed out, the naturalization of justice as exclusively a national matter happened despite economic structures across territorial borders and geo-political links between states that systematically disadvantaged people in countries that were not 'European settler' states, see Gurminder K Bhambra, *Rethinking Modernity: Postcolonialism and the Sociological Imagination* (Palgrave Macmillan 2007); Julian Go, *Postcolonial Sociology* (Emerald Publishing 2013).

[2] David Held, *Democracy and Global Order: From the Modern State to Cosmopolitan Governance* (Polity Press 1995); Nancy Fraser, *Scales of Justice: Reimagining Political Space in a Globalizing World* (Polity Press 2008).

Kate Nash, *Human Rights, Global Justice, and the Limits of Law* In: *The Limits of Human Rights*. Edited by: Bardo Fassbender and Knut Traisbach, Oxford University Press 2019. © The Several Contributors.
DOI: 10.1093/oso/9780198824756.003.0005

Human rights may seem to be the 'natural', or at least the inevitable language within which to address issues of global justice. In fact, however, human rights have themselves been 'globalizing'. In 1948, the Universal Declaration of Human Rights (UDHR) was not much more than a rhetorical flourish in the margins of the UN Charter, and state leaders signed up to human rights conventions in the 1970s knowing that there were no mechanisms through which they could be held accountable for failing to respect them. Although the UN Charter stresses co-operation and respect for human rights, it established 'equality between sovereigns' (or more accurately inequality) and promised that the UN would not interfere in 'matters which are essentially within the domestic jurisdiction of any state'.[3]

Human rights have been globalizing in that they have become the focus of greater interconnectedness across national borders. There are now mechanisms at the UN through which pressure has been brought on states—legal (in the International Criminal Court (ICC), for example), moral (through periodic country reports on compliance with international human rights treaties), economic (through targeted sanctions), and even military (the controversial 'humanitarian interventions' given a firmer legal basis by the 'Responsibility to Protect' in 2005). Sources of international law have become more transnational: non-governmental organizations (NGOs) and intergovernmental organizations (IGOs) participate in formulating the content of international treaties, *jus cogens* emerged post-Second World War as a new form of customary international law, customary international law is now drawn on in national courts.[4] As a result of such changes some theorists have gone so far as to talk about the emergence of 'cosmopolitan law'. Cosmopolitan law is defined as international law that reaches *inside states*, depending for its legitimacy on multi-scalar networks of authority to enforce claims against human rights violators regardless of the national citizenship of the claimant, and even regardless of where the violations took place.[5] Does the globalization of international law mean that human rights are increasingly becoming a matter of technocratic, rational-legal bureaucratic administration, above the political fray—for better or for worse?[6]

---

[3] Article 2(7) UN Charter. Although equal in sovereignty, states are nevertheless formally as well as informally unequal at the UN, see Jack Donnelly, 'Sovereign Inequalities and Hierarchy in Anarchy: American Power and International Society' (2006) 12 European Journal of International Relations 139.

[4] Louis Henkin, 'Human Rights and "State Sovereignty"' (1995/1996) 25 Georgia Journal of International and Comparative Law 31; Robert McCorquodale, 'International Community and State Sovereignty: An Uneasy Symbiotic Relationship' in Colin Warbric and Stephen Tierney (eds), *Towards an 'International Legal Community'? The Sovereignty of States and the Sovereignty of International Law* (British Institute of International and Comparative Law 2006) 241; Saskia Sassen, *Territory, Authority, Rights: From Medieval to Global Assemblages* (Princeton University Press 2006).

[5] David Held, 'Law of States, Law of Peoples: Three Models of Sovereignty' (2002) 8 Legal Theory 1.

[6] Costas Douzinas, *The End of Human Rights: Critical Legal Thought at the Turn of the Century* (Hart Publishing 2000).

II. ... THROUGH STATES

Despite the opening up of international law to new influences and new modes of enforcement, it is still overwhelmingly dependent on states. International law remains unpredictable in its application, to the point where its cosmopolitanization is better understood as the hope for an new ideal, extrapolated from examples (such as convictions resulting from the application of humanitarian law at the ICC, treaties drafted with the co-operation of NGOs, like the Declaration on the Rights of Indigenous Peoples, law used in national courts against corporations, like the Alien Tort Claims Act in the United States) which are invariably specific and appear limited outside the context of grand, epochal theory.[7] Cosmopolitan law seems more aspiration than fact, more hope for the future than hard-headed analysis of specific changes in the present. In fact, it can be argued that international law will never become a predictable, routinely applied set of coherent and consistent rules precisely because, in the absence of global consensus on fundamental norms, and without a final authoritative law-maker and enforcer at the global scale, states remain the most important actors in making and institutionalizing international human rights law.[8] Most importantly, from a sociological perspective, respect for human rights depends on the political strategies through which state formations are reproduced, challenged or transformed.

States are distinctive forms of organization. In very general terms, states are unique in their capacities to concentrate and distribute resources, both material and moral. States are structured and reproduced through political strategies that make use of military and economic resources and moral resources of legitimation that can never be fully controlled. Except perhaps in conditions of extreme authoritarianism there is inevitably political conflict within states and across nominal boundaries that separate states from civil societies and from each other. State officials try to influence how resources are collected and concentrated 'in the name of the State' and how they are used; and they try to block the ambitions and projects of others with designs on the same resources. Officials acting in the name of states are, therefore, exceptionally dangerous—well-equipped to benefit from torture, rape, and murder, and from turning funds that are ostensibly collected for public benefit through taxes and international aid to their own purposes. At the same time, states are crucial to the realization of human rights in practice. It is only states that have the resources to deliver the extensive range of rights that are already encoded in international human rights law, as well as in demands that have not yet reached that status. Even the ICC and the Responsibility to Protect, which do

---

[7] See Kate Nash, *The Political Sociology of Human Rights* (Cambridge University Press 2015) (hereafter Nash, *Political Sociology of Human Rights*).
[8] Stephen D Krasner, 'The Hole in the Whole: Sovereignty, Shared Sovereignty and International Law' (2004) 25 Michigan Journal of International Law 1075.

point definitively beyond the UN definition of sovereignty as 'non-interference in domestic affairs', depend on the resources provided by states. States are at the same time the violators *and* the guarantors of human rights.

The ideal-type of the state through which respect for human rights is to be realized is the juridical or Rule of Law state. The juridical state is one in which officials who act 'in the name of the state' are organized and constrained by law; and in which law is made through proper procedures. When a politician ratifies a human rights treaty (at least as far as it is assumed that their action is sincere) what is presupposed is that she or he is embedded in legal and bureaucratic structures (or will be soon) to ensure that what has been promised will be respected in practice. It is Northwestern European settler states which most resemble the ideal-type of the juridical state.[9] In fact, the ideal-type itself is based on analyses of the long (and itself idealized) historical formation of European states. Although the ideal-type of the juridical state is problematic in many respects—especially because it is very far from existing in most of the world—as an ideal it has significant influence in human rights circles. In Northwestern states it tends to be assumed that 'getting the law right' is foundational for human rights—and strategic litigation in courts is the most valuable lever by which respect for human rights can be realized. In fact, however, even in Northwestern states, even in the circumstances that most closely those of the ideal-type of the juridical state, realizing respect for human rights always requires a good deal more than getting the law right.

The key material resources on which states depend, and which state officials cannot fully control, are military and economic force. The juridical state is defined as such (most famously in the work of Max Weber) by its monopoly on violence within its territory.[10] In fact, no state has ever had an army and police force that fully monopolized the means of violence within its territory. How state officials create and make use of military resources to realize their projects, how they respond to armies and armed militias that appear to threaten or to strengthen their position, and how their decisions are encouraged or constrained by other actors nationally and internationally: these are all crucial to how states guarantee or violate human rights. In the juridical state, use of force is largely constrained by law. Very often, however, decisions are taken that are legally considered 'exceptional'. All states allow themselves the *legal* possibility of making exceptions when faced with dangers to national security. Infringements of civil rights within Northwestern states in what has become virtually a permanent 'state of emergency' in the global war

---

[9] As a result of different, though interlinked, histories of state formation, states are not all structured in the same way in relation to other states, international institutions, and national civil societies. There are few states in the world that resemble the juridical state—and even the Northwestern states of the United States, Western Europe, and Australasia differ from the ideal-type. I discuss differences in state structures that are relevant to the possibilities of realizing human rights in Nash, *Political Sociology of Human Rights* (n. 7).

[10] Max Weber, 'Politics as a Vocation' in Hans Heinrich Gerth and Charles Wright Mills (eds), *From Max Weber: Essays in Sociology* (first published 1948, Routledge 1991) 77.

on terror have been very well-documented in recent years, with laws in the United States and Europe enabling racial profiling, detention without charge, and extensive surveillance over citizens and non-citizens. In addition, we have seen the civil rights of unauthorized migrants into Northwestern states violated when they are incarcerated in prison-like facilities without due process of law—a violation that has been ruled legal in the European Court of Human Rights (ECtHR).[11] Outside states' territories, violations of human rights are also very evident, and often legally permitted within the state as the prerogative of the executive, the defender of state security. It is rare that they are considered by constitutional courts within states. To some extent this legal sanctioning of human rights violations is what is changing with the globalization of international human rights law: heads of state and military leaders can now be prosecuted for torture, disappearances, summary executions, and war crimes in international courts. On the other hand, the administration of law in international courts is extremely uneven. There is clearly no question of prosecuting George Bush or Tony Blair for the part they played in the illegal invasion of Iraq, and to date it is striking that it is *only* African leaders who have been prosecuted in the ICC since it was established in 2002. Where the administration of human rights in international courts is so uneven, it looks more like another way of doing geo-politics than law administered by rational-legal institutions.

States are also organizations that rely on the centralization and redistribution of economic resources which state officials cannot fully control. The exceptional capacities of states, and the degree to which they depend on or are autonomous from the owners of capital, has long been debated in the Marxist tradition.[12] Neo-liberal public policies clearly show that the enjoyment of all rights depend on structures that go far beyond the juridical state and the rule of law. They depend on how governments deal with global capitalist elites in national economic policies, how transnational corporations are treated, and how markets, including financial markets, are created and regulated nationally and internationally. It is not just social and economic rights and workers' rights that depend on economic policy. Civil and political rights are also expensive to organize in practice: training and paying police properly, ensuring that people arrested have access to a fair trial, arranging fair and free elections. Tight limits on public spending also have an impact on civil rights. Cuts to legal aid in the United Kingdom, for example, which mean that people on low incomes are now less likely to have access to legal representation in court, exacerbate inequalities in rights to a fair trial.[13]

---

[11] Marie-Bénédicte Dembour, *When Humans Become Migrants: Study of the European Court of Human Rights with an Inter-American Counterpoint* (Oxford University Press 2015) 378–81.
[12] See Bob Jessop, *State Theory: Putting the Capitalist State in its Place* (Polity Press 1990).
[13] Owen Boycott, 'Legal aid cuts creating two-tier justice system, says Amnesty', *The Guardian* (London, 11 October 2006) <http://www.theguardian.com/law/2016/oct/11/legal-aid-cuts-two-tier-system-amnesty-international-law-justice> accessed 31 January 2019.

Finally, in addition to material resources, state officials also rely on *moral* resources to carry out their political projects. Officials rely—to a greater or lesser extent in different cases—on authority to act 'in the name of the state', to make use of the state's resources and capacities in ways that are considered justified or legitimate. There is a variety of types of authority.[14] What we are interested in here is 'popular authority', paradigmatic of democracy. 'Popular authority' rests *not* on *transcending* politics, either in law or in moral claims, but on representing the people. A key source of authority to act 'in the name of the state' today is that which is claimed by politicians elected to be the voice of 'we the people'.

III. TWO SOVEREIGNTIES

If it seems odd to think of states as the *guarantors* of human rights, that is because states tend to be seen as *obstacles* to the realization of respect for human rights in practice. State sovereignty, the principle that there should be no outside interference in the affairs of states or in what goes on inside their territories, is generally seen as a problem for the realization of human rights: it must be overridden or transformed so that everyone, no matter where they are born or where they are living, can enjoy universal human rights.[15] Much of what counts as cosmopolitan law is an attempt to limit—or as theorists of cosmopolitanism would prefer, to 'share'—state sovereignty (with the European Union (EU) being the chief example of how such sharing is already working in practice).[16]

In terms of international human rights law, however, what difference does it make to discussions over sovereignty when we note that *popular* sovereignty is itself a human right? Article 1 of both International Covenants states that:

> All peoples have the right of self-determination. By virtue of that right they freely determine their political status and freely pursue their economic, social and cultural development.

The covenants came into effect in 1976, and Article 1 is large part a product of de-colonization, which was already well underway by this time. It codifies respect for the national self-determination of citizens in *all states*. As we have noted, the priority of citizens as the bearers of human rights had already been proclaimed in the great eighteenth-century declarations of human rights. Although citizenship was not extended to all adults within Northwestern states until the twentieth

---

[14] See Nash, *Political Sociology of Human Rights* (n. 7).
[15] Daniel Levy and Natan Sznaider, *The Holocaust and Memory in the Global Age* (Temple University Press 2006).
[16] Thomas W Pogge, 'Cosmpolitanism and Sovereignty' (1992) 103 Ethics 48.

century, and people in states that were European colonies never had citizenship rights, the *principle* that the law is only legitimate if it is 'we the people' who give it to ourselves was already established as the basis of democracy early in modernity. It is as the confirmation of this common-sense principle of democracy, and at the same time its extension to peoples liberated from empire, that national self-determination appears in international human rights law.

There is, then, a paradox at the heart of the project of globalizing human rights. On the one hand, human rights are universal, the lives, freedoms, capacities, the dreams of all human beings on the planet must be treated as of equal value if there is to be global justice. On the other hand, citizens have priority: it is citizens who 'give the law to themselves', at the same time giving legitimate authority to elected politicians to represent them, their interests and values, hopes, dreams and fears, at home and abroad. *State* sovereignty, generally seen as an obstacle to the realization of universal human rights, is entangled with *popular* sovereignty: it is only national citizens who should decide on the content, value, and reach of human rights law that constrains the democratic state.

IV. THE CITIZEN/HUMAN PARADOX

The citizen/human paradox is at the heart of human rights. It is encoded in international human rights law itself, which therefore pulls in quite opposite directions. Moreover, the citizen/human paradox is not just a paradox *in* law; it is a paradox on which international human rights law itself *depends*. If it is only states that have capacities to deliver the extensive range of rights encoded in international human rights law, and if it is only citizens who can legally will the law by which state actions should be constrained, human rights can only be fully realized when citizens will law that binds their state to respect the universal rights of citizens and non-citizens alike.

The citizen/human paradox has several consequences for international human rights law and its limits. First, it follows that political conflicts over what is owed to citizens and what is owed to non-citizens, whether resident on the territory or not, are inherent to the realisation of respect for human rights. Globalization involves interconnections and at the same time inequalities of political influence (that often map onto and reproduce colonial inequalities). Many campaigns for human rights within the national frame concern the rights of non-citizens, of migrants and refugees. Some campaigns try to build solidarity in which voters in one country use their influence over the state of which they are citizens to address violations elsewhere.[17] Sometimes it is states which are themselves violating the rights

---

[17] This type of campaign is what is analysed in the 'boomerang model': activists make connections across borders (in transnational advocacy networks) to influence one (or more) state(s) to put pressure on another to alter policies, legislation, and practices that violate rights, see Margaret E Keck

of non-citizens in other territories. In all these cases, campaigns are mobilized to convince voters of their responsibilities towards fellow humans who happen not to be fellow citizens.

Secondly, conflicts concerning what is due to citizens and what is due to non-citizens results in the politicization of human rights law. This politicization is currently very evident in the United Kingdom, where the Prime Minister at the time of writing, Theresa May, leads a party which—before the Brexit referendum, and when she was Home Secretary, responsible for the domestic legal system—has committed itself to leaving the European Convention of Human Rights (ECHR) if the Council of Europe does not agree with the government's proposed reforms of national human rights law. These commitments followed a long campaign against human rights law on the part of right-wing newspapers.[18] It is not just on the side of conservatism, however, that human rights law is politicized. Human rights NGOs that support 'test cases' are engaged in strategic litigation intended to establish a new interpretation of legislation or to prompt new law that will steer the polity in a different direction. As Conor Gearty argues, it is telling that in the highest national and international courts judgments are always made by several judges: highly contentious interpretations of law are settled by 'a show of hands'. In such cases, legal judgments look less like finding the truth of the law and much more like a political (even a quasi-democratic) decision.[19]

Thirdly, it follows from the citizen/human paradox that human rights is not a language through which nationalism is likely to be replaced by cosmopolitanism any time soon. Most of us who are interested in human rights are more likely to identify as cosmopolitans than as nationalists. We are very familiar with the dangers of nationalism and the xenophobia and cultural racism to which it is aligned that give rise to a range of 'human rights wrongs', from discrimination through personal and state violence, ultimately to genocide. We are more likely to identify as favouring a world in which papers and passports are irrelevant, and to wish to live in cities where differences of language and customs are a matter of interest and enjoyment rather than fear and hatred.[20]

However, as Craig Calhoun argues, nationalism has also been, and remains, an often-overlooked source of solidarity which, through commitment to public institutions and civic values, is one of the conditions of democracy itself.[21] In one respect it is true that 'national' is no more than an administrative category; it is

---

and Kathryn Sikkink, *Activists Beyond Borders: Advocacy Networks in International Politics* (Cornell University Press 1998).

[18] Kate Nash, 'Politicising Human Rights in Europe: Challenges to Legal Constitutionalism from the Left and the Right' (2016) 20 The International Journal of Human Rights 1295 (hereafter Nash, 'Politicising Human Rights').
[19] Conor Gearty, *Can Human Rights Survive?* (Cambridge University Press 2006) 88–9.
[20] Michael Ignatieff, *Blood and Belonging: Journeys into the New Nationalism* (Vintage 1994) 7–9.
[21] Craig Calhoun, *Nations Matter: Culture, History, and the Cosmopolitan Dream* (Routledge 2007).

'a collectivity existing within a clearly demarcated territory, which is subject to a unitary administration'.[22] However, as Calhoun argues, to consider 'national' solely in bureaucratic terms is to ignore 'banal nationalism', the everyday reproduction—which is at the same time the continual changing—of common understandings of who makes up 'we the people' and how we orient ourselves towards those who are not (sometimes not yet) included as citizens. As Calhoun puts it: 'Distinctive national self-understandings are produced and reproduced in literature, film, political debate—and political grumbling, political jokes, and political insults. These structure the ways in which people feel solidarity with each other (and distinction from outsiders).'[23] Solidarity need not mean uniformity; reflexively multi-cultural polities can surely also be solidaristic. Shared understandings may be hateful or they may accommodate and take pleasure in differences, they may be open-minded and generous or fearful and closed-minded—perhaps more likely, they may be ambivalent and contradictory. But it is important to recognize that such understandings are, in part, the basis on which human rights will founder and fail, or find fruitful ground in which to flourish.

There is much debate over the rise of national-populism in Europe and the United States, today. If we take the Brexit vote as an example of national-populism, it is clear from the rhetoric that was used by leading 'leavers' and from the rise in hate crimes that have followed the vote to leave the EU that xenophobia and racism are part of the reaction to immigration that is being fuelled by right-wing nationalist parties. However, it also seems that there are concerns about social justice at work too. National-populism is not just hostile to migrants, it is also against elites (even if its political representatives need not themselves come from impoverished or marginalized backgrounds). In part the Brexit vote also represents disaffection with neo-liberal economic policies: it represents desires for social protection from global 'free markets' (in a similar way to the movements analysed by Polanyi in response to nineteenth-century liberalism).[24] Not having been educated at university and working in a semi-skilled or unskilled job were factors (along with being over fifty and living outside a big city) that made it more likely that an individual would vote to leave the EU. At the same time, it seems very evident in the United Kingdom that the vote to leave the EU is also a challenge to the globalization of human rights. It is consistent with the long-running campaign against human rights by right-wing newspapers, which incessantly repeat stories about the freedoms and privileges allowed to foreign criminals, terrorists, and 'bogus asylum-seekers' by the judiciary, national and European, as well as with Tory party rhetoric against

---

[22] Ibid, 58, quoting Anthony Giddens, *The Nation-State and Violence* (University of California Press 1987) 116.
[23] Ibid, 156.
[24] Karl Polanyi, *The Great Transformation: The Political and Economic Origins of Our Time* (Beacon Press 2001).

European human rights law.[25] The association of human rights with Europe, with undesirable migrants, and with the curbing of parliamentary sovereignty also played a part in the United Kingdom's vote to leave the EU.

Ignorance and lies are serious problems. If it is how officials acting 'in the name of the state' organize military, economic, and moral resources that ultimately impacts on the life chances of citizens and non-citizens, within the territory or in other parts of the world, how well-informed and how effective in targeting particular political projects are the voters who decide how government should represent 'we the people'? For the most part—and especially when it is a matter of foreign policy (which quite often depends on executive decisions and which is also often covert), law, or economic policy (the details of which are apparently difficult for professionals themselves to understand)—the answer is clearly 'not very'. Multilateralism and the co-operation of states in IGOs, which is itself essential to global justice, surely exacerbates the problem. The difficulty of democracy in such a complex world is too big to go into here. What is clear, however, is that there must be mediators between democratically elected governments and 'the people'. It is political parties that play this role most obviously, and perhaps more importantly where human rights and matters of global justice are concerned, NGOs linked into transnational advocacy networks. NGOs are needed to mediate the expertise that is indispensable to understanding issues of global justice, to make voters aware of consequences of their government's actions that they could not otherwise know, and to mobilize campaigns that move people to action—not only in their own interests but also on behalf of strangers, whether citizens or not—to influence the political projects of state officials.

Nationalist hostility to human rights, and to those who claim them, must be challenged through formal political channels and in the courts, but perhaps even more importantly, it must be challenged in the media and in everyday life. In terms of the cultural politics of human rights, the political party Podemos, which achieved a meteoric electoral success in Spain in recent years, is instructive. Podemos has unapologetically adopted populist rhetoric, and tried to engage voters through national identification. However, it does not demonize non-nationals or minorities, and as well as demanding better conditions of entry and work for migrants, at the same time it also makes use of human rights language to demand the social and economic rights with which many of those tempted by right-wing populism are concerned in Spain. Podemos is an example of a political party which has both engaged with the state, suggesting structural changes to Spanish and European Union government, and with nationalist identifications in Spanish civil society, setting up discussion groups in housing projects and workplaces, and reaching new audiences through debates on TV.[26]

---

[25] See Nash, 'Politicising Human Rights' (n. 18); Conor Gearty, *On Fanstasy Island: Britain, Europe, and Human Rights* (Oxford University Press 2016).
[26] Ibid.

V. HUMAN RIGHTS ARE POLITICAL

In conclusion, then, political sociology enables us to understand how human rights are necessarily political. International human rights law can never simply be technocratic as long as democracy is also an aspiration, and as long as the world is organized by and through states. What is most important to whether human rights are violated or respected, at home and abroad, are fundamental structures of states and civil societies, and the political strategies of officials who make use of the exceptional material and moral resources of states. Sociological analysis takes us far beyond concerns with encoding and administering human rights in international human rights law. Beyond law it is necessary to consider not just politics in formal settings, in parliaments and in the committee rooms and corridors of IGOs, but also the cultural politics, the definitions of 'us' and 'them', 'human' and 'rights' that are represented in mainstream and social media, in popular culture, in music and film, and in conversations in meeting places, streets, and shops.

As Hannah Arendt argued at the very beginning of the contemporary human rights regime in the 1950s, it is in political community that people gain the 'the right to rights', which then allows them to appear in public as worthy of justice.[27] In a world organized through states in which 'we the people' have at least some say over how officials use the considerable resources concentrated in national states, for good or for ill, the political community within which a person may appear as having the 'right to rights' is almost invariably the nation. What is important, then, for global justice, is that 'we the people' do not only turn inwards, to each other; we must also turn outwards, to listen to the stories of those who barely have a voice in our everyday worlds. If human rights are to be of relevance, the paradox of the citizen/human must be confronted.

Bibliography

Arendt H, *Origins of Totalitarianism* (Harcourt Brace 1979)
Bhambra G, *Rethinking Modernity: Postcolonialism and the Sociological Imagination* (Palgrave Macmillan 2007)
Boycott O, 'Legal aid cuts creating two-tier justice system, says Amnesty', *The Guardian* (London, 11 October 2006) <http://www.theguardian.com/law/2016/oct/11/legal-aid-cuts-two-tier-system-amnesty-international-law-justice> accessed 31 January 2019
Calhoun C, *Nations Matter: Culture, History, and the Cosmopolitan Dream* (Routledge 2007)
Dembour MB, *When Humans Become Migrants: Study of the European Court of Human Rights with an Inter-American Counterpoint* (Oxford University Press 2015)
Donnelly J, 'Sovereign Inequalities and Hierarchy in Anarchy: American Power and International Society' (2006) 12 European Journal of International Relations 139

---

[27] Hannah Arendt, *Origins of Totalitarianism* (Harcourt Brace 1979).

Douzinas C, *The End of Human Rights: Critical Legal Thought at the Turn of the Century* (Hart Publishing 2000)

Fraser N, *Scales of Justice: Reimagining Political Space in a Globalizing World* (Polity Press 2008)

Gearty C, *Can Human Rights Survive?* (Cambridge University Press 2006)

Gearty C, *On Fanstasy Island: Britain, Europe, and Human Rights* (Oxford University Press 2016)

Go J, *Postcolonial Sociology* (Emerald Publishing 2013)

Held D, *Democracy and Global Order: From the Modern State to Cosmopolitan Governance* (Polity Press 1995)

Held D, 'Law of States, Law of Peoples: Three Models of Sovereignty' (2002) 8 Legal Theory 1

Henkin L, 'Human Rights and "State Sovereignty"' (1995/1996) 25 Georgia Journal of International and Comparative Law 31

Ignatieff M, *Blood and Belonging: Journeys into the New Nationalism* (Vintage 1994)

Jessop B, *State Theory: Putting the Capitalist State in its Place* (Polity Press 1990)

Keck M and Sikkink K, *Activists Beyond Borders: Advocacy Networks in International Politics* (Cornell University Press 1998)

Krasner SD, 'The Hole in the Whole: Sovereignty, Shared Sovereignty and International Law' (2004) 25 Michigan Journal of International Law 1075

Levy D and Sznaider N, *The Holocaust and Memory in the Global Age* (Temple University Press 2006)

McCorquodale R, 'International Community and State Sovereignty: An Uneasy Symbiotic Relationship' in Warbric C and Tierney S (eds), *Towards an 'International Legal Community'? The Sovereignty of States and the Sovereignty of International Law* (British Institute of International and Comparative Law 2006) 241

Nash K, *The Political Sociology of Human Rights* (Cambridge University Press 2015)

Nash K, 'Politicising Human Rights in Europe: Challenges to Legal Constitutionalism from the Left and the Right' (2016) 20 The International Journal of Human Rights 1295

Pogge TW, 'Cosmpolitanism and Sovereignty' (1992) 103 Ethics 48

Polanyi K, *The Great Transformation: The Political and Economic Origins of Our Time* (Beacon Press 2001)

Sassen S, *Territory, Authority, Rights: From Medieval to Global Assemblages* (Princeton University Press 2006)

Weber M, 'Politics as a Vocation' in Gerth HH and Mills CW (eds), *From Max Weber: Essays in Sociology* (first published 1948, Routledge 1991) 77

4
Human Rights beyond the Double Bind of Sovereignty
A Response to Kate Nash

Mark Goodale

In Kate Nash's insightful essay on the limits of human rights, she argues that 'there is a paradox at the heart of the project of globalizing human rights'. This is the paradox created by the difference between a particular liberal conception of individuals *qua* (natural) rights bearers and the postwar political and legal system within which this conception was given shape and form. This was a system based on two kinds of sovereignties, both of which work to undermine the cosmopolitan and universalist imperatives of human rights. At the wider level, *state* sovereignty requires non-interference in state affairs and is the Westphalian bedrock of the postwar settlement, one in which nation states stand in an equal relation to one another through a kind of collective pact of negative liberty. Of course, even at a formal level, the postwar international system is not based on a complete and equal form of state sovereignty, since the most powerful institution in the United Nations (UN)—the bloc of permanent members of the Security Council—gives to each of the five countries a political super-sovereignty through which the principles of the Atlantic Charter have at times been warped, manipulated, or ignored.

Below state sovereignty, as Nash explains, the idea of human rights is menaced by an even more eroding particularity: what she describes as *popular* sovereignty. Here, at least for democratic states, compliance with universal norms through the sovereign state is dependent on the vicissitudes of majority consent by citizens of each nation state. The working of these two sovereignties against the postwar vision of a transnational culture of global belonging creates a double bind. On the one hand, global justice is supposed to depend on universal human rights, or, as the Preamble to the Universal Declaration of Human Rights (UDHR) puts it, human rights are conceived as the 'foundation of freedom, justice and peace in the world'. On the other hand, as Nash's essay argues, the same international system that made human rights the precondition for global justice did so in a way that ensured that human rights would never be fully realized in practice, that the 'promotion of universal respect for and observance of human rights and fundamental freedoms' (to sample again from the UDHR's Preamble) would often be limited to the level of well-meaning humanitarian rhetoric.

As Nash explains, this 'citizen/human paradox' has three major long-term implications for the future of human rights. First, it ensures that a bright and often brutal line will continue to be drawn between citizens and non-citizens, since it is only citizens who get to enjoy universal human rights rendered into domestic law. On the day that I write this (18 April 2018), a caravan of Central American asylum seekers has just arrived to the bizarre border region between Mexico and the United States, a dystopian Pacific beach on which a high steel border wall stretches offshore into the roiling surf line, daring those coming north (always north, never south) to *just try and swim around it*. The embodied implication is that the lives of the universal human rights bearing citizens on the northern side of the beach wall are worth more than the universal human rights bearing lives of the non-citizens to the south because they are different kinds of lives, they are first American citizen lives.

Second, in managing this paradox in practice, as Nash explains, both states and transnational actors must infuse human rights with self-interested content; the relation of human rights to national law and development policy becomes one in which the meaning of human rights itself is refashioned in terms of the interests of national and transnational elites. To call this effect the 'politicization of human rights law', as Nash does, is very different than to say, as scholars like Michael Goodhart have done, that human rights must be understood first and foremost as a framework for making political claims—ideally on behalf of vulnerable populations or in the interests of progressive change.[1] Instead, 'political' here means something more like 'cynical appropriation' or 'rhetorical manipulation'. Either way, the practice of human rights in terms of its paradoxical historical and conceptual core bears little relation to the universalizing and apolitical aspirations of its postwar origins.

And finally, Nash argues that the paradox underlying contemporary human rights demonstrates precisely why 'human rights'—understood as it is, not as it is sometimes imagined to be—should not be counterposed to nationalism through a false dialectic that envisions cosmopolitan human rights in opposition to culture, regional identity, and populism. This is perhaps the most radical argument in Nash's essay: that in making the state the anchor around which the postwar human rights system revolves, the very concept of human rights itself was fundamentally altered—it was, one might say, nationalized. Even more, she suggests that the nationalization of human rights, the denuding in practice of its cosmopolitan origins, is most pronounced in the area of social and economic, rather than civil and political, human rights. Using the case of the Spanish political and social party

---

[1] Michael Goodhart, 'Human Rights and the Politics of Contestation' in Mark Goodale (ed.), *Human Rights at the Crossroads* (Oxford University Press 2013) 31.

Podemos as a point of reference, Nash argues that social and economic rights demand localized and granular commitments on the part of communities—national, linguistic, social—that run counter to the abstract liberal idealism that grounds civil and political human rights. On this innovative reading, social and economic human rights become an alternative normative means through which concrete social justice movements can take shape beyond the narrowness of cultural affiliation or political party but well below the level of the fictive kin group that the UDHR describes as 'all members of the human family'.

I.

In what remains, I would only add two elements to Nash's framework for understanding the relationship between the state, political legitimacy, conceptions of belonging, and the future of human rights: the first, historical; the second, critical theoretical. In beginning her essay with an extract from the 1789 Declaration of the Rights of Man and of the Citizen, Nash reminds us that the history of human rights has always been marked by philosophical and political dilemmas. Indeed, although Jean-Jacques Rousseau was influenced by the late-eighteenth century writings of John Locke, Rousseau's major contribution (1762) to social contract theory was a deep and radical departure from the principles developed by what Nancy Hirschmann has called the 'father of liberalism'.[2]

Whereas Locke had emphasized the importance of individuals exercising their natural rights in concert with other normatively windowless 'monads'[3] in order to form political communities, particularly for the defence of private property, Rousseau had given priority to something quite different: *la volonté générale*, or the General Will. Although one of Rousseau's most well-regarded contemporary interpreters, Maurice Cranston, has argued that the 'general will is a normative concept',[4] its troubled afterlives have revealed both its essential ambiguity and its relation to concepts of national identity, the people, and race. Indeed, the fact that the French Declaration makes the quasi-mystical concept of the general will its key principle while the relatively contemporaneous American Declaration of Independence divides the source of right between a divine creator and the consent of the governed, goes some way towards explaining the quite different political and legal histories in France and the United States over the succeeding centuries.

---

[2] Nancy Hirschmann, *Gender, Class, and Freedom in Modern Political Theory* (Princeton University Press 2007).
[3] Mark Goodale, 'The Misbegotten Monad: Anthropology, Human Rights, Belonging' in Danielle Celermajer and Alexandre Lefebvre (eds), *The Subject of Human Rights* (Stanford University Press forthcoming).
[4] Maurice Cranston, 'Introduction' in Jean-Jacques Rousseau, *The Social Contract* (first published 1782, Penguin Books 1968) 37.

Nevertheless, the key point is that the French Declaration, which, as Nash rightly emphasizes, exercised an inordinate influence on the global history of human rights, was grounded in a vague philosophy that neither gave priority to the individual nor to the sum total of individuals acting as a collective. Rather, the general will preceded individuals and was imagined to act as an ever-present check on individual liberty (something that has caused scholars to view Rousseau as either an 'early-fascist or early-communist, at all events a totalitarian'[5]).

Thus, from the very beginning, as it were, the 'principles [that] ... subsequently became so taken-for-granted as to be invisible', that is, that 'humans have rights as such', as Nash puts it, were to a large extent both anti-individualist and anti-universalist. Despite the fact that the French Declaration begins with the recognizably abstract statement that 'men are born and remain free and equal in rights', this assertion is quickly belied by the antecedence and normative preeminence of the general will, as we have seen. But as the history of the French Revolution and the nineteenth century would reveal, it was the coequality in the Declaration of 'man' (which meant men, and only some men at that) and 'citizen' that would prove to be so problematic for both the history and contemporary understanding of human rights. This was not only because 'citizen' implied a member of a particular political community and not simply a member of the imagined 'human family', although this was true enough. It was because 'citizen' became a keyword that gestured towards socialist politics, the redistribution of economic resources, and eventually the purging of elites. During the Paris Commune of 1871, most notably, *citoyen/citoyenne* became alternately a badge of honour and a brutal epithet that marked a dividing line between rebellion and mass atrocity.[6]

This tension between the violence of differentiated belonging and the aspirations of human rights carried over into the twentieth century and shaped global history in important ways up to the Second World War and the eventual adoption of the UDHR in its aftermath. For example, to keep with the French experience, the French Third Republic (1870–1940) saw the French colonial empire expand considerably on the basis of an ideology which attempted to reconcile republicanism with colonial domination. This tortured linkage was made most influentially by the Breton philologist Ernest Renan, who supported both the rights of citizenship and self-determination at the same time in which he was a leading advocate for the French empire's *mission civilisatrice* on the basis that the French occupied a higher place within a hierarchy of races compared to colonized populations.[7] Thus, right up until the years in which the UDHR was drafted, what Nash describes as the 'citizen/human paradox' had become deeply intertwined with the full history of

---

[5] Ibid, 34.

[6] John Merriman, *Massacre: The Life and Death of the Paris Commune of 1871* (Yale University Press 2014).

[7] Gilles Manceron, *Marianne et les colonies: Une introduction à l'histoire coloniale de la France* (La Découverte 2003).

human rights itself, a history marked by contradiction, colonial justification, and nationalist terror.

During what I have called elsewhere the 'prehistory' of human rights,[8] that is, the roughly two years from the creation of the Commission on Human Rights to the adoption of the UDHR in December 1948, these tensions played out within the processes—both deliberate and chaotically ad hoc—that were the basis for producing a declaration of human rights for the new international order. Even among those who had agreed to participate in a supposedly global survey on the principles of human rights undertaken by the United Nations Educational, Scientific and Cultural Organization (UNESCO), a survey whose results were intended to shape the content of what became the UDHR, the question of the relationship between the individual and the collective, between negative and positive rights, and between the state and society, were treated in widely divergent ways.

Yet even across this philosophical diversity, there was at least one important trend among the UNESCO responses: a general puzzlement, which was expressed at times with poetic outrage (e.g. by TS Eliot), that the several institutions of the embryonic international system were insisting on a *bill of human rights* as the foundation for the future. As Morris L Ernst, one of the founders of the American Civil Liberties Union (ACLU), put it at the time, 'it seems to me that we are finished with the era of passing general resolutions in regard to liberty and freedom'.[9] And for the many traditional leftists at mid-twentieth century—both those who participated in the UNESCO survey and otherwise—there was no question about the validity of human rights in relation to the socialist and communist systems that followed from the Russian Revolution. For them, human rights was a late-eighteenth-century solution to the problems of feudalism that had no contemporary relevance in the face of global inequality and the structural violence of capitalist accumulation.

II.

Finally, beyond the historical, I would make a critical theoretical observation in relation to Nash's essay. To return to Nash's invocation of the Spanish political and social party Podemos, what interests me here is not its 'meteoric electoral success in Spain in recent years', as revealing as this might be. Rather, it is the fact, as Nash also underscores, that its ideological platform is both infused with principles that align with human rights advocacy and grounded in national, regional, local, and, indeed, ecological specificities. In this sense, the rise of Podemos carries important lessons for the future of human rights, since its hybrid positions suggest that

---

[8] Mark Goodale (ed.), *Letters to the Contrary: A Curated History of the UNESCO Human Rights Survey* (Stanford University Press 2018).
[9] Quoted in ibid, 299.

human rights norms must be vernacularized in terms that are immediately recognizable and woven into relevant histories. This becomes all the more important in an era in which anti-human rights politics makes its claims on people's hearts (and sometimes on their minds) precisely on the basis of its deep relevance, whether for the protection of culture, or on behalf of national interests, or at the service of economic security.

Indeed, in Podemos's dizzyingly elaborate 394-point programme—one that bears all the marks of a movement led by academics with a certain affinity for the organizational zeal of the Fourth International—'human rights' are mentioned only three times, and then only in the context of quite specific and nationally embedded—that is, non-universal—justice demands: Point 260 calls for the creation of a government human rights office; Point 261 draws attention to the importance of the human rights to memory and truth in light of Spanish history; and Point 316 calls for the 'reestablishment of the right to migration [and] respect for human rights on the southern border', also a direct reference to an ongoing national conflict.[10] Yet across the remaining 391 points of Podemos's platform, one can discern the spirit of human rights promotion comingled with a wide range of ideological orientations. The result is a formidable politics of counterhegemonic resistance that, as Nash puts it, 'does not demonize non-nationals or minorities ... at the same time it also ... demand[s] the social and economic rights with which many of those tempted by right-wing populism are concerned in Spain'.

III.

In light of these various implications, we therefore arrive at several conclusions regarding the future of human rights understood in terms of both limits and possibilities. As Nash's essay convincingly argues, the orthodox account of human rights that 'rose and fell'[11] during the first two decades of the post-Cold War did so in part because it was grounded in certain conceptual dilemmas, which played out by weakening human rights in legal and political practice. A reformulated human rights would be one that recognized these limitations and sought to move beyond them. An important first step would be to leave to the side the universalist orientation of human rights in favour of vernacularized projects—as with Podemos—that retained the progressive vision of human rights translated into concrete and historicized categories. Most radically, this would imply the normative abandonment of *universal* human rights itself in exchange for *plural* human rights. This is not an

---

[10] Podemos, *Programa 2016* <http://www.lasonrisadeunpais.es/programa/> accessed 31 January 2019.

[11] Lori Allen, *The Rise and Fall of Human Rights: Cynicism and Politics in Occupied Palestine* (Stanford University Press 2013).

arid recipe for relativism, however, but rather the suggestion that the articulation of rights for all humans necessarily imposes constraints that have rendered human rights, as Moyn has put it, 'not enough'.[12]

Bibliography

Allen L, *The Rise and Fall of Human Rights: Cynicism and Politics in Occupied Palestine* (Stanford University Press 2013)

Cranston M, 'Introduction' in Rousseau JJ, *The Social Contract* (first published 1782, Penguin Books 1968)

Goodale M (ed.), *Letters to the Contrary: A Curated History of the UNESCO Human Rights Survey* (Stanford University Press 2018)

Goodale M, 'The Misbegotten Monad: Anthropology, Human Rights, Belonging' in Celermajer D and Lefebvre A (eds), *The Subject of Human Rights* (Stanford University Press *forthcoming*)

Goodhart M, 'Human Rights and the Politics of Contestation' in Goodale M (ed.), *Human Rights at the Crossroads* (Oxford University Press 2013) 31–44

Hirschmann N, *Gender, Class, and Freedom in Modern Political Theory* (Princeton University Press 2007)

Manceron G, *Marianne et les colonies: Une introduction à l'histoire coloniale de la France* (La Découverte 2003)

Merriman J, *Massacre: The Life and Death of the Paris Commune of 1871* (Yale University Press 2014)

Moyn S, *Not Enough: Human Rights in an Unequal World* (Belknap Press 2018)

Podemos, *Programa 2016* <http://www.lasonrisadeunpais.es/programa/> accessed 31 January 2019

---

[12] Samuel Moyn, *Not Enough: Human Rights in an Unequal World* (Belknap Press 2018).

5
Emergencies and Human Rights
A Hobbesian Analysis

*David Dyzenhaus**

Salus populi suprema lex esto—may the safety of the people be the supreme law. If Cicero's maxim is correct, human rights do have limits. When the safety or welfare of the people is under threat because of a situation of emergency, the law that governs is not the law, including the law of human rights if the law happens to enshrine such rights. Rather, a political judgment governs about what it takes to secure the safety of the people. Human rights are therefore neither inalienable nor illimitable since some body or person may legitimately strip people of their legal rights or severely limit the rights in at least one kind of situation, the situation of an emergency.

Thus interpreted, Cicero's maxim has had a deep influence on political and legal thought that reaches into the present. It is regarded as the key to the Roman institution of dictatorship in which in times of emergency one person was for a limited period given otherwise unlimited power to respond to the emergency as he saw fit. In particular, the maxim and its institutional context are central to the 'reason of state' or 'sovereign prerogative' tradition that stretches from Machiavelli through Carl Schmitt and his claim that '[s]overeign is he who decides on the state of exception'[1] to contemporary political thinkers such as Girgio Agamben.

In Schmitt's view, political order has to be understood as 'autonomous'. The 'political' in his theory is the site of an existential struggle between friend and enemy, resolved by the decision of the sovereign made on the basis of a vision of the substantive homogeneity of the *Volk*, whose mark of success is that he attracts their acclaim.[2] Sovereign authority is precisely the unmediated coercive power that reveals itself in an emergency.

Liberals will reject Schmitt's idea of the autonomy of the political and its vision of community. But the claim about sovereign authority in times of emergency,

---

* I thank Thomas Poole and Knut Traisbach for comments on a draft, the audience at a Max Weber lecture at the European University Institute for their questions, and for discussion the participants in the Berlin Colloquium on Global and Comparative Public Law of the Wissenschaftszentrum für Sozialforschung and in the Gosepath Seminar for Practical Philosophy at the Free University, Berlin.

[1] Carl Schmitt, *Political Theology: Four Chapters on the Concept of Sovereignty* (MIT Press 1988) 14 (hereafter Schmitt, *Political Theology*).
[2] Carl Schmitt, *The Concept of the Political* (Rutgers University Press 1976).

which Schmitt takes as evidence for his account of the political, reaches into the heart of their liberal constitutionalist tradition. This is exemplified in the fact that John Locke made Cicero's maxim his epigraph for *The Second Treatise of Human Government*.[3] Locke extolled the virtues of the rule of law—of the advantages to liberty of life under 'settled, standing' legislated rules common to all in contrast to 'the inconstant, uncertain, unknown, arbitrary will of another man'.[4] But he also insisted that in emergencies the government had to have a prerogative or legally unconstrained power to 'act according to discretion, for the publick good, without the prescription of the Law, and sometimes even against it'.[5] It might well seem to follow that, as the editor of a recent illuminating collection *Human Rights in Emergencies* puts it, '[p]ublic emergencies ... present the ultimate test for human rights theory in its practical application'.[6]

I will argue not only that the safety of the people may not be *legitimately* secured by acting outside of law, but also that the safety of the people *cannot* be secured by acting outside of law since the 'safety of the people' is itself a juridical concept. But I wish to push the argument even further to the claim that human rights are part of the law to which political authorities are always subject. That claim will, however, seem implausible because of the various ways in which the legal entitlement to human rights seems to be relative.

First, the idea that political authorities must respect human rights as legal entitlements is usually taken to have traction in the practice of states only in the postwar period. Even if we think now that all human beings are entitled to such rights, we should recognize that they are relative at least in the sense they are legal entitlements only in our own time. Second, even in our own time, there are states in which human rights are not legal entitlements or, if they are, the states pay at best lip service to them. Hence, we might say that such rights are also relative to place in that your legal entitlement to such rights depends very much on where you happen to find yourself.

Third, even if you happen to live somewhere where human rights are legal entitlements, and respected as such, you may find that the respect is conditional on the state not confronting an emergency. Indeed, this conditionality seems to be given formal recognition in the many legal regimes of human rights that make explicit provision for the state to derogate in times of emergency from at least some of the rights enumerated in the regime, an echo of similar provisions in international human rights regimes. Hence, there is yet another sense in which human rights seem relative. They are enjoyed as legal entitlements only in normal times.

---

[3] John Locke, *Second Treatise of Government* (Hackett 1980).
[4] Ibid, paras 22 and 137.
[5] Ibid, para. 160.
[6] Evan J Criddle, 'Introduction: Testing Human Rights Theories During Emergencies' in Evan J Criddle (ed.), *Human Rights in Emergencies* (Cambridge University Press 2016) 1, 11 (hereafter Criddle (ed.), *Human Rights in Emergencies*).

This third kind of relativism seems the most troubling of the three. It differs from the relativisms of time and place in that it is political relativism: it relativizes human rights not only to normality but even further to political judgment about normality. It makes it appropriate to recognize that even when human rights are properly observed legal entitlements, they enjoy this status on condition that the safety of the people is not imperilled. It follows that even if the safety of the people is a juridical concept, human rights are not. It is for this reason that public emergencies seem to 'present the ultimate test for human rights theory in its practical application'.

I shall argue that these relativist concerns can be overcome once we understand that the juridical concept of the safety of the people includes respect for the human rights of the individuals who make up what we can think of as the 'jural community': the political community of legal subjects bound together by the rule of law. It follows that emergencies do not so much expose limits to human rights as show how human rights constitute the jural community. Rather than emergencies telling us how human rights will or may legitimately be limited, they tell us how human rights shape the way in which states respond to emergencies because of the onus of justification states bear to the subjects who make up the jural community. Justification is always justification in terms of such rights.

This last claim will appear worryingly ambiguous between the vacuous claim that political justification by definition satisfies human rights and the too robust claim that a political justification counts as such only when it meets the standard set by human rights.

In the vacuous claim, the safety of the people is the supreme human right, and in times of emergency a political judgment about it trumps all other claims. In the too robust claim, Cicero's maxim is opposed by one of it naïve Latin counterparts: *fiat justitia, ruat caelum*—let justice be done, though the heavens fall.

My argument navigates between these two pitfalls by going backwards in time. Section I seeks to clarify the problem at stake in this debate through a discussion of two essays by a remarkable philosopher, Bernard Williams, 'Realism and Moralism in Political Theory' and 'Human Rights and Relativism'.[7] Williams follows Thomas Hobbes in arguing that the mark of 'the political' lies in a society finding a solution to the problem of how to create order. He also argues that a political order differs from a mere coercive order in that it seeks to satisfy the 'Basic Legitimation Demand', which places the state under an onus of justification to those subject to its power. This argument connects to the essay on human rights because it suggests

---

[7] Bernard Williams, 'Realism and Moralism in Political Theory' in Geoffrey Hawthorn (ed.), *Bernard Williams—In the Beginning was the Deed: Realism and Moralism in Political Argument* (Princeton University Press 2005) 1 (hereafter Williams, 'Realism and Moralism in Political Theory') and Bernard Williams, 'Human Rights and Relativism' in Hawthorn (ed.), ibid, 62 (hereafter Williams, 'Human Rights and Relativism').

that one way in which human rights are *not* relative is that political justification is always in terms of the human rights of those subject to the state in a way that avoids the pitfalls of being vacuous or too robust.

However, as I show in section II, the avoidance is not on the basis of a philosophical answer to the problem Williams's essays illuminate. Rather, the answer lies in putting in place the kind of institutional structure of legality required for the state to discharge its onus of justification.[8] Despite Williams's dismissal of Hobbes's own solution to the problem of order, it is to be found in the legal order Hobbes envisaged on the cusp of the development of the modern state. Within that structure, we can understand the non-relative way in which human rights are constitutive of legal order and so shape how the state must respond to emergencies. In situations of emergency when the survival of the state is at risk, human rights can ensure the cohesion of the jural community by maintaining the onus of justification. If in situations of emergency the basic (human) right to justification is forfeited, the political order dismantles from within by becoming a coercive order.

In the third and final section, I shall return to the Roman and thus deep historical roots of this institutional structure in light of a revisionist account of how we should understand Cicero's maxim. These roots help to illuminate why human rights, while not being able to avoid the challenge posed by states of emergencies, can—normatively and politically—limit both discourses and practices associated with reason of state by maintaining a basic requirement of justification of sovereign authority. This basic legitimation demand is constitutive of a political order as a jural community and affords an understanding of the autonomy of the political that is both realistic and distinct from Schmitt's.

---

[8] This is the major difference between my Williams-inspired argument and Rainer Forst's influential account of the right to justification in various works, e.g. Rainer Forst, *The Right to Justification: Elements of a Constructivist Theory of Justice* (Columbia University Press 2012) and Rainer Forst, *Justification and Critique* (Polity Press 2014). While I find many points of contact between his work and mine, his account of the right to justification depends on the quest for a transcendental philosophical basis for the right that is not only, in my view, misguided, but also has the consequence of importing considerations that require the too robust claim. See, e.g., *The Right to Justification*, 203–28, where he says at 220–1 that his 'moral constructivism' has to find a 'level' which 'shows that moral persons, both in a given context and beyond it, must grant certain rights to one another, rights that they *owe* one another, in a moral sense' (emphasis in the original). As Forst makes plain on these pages, his theory thus seeks an even stronger transcendental grounding than that provided by Jürgen Habermas, one that has a 'core content' 'prior to political justice', ibid (compare *Justification and Critique*, 38–70 and 46–7.) For trenchant criticism, see Lois McNay, 'The Limits of Justification: Critique, Disclosure and Reflexivity' (2016) European Journal of Political Theory 1. My own view, in contrast, is pragmatic both in that it is based on practice and experience and makes successful practice the test of whether it should continue to be held. It is inspired by Etienne Mureinik's articulation of legal culture as a 'culture of justification', see Etienne Mureinik, 'A Bridge to Where? Introducing the Interim Bill of Rights' (1994) 10 South African Journal on Human Rights 31, 32 as elaborated in David Dyzenhaus, 'Law as Justification: Etienne Mureinik's Conception of Legal Culture' (1998) 14 South African Journal on Human Rights 11.

I. LEGITIMACY, JUSTIFICATION, AND HUMAN RIGHTS

Central to Williams's essays is the thought that political theory should start with the Hobbesian question of how to secure 'order, protection, safety, trust, and the conditions of cooperation'.[9] This, he says, is the 'first' political question because 'solving it is the condition of solving, indeed posing, any others'.[10] But 'first' should not be understood as implying that the question 'once solved ... never has to be solved again' because 'a solution to the first political question is *required all the time*'.[11]

According to Williams, it is a necessary condition of legitimacy that the state solves the first political question, which means that it must satisfy 'the Basic Legitimation Demand' (BLD) that every legitimate state must satisfy if it is to show that it wields authority rather than sheer coercive power over those subject to its rule. To meet that demand the state 'has to be able to offer a justification of its power *to each subject*', which means to every individual in its power, 'whom by its own lights it can rightfully coerce under its laws and institutions'.[12]

Williams regards legitimacy as a matter of actual acceptance of a political order's legitimacy by those subject to it. He thus opposes liberal political theories that make morality prior to politics, either by taking politics to be the instrument of the moral or as structurally constrained by moral principles. In contrast to these versions of 'political moralism', he advocates 'political realism' which he thinks gives a 'greater autonomy to distinctively political thought'.[13] In general, he insists on the autonomy of 'the political'—a deliberate echo of Schmitt.[14] What counts as legitimate in a particular political order is relative to what is accepted in that order, not what some theory has determined as the moral standards which any order has to meet to count as legitimate; for example, and as many liberals would argue, that its laws respect some predetermined list of human rights.

Williams's opposition is not, however, to liberalism as such. Rather, he sees liberalism as providing a candidate for answering the BLD, one that developed at a particular time and confined to a small number of existing states. While liberals are entitled to claim that their answer to the BLD is—at least in their societies—the best possible answer, they should not do so by building the assumptions of their moral theory into political theory itself. Rather, their theory provides a historically contingent answer to the first political question.

---

[9] Williams, 'Realism and Moralism in Political Theory' (n. 7) 3.
[10] Ibid and Williams, 'Human Rights and Relativism' (n. 7).
[11] Williams, 'Human Rights and Relativism' (n. 7) and Williams, 'Realism and Moralism in Political Theory' (n. 7) 3 (emphasis in the original).
[12] Williams, 'Realism and Moralism in Political Theory' (n. 7) 4 (emphasis in the original).
[13] Ibid 3.
[14] See also his remarks in Bernard Williams, 'From Freedom to Liberty: The Construction of a Political Value' in Geoffrey Hawthorn (ed.), *Bernard Williams—In the Beginning was the Deed: Realism and Moralism in Political Argument* (Princeton University Press 2005) 75, 77–8.

Part of the problem Williams thus sees with the lack of realism in liberal political theory is that its claim that only liberal states are legitimate makes it relevant only to a small number of states and to quite recent times. In other words, if an understanding of legitimacy is central to political theory, liberalism is too reductive in that it reduces legitimacy to correspondence with a set of values that make up one or other liberal position. And that reduction does not so much offer an understanding of the concept of legitimacy as eliminate it from political theory altogether. It puts in place the too robust sense of justification because a claim that a measure is legitimate in political theory is a claim that it should be accepted despite the fact that its content is not in accord with a particular moral position.

But Williams also seems to suppose that realists should accept that political relativism is right, which might make his position prey to a different kind of reductivism. He emphasizes that a political order to keep itself distinct from what he calls an 'unmediated coercive power' must avoid its solution to the problem of achieving order becoming part of the problem; for example, if it resorts to 'the most blatant denials of human rights, torture, surveillance, arbitrary arrest, and murder'.[15] But he also says that we should recognize that a state may engage its enemies in ways that we find discomfiting but have an authentic claim to be legitimate:

> Thus what is in its terms a legitimate order may use what we would regard as cruel and unusual punishments; it is significant that, not surprisingly, they make no secret of this. They or others may use, rather less openly, ruthless methods against subversives or threatening revolutionaries. Are such measures in themselves violations of human rights? If they are, are they violations justified by emergency?[16]

He continues:

> Any state may use such methods in extremis, and it is inescapably true that it is a matter of political judgement, by political actors and commentators, whether given acts are part of the solution or of the problem. Liberal states make it a virtue—and it is in indeed a virtue—to wait as long as possible before using such solutions, because they have the constant apprehension that those solutions will become part of the problem, Liberal states are well-regarded, and rightly so, for showing this restraint. They should be less well regarded, as the writings of Carl Schmitt may remind us, if they turn this into the belief that the only real sign of virtue is to wait too long.[17]

---

[15] Williams, 'Human Rights and Relativism' (n. 7) 69.
[16] Ibid, 70.
[17] Ibid, 70; see William E Scheuerman, 'Human Rights Lawyers v. Carl Schmitt' in Criddle (ed.), *Human Rights in Emergencies* (n. 6) 175.

If 'such methods' refers to 'blatant denials of human rights', Williams would be committed to the view that human rights are expendable luxuries. In addition, this second invocation of Schmitt may seem ominous, since he is notorious for claiming that the state is legally unlimited in its response to emergencies and that ideas like 'human rights' are vacuous tropes of liberal thought.

On the one hand, Williams's realism should incline him more to the vacuous claim and thus to a different kind of reductivism in which justification becomes whatever happens to be accepted as such, whatever its content. But, on the other hand, he is also willing to countenance that the BLD is a moral principle, as long as one understands that it is inherent in politics, that is, in the Hobbesian political question.[18] As he puts it, Hobbes did not

> think that a ... [legitimate] state could be identical with a reign of terror; the whole point was to save people from terror. It was essential to his construction, that is to say, that the state—the solution—should not become part of the problem. This is an important idea: it is part of what is involved in a state's meeting ... the Basic Legitimation Demand ....[19]

In addition, Williams recognizes that successful domination may make it the case that legitimation demands simply do not arise. For example, a group might accept the dominant ideology that deems it to be inferior and so justifiably relegated to a subordinate position in the society. And so he introduces a second principle, the 'critical theory principle' that 'the acceptance of a justification does not count if the acceptance itself is produced by the coercive power which is supposedly being justified'.[20]

These two essays thus preserve a tension between the idea that acceptance by the subjects of rule suffices for legitimacy and the idea that the critical theory principle can give us reason to doubt that a regime is legitimate despite the fact that it is generally accepted as such by those subject to it. Put in terms of the classical debate in political theory, Williams rejects the distinction between *de facto* and *de jure* authority, but suggests that an authority in fact must always strive for legitimacy and will achieve it only on condition that it does not blatantly abuse human rights.

That tension will seem to some if not many to make his theory incoherent. But it indicates rather that philosophy can only get us as far as seeing clearly what the tension is that has to be resolved. It cannot provide a solution that resolves that tension without resorting to unrealistic transcendental arguments. Williams says of emergency situations that 'there is always room for argument in such cases' but takes it to be a virtue of his account that it is at least clear 'what the argument is

---

[18] Williams, 'Realism and Moralism in Political Theory' (n. 7) 3.
[19] Ibid, 4.
[20] Ibid, 8.

about'.[21] The clarity resides, in my view, in seeing that this is the tension that has to be addressed and moreover addressed publicly. I shall now try to show that Hobbes not only, as Williams suggests, correctly posed the first political question of how to achieve order, but also sketched the institutional structure that permits a political community to work through that tension in the requisite public fashion.

II. HOBBES AND THE BASIC LEGITIMATION DEMAND

As I indicated, Williams does not take more from Hobbes than his posing of the first political question because he considers Hobbes made the mistake of supposing that the absence of disorder is a sufficient condition of legitimacy when it is only a necessary one.[22]

But, while Williams recognizes that Hobbes not only posed the first question, but also did so in a way that requires seeing that BLD is inherent in it, he does not pause to examine how Hobbes himself went about answering the question.[23] As a result, he does not appreciate that for Hobbes the primary way that a political order is distinguished from an *unmediated* coercive order is precisely in that law plays the mediating role. Law's role in transforming might into right constitutes a special kind of political community—a jural community.[24]

In Hobbes's political theory, the state is created by a covenant between individuals in the state of nature who thereby unify themselves into one person.[25] The state cannot by itself act, so it has to be represented by the sovereign person (if one) or persons (if a group) and in the act of covenanting the individuals authorize the sovereign to secure the common peace and their safety. Since he acts in their name, he acts as an artificial not a natural person, so there must be a way of distinguishing acts done by the sovereign in his public capacity from acts done by the individual or individuals who make up the sovereign in their private capacity. The marks of public authority attach to the way that the sovereign communicates with his subjects, which is through a public order of law. Those subject to the sovereign's

---

[21] Williams, 'Human Rights and Relativism' (n. 7) 72.

[22] Williams, 'Realism and Moralism in Political Theory' (n. 7) 3.

[23] Williams is hardly alone in his inattention to Hobbes's legal theory. It is characteristic of nearly all Hobbes scholars.

[24] Although Williams barely discusses law, it is clear that he regards law and the rule of law as part of the answer to the first political question, see his remarks about Habermas in Williams, 'Realism and Moralism in Political Theory' (n. 7) 15–16.

[25] This section summarizes a view of Hobbes I have developed in several places, e.g., David Dyzenhaus, 'Hobbes on the Authority of Law' in David Dyzenhaus and Thomas Poole (eds), *Hobbes and the Law* (Cambridge University Press 2012) 186 (hereafter Dyzenhaus, 'Hobbes on the Authority of Law' and Dyzenhaus and Poole (eds), *Hobbes and the Law*). The account below is primarily an account of the argument in Thomas Hobbes, *Leviathan* (Cambridge University Press 2014) (hereafter Hobbes, *Leviathan*).

laws must understand that they own all his laws since they are ultimately the authors of the law. Put differently, since the sovereign always acts with right, *de jure*, they cannot accuse him of injustice because that would be to claim that he acted without the right he has through their authorization.

Hobbes emphasizes that as long as one is in a condition of subjection to a sovereign's laws, it does not matter how that condition came about: the subject will be deemed to have consented to the sovereign's rule. *De facto* authority is *de jure*. In addition, since such subjection permits the escape from the situation of continual emergency in which individuals find themselves in the state of nature, Hobbes often uses the threat of a return to the state of nature as an inducement to subjects to understand their obligation of obedience to the sovereign's laws, whatever their content. His argument may thus seem to present a 'once and for all' and highly authoritarian solution to the question of how to secure order, rather than, as Williams suggests, one that is provided 'all the time'.

It is, however, important, to see that the covenanting individuals do more than create the state; they also transform themselves from natural individuals into legal subjects. With that transformation, they establish a relationship of reciprocity between subject and sovereign: the 'mutuall Relation between Protection and Obedience', as Hobbes puts it in the last paragraph of *Leviathan*.[26] That relationship is between two kinds of artificial person—the person of the sovereign and the persons who are legal subjects, and for Hobbes it is the mark of the political—of the fact that a political order has been established in which rule is by right and the natural realm of rule by might has been left behind.

Put differently, a political order is characterized by authority relationships by contrast with unmediated coercive power. The point is not that a political order can do without coercive power, only that it wields power in a way that makes plausible a claim to have been authorized by those who are subject to that power. Any exercise of coercive power by the state must therefore be recognizable as an authoritative act, which entails that it must meet two conditions of public authority. The first is formal—the 'validity proviso' that any exercise of power must show a legal warrant in a law that has been made in accordance with the order's formal public criteria for recognizing a law. The second condition is substantive. Any exercise of power must meet the 'legality proviso': the laws the sovereign makes have to be interpreted, and so must be interpretable, in light of Hobbes's extensive list of the laws of nature.[27]

In large, complex societies, the exercise of sovereignty will require officials to implement the laws and subordinate judges to provide authoritative interpretations of the law. These officials are a necessary part of the exercise of sovereign authority since it is they who ensure that the general laws that the sovereign enacts are appropriately applied to subjects.

---

[26] Hobbes, *Leviathan* (n. 25) 491.
[27] See Dyzenhaus, 'Hobbes on the Authority of Law' (n. 25).

While the sovereign *qua* ultimate legislator and judge is not accountable to his subjects for infractions of the laws of nature, his subordinate officials—including judges—must seek to show that the law as it is applied in particular cases is consistent with the laws of nature, notably the law that commands that subjects be treated equitably. That puts an onus of justification on officials which, if it cannot be discharged, raises the question whether the subject is within the reciprocal relationship of protection and obedience, and so implies that the relationship is not political but one of hostility or unmediated coercion between more and less powerful natural individuals. Put differently, while Hobbes's solution to the first political question is the injunction, 'Obey the law, whatever its content', it is far from unmediated coercion. It is coercion mediated by legal right because the content has to be put into legal form and then applied and interpreted in a way that discharges the onus of justification.

Hobbes's solution is not then a once and for all one. Subjects are entitled to a justification of how a law applies to them as members of a jural community in which each individual enjoys equal freedom before the law. If the only possible interpretation of the state's response is that it outlaws a subject by ejecting him or her from the jural community that person is in the emergency condition of the state of nature from which entry into the political is supposed to be an escape. The solution, as we have seen Williams say, becomes the problem.

Thus, if the political relationship between sovereign and subject is to be maintained, it has to shape the way in which the state responds to threats, including threats that, in the opinion of those who hold sovereign office, rise to the level of a public emergency. For when states respond to emergencies, they must continue to meet the two conditions of public authority lest they change the relationship between officials and subjects from a civil-society one of authority mediated by law to a state-of-nature one of unmediated coercion. For Hobbes, in contrast to Locke, the sovereign may not act against the law without ceasing to be sovereign.[28]

In this shaping, what we would today call human rights play a role. Hobbes, of course, does not talk of 'human rights'. But he insists from the beginning of *Leviathan* that the individual human being as such is the subject of political order. Moreover, he does have a category of 'inalienable rights', the rights that follow from one's right to preserve oneself.[29] Indeed, he makes it clear that this right carries

---

[28] This claim requires me to treat as an aberration Hobbes's claim in *Leviathan* (n. 25) 153 that the sovereign can act purely on the basis of power rather than law, as well as Hobbes's reliance on the biblical story of David and Uriah in the same chapter at 148. For the argument as to why one should take this position, see David Dyzenhaus, 'How Hobbes Met the "Hobbes Challenge"' (2009) 72 Modern Law Review 488, 493–6. For a view of Hobbes that sees him as moving between the constitutionalist and reason of state traditions, see Thomas Poole, 'Hobbes on Law and Prerogative' in Dyzenhaus and Poole (eds), *Hobbes and the Law* (n. 25) 68.

[29] See the marginal note 'not all rights are alienable' in Hobbes, *Leviathan* (n. 25) 93 and see further 150–1.

over into the civil condition so that the subject has the right to resist punishment, even when the violence of punishment is fully mediated by law.[30]

Hobbes's theory of punishment is peculiar but instructive for an understanding of the requirement of justification. On the one hand, it has at its core a distinction between punishment and hostility where the former requires that the person has been convicted in a fair trial of a crime set out in a prior general law, and is proportionate in that it is aimed at reforming the individual and deterring others, not at revenge. On the other hand, Hobbes insists that while subjects must be taken to have authorized the institution of punishment in general, no one can be taken to have authorized the sovereign to punish him or her in particular, so that the subject who is about to be punished is entitled to resist. At that moment, the subject is in a relationship of unmediated power or hostility with the sovereign or his officials.

Hobbes's theory of punishment thus presents a double optic on the violence necessary to maintain order.[31] There is the private optic of the about-to-be-punished individual who is in a kind of mini-state of nature vis à vis the officials. But there is also the public optic of fellow subjects for whom it is very important to observe that the individual got all of the protections afforded by the rule of law before being subject to coercion.[32]

The tension between the two optics comes about because Hobbes's subject is the bearer of human rights. There is only one pre-political right, the right that every human has to self-preservation, including the right to judge for oneself how to exercise that right. In the state of nature, it is a worse than useless right since its existence contributes to the precariousness of that state, so it is rational for individuals to authorize a sovereign to govern them. It is thus also rational for anyone subject to such government to understand that he or she should be taken to have consented so to be governed. But it is rational only as long as the reciprocal relationship between protection and obedience is maintained in which protection is of the subject understood as a person who is free and equal before the law.

Hence, the pre-political right to preserve oneself survives into the civil condition in two ways, first as a political right, for Hobbes the right of rights, which is the right to demand a justification from public officials for any exercise of coercive power in terms of the reciprocal relationship between protection and obedience. Second, it survives as setting the limit of that political relationship by marking

---

[30] Ibid, ch. 27.
[31] I owe these insights to the work of Alice Ristroph, e.g. 'Criminal Law for Humans' in Dyzenhaus and Poole (eds), *Hobbes and the Law* (n. 25) 97. It is important to keep in mind that the right to resist punishment is about resistance to state coercion. If, e.g., hospitals during an epidemic do not have the resources to treat all those afflicted, those who fall outside of the groups who are considered treatable are not entitled to try to get access to the resources by force. If tried and convicted for breaking the law that governs access to such resources, they will be entitled to resist punishment. But at that point their position is no different from that of any criminal who is subject to punishment.
[32] On the importance of publicity in Hobbes, see Jeremy Waldron, 'Hobbes and the Principle of Publicity' (2001) 82 Pacific Philosophical Quarterly 447.

the point where justification runs out and political order turns into unmediated coercion.

Hobbes, then, is one of the founders of the modern political discourse of constitutionalism about the reciprocal relationship between, on the one hand, the sovereign person of the state and the officials who implement and interpret the law and, on the other hand, the persons who are subject to the law. The sovereign as an artificial person speaks to the subjects through law and legal language has its own grammar that requires that subjects be addressed in a way that respects them as bearers of what we today call human rights. As a result, the officials who apply the law to that person are under an onus of justification that requires them to demonstrate why the law as it applies is respectful of such rights. And this is the case even when the state is thought by those who wield public power to be under severe threat.

Hobbes's position is a realist one in that legitimacy depends on what people in a particular time and place actually accept. As he said in *Behemoth*, 'the Power of the mighty has no foundation but in the opinion and the beleefe of the people'.[33] But it is not reductive in either of the two ways sketched above. In that same book, as elsewhere,[34] Hobbes makes it clear that a sense of duty, not fear of coercion, underpins the maintenance of civil society. He asks: 'For if men know not their duty, what is there that can force them to obey the laws? An army you will say? But what shall force the army?'[35]

But Hobbes is not a total realist in that his theory is built on an assumption of political morality.[36] Hobbes tries to put the right to preserve oneself which each individual enjoys equally in terms of facts about individuals in a state of nature—the fact of our more or less equal intellectual abilities and the fact of our more or less equal physical abilities to harm each other.[37] But, as Kinch Hoekstra has argued, the role that equality plays for Hobbes in civil society shows that in his theory 'it is less a matter that we are equals because we can destroy one another if we are so inclined, and more that we must acknowledge one another as equals because we will otherwise be inclined to destroy one another'.[38] In other words, Hobbes builds into his political theory a normative presupposition of equality that subsequently informs his understanding of the kind of protection or safety that the sovereign must supply his subjects for them to be able to accept that he governs in their name.

---

[33] Thomas Hobbes, *Behemoth or the Long Parliament* (University of Chicago Press 1990) 16 (hereafter Hobbes, *Behemoth*).

[34] For example, Hobbes, *Leviathan* (n. 25) 232: 'And the grounds of these Rights, have the rather need to be diligently, and truly taught; because they cannot be maintained by any Civill Law, or terrour of legal punishment.'

[35] Hobbes, *Behemoth* (n. 33) 58–9.

[36] For illuminating discussion of Hobbes's realism, see Robin Douglas, 'Hobbes and Political Realism' (2016) European Journal of Political Theory 1.

[37] Hobbes, *Leviathan* (n. 25) 86–7.

[38] Kinch Hoekstra, 'Hobbesian Equality' in Sharon A Lloyd (ed.), *Hobbes Today: Insights for the 21st Century* (Cambridge University Press 2013) 76, 77.

That presupposition was radical in his time. *Leviathan* is best read as an invitation to an audience who had just survived a civil war fought over, in part, that very presupposition. It invites them to attempt to build a society on the foundation of this presupposition—on the promise that the experience of living in such a society will show that individuals with very different gods and demons can coexist peacefully as long as they acknowledge each other as equals. It is that acknowledgement that requires the political idea of legitimacy—the idea that one should accept the legitimacy of a public order of laws not because one morally approves of their content, but because they can be justified as not undermining one's equal status before the law at the same time as they afford the conditions of peaceful interaction.

The vindication of the promise does not depend on any transcendental argument about why one must accept that presupposition. It rests on the appeal to the kind of experience that will result from adopting it as one's foundational presupposition. But once adopted, certain things do follow, for example, the need to establish the institutional structures that will make such experience possible; notably, the legal institutions that ensure that legal subjects can get answers to the question—'But how can that be law for me?'

Because it rests on an appeal, a kind of bet based on past experience about how future experience will turn out if one regulates public life on the basis of the presupposition, it may seem vulnerable to what we can think of as the Schmittian challenge: The constitutionalist commitment to the rule of law cannot survive an emergency, which will then reveal the falsity of the presupposition. And it is to that challenge that I now turn.

III. CONSTITUTIONALISM VERSUS REASON OF STATE

Constitutionalism is not the only modern political discourse. As I suggested at the beginning, there is also the discourse associated with Machiavelli and Schmitt of 'reason of state' and prerogative, in which sovereign authority is precisely the unmediated coercive power that reveals itself in an emergency. At least in Schmitt, and in deliberate contrast to the constitutionalist tradition, the essential political relationship is one of hostility between friend and enemy and the normative force of a sovereign decision comes from its ability to eradicate conflict from a territory by establishing the substantive homogeneity of the people of that territory. The criterion of membership of the people is substantive rather than formal and legal and the solution to the first political question is a once and for all one. Once a 'concrete order', to use Schmitt's term, is established, the function of law is as a top down instrument of rule and the sovereign can decide to rule otherwise according to his judgement about what is necessary to secure the safety of the people.[39]

As I also suggested, Cicero's maxim and the Roman constitutional context in which in times of emergency the consuls gave a dictator authority to do whatever in his judgement seemed necessary to restoring the safety of the people figure large in this tradition. But in *Crisis and Constitutionalism: Roman Political Thought from the Fall of the Republic to the Age of Revolution*, Benjamin Straumann argues that this maxim and its context have long been misinterpreted.[40] Cicero did not mean that the maxim placed consuls above the law. Rather, he offered a supreme principle that governed their conduct in accordance with the law, for the consuls remained subject to law in at least the sense that they were subject to fundamental or constitutional law.[41]

Straumann's point is not confined to getting Cicero right. Rather, the correct interpretation of the maxim enables an understanding of the institution of emergency dictatorship within the Roman legal order as subject to law, or, as we say today, subject to the rule of law. And since the maxim is taken to stand for the alleged truism that in times of emergency one or other political authority within the state structure may legitimately act unconstrained by law, the correct interpretation helps to make a wider point about legal order in general. The safety of the people cannot be legitimately secured by acting outside of law.

Straumann's study shows that central to the Roman constitutionalist mode of responding to crises was the preservation of, first, the institution of *provocatio*—the citizens' right of appeal against decisions which affected them negatively by those who held high office—and, second, of the principal legislative institutions of the state and their modes of law-making. Such preservation was seen as a matter of the higher order or natural law that expressed the normative core of the republican idea of 'the people' of a political and legal order.[42]

In particular, Straumann brings to the surface the Roman idea of political community as a jural community. As he explains, the jural conception of politics emerged against a backdrop of the decay of Roman political institutions that made vivid the possibility of the disintegration of society into the anarchy of a state of nature and so raised as urgent questions the location of sovereignty in—as well as the fundamental commitments of—the political order. Simply put, the question was raised of the nature of the Roman political order. The Roman answer, as formulated principally by Cicero, rejected Greek theories that asserted a continuity between

---

[39] Carl Schmitt, *Über die drei Arten des rechtswissenschaftlichen Denkens* (Hanseatische Verlagsanstalt 1934).
[40] Benjamin Straumann, *Crisis and Constitutionalism: Roman Political Thought from the Fall of the Republic to the Age of Revolution* (Oxford University Press 2016) 35 et seq. (hereafter Straumann, *Crisis and Constitutionalism*).
[41] Ibid, 36.
[42] Ibid, 129–39.

ethics and politics such that there is some highest ethical good at which politics aims. Instead, it was based on the argument that politics is limited by 'law-like constitutional principles' so that the highest officers of state are in charge of 'the people' only because it is the case that these principles are in charge of the officers.[43]

In addition, Straumann sketches the trajectory of these ideas through Bodin to Hobbes to the present. As in Hobbes who finished *Leviathan* at a time when civil war had made vivid the possibility of the disintegration of his society into anarchy, the point of political theory is to establish the principles of order that mark the distinction between a condition in which individuals are subject to unmediated coercive power and a civil condition in which they interact with each other within a stable and secure framework of laws.

A mark of this conception of the political is, then, that political order is always legal order, in that the subjects of the law can demand of officials that they justify their coercive acts by showing that there is a basis or warrant in the law for these acts, not only in the positive or enacted law of the order, but also (where relevant) in the constitutional principles of that order. These principles will come more to the fore in times of stress and it is not the case that their application will be uncontroversial. But even when there is deep controversy over their application, they are still considered as the principles that constitute the political realm, so that the disagreements are to be worked out within the institutional structures of that realm.

That the Roman legal order already has this conception is significant. As Straumann shows, the jural conception was first conceived by the Romans, and no one would accuse the Romans of liberalism. As a result, the jural conception of politics is not liberal, except in the following sense. The very idea that individuals do not have to consider themselves as striving to achieve some highest ethical good, but simply as members of a community in which coercive state action has to be justified as being in accordance with law may in our era favour liberal ideologies over others. Indeed, the claim that authority is a matter of reasoned justification is strongly associated with both liberalism and the constitutionalist tradition.

But notice that that claim opens up the prospect of a realm of politics which is independent of any conception of the highest ethical good for individuals, and that the alternatives in the reason of state tradition are all about closing down political conflict by a legally unconstrained decision. Somewhat ironically, one can consequently argue that if Schmitt is right that political theory needs a conception of the autonomy of the political, it is to be found in the constitutionalist tradition that was first articulated by Roman political theorists and jurists.

Even more important is that the constitutionalist tradition established both the right to reasoned justification as the mark of the political relationship and that an institutional structure be put in place that seeks to ensure that such justification

---

[43] Ibid, 25.

is available. As Straumann shows, in the hands of Bodin and Hobbes the ruling out of a constitutional right of resistance is matched by the installation within the political order of the legal institutions of a well-ordered society, one that militates against a sovereign's need to resort to the secret policies and acts of illegal violence that form part of the *arcana* or 'dark matter'[44] that is the stuff of the reason of state tradition.[45]

The constitutionalist tradition cannot of course claim to have eliminated such dark matter from any particular legal order. Rather, its ambition is to strive for its elimination through a continual process of experimentation in light of experience. It is deeply pragmatic in spirit and in the latter half of the twentieth century has developed an apparatus both internationally and domestically around human rights regimes that is immensely complex in comparison to the constitutional instruments that typified the period before the Second World War, let alone those of the Roman Republic. It includes distinctions between derogable and non-derogable rights, different kinds of supervisory bodies at the international and national levels, doctrines of deference, proportionality, reasonableness, margin of appreciation, and so on.[46]

But all this complexity can be distilled down to the constitutional fundamentals of the Roman political and legal order: the subject's right of appeal to a body independent of the official who wields coercive power and the claim that the law—both enacted law and constitutional principle—is in charge of the officials, no matter how elevated their office. These two fundamentals make up the necessary institutional basis of the political right of rights, the subject's right in virtue being subject to state coercive power to have justified any exercise of such power.

The question whether a subject's human rights have been violated thus depends ultimately not so much on whether an official has violated a right on a prior list of rights each with a determinate content, but on the answer to the BLD that is given within the institutional structures of the order. The content of rights and their limits will thus vary from order to order and across time. But that does not make human rights subjective or relative in any interesting fashion. It just makes their content contingent on the justificatory processes within particular societies in which what counts is actual acceptance, though under the scrutiny of the critical theory principle that requires suspicion 'if the acceptance itself is produced by the coercive power which is supposedly being justified'.

Note that the critical theory principle can to some large extent be institutionalized through legal mechanisms that require public reasons and independent

---

[44] See Thomas Poole, *Reason of State: Law, Prerogative and Empire* (Cambridge University Press 2015) 56, arguing that Hobbes thought that the sovereign must have capacities to act extra-legally and that these make up the 'dark matter of Hobbes's constitutional universe'. See also Thomas Poole, 'The Law of Emergency and Reason of State' in Criddle (ed.), *Human Rights in Emergencies* (n. 6) 148.

[45] See Straumann, *Crisis and Constitutionalism* (n. 40) 306–7.

[46] See the chapters in Part 1 of Criddle (ed.), *Human Rights in Emergencies* (n. 40).

checks on both the accuracy and cogency of the reasons. But in order to think such a process worth undertaking, one has to adopt as a regulative assumption of institutional design that the point is to channel coercive power so that is it mediated in a way that enables its application to be justified. Proponents of this tradition do not, as Schmitt charged, face the option of either ignoring emergencies or suspending their deepest commitments.[47] Rather, they require a 'progressive realization of constitutionalism' in a bid to keep the solution from reintroducing the problem.[48]

Difficult questions remain: What does the rule of law and of human rights actually require of states in terms of justification? Who decides whether the onus of justification has been fulfilled? In particular, who interprets the constitution in situations of emergency? Who balances conflicting human rights (the right of the people to safety versus individual rights)? How do human rights impose limits on possible justifications? But in this light, Schmitt's challenge to the constitutionalist tradition has to be reformulated.

It is no longer the challenge that the sovereign may act extra-legally and so disregard legal entitlements to human rights. Rather, it is that the requirement that the sovereign act legally stretches the language of legality to the point where law's controls become merely formal and the claim to comply with human rights becomes vacuous. The question becomes one of how the state responds to what I have called in other work the 'compulsion of legality'—that it is a necessary condition of legitimate state action that the public officials who perform the action have a legal warrant.[49]

I sketch in that work the two very different 'cycles of legality' the compulsion of legality can set in motion. In one 'virtuous cycle', the institutions of legal order co-operate in devising controls on public actors that ensure that their decisions comply with the principle of legality, understood as a substantive conception of the rule of law. In the other 'empty' cycle, the content of legality is understood in an ever more formal and vacuous manner, resulting in the mere appearance or even the pretence of legality.

With this second cycle, the compulsion of legality may conclude in the subversion of the kinds of values associated with a conception of the rule of law oriented

---

[47] Schmitt, *Political Theology* (n. 1) 14.
[48] Carl J Friedrich, *Constitutional Reason of State* (Brown University Press 1957) 90. Friedrich, who had observed the travails of the Weimar Republic as a student in Germany before he embarked on a career that made him one of the United States' most influential political scientists, wrote that while the Kantian solution of a world state was unattainable, there was nevertheless something to be learned from it. It had 'the advantage of providing a developmental model and a pragmatic, if not a practical projection into the future, by which concrete political action programs may be inspired and policy shaped', ibid, 89. For an exploration of similar ideas in the international domain, see Evan J Criddle and Evan Fox-Decent, *Fiduciaries of Humanity: How International Law Constitutes Authority* (Oxford University Press 2016).
[49] For an extensive treatment of these themes, see David Dyzenhaus, 'Preventive Justice and the Rule of Law Project' in Andrew Ashworth, Lucia Zedner, and Patrick Tomlin (eds), *Prevention and the Limits of the Criminal Law* (Oxford University Press 2013) 91.

to the protection of human rights. One gets what a UK judge memorably described as a 'thin veneer of legality' over the 'reality' of 'executive decision-making, untrammelled by any prospect of effective judicial supervision'.[50] But while the prospect of the empty cycle presents a constant risk, it is more than matched by the opportunity that the virtuous cycle presents. As lawyers, judges, and social activists in Trump's United States have shown, what it takes for the virtuous cycle to unfold is commitment and hard work in particular cases and contexts, all done within the jural community that is 'the people' of the modern state.

Bibliography

Criddle EJ, 'Introduction: Testing Human Rights Theories During Emergencies' in Criddle EJ (ed.), *Human Rights in Emergencies* (Cambridge University Press 2016) 1

Criddle EJ and Fox-Decent E, *Fiduciaries of Humanity: How International Law Constitutes Authority* (Oxford University Press 2016)

Douglas R, 'Hobbes and Political Realism' (2016) European Journal of Political Theory 1

Dyzenhaus D, 'Law as Justification: Etienne Mureinik's Conception of Legal Culture' (1998) 14 South African Journal on Human Rights 11

Dyzenhaus D, 'How Hobbes met the "Hobbes Challenge"' (2009) 72 Modern Law Review 488

Dyzenhaus D, 'Hobbes on the Authority of Law' in Dyzenhaus D and Poole T (eds), *Hobbes and the Law* (Cambridge University Press 2012) 186

Dyzenhaus D, 'Preventive Justice and the Rule of Law Project' in Ashworth A, Zedner L, and Tomlin P (eds), *Prevention and the Limits of the Criminal Law* (Oxford University Press 2013) 91

Forst R, *The Right to Justification: Elements of a Constructivist Theory of Justice* (Columbia University Press 2012)

Forst R, *Justification and Critique* (Polity Press 2014)

Friedrich CJ, *Constitutional Reason of State* (Brown University Press 1957)

Hobbes T, *Behemoth or the Long Parliament* (University of Chicago Press 1990)

Hobbes T, *Leviathan* (Cambridge University Press 2014)

Hoekstra K, 'Hobbesian Equality' in Lloyd SA (ed.), *Hobbes Today: Insights for the 21st Century* (Cambridge University Press 2013) 76

Locke J, *Second Treatise of Government* (Hackett 1980)

McNay L, 'The Limits of Justification: Critique, Disclosure and Reflexivity' (2016) European Journal of Political Theory 1

Mureinik E, 'A Bridge to Where? Introducing the Interim Bill of Rights' (1994) 10 South African Journal on Human Rights 31

Poole T, 'Hobbes on Law and Prerogative' in Dyzenhaus D and Poole T (eds), *Hobbes and the Law* (Cambridge University Press 2012) 68

Poole T, *Reason of State: Law, Prerogative and Empire* (Cambridge University Press 2015)

Poole T, 'The Law of Emergency and Reason of State' in Criddle EJ (ed.), *Human Rights in Emergencies* (Cambridge University Press 2016) 148

---

[50] Justice Sullivan in *Re MB* [2006] EWHC 1000 (Admin), [2006] HRLR para. 103.

Ristroph A, 'Criminal Law for Humans' in Dyzenhaus D and Poole T (eds), *Hobbes and the Law* (Cambridge University Press 2012) 97
Scheuerman WE, 'Human Rights Lawyers v. Carl Schmitt' in Criddle EJ (ed.), *Human Rights in Emergencies* (Cambridge University Press 2016) 175
Schmitt C, *Über die drei Arten des rechtswissenschaftlichen Denkens* (Hanseatische Verlagsanstalt 1934)
Schmitt C, *The Concept of the Political* (Rutgers University Press 1976)
Schmitt C, *Political Theology: Four Chapters on the Concept of Sovereignty* (MIT Press 1988)
Straumann B, *Crisis and Constitutionalism: Roman Political Thought from the Fall of the Republic to the Age of Revolution* (Oxford University Press 2016) 35
Waldron J, 'Hobbes and the Principle of Publicity' (2001) 82 Pacific Philosophical Quarterly 447
Williams B, 'Realism and Moralism in Political Theory' in Hawthorn G (ed.), *Bernard Williams—In the Beginning was the Deed: Realism and Moralism in Political Argument* (Princeton University Press 2005) 1
Williams B, 'Human Rights and Relativism' in Hawthorn G (ed.), *Bernard Williams—In the Beginning was the Deed: Realism and Moralism in Political Argument* (Princeton University Press 2005) 62
Williams B, 'From Freedom to Liberty: The Construction of a Political Value' in Hawthorn G (ed.), *Bernard Williams—In the Beginning was the Deed: Realism and Moralism in Political Argument* (Princeton University Press 2005) 75

6
Reason, Faith, and Feelings
A Response to David Dyzenhaus

Conor Gearty

I. THE FLIGHT FROM REASON

The United Kingdom's European Union (Withdrawal) Act 2018 allows a 'Minister of the Crown' to make by way of regulation 'such provision as the Minister considers appropriate to prevent, remedy or mitigate—(a) any failure of retained EU law to operate effectively, or (b) any other deficiency in retained EU law, arising from the withdrawal of the United Kingdom from the EU'.[1] Such regulations may make 'any provision that could be made by an Act of Parliament'.[2] Various constraints on the breadth of this blanket empowerment appear but these are then rather undermined by the later, extraordinary section 9(1) which deals with the power to make regulations before 'exit day' if such regulations are 'consider[ed] appropriate for the purposes of implementing the withdrawal agreement' that is concluded before departure. Section 9(2) of the original Bill declared not only that such regulations 'may make any provision that could be made by an Act of Parliament' but also that this extended to 'modifying this Act'.[3] Some light parliamentary scrutiny was also promised then[4] but of course this could have itself been dispensed with after just one whipped vote as could the caveats constraining the powers taken under the clause on changes necessitated by withdrawal. New taxes, retrospective laws, disruption of the Good Friday Agreement, repeal of the Human Rights Act—all were just one statutory instrument away from uncontrolled ministerial attention—but are now explicitly excluded in the Act.[5] Nevertheless the elimination of the availability of EU Charter rights in UK law post Brexit[6] and the removal of the right to sue for damages under the EU rule in *Francovich*[7] are signs that the pessimists

---

[1] European Union (Withdrawal) Act 2018, s. 8(1) <http://www.legislation.gov.uk/ukpga/2018/16/pdfs/ukpga_20180016_en.pdf> accessed 31 January 2019.
[2] Ibid, ss 8(5) and 9(2).
[3] European Union (Withdrawal) Bill <https://publications.parliament.uk/pa/bills/lbill/2017-2019/0079/18079.pdf> accessed 31 January 2019.
[4] Ibid, sch. 7 para. 7(2)(g).
[5] European Union (Withdrawal) Act 2018, ss 8(7) and 9(3).
[6] Ibid, s. 5(4).
[7] Ibid, sch. 1 para. 4.

Conor Gearty, *Reason, Faith, and Feelings: A Response to David Dyzenhaus* In: *The Limits of Human Rights*. Edited by: Bardo Fassbender and Knut Traisbach, Oxford University Press 2019. © The Several Contributors.
DOI: 10.1093/oso/9780198824756.003.0008

about what Brexit entails for human rights may not on this occasion be alarmist. This is the kind of measure that could only be contemplated in times of extreme emergency, even if the characterization is (so far) carefully avoided by government.

This short reflection on David Dyzenhaus's excellent essay on emergencies and human rights is not a platform for yet more polito-legal polemics on the departure of the United Kingdom from the EU. Whatever happens to Brexit, the Act and the preceding versions of the Bill throw into sharp relief something quite dramatic that is taking place in democratic polities across the world—a conscious flight from reason, a rejection of the need to drive policy on the basis of arguments recognizable to those writing in the 'liberal and constitutionalist tradition' as Dyzenhaus terms it.[8] Indeed the very non-deployment of the language of emergency is a proof of sorts that we have moved beyond reason: there is no emergency because we say there is none. Brexit will work because Brexit will work. Arguments against are the work of naysayers to be rejected not because of their content but because of the perfidious experts who articulate them. Because the destination is unknown of course blanket powers are needed. Reason welcomes scrutiny; unreason seeks protection from it. As the government put it explaining the change '[w]hilst Parliament has remained sovereign throughout our membership of the EU, it has not always felt like that'.[9]

It is not surprising that those who subscribe to this approach to politics, whether they be in Britain, Hungary, Poland, the United States, or anywhere else, invariably become very exercised by the threat posed by the courts to their grand schemes. Courts stand for exactly that which they have chosen to reject. Both Poland and Hungary have sought to redraw the boundary between the executive and judicial branches in favour of the former.[10] Many of President Trump's nominations to the federal bench have been almost comically inept.[11] Very early on in the Brexit process the UK Prime Minister Mrs Theresa May made any recourse to the jurisdiction of the European Court of Justice (ECJ) a red line past which no British Brexit negotiator would cross.[12] Similar antagonism to the European Court of Human Rights

---

[8] David Dyzenhaus, 'Emergencies and Human Rights: A Hobbesian Analysis' in Bardo Fassbender and Knut Traisbach (eds), *The Limits of Human Rights* (Oxford University Press 2019) 89, 89 (hereafter Dyzenhaus, 'Emergencies and Human Rights').

[9] HM Government, *The United Kingdom's Exit from and New Partnership with the European Union* (Cm 9417, 2017) para. 2.1 <https://www.gov.uk/government/uploads/system/uploads/attachment_data/file/589191/The_United_Kingdoms_exit_from_and_partnership_with_the_EU_Web.pdf> accessed 31 January 2019.

[10] Kim Lane Shepple and Rui Tavares, 'The Rule of Law Challenge in Europe: From Hungary to Poland' [2016] Green European Journal <https://www.greeneuropeanjournal.eu/the-rule-of-law-challenge-in-europe-from-hungary-to-poland/> accessed 31 January 2019.

[11] Charlie Savage, 'Poor Vetting Sinks Trump's Nominees for Federal Judge' *The New York Times* (New York, 18 December 2017) <https://www.nytimes.com/2017/12/18/us/politics/matthew-petersen-judge-nominee-withdraws-trump.html> accessed 31 January 2019.

[12] The Rt. Hon. Theresa May, 'The Government's Negotiating Objectives for Exiting the EU' (Speech on a Plan for Britain, 17 January 2017) <https://www.gov.uk/government/speeches/the-governments-negotiating-objectives-for-exiting-the-eu-pm-speech> accessed 31 January 2019.

had even led her (when Home Secretary) to suggest that the United Kingdom withdraw from the European Convention on Human Rights (ECHR), joining only Belarus outside this wider European framework of judicial accountability.[13] The UK courts themselves have not been above suspicion of betrayal when they have engaged in local human rights analysis and, infamously, in the winter of 2016/17 they drew vast abuse when they interpreted domestic law in a way that made parliamentary authorization of withdrawal from the EU a constitutional necessity.[14] As with the anti-Brexit experts, in none of these cases or jurisdictions has it been the legal reasoning deployed that has been the issue so much as it has been the supposed unconstitutional brazenness of the judgments, the fact that they have happened at all rather than what they have said.[15]

Dyzenhaus writes about 'a situation of emergency' leading to a 'political judgement ... about what it takes to secure the safety of the people' and argues for the importance of law as a way of holding to account decisions taken on this basis. In demanding a role for justification even in emergencies, Dyzenhaus seeks to steer a middle path 'between the vacuous claim that political justification by definition satisfies human rights and the too robust claim that a political justification counts as such only when it meets the standard set by human rights'. He finds his desired *via media* in insisting that 'political justification' should be characterized 'in terms of the human rights of those subject to the state', with 'an institutional structure of legality' being put in place to ensure that the state discharges 'its onus of justification' in this regard. The flight from reason with which this short comment started looks at first glance impossible to reconcile with Dyzenhaus's demand for a human rights justification for law generally and emergency law in particular. But if we jump too readily to this conclusion we risk missing two features of the key concepts in Dyzenhaus's scheme that together affect its application: first, the malleability of what human rights can be said to entail and second, the capacity of justification to reach beyond a socio-political legal ('liberal constitutionalist') environment in which (Dyzenhaus's) rationality is taken for granted. Another way of putting these two points is to say that human rights are less demanding than they sound while justification is less enamoured of reason than we might have supposed. As a result, it follows that if choices have to be made between the

---

[13] Anushka Asthana and Rowena Mason, 'UK must leave European convention on human rights [sic!], says Theresa May' *The Guardian* (London, 25 April 2016) <https://www.theguardian.com/politics/2016/apr/25/uk-must-leave-european-convention-on-human-rights-theresa-may-eu-referendum> accessed 31 January 2019.
[14] *R (Millar) v. Secretary of State for Exiting the European Union* [2017] UKSC 5. On press coverage see among many examples Guy Adams, *Daily Mail* (London, 2 December 2016) <http://www.dailymail.co.uk/news/article-3995754/The-judges-people-week-11-unaccountable-individuals-consider-case-help-thwart-majority-Brexit-Mail-makes-no-apology-revealing-views-links-Europe.html> accessed 31 January 2019.
[15] See generally Conor Gearty, *On Fantasy Island: Britain, Europe, and Human Rights* (Oxford University Press 2016).

two extremes that Dyzenhaus believes he is steering between, his middle ground is more likely to produce—in the current climate of post-rational politics—a tilt towards the political justification (his 'vacuous claim') than its legally weighted ('too-robust') rival.

II. LAND

A good place to start in developing this short point is the well-known *Belmarsh* case, involving the detention of suspected international terrorists in the United Kingdom in the immediate aftermath of the attacks by Al-Qaida on the United States on 11 September 2001.[16] The decision in the UK's most senior court is famous both for its ringing endorsement of the principles of liberty and non-discrimination which had at that point only recently been introduced explicitly into UK law via that country's Human Rights Act 1998, and also for its denial that the emergency opt-outs permitted by that legislation should go unsupervised by the judicial branch. For the majority of the House of Lords the key failure of the law before it was its division of the population into 'foreign' and 'non-foreign' suspected terrorists.[17] This made perfect sense from the perspective of the deliberately universal nature of the rights legislation under which the case fell to be decided. Nationality is not a permitted basis for justification. Rather than argue directly that it was—bound to be a losing game—defenders of the detention regime sought to take the matter away from the courts, the Attorney General submitting 'that as it was for Parliament and the executive to assess the threat facing the nation, so it was for those bodies and not the courts to judge the response necessary to protect the security of the public'.[18] Since these 'were matters of a political character calling for an exercise of political and not judicial judgment', it was 'not for the courts to usurp authority properly belonging elsewhere'.[19]

Dyzenhaus sees Carl Schmitt as characterizing '[s]overeign authority [as] precisely the unmediated coercive power that reveals itself in an emergency', but does this inevitably obliterate the need for justification, or simply change the shape it must take? The point of the government's legal argument in the *Belmarsh* case was not to deny the need for justification altogether, but rather to argue that a different kind of rational explanation was called for, one that did not necessarily engage in a court's vision of what reason entailed but which constructed its version of what made sense in a different way, acknowledging and accommodating the strength of public feeling, responding to a perceived need to be seen to act, and (as Lord

---

[16] *A (FC) and others (FC) v. Secretary of State for the Home Department* [2004] UKHL 56; [2005] 2 AC 68.
[17] See especially Baroness Hale para. 238.
[18] Lord Bingham para. 37.
[19] Ibid.

Bingham put it) 'to make legislative choices ... when (as is often the case) the interests of one individual or group have to be balanced against those of another individual or group or the interests of the community as a whole'.[20] That argument was rejected—but this did not mean that they produced no justifications, only that they had explanatory power to which the judges were deaf. As the *Belmarsh* dissentient Lord Walker put it: 'It is not suggested that the Secretary of State or any of his officials has given misleading or disingenuous reasons for their actions. What is said is that they have asked themselves the wrong questions, and have reached irrational and disproportionate answers.'[21]

In the *Belmarsh* case the human rights demands held fast, resisting in the name of the 'liberal-constitutionalist tradition' with its commitment to universalist rights a rationale—rooted in national security—that made a different kind of sense. The law that the judgment ruled incompatible with human rights[22] had only been required to be enacted because of earlier human rights rulings from the European Court of Human Rights in Strasbourg that had denied the authorities the power to expel foreigners where this would have created a serious risk of their being killed and/or subjected to torture, or inhuman or degrading treatment.[23] Later cases extended the protection of human rights to foreigners harmed by the actions of military forces abroad.[24] With the possible exception of the prisoners' voting case of *Hirst v. United Kingdom (No. 2)*,[25] no decisions have done more to cause the ideal of human rights and its judicial defenders to be drawn into political controversy, and to face widespread criticism. The rational justification of human rights sits at odds with feelings of patriotism and of national anxiety that supply a different range of justifications for the actions taken, the disregard of which (while making perfect sense in the world of its own reasoning) has been what has made an anti-Strasbourg and anti-rights sentiment so powerful in recent years in the United Kingdom. The result has been the thinnest of thin legal mediations of the executive's coercive capacity, in the shape of administrative powers given to the executive by parliament after the *Belmarsh* reverse. It was in commenting on one such scheme that Justice Sullivan made his comment about the 'thin veneer of legality' with which quote Dyzenhaus concludes his essay.[26] This is what happens when a justification rejected by the legal community is understood all too well and accepted within the political sphere.

---

[20] Ibid, para. 38.
[21] Lord Walker para. 193.
[22] Anti-terrorism, Crime and Security Act 2001 pt. IV.
[23] See most famously *Chahal v. The United Kingdom*, App. No. 22414/93, 15 November 1996.
[24] *Al-Skeini and Others v. The United Kingdom*, App. No. 55721/07, 7 July 2011.
[25] *Hirst v. The United Kingdom (No. 2)*, App. No. 74025/01, 6 October 2005.
[26] Dyzenhaus, 'Emergencies and Human Rights' (n. 8) 105.

III. COMMUNITY

A second kind of rationality that does not resonate with liberal constitutionalism and which as a result inevitably loses out in the same way when justification is demanded is that variant of reason which roots itself in religious belief. It is of course right to acknowledge that some frameworks of institutionalized faith consciously eschew any engagement with the rational and/or seek deliberately to minimize its influence, but this is not true of all. To take one important example, the Roman Catholic Church positively glories in the confidence that its commitment to reason gives it, enabling it in particular to engage in what it considers to be a strong critique of the effect on freedom of secular society.[27] But this has taken it into territory that is unrecognizable as justificatory so far as the assumptions of contemporary liberal democracy are concerned. As our understanding of what is entailed in being a free human changes, so our impatience grows with defences mounted by the old order, however well argued, however widely accepted these might have been in the past. Where once we all saw reason now those in the vanguard of change see obstructive, out-of-date pedantry.

There are many examples but one of the best perhaps is the tremendous success of the argument that gay men (and women) should not be restricted so far as their private, consensual, and adult sexual relations are concerned. In the early days of the articulation of this entitlement as part of the right to respect for privacy before the European Court of Human Rights, it was still possible to argue, as the Irish judge Justice Walsh did in dissent in *Dudgeon v. The United Kingdom*[28] that Lord Devlin had been right in his debate in the 1960s with HLA Hart[29] 'that as the law exists for the protection of society it must not only protect the individual from injury, corruption and exploitation but it [Judge Walsh now quoting Devlin directly] "must protect also the institutions and the community of ideas, political and moral, without which people cannot live together. Society cannot ignore the morality of the individual any more than it can his loyalty; it flourishes on both and without either it dies" '.[30] Now of course there is no going back to these unsympathetic times or reversal of this trend towards sexual freedom, and there is much in Judge Walsh's judgment that reads even more offensively today than it did at the time (1981).[31] But the core point here transcends its particular circumstances in its assertion that if 'the State has a valid interest ... in the preservation of the moral ethos of its

---

[27] See Denys Turner, *Thomas Aquinas: A Portrait* (Yale University Press 2013), brilliantly reviewed by Terry Eagleton, 'Disappearing Acts' (2013) 35 London Review of Books 39 <https://www.lrb.co.uk/v35/n23/terry-eagleton/disappearing-acts> accessed 31 January 2019.

[28] *Dudgeon v. The United Kingdom*, App. No. 7525/76, 22 October 1981 (hereafter *Dudgeon v. The United Kingdom*).

[29] Patrick Devlin, *The Enforcement of Morals* (Oxford University Press 1959); Herbert LA Hart, *Law, Liberty, and Morality* (Stanford University Press 1963).

[30] *Dudgeon v. United Kingdom* (n. 28) Partially Dissenting Opinion by Judge Walsh para. 9.

[31] Ibid, paras 13 and 14.

society, then the State has a right to enact such laws as it may reasonably think necessary to achieve [this object]'.[32] And this is even if the occasional individual gets knocked back as a result. We may disagree with this outlook but it is hard to dismiss it as entirely without justification (even if the justification is not ours).

The issue appears in an updated shape in the difficult debate gripping much of Europe over how much licence to allow the expression of religious faith in the public square, an issue treated as a life or death matter for Europe by at least some commentators.[33] Many of the judicial interventions on the question appear relaxed about Judeo-Christian manifestations of religious faith but distinctly anxious—hostile even—to Moslem equivalents. This immediately subverts justification when viewed from a human rights point of view: how can you possibly choose between religions? But recalling Walsh/Devlin, and going deliberately under the surface of the issue, why shouldn't Europe preserve its Judeo-Christian shape even if it is at some cost to the life-opportunities of the new arrivals? This bit of the world has a certain way of doing things and while it welcomes others it does so on its terms: no 'melting pot' can be allowed ruin the food for everybody. We may deplore the position, but it is not one that presents as wholly unjustified.[34]

The European Court of Human Rights found itself confronted by exactly this dilemma in *SAS v. France*.[35] The applicant complained that France's decision fully to restrict her wearing of the niqab and burqa in public violated her right to manifest her religion or belief and her right to be able to enjoy this right in a non-discriminatory way. Both rights are embedded in the European Convention on Human Rights and Fundamental Freedoms the interpretation of which it is the duty of this European-wide Strasbourg court to interpret. Of course there are permitted exceptions, through which gateway a test of proportionality has been able to embed itself in the Court's jurisprudence. And a feature (inevitably) of the test of proportionality, routinely applied, is justification. But by reference to what? Which societal goals permit the shift away from individual rights? How can a rights' instrument justify such an intrusion into the private life of an individual, where no discrimination is permitted without a reason recognizable to the Court, but where the true reason for the regulatory intervention (keeping Europe's values in their proper shape) cannot be articulated, or if put into words cannot be accepted by the judges?

The Grand Chamber found an answer in expanding one of the explicit grounds of legitimation, a conventional liberal one about 'the protection of the rights and freedoms of others', into something capable of encompassing a demand that all whose within a jurisdiction show 'respect for the minimum requirements of life

---

[32] Ibid, para. 14.
[33] Douglas Murray, *The Strange Death of Europe: Immigration, Identity, Islam* (Bloomsbury Publishing 2017).
[34] Ronan McCrea, 'The Ban on the Veil and European Law' (2013) 13 Human Rights Law Review 57.
[35] *SAS v. France*, App. No. 43835/11, 1 July 2014.

in society', or 'living together' as the government put it in the course of making their case.[36] The Court understood 'the view that individuals who are present in places open to all may not wish to see practices or attitudes developing there which would fundamentally call into question the possibility of open interpersonal relationships, which, by virtue of an established consensus, forms an indispensable element of community life within the society in question'.[37] As a result it 'was able to accept that the barrier raised against others by a veil concealing the face is perceived by the respondent State as breaching the right of others to live in a space of socialisation which makes living together easier'.[38] Having developed this new basis for restricting freedom, the majority was then able fairly easily to deploy reasons to justify its finding that the ban was proportionate,[39] in a way that would not have been possible had the test been against the needs, say, of 'public safety'.[40] In a similar way the discrimination claim was blunted by the existence of the 'objective and reasonable justification' that had denied the Article 9 claim. The reasoning behind both was only convincing because the initial starting point had been fixed to make it so. Even with something so rational as justification there is no avoiding the deeper political structure that determines what works under this umbrella and what does not.

IV. JUSTIFICATION BY FAITH

The forces of political passion are not so easily dispersed by reason as believers in human rights might hope and suppose; rather they bend the 'institutional structure of legality'[41] sought by Dyzenhaus into a shape which makes their demands amenable to (rather than blocked by) his regime of human rights justification, what he describes at the end of his essay as the 'empty cycle' rather than the 'virtuous' one in which he believes. Giving the flight from constitutional liberalism the benefit of the doubt, can it be that this liberal approach to constitutional government generates only one of the shapes that justification can take, one among many rather than *the* one *primus inter pares*? Maybe 'feelings' produce their own kind of reason which delivers justification in its own terms, terms that we constitutionalists might not like perhaps but not the less justifications for that? And this justification is then processed through the legal/human rights realm to deliver outcomes that appear human rights compatible but which in practice are pale reflections of what human rights (and the principle of legality) should demand. If we legal

---

[36] Ibid, para. 122.
[37] Ibid.
[38] Ibid.
[39] Ibid, paras 140–59.
[40] Ibid, para. 139.
[41] Dyzenhaus, 'Emergencies and Human Rights' (n. 8) 92.

rationalists describe as unreasoned the intense feelings that are driving change in (to us) so many unattractive ways around the world, is this not because there is no justification at all but rather because what a justification there is comes out of an altogether different socio-political tradition, one that terrifies more than it amuses?

Bibliography

Adams G, *Daily Mail* (London, 2 December 2016) <http://www.dailymail.co.uk/news/article-3995754/The-judges-people-week-11-unaccountable-individuals-consider-case-help-thwart-majority-Brexit-Mail-makes-no-apology-revealing-views-links-Europe.html> accessed 31 January 2019

Asthana A and Mason R, 'UK must leave European convention on human rights [sic!], says Theresa May' *The Guardian* (London, 25 April 2016) <https://www.theguardian.com/politics/2016/apr/25/uk-must-leave-european-convention-on-human-rights-theresa-may-eu-referendum> accessed 31 January 2019

Devlin P, *The Enforcement of Morals* (Oxford University Press 1959)

Dyzenhaus D, 'Emergencies and Human Rights: A Hobbesian Analysis' in Fassbender B and Traisbach K (eds), *The Limits of Human Rights* (Oxford University Press 2019) 89

Eagleton T, 'Disappearing Acts' (2013) 35 London Review of Books 39 <https://www.lrb.co.uk/v35/n23/terry-eagleton/disappearing-acts> accessed 31 January 2019

Gearty C, *On Fantasy Island: Britain, Europe, and Human Rights* (Oxford University Press 2016)

Hart HLA, *Law, Liberty, and Morality* (Stanford University Press 1963)

May T, 'The Government's Negotiating Objectives for Exiting the EU' (Speech on a Plan for Britain, 17 January 2017) <https://www.gov.uk/government/speeches/the-governments-negotiating-objectives-for-exiting-the-eu-pm-speech> accessed 31 January 2019

McCrea R, 'The Ban on the Veil and European Law' (2013) 13 Human Rights Law Review 57

Murray D, *The Strange Death of Europe: Immigration, Identity, Islam* (Bloomsbury Publishing 2017)

Savage C, 'Poor Vetting Sinks Trump's Nominees for Federal Judge' *The New York Times* (New York, 18 December 2017) <https://www.nytimes.com/2017/12/18/us/politics/matthew-petersen-judge-nominee-withdraws-trump.html> accessed 31 January 2019

Shepple KL and Tavares R, 'The Rule of Law Challenge in Europe: From Hungary to Poland' [2016] Green European Journal <https://www.greeneuropeanjournal.eu/the-rule-of-law-challenge-in-europe-from-hungary-to-poland/> accessed 31 January 2019

Turner D, *Thomas Aquinas: A Portrait* (Yale University Press 2013)

PART II
LIMITS OF FUNCTIONS, LIMITS OF USES: ACTORS AND PRACTICES

7
Being a Realist about Human Rights

Christian Reus-Smit

There are two kinds of limits to human rights. The first are philosophical and concern the limits of human rights as moral values. Human rights treat the individual as the primary unit of moral concern and struggle to accommodate the moral integrity and associated rights of collectivities. By framing moral debate in terms of rights, they reduce discussions of responsibility to the correlative duties that attend particular rights. And rooted in Western philosophical thought, human rights are far from universal: indeed, they are inherently particular (or so the argument goes). The second kind of limits are political. Irrespective of their value and standing as moral values, human rights are limited by the realities of power and interest. Human rights matter when, and only when, powerful actors say they do, and historically this has been rare. Nothing more than the musings of idealists, human rights are forever assailed by, and dependent upon, might in the service of self-interest.

This chapter is concerned with the political limits to human rights, but as we shall see, grasping these correctly depends in part on understanding human rights as distinctive kinds of moral values. The principal account of these limits is advanced by realists, whose self-designation already signals an abiding moral scepticism. Three elements of their thought confine human rights to the political margins. The first is their characterization of international relations as a struggle for power in which 'the strong do what they have the power to do and weak accept what they have to accept'.[1] The second is their default materialism.

While states can have diverse interests, the realization of these always depends on power, and the ultimate sources of power are guns and money. The third element is their conception of agency. Not only are states the primary actors, the only states that matter are great powers, whose standing as such derives primarily from their material capacities. In this realist world view, the efficacy of human rights is severely circumscribed. Only on those rare occasions when they rise high in a dominant state's hierarchy of interests will they have any political traction.

Widespread as this view is, it fundamentally misunderstands the political limits to human rights. Nothing I say here questions the ubiquity of power struggles

---

[1] Thucydides, *History of the Peloponnesian War* (Penguin 1972) 401–2.

Christian Reus-Smit, *Being a Realist about Human Rights* In: *The Limits of Human Rights* Edited by: Bardo Fassbender and Knut Traisbach, Oxford University Press 2019. © The Several Contributors.
DOI: 10.1093/oso/9780198824756.003.0009

in world politics or challenges the notion that states seldom rank human rights among their primary interests. Human rights are always subject to the vicissitudes of power, and if their success depended on great powers they would seldom escape the realm of wishful thinking. My point is different, though. The realist account misunderstands the nature of power, naively privileges the material sources of that power, and is blind to revolutionary forms of agency in world politics. Rights revolutions have transformed the international political landscape over the past three centuries, yet blinkered by these misconceptions, realists have little if anything to say about these transformations. Being a 'realist' about human rights requires abandoning these misconceptions and understanding power and agency in very different ways.[2]

The following discussion is divided into five parts. I begin by exploring the conventional realist position in greater detail, and then seek to reconceive power and agency by enlisting the concept of 'protean power' pioneered in a book edited by Peter Katzenstein and Lucia Seybert. In contrast to 'control power', which involves mastery under conditions of calculable risk, protean power is the product of innovation under conditions of uncertainty.[3] Most of our theories assume a world of risk, but in reality uncertainty is ubiquitous in world politics. Moreover, uncertainty is greatly accentuated by meaning indeterminacy and institutional complexity, conditions that commonly accompany the politics of rights. Part III explores the relationship between order, rights, and uncertainty, and the remainder of the chapter illustrates this relationship with a critique of recent accounts of the post-1945 politics of human rights.

I. REALIST SCEPTICISM

For their proponents, human rights are fundamental values: their protection is essential to the moral and physical well-being of individuals, and their recognition and advancement is the primary measure of political legitimacy. Yet in the realist world view, two other values take precedence: the prudent pursuit of the national interest, and the preservation of international order. Both derive from the structural realities of international relations. The most fundamental of these

---

[2] The argument advanced here draws on ideas developed in my other works, particularly Christian Reus-Smit, *Individual Rights and the Making of the International System* (Cambridge University Press 2013) (hereafter Reus-Smit, *Individual Rights*); Christian Reus-Smit, 'Protean Power and Revolutions in Rights' in Peter J Katzenstein and Lucia A Seybert (eds), *Power in Uncertainty: Exploring the Unexpected in World Politics* (Cambridge University Press 2018) 59; and Christian Reus-Smit, 'The Battle Rages On: The Struggle for Human Rights Enters a New Era', *Foreign Affairs* (New York, 9 June 2014) <http://www.foreignaffairs.com/articles/141555/christian-reus-smit/the-battle-rages-on> accessed 31 January 2019.

[3] Lucia A Seybert and Peter J Katzenstein, 'Protean Power and Control Power: Conceptual Analysis', in Lucia A Seybert and Peter J Katzenstein (eds), *Protean Power: Exploring the Uncertain and Unexpected in World Politics* (Cambridge University Press 2018) 3.

was emphasized by Hans Morgenthau when he argued that 'International politics, like all politics, is a struggle for power'.[4] Morgenthau attributed this to the inherent human will to dominate, while Kenneth Waltz and others have stressed the anarchic nature of the international system. Either way, the desire for power, and the struggle this generates, is considered a defining characteristic of international relations. Power is understood here in almost exclusively material terms. The power of a state is the capabilities of that state, determined by the material resources it commands. The distribution of power in an international system is, in turn, the distribution of capabilities (*qua* material resources) across that system. The principal units in such a system are sovereign states, and most of these are discounted in the realist world view. Where the struggle for power prevails, only the most powerful matter: hegemons first, great powers second.

When international relations are conceived in this way, human rights are at best secondary, even tertiary, values. The national interest is the highest value, and its prudent pursuit is at a premium. The only collective value of any note is international order, as some modicum of peace and stability is valued by all but the most revolutionary powers. Realists do not, of course, deny the existence of the increasingly elaborate international human rights regime. They deny, however, that these rules and norms alter in any way the fundamental dynamics of international relations. To begin with, once we dispense with the notion that there was ever a golden age of sovereignty, when states enjoyed supreme authority within their borders and denied any higher authority beyond, international conventions that compromise states' Westphalian sovereignty are just another example of the 'organized hypocrisy' that is sovereignty.[5] Second, these rules and norms are almost always the product of three things: convergent state interests, rational bargaining, and coercion. States can accept human rights treaties because they are unlikely to violate them, so they are low cost; because they value human rights or receive side-payments to comply; or they have been subject to coercion. Given all of this, Jack Goldsmith and Eric Posner hold 'that modern multilateral human rights treaties have little exogenous influence on state behavior'.[6] The importance of side-payments and coercion point to an additional feature of international human rights—their dependence on great and powerful friends. In the end, human rights make a difference only when powerful states say they do, and even then, realists caution against trusting great powers who cloak their actions in moral garb, human rights included.

---

[4] Hans J Morgenthau, *Politics Among Nations: The Struggle for Power and Peace* (6 edn, McGraw Hill 1985) 31.
[5] Stephen D Krasner, *Sovereignty: Organized Hypocrisy* (Princeton University Press 1999) 105–26 (hereafter Krasner, *Sovereignty*).
[6] Jack L Goldsmith and Eric A Posner, *The Limits of International Law* (Oxford University Press 2006) 108.

II. POWER AND AGENCY RECONCEIVED

The authority of realism rests, in significant part, on the determination of realists to stare the harsh realities of international relations in the face; to see power wherever it lies, to expose interests behind rhetoric, and to admit the primacy of some over others. Yet for all this, realists are constantly bemoaning irrational state behaviour (as though leaders hadn't grasped the theory) and hastily constructing post-hoc explanations for international events that surprised them as much as everyone else: the end of the Cold War being the classic example. This is not because their focus on power and differential agency was wrong, though: it's because they misconceived these. Power is more complex than the distribution and deployment of material capabilities, and complex forms of power generate and enable complex forms of agency.

In their volume, *Protean Power: Exploring the Uncertain and Unexpected in World Politics*, Katzenstein and Seybert distinguish between 'control' and 'protean' power. The first involves control under conditions of calculable risk; the second is a product of innovation under conditions of uncertainty. Realists, like most International Relations scholars, focus exclusively on control power. As good Weberians, they see power as the ability of A to get B to do what A wants, and the risks this entails are calculable: the distribution of capabilities can be assessed, and the configuration of interests determined. The problem, Katzenstein and Seybert argue, is that world politics is not simply a realm of calculable risk: it is also characterized by often intractable uncertainties. Faced with such uncertainties, actors innovate in the pursuit of immediate, localized objectives. This innovation, however, generates protean power, often transforming social orders in unexpected ways. This power is not possessed or wielded by individual or collective actors; it is an unintended consequence of creative responses to uncertainty, often accentuating that uncertainty. International history is replete with unanticipated, often revolutionary, developments, and recent history offers many examples. The fact that we are repeatedly surprised by these events, Katzenstein and Seybert argue, is due to our misconception of world politics as a realm of risk not uncertainty, and our failure to grasp the workings of protean as well as control power.

Katzenstein and Seybert distinguish between two kinds of uncertainty: operational and radical. The first, which consists of known unknowns, can, with sufficient knowledge, be transformed into the world of risk. Radical uncertainty, by contrast, is characterized by unknown unknowns. More than this, many of these unknowns are unknowable. This kind of uncertainty is thus more than a cognitive condition, a lack of knowledge: it is an inherent and intractable feature of complexity.

Radical uncertainties are especially pronounced in highly complex institutional environments, such as that prevailing today at the global level. This is for two reasons. First, all institutional environments comprise webs of intersubjective meanings that constitute identities and structure action. Yet these meanings are inherently indeterminate—they are open to multiple, often contradictory, interpretations. Even codified legal rules are now understood to be indeterminate, a function of the 'semantic openness of legal speech'.[7] Second, in complex institutional environments actors never navigate one institution at a time; they navigate numerous overlapping institutions simultaneously. This is partly why individuals have multiple social identities, why they forum shop to realize the best institutional outcomes, and why the proliferation of regimes in the same issue area can generate normative conflict, undermining effectiveness. In relatively sparse institutional environments, the radical uncertainty that attends meaning indeterminacy is always present. It is accentuated dramatically, however, under conditions of high institutional density, where the sheer multiplicity of meanings layers uncertainty upon uncertainty.

Power can be exercised for many purposes, but the construction and determination of political orders, including international orders, is among the most fundamental, as political orders frame the play of politics, their institutions defining the principal agents and the bounds of acceptable action. When scholars consider the power that shapes orders, they emphasize control power, whether in its compulsory, institutional, or structural forms.[8] Yet all but the most diehard realists acknowledge that political orders—international or otherwise—rest on more than material might; their stability and efficacy also depends on legitimacy, on the perception of those subject to them that they are 'desirable, proper, appropriate within some socially constructed system of norms, values, beliefs, and definitions'.[9] The opens the door, however, to a very different kind of power. An order's legitimacy depends on prevailing intersubjective meanings—norms, values, and beliefs—but these meanings defy control, as they are inherently indeterminate and often embedded in multiple, overlapping, and at times contradictory institutions. The imperative of legitimacy, and the dependence of this legitimacy on indeterminate, institutionalized meanings, thus renders the politics of order a realm of risk and uncertainty, and the currents of radical uncertainty diminish the efficacy of control power while accentuating protean power.

---

[7] Martti Koskenniemi, *From Apology to Utopia: The Structure of International Legal Argument* (Cambridge University Press 2005) 590–6.
[8] On the differences between these forms of control power, see Michael Barnett and Raymond Duvall, 'Power in Global Governance' in Michael Barnett and Raymond Duvall (eds), *Power in Global Governance* (Cambridge University Press 2005) 1–32.
[9] Mark C Suchman, 'Managing Legitimacy: Strategic and Institutional Approaches' (1995) 20 The Academy of Management Review 571, 574.

III. ORDERS, RIGHTS, AND UNCERTAINTY

Any discussion of the rights of individuals has to be made with reference to political orders. Not only do claims to rights emerge within the context of such orders—as claims about the powers and freedoms that individuals rightfully enjoy within and against prevailing institutions—but political orders, international and domestic, are usefully conceived as aggregations and distributions of individual and institutional rights. In sovereign political orders, absolutist orders define and allocate rights in one way, and democratic orders do so in another. The same is true of international orders. Building on my previous work, I define such orders as systemic configurations of political authority, comprising multiple units of authority, arranged according to some principle of differentiation.[10] This principle might be empire, heteronomy, sovereignty, or some combination thereof. The crucial thing for our purposes is that imperial orders delineate and distribute rights differently from heteronomous orders, and both do so differently from orders of sovereign states.

A key challenge for all political orders is sustaining the legitimacy of the prevailing definition and allocation of rights. Rights are legitimate powers and freedoms, and they define how individuals stand in relation to one another, how individuals and collectivities relate, and how both stand in relation to political institutions. When prevailing distributions of rights are deemed legitimate, these relations enjoy a stability that coercion along cannot deliver. When they are challenged, however, orders can fall into crisis, at times leading to revolutionary change. Examples abound. Magna Carta, the Peace of Westphalia, the American and French Revolutions, the collapse of Europe's territorial empires, the fall of the Berlin Wall: all involved crises in the prevailing allocation and distribution of rights and the organizations of political authority these licensed and constituted.

The clash between two kinds of individual rights have been especially prominent in such crises: special and general rights.[11] Both are the rights of sole persons, not collectivities, but they differ in crucial ways. Special rights are rights that are rooted in custom, contract, or social standing. The rights one gains when signing a contract to buy a house are a good example. The contract gives both the vendor and the purchaser certain rights, but they have these rights only by virtue of the contract. Another example is the feudal rights held by European lords and peasants, rights they held because of their respective positions within medieval hierarchies. These rights contrast markedly with general individual rights. These are rights an individual has by virtue of their status as an integral moral being with inherent capacities that warrant protection. Human rights are the quintessential example

---

[10] Christian Reus-Smit, 'The Liberal International Order Reconsidered' in Rebekka Friedman, Kevork Oskanian, and Ramon Pacheco-Pardo (eds), *After Liberalism* (Palgrave Macmillan 2013) 167, 169.
[11] Reus-Smit, *Individual Rights* (n. 2) 36–7.

of such rights: individuals have them simply because they are human, not because of custom, contract, or social standing. Such rights are inherent and inalienable; one has them whether or not they are recognized or protected. Indeed, it is when they are denied and violated that they are most important. The crucial thing to note, however, is that for most of the history of general individual rights they were thought not to apply to all biological humans: adherents of other faiths, unpropertied men, 'barbarians' and 'savages', peoples of colour, women, indigenous peoples, homosexuals, and transsexuals, all have at one time or another been excluded from the category of entitled moral beings. Only in the second half of the twentieth century did the 'zone of application' come close to applying to all biological humans.[12]

General individual rights pose a particular problem for political orders. I argued above that orders rest not only on material might but also legitimacy. Yet constructing and sustaining such legitimacy is at best only partially amenable to control power, as judgements of legitimacy are made with reference to prevailing norms, values, and beliefs which are inherently indeterminate and often embedded in complex institutional environments. General individual rights are an especially pronounced example. Central to such rights is the idea of the integral moral being; the individual person endowed with the requisite capacities that warrant the protection and empowerment of such rights. Yet who constitutes such a person is inherently subjective. Short of all biological humans, and even this is contested, there is no way to define objectively who qualifies as an worthy moral being. Furthermore, because such rights ordain individuals with legitimate powers and freedoms, their unequal distribution generates contention, often struggle. Campaigns for general individual rights, whether waged against regimes of special rights or the maldistribution of general rights, thus breed contentious politics. This politics is complicated by the existence of overlapping institutions which give uneven recognition to different kinds of rights and afford different opportunities for the advancement of rights claims.

Two things follow from this argument about orders, rights, and uncertainty. First, Stephen Krasner's oft-quoted claim that the existence of multiple, indeterminate international norms, with no authoritative mechanisms for their interpretation, favours the exercise of control power is wrong, or at best overstated.[13] Meaning indeterminacy and institutional complexity creates space for innovation in the cracks and contradictions of an order creating new dynamics of protean power. The legitimacy of political orders depends on the robustness of their rights regimes, yet although these regimes can be codified and institutionalized they cannot be controlled, especially when claims to individual rights enter the

---

[12] Axel Honneth, *The Struggle for Recognition: The Moral Grammar of Social Conflicts* (MIT Press 1995) 113; see also Lynn Hunt, 'Humanity and the Claim to Self-Evidence' in Bardo Fassbender and Knut Traisbach (eds), *The Limits of Human Rights* (Oxford University Press 2019) 39, 48–52.

[13] Krasner, *Sovereignty* (n. 5) 6.

political arena. Second, because meaning indeterminacy and institutional complexity render the political terrain radically uncertain, creating space for innovation by notionally weak actors and generating new currents of protean power, revolutions in rights almost always come by surprise. They are always the result of fraught, protracting struggle, but their victories happen suddenly, transforming political orders in ways, and with timing, previously unimaginable to those previously considered the 'powerful' and the 'weak'.

IV. THE NEW SCEPTICISM

For two decades after the end of the Cold War there was widespread confidence that human rights were gaining ever greater traction globally: democracy was spreading, states of all complexions reaffirmed their commitments to human rights norms, new international judicial institutions were established, and the doctrine of the Responsibility to Protect (R2P) was moving from a principle to a norm. In recent years, however, this optimism has receded as autocracies rebound, new divisions over human rights emerge, the objectivity and efficacy of the International Criminal Court (ICC) is questioned, and colossal humanitarian failures like Syria put a pale over R2P. This creeping pessimism has been accompanied by a new wave of scholarship that proclaims the end of the human rights era.[14]

In this scholarship, the human rights era was remarkably brief, from the 1970s to roughly 2008. Conventional wisdom long held that human rights became important in world politics after 1945. Shocked into action by the Nazi Holocaust, the international community defined promotion and respect for human rights as a central purpose of the United Nations (UN), adopted both the Universal Declaration of Human Rights (UDHR) and the Convention on the Prevention and Punishment of the Crime of Genocide in 1948, and passed the two legally binding International Covenants on human rights in 1966. Yet the significance of all of this has been greatly exaggerated, the new wave of scholarship suggests. After 1945 international commitment to human rights was lukewarm at best, the ideologies of nationalism and socialism had far greater political purchase, and there was little if anything by way of a global human rights movement.

The 1970s were a turning point. In the decades that followed, three key developments unfolded. Central to the new accounts is the rise of transnational advocacy organizations, especially Amnesty International. By forging a direct link between

---

[14] See Samuel Moyn, *The Last Utopia: Human Rights in History* (Harvard University Press 2010) (hereafter Moyn, *Last Utopia*); Mark Mazower, *No Enchanted Palace: The End of Empire and the Ideological Origins of the United Nations* (Princeton University Press 2009) (hereafter Mazower, *No Enchanted Place*); Aryeh Neier, *The International Human Rights Movement: A History* (Princeton University Press 2012); and Stephen Hopgood, *The Endtimes of Human Rights* (Cornell University Press 2013) (hereafter Hopgood, *Endtimes*).

concerned individuals (largely in the West) and political prisoners, Amnesty took human rights advocacy out of the remote halls of the UN and seeded a global social movement. In time the fundraising imperative drove the professionalization of such organizations, giving the movement a permanent transnational organizational architecture. The second development was the human rights turn in American foreign policy, instigated by the Carter Administration. Honoured as often as not in the breech, human rights nonetheless assumed far greater prominence in US policy, a prominence that persisted beyond the fall of the Berlin Wall and through the (seemingly fleeting) unipolar moment. The global promotion of human rights was thus enabled and empowered by engaged hegemony. The final development was the construction of key international institutions, most notably the Tribunals for Rwanda and the former Yugoslavia and the International Criminal Court. In the decades following the Second World War efforts focused on codifying international rights norms, but now the action turned to enforcement, to punishing even heads of state for gross human rights violations.

This highpoint is said to have passed, though. All of the key developments have run their course, Stephen Hopgood contends. American power is declining, and as autocratic, non-Western states grow in power and confidence, the idea of a global consensus on human rights—of a set of norms that have steadily diffused—is being replaced by the sober realization that they may be partial, precarious, and divisive. The great transnational advocacy organizations are in trouble as well. Their business models relied on the mutually reinforcing convergence of American and European political power and engaged Western middle classes. But as global power shifts, Amnesty, Human Rights Watch, and other global non-governmental organizations (NGOs) are scrambling to engage the Global South. The gloss has also gone off key institutional developments. The ICC is now well established, but it is caught between liberal accusations of flawed legal procedures and claims of Western bias from the non-Western world. The doctrine of the R2P, which until the Libyan intervention appeared to be a rapidly consolidating international norm, has been undermined by the conduct of the Libyan campaign, inaction in Syria, Russia's cynical abuse of the principle in Georgia and the Crimea, and the loss of any chance of consensus in the Security Council.[15]

Two things are worth noting about this new scepticism. First, it repeats, in modified form, the realist account of the political limits of human rights—they matter when great powers say they do. The claimed apogee of human rights spans Carter's engaged foreign policy through to the end of the unipolar moment: American power and commitment was fundamental. The agency of transnational advocacy groups also has a central place in these accounts, but these are always Western groups, and only reinforce the idea that Western hegemony was crucial. Second,

---

[15] Hopgood, *Endtimes* (n. 14) vii–xv.

and following from this, although the new scepticism shifts the origin of the human rights era from 1945 to the 1970s, it replicates the Western chauvinism that accompanies most accounts of human rights—human rights are a Western project, reflecting Western values, enabled by Western power. This narrative, echoed in most textbooks on the subject, is not only gratifying to those in the West but useful to autocrats elsewhere who have an interest in casting human rights as a hegemonic imposition and denying their universality.

V. TO CUT A LONG STORY SHORT

The period from the 1970s to 2000s indeed saw notable human rights developments, and few would deny the importance of transnational activism enabled by a more engaged hegemon. But in isolating and privileging these developments, the new sceptics mistake a fragment of the story for the story itself. Human rights, as we saw above, are a species of general individual rights, and their history is intelligible only if placed within the history of this broader genus of rights. Furthermore, because political orders are structured and sustained by regimes of rights, the legitimacy of such orders is often the focus of struggles for individual rights. An adequate history of human rights must, therefore, locate them within the larger history of the politics of individual rights and the changing nature of the international political order. Such a history reveals very different power dynamics than commonly emphasized, however, and very different patterns of agency.

Two momentous developments occurred in the decades following the Second World War. The first was a dramatic transformation in the nature of the international political order. The old order that combined sovereignty in the core with empire abroad was replaced by the world's first universal system of sovereign states, fundamentally reconfiguring political authority across the globe. The second was the negotiation of the key instruments of the international human rights regime, most notably the UDHR and the two legally binding International Covenants. To justify their privileging of the period after 1970, the new sceptics downplay the significance of these earlier developments in the regime, and as part of this, deny that these developments were connected with post-1945 decolonization, the process driving changes in the international political order. The first move involves all sorts of contortions, though: like Samuel Moyn's claim that human rights only mattered politically when they inspired a global social movement, and Mark Mazower's curious claim that after negotiating the UDHR states gave up on a legally binding convention, ignoring altogether the two Covenants.[16] The negotiation of the Declaration and Covenants was far from insignificant,

---

[16] Moyn, *Last Utopia* (n. 14) 8; Mazower, *No Enchanted Palace* (n. 14) 133.

though. Among other things, they provide key legal foundations for all subsequent human rights institutions. More importantly for our purposes, their negotiation and post-1945 transformations in the international political order were deeply interconnected.

The transformation from the old sovereign-imperial order to universal sovereignty was the product not only of the near simultaneous collapse of Europe's empires but of the dramatic collapse of the institution of empire itself. In the space of a few decades, empire went from an entirely legitimate form of rule to a 'crime'. The old order suffered a terminal crisis of legitimacy, leaving Europe's empires, already weakened by world war and assailed by anti-colonial movements, without the moral rationales of 'civilizing mission' and 'sacred trust'. After 1960, when this normative revolution was complete, the collapse of the old order accelerated. Between 1946 and 1960 the rate of decolonization was 1.26 new states per year; between 1960 and 1975 it was 3.86.[17] Three decades after the Second World War Europe's empires were all but gone, hierarchy assumed more shadowy forms, and 'empire' became a term of opprobrium.

This revolution was driven by the politics of individual rights. The first thing to note, however, was that this politics played out in a highly complex institutional environment. Prior to the twentieth century, anti-colonial struggles took place largely within the confines of empires themselves, with some spill over into society of states. Early nineteenth-century struggles against the Spanish Empire are a case in point. After the First World War, the institutional environment became more complex, as the League of Nations added another institutional layer, principally through the Mandate system. The UN added greatly to this complexity. Key here were its fledging human rights bodies and the gradual negotiation of international human rights norms. In the wake of the Second World War, therefore, the imperial powers, post-colonial states, and anti-colonial forces faced a highly variegated institutional context, comprising intra-imperial, international, and supranational elements.

Within this environment new opportunities for normative innovation emerged, and the potential for control dissipated. The principal site for such innovation was the UN's human rights bodies and the negotiation of the two International Covenants. It was there that the right to self-determination was redefined and rehabilitated, undercutting the legitimacy of empire. Prior to the Second World War, this was a right enjoyed by ethnically defined nations, and one restricted to those emerging from the wrecks of the Austro-Hungarian, German, and Ottoman Empires. It didn't apply to 'barbarian' or 'savage' peoples in Europe's remaining empires, and even if it did, the multiethnic composition of most colonies made it hard for them to qualify as ethnic-nations. This understanding of

---

[17] Reus-Smit, *Individual Rights* (n. 2) 154.

self-determination was shattered, first, by the failure of the interwar minority treaties to prevent widespread ethnic cleansing, and second, by the Nazi campaign for an ethnically homogeneous greater Germany, widely seen as a perverse consequence of the ethnic right to self-determination. After the Second World War this right had to be redefined and rehabilitated if it was to be of any use to colonial peoples.

Post-colonial states achieved this by grafting the right to self-determination to emerging human rights norms. Contrary to conventional accounts, these states played a crucial role in the negotiation of these norms.[18] While the Soviet Union insisted on the priority of economic and social rights, they insisted that civil and political rights take precedence. And while leading Western powers opposed the right of individuals to petition UN bodies, post-colonial states were consistently in support. Indeed, the Optional Protocol to the International Covenant on Civil and Political Rights would not exist without their efforts. Most importantly, post-colonial states successfully opposed two proposals pushed by leading Western states. The first was a 'federal state' clause that would have reduced the obligations of such states to uphold human rights within their provinces; the second was a 'colonial' clause that would have freed imperial powers of obligations to protect and promote human rights in their colonies. If these proposals had succeeded, large sectors of humanity would have been outside the reach of international human rights norms. In no small sense, therefore, post-colonial states universalized human rights. Or put differently, they put the 'human' in human rights.

It was in this context that post-colonial states in the UN resuscitated the right to self-determination. If the right was to apply to all colonial peoples outside Europe, and if multiethnic peoples, not just ethnically defined nations, were to qualify, it had to be reconstructed on universalist foundations. Post-colonial states did this by grafting it to the human rights norms they were busy negotiating. Successfully calling for the insertion of the right to self-determination in Article 1 of both Covenants, they argued that 'no basic human rights could be ensured unless this right were ensured'.[19] In 1952 this connection was stressed in General Assembly Resolution 637 (A): 'the right of peoples and nations to self-determination is a prerequisite for the enjoyment of all fundamental human rights'.[20] Moyn claims that this shows the secondary nature of human rights, insisting that post-colonial states attached more value to the collective right. This misunderstands what they meant

---

[18] See Christian Reus-Smit, 'Human Rights and the Social Construction of Sovereignty' (2001) 27 Review of International Studies 4, 519–38; Christian Reus-Smit, 'Struggles for Individual Rights and Expansion of the International System' (2011) 65 International Organization 2, 207–42; and Reus-Smit, *Individual Rights* (n. 2).
[19] United Nations, *Yearbook of the United Nations 1951* (UN Office of Public Information 1951) 485.
[20] The right of peoples and nations to self-determination, GA Res. 637 (VII) (16 December 1952) preamble.

by 'prerequisite', though. They didn't mean that it had normative priority, only that it was a necessary precondition.[21]

VI. CONCLUSION

Realist accounts of the limits of human rights hold that the might and interests of dominant states define the realm of political possibility. No amount of diffusion and persuasion will give human rights political teeth; only committed states with the requisite material capabilities can give human rights this bite. Conversely, struggles for rights arrayed against mighty states, willing to flex their control power, are destined to fail. Parsimonious as this thesis is, though, it so simplifies power and agency in the politics of human rights as to render it naively unrealistic. If it were true, revolutions in rights would never happen, or only with support of enlightened great powers, and realists (and others) would never be caught by surprise.

The limits of human rights *are* affected by power and agency, but both are considerably more complex than realists imagine or acknowledge. World politics is not simply a realm of calculable risk amenable to the exercise of control power; it is also a realm of uncertainty—often radical uncertainty—that privileges innovation and generates transformative currents of protean power. International political orders form the political architecture of world politics, but such orders are institutionally highly complex, greatly accentuating the meaning indeterminacy inherent to all rules, norms, and intersubjective beliefs and values. This is especially relevant to the politics of rights. Political orders, international or otherwise, rest on regimes of rights, and the legitimacy of these regimes is central to their stability and longevity. Yet these rights, and their political legitimacy, defy control: not only are they often embedded in a range of overlapping institutions, their meanings can be narrated by political elites but not controlled. This is clearly apparent in the crisis of the old sovereign-imperial order, where the regime of unequal entitlements that held it together was challenged by claims to general individual rights, the meaning and applicability of which the imperial powers and their Western allies failed to control.

In the end, being a realist about human rights means at least three things. First, it means understanding that political orders of all varieties rest not only on material might but on legitimacy as well. Moreover, an order's legitimacy cannot be commanded by elites; it is ordained by its constituents, whose judgements are informed by prevailing norms and values. Second, political orders rest on regimes of rights, and the resilience of orders depends on the legitimacy of these regimes. The realist eye should be alert to the fact that hierarchical political orders that rest on regimes of unequal special rights, such as empires and autocracies, are

---

[21] Reus-Smit, *Individual Rights* (n. 2) 169–70.

vulnerable to claims for the recognition of general individual rights. Not only do these rights challenge directly special rights regimes, but their meaning defies control. Third, the definition and mobilization of general individual rights has never been the preserve of the materially powerful. Historically, subjugated peoples have been the crucial agents, innovating in the cracks and contradictions of complex institutional environments. Those who insist that human rights became important to world politics after 1970 ignore how these realities shaped world politics prior to then, and their proclamation of the end of human rights depends on ignoring them again.

Bibliography

Barnett M and Duvall R, 'Power in Global Governance' in Barnett M and Duvall R (eds), *Power in Global Governance* (Cambridge University Press 2005) 1

Goldsmith JL and Posner EA, *The Limits of International Law* (Oxford University Press 2006)

Honneth A, *The Struggle for Recognition: The Moral Grammar of Social Conflicts* (MIT Press 1995)

Hopgood S, *The Endtimes of Human Rights* (Cornell University Press 2013)

Hunt L, 'Humanity and the Claim to Self-Evidence' in Fassbender B and Traisbach K (eds), *The Limits of Human Rights* (Oxford University Press 2019) 39

Koskenniemi M, *From Apology to Utopia: The Structure of International Legal Argument* (Cambridge University Press 2005)

Krasner SD, *Sovereignty: Organized Hypocrisy* (Princeton University Press 1999)

Mazower M, *No Enchanted Palace: The End of Empire and the Ideological Origins of the United Nations* (Princeton University Press 2009)

Morgenthau HJ, *Politics Among Nations: The Struggle for Power and Peace* (6 edn, McGraw Hill 1985)

Moyn S, *The Last Utopia: Human Rights in History* (Harvard University Press 2010)

Neier A, *The International Human Rights Movement: A History* (Princeton University Press 2012)

Reus-Smit C, 'Human Rights and the Social Construction of Sovereignty' (2001) 27 Review of International Studies 519

Reus-Smit C, 'Struggles for Individual Rights and Expansion of the International System' (2011) 65 International Organization 207

Reus-Smit C, 'The Liberal International Order Reconsidered' in Friedman R, Oskanian K, and Pacheco-Pardo R (eds), *After Liberalism* (Palgrave Macmillan 2013) 167

Reus-Smit C, *Individual Rights and the Making of the International System* (Cambridge University Press 2013)

Reus-Smit C, 'The Battle Rages On: The Struggle for Human Rights Enters a New Era' *Foreign Affairs* (New York, 9 June 2014) <http://www.foreignaffairs.com/articles/141555/christian-reus-smit/the-battle-rages-on> accessed 31 January 2019

Reus-Smit C, 'Protean Power and Revolutions in Rights' in Katzenstein PJ and Seybert LA (eds), *Protean Power: Exploring the Uncertain and Unexpected in World Politics* (Cambridge University Press 2018) 59

Seybert LA and Katzenstein PJ, 'Protean Power and Control Power: Conceptual Analysis' in Katzenstein PJ and Seybert LA (eds), *Protean Power: Exploring the Uncertain and Unexpected in World Politics* (Cambridge University Press 2018) 3

Suchman MC, 'Managing Legitimacy: Strategic and Institutional Approaches' (1995) 20 The Academy of Management Review 571

Thucydides, *History of the Peloponnesian War* (Penguin 1972)

8
Political Limits of International Human Rights
A Response (or a Rejoinder) to Christian Reus-Smit

Başak Çalı

Political limits of international human rights is a well-trodden discourse in human rights studies. It is also one that brings together approaches that would otherwise not normally be considered together. International relations realists and critics of Western imposition and hegemony join forces when the political limits of international human rights come to the fore.[1] Realists characterize advocates of international human rights as naive in their understanding of how power operates in world politics and hold that international human rights lack any independent effects of their own, as power dynamics ultimately determine and shape what can be achieved through international human rights and related advocacy. International human rights are not likely to have any effect if they do not overlap with the interests of states.[2] When they work, they will merely represent or serve the interests of powerful states.[3] Critics of Western hegemony also echo this. They hold that international human rights merely operate as tools of Western imposition of values, as Western states and Western civil society are the original authors of what really counts as international human rights. Evidence for this is often found in the lack of attention paid to economic, social, and cultural rights as parts of the international human rights imaginary and practice, as well as the inability of international human rights to meaningfully contribute to debates about the negative human rights effects of neo-liberal economic policies.[4]

---

[1] Tony Evans, *The Politics of Human Rights: A Global Perspective* (2nd edn, Pluto Press 2005); Makau Mutua, *Human Rights: A Political and Cultural Critique* (University of Pennsylvania Press 2002); Eric A Posner, *The Twilight of Human Rights Law* (Oxford University Press 2014) (hereafter Posner, *Twilight*); Stephen Hopgood, *The Endtimes of Human Rights* (Cornell University Press 2013).
[2] Posner, *Twilight* (n. 1).
[3] Samuel Moyn, *The Last Utopia: Human Rights in History* (Harvard University Press 2010).
[4] John Linarelli, Margot E Salomon, and Muthucumaraswamy Sornarajah, *The Misery of International Law: Confrontations with Injustice in the Global Economy* (Oxford University Press 2018).

Başak Çali, *Political Limits of International Human Rights: A Response (or a Rejoinder) to Christian Reus-Smit* In: *The Limits of Human Rights*. Edited by: Bardo Fassbender and Knut Traisbach, Oxford University Press 2019. © The Several Contributors.
DOI: 10.1093/oso/9780198824756.003.0010

In this response piece to Christian Reus-Smit's 'Being a Realist about Human Rights', I expand on his critique of the portrayal of those who identify political limits to human rights through the lens of realism. In this respect, this chapter is a rejoinder to Reus-Smit's chapter rather than a counter-point. Ultimately I am in agreement with Reus-Smit and his argument that the realist position on the political limits of international human rights imposes a blanket and static conception of power. This, in particular, lacks nuance and fails to identify the specific contours of the political limits of international human rights currently at work in international politics. I also agree with Reus-Smits' characterization of what he calls 'the new sceptics' of human rights[5] who reduce international human rights to a project of the West, its states, and its non-governmental organizations (NGOs).

I also hold, however, that the political limits of international human rights need to be framed by moving the debate from what Baxi calls modern human rights to contemporary human rights.[6] Modern human rights are often characterized as a 'gift of the West to the rest'[7] with certain logics that exclude particular categories of rights and violations and prioritize others. In contrast, 'contemporary human rights' focuses on a multi-authored concept of international human rights practice. In the contemporary conception, individuals and groups invoke human rights in inclusive ways to challenge and contest states, whether they are in the West or in the rest, through recourse to legal and non-legal forms of organized action and contestation in multiple fora, be they domestic or transnational. This shift in the framing of what we mean by international human rights lends support to the argument that realism not only simplifies the political limits of international human rights, it also misrepresents them. This applies, in particular, to their transformative and empowering potential. It does not, however, deny *tout court* that international human rights have political limits. Political limits to contemporary international human rights practices do exist, but not in the ways that realists, old or new, may have us believe. I locate political limits to contemporary human rights in two places. First, there is the constant pushback from states about the boundaries of international human rights with a particular emphasis on the legitimacy of democratic decision-making nationally. Secondly, I highlight the political and institutional difficulties faced by international human rights practice in responding to the shifts of de facto authority from states to private corporate powers. The latter political limit is not reducible to the hegemony of Western states. The lack of appetite to regulate corporate power at the global level cannot only be associated with Western corporate power,[8] but manifests itself as a current structural and institutional limitation.

---

[5] Christian Reus-Smit, 'Being a Realist about Human Rights' in Bardo Fassbender and Knut Traisbach (eds), *The Limits of Human Rights* (Oxford University Press 2019) 121, 130–32 (hereafter Reus-Smit, 'Being a Realist').

[6] Upendra Baxi, *The Future of Human Rights* (Oxford University Press 2002) 24–42.

[7] Ibid, 24.

[8] William Burke-White, 'Power Shifts in International Law: Structural Realignment and Substantive Pluralism' (2015) 56 Harvard International Law Journal 1.

My rejoinder is in three parts. First I lay out my main points of agreement with Reus-Smit's analysis of realist and Western hegemony perspectives on the political limits of human rights and his defence of protean power as a framework for empirical analysis of international human rights developments between 1945 and the 1970s. In section II, I argue that what is missing in realist objections is not only an adequate conception of power. The objections pay inadequate attention to the distinction between modern human rights and contemporary human rights. The latter emphasizes the agency of individuals and communities. It does not regard them as victims of human rights violations whose faith rests with gaining support from Western powers, but as authors themselves of international human rights, often against Western hegemonic understandings. International human rights, as part of broader political contestations, are not only determined by powerful states, but also by third party adjudicators, interpreters, individual and civil society groups in diverse institutional settings. I take the example of regional human rights courts and their role, alongside individuals and civil society groups, in co-authoring international human rights to elucidate this point. In section III, I argue that we should look for the political limits of human rights not in the power struggles between states, but in the health of human rights institutions in their responses to the needs of contemporary human rights movements and the uncertainties associated with corporate power as a new form of social organization that supersedes sovereign states.

I. REALISM ABOUT INTERNATIONAL HUMAN RIGHTS: A SIMPLE STORY LINE

Reus-Smit outlines two forms of realist criticism of international human rights. First, he describes what may be termed as a generic realist view on international human rights, based on the core premises of realist international theory. Then there is the new form of realist criticism, where the political limits of international human rights are firmly located in their mirroring of Western hegemony.

The message of the generic realist view on international human rights is communicated loud and clear. It centres on the fact that international human rights are a subset of norms and, as such, they share the common position of all norms in international relations. They only have consequences for the international order as a whole when the interests of the most powerful states, power understood as material power, converge to say that they do. Most fine-grained realist analysis of the place of international human rights and international human rights law are variations of these arguments. States ratify international human rights treaties when they think it is in their self-interest, not because they have an inherent normative commitment to human rights as such. They comply with international human rights treaties when it benefits them and flout these commitments easily when their self-interests dictate otherwise. States further seek to use international human rights to criticize other states or to intervene in their internal affairs when it is in line with their interests. International human rights can be mobilized for international intervention when the most powerful states see such intervention aligned with their interests.

The new realist forms of criticism take their cue from these general premises, but also specifically focus on the role of Western hegemony. This perspective proposes that human rights have become a *lingua franca* through their use by Western hegemonic powers. It also proposes that international human rights reflect the preferences of Western states with their traditionally strong emphasis on civil and political rights, at the expense of economic, social, and cultural rights. The Western international human rights movement, often viewed through the prism of Amnesty International and Human Rights Watch, is also invoked to hold that the international human rights movement, too, is a reflection of the Western hegemony's dominance in shaping global international human rights discourse.

Reus-Smit criticizes both the generic and the new forms of realism, offering an analysis of the political limits of international human rights by focusing on their conception of power and agency in international relations. In particular, he holds that power in international relations cannot be reduced to material and static notions of power as control under conditions of calculable risk. Instead, he underlines, together with Katzenstein and Seybert, that world politics is not a domain of calculable risk but of deep uncertainty. It is one where actors innovate with a view to advance their short-term goals in complex and overlapping institutional environments.[9] The relationship between uncertainty and innovation gives rise to protean power whose operation is not predetermined by static interests and their comparative material advantage. Rather, it is informed by contestation, struggle for new meanings, and the creation of new forms of this power. Turning to the critique of international human rights as reflecting Western hegemonic visions, Reus-Smit underlines that the history of international human rights law shows that these Western hegemonic visions were disturbed in many critical junctures prior to human rights becoming the *lingua franca* of the West in 1970s. This was though the emergence of protean powers in the international system after the end of Second World War and in the subsequent processes of decolonization.

---

[9] Reus-Smit, 'Being a Realist' (n. 5).

II. MODERN VERSUS CONTEMPORARY INTERNATIONAL HUMAN RIGHTS: AN EVEN MORE COMPLEX STORY ON POLITICAL LIMITS

I join forces with Reus-Smit's analysis and his scepticism about the simple storyline of realism and those who find the limits of international human rights in the hegemony of Western states and organizations. In fact, the reality is more complex, not only with respect to the global history of human rights, but also its present and possible future. A core aspect of this complexity lies in the institutionalization of international human rights law through the creation of wide-ranging international human rights institutions, including regional human rights commissions and courts as well as monitoring bodies under the auspices of the UN. First in Europe, then in the Americas and in Africa, the creation of regional human rights courts and commissions, has altered our understanding of what international human rights stand for. Allowing individuals to bring forward international human rights claims means that dominant views about international human rights and their role in domestic and international politics have been continuously contested and reinterpreted. This disturbs the view that Western states have been the sole authors of international human rights.

The processes for states to agree to submit themselves to the authority of these institutions were long winded in all regions. Yet, at different junctures in various regions, these institutions have become part of the complex terrain of international politics. It is now an established norm that individuals and civil society organizations can bring cases against states about their duties to respect and protect human rights, and this has led to thousands of human rights cases at the international level. The UN has replicated this trend of allowing individuals to pursue cases before its human rights treaty bodies. Even in the most neglected domain, economic and social rights, there are now three dedicated treaty bodies which allow for individual complaints: the Committee on Economic Social and Cultural Rights, the Committee on the Elimination of All Forms of Discrimination against Women, and the Committee on the Rights of Peoples with Disabilities. This institutionalization leads to an understanding of international human rights, not as a domain of interstate politics where one state waves a human rights document at the other, or where Western states stand and point fingers, but where international advocates, from all around the world, seek authoritative interpretations of international human rights as a way to challenge all states. Thus we are able, for example, to understand the scope of torture[10] or unlawful killings[11] or the duty not to extradite an individual to face the death penalty in another state[12] through cases brought by

---

[10] *Ireland v. The United Kingdom*, App. No. 5310/71, 18 January 1978.
[11] *McCann and others v. The United Kingdom*, App. No. 18984/91, 27 September 1995.
[12] *Soering v. The United Kingdom*, App. No. 14038/88, 7 July 1989.

individuals against one Western state—the United Kingdom. International human rights advocates around the globe have also been able to challenge preexisting conceptions of international human rights and the power relations embedded in them. The indigenous peoples' rights jurisprudence of the Inter American Court of Human Rights and the African Commission on Human Rights are two examples of what Reus-Smit may see as operations of protean social power in complex, contemporary supranational settings.

The realist sceptics would be quick to point out that this multi-authored institutional revolution in international human rights does not change the fact that compliance with international human rights cases is far from perfect and states will continue to fail to comply with human rights judgments. The empirical analyses of compliance with human rights judgments, however, does not fully back up the realist position. It shows rather that compliance deficiencies have multiple causes and protean power is also at work in the course of compliance dynamics, and not only at the level of international human rights claim-making.[13] What is more, institutionalized forms of international human rights, which evolve through the proliferation of new cases, have wider effects beyond the more narrow focus on compliance in demonstrating how international human rights shapes international politics.[14]

Conceptualizing international human rights as mirrors of Western hegemonic interests or as tools of interstate politics is thus based on a very static view of international human rights and focuses on their presence or existence in texts rather than how they are brought to life through claims made by individuals and civil society against states, including the world's most powerful. The focus on international human rights as an element of the foreign policy of Western states fits better with how the United States sees international human rights. It is, by choice, the most isolated state from international institutional accountability through refusing to accept any oversight above and beyond its own Supreme Court. To see international human rights from this perspective skews the larger picture of how contemporary practices of international human right have altered the dynamics of political calculation in other parts of the world.

III. POLITICAL LIMITS OF CONTEMPORARY INTERNATIONAL HUMAN RIGHTS

The ability of individuals to claim and shape international human rights through supranational institutions is not a mono-directional development that leads to

---

[13] Laurence R Helfer and Erik Voeten, 'International Courts as Agents of Legal Change' (2014) 68 International Organization 77.

[14] Robert L Howse and Ruti Teitel, 'Beyond Compliance: Rethinking Why International Law Really Matters' (2010) 1 Global Policy 127.

more buy-in from states seeking to shape their interests and legitimacy in the mirror image of international human rights law. A dominant discussion in the past decade has instead focused on the growing backlash against international human rights courts and their willingness to incorporate contemporary rights claims in the imaginary of international human rights at the expense of state sovereignty.[15] This backlash takes the form of states shutting down international courts, threats or actual withdrawals from international human rights regimes,[16] and political pressure placed on human rights courts to retreat from dynamic interpretations of international human rights justified on the grounds that domestic institutions, be they parliaments or constitutional courts, enjoy more democratic legitimacy in determining the boundaries of human rights than international courts.[17] This political pushback is a sign of unresolved tensions between democratic self-determination within a single political community and international human rights, not an endorsement of the realist view on the limits of international human rights. It is built on the normative qualities of democratic regimes and their right to make their own decisions, rather than the use of might to enforce their world views. The assertion of the normative democratic identity of states as justification for the political limits of international human rights, however, is not always an altruistic defence of democracy. At times, it is based on hostile attitudes towards migrants or asylum seekers as seen in Europe. What we are witnessing, therefore, is a series of ongoing contestations, not based on power-based concerns but on normative concerns, concerning the political limits of international human rights.

Moving further away from the well-known realist critiques of political limits to international human rights brings us to the question of whether the rise of economic power, often in ways that surpasses sovereignty, as the basis of the international order, and the lack of institutional settings for protean forms of power to challenge these new actors, can be framed as a new political limit to international human rights. Holding multinational corporations accountable for their adverse human rights impacts faces political and institutional resistance in many parts of the world. Corporate entities, unlike state powers, hide behind the domestic regulations of each and every individual state, and to address their contribution to the decay of international human rights protection requires going beyond the statist focus of international human rights. If we accept that the institutionalization of international human rights has allowed and increased the opportunities for protean forms of power to influence legitimate conceptions of state authority,

---

[15] Mikael Rask Madsen, 'The Challenging Authority of the European Court of Human Rights: From Cold War Legal Diplomacy to the Brighton Declaration and Backlash' (2016) 79 Law and Contemporary Problems 141.
[16] Consider, e.g., the Venezuelan withdrawal from the Inter-American Court of Human Rights and the UK threats of withdrawal from the jurisdiction of the European Court of Human Rights.
[17] Başak Çalı, Anne Koch, and Nicola Bruch, 'The Legitimacy of Human Rights Courts: A Grounded Interpretivist Analysis of the European Court of Human Rights' (2013) 35 Human Rights Quarterly 955.

resistance to new forms of contemporary human rights claims that seek to do the same for corporate forms of power emerges as a new political limit. This pressing issue of our age needs to receive more attention than the idea that modern human rights are an outpost of Western hegemony.

IV. CONCLUSION

International human rights are not merely the domain of one state criticizing the human rights practices in another, nor a Western NGO speaking on behalf of human rights holders in the Global South. Realist criticisms of human rights, as prevalent as they are, limit our understanding of what contemporary international human rights are, who has agency in contesting and defining them, and what notion of the political is appropriate in assessing the limits of international human rights. A turn away from realism allows us to study the relationship between institutional settings and their ongoing use by protean powers and the feedback effects that these create on the political limits of international human rights as well as its political futures. This research agenda calls for closer attention to be paid to how normative concerns, such as those found in the defence of democracy, have become new political limits for international human rights. It also demands that we analyse how corporate power, shielded not only by the West but also by the rest, raises urgent questions about the political limits of international human rights.

Bibliography

Baxi U, *The Future of Human Rights* (Oxford University Press 2002)

Burke-White W, 'Power Shifts in International Law: Structural Realignment and Substantive Pluralism' (2015) 56 Harvard International Law Journal 1

Çalı B, Koch A, and Bruch N, 'The Legitimacy of Human Rights Courts: A Grounded Interpretivist Analysis of the European Court of Human Rights' (2013) 35 Human Rights Quarterly 955

Evans T, *The Politics of Human Rights: A Global Perspective* (2nd edn, Pluto Press 2005)

Helfer LR and Voeten E, 'International Courts as Agents of Legal Change' (2014) 68 International Organization 77

Hopgood S, *The Endtimes of Human Rights* (Cornell University Press 2013)

Howse RL and Teitel R, 'Beyond Compliance: Rethinking Why International Law Really Matters' (2010) 1 Global Policy 127

Linarelli J, Salomon ME, and Sornarajah M, *The Misery of International Law* (Oxford University Press 2018)

Madsen MR, 'The Challenging Authority of the European Court of Human Rights: From Cold War Legal Diplomacy to the Brighton Declaration and Backlash' (2016) 79 Law and Contemporary Problems 141

Moyn S, *The Last Utopia: Human Rights in History* (Harvard University Press 2010)
Mutua M, *Human Rights: A Political and Cultural Critique* (University of Pennsylvania Press 2002)
Posner EA, *The Twilight of Human Rights Law* (Oxford University Press 2014)
Reus-Smit C, 'Being a Realist about Human Rights' in Fassbender B and Traisbach K (eds), *The Limits of Human Rights* (Oxford University Press 2019) 121

9
Human Rights Bodies and the Structure of Institutional Obligation

Jan Klabbers

I. INTRODUCTION

A few years ago, six European human rights experts found themselves in a room trying to identify which of a group of ninety students had written the best master's thesis that academic year within the framework of the institution all were affiliated with. Soon, a strong consensus emerged that among the main contenders was a thesis on the relationship between human rights and the market, more specifically a thesis making the argument that states have a human rights-based obligation to regulate markets. While five of the six experts lauded the merits of the thesis, the sixth was hesitant: he pointed out (to everyone's surprise) that the thesis was marred by the fact that it said nothing about the positive contributions many companies make to human rights these days.[1]

The other five experts were momentarily baffled. After all, while admittedly markets are populated by companies, the thesis was not about the role of companies, whether positive or negative; it made an entirely different kind of argument, on a different level of abstraction, and the argument of the thesis would stand even if, to paraphrase James Madison, all companies are angels. The thesis was concerned with controlling the invisible hand, not with controlling any particular market actor.

The sixth expert was, arguably, the most senior and well-known of the experts assembled in the room, at least in the human rights community, and with impeccable human rights credentials. As it happens, as the institution's president he was also responsible for the fund-raising activities of the programme in the framework of which the thesis was written, and this fund-raising depends, in part, on the generosity of companies. Moreover, this sixth expert was no doubt concerned about the negative effect on the employment of graduates of the programme if the programme were seen to be overly critical of the role of companies when it comes to

---

[1] Full disclosure (well, relatively full): I was one of those six individuals, and the thesis at issue had been written under my supervision. No sour grapes though: eventually the thesis was selected as the best of that academic year—for what it is worth.

Jan Klabbers, *Human Rights Bodies and the Structure of Institutional Obligation* In: *The Limits of Human Rights*. Edited by: Bardo Fassbender and Knut Traisbach, Oxford University Press 2019. © The Several Contributors.
DOI: 10.1093/oso/9780198824756.003.0011

human rights. Wearing his institutional hat, the sixth expert was worried not so much about such things as the freedom of speech or academic freedom of the student who had written the thesis, but rather more about the institutional interest in securing funding and securing employment opportunities for its graduates. And on at least one conception of ethics—a consequentialist conception—this is what he should be concerned about: the interests of future generations of students easily trump the current interest of a single student on any such consequentialist analysis, especially considering that what was at stake was merely a bonus to begin with. This merely concerned publication of the master's thesis of a student who had already passed all exams, whose work had already been graded, and who was certain to receive the degree the next day. On the other hand, the institutional interest may be difficult to reconcile with the very idea for which the institution was set up: surely, if human rights mean anything, they exist precisely to protect individuals against the enforcement of perceived institutional interests, so there is more than a little irony involved in seeing the president of a human rights institution actively promoting institutional interests.

The anecdote may be trivial, but it neatly illustrates some of the tensions involved in the institutionalization of any human activity. The moment an activity comes to form part of the mandate of an institution (any activity, and any institution), a tension starts to occur between the substantive interests behind the activity, and the institutional interests.[2]

This can be observed with respect to all sorts of institutions. Universities, for example, are no longer concerned with education, research, and learning, but with moving up the rankings and acquiring external funding. My own employer, the University of Helsinki, spent a lot of time defining institutional values a decade ago (we agreed on such fairly common sense values as gender equality, basic human rights, and environmental sustainability, against the uncontested background of the idea of education as a public task), but is currently happily engaged in charging tuition fees to non-EU students and doing business with China—ostensibly to export the Nordic Rule of Law to China, less ostensibly to boost the budget: doing business with China generates resources in order to do further business with China. Even more problematic perhaps, at least in light of those substantive values formulated a decade ago, are plans to have the private arm of the University offer tailor-made teaching programmes to Kuwait—it will be interesting to see how this can be reconciled with, say, gender equality. And on some level it is difficult to blame the University: with public funding having gone

---

[2] To be sure, there are other aspects to be considered, and one is that to the extent that institutions embody traditions and social practices, they offer an alternative to egotism and atomism. Such an approach may owe something to Alasdair McIntyre, *After Virtue: A Study in Moral Theory* (2nd edn, Duckworth 1985); a more recent manifesto is Hugh Heclo, *On Thinking Institutionally* (Paradigm Publishers 2008).

through dramatic budget cuts and with an ever-spreading market ethos affecting public offices, the move to China and Kuwait hardly comes as a surprise and might even, in the eyes of the policy-makers, be considered necessary to safeguard the future of the institution.

Likewise, many football clubs have become industries, aiming to make a profit through buying and selling players rather than trying to win prizes, never mind nurturing the interest in the game for its own sake, or teaching youngsters about such things as fair play.[3] Human rights institutions are no exception: here too, substantive and institutional interests may come to diverge, perhaps even collide.

What is good for the institution may come to diverge from what is good for the matter at hand, a phenomenon political realists long ago internalized with respect to the institution of the state, and typically refer to as 'raison d'État'. In the same vein, scholars of public administration long ago realized that bureaucratic agencies can and will be involved in turf wars: they fight not over their mandates per se, but over a bigger share of the national budget, or a bigger set of responsibilities. *Mutatis mutandis*, much the same applies to non-governmental organizations (NGOs), who are often driven by a combination of substantive passion and an institutional interest: in order to receive continued funding, these need to show that they are active and successful—in relative isolation from what they were originally set up for. This, in turn, implies that their work often becomes measured in quantifiable units which, in turn, may exist in relative isolation from what the original inspiration was. In this way, an NGO set up to help the victims of rape in internal armed conflict may well become an institution engaged in bringing as many cases as possible to the European Court of Human Rights: after all, bringing a case provides an objective yardstick, far more so than the more elusive practices associated with post-traumatic care.

This chapter aims to provide, in section II, an overview of the various types of human rights institutions in existence (without any pretence of being exhaustive). Section III will discuss the inevitability of institutionalization and some of its pitfalls, while section IV provides some selected examples, from the human rights sphere, illustrating the tension between individual and collective interests. Section V concludes. The main argument running through this chapter will be that institutionalization affects the structure of ethical and legal obligation, and that this, in turn, affects human rights institutions.

---

[3] One is reminded of Albert Camus' well-known claim that whatever he learned about morality, he learned from football. On Camus' ethics, see Jan Klabbers, 'The Passion and the Spirit: Albert Camus as Moral Politician' (2016) 1 European Papers 13 <http://europeanpapers.eu/en/system/files/pdf_version/EP_eJ_2016_1_4_Article_Jan_Klabbers_0.pdf> accessed 31 January 2019.

II. HUMAN RIGHTS INSTITUTIONS

There is no denying the circumstance that human rights have become institutionalized, and (if an apparent mixing of metaphors is allowed) have become an industry of sizeable proportions.[4] This is first and foremost visible in the explosion of formal state-endowed human rights institutions, ranging from a number of international courts and tribunals to domestic bodies tasked with supervising the application of human rights in one form or another, such as the Dutch Human Rights College, the successor of a Commission on Equal Treatment.[5] It is not a court per se, but scrutinizes human rights practices in the Netherlands and provides advisory opinions on how to proceed or how to remedy the situation.

The Human Rights College was set up in answer to a call by the United Nations (UN) that every UN member state should have its own human rights institution. It follows a set of internationally prescribed principles,[6] and is affiliated with similar institutions through both the UN and the European Network of National Human Rights Institutions, while in Europe the corresponding institution of the EU (the Fundamental Rights Agency) also plays something of a complementary role. Organs of this nature exist in many states, as do similar institutions such as ombudspersons, children's rights committees, non-discrimination watchdogs, etc.

In addition, on the international plane as well many human rights institutions exist. These include well-established courts such as the European Court of Human Rights, an institution comprising forty-seven (!) judges and some 650 registry staff, with an annual budget of a little under 70 million euros.[7] But there are also smaller, or more specific, human rights related tribunals, such as the three-person Human Rights Advisory Panel investigating human rights complaints in Kosovo. Within the UN system, many substantive treaties for the protection of human rights come with their own monitoring body, which may (dependent on their precise mandate) entertain interstate complaints, initiate investigations, conduct on-site inspections, promulgate general statements, or even entertain complaints from individuals. And where individual responsibility can be assigned to violations of norms for the protection of the individual, international and hybrid criminal tribunals have been set up, usually with a very specific mandate—the Special Tribunal for Lebanon may be on the extreme end of the spectrum, set up as it is to investigate a single attack in Lebanon leading to the death of twenty-two or twenty-three[8] individuals. These

---

[4] The mixing of metaphors is only apparent: industries too demonstrate all the characteristics of bureaucracies.

[5] See <http://www.mensenrechten.nl> accessed 31 January 2019.

[6] These are known as the Paris Principles, National institutions for the promotion and protection of human rights, GA Res. 48/134 (20 December 1993).

[7] The figures are culled from the Court's website <http://www.echr.coe.int> and <https://www.echr.coe.int/Documents/Budget_ENG.pdf> accessed 31 January 2019.

[8] Both numbers can be found on the tribunal's website <https://www.stl-tsl.org> accessed 31 January 2019.

courts too form considerable bureaucracies: the Special Tribunal for Lebanon, for example, not only has its premises and staff in the Netherlands, but also has a Beirut Office and a New York Liaison office, together employing some 450 people. Its total budget for 2016 is set at 62.8 million EUR, only marginally less than that of the European Court of Human Rights.[9]

And then there can be, on the international level, both administrative and political organs devoted to human rights. The most well-known example of the latter is the Human Rights Council of the UN, successor to the much-maligned Commission on Human Rights.[10] Forty-seven of the UN's member states are represented on it for a limited period of time, and its main tasks include monitoring and debating. A particular background 'in human rights' (whatever that may mean) does not seem to be among the prerequisites, neither for member states nor for office holders. At the time of writing membership includes such human rights stalwarts as China and the Russian Federation, as well as some other states with well-recorded human rights issues, such as Indonesia (with a notable fondness for the death penalty), Saudi Arabia (particularly memorable on women's rights), Nigeria (embracing indigenous peoples and young girls), and Qatar (offering warm welcomes to migrant workers). The Council President for 2015–16 was the South Korean diplomat Choi Kyonglim, whose main expertise is international trade governance.[11] His successor was El Salvador's Joaquín Alexander Maza Martelli, whose background is in all-round diplomacy and foreign policy.[12]

Administratively, the most important entity in the UN system is the UN's Office of the High Commissioner for Human Rights (OHCHR), which in late 2013 employed more than 1,000 people in various offices around the globe, and another 689 human rights officers in various peacekeeping missions. The budget is taken care of in part by the UN, in part by voluntary contributions from UN member states, and seems to hover around USD 200 million per year.[13]

The institutionalization of human rights also takes place without the formal involvement of governments. There exist many NGOs devoted to human rights in one way or another. The most well-known of these are Amnesty International and Human Rights Watch, but there are many, many others, occupying themselves with all sorts of human rights issues. Thus, there are NGOs devoted the children's rights, national and internationally operating, ranging from a Dutch NGO such as

---

[9] See the Tribunal's Seventh Annual Report (2015–16) <http://www.stl-tsl.org/en/documents/president-s-reports-and-memoranda/4833-seventh-annual-report-2015-2016> accessed 31 January 2019.

[10] See generally Jan Klabbers, 'Reflections on the Politics of Institutional Reform' in Peter Danchin and Horst Fischer (eds), *United Nations Reform and the New Collective Security* (Cambridge University Pres 2010) 76, especially 84–7.

[11] See <https://www.ohchr.org/EN/HRBodies/HRC/Pages/Presidency10thCycle.aspx> accessed 31 January 2019.

[12] See <https://www.ohchr.org/EN/HRBodies/HRC/Pages/Presidency11thCycle.aspx> accessed 31 January 2019.

[13] See <https://www.ohchr.org/EN/AboutUs/Pages/FundingBudget.aspx> accessed 31 January 2019.

Kidsrights Foundation to the classic Swiss-based Terre des Hommes. Some of these are highly specialized, focusing on a single aspect of children's rights (child labour, circumcision), whereas others have a more general brief. These NGOs themselves are (sometimes heavily) institutionalized: they will have a secretariat, headed by a secretary-general or some suchlike officer, and may have organs where experts, donors, or other major stakeholders come together. Amnesty International, for example, is run by a Secretary-General; has a number of directors for positions such as campaigning, fundraising, or information; the Secretary-General has as a sounding board a global council involving the likes of Sir Richard Branson, novelist Paulo Coelho, and artist Yoko Ono, while broad policy is determined by an international board.[14] It also has the odd organizational scandal, most famously so when the previous Secretary-General negotiated a generous severance package upon her second term in office coming to an end.[15]

There are also institutions, whether NGOs or otherwise, bringing two or more types of interests together, bringing together a number of institutions and forming a new institution in the process. The anecdote with which this chapter started provides an example, relating as it does to an educational human rights entity (the European Inter-University Centre, EIUC) set up by a number of smaller educational human rights entities, typically affiliated with universities from the EU's member states. In addition, many of these same university institutes collaborate in the Association of Human Rights Institutes, set up in 2000 and having a structure comprising a Chairperson, a Secretariat, and an Executive Committee.[16]

Processes of institutionalization, complete with an identifiable 'raison d'institution', can thus also be discerned outside governmental circles, and a firm reminder of this came when the NGO set up by Finland's former President Martti Ahtisaari, Crisis Management Initiative (CMI), announced that a successor to Ahtisaari had been found. This successor is Finland's former Foreign Minister and Prime Minister Alexander Stubb. Contrary to Ahtisaari, who is comfortable working away from the spotlight, Stubb is known as someone who is rather keen on the spotlights. If Ahtisaari is a social-democrat, a former school teacher, and former UN civil servant, Stubb by contrast represents the conservative party, and has been a politician for most of his professional life. Where it may be argued that Ahtisaari's low-key profile helps him in his role as mediator, Stubb is possibly too fond of the spotlight to be a successful mediator. Still, the initial surprise upon hearing the news faded away quite quickly upon realizing that the most important task of the leadership of CMI is not substantive, but institutional: Stubb can be expected to have access to the corridors of Finnish political power, and that is where

---

[14] See <https://www.amnesty.org/en/about-us/how-were-run/structure-and-people/> accessed 31 January 2019.
[15] See <https://www.ngo-monitor.org/reports/the_irene_khan_affair/> accessed 31 January 2019.
[16] See <http://new.ahri-network.org/sample-page/> accessed 31 January 2019.

the funding can be found to secure CMI's survival. Never mind whether he is any good at mediating in conflict situations; what matters is that he can be expected to be very good at furthering the interests of CMI.

III. INSTITUTIONALIZATION

Institutionalization is, it seems, an inevitable part of human activity.[17] Whenever people wish to do things together, or need to do things together, or even think they wish or need to do things together, they face two basic options.[18] Either they conclude a convention to do things together, or they set up an institution to do things together.[19] Those conventions, moreover, may over time institutionalize as well: the co-operation becomes regular, and someone is hired to keep the records, or to take notes, or to help out in other ways. Some of these institutions remain somewhat abstract (think of the institution of money, or the institution of marriage); others may occupy a building, adopt a logo, and acquire legal personality of some kind or other (think of the United Nations, or the BBC). Some are set up around some sort of foundational myth (this applies in particular to states,[20] i.e. institutions thought to be based on some common trait[21]), but most are set up with some kind of function in mind. This can usually be an instrumental function (the World Health Organization (WHO) serves the cause of global health promotion), but can also manifest a political instrumentalism: an institution may well be created because a distinguished politician needs a final plum position before retirement, or can only be persuaded to step down in exchange for heading a newly created institution.

Either way, institutions play a vital role in society, as highlighted by Elster: values and resources (political, economic, social, material, cultural) tend to be distributed by institutions.[22] Institutions decide on who shall receive welfare; institutions decide who shall perform military service, or who shall receive a kidney transplant or

---

[17] Mary Douglas puts it strongly in the closing sentence of her celebrated monograph: 'For better or worse... individuals... have no other way to make the big decisions except within the scope of institutions they build.' See Mary Douglas, *How Institutions Think* (Syracuse University Press 1986) 128.

[18] This section is inspired by Seamas Miller, *The Moral Foundations of Social Institutions: A Philosophical Study* (Cambridge University Press 2010) who proposes that institutions tend to be created to facilitate the pursuit of collective ends by individuals.

[19] This discounts the possibility of incidental, ad hoc joint action, as when two individuals come together on the dance floor, or when a bunch of robbers burgle a house in a one-time event.

[20] But not exclusively to states: companies too may owe much to original mythology (Henry Ford and the Ford Motor Company, Apple and Steve Jobs) and so may other actors. Even the UN would possibly not be the same without the reification of Dag Hammarskjöld. For a fine study of Hammarskjöld's ethics, see Manuel Fröhlich, *Political Ethics and the United Nations: Dag Hammarskjöld as Secretary-General* (Routledge 2008).

[21] The seminal study is Benedict Anderson, *Imagined Communities* (2nd edn, Verso 1991) but the point is of more ancient provenance: see already Ernest Renan, *Qu'est-ce qu'une nation?* (first published 1882, Flammarion 2011).

[22] Jon Elster, *Local Justice: How Institutions Allocate Scarce Goods and Necessary Burdens* (Russell Sage Foundation 1992).

be eligible for a visa or green card. In principle, many of these decisions could be left to a single decision-maker, but if so, many of us would worry about nepotism, arbitrary treatment, discrimination. Hence, it is not just the case that institutions well-nigh inevitably arise wherever humans wish to do things together, it is also the case that these institutions carry the promise of doing things better (i.e. with greater fairness) than would otherwise be the case.

Still, nothing is without its price, and this applies to institutions as well. Institutionalization comes with two (possible) expenses. The first is well-known, oft-lamented, and oft-exaggerated and, at the end of the day, not particularly interesting: institutionalization often implies a certain lack of efficiency. While a single judge (Dworkin's Hercules comes to mind[23]) might be able to take decisions quickly and wisely, Hercules cannot be fully trusted—after all, what if his nephew stands trial before him? Hence, a college of judges is deemed advisable, but this inevitably means that the judges will need to communicate with each other, compare notes, and perhaps negotiate the outcome, while in many cases judgments are open to appeal or cassation with different, higher-ranked colleges of judges. While this is thought to lead to better decisions, it nonetheless takes time and creates some duplication of effort.[24] And what applies to judges applies to all administrators, perhaps even *a fortiori*.[25]

The second cost is more interesting: it entails that the institution itself enters the equation in normative questions.[26] With a single decision-maker, one might always ask the question whether a decision to act in a particular way is or is not legally or ethically acceptable or appropriate, and such question can typically be answered under reference to some existing rule. Thus, the question whether an individual who spreads cholera through negligence should pay compensation to the victims can often be answered in fairly straightforward manner: the only actors to consider are the actor, and the victims, and the only question to ask is whether the causal connection between the two is strong enough to warrant liability. What emphatically does not enter the picture is the effect that a finding of liability will have on the actor—if found negligent, then he or she shall pay compensation, even if this will lead to bankruptcy or insolvency.

But things are different where an institution is involved and accused of being negligent, for while the individual might be considered dispensable, the institution

---

[23] Legal philosopher Ronald Dworkin devised a mythical, all-knowing judge, named Hercules, who would always be able to find the single right answer to any legal question. See, e.g., Ronald Dworkin, *Law's Empire* (Fontana 1986).

[24] It cannot per se be said to be less efficient though, as it is possible that the enhanced quality of decision-making more than compensates for the losses involved in terms of time and energy.

[25] Judges, after all, are often held uniquely qualified to take some kinds of decisions, especially those with legal elements. For a critique, see John Hart Ely, *Democracy and Distrust: A Theory of Judicial Review* (Harvard University Press 1980).

[26] See generally also Jeremy Waldron, *Political Political Theory: Essays on Institutions* (Harvard University Press 2016).

is not so considered: it was created for a reason, and that reason (the institutional function) continues to exist even if the institution itself does not. Thus, if the UN through negligence brings cholera somewhere, one cannot simply apply the above logic involving merely the actor and the victims, for what if the UN were to go bankrupt? Or if the UN were to decide that in the future it will not engage in peacekeeping anymore, out of fear for being prosecuted and the public relations fall-out? Things might not come to head in this extreme manner, but what is possible (and has arguably already occurred) is that the UN, in order to protect itself, might become markedly more reluctant to intervene when it is needed than might otherwise be the case.[27]

In other words, the involvement of institutions changes the structure of situational ethics: wherever an institution is involved, the institutional interest (however perceived) enters the picture, and cannot simply be ignored or defined away.[28] And this is so not because of the interest of the institution in and of itself, but because the institution carries the promise of further benevolent or necessary action. Hence, evaluating its behaviour of today should take into account the promise it offers with respect to the future. The philosopher Bernard Williams generalized and summarized the position well when observing that a particular deformation of political life (and institutions, of course, inherently mark political life) 'consists in the inability to consider a question on its merits because one's attention is directed to the consequences of giving ... a particular answer'.[29]

This attitude is well-engrained in our institutions. With respect to international organizations, it is often referred to as functionalism: the functioning of the organization should not be impeded, and anything it does should be tested against its main task.[30] In other settings (courts and tribunals for example) it is referred to as 'structural bias',[31] but either way, the idea is much the same: the institution is set up to accomplish a certain end, and this end colours all its activities. As Graeber puts it: 'bureaucracy is the first and only social institution that treats the means of doing things as entirely separate from what it is that's being done'.[32] Thus, a trade panel can be expected to analyse matters before it through the prism of its function

---

[27] See Michael Barnett and Martha Finnemore, *Rules for the World: International Organizations in Global Politics* (Princeton University Press 2004).

[28] This not the same as saying that responsibility tends to 'leak away' in organizations, a well-known phenomenon brilliantly discussed in, e.g., Robert Jackall, *Moral Mazes: The World of Corporate Managers* (first published 1990, Oxford University Press 2010).

[29] See Bernard Williams, 'Politics and Moral Character' in Stuart Hampshire (ed.), *Public and Private Morality* (Cambridge University Press 1978) 55, 68 (hereafter Hampshire (ed.), *Public and Private Morality*).

[30] See Jan Klabbers, 'The EJIL Foreword: The Transformation of International Organizations Law' (2015) 26 European Journal of International Law 9.

[31] See, e.g., Martti Koskenniemi, 'The Fate of Public International Law: Between Technique and Politics' (2007) 70 Modern Law Review 1.

[32] His use of the term 'bureaucracy' is close enough to my use of 'institution'. See David Graeber, *The Utopia of Rules: On Technology, Stupidity, and the Secret Joys of Bureaucracy* (Melville House 2015) 165.

in trade; a human rights court, by the same token, can be expected to prioritize human rights protection over other, possibly competing concerns.

But it goes further than this, in that it also entails that the institution can almost invariably defend itself by referring to its function.[33] This is how the World Bank, for quite some time, defended itself against charges that its acts would end up stimulating or facilitating human rights violations: it could reply, and not without some cogency, that it was set up to stimulate development, not human rights; and that it was not even allowed to take human rights into account as it should only take economic factors into account in its decision-making, in accordance with its constitution.

This makes it extremely difficult to evaluate, let alone criticize, institutions in general. Several factors conspire here. The first is that the institutional interest needs to be conceived of in flexible ways. Institutions—public institutions, at any rate—typically are the result of some kind of delegation (either from below, as with international organizations created by member states, e.g., or from above, as with entities set up by national governments to perform a functional task), and can only do their work if they are not micro-managed: some degree of discretion is necessary, for otherwise the act of delegation becomes pointless. But as soon as discretion enters the picture, it follows that the institution can take on a life of its own, and (dependent on its leadership) it might start to push the boundaries of that discretion just a little, and then a little bit more still. As a result, it might over time become difficult to tell—barring extreme cases—whether the institution sticks to its tasks, or whether it transgresses its tasks; whether it acts within its powers, or whether it acts *ultra vires*. What is more, if all relevant stakeholders agree that a certain action is necessary in the furtherance of the organizational function, then the question of whether the action is *ultra vires* does not seem particularly relevant anymore; it will come across as the desperate appeal by the formalist, clinging to something that has long since passed.

Second, if it is the case that the relevant factor to include is the promise carried by the institution rather than the institution itself, any analysis will have to remain speculative: one cannot judge the UN only on what is has done; one cannot predict with ironclad certainty how it will respond to a finding of liability—at best one can speculate that a finding of liability will have certain effects, but one cannot be certain that these effects will manifest themselves.

A third factor is that given the fact that the structural bias is indeed structural, it is difficult, well-nigh impossible, to escape from it—and as a result it is difficult to find fault with it too. The trade expert is conditioned to think and breathe 'trade': if

---

[33] Thomas Nagel expresses much the same when suggesting that 'public decisions will be justifiably more consequentialist than private ones', precisely because the institution and the promise it carries are implicated. See Thomas Nagel, 'Ruthlessness in Public Life' in Hampshire (ed.), *Public and Private Morality* (n. 29) 75, 84.

to a man with a hammer everything looks like a nail, the trade lawyer will view a new piece of labour legislation, or an environmental protection decree, or an economic boycott, in terms of its effects on trade. What is more, she is entirely justified in doing so, as her brief is precisely to gauge the trade effects of labour legislation, environmental protection decrees, and economic boycotts: if she is tasked to interpret trade rules, this is what she will do—her institutional affiliation and professional training demand nothing less.[34] And the same applies to the environmental expert, the labour expert, the security expert.

There is a further factor here, less obvious perhaps but still relevant, and that is that once the experts start talking amongst themselves, there is often no settled possibility of intervening within the same vocabulary and from the same perspective. All one can do is evaluate from a different angle. If the trade experts are united that a particular trade measure is incompatible with a general trade rule, it is difficult for the non-trade experts to tell the experts that they are wrong on their own turf. The best the non-expert can do is appeal to some other set of standards: maybe the experts followed the wrong procedure, maybe the outcome of their reasoning is ethically problematic or creative of political problems down the road; but they are unlikely to be able to tell the experts that they were wrong on the issue of trade itself.

IV. THREE ILLUSTRATIONS

Human rights agencies, however precisely conceived, cannot escape the mechanics of institutionalization either and, more importantly, cannot resist many of the temptations that institutionalization offers. Institutionalization often involves re-centring the institutional interest, shifting attention away from the substantive interest or philosophy that stimulated the creation of the institution to begin with. There is no doubt that numerous examples could be found, involving numerous institutions (and always mindful of the cautionary tale about throwing the first stone). Still, this section will discuss (and superficially so) merely three examples, which together provide a fine overview of the sort of issues emerging and the strategies institutions may develop to cope with them.

The first example is drawn from the United Nations, formally tasked with achieving international cooperation to promote and encourage respect for human rights, in the convoluted words of Article 1, paragraph 3, of the UN Charter. Since the mid-1950s, the UN has been actively engaged in peacekeeping: interjecting neutral soldiers, drawn from various member states, into conflict zones. Sadly, over the years it has become clear that sometimes peacekeepers themselves engage in

---

[34] On trade experts, see Erin Hannah, James Scott, and Silke Trommer (eds), *Expert Knowledge in Global Trade* (Routledge 2016).

unwarranted activities, ranging from committing torture to organizing drugs or people trafficking. So too during a mission in the Central African Republic where, it seemed, large numbers of peacekeepers had engaged in sexual abuse of local women and even children.

Things started to come to light in the spring of 2014, when the first reports of illicit activities involving in particular abuse of young boys became public.[35] A young female human rights officer with the OHCHR starts to work on the matter, together with a colleague from UNICEF, and after conducting interviews with individuals affected by abuse, they issued a report. This was sent to a number of higher-ranking officials, one of whom, a Swedish official named Anders Kompass, passed it on to the French authorities, who then started an investigation.

It is here that the institutional reflex for self-preservation made its appearance. Once the French authorities started their investigation, they were told that all contact with the UN should pass via UN lawyers. Kompass, in the meantime, briefed his superiors; as a result, OHCHR initiated an internal investigation against him, charging him with leaking sensitive materials and breaking protocol. Official UN reports, incidentally, failed to mention the matter, and the investigations of the human rights officer who started all this were questioned. Kompass was asked to resign, which he refused to do. He was then suspended, and took OHCHR to the UN dispute tribunal. The UN dispute tribunal was not particularly impressed with how the UN has handled things, and held that Kompass's suspension was at least *prima facie* unlawful.[36]

In the course of 2015, further stories of misbehaviour by peacekeepers in the Central African Republic came to light, with soldiers from various troop-contributing countries being involved. This continued for much of 2016, and in June of that year Kompass eventually handed in his resignation. In the meantime, in June 2015, the UN had set up an independent panel to investigate claims about sexual abuse in the Central African Republic, with the panel issuing its report in December 2015.[37] In its wake, in February 2016 the UN appointed a special coordinator on improving its response to sexual exploitation and abuse. Still, new allegations keep coming to light.

The entire unsavoury episode suggests, not for the first time, that when the institutional interest is under attack, the UN closes the ranks and circles the wagons. Instead of taking the allegations seriously, the first reflexive response is invariably to protect the organization—and equally invariably, this backfires.

---

[35] Much of what follows is culled from <http://archive.crin.org/en/home/campaigns/transparency/uncover.html> accessed 31 January 2019.

[36] See *Kompass v. Secretary-General of the United Nations*, Case no. UNDT/GVA/2015/126, 5 May 2015.

[37] See Marie Deschamps, Hassan B Jallow, and Yasmin Sooka, *Taking Action on Sexual Exploitation and Abuse by Peacekeepers: Report of an Independent Review on Sexual Exploitation and Abuse by International Peacekeeping Forces in the Central African Republic* (17 December 2015) <www.un.org/News/dh/infocus/centafricrepub/Independent-Review-Report.pdf> accessed 31 January 2019.

In principle, one would think that an organization that owes its existence in part to ideals about justice and human rights, could and perhaps should be mindful of this part of its mandate. While, admittedly, human rights do not occupy a very prominent place in the UN Charter, nonetheless the International Court of Justice (ICJ) could point out in 1954 that an organization devoted to justice should itself be seen to be acting justly, and provide access to justice if and when warranted. The ICJ did so on the occasion of having to form an opinion on the legality of the creation of the UN Administrative Tribunal, a tribunal set up to protect the staff of the UN against management.[38] During the high tide of McCarthyism, the witch hunt against (largely imaginary) communist spies in the United States, several UN employees were accused of falling into this category. Instead of standing in front of his employees and offering them protection, however, then Secretary-General Trygve Lie quickly decided to dance to McCarthy's tune, and fired the staff members concerned, or refused to extend their contracts.[39]

More generally, whenever there is a possible accusation going against the UN, whether it concerns a book by staff members exposing some internal issues[40] or whether the global community is upset by the imposition of sanction by the Security Council or the outbreak of cholera linked to peacekeepers, the UN's first response is to be non-responsive.

But the UN is far from the only example—even human rights courts, the guardians of the human rights spirit, sometimes fall prey to institutional temptations. One thing human rights courts (and other monitoring bodies) need to contend with is the lure of the indicator. Many of the recognized human rights—in particular, but not exclusively, social and economic rights—are difficult to enforce in pure form. A right to water cannot mean that someone is placed on every street corner with a jug of clean water; a right to life cannot prevent people from getting killed. Hence, to guarantee such rights often means resorting to procedural criteria: the right to water is broken down into questions about equal access to water, whether authorities have a water strategy, whether procedures exist locally in case access to water is denied, etc. This, in turn, may lead to the curious situation that where all the formal boxes are ticked, the right to water is seen as guaranteed, even in extreme cases of drought: as long as people have equal access to whatever water there is and as long as procedures exist, it matters less whether there actually is any water. What is more, this proceduralization of rights might therewith manage to mask unsavoury political or economic developments: the right to water *qua* right

---

[38] See Effect of Awards of Compensation made by the United Nations Administrative Tribunal (Advisory Opinion of 13 July 1954) [1954] ICJ Rep 47.
[39] In his memoirs, Lie maintained that he had done the right thing, was supported by independent legal advice, and had in no way 'packed' the Commission of Jurists that advised him on the matter. See Trygve Lie, *In the Cause of Peace: Seven Years With the United Nations* (MacMillan 1954) 398–400.
[40] See Kenneth Cain, Heidi Postlewait, and Andrew Thomson, *Emergency Sex (and Other Desperate Measures): A True Story from Hell on Earth* (Hyperion 2004).

is not automatically affected by the existence of a private monopoly controlling the water supply.[41] Likewise, the case law of the European Court of Human Rights pays considerably less attention to the great moral issues it could involve (think abortion or euthanasia) than it does to procedural issues once an individual has died in captivity or pursuit. In a sense, therewith, there is something in the very structure of many rights that compels proceduralization, and makes that human rights institutions have a hard time escaping what may be termed human rights technocracy.

Human rights courts have also had to grapple with two elements of bureaucracy that pull in different directions. On the one hand, ever since Weber it is realized that institutionalization goes hand in hand with a form of hierarchy,[42] and this places international tribunals almost naturally at the juridical apex—it would be decidedly counterintuitive to appeal decisions of an international court before a local court in some remote village. Yet, the sheer volume of cases thus potentially making their way upwards means that some rationalization is required. This can take the form of pilot judgments, but before the European Court of Human Rights has also taken the form of the margin of appreciation doctrine: in issues of morality (and this is what many human rights issues are, of course), local authorities are deemed better placed to determine what is acceptable than distant judges tucked away in Strasbourg.[43] As a result, practices that might be in tension with common intuitions about human rights have nonetheless been deemed agreeable. This has no doubt reduced the workload of the Court but also, and more importantly probably, increased its legitimacy in the eyes of the states that are parties to the European Convention—they are told, in so many words, that Strasbourg is unlikely to intervene in their everyday practices. And this, in turn, has no doubt helped to cement and guarantee the institutional position and interests of the European Court of Human Rights.

And then there may be cases where a human rights court makes a decision which is technically defensible and yet seems very wrong, precisely from the point of view of the *esprit* of human rights, and the disjunction seems to result precisely once again from institutional concerns. One example is the 2013 judgment by the European Court of Human Rights in *Perincek v. Switzerland*, confirmed by the Grand Chamber in 2015.[44] Mr Perincek had been convicted in Switzerland for denying the Armenian genocide; he appealed to the Strasbourg Court that his

---

[41] In the same vein, Norrie once astutely observed that all the hoopla about the adoption of the Human Rights Act in the United Kingdom nonetheless left the Thatcherite economy intact. See Alan Norrie, 'Criminal Justice, Judicial Interpretation, Legal Right: On Being Sceptical about the Human Rights Act 1998' in Tom Campbell, Keith D Ewing, and Adam Tomkins (eds), *Sceptical Essays on Human Rights* (Oxford University Press 2001) 261, 268.

[42] Max Weber, *Economy and Society* (Roth and Wittich eds, University of California Press 1978).

[43] George Letsas, *A Theory of Interpretation of the European Convention on Human Rights* (Oxford University Press 2007).

[44] See *Perincek v. Switzerland*, App. No. 27510/08, 17 December 2013 and 15 October 2015. For commentary, see Jan Klabbers, 'Doing Justice? Bureaucracy, the Rule of Law and Virtue Ethics' (2017) 6 Rivista di Filosofia del Diritto 27.

freedom of speech had been curtailed, and the Court agreed. In pitting the case as one of freedom of speech versus genocide denial, the Court came close to genocide denial itself: it strongly suggested that what had taken place in Armenia a century earlier, the slaughter of up to one and a half million people, was not really genocide, or at least had not generally been recognized as such. In doing so, the Court displayed a stunning lack of empathy, fundamentally at odds with the very idea of human rights. There seems to be no plausible legal, let alone ethical, explanation for the Court's attitude, all the more so as the separate opinion of two of its judges had pointed to a far more elegant way out.[45] The one remaining possibility then is an institutional explanation: with the Court's position under threat, with subsidiarity being mooted at the 2012 Brighton meeting of the parties to the Convention and finding formal confirmation in Protocol No. 15, and amidst persistent rumours of possible withdrawal by the United Kingdom, perhaps the Court felt the need to firmly re-establish its credentials at least when it comes to classic civil and political rights (so central to the United Kingdom's tradition of political theory) by clamping down on possible violations of the freedom of speech, if necessary at the expense of other rights. If so, then it would seem considerations relating to the institutional interest prevailed over people of flesh and blood.

The third example similarly illustrates how the promise associated with the institution came to overshadow the work of the institution itself. In 1999, NATO bombers dropped bombs on Belgrade, in order to induce the Serbian authorities to stop the ugly practice of ethnic cleansing taking place in Kosovo, a territory nominally forming part of Serbia but wishing to break away. NATO's bombers did not have the benefit of acting upon authorization by the Security Council, and thus there was a strong possibility that the behaviour was not in accordance with international law. Consequently, the prosecutor of the International Criminal Tribunal for the Former Yugoslavia (ICTY), set up a few years earlier to deal with atrocities taking place in the former Yugoslavia, was urged by some to start legal proceedings: bombing a city without Security Council authorization constitutes at least *prima facie* evidence of aggression, perhaps even of genocide, no matter how justifiable it may seem upon further reflection.[46]

The ICTY prosecutor, however, decided not to start proceedings involving the NATO bombings. In her memoires she explains the reasons behind the decision. It was not, so she assures her readers, because she supported the bombings, although as a matter of fact she did. Instead, she realized that she hit a wall. NATO

---

[45] Judges Sajo and Raimondi suggested in their separate opinion to the 2013 decision (n. 44) that the case be best seen as one involving the principle of legality: since similar cases had never resulted in a criminal conviction, Perincek should not have been convicted either. This has the great benefit of not having to weigh one right against another.

[46] For an argument along these lines, commenting on a set of decisions by the ICJ, see Martti Koskenniemi, 'Evil Intentions or Vicious Acts: What is *Prima Facie* Evidence of Genocide?' in Matti Tupamäki (ed.), *Liber Amicorum Bengt Broms* (ILA 1999) 180.

and its member states refused to co-operate, and even China, one of the victims (the Chinese embassy in Belgrade had been hit, apparently by mistake) did not provide the ICTY with any information. But the clincher was, again, the future prospect: Del Ponte realized quickly that not only an investigation into NATO's acts was doomed to fail, but that if she were to persist, it would also jeopardize further investigations by the ICTY: NATO and its members could refuse any further co-operation and, truth be told, she had already often encountered their reluctance to assist with prosecutions—she often refers to the *muro di gomma* ('wall of rubber') thrown up by Western leaders. Moreover, the ICTY staff was dependent on NATO for its safety when operating in Bosnia or Kosovo. Without NATO support, in other words, the entire ICTY was doomed to fail.[47]

V. TO CONCLUDE

The ancient Romans already realized that wherever there is a society, there will be law; they could have added a second paragraph, to the effect that wherever there is a society, there will be institutions. Institutions come in all sizes and shapes, they can be public and private, or the result of delegation downwards or upwards, and national legal systems usually recognize a bunch of them as legal persons, from limited liability companies to charities, and from partnerships to associations. Human action, so it seems, cannot escape institutionalization.

In this light, it is no surprise perhaps that institutions are being studied by a variety of academic disciplines, from political science to anthropology, from law to sociology, from ethics to economics. But what is perhaps surprising is that little of this has resulted in cross-disciplinary understandings—there is no discipline of 'institutionalism' studying institutions from different perspectives; perhaps the closest are the disciplines of business administration and public administration, but these very labels already manifest a certain fragmentation.[48]

Perhaps for the lawyer as well as the ethicist, one of the more interesting aspects of institutionalization is the interplay between individual and collective obligation. Without prejudice to the question whether institutions can be moral agents,[49] at the very least it would seem that the obligations of individuals cannot automatically be transposed to institutions—the institution intervenes in the relevant legal (or ethical) relationship, and transforms the normative landscape. This in turn

---

[47] See Carla del Ponte with Chuck Sudetic, *Mevrouw de aanklager* (De Bezige Bij 2008) especially 91–9. The book was originally published in Italian, in 2008, as *La Caccia: Io e i criminali di guerra* (Feltrinelli 2008).

[48] In fact, there is not even much sustained and comprehensive legal thinking on bureaucracy and institutionalization. A valiant attempt is Meir Dan-Cohen, *Rights, Persons, and Organizations: A Legal Theory for Bureaucratic Society* (University of California Press 1986).

[49] For a useful collection, see Toni Erskine (ed.), *Can Institutions Have Responsibilities? Collective Moral Agency and International Relations* (Palgrave MacMillan 2003).

raises hosts of other questions: for example, are individuals allowed to act in perfidious ways due to their institutional roles?[50] Should individuals in position of authority incur responsibility for the acts of the institutions they are leading?[51] What at any rate is the relationship between individuals, their beliefs, and their roles within institutions?[52]

What makes things more interesting still for the human right expert is that there is a strong tension between the existence of individual human rights, and the institutionalization processes characterizing political life, including institutionalization of the protection of those human rights. And as noted above, it is not invariably the case that in case of conflict, the spirit of human rights prevails; often enough, the pressures emanating from the institution and its interests, including the promise of a better tomorrow supposedly associated with the institution, prevail. This then helps frame the standard institutional dilemma: institutions help deliver substance, but at the expense of undermining the very idea they are supposed to help deliver.

As a result, the most successful institutions (in terms of longevity and public trust) are those which manage to remind themselves of their initial tasks and do not get side-tracked by the smell of success and the call for institutional expansion. This may be a matter of building in 'constitutional irritants';[53] it may also be a matter of responsible leadership.[54]

Bibliography

Anderson B, *Imagined Communities* (2nd edn, Verso 1991)
Applbaum AI, *Ethics for Adversaries: The Morality of Roles in Public and Professional Life* (Princeton University Press 1999)
Barnett M and Finnemore M, *Rules for the World: International Organizations in Global Politics* (Princeton University Press 2004)
Cain K, Postlewait H, and Thomson A, *Emergency Sex (and Other Desperate Measures): A True Story from Hell on Earth* (Hyperion 2004)
Dan-Cohen M, *Rights, Persons, and Organizations: A Legal Theory for Bureaucratic Society* (University of California Press 1986)
Douglas M, *How Institutions Think* (Syracuse University Press 1986)

---

[50] See, e.g., David Luban, *Lawyers and Justice: An Ethical Study* (Princeton University Press 1988); Arthur Isak Applbaum, *Ethics for Adversaries: The Morality of Roles in Public and Professional Life* (Princeton University Press 1999).

[51] See, e.g., Dennis F Thompson, *Political Ethics and Public Office* (Harvard University Press 1987), and Dennis F Thompson, *Restoring Responsibility: Ethics in Government, Business, and Healthcare* (Cambridge University Press 2005).

[52] See, e.g., Robert S Downie, *Roles and Values: An introduction to Social Ethics* (methuen 1971).

[53] The notion is developed in a slightly different context (or is it?) by Gunther Teubner, *Constitutional Fragments: Societal Constitutionalism and Globalization* (Oxford University Press 2012).

[54] For a (conservative) argument along these lines, see Larry D Terry, *Leadership of Public Bureaucracies: The Administrator as Conservator* (2nd edn, Sharpe 2003).

Downie RS, *Roles and Values: An Introduction to Social Ethics* (Methuen 1971)
Dworkin R, *Law's Empire* (Fontana 1986)
Elster J, *Local Justice: How Institutions Allocate Scarce Goods and Necessary Burdens* (Russell Sage Foundation 1992)
Ely JH, *Democracy and Distrust: A Theory of Judicial Review* (Harvard University Press 1980)
Erskine T (ed.), *Can Institutions Have Responsibilities? Collective Moral Agency and International Relations* (Palgrave MacMillan 2003)
Fröhlich M, *Political Ethics and the United Nations: Dag Hammarskjöld as Secretary-General* (Routledge 2008)
Graeber D, *The Utopia of Rules: On Technology, Stupidity, and the Secret Joys of Bureaucracy* (Melville House 2015)
Hannah E, Scott J, and Trommer S (eds), *Expert Knowledge in Global Trade* (Routledge, 2016)
Heclo H, *On Thinking Institutionally* (Paradigm Publishers 2008)
Jackall R, *Moral Mazes: The World of Corporate Managers* (first published 1990, Oxford University Press 2010)
Klabbers J, 'Reflections on the Politics of Institutional Reform' in Danchin P and Fischer H (eds), *United Nations Reform and the New Collective Security* (Cambridge University Pres 2010) 76
Klabbers J, 'The EJIL Foreword: The Transformation of International Organizations Law' (2015) 26 European Journal of International Law 9
Klabbers J, 'The Passion and the Spirit: Albert Camus as Moral Politician' (2016) 1 European Papers 13 <http://europeanpapers.eu/en/system/files/pdf_version/EP_eJ_2016_1_4_Article_Jan_Klabbers_0.pdf> accessed 31 January 2019
Klabbers J, 'Doing Justice? Bureaucracy, the Rule of Law and Virtue Ethics' (2017) 6 Rivista di Filosofia del Diritto 27
Koskenniemi M, 'Evil Intentions or Vicious Acts: What is Prima Facie Evidence of Genocide?' in Tupamäki M (ed.), *Liber Amicorum Bengt Broms* (ILA 1999) 180
Koskenniemi M, 'The Fate of Public International Law: Between Technique and Politics' (2007) 70 Modern Law Review 1
Letsas G, *A Theory of Interpretation of the European Convention on Human Rights* (Oxford University Press 2007)
Lie T, *In the Cause of Peace: Seven Years With the United Nations* (MacMillan 1954)
Luban D, *Lawyers and Justice: An Ethical Study* (Princeton University Press 1988)
McIntyre A, *After Virtue: A Study in Moral Theory* (2nd edn, Duckworth 1985)
Miller S, *The Moral Foundations of Social Institutions: A Philosophical Study* (Cambridge University Press 2010)
Nagel T, 'Ruthlessness in Public Life' in Hampshire S (ed.), *Public and Private Morality* (Cambridge University Press 1978) 75
Norrie A, 'Criminal Justice, Judicial Interpretation, Legal Right: On Being Sceptical about the Human Rights Act 1998' in Campbell T, Ewing KD, and Tomkins A (eds), *Sceptical Essays on Human Rights* (Oxford University Press 2001) 261
del Ponte C with Sudetic C, *Mevrouw de aanklager* (De Bezige Bij 2008)
Renan E, *Qu'est-ce qu'une nation?* (first published 1882, Flammarion 2011)
Terry LD, *Leadership of Public Bureaucracies: The Administrator as Conservator* (2nd edn, Sharpe 2003)
Teubner G, *Constitutional Fragments: Societal Constitutionalism and Globalization* (Oxford University Press 2012)
Thompson DF, *Political Ethics and Public Office* (Harvard University Press 1987)

Thompson DF, *Restoring Responsibility: Ethics in Government, Business, and Healthcare* (Cambridge University Press 2005)
Waldron J, *Political Political Theory: Essays on Institutions* (Harvard University Press 2016)
Weber M, *Economy and Society* (Roth and Wittich eds, University of California Press 1978)
Williams B, 'Politics and Moral Character' in Hampshire S (ed.), *Public and Private Morality* (Cambridge University Press 1978) 55

10
Dissecting the Institution
A Response to Jan Klabbers

Rosa Freedman and Ruth Houghton

Investigating the impact of institutionalism on human rights is a much-needed project, and for that reason Jan Klabbers' contribution to this collection is welcomed. Institutionalism is concerned with the functioning of an institution; its internal structures and processes. The contested effects of *institutionalization*—or the proliferation of international institutions—on international law are well-documented; on the one hand it has given rise to an idea of centralization, and on the other it has led to the fragmentation of international law into separate legal orders, with competing institutional drivers, such as powers and jurisdiction, funding, and decision-making processes.[1] International law scholars have previously considered the impact of institutional factors on judicial bodies and tribunals, such as the deference to member states at the International Court of Justice (ICJ) so as to ensure the longevity of its roles in dispute settlement between states.[2] Within human rights, institutionalism and the extraneous effects of decision-making being made by an institution are not as frequently discussed. In this chapter, then, Klabbers makes an important contribution by highlighting the need to examine the functioning of human rights institutions in order to consider the effects they have on the content of human rights norms. In response to Klabbers opening the door on this important area, we will use this comment piece to emphasize the need to differentiate clearly between institutions and actors, and indeed between different types of institutions and different types of actors, in order to explore systematically any impact on how international human rights law is developed and implemented. To do so, we will focus on a few of the examples Klabbers uses, demonstrating why a

---

[1] For a discussion on centralization, see Richard Collins, *The Institutional Problem in Modern International Law* (Hart Publishing 2016) 199.

[2] Ruth Mackenzie and Philippe Sands, 'International Courts and Tribunals and the Independence of the International Judge' (2003) 44 Harvard International Law Journal 271; Ruth Mackenzie, Cesare PR Romano, Yuval Shany, and Philippe Sands, 'The Project on International Courts and Tribunals (PICT)' in Ruth Mackenzie, Cesare PR Romano, Yuval Shany, and Philippe Sands (eds), *Manual on International Courts and Tribunals* (Oxford University Press 2010) vii; Gleider I Hernández, 'Impartiality and Bias at the International Court of Justice' (2012) 1 Cambridge Journal of International and Comparative Law 183, 190 (hereafter Hernández, 'Impartiality and Bias').

Rosa Freedman and Ruth Houghton, *Dissecting the Institution: A Response to Jan Klabbers* In: *The Limits of Human Rights*. Edited by: Bardo Fassbender and Knut Traisbach, Oxford University Press 2019. © The Several Contributors.
DOI: 10.1093/oso/9780198824756.003.0012

more nuanced discussion of the institutions and actors would allow greater understanding of the effect—if any—of institutionalism.

As Klabbers explains, one clear manifestation of institutionalism can be seen when an institution prioritizes its own interests over the interests or rights of others. When the United Nations (UN) closed ranks with respect to the outbreak of cholera in Haiti and used a procedural bar to undermine the fundamental rights of cholera victims to access a court and a remedy, it is clear how institutionalism—the need to protect the institution—worked. But what is missing here is what arms of the 'UN' were unresponsive and how that was proceduralized and justified. Closing ranks to protect an institution necessitates an interplay between individuals working at the UN and reliance on particular policies, mandates, and processes. Interviews contained in a forthcoming piece by Rosa Freedman and Nicolas Lemay-Hérbert demonstrate that there were a number of actors within and parts of the UN that wanted to resolve the Haiti cholera claims, and that the Office of Legal Affairs—one small but powerful part of the UN—dictated that they all adhere to the closing of ranks.[3] Klabbers' study of institutionalism here would be enhanced by an explicit statement on the distinction between the institution, its different parts, and the actors involved.

Understanding how institutionalism impacts upon international human rights law requires a systematic appraisal of the different types of international human rights institutions: their functions (judicial, bureaucratic, political); their membership criteria; and their decision-making processes (e.g. voting rules and practices). Within the UN human rights system alone—ignoring regional and national human rights mechanisms—there are a plethora of different institutions: the quasi-judicial role played by the treaty monitoring bodies; the political forum of the UN Human Rights Council; the Secretariat, serving the interests of member states; and the Special Procedures (e.g. Special Rapporteurs, Independent Experts, and Working Groups). Each type of institution has its own working methods, types of powers, forms of activity, mandates, indicators of success, and abilities to affect laws or practice or both. Comparing one type with another without explicitly recognizing and addressing those differences is akin to comparing apples and pears. Institutional drivers will be different depending on which human rights institution is being assessed. We shall clearly lay out our marker at this stage: we understand institutionalism to be concerned primarily with institutional markers. Of course, institutions are populated by the individuals that work there and others who interact with the institutions, but decisions made by those people are not institutionalism per se. And while we would be very interested in picking up on Klabbers' focus on

---

[3] See Rosa Freedman and Nicolas Lemay-Hérbert, 'The Security Council in Practice: Haiti, Cholera, and the Elected Members of the United Nations Security Council' (2019) 32 Leiden Journal of International Law, forthcoming. Klabbers does highlight the role of the UN lawyers with respect to allegations about sexual assault by peacekeepers.

the impact that individuals may have on human rights, systematically studying the role of individual actors on human rights—something we cannot do justice in this short commentary—is not sufficient to understand the effect of institutionalism.

I. INDIVIDUALS AND THE INSTITUTION

We would first like to discuss one example that Klabbers draws upon. People who work at the institutions select the direction of travel. Whether it is ambassadors with particular interests in human rights—or those who have no interest at all—individual judges or part-time pro bono experts, the human rights institutions rely upon and are shaped by the people who work within them. Klabbers touches upon this when he discusses, in his chapter, how judges in the European Court of Human Rights might impact upon how the law is developed and applied. It would be interesting to consider the respective impact of the various roles these different types of actors have; that is, what genuine scope there is for an individual actor to develop human rights norms. If we were exploring the effects of individual actors, we would also need to unpack the effect of paid versus pro bono employment, the nature of different roles, and the levels of independence afforded by different governments (even if roles are supposedly independent from national interference). All of these are key factors when analysing and unpacking how institutional actors, individually and collectively, impact upon human rights.

We particularly like talking about Special Procedures because it is the 'crown jewel' of the UN human rights system.[4] Special Procedures mandate holders are appointed for fixed terms as part-time, unpaid, independent experts. Some of those individuals have received (informal) support from their home states during their campaigns, while others have run wholly independently; some are lawyers, some civil society members, some specialists in specific areas, and some academics; some are UN insiders, and some have never previously set foot in a UN human rights body. They hail from across the world—by passport, at least. During their term in office they can shape their mandates. They may request to visit any country, and they may take up any thematic issue they deem relevant. They are independent of all entities, including their home states (though note the issue of funding mentioned above), the UN, and the Secretariat, and perform the role in their 'spare' time. As such, it is clear that the personality and personal interests of the experts are able to—and do—shape the contours of the mandate and therefore the human right itself.

---

[4] Kofi Anan, 'Statement at Time Warner Centre' (New York, 8 December 2006) <http://www.un.org/sg/en/content/sg/speeches/2006-12-08/urging-end-impunity-annan-sets-forth-ideas-bolster-un-efforts-protect> accessed 31 January 2019.

There are too many excellent examples for us to be able to begin to explain the impact of the personalities of some UN Special Procedures mandate holders on the development of human rights.[5] We would encourage readers to look into why the mandate on cultural rights was created—spoiler alert: Cuba intended it to be used as a mechanism for undermining universality of fundamental rights[6]—and then contrast those intentions with what Farida Shaheed and Karima Bennoune have done to advance women's rights, cultural heritage, and minority rights using their platforms as successive holders of that mandate.[7] Philip Alston has recently used his mandate on human rights and extreme poverty to scrutinize the most powerful countries and their approach to the most vulnerable in their societies,[8] while Olivier de Schutter chose to shine the spotlight on obesity in a developed country when holding the mandate on the right to food.[9] Others have used their mandates for purposes somewhat less connected to human rights, such as when Jean Ziegler used his mandate (on the right to food) to compare Israelis with Nazis,[10] or—as Sir Nigel S Rodley pointed out—when the Special Rapporteur on the former Yugoslavia argued in favour of immunity for the Serbian President Slobodan Milosovic, which was at odds with the policy against impunity for human rights violations.[11]

Clearly, even just within this one part of the international human rights system the role of the individual depends on many factors. At the very least, we would advise taking into account the individual actor's role, employment status, personality traits, nationality, academic background, formal training (e.g. in law) or expertise, work experience, and potential connections, amongst others.[12] But to account for

---

[5] See, e.g., Jessie Hohmann, 'Principle, Politics and Practice: The Role of UN Special Rapporteurs on the Right to Adequate Housing in the Development of the Right to Adequate Housing in International Law' in Aoife Nolan, Rosa Freedman, and Thérèse Murphy (eds), *The United Nations Special Procedures System* (Brill 2017) 271.

[6] For a discussion on Cuba's involvement with mandates on cultural rights see Rosa Freedman and Jacob Mchangama, 'Expanding or Diluting Human Rights?: The Proliferation of United Nations Special Procedures Mandates' (2016) 38 Human Rights Quarterly 164, 184–5.

[7] See Report of the Special Rapporteur in the field of cultural rights (Farida Shaheed), GA Res. A/67/287 (10 August 2012); Report of the Special Rapporteur in the field of cultural rights (Karima Bennoune), GA Res. A/72/155 (17 July 2017).

[8] Report of the Special Rapporteur on extreme poverty and human rights on his mission to the United States of America (Philip Alston), GA Res. A/HRC/38/33/ Add. 1 (4 May 2018).

[9] Report submitted by the Special Rapporteur on the right to food (Olivier De Schutter), GA Res. A/HRC/19/59 (26 December 2011).

[10] Alan Johnson, 'Appointment with farce' *The Guardian* (London, 5 April 2008) <http://www.theguardian.com/commentisfree/2008/apr/05/appointmentwithfarce> accessed 31 January 2019. See also Nigel S Rodley, 'On the Responsibility of Special Rapporteurs' (2011) 15 The International Journal of Human Rights 319, 320: '[T]he first special rapporteur on the right to food, Jean Ziegler, who apparently referred to the thousands dying from malnutrition in Brazil, which he was visiting, as genocide' (hereafter Rodley, 'Responsibility of Special Rapporteurs').

[11] Ewen MacAskill and Ian Traynor, 'Fury as UN envoy suggests war crimes amnesty for Milosovic' *The Guardian* (London, 5 October 2000); Rodley, 'Responsibility of Special Rapporteurs' (n. 10) 320.

[12] This is an indicative list and not an exhaustive list. Some of these things Hernández has considered with respect to the judges at the ICJ (importantly, the role of their homogenous legal training). Hernández, 'Impartiality and Bias' (n. 2).

the impact of institutionalism would necessitate an understanding of the creation of the mandate (and the flexibility of the mandate), potential accountability mechanisms, and funding. Indeed, Inga T Winkler and Catarina de Albuquerque have shown how funding streams—and in particular, informal funding—shape how the right to water is applied: projects that promote the right to water, rather than identify violations or protect against violations of the right are more likely to be funded by philanthropic donors.[13] And while external funding does need to be transparently documented on a mandate holder's website, there are many instances where funders (governments, charities, or private organizations) have only granted the money if mandate holders use it to focus on particular themes.

Studying the personal choices of individual actors, and the impacts of their personalities on the decision-making of human rights institutions, is another worthy project, but even that would not be sufficient to understand and interrogate how institutionalism affects human rights.[14] Klabbers gives the example of one academic judging an essay competition, highlighting that the individual's concern with the funding of a human rights-related programme affected his judgement, but that—like the personality of a Special Procedures mandate holder—is a question of personality and personal concerns, rather than an institutional driver. Some individuals may wear their 'institutional-hat', but others leave such hats at the door.

II. INSTITUTIONALISM: THE STRUCTURE AND FUNCTION OF AN INSTITUTION

Institutionalism, as we understand it, is the way in which the structure and function of an institution shapes decision-making and has negative or positive effects on the content of human rights norms. Keeping the focus on the UN, we would like to turn to the UN Human Rights Council to unpack and demonstrate, albeit briefly, how institutionalism might be explored. The Council is often criticized for facilitating the inclusion of known human rights abusers as part of its membership. The criteria for election are weak and, as Klabbers demonstrates, this leads to problematic membership. Focusing on individual members is only part of the story; Freedman has shown how the groups of member states forge practices that negatively politicize the work of the Council.[15] It is the institutional make-up of

---

[13] See Inga T Winkler and Catarina de Albuquerque, 'Doing It All and Doing It Well? A Mandate's Challenges in Terms of Cooperation, Fundraising and Maintaining' Independence' in Aoife Nolan, Rosa Freedman, and Thérèse Murphy (eds), *The United Nations Special Procedures System* (Brill 2017) 188.

[14] Hernández draws a distinction between the function of the judge and the function of the court. Hernández, 'Impartiality and Bias' (n. 2) 190.

[15] Rosa Freedman, *The United Nations Human Rights Council: A Critique and Early Assessment* (Routledge Research in Human Rights Law 2013) (hereafter Freedman, *Human Rights Council*); see also Rosa Freedman and Ruth Houghton, 'Two Steps Forward, One Step Back: Politicisation of the Human Rights Council' (2017) 17 Human Rights Law Review 753.

the Council that facilitates these negative practices. Created as a political body, the Council's forty-seven member states are elected from regional groups; an attempt to ensure geographical representation.[16] There are thirteen seats for states from the Group of African states, thirteen seats for the Group of Asian states, six seats for the Group of Eastern European states, eight for the Group of Latin American and Caribbean states, and seven for the Group of Western European and other states.[17] One of the results of this set-up is the power of regional groupings to shape proceedings at the Council. Regional groups, or political blocs, such as the African Group, the Organization of Islamic Cooperation (OIC), the Western European and Others Group (WEOG), and the Non-aligned Movement (NAM) use tactics such as bloc voting, the repetition of positions, and statements of allegiance to undermine the work of the Council. The Council's forum nature—its drive to offer a discursive environment—and the regional distribution of members facilitates the use of bloc tactics. Nothing in the Council's mandate or its institutional building package creates a bulwark against these practices.

The 'talking-shop' nature of the Council has affected the implementation of human rights norms. Certain states are shielded from criticism because allied states use valuable Council time and resources to praise the state instead; for example, at the Special Session on Sri Lanka, its allies rallied round to write a resolution that put forward the government's version of events, praised state forces, and pointed the finger only at abuses committed by the Liberation Tigers of Tamil Eelam (LTTE).[18] Delays on resolutions with respect to protections for LGBT+ persons, focusing on 'the family' and 'traditional values', or the lengthy insistence that defamation of religion might be a right created smoke-screens that meant states were able to continue to violate rights. Similar tactics also have a negative impact on the content of norms, with a recent example being the amendment to Resolution 32/2 that sets the precedent for cultural relativism to be enshrined in relation to the fundamental rights of LGBT+ individuals not to be subject to state-sponsored or condoned violence or discrimination.

Observing the EU at the Council offers an additional layer of institutionalism. EU member states at the Council are driven by the EU position,[19] and thus can fail to weigh in on certain countries' violations of human rights, such as the silence from the EU on the crisis in Darfur.[20] EU states agree to uphold a unified position—it is not just a choice on the part of a delegation—and as such, this is

---

[16] Human Rights Council, GA Res. 60/251 (3 April 2006) para. 7.
[17] Ibid.
[18] Assistance to Sri Lanka in the promotion and protection of human rights, HRC Resolution S-11/1 (27 May 2009).
[19] Article 34(1) of Treaty on European Union (TEU) states that EU member states 'shall coordinate their action in international organisations and ... shall uphold the common positions in such forums'; see Karen E Smith, 'Speaking with One Voice? European Union Co-ordination on Human Rights Issues at the United Nations' (2006) 44 Journal of Common Market Studies 113.
[20] See Freedman, *Human Rights Council* (n. 15).

an effect of institutionalism that comes about due to the internal structures of the institution and its members. Many an opportunity to promote, protect, or develop human rights has been missed owing to the need for constant internal EU negotiation, or the adherence to a common position that often reflects the lowest common denominator.

Drawing a distinction between the actors that work in the institution and the institution itself is fundamental when considering potential reforms. You can take the individual out of the institution, but this might have minimal impact if the institution's processes, powers, and funding are such that it facilitates abuses by individuals.

Bibliography

Anan K, 'Statement at Time Warner Centre' (8 December 2006) <http://www.un.org/sg/en/content/sg/speeches/2006-12-08/urging-end-impunity-annan-sets-forth-ideas-bolster-un-efforts-protect> accessed 31 January 2019

Collins R, *The Institutional Problem in Modern International Law* (Hart Publishing 2016)

Freedman R, *The United Nations Human Rights Council: A Critique and Early Assessment* (Routledge Research in Human Rights Law 2013)

Freedman R and Mchangama J, 'Expanding or Diluting Human Rights?: The Proliferation of United Nations Special Procedures Mandates' (2016) 38 Human Rights Quarterly 164

Freedman R and Houghton R, 'Two Steps Forward, One Step Back: Politicisation of the Human Rights Council' (2017) 17 Human Rights Law Review 753

Freedman R and Lemay-Hérbert N, 'The Security Council in Practice: Haiti, Cholera, and the Elected Members of the United Nations Security Council' (2019) 32 Leiden Journal of International Law, forthcoming

Hernández GI, 'Impartiality and Bias at the International Court of Justice' (2012) 1 Cambridge Journal of International and Comparative Law 183

Hohmann J, 'Principle, Politics and Practice: The Role of UN Special Rapporteurs on the Right to Adequate Housing in the Development of the Right to Adequate Housing in International Law' in Nolan A, Freedman R, and Murphy T (eds), *The United Nations Special Procedures System* (Brill 2017) 271

Johnson A, 'Appointment with farce' *The Guardian* (London, 5 April 2008) <http://www.theguardian.com/commentisfree/2008/apr/05/appointmentwithfarce> accessed 31 January 2019

MacAskill E and Traynor I, 'Fury as UN envoy suggests war crimes amnesty for Milosovic' *The Guardian* (London, 5 October 2000)

Mackenzie R and Sands P, 'International Courts and Tribunals and the Independence of the International Judge' (2003) 44 Harvard International Law Journal 271–85

Mackenzie R, Romano CPR, Shany Y, and Sands P, 'The Project on International Courts and Tribunals (PICT)' in Mackenzie R, Romano CPR, Shany Y, and Sands P (eds), *Manual on International Courts and Tribunals* (Oxford University Press 2010) vii

Rodley NS, 'On the Responsibility of Special Rapporteurs' (2011) 15 The International Journal of Human Rights 319

Smith KE, 'Speaking with One Voice? European Union Co-ordination on Human Rights Issues at the United Nations' (2006) 44 Journal of Common Market Studies 113

Winkler IT and de Albuquerque C, 'Doing It All and Doing It Well? A Mandate's Challenges in Terms of Cooperation, Fundraising and Maintaining' Independence' in Nolan A, Freedman R, and Murphy T (eds), *The United Nations Special Procedures System* (Brill 2017) 188

11
Differentiating Fundamental Rights and Economic Goals

Aryeh Neier

Some aspects of the way that we conduct our lives in relation to others are so fundamental that we think of them as human rights. That is, they are intrinsic and essential aspects of our existence. Moreover, we recognize that they are not only important to us as individuals but that others in greatly varied circumstances in different parts of the world also cherish them. Concern for them is so widespread that protection for them should be universal. Indeed, since the adoption of the Universal Declaration of Human Rights (UDHR) by the United Nations (UN) in 1948, they have been globally accepted as universal. These are rights that help to define us as human.

A particular concern is protecting human rights against the exercise of government power. We recognize that governments require extensive powers in order to provide for public safety and to promote public welfare. Yet we also insist that effective restraints are needed to prevent governments from crossing the lines that we draw to safeguard human rights. To be effective those restraints must have the force of law.

The broad general areas in which we attempt to protect human rights may be grouped under the broad headings of liberty, dignity, equality, fairness, humanity,[*] and autonomy. In some cases, we have come to believe that absolute rules are required. For example, our commitment to liberty is such that there is no circumstance in which slavery may be tolerated. Similarly, our commitment to dignity forbids any use of torture. In other areas, however, we recognize that there are competing considerations that should be taken into account and that protections may not be absolute. Limits on certain rights may be accepted to the extent that is absolutely necessary to protect the rights of others, to ensure public safety and to provide for military necessity. For example, our concern for autonomy makes us value individual privacy but does not exclude the possibility of searches of our persons and our property that are needed to ensure the safety of others and that are duly

---

[*] Inclusion of the concept of humanity in this list reflects the convergence that has taken place between commitment to the principles of international human rights law and commitment to the principles of international humanitarian law, or the laws of war.

Aryeh Neier, *Differentiating Fundamental Rights and Economic Goals* In: *The Limits of Human Rights*. Edited by: Bardo Fassbender and Knut Traisbach, Oxford University Press 2019. © The Several Contributors.
DOI: 10.1093/oso/9780198824756.003.0013

authorized. Our commitment to humanity makes us prohibit deliberate attacks on civilians in armed conflict, or attacks that are indiscriminate and that do not distinguish between combatants and civilians. On the other hand, they do not rule out attacks on military targets that have the unintended effect of causing civilian casualties that are not out of proportion to their military value. The extent to which rights that are conditional may be limited, and the procedures employed to determine those limits, are ongoing subjects for disagreement and debate among those who are committed to the broad protection of rights.

The fact that human rights may be protected by imposing restraints on the exercise of power helps to ensure that they are universal in application and effect. Variations in protections are not justified by differences in resources. Legal restraints on the government of a poor country are just as capable of enforcing a prohibition on slavery or torture as the legal restraints on the government of a wealthy country. There may be limits on a poor country's ability to promote fairness by providing legal assistance to indigent defendants, or to uphold dignity by providing decent prison conditions. Yet it is not beyond the capacity of even the poorest governments to assure substantial fairness in criminal trials or to assure that prison conditions do not descend to the level of gross violations of human dignity. Every government, everywhere, at all times, can be and should be held accountable for the protection of human rights.

I. ECONOMIC GOALS

It is, of course, also the case that all human beings require certain economic benefits such as food, water, shelter, clothing, education, and health care. So far as these are concerned, however, economic resources inevitably play a part. These benefits, or goals, cannot be secured merely by placing restraints on governments. Rather, they must be obtained in some cases by requiring that governments should make difficult choices in their use of their resources. For example, in a country with extremely limited resources, it may require a substantial struggle to make sure that all children are able to obtain a primary school education. On the other hand, in a wealthy country, the critical question may be whether higher education is universally available. There are likely to be substantial political complexities in making decisions about resources that go far beyond those involved in imposing legal restraints on the exercise of governmental powers. Addressing such questions that involve the allocation of scarce resources is generally at the heart of the political process in any country.

It does not denigrate the significance of these economic benefits, or goals, to suggest that they are in a somewhat different category than those I prefer to think of as human rights. Addressing these economic issues should be a matter of foremost concern in the making of public policy. It is not helpful to their resolution to suggest that they can be addressed effectively by legal prohibitions on the powers of government such as those that are used to uphold our commitments to liberty and dignity.

Advocacy is required to promote both civil and political rights and economic and social goals. For the most part, however, the advocacy that is needed takes place in different venues, by different means, and in accordance with different criteria. In many cases, it is probably desirable that different entities should engage in the advocacy that is required.

Advocacy with respect to civil and political rights generally involves trying to persuade governments to adhere to norms that they purport to accept. Few governments acknowledge that they engage in such practices as torture, or extrajudicial executions, or disappearances, or the intentional or indiscriminate infliction of casualties on civilians in armed conflicts. Accordingly, these issues may be addressed by advocates through such means as the documentation of abuses, the dissemination of the information publicly, public campaigns that attempt to embarrass the officials responsible, and, at times, through litigation. Another means to address these issues is by holding accountable the officials responsible for the most egregious abuses by making them the targets of publicly sponsored investigations such as 'truth' commissions; and, in the most serious cases, such as those that may involve the extensive practice of torture or the commission of war crimes, by criminal prosecutions before domestic or international tribunals.

Advocacy with respect to social and economic goals generally requires persuading governments to engage in redistribution of their resources, such as providing additional funds for such benefits as health care or housing; and by reallocating the burdens of a society, such as taxes. The criteria are different because there are no universally applicable standards by which to measure the practices of governments with respect to these matters. What constitutes decent housing, or an income adequate to meet the necessities of life, for example, varies greatly from country to country, and also within countries. Similarly, the apportionment of taxes fairly will vary greatly depending on the economic circumstances of different societies. Again, most advocacy with respect to economic and social goals must take place through the political process and ordinarily requires that legislative bodies should set priorities, make choices and engage in trade-offs. In a wealthy country such as the United States, the residents of Flint, Michigan should be able to obtain clean, safe drinking water and the residents of Detroit, Michigan ought to be able to obtain jobs, pensions, and decent housing. No one should be denied the opportunity to obtain a university education because they cannot afford the cost. All should be provided with publicly supported health care, including the costs for expensive forms of treatment that may be required to save lives or to maintain a good quality of life. And so on. In practice, however, even in a country as well off as the United States, it is unlikely that all these goals can be achieved simultaneously. The political processes required to achieve all these goals probably require setting limits on other economic benefits that are provided to other segments of society, such as high expenditures to subsidize cultural centres or sports arenas, or to build new highways; or imposing significant increases in taxes on businesses or wealthy individuals; or some combination of the two. In a poor country such as Sierra Leone or Haiti, choices may have to be made between such urgent concerns as providing adequate food, clean water, primary health care, and early childhood education for all. The form of advocacy required to achieve these results consists primarily of political organizing over an extended period, and the venue in which advocacy must be focused in a democracy is the legislature. Redistribution cannot simply be decreed by an executive official or ordered by a court. Where citizens are able to exercise their rights to take part in self-government, the process must take place in a manner that enjoys democratic legitimacy.

Aside from protecting public safety, dealing with the fair distribution of economic benefits and burdens is the foremost responsibility of a democratic political process. Accordingly, those espousing economic and social goals involving more equitable arrangements must develop the political capacity and engage in the political effort needed to do so effectively. As there is often substantial disagreement over what is fair, and over how best to go about promoting fairness, the political processes by which such matters are resolved are likely to be complex and drawn out. Those are among the reasons that I prefer to refer to 'goals' rather than 'rights' when referring to economic redistribution.

II. UPHOLDING THE RIGHTS OF THE UNPOPULAR

Protecting civil and political rights often requires upholding the rights of persons who are highly unpopular such as those accused of violating the criminal law; or adherents of dissident political or religious views; or members of racial, religious, or sexual minorities that suffer from prejudice. To prevail in upholding their rights, it is not necessarily essential to transform public attitudes towards them. Rather, what is needed is to secure public acceptance that certain rights should be respected for all, including those who are looked down upon by others, and even for those who may be most hated or despised. For example, even an accused mass murderer or child molester should be entitled to the right to counsel and the right to a fair trial. The autonomy of a transgender person should be respected even when it involves a sensitive issue such as the choice of a bathroom. Civil and political rights should be vindicated even in circumstances in which public attitudes towards the beneficiaries remain hostile. What is necessary to vindicate civil and political rights is to persuade key officials, such as those exercising executive authority, or judges, that universal norms should be upheld in all cases. They should protect civil and political rights even when taking such action is highly unpopular.

On the other hand, prevailing in efforts to redistribute resources, as by extending such expensive health benefits to all as potentially life-saving advanced medical interventions (organ transplants, kidney dialysis, treatment for rare forms of cancer, etc.) or providing all with sufficient income for a decent life, is only likely to succeed if advocates can win substantial popular support. In a democratic society, those officials who raise taxes or undertake major new spending programmes that eliminate or reduce the benefits that have been available to some in order to provide benefits to others, or that increase taxes for some as a means of redistribution, cannot do so unilaterally. Obtaining support involves not only securing wide agreement that redistribution is desirable, but also negotiating agreement on specific measures. In the absence of such support, public officials probably will not hold on to their offices for long. Redistribution is likely to fail unless it can obtain the backing of a large share of the electorate.

III. CONFLICTS BETWEEN ECONOMIC GOALS

It should also be recognized that measures to promote economic and social goals that involve the equitable distribution of resources may conflict with each other. For example, the world's most populous countries, China and India, have both made immense headway in recent years in lifting many millions of their citizens out of poverty. This has been achieved through rapid industrialization that has been made possible by the availability of relatively inexpensive and plentiful fossil fuels, mainly coal. Yet a consequence of their consumption of vast amounts of coal is very high levels of air pollution that have contributed to great increases in pulmonary diseases, heart diseases, and cancer. New Delhi and Beijing both suffer from extreme air pollution. Without the extensive consumption of coal, many more persons in China and India would remain impoverished. On the other hand, because of large scale consumption of coal, many more persons in China and India suffer from damage to their health that shortens their lives. The policies that are effective in lifting a large number of persons out of poverty may simultaneously have the adverse effect of significantly shortening their life expectancy. It is impossible to resolve such a conflict by generalized assertions that a right to a decent income or a right to health takes precedence. Both of these goals are immensely important. Rather, it is necessary to try to achieve the best possible balance through the political process—again, preferably a democratic political process. Through such a process, it might be decided that the best approach is deferring the improvement of income for large numbers of people until alternative sources of energy are available, such as wind power or solar power. On the other hand, many of those condemned to live in poverty for more extended periods might favour contrary positions. The resolution of such questions ought to be the result of a political process. By their nature, however, civil and political rights tend not to involve such conflicts. The rights to speak or to worship freely, to obtain a fair trial, to not be punished cruelly, and to obtain the equal protection of the laws generally do not conflict with each other. There may be a small number of relatively minor issues on which there appear to be conflicts, but these can be readily resolved in judicial proceedings. The conflicts involving economic and social goals, on the other hand, tend to involve matters that should, and do, loom large in the political process.

Resolving conflicts involving economic and social goals requires striking a balance. Yet it would be disastrous for the protection of civil and political rights such as freedom of speech to strike a balance between an individual's right to express herself peacefully and a government's interest in promoting social harmony. It would severely undercut due process of law if the right to a fair trial were balanced against the state's need to detain indefinitely those it suspects of terrorism without presenting in court the evidence that is needed to secure a criminal conviction. It would negate the right to equal protection of the laws if it were balanced against the interest of the police in controlling crime by stopping and searching members of a racial group suspected of disproportionate involvement in crime. Balancing, which is indispensable where economic and social goals are concerned, is anathema to advocates of civil and political rights.

Another factor that differentiates civil and political rights from economic and social goals is that the former lend themselves to protection on an individual basis. That is, every time one person's right to speak freely or not be to be tortured is vindicated, it is an advance for civil and political rights. In contrast, economic and social goals that involve redistribution generally must be advanced collectively. Providing additional economic benefits to one person or imposing an increased tax burden on a single individual does not promote the equity that is sought by advocates of redistribution. It is only measures that promote collective redistribution that further economic goals. Though litigation may be a means to protect civil and political rights collectively in circumstances in which class actions are possible, or in legal systems where precedents help determine the outcome of future cases, it is more often a means of vindicating rights on a case by case basis. On the other hand, action by a legislative body tends to be more effective in promoting goals that require collective implementation.

To point out that the advocacy of civil and political rights generally takes place in different venues, by different means, and in accordance with different criteria than the advocacy of economic and social goals, is not to suggest a hierarchy. All should be able to speak freely and to be treated equally. They should also be able to obtain health care and decent housing. Freedom of speech and health care are both necessities, but they are different and neither takes precedence over the other. In some circumstances, they may be complementary. For example, when I am sick, I need health care. But I also need to be able to speak and organize to express my need for health care and to try to be sure that I obtain care that is of high quality and suited to my needs on terms that I find satisfactory. Yet if we recognize that the right to speak and the right to obtain health care must usually be pursued in different venues and by different means and in accordance with different criteria, it seems appropriate to question whether they should be pursued simultaneously by the same advocates.

I believe there is a strong case that advocacy of civil and political rights and advocacy of social and economic goals do not go hand in hand. Readiness to champion the rights of all, including the most despised members of society, is crucial in upholding civil and political rights. If the disfavoured can be silenced, everyone's freedom of speech is threatened. If a suspect in a terrorism case is subject to torture, justifications for extending the practice of torture will pass muster. Inevitably, however, many persons will associate those who champion the rights of the despised with those whose rights they uphold. Proponents of civil and political rights have to recognize and accept that they themselves may become highly unpopular. It goes with the territory. This often makes them ill-suited to persuade the general public, or a democratically elected legislative body, to redistribute resources or to shift the tax burden. To succeed as advocates of redistribution, it is not helpful to generate ill will by taking up the causes of those who may be looked down upon by most persons. Yet it would undercut the defence of civil and political rights if advocacy in that arena is guided by the need of the advocates to secure the popular support that is needed to promote economic redistribution effectively.

There are times when civil and political rights can be vindicated through advocacy by those directly affected by denials of rights. For example, if a university attempts to suppress the expression of unpopular political views by a member of its faculty, the protests of other members of the faculty or of students at that university may be effective in protecting freedom of speech. At other times, however, it is only advocacy by persons unconnected to those whose rights are violated and who engage in the protection of rights solely because of their commitment to the principles at stake that is likely to be effective. An example might be advocacy on behalf of an accused criminal who was coerced to confess; or advocacy on behalf of an inmate of a mental hospital who objects to being subjected to electroconvulsive therapy. In contrast, effective advocacy of economic redistribution almost always requires extensive organizing among those who would be directly affected. The likelihood is remote that significant reforms involving the availability of health care, education, housing, increased income levels, or other such benefits will take place solely through benign efforts by those not directly affected. As the beneficiaries of economic redistribution usually must act in their own interests to prevail in such struggles, it is likely that they will face resistance from others who see their interests threatened. By their nature, such struggles are part of the political process. Of course, some of those who get involved may take positions that are motivated primarily by principles rather than self-interest. Indeed, in some cases, the participants may include those who take stands that seem to run counter to their own interests. When they do so, it is likely to be in the context of a political process in which many of the other participants are intent on advancing their own interests. The democratic process, by its nature, tends to involve advocacy in which both principles and self-interest play a role. On the other hand, the processes in which civil and political rights are protected generally require that self-interest should be put aside in order to make sure that principles are upheld.

One factor that may make some proponents of redistribution of economic resources and burdens to promote fairness eager to engage in advocacy in the same venues where civil and political rights are protected, and in accordance with comparable criteria, is that this seems easier than relying on the political process. The political organizing required to succeed in the political process is difficult; it must take place over an extended period; and there is no guarantee of success. Those with opposing interests may be well established and often are in a position to outspend those seeking more equitable distribution. Prevailing by such means as judicial decision-making, as may be possible in matters involving civil and political and rights, may appear to be far less onerous. Yet such efforts to evade, or circumvent, the political process are unlikely to succeed. For the most part, courts are acutely sensitive to the limits on their powers. Judges are aware that they rely on the other branches of government to enforce their decisions. Accordingly, they must be concerned about the democratic legitimacy of their actions. They may be able to deal with economic redistribution when matters come before them in which invidious discrimination on the basis of such criteria as race or ethnicity are involved, such as refusal to pave the streets or provide for sewage disposal only in urban neighbourhoods populated by racial minorities. Overturning such invidious practices may meet the criterion of legitimacy. Even in such circumstances, however, courts have done poorly in providing redistribution. In the United States, for example, it is usually necessary for the victims of racial discrimination to prove an intent to discriminate; a mere showing of discriminatory effect, or disparate impact, is generally insufficient to secure a judicial remedy. Even when courts are willing to address redistribution to promote fairness, it is usually necessary to rely on the political process to secure compliance with judicial decisions on such matters. This is likely to involve the same difficulties as would be encountered if it were recognized at the outset that economic redistribution must take place through the political process. A favourable court decision may or may not be helpful. Sometimes it arouses a backlash focusing on what is seen as judicial usurpation of power.

Vindicating civil and political rights is an ongoing struggle because new rationales and new pressures for officials to place limits on those rights arise all the time. Also, public officials may engage in demagoguery on such matters for their own political purposes or may genuinely believe that civil and political rights should be restricted. Similarly, the attempt to promote the more equitable distribution of economic resources and burdens is also an ongoing struggle, but for different reasons. In the latter case, the reasons often involve efforts by some segments of society to seek advantages for themselves that have the effect of disadvantaging others. When new issues arise involving civil and political rights, it is generally possible for advocates to try to resolve them by measuring them in accordance with established principles. Prevailing in such matters may be difficult, but it is usually not because it is difficult to discern how those principles should be applied. On the other hand, when it comes to dealing with new developments involving economic issues, such as proposals to alter the tax structure, there may be disagreements in good faith between those who voice opposing views about their impact on fairness.

Finally, it is important to recognize that opponents of economic redistribution to promote fairness often argue that a consequence of such redistribution is that it reduces incentives for economic gain that ultimately provide economic benefits for all. It is possible to dismiss some such arguments as bad faith attempts to provide a rationale for gross inequities. Yet not all such arguments can be or should be readily dismissed. It is evident that private gain is a powerful incentive for a great deal of economic activity that has beneficial consequences for many persons. The troublesome question is where to draw the line. How should a society promote the entrepreneurial spirit needed to make economic advances and, simultaneously, promote economic fairness? What is apparent is that the line cannot be fixed for all time. It must be adjusted in accordance with changing economic circumstances. The only way to draw the line and to keep redrawing it is through the political process. Here again, it is the political process that is the appropriate venue for dealing with economic and social goals while it is such means as 'naming and shaming' by documenting abuses and, in some cases, the judicial process, that are appropriate means for protecting civil and political rights.

12
Advocating for Social and Economic Rights—Critical Perspectives
A Response to Aryeh Neier

*Jeremy Perelman**

Are social and economic rights (SER) 'real' rights, or do they belong to different categories of interests, benefits, or policy goals which individuals and polities can aspire to? Should they be enshrined in higher level domestic or transnational constitutional orders and, if so, with the same normative value as civil and political rights (CPR)? Do courts have the democratic legitimacy and competence to adjudicate them and to require from governments that they allocate scarce resources for their realization? Should human rights and social justice advocates focus their resources, skills, and energies on advocating for the realization and enforcement of these rights and their respective normative and political goals? In his carefully worded essay, Aryeh Neier addresses these long-debated questions in ways that many human rights advocates and scholars alike have read as provocative or even '*passé*'.[1] SER, it is argued, have been enshrined in the Universal Declaration on Human Rights (UDHR) and the International Covenant on Economic, Social and Cultural Rights (ICESCR) as well as in regional and domestic instruments. They have been re-declared as interdependent and as indivisible from CPR since the post-Cold War Vienna Declaration and Programme of Action in 1993. An increasing number of jurisdictions have since then given them constitutional or equivalent legal status, supported by sophisticated constitutional theories. Treaty monitoring bodies and regional and domestic courts have recognized them as

---

* The author is most thankful to Aryeh Neier whose commitment to his vision of human rights he respectfully admires. He is also very grateful to the editors for their immense work and patience in bringing such a wide-ranging group of scholars within one single volume.

[1] See, e.g., Margot E Salomon, 'Human Rights Are Also About Social Justice' (Open Democracy, 25 July 2013) <https://www.opendemocracy.net/en/openglobalrights-openpage/human-rights-are-also-about-social-justice/> accessed 31 January 2019; Alicia Eli Yamin and Ignacio Saiz, 'Human Rights and Social Justice: The In(di)visible Link' (Open Democracy, 30 July 2013) <https://www.opendemocracy.net/en/openglobalrights-openpage/human-rights-and-social-justice-indivisible-link/> accessed 31 January 2019 (hereafter Yamin and Saiz, 'Human Rights and Social Justice'); César Rodríguez-Garavito, 'Against Reductionist Views of Human Rights' (Open Democracy, 30 July 2013) <https://www.opendemocracy.net/en/openglobalrights-openpage/against-reductionist-views-of-human-rights/> accessed 31 January 2019.

Jeremy Perelman, *Advocating for Social and Economic Rights—Critical Perspectives: A Response to Aryeh Neier* In: *The Limits of Human Rights*. Edited by: Bardo Fassbender and Knut Traisbach, Oxford University Press 2019. © The Several Contributors.
DOI: 10.1093/oso/9780198824756.003.0014

justiciable and offered increasingly fine-grained interpretations of the obligations and duties that can be derived from their legal articulations. Important and celebrated judicial decisions have led to real-world change in the realms of education, food, health care, and housing in both developing and developed countries. Finally, non-governmental organizations (NGOs) and social movements around the world have drawn on the SER rhetoric in their advocacy strategies to build power and leverage change for social justice.

There persist, however, in Neier's words, crucial questions addressed to those very same advocates and scholars who are critical of his argument that remain only partially answered. In the following comment, I will begin by situating Neier's argument within a set of critiques addressed to SER and their implementation (section I). I will then point to key responses which have been developed to rebuke some of these critiques (section II). I will finally revisit the critique of SER from the perspective of the history and fundamental structure of the human rights framework and point to approaches aimed at taking this critique seriously (section III).

I. Conceptual and Pragmatic Considerations: SER as Rights and as Political Strategies

A. SER as Rights

At the core of Neier's argument is a *conceptual*, liberal critique of SER. While Neier is careful to point out throughout his essay that he personally favours redistributive policies, such an aspiration belongs to the realm of policy goals, rather than rights. For Neier, rights are to be understood in classical liberal fashion, in which they delimit justifications for restraining individual liberty and constitute the normative foundation for individual claims in relation to a duty-bearer. In the case of human rights, the duty-bearer is the state and its obligations are derived from fundamental principles of human dignity and liberty.[2] Neier draws here on both positivist and neo-Kantian liberal rights-based arguments to suggest that these principles have been granted universal legal recognition and constitute inherent, non-disputable principles of a democratic polity which may not be contingent on cultural or material constraints.

Neier conceives liberty in primarily negative terms.[3] Rights protect the individual's private sphere against the interference of public power, including

---

[2] Neier uses mostly these terms throughout his text, but points to the principles of 'liberty, dignity, equality, fairness, humanity, and autonomy', see Aryeh Neier, 'Differentiating Fundamental Rights and Economic Goals' in Bardo Fassbender and Knut Traisbach (eds), *The Limits of Human Rights* (Oxford University Press 2019) 175 (hereafter Neier, 'Differentiating').

[3] See Isaiah Berlin, 'Two Concepts of Liberty' in Isaiah Berlin (ed.), *Four Essays on Liberty* (Oxford University Press 1969) 118; Frederick Schauer, 'A Comment on the Structure of Rights' (1992–93) 27 Georgia Law Review 415.

democratically legitimated public power. While valuable from an ideological or policy perspective, SER are of a different *nature* than CPR and imply different sets of duties on the state. While Neier also recognizes positive features of state duties attached to CPR, these rights constitute a distinct category grounded on fundamental principles which principally imply negative duties of non-interference by the state in individual autonomous spheres. SER, at their core, 'cannot be secured merely by placing restraints on governments' because they 'inevitably' involve economic resources and they impose primarily positive duties on the state. For Neier, therefore, only CPR ought to be understood as human rights, ideally enshrined in constitutions and protected by an independent judiciary as individual trumps against majoritarian will and against discriminatory, authoritarian, or collectivist approaches embedded in state power.

Neier's contention reflects different sets of arguments which often overlap but ought to be distinguished. A first set of critiques relates to the *vagueness* of SER and raises questions about their nature as legal or even moral rights and their enforceability. SER are said to lack the 'clarity of definition' and prioritization of duties required for their qualification as legal rights and their enforcement as individual claims. Unlike well-defined CPR, which involve clear and immediate duties of non-interference regardless of a state's resources, SER are subject to a broad, vaguely defined, and necessarily contingent obligation of progressive realization commensurate with the state's available resources. Furthermore, Neier points out repeatedly that SER, because they promote economic equity, correspond to claims usually representative of collective and therefore harder to delimit interests.

Related to debates about their nature as rights, a long-standing set of arguments focuses on whether SER ought to be *constitutionalized* and granted supralegislative value and, if so, which normative value they should have vis-à-vis CPR. While Neier engages only indirectly with this debate, it has and continues to animate constitutional scholars and political thinkers.[4] A central line of argumentation suggests that to be granted constitutional protection, rights must be enforceable in courts and submitted to a relatively high level of scrutiny within a process of judicial review. Related to the question of enforceability on the basis of their lack of clarity is thus the question of SER's justiciability, which Neier addresses on the basis of two sets of arguments.

The first is based on *separation of power* or countermajoritarian principles of liberal democratic and constitutional theory. Courts, it is argued, lack the democratic

---

[4] See, e.g., Mark Tushnet, *Weak Courts, Strong Rights: Judicial Review and Social Welfare Rights in Comparative Constitutional Law* (Princeton University Press 2008); William E Forbath, 'Constitutional Welfare Rights: A History, Critique and Reconstruction' (2001) 69 Fordham Law Review 1821; Frank I Michelman, 'Constitutionally Binding Social and Economic Rights as a Compelling Idea: Reciprocating Perturbations in Liberal and Democratic Constitutional Visions' in Helena Alviar García, Karl Klare, and Lucy A Williams (eds), *Social and Economic Rights in Theory and Practice: Critical Inquiries* (Routledge 2015) 277 (hereafter Alviar García, Klare, and Williams (eds), *Social and Economic Rights*).

legitimacy to conduct this high-level judicial review of state policies and adjudicate SER, which involves trade-offs in the allocation and prioritizing of necessarily limited public resources. 'Only the elected representatives of the people,' Cass Sunstein once famously argued,[5] 'should be allowed to make these difficult choices.' Confining such choices to the judicial sphere would exclude policy-making from public debate, as courts would engage in the necessarily political process of allocating resources in order to uphold and balance rights. While recognizing limitations to the absolute nature of state duties under CPR and the existence of conflicting considerations such as public order, Neier suggests that conflicts in the CPR sphere tend to relate to minor issues which can be resolved by courts. While it is 'anathema' for CPR defenders, for Neier, the process of balancing would be at the heart of SER adjudication and imply stark choices on issues that 'loom large in the political process'.[6] Going further, this line of critique often adopts a more explicitly ideological argument, suggesting that because implementing SER necessarily involves resource allocation and therefore positive, redistributive state intervention in economic policy-making, adjudicating SER would translate to compelling governments to interfere in free markets. While not explicitly endorsing this line of reasoning, Neier points in the final paragraph of his essay to the value of welfarist arguments against redistributive policies and suggests that 'drawing the line' between economic efficiency and fairness is inherent to the *political* process, rather than the realm of judicial review.

The second line of arguments related to the justiciabilty of SER relates to the *competence* of the judiciary to exercise judicial review on SER. Even if SER were to be accepted as rights and constitutionalized, and one recognized courts' democratic legitimacy to adjudicate them, judges themselves may be reluctant to do so on the basis of the technical difficulty of identifying and imposing positive duties on the state within the confines of the judicial process. As suggested by Neier, courts may not have the capacity and bureaucratic skills or tools to determine state duties or to articulate remedies in cases relating to complex social policy-making processes. This technical lack of capacity, it is argued, may further undermine the judiciary's legitimacy.

B. SER as Political Strategies

A widely respected and celebrated lawyer who played a central role in the development of the human rights movement both in the United States and internationally, Neier complements his conceptual misgivings about SER with strategic

---

[5] Cass Sunstein, 'Against Positive Rights: Why Social and Economic Rights *Don't* Belong in the New Constitutions of Post-Communist Europe' (1993) 2 East European Constitutional Review 35.
[6] Neier, 'Differentiating' (n. 2) 179.

considerations about advocacy. Throughout his argumentation Neier insists on the value of social and economic benefits and goals, pointing out that his argument does not imply a hierarchy between those benefits and the set of principles he qualifies as rights. His argument is that because there is a difference in nature between two sets of interests—one based on fundamental, universally accepted principles that belong to the category of human rights and another set of interests which do not belong to this category—*advocacy* for CPR ought to take place in 'different venues, by different means, and in accordance with different criteria' than the advocacy for economic and social goals.[7] Advocacy on behalf of those valuable goals ought to be undertaken by different actors than human rights defenders. Saying so, Neier argues, is not to denigrate those goals and their advocates. While highlighting his own ideological preference for redistributive and social policies, Neier suggests that achieving such goals cannot rely on tactics and methods used by CPR advocates, meant and designed to place constraints on governments. Human rights advocates should thus *only* be in the business of advocating for the implementation of CPR, draw on their well-honed methods of rigorously documenting human rights violations and adopting naming and shaming strategies to engage policy-makers, and, when needed or possible, use litigation.

The latter is, in particular for Neier, not well adapted to SER advocacy, both conceptually and practically. Because advocating for SER involves economic redistribution, it aims at shifting resource allocation in favour of collective, rather than individual, interests. Targeting policy-makers and legislative bodies, rather than courts, is therefore more effective. Courts may not be willing, due to judicial deference, or able to achieve social justice goals, if unaccompanied by or entirely circumventing engagement with the political process.[8] One may add that relying on courts as 'activists' may even backfire strategically. And Neier suggests that advocates ought to engage in 'political organizing over an extended period' and coalition-building in order to win popular support for redistribution. This stands in contrast with the protection of CPR, which often imply vindication of fundamental principles against hostile democratic majorities. Neier is particularly insistent on this point. It relates for him to the difference in the nature of claims attached to CPR and SER and the pragmatic effectiveness of advocacy strategies to achieve their respective political goals.

---

[7] Ibid, 177 and 180.

[8] Ibid, 182; although not explicitly endorsed by Neier, the argument relates here to long-standing critiques of the empirical impact of court decisions on social change; see, e.g., Gerry Rosenberg, *The Hollow Hope: Can Courts Bring About Social Change?* (2nd edn, The University of Chicago Press 2008). On the limits of court-centred SER advocacy and the salience of 'political' lawyering, see William E Forbath, Zackie Achmat, Geoff Budlender, and Mark Heywood, 'Cultural Transformation, Deep Institutional Reform, and ESR Practice: South Africa's Treatment Action Campaign' in Lucie E White and Jeremy Perelman (eds), *Stones of Hope: How African Activists Reclaim Human Rights to Challenge Global Poverty* (Stanford University Press 2011) 51 (hereafter White and Perelman (eds), *Stones of Hope*); see also Malcom Langford, César Rodríguez-Garavito, and Julieta Rossi (eds), *Social Rights Judgments and the Politics of Compliance: Making it Stick* (Cambridge University Press 2017).

A division of labour between advocates of CPR and SER, Neier suggests, is thus necessary because upholding CPR often means upholding principles against democratic will and because those who do so, as Neier well knows,[9] are likely to be unpopular. As such, they often need to be 'unconnected' to rights holders and are therefore not ideally placed to engage in the organizing of social movements and political coalition-building for economic redistribution that SER advocacy requires. Such organizing, Neier suggests, is challenging as it is at the core of the necessarily complex political process.

II. SER AS RIGHTS AND POLITICAL STRATEGIES: RESPONSES FROM THE FIELDS

These arguments, whether at the conceptual or strategic levels, have generated a wide range of counter-arguments. They range from moral and political philosophy to constitutional theory and from doctrinal to empirical as well as strategic, advocacy-focused considerations. Some of these responses even have been directly addressed to Neier.

A. The Positivist Answer: SER as International Law

One set of responses draws on straightforward positivist arguments, used at times as a preamble to more theoretical or ideological responses. They suggest that SER are an indivisible part of the corpus of international human rights law. While not universally adopted, the ICESCR has 169 state parties and is part of the international bill of human rights, along with the International Covenant on Civil and Political Rights (ICCPR) and the UDHR, the latter of which includes a range of SER (Articles 22, 25, 26, notably) and has for some scholars acquired customary international law status.[10] Governments have thus internationally agreed to binding SER obligations which include the development of policies and implementation of SER and which cannot be derogated because of changing economic conditions. SER are not gifts, luxuries, or aspirations but rights in their own terms which are justiciable and demand remedies when violated. Human rights advocates ought to not be deterred by considerations such as Neier's about the nature of rights and consider that it is mostly a matter of time until SER instruments are

---

[9] Aryeh Neier, *Defending My Enemy: American Nazis, the Skokie Case, and the Risks of Freedom* (2nd edn, International Debate Education Association 2012).

[10] See, e.g., Margot E Salomon, *Global Responsibility for Human Rights: World Poverty and The Development of International Law* (Oxford University Press 2007).

enforced just like internationally protected CPR. Those rights, it is argued, were not 'clearly defined' in 1948 either. Normative clarification and legal interpretation by treaty-monitoring bodies and regional institutions will eventually clarify and widen the recognition of SER as justiciable rights and enable their enforcement. To back this set of arguments, advocates point to the inclusion of SER in an increasing number of constitutions, particularly in the global South. They celebrate developments including but not limited to judicial 'victories' in jurisdictions such as South Africa, India, or more recently Latin America.

B. Theoretical Rejoinders

With regard to Neier's contention about the nature of rights, a series of arguments have been articulated about the nature of SER as either moral or legal rights. A key contribution is Martha C Nussbaum's and Amartya Sen's capabilities approach, which continues to play an important role in the context of debates around SER both in terms of theories of justice and in relationship to the process of development.[11] In the field of development, Sen has made a key contribution against the long-standing view that suggests necessary trade-offs between development conceived as economic growth and human rights. He was a vocal critic of welfarist approaches to development that focused on and prioritized economic growth and a free market-based allocation of resources. He also took issue with cultural relativist arguments against the universality of CPR and empirical claims about their impediment to growth. Following these critiques, Sen conceptualizes CPR and SER as indivisible and interdependent ends and means of development. In what can be used here as a rebuke to Neier's last paragraph, in which he seems to adopt a consequentialist perspective to question the effects of redistributive policy on aggregate welfare, Sen makes a strong case for SER based on both deontological and instrumental terms.[12] He characterizes SER however as 'meta-rights' which should not be limited conceptually to legal understandings and strategies, concurring here partly with Neier.[13] Sen also makes a strong case for the conceptual and instrumental *interdependence* between both sets of rights. Drawing on a positive conception of liberty and partly echoing here Karl Marx's critique of liberal understandings of rights related to a public/private distinction, he points to the argument that one 'cannot eat' civil, political, and liberal market rights. There is, therefore,

---

[11] Amartya Sen, *Development as Freedom* (Oxford University Press 1999).
[12] For an extensive discussion see Jeremy Perelman, *The Rights-ification of Development: Global Poverty, Human Rights and Globalization in the Post-Washington Consensus* (Cambridge University Press forthcoming) (hereafter Perelman, *The Rights-ification of Development*).
[13] Amartya Sen, 'Elements of a Theory of Human Rights' (2004) 32 Philosophy & Public Affairs 315 where he highlights the political salience of SER as abstract 'meta rights' to a set of policies and warns against fitting them into the 'juridical cage' of legal rights; he suggests instead focusing on agitation, monitoring, and other strategies to foster political support.

a need to uphold SER-grounded investments in social policy, including through policies that involve regulation and taxation encroachments on private property rights.

Beyond Sen, this argument can be found in numerous responses to Neier's contention that human rights ought to remain exclusively about protecting an individuals' private sphere by upholding negative duties as constraints on government. Some of these responses draw on visions of a liberal democratic welfare state in which CPR function as normative trumps on the will of elected majorities. SER, on the other hand, function as equally necessary normative breaks addressing another source of power that can't be left aside of the liberal rights paradigm: that of free markets and private actors. In some versions, this implies minimal safety nets for the most disadvantaged individuals within society. In others, it points to more substantive forms of redistributive policies and extended regulatory frameworks.

With regard to debates about the constitutionalization of SER and separation of power arguments, a range of liberal constitutional scholars have suggested that enforceability is not and should not be a condition for granting constitutional, supra-legislative value to these rights. Furthermore, many have argued that the 'vagueness' of SER, rather than being a limitation, offers democratic grounding for policy-making. Granting SER constitutional value, it is suggested, can establish a constitutional-interpretive framework for broader democratic debates and political public reasoning in decision-making. Courts adjudicating SER thus become spaces in which cultures of justification are created[14] and open, Habermasian dialogic forms of democratic politics can take place in the public eye.[15] Going further and writing from a more critical perspective, scholars such as Karl Klare have argued against lingering separation of power arguments and claim that these arguments are embedded in a restrictive understanding of distribution and democracy.[16] More 'advanced' democratic theories suggest institutional roles for courts in robustly enforcing SER and mandating governments to implement social policies, including in contexts in which such enforcement may involve ruling against 'hostile' coalitions or majorities, thereby countering Neier's contention.[17] Indeed one may argue that Neier's contention that the appropriate focus and locus for advocating and implementing SER is the legislature (i.e. an implementation through the 'political process' and by winning popular support in a democratic

---

[14] See Etienne Mureinik, 'A Bridge to Where? Introducing the Interim Bill of Rights' (1994) 10 South African Journal of Human Rights 31, 32.

[15] See, e.g., Katharine Young, *Constituting Economic and Social Rights* (Oxford University Press 2012).

[16] For a critical perspective on the argument, articulated by Neier, that distribution only occurs through public regulation (such as taxation to finance a SER-mandated social policy) and pointing to the distributive features of allegedly 'neutral' private law regimes and their adjudication, see Duncan Kennedy, 'The Stakes of Law, or Hale and Foucault!' (1991) 15 Legal Studies Forum 327.

[17] Karl Klare, 'Critical Perspectives on Social and Economic Rights, Democracy and Separation of Powers' in Alviar García, Klare, and Williams (eds), *Social and Economic Rights* (n. 4) 3 (hereafter Klare, 'Critical Perspectives'), citing 'deliberative', 'empowered', 'experimentalist', 'participatory', 'postliberal', 'radical', 'substantive', or 'thick' understandings of democracy.

system) assumes a functioning representative system. It also presupposes a political economy in which the poor (and sometimes the democratic majority *tout court*) are not impeded to effectively further their interests through the political process. Contemporary examples of economic elites co-opting the political system in both developing and developed democratic countries present significant challenges to the empirical reality of this vision.[18]

C. Doctrinal Rejoinders: The Structure of Rights and the Respect, Protect, and Fulfil Trilogy

A central argument often used in contemporary human rights commentary to refute arguments such as Neier's about the fundamental conceptual and ideological distinction between CPR and SER characterizes both sets of rights as generating a *common* set of obligations and duties on states—also known as the 'respect, protect, and fulfil' trilogy.[19] As a significant doctrinal development, it reflects an effort from within the human rights movement to articulate a 'comprehensive' framework that can overcome entrenched arguments about the CPR/SER divide. It seeks to answer the 'vagueness', justiciability, and enforceability critiques against SER and has emerged as the dominant contemporary articulation of international human rights law. It operates as an analytical device aimed at clarifying and streamlining the normative content of the human rights law corpus as a whole. At the same time, it seeks to 'concretize' and 'operationalize' human rights norms, in particular SER.

A now well-established doctrinal construct, the trilogy gained political traction following the post-Cold War re-unification of the 'indivisible' human rights legal framework.[20] Its theoretical underpinnings can be related to Henry Shue's influential *Basic Rights*,[21] which develops a primarily analytical argument that counters systematic distinctions between security/liberty/negative (civil and political) and subsistence/welfare/positive (economic, social, and cultural) rights and duties. Shue's vision, however, also implies a strong version of the idea that expansive entitlements to material goods are a necessary foundation for any engagement in liberal democracy and potentially a foundation for global redistributive justice.[22]

---

[18] For a proposal to overcome such a political economy in the US context, see Joseph Fishkin and William E Forbath, 'The Anti-Oligarchy Constitution' (2014) 94 Boston University Law Review 671.
[19] See, e.g., Olivier de Schutter, *International Human Rights Law: Cases, Materials, Commentary* (2nd edn, Cambridge University Press 2014) 18–19 and 280–91.
[20] Committee on Economic, Social and Cultural Rights (ICESCR) General Comment No. 12, 'The Right to Adequate Food (art 11)' E/C.12/1999/5, para. 15.
[21] Henry Shue, *Basic Rights: Subsistence, Affluence, and U.S. Foreign Policy* (2nd edn, Princeton University Press 1996).
[22] Thomas Pogge, 'Shue on Rights and Duties' in Charles R Beitz and Robert E Goodin (eds), *Global Basic Rights* (Oxford University Press 2009) 113.

The obligation to 'respect' entails the classic liberal negative obligation for states not to interfere in the sphere of private life and market relations. Respecting SER thus implies that states should *refrain from* taking any measure that would prevent access to a social good, which is essentially conceived as being produced, accessible, and distributed through market mechanisms at the national level. The obligation to 'protect' SER involves an active obligation to prevent violations by third parties through regulation or legislation in form of preventive measures and deterring sanctions, but also the provision of remedies to victims of infringements by private parties. The obligation to 'fulfil', defined under now common doctrinal interpretation by the Committee on Economic, Social and Cultural Rights as the obligation to 'facilitate, promote, and provide', entails that states have an obligation to move towards the full realization of SER by adopting legislative, administrative, budgetary, judicial, and other measures. The obligation to provide has largely been framed, almost classically by now, as applying to *both* SER and CPR and as potentially requiring in both cases the allocation of state resources. A right to a fair trial, for instance, may involve significant budgetary expenditure, such as the funding of a legal aid system guaranteeing fair access to trial to those who are not able to afford a lawyer.[23] Neier gives a nod to this argument,[24] but points to the difference in the scale of expenditures implied by obligations to fulfil CPR, especially in their remedial judicial interpretation, vis-à-vis expenditures related to 'large-looming' SER.

As a rejoinder to Neier's contention that the obligation to 'respect' constitutes the exclusive core of human rights obligations and that SER necessarily involve positive duties and resource allocations linked to the obligations to 'fulfil' and 'provide', human rights advocates don't always highlight the argument that the fulfilment of CPR may also involve budgetary resources. Often they prefer to show how existing case law on SER involves primarily a violation of the obligation to 'respect', for instance in cases of forced evictions in the context of the right to housing. They also stress that human rights are key in light of increasingly private sources of power which can be restrained by emphasizing states' obligations to 'protect' against the interference of private actors. And they highlight doctrinal arguments related to the trilogy suggesting that it incorporates a transversal/horizontal and immediate requirement on state behaviour, namely the obligation of non-discrimination. Advocates thus often highlight the 'protective' features of the SER framework, rather than its redistributive features, which they often present as the socio-democratic 'last resort' palliative for market failures. However, the same advocates also insist, often at the same time, that SER are and should be about social justice and that this entails substantive fiscal redistribution based on extended interpretations of the obligations to 'fulfil' and 'provide'.

---

[23] *Airey v. Ireland*, App. No. 6289/73, 9 October 1979.
[24] Neier, 'Differentiating' (n. 2) 176.

Finally, in order to counter arguments that criticize the vagueness and enforceability of SER and stress instead the universality and immediacy of minimum CPR standards, many draw on two doctrinal interpretations. The first is the doctrine of a 'minimum core' that also exists in all SER as an immediate requirement and for which thus the progressive realization framework does not apply.[25] The second is the obligation of non-retrogression attached to the obligation to 'fulfil' derived from the ICESCR.[26] Both interpretations have served as a basis for the articulation of various versions of human rights-based approaches to development or for the 2012 Guiding Principles on Extreme Poverty and Human Rights, which aim to constrain and guide trade-offs in social policy-making.

III. REVISITING AND TRANSCENDING CRITIQUE: THE LIMITS OF THE HUMAN RIGHTS FRAMEWORK AND BEYOND

Whether at the theoretical or doctrinal level, these responses to Neier's longstanding argument seem to be widely shared within the human rights field. They remain, however, vulnerable to a set of critiques about the underlying features of the human rights framework which come from different traditions than Neier's.

Critical and post-realist legal scholars have long questioned human rights as a viable framework for social justice.[27] They point to its liberal,[28] individualistic, and formalist features which focus on negative obligations of the nation state, rather than imposing strong positive redistributive duties. These scholars highlight how the human rights framework entrenches the public–private divide by configuring power relations as a limited dichotomy between suffering subjects on the one hand and the state on the other. This neglects horizontal private relations as well as the broader social, legal, and institutional contexts in which other state–individual relations take place. Although it is strongly opposed to Neier's questioning of redistributive policies on the basis of 'efficiency', the critique of human rights as a formalist framework partly links with Neier's contention that the claiming and

---

[25] For a critical analysis, see Katharine Young, 'The Minimum Core of Economic and Social Rights: A Concept in Search of Content' (2008) 33 Yale Journal of International Law 113.

[26] Committee on Economic, Social and Cultural Rights (ICESCR) General Comment No. 3, 'The Nature of States parties obligations (art 2(1))' E/1991/23, para. 9.

[27] See notably Duncan Kennedy, 'The Critique of Rights in Critical Legal Studies' in Wendy Brown and Janet Halley (eds), *Left Legalism, Left Critique* (Duke University Press 2002) 178; Klare, 'Critical Perspectives' (n. 16); for an excellent recent typology of critical perspectives on human rights, see Karen Engle, 'Human Rights Consciousness and Critique' in Didier Fassin and Bernard E Harcourt (eds), *A Time for Critique* (Columbia University Press 2019) 91.

[28] On the liberal origins of SER articulated in the 1790s' revolutionary France, which dismisses the classic genealogy of SER as 'second generation' rights linked to socialist ideas, see Charles Walton, 'The French Revolution: A Redistributive Crisis' in Virginie Martin and Guillaume Mazeau (eds), *L'Histoire en Liberté: Mélanges pour Jean-Clément Martin* (Publications de la Sorbonne forthcoming).

especially the judicial adjudication of SER may not sufficiently address key policy choices of, for instance, developing countries that face trade-offs between alleviating poverty and fighting climate change. Indeed, the critique suggests that the human rights framework on its own cannot provide a blueprint for deciding between conflicting considerations. This is so because the framework itself reflects conflicting interests and entails political struggles. There are intrinsic tensions *between* rights which may be claimed in radically conflicting ways according to different interests. Finally, and again partly overlapping analytically with Neier's suggestions although coming from a different ideological perspective, this strand of critique also points to the demobilizing features of human rights advocacy.[29] This argument suggests that the strong focus in advocacy on formalistic legal technicalities draws energy away from the necessary political process involved in social change and blinds to other avenues for transformative change such as engaging in political mobilization and social movements linked to distributive economic analysis.

Partly inspired by critical legal scholars, Third World Approaches to International Law (TWAIL) scholars have turned to history and post-colonial analyses to critique human rights as an imperialistic project that promotes allegedly universal but ultimately Western capitalist interests and values. Human rights are seen as crowding out other past or contemporary normative frameworks and ideas, including alternative articulations of rights about livelihood, social change, and emancipation from empire and capital. It is argued that the emancipation that animated anti-colonial movements arguably went beyond aspirations to national self-rule and individual rights within the confines of the liberal welfare state. And that it continues today to frame social movements in the Global South around open-ended, solidaristic approaches of resistance to neo-liberal violence.[30]

In his historical analysis of the crystallization of human rights as international law, Samuel Moyn also draws attention to 'progressive', although much less open-ended moments of history in which human rights might have related to their original emancipatory promise. He points in particular to a politically fluid pre-1948 moment,[31] marked notably in the United States by Franklin D Roosevelt's vision emphasizing a 'freedom from want'. This was a New Deal-inspired version of SER rhetoric which was related to the 'freedom from fear' and embedded in a liberal, socio-democratic welfare state. Moyn argues that this moment ended up vanishing through Cold War tensions and that the evolution of the modern human rights movement in the 1970s gave rise to a 'minimalist' utopia, rather than proclaiming revolutionary change. In his latest work,[32] Moyn keeps examining the roads not

---

[29] David Kennedy, *The Dark Sides Of Virtue: Reassessing International Humanitarianism* (Princeton University Press 2004).
[30] See Makau Mutua, *Human Rights: A Political and Cultural Critique* (University of Pennsylvania Press 2008).
[31] Samuel Moyn, *The Last Utopia: Human Rights in History* (Harvard University Press 2010).
[32] Samuel Moyn, *Not Enough: Human Rights in an Unequal World* (Belknap Press 2018).

taken by the human rights movement, in particular with regard to substantive understandings of equality. While highlighting that the modern human rights movement isn't intrinsically ideologically correlated to neo-liberalism or responsible for its rise,[33] Moyn argues that the movement has failed to do 'enough' to address its social and economic consequences. First of all, it adhered to calls such as Neier's and largely dismissed SER until very recently. And when it finally started to take SER more seriously, the movement focused on 'horizontal' economic inequalities through a non-discrimination lens. It drew on a 'sufficiency' framework aimed at ensuring minimum thresholds for SER realization in terms of safety nets. Thereby, one may add, it adhered to the liberal 'protective' and 'last resort' foundations of the respect–protect–fulfil trilogy. In doing so, it left out rising 'vertical' inequalities of wealth and income and ignored a more substantive 'equality' framework based on SER as a strong normative call for domestic and global redistributive justice. Thus, for Moyn, both the crystallization of human rights into legal institutions and the use of SER by advocates have served to reinforce a neo-liberal global political economy.

Moyn's arguments are contentious. They have generated an important backlash from human rights actors and scholars, in part because he ignores the wide range of human rights practices that constitute the human rights movement beyond large Western human rights NGOs. He also downplays the currency and reality of life-saving human rights practices on the ground, where local human rights actors are often the first responders to the violence of neo-liberal globalization. His work, however, seems to have hit a nerve, similarly to David Kennedy's *The Dark Side of Virtue* a decade ago. While important responses still need to be articulated, the critique cannot be entirely dismissed. The human rights movement *is* often limited in its capacity or willingness to confront the neo-liberal political economy head on, for instance, by challenging the underlying background rules—of trade, intellectual property, investment, and development—that govern globalized modes of economic production. Indeed, a close analysis of various efforts by human rights advocates to 'stretch' doctrinal and political understandings of SER to develop and operationalize human rights-based approaches to development and poverty alleviation are revealing. Another example are recent efforts to adapt the human rights framework to risk-management approaches such as the UN Guiding Principles on Business and Human Rights in order to 'civilize' globalization. These initiatives all point to the limited ability to challenge the structural features of neo-liberal globalization *as* development and to move beyond minimum standards, safety nets,

---

[33] See also Peter Rosenblum, 'When Splitters become Lumpers: Pitfalls of a Long History of Human Rights' (Law and Political Economy, 10 August 2018) <https://lpeblog.org/2018/08/10/when-splitters-become-lumpers-pitfalls-of-a-long-history-of-human-rights/> accessed 31 January 2019 (hereafter Rosenblum, 'When Splitters become Lumpers').

and process-oriented compensatory frameworks to address widespread SER violations.[34]

Lastly, another important strand of critique relates to empirical analyses of SER advocacy and adjudication.[35] Close analyses of the political economy of Latin American social rights constitutionalism and the emergence of what many like to call the judicialization of politics and public life have shown that court-led compromises can tamper an otherwise accepted version of neo-liberal extractive capitalism.[36] But they have also shown how, for example in Colombia, judicial adjudication of constitutionally recognized SER benefits not the poor but mainly middle- or upper middle-class segments of the population.[37]

IV. CONCLUSION

While drawing on markedly different ideological and analytical groundings, Neier's critique of SER and more generally that of critical legal scholars, TWAIL, or Samuel Moyn have one element in common: they have pushed human rights advocates to respond to the critiques and to articulate more specifically the politics of their practice. Critique about the limits of human rights has this crucial role of situating and questioning practice within broader, underlying, or occluded dynamics and structures. Suggestions that one's practice should not lie within the realm of human rights, that it has implicit dark sides or is 'not enough' ought to push any thoughtful practitioner to aspire to make a strong case that her action falls squarely in what a more broadly articulated notion of human rights practice is, can, and should be about, or that she can do 'more', if not 'better'. Many scholars, advocates, and scholars-practitioners have in fact just done so. For there is indeed more to the human rights movement on the ground than meets the critical American eye.

Scholars have argued for designing 'smarter'[38] SER strategies that take critique on board or that draw on the savvy work of African SER advocates who both take stock of and work through critique to deploy SER language in more strategic and pragmatic ways. Pertinent examples are multilevel grassroots and transnational campaigns aimed at prefiguring institutional innovation for the provision of social goods. Such campaigns engage in the political work Neier describes as typically needed to achieve socio-economic 'goals'. Beyond debates about their nature and

---

[34] For an extended analysis, see Perelman, *The Rights-ification of Development* (n. 12).

[35] Alviar García, Klare, and Williams (eds), *Social and Economic Rights* (n. 4); Malcolm Langford, 'Critiques of Human Rights' (2018) 14 Annual Review of Law and Social Science 69.

[36] Daniel M Brinks and William Forbath, 'The Role of Courts and Constitutions in the New Politics of Welfare in Latin America' in Randall Peerenboom and Tom Ginsburg (eds), *Law and Development of Middle-Income Countries: Avoiding the Middle-Income Trap* (Cambridge University Press 2014) 221.

[37] David Landau, 'The Reality of Social Rights Enforcement' (2011) 53 Harvard International Law Journal 190.

[38] Klare, 'Critical Perspectives' (n. 8) 12.

value as rights, they recognize the salience of the human rights *discourse* to crystallize aspirations for social and economic justice. They do so by grounding a social-movement infused human rights praxis in explicit visions of redistributive politics beyond traditional forms of state-oriented human rights strategies.[39] Importantly, their work draws on *both* legal and non-legal strategies and on SER language when and if useful. SER are thus seized, vernacularized, and hybridized with other normative framings that can catalyze social movement and generate political power.[40]

Is this kind of practice representative? Large international human rights organizations have somewhat refined their SER advocacy over the past decade. Innovative UN Special Rapporteurs have 'stretched' the SER framework to generate dynamic levers of accountability that can be seized by political and social movements. They also established links to other spheres of norm-building and policy-making. Specialized SER organizations have employed both legal and non-legal strategies and developed innovative, pluri-disciplinary methods akin to the 'rigorous and systematic' documentation Neier presents as CPR work to identify systematic policy failures and/or abuses. They have linked these methods with legal and policy-oriented strategies, have established alliances with local social and labour movements, and have recognized coalition-building and local bottom-up political organizing as key to generating 'transformative change'.[41] Other advocates have preferred to shun strategies based on human rights law, institutions, or even language. Instead, they have engaged other technical areas of law that underpin globalized economic production and business practices such as global manufacturing supply chains, foreign direct investment, and transnational natural resources extraction. In this context, they designed advocacy strategies to influence corporate behaviour and generate sustained human and labour rights compliance.[42]

To go beyond Neier's critique and address Samuel Moyn's call for a shift 'back' towards the paradigm of equality in SER advocacy, is this, can this, be 'enough'? The increasing defiance towards the democratic rule of law and the liberal human rights paradigm and the emergence of a post-liberal order represent a momentous challenge. As I mentioned before, while this defiance takes many forms and is linked to a variety of factors, it is crucial for human rights advocates to 'listen' to critique. Rejecting critique because it might undermine the already jeopardized legitimacy of the human rights framework and movement seems ill-advised. Advocates ought to take stock of the critique and apply in turn a critical, scrutinizing eye to both the critique *and* the counter-arguments. They need to probe how much the articulated responses have effectively generated change on the ground and assess

---

[39] White and Perelman (eds), *Stones of Hope* (n. 8).
[40] For a similar argument, see Rosenblum, 'When Splitters become Lumpers' (n. 33).
[41] Yamin and Saiz, 'Human Rights and Social Justice' (n. 1).
[42] Rosenblum, 'When Splitters become Lumpers' (n. 33); Perelman, *The Rights-ification of Development* (n. 12).

in what directions this change pointed and which limits persist because of the entrenchment and political economy of neo-liberalism.

Going beyond the promise of international human rights law,[43] progressive scholars and activists ought to recognize the salience of SER language in framing campaigns for social justice despite the shortcomings of the human rights framework.[44] This is all the more important at a moment when there is perhaps a political opening precisely because of the return of inequality as a predominant phenomenon in the Global North and increasingly also in the Global South. There seems to be a window of opportunity for human rights defenders and social justice advocates to seize and re-articulate a rhetoric which, despite all the critique, keeps resonating on the ground. This SER-based rhetoric should be clearly articulated around the tools of distributive analysis and the substantive language of distributive justice, rather than on exclusively formalistic grounds of non-discrimination, participation, free and prior consultation, or transparency.

Recent initiatives targeting fiscal (in)justice, addressing economic inequalities directly in human rights terms or engaging policy arenas such as trade, finance, investment, or intellectual property are encouraging. The fact that Human Rights Watch, the organization Neier helped to found, is opening a position on 'human rights and inequality' is quite revealing. But these various initiatives ought to be scrutinized in light of whether and how they can best serve the kind of work that Neier points out as implicitly linked to the work of social justice. They need to look hard at whether and how they can serve not the edifice of SER and the justification of expertise-driven practice but the demands for social and economic justice in the age of entrenched neo-liberalism and rising populism. Again, this implies a readiness to take critique *on board* and to develop critically informed practices. Such practices would not reject SER but ally with them and, most importantly perhaps, allow its rhetorical and progressive political potential to be *seized by* local and transnational movements for social justice. These movements and their demands may well be articulated in languages other than rights talk and may address such diverse areas as work, distribution, cultural and/or social relegation, climate change, or religion. The future of human rights work is increasingly about such new, hybridized languages, methods, and strategies for social justice.[45]

---

[43] John Linarelli, Margot E Salomon, and Muthucumaraswamy Sornarajah, *The Misery of International Law: Confrontations with Injustice in the Global Economy* (Oxford University Press 2018).

[44] See, e.g., Paul O'Connell, 'On the Human Rights Question' (2018) 40 Human Rights Quarterly 962.

[45] César Rodríguez-Garavito, 'Reimagining Human Rights' (2017) 13 Journal of International Law and International Relations 10.

Bibliography

Berlin I, 'Two Concepts of Liberty' in Berlin I (ed.), *Four Essays on Liberty* (Oxford University Press 1969) 118

Brinks DM and Forbath W, 'The Role of Courts and Constitutions in the New Politics of Welfare in Latin America' in Peerenboom R and Ginsburg T (eds), *Law and Development of Middle-Income Countries: Avoiding the Middle-Income Trap* (Cambridge University Press 2014) 221

Engle K, 'Human Rights Consciousness and Critique' in Fassin D and Harcourt BE (eds), *A Time for Critique* (Columbia University Press 2019) 91 edn

Fishkin J and Forbath WE, 'The Anti-Oligarchy Constitution' (2014) 94 Boston University Law Review 671

Forbath WE, 'Constitutional Welfare Rights: A History, Critique and Reconstruction' (2001) 69 Fordham Law Review 1821

Forbath WE, Achmat Z, Budlender G, and Heywood M, 'Cultural Transformation, Deep Institutional Reform, and ESR Practice: South Africa's Treatment Action Campaign' in White LE and Perelman J (eds), *Stones of Hope: How African Activists Reclaim Human Rights to Challenge Global Poverty* (Stanford University Press 2011) 51

Kennedy D, *The Dark Sides of Virtue: Reassessing International Humanitarianism* (Princeton University Press 2004)

Kennedy D, 'The Stakes of Law, or Hale and Foucault!' (1991) 15 Legal Studies Forum 327

Kennedy D, 'The Critique of Rights in Critical Legal Studies' in Brown W and Halley J (eds), *Left Legalism, Left Critique* (2002) 178

Klare K, 'Critical Perspectives on Social and Economic Rights, Democracy and Separation of Powers' in Alviar García H, Klare K, and Williams LA (eds), *Social and Economic Rights in Theory and Practice: Critical Inquiries* (Routledge 2015) 3

Landau D, 'The Reality of Social Rights Enforcement' (2011) 53 Harvard International Law Journal 190

Langford M, 'Critiques of Human Rights' (2018) 14 Annual Review of Law and Social Science 69

Langford M, Rodríguez-Garavito C, and Rossi J (eds), *Social Rights Judgments and the Politics of Compliance: Making it Stick* (Cambridge University Press 2017)

Linarelli J, Salomon ME, and Sornarajah M, *The Misery of International Law: Confrontations with Injustice in the Global Economy* (Oxford University Press 2018)

Michelman FI, 'Constitutionally Binding Social and Economic Rights as a Compelling Idea: Reciprocating Perturbations in Liberal and Democratic Constitutional Visions' in Alviar García H, Klare K, and Williams LA (eds), *Social and Economic Rights in Theory and Practice: Critical Inquiries* (Routledge 2015) 277

Moyn S, *The Last Utopia: Human Rights in History* (Harvard University Press 2010)

Moyn S, *Not Enough: Human Rights in an Unequal World* (Belknap Press 2018)

Mureinik E, 'A Bridge to Where? Introducing the Interim Bill of Rights' (1994) 10 South African Journal of Human Rights 31

Mutua M, *Human Rights: A Political and Cultural Critique* (University of Pennsylvania Press 2008)

Neier A, *Defending My Enemy: American Nazis, the Skokie Case, and the Risks of Freedom* (2nd edn, International Debate Education Association 2012)

Neier A, 'Differentiating Fundamental Rights and Economic Goals' in Bardo Fassbender and Knut Traisbach (eds), *The Limits of Human Rights* (Oxford University Press 2019) 175

O'Connell P, 'On the Human Rights Question' (2018) 40 Human Rights Quarterly 962

Perelman J, *The Rights-ification of Development: Global Poverty, Human Rights and Globalization in the Post-Washington Consensus* (Hart Publishing forthcoming)

Pogge T, 'Shue on Rights and Duties' in Beitz CR and Goodin RE (eds), *Global Basic Rights* (Oxford University Press 2009) 113

Rodríguez-Garavito C, 'Reimagining Human Rights' (2017) 13 Journal of International Law and International Relations 10

Rodríguez-Garavito C, 'Against Reductionist Views of Human Rights' (Open Democracy, 30 July 2019) <https://www.opendemocracy.net/en/openglobalrights-openpage/against-reductionist-views-of-human-rights/> accessed 31 January 2019

Rosenberg G, *The Hollow Hope: Can Courts Bring About Social Change?* (2nd edn, The University of Chicago Press 2008)

Rosenblum P, 'When Splitters become Lumpers: Pitfalls of a Long History of Human Rights' (Law and Political Economy, 10 August 2018) <https://lpeblog.org/2018/08/10/when-splitters-become-lumpers-pitfalls-of-a-long-history-of-human-rights/> accessed 31 January 2019

Salomon ME, *Global Responsibility for Human Rights: World Poverty and The Development of International Law* (Oxford University Press 2007)

Salomon ME, 'Human Rights Are Also About Social Justice' (Open Democracy, 25 July 2013) <https://www.opendemocracy.net/en/openglobalrights-openpage/human-rights-are-also-about-social-justice/> accessed 31 January 2019

Schauer F, 'A Comment on the Structure of Rights' (1992–93) 27 Georgia Law Review 415

de Schutter O, *International Human Rights Law: Cases, Materials, Commentary* (2nd edn, Cambridge University Press 2014)

Sen A, *Development as Freedom* (Oxford University Press 1999)

Sen A, 'Elements of a Theory of Human Rights' (2004) 32 Philosophy & Public Affairs 315

Shue H, *Basic Rights: Subsistence, Affluence, and U.S. Foreign Policy* (2nd edn, Princeton University Press 1996)

Sunstein C, 'Against Positive Rights: Why Social and Economic Rights Don't Belong in the New Constitutions of Post-Communist Europe' (1993) 2 East European Constitutional Review 35

Tushnet M, *Weak Courts, Strong Rights: Judicial Review and Social Welfare Rights in Comparative Constitutional Law* (Princeton University Press 2008)

Walton C, 'The French Revolution: A Redistributive Crisis' in Martin V and Mazeau G (eds), *L'Histoire en Liberté: Mélanges pour Jean-Clément Martin* (Publications de la Sorbonne forthcoming)

Yamin AE and Saiz I, 'Human Rights and Social Justice: The In(di)visible Link' (Open Democracy, 30 July 2013) <https://www.opendemocracy.net/en/openglobalrights-openpage/human-rights-and-social-justice-indivisible-link/> accessed 31 January 2019

Young K, 'The Minimum Core of Economic and Social Rights: A Concept in Search of Content' (2008) 33 Yale Journal of International Law 113

Young K, *Constituting Economic and Social Rights* (Oxford University Press 2012)

PART III
LIMITS OF SCOPE, LIMITS OF RECOGNITION: THE CASE OF WOMEN'S RIGHTS

13
Between the Margins and the Mainstream
The Case of Women's Rights

*Hilary Charlesworth and Christine Chinkin**

I. INTRODUCTION

The area of women's rights is one of the most contested in the field of human rights. Women's groups have struggled over the past century for legal recognition and guarantee of their rights. From the earliest days of international institutional organization, women have targeted the international arena as a site of emancipation.[1] Despite normative successes, limits—both theoretical and practical—have quickly emerged in each apparent step forward, generating campaigns for further developments. This process has created a complex geography of actors, sites, and mechanisms that now co-exist, with overlapping agendas and unclear conceptual linkages between them.

Over the past century, two major strands of activity have emerged in international regimes for the protection of women: one developed through human rights institutions, the second through the United Nations Security Council. This chapter first charts this landscape and its conceptual limits. It describes how campaigns for recognition of women's rights oscillate between preferring specialist institutions for women, with the risk of marginalization, on the one hand and insisting that mainstream, or apparently general, international institutions recognize women's lives on the other. This movement between the margins and the mainstream has both progressive and conservative elements, but the structural bases of women's disadvantage rarely attract attention.

II. THE HUMAN RIGHTS FIELD

The first strand commenced with the formal international articulation of the prohibition of discrimination on the basis of sex in the UN Charter in 1945.[2] This

---

* Christine Chinkin thanks the UK Arts and Humanities Research Council for funding a research project on *A Feminist International Law of Peace and Security*, under which this chapter was written.

[1] Arvonne Fraser, 'Becoming Human: The Origins and Development of Women's Human Rights' (1999) 21 Human Rights Quarterly 853.

[2] Charter of the United Nations (adopted 26 June 1945, entered into force 24 October 1945), Articles 1(3), 55, 56.

Hilary Charlesworth and Christine Chinkin, *Between the Margins and the Mainstream: The Case of Women's Rights*. In: *The Limits of Human Rights*. Edited by: Bardo Fassbender and Knut Traisbach, Oxford University Press 2019. © The Several Contributors.
DOI: 10.1093/oso/9780198824756.003.0015

was reaffirmed in the International Bill of Human Rights,[3] but these provisions had little impact in mainstream jurisprudence or practice. From its outset, the UN human rights system was supplemented by the work of the UN Commission on the Status of Women (CSW). CSW was created because women delegates in the Sub-Commission on Women of the Commission on Human Rights demanded separate status as they feared their concerns would be subsumed by the Commission, an early illustration of the tension between specialist domains and general institutions.[4] CSW drafted treaties dealing with specific issues of women's rights: on the political status of women,[5] the nationality of married women,[6] and the age of marriage.[7] Other treaty regimes protected women in specific contexts, such as against rape in armed conflict,[8] trafficking,[9] and in the workplace.[10]

The lack of impact of the general prohibition on sex discrimination and the restricted subject matter of the specialized treaties prompted the adoption by the UN General Assembly of the Declaration on the Elimination of Discrimination against Women in 1967,[11] which recognized the continuing 'considerable discrimination against women'.[12] This was followed in 1979 by the Convention on the Elimination of All Forms of Discrimination against Women (CEDAW).[13] The Convention emerged from the UN Decade for Women (1975–85). The Decade was marked by deep tensions between women from different political and economic systems. For

---

[3] Universal Declaration of Human Rights, GA Res. 217 A (III) (10 December 1948) [1948–49] UN Yearbook 535, Article 2; International Covenant on Civil and Political Rights (adopted 16 December 1966, entered into force 23 March 1976) 999 UNTS 171, Article 2(1) (hereafter ICCPR); International Covenant on Economic, Social and Cultural Rights (adopted 16 December 1966, entered into force 3 January 1976) 993 UNTS 3, Article 2(2) (hereafter ICESCR).

[4] Hilka Pietilä, *The Unfinished Story of Women and the United Nations* (United Nations Non-Governmental Liaison Service 2007) 13.

[5] Convention on the Political Rights of Women (adopted 31 March 1953, entered into force 7 July 1954) 193 UNTS 135.

[6] Convention on the Nationality of Married Women (adopted 20 February 1957, entered into force 11 August 1958) 309 UNTS 65.

[7] Convention on Consent to Marriage, Minimum Age for Marriage and Registration of Marriages (adopted 10 December 1962, entered into force 9 December 1964) 521 UNTS 231.

[8] Convention relative to the Protection of Civilian Persons in Time of War (Geneva Convention IV) (adopted 12 August 1949, entered into force 21 October 1950) 75 UNTS 287, Article 27; Additional Protocol to the Geneva Conventions of 12 August 1949, and relating to the Protection of Victims of International Armed Conflicts (Additional Protocol I) (adopted 8 June 1977, entered into force 7 December 1978) 1125 UNTS 3, Article 76.

[9] See Convention for the Suppression of the Traffic in Persons and of the Exploitation of the Prostitution of Others (adopted 21 March 1950, entered into force 25 July 1951) 96 UNTS 271, which consolidated earlier treaties.

[10] See, e.g., Convention concerning Equal Remuneration for Men and Women Workers for Work of Equal Value (adopted 29 June 1951, entered into force 23 May 1953) 165 UNTS 304; Convention concerning Discrimination in respect of Employment and Occupation (adopted 25 June 1958, entered into force 15 June 1960) 362 UNTS 31. These are included in the International Labour Organisation's eight fundamental conventions.

[11] Declaration on the Elimination of Discrimination against Women, GA Res. 2263 (XXII) (7 November 1967) (hereafter Declaration on the Elimination of Discrimination against Women).

[12] Ibid, preamble.

[13] Convention on the Elimination of All Forms of Discrimination against Women (adopted 18 December 1979, entered into force 3 September 1981) 1249 UNTS 13 (hereafter CEDAW).

example, women activists from the Eastern bloc located the source of women's disadvantage in the free market economy, while American women's groups focused on inequality of opportunity within capitalism.[14] For their part, women from the Global South regarded the continuing effects of colonial domination and economic disparity with the North as critical factors in their situation. The Convention shows traces of these tensions,[15] but does not resolve them. It contains a broad definition of discrimination,[16] and requires states to take legal and other measures to ensure the practical realization of the principle of sex equality.[17] The treaty covers a range of areas in public and private life where state parties must work to eliminate discrimination against women and requires 'appropriate measures' for the 'full development and advancement of women'.[18] In drafting the Convention, the CSW drew upon the expertise of its members, mainly women delegates, but followed the structure of the mainstream human rights treaties, especially in the creation of an expert, independent monitoring committee.

As of September 2019, the Convention had 189 states parties. Despite almost universal state participation in the treaty, its effectiveness has been undermined by states' reluctance to implement it, manifested for example through far-reaching reservations.[19] Monitoring of the Convention was initially limited to state reporting; in 1999, adoption of an Optional Protocol introduced an inquiry procedure and provided for individual communications with respect to those states that accepted the Protocol.[20] These procedures have allowed the Committee on the Elimination of Discrimination against Women (CEDAW Committee) to develop jurisprudence in specific contexts, albeit in a small number of cases.[21]

The norms of the Convention have been developed both through the Convention's specialist monitoring body and through mainstream institutions. Since its inception in 1982, the Committee has been active in interpreting the treaty as a 'dynamic instrument',[22] primarily through its General Recommendations.

---

[14] See Kristen Ghodsee, 'Revisiting the United Nations Decade for Women: Brief Reflections on Feminism, Capitalism and Cold War Politics in the Early Years of the International Women's Movement' (2010) 33 Women's Studies International Forum 3.
[15] See, e.g., CEDAW (n. 13), whose preamble references to the new international economic order.
[16] Ibid, Article 1.
[17] Ibid, Article 2.
[18] Ibid, Article 3.
[19] Jane Connors, 'Article 28: Reservations' in Marsha A Freeman, Christine Chinkin, and Beate Rudolf (eds), *The UN Convention on the Elimination of All Forms of Discrimination against Women: A Commentary* (Oxford University Press 2012) 565.
[20] Optional Protocol to the Convention on the Elimination of All Forms of Discrimination against Women (adopted 10 December 1999, entered into force 22 December 2000) 2131 UNTS 83.
[21] See Alice Edwards, 'Displacement, Statelessness and Questions of Gender Equality and the Convention on the Elimination of All Forms of Discrimination against Women' (2009) United Nations High Commissioner for Refugees Background Paper 2009/02 <https://www2.ohchr.org/english/bodies/cedaw/docs/unhcr_cedaw_background_paper4.pdf> accessed 31 January 2019.
[22] UN Committee on the Elimination of Discrimination against Women (hereafter CEDAW Committee) General Recommendation no. 28, 'Core obligations of States parties (art 2)' CEDAW/C/GC/28, para. 2 (hereafter CEDAW Committee General Recommendation no. 28).

Although the Convention has no provision on violence, the CEDAW Committee has interpreted it to encompass gender-based violence against women and girls as a form of discrimination within Article 1 and asserted states' obligations to address such violence whether committed by state or non-state actors.[23] It has recognized the potential limits of the idea of 'sex-based' discrimination, explaining that this also encompasses discrimination based on the 'socially constructed identities, attributes and roles for women and men', which is 'gender-based discrimination'.[24] The Committee has also acknowledged women's diversity and the inextricable linkage of sex and gender-based discrimination against women with other factors that adversely affect women's access to rights 'such as race, ethnicity, religion or belief, health, status, age, class, caste, and sexual orientation and gender identity'.[25]

The work of the CEDAW Committee has appeared marginal to the mainstream human rights institutions. The initial meeting place of the CEDAW Committee in New York and Vienna, serviced by the UN Division for the Advancement of Women rather than the Human Rights Division, kept it physically apart from the other human rights treaty bodies. In 2008 meetings of the CEDAW Committee moved to Geneva and, like the other treaty bodies, it came within the Office of the High Commissioner for Human Rights (OHCHR). The human rights treaty bodies at first paid little attention to the prohibition of sex-based discrimination within their texts, perhaps thinking that the existence of the CEDAW Committee reduced their responsibility for addressing issues relating to women. The adoption of the policy of gender mainstreaming throughout UN activities, as urged by the Vienna Programme for Action and Beijing Platform for Action,[26] had little immediate impact on human rights law,[27] until the adoption of General Comment no. 28 by the UN Human Rights Committee in 2000[28] and General Comment no. 16 by the UN Committee on Economic, Social and Cultural Rights in 2005.[29] Other treaty bodies and special procedures have adopted similar

---

[23] CEDAW Committee General Recommendation no. 19, 'Violence against women' HRI\GEN\1\Rev.1, para. 7 (hereafter CEDAW Committee General Recommendation no. 19).
[24] CEDAW Committee General Recommendation no. 28 (n. 22) para. 5.
[25] Ibid, para. 18.
[26] Vienna Declaration and Programme for Action, A/CONF.157/23 (25 June 1993) part II, para. 37; Beijing Declaration and Platform for Action, A/CONF.177/20 (15 September 1995) para. 221 (hereafter Beijing Declaration and Platform for Action).
[27] Anne Gallagher, 'Ending the Marginalization: Strategies for Incorporating Women into the United Nations Human Rights System' (1997) 19 Human Rights Quarterly 283; for a critique of the policy of gender mainstreaming see Sari Kouvo, 'The United Nations and Gender Mainstreaming: Limits and Possibilities' in Doris Buss and Ambreena Manji (eds), *International Law: Modern Feminist Approaches* (Hart Publishing 2005) 237.
[28] HR Committee (ICCPR) General Comment no. 28, 'The Equality of Rights Between Men and Women (art 3)' CCPR/C/21/Rev.1/Add.10.
[29] Committee on Economic, Social and Cultural Rights (ICESCR) General Comment no. 16, 'The equal right of men and women to the enjoyment of all economic, social and cultural rights (art 3)' E/C.12/2005/4.

statements.[30] The overall take-up of gender mainstreaming by human rights bodies has been, however, patchy and inconsistent.[31]

UN institutions have supplemented the normative regime for the protection of women's rights. For example, despite the tensions between women described above, women activists largely found common cause in seeking recognition of violence against women as a violation of human rights. Significant success was achieved in the early 1990s through the World Conference on Human Rights in Vienna, adoption of the General Assembly Declaration on Elimination of Violence against Women[32] and mandating the Special Rapporteur on Violence against Women—the first human rights special procedure to be focused exclusively on women's rights.[33] Tensions re-emerged at the Fourth World Conference on Women, held in 1995 in Beijing, where feminization of poverty was the primary concern of women from the Global South and there were sharp divisions over inclusion of any reference to sexual orientation.[34] The Declaration and Platform for Action identified twelve critical areas of concern for women's rights, including women and poverty, violence against women, human rights of women and, as discussed below, women and armed conflict. In the decades since Beijing other UN institutions have continued to address violence against women,[35] and non-discrimination against of LGBTI persons has slowly entered the lexicon.[36]

Regional institutions have also played a significant role in extending the scope of women's human rights through interpretation of their general human rights treaties[37] and through the adoption of specialist ones. Both the Inter-American

---

[30] See, e.g., Report of the Special Rapporteur on Torture and Other Cruel, Inhuman or Degrading Treatment or Punishment (Manfred Nowak), 'Strengthening the protection of women from torture' GA Res. A/HRC/7/3 (15 January 2008); see also Report of the Special Rapporteur on Torture and Other Cruel, Inhuman or Degrading Treatment or Punishment (Juan E Méndez), 'Gender perspectives on torture and other cruel, inhuman and degrading treatment or punishment' A/HRC/31/57 (5 January 2016).

[31] Christine Chinkin, 'Gender and Economic, Social, and Cultural Rights' in Eibe Riedel, Giles Giacca, and Christophe Golay (eds), *Economic, Social and Cultural Rights in International Law: Contemporary Issues and Challenges* (Oxford University Press 2014) 134.

[32] Declaration on the Elimination of Violence against Women, GA Res. 48/104 (20 December 2003).

[33] The special rapporteur on violence against women, its causes and consequences was originally mandated by Commission on Human Rights Res. 1994/45 (4 March 1994) E/CN.4/RES/1995/86.

[34] For discussion of the 'trade-off' leading to erasure of sexual orientation see Dianne Otto, 'Lesbians? Not in My Country. Sexual Orientation at the Beijing World Conference on Women' (1995) 20 Alternative Law Journal 288.

[35] See, e.g., Commission on the Status of Women, UN Economic and Social Council, 'Agreed Conclusions: The Elimination and Prevention of All Forms of Violence against Women and Girls' E/CN.6/2013/L.5 (19 March 2013); HR Council Res., 'Accelerating efforts to eliminate violence against women: preventing and responding to violence against women and girls, including indigenous women and girls' A/HRC/RES/32/19 (30 June 2016).

[36] See, e.g., CEDAW Committee General Recommendation no. 28 (n. 22) para. 18; CEDAW Committee General Recommendation no. 35, Updating General Recommendation no. 19, 'Gender-based violence against women' CEDAW/C/GC/35, para. 12.

[37] For example, the European and Inter-American human rights courts have interpreted provisions of the European Convention on Human Rights and Fundamental Freedoms and Inter-American Convention on Human Rights, respectively, as applying to rape and domestic violence. Cases include *MC v. Bulgaria*,

human rights system and the Council of Europe have adopted specific treaties dealing with violence against women,[38] and the African Union has adopted a Protocol to the African Charter on Human and Peoples' Rights dealing with the rights of women and more generally addressing the gaps in CEDAW for application throughout Africa.[39]

This account of the development of the international protection of women's human rights illustrates the to and fro between the margins—the specialist women's bodies and instruments—and the mainstream international institutional work. But this complex landscape has clear limits. Many of the relevant instruments are legally non-binding, and regional treaties are geographically restricted. At a normative level, CEDAW's broad notion of equality—extending to both equality of treatment and equality of outcome—is limited conceptually by its general requirement of a male comparator. In other words, the Convention's standard of equality is that of male lives and experience. This account of equality thus excludes human rights violations that have no counterpart in men's lives, such as women's reproductive rights.[40] Another normative limitation is that the exclusive focus on the categories of men and women emphasizes the significance of biological sex and heterosexual relations. Further, women's rights are frequently seen as in opposition to other rights, such as those to property, to freedom of movement, the right to a fair trial, or to religious freedom.

Attempts to guarantee women's human rights also encounter resistance in arguments that women's equality is destructive to societal structures. For example, the UN Human Rights Council has debated the relationship of human rights and 'the traditional values of humankind'.[41] This agenda item was promoted by Russia, responding to its own declining population and high rate of family breakdown. It has been supported by the Russian Orthodox Church, which blames these phenomena on the women's and gay rights movements.[42] Other socially conservative

---

App. No. 39272/98, 4 December 2003; *Opuz v. Turkey*, App. No. 33401/02, 9 June 2009; *González v. Mexico (Cotton Field)*, Inter-American Court of Human Rights Series C no. 205, 16 November 2009.

[38] Inter-American Convention on the Prevention, Punishment and Eradication of Violence against Women (Convention of Belém do Pará) (adopted 6 September 1994, entered into force 5 March 1995) 33 ILM 1534; Council of Europe Convention on Preventing and Combating Violence against Women and Domestic Violence (Istanbul Convention) (adopted 11 May 2011, entered into force 1 August 2014) CETS no. 210.
[39] Protocol to the African Charter on Human and Peoples' Rights on the Rights of Women in Africa (Maputo Protocol) (adopted 11 July 2003, entered into force 25 November 2005) CAB/LEG/66.6 integrates a prohibition on violence against women throughout.
[40] We have discussed this in greater detail in Hilary Charlesworth and Christine Chinkin, 'The New United Nations "Gender Architecture": A Room with a View?' (2013) 17 Max Planck Yearbook of United Nations Law 1.
[41] See, e.g., HR Council Res., 'Promoting human rights and fundamental freedoms through a better understanding of traditional values of humankind' A/HRC/Res/12/21 (12 October 2009) (hereafter HR Council Res. 12/21).
[42] See Kristina Stoeckl, *The Russian Orthodox Church and Human Rights* (Routledge 2014) 109. HR Council Res. 12/21 (n. 41).

movements such as pro-life groups in the United States have similarly lent support. Human rights non-governmental organizations (NGOs) have in contrast contributed significant critique to the traditional values debate in the Human Rights Council.[43] These issues have polarized the Council, essentially putting Western European states and some allies in opposition to Russia, other Eastern European states, and states with large Muslim populations. Debates have continued over several years, expert workshops have convened and studies have been prepared on the content of 'traditional values of humankind' and on the relationship between individual responsibilities and state obligations and between individual and family rights. In 2012 a report from the Human Rights Council's Advisory Council noted that, while some traditional values were the foundation for human rights, others justified discrimination and subordination. The report emphasized the primacy of international human rights standards.[44]

In another line of thinking that potentially limits women's human rights, the Council has adopted resolutions each year since 2014 on the protection of the family, calling on states to adopt 'family-friendly laws and policies'.[45] The family is presented as 'the fundamental group of society and the natural environment for the growth and well-being of all its members'.[46] The resolutions also refer repeatedly to the 'increasing vulnerabilities' of the family unit, implying that the family is endangered by the recognition of the rights of women, of same sex couples, and of sexual and gender minorities. In other words, the traditional patriarchal family unit requires protection from challenges to its structure. These resolutions do not define the concept of a family, but their use of the term 'the family', rather than the plural form 'families', has been understood as a code for 'traditional' family groups, specifically those formed by heterosexual couples.[47] This impression is reinforced by the image of the family as a 'natural' phenomenon and as a guardian of the social fabric, playing 'a crucial role in the preservation of cultural identity, tradition, morals, heritage and the values system of society'.[48] These resolutions contrast

---

[43] HR Council, 'Summary of Information from States Members of the United Nations and Other Relevant Stakeholders on Best Practices in the Application of Traditional Values while Promoting and Protecting Human Rights and Upholding Human Dignity: Report of the United Nations High Commissioner for Human Rights' A/HRC/24/22 (17 June 2013). These groups included Article 19, ARC International, and the International Service for Human Rights.

[44] HR Council, 'Study of the Human Rights Council Advisory Committee on Promoting Human Rights and Fundamental Freedoms through a Better Understanding of Traditional Values of Humankind' A/HRC/AC/22/71 (6 December 2012).

[45] HR Council Res. 29/22, A/HRC/RES/29/22 (22 July 2015) (hereafter HR Council Res. 29/22); HR Council Res. 32/23, A/HRC/RES/32/23 (18 July 2016).

[46] HR Council Res. 29/22 (n. 45), preamble.

[47] Pooja Patel and Sarah Brooks, 'Protection of the Family Resolution Increases Vulnerabilities and Exacerbates Inequalities' (International Service for Human Rights, 19 June 2015) <http://www.ishr.ch/news/protection-family-resolution-increases-vulnerabilities-and-exacerbates-inequalities> accessed 31 January 2019.

[48] HR Council Res. 29/22 (n. 45).

with a 2016 report from the Office of the High Commissioner for Human Rights,[49] which endorses a broad notion of family, including those of same-sex couples[50] and elaborates the human rights attaching to individuals within a family, particularly to equality.[51]

One of the problems in promoting the protection of the family in human rights institutions is that it implies that the preservation of the family is more important than respecting the human rights of individuals within the family. For example, it could undermine the claims of women and girls to equal rights to property and inheritance. The CEDAW Committee and special procedures of the Human Rights Council, particularly the Special Rapporteur on Violence against Women, have over the past decades emphasized the family as a site of violence against women.[52] Protection of the family can thus obscure the way that it promotes certain pathologies in power relationships. A 2015 resolution of the Human Rights Council refers briefly and generally to the principle of equality between women and men and respect for the human rights of all family members,[53] but it gives much greater priority to maintenance and support for the family. It indeed assumes that protection of the family will promote the human rights of its members.[54]

The protection of the family initiative illustrates the intensity of the politics over the assertion of universal human rights on the one hand and the claims of tradition and culture on the other. The latter are especially limiting factors in the case of women's human rights. The backlash against women's rights was a major reason for the decision not to hold a 'Beijing plus 20' conference in 2015. It is evident also in the 2017 United States' reinstatement and expansion of the 'global gag' rule which precludes overseas funding for organizations that provide counselling about abortion, or advocate the liberalization of abortion laws.[55] Human rights is a public discourse regulating relationships between the state and individuals, while for many women, their lives and experience of rights (or their violations) still rest in the private domain. Even where women participate in public life, their enjoyment of rights may be curtailed

---

[49] HR Council, 'Protection of the Family: Contribution of the Family to the Realization of the Right to an Adequate Standard of Living for its Members, particularly through its Role in Poverty Eradication and Achieving Sustainable Development' A/HRC/31/37 (29 January 2016) (hereafter HR Council, 'Protection of the Family').

[50] Ibid, paras 24–7.

[51] Ibid, paras 22–3, 28–47.

[52] See, e.g., CEDAW Committee General Recommendation no. 19 (n. 23), especially para. 23; Report of the Special Rapporteur on Violence against Women, its Causes and Consequences (Yakin Ertürk), 'Intersections between Culture and Violence against Women' A/HRC/4/34 (17 January 2007); Report of the Special Rapporteur on Violence against Women, Its Causes and Consequences (Rashida Manjoo), 'Addendum; Mission to Afghanistan' A/HRC/29/27/Add.3 (12 May 2015) para. 13; see also HR Council, 'Report of the Working Group on the issue of discrimination against women in law and in practice' A/HRC/29/40 (2 April 2015).

[53] HR Council Res. 29/22 (n. 45) paras 9, 14–15.

[54] Ibid, para. 20.

[55] President Donald J Trump, 'Presidential Memorandum Regarding the Mexico City Policy' (White House Office of the Press Secretary, 23 January 2017) <http://www.whitehouse.gov/the-press-office/2017/01/23/presidential-memorandum-regarding-mexico-city-policy> accessed 31 January 2019.

in the private sphere, for instance through domestic or intimate partner violence. Resurgence of the notion of the primacy of the family represents a privatizing of rights that threatens the provision for equality within the family in CEDAW Article 16.

Both the traditional values and protection of the family initiatives are in tension with Article 5(a) CEDAW which requires states '[t]o modify the social and cultural patterns of conduct of men and women, with a view to achieving the elimination of prejudices and customary and all other practices which are based on the idea of the inferiority or the superiority of either of the sexes or on stereotyped roles for men and women'. Article 5 is based on the recognition that women cannot enjoy their rights unless such practices are eliminated. The CEDAW Committee has applied Article 5 as a tool for enhancing equality, seeking to make more concrete its somewhat abstract wording.[56] The Human Rights Council initiatives also undermine the reiteration by the Beijing Platform for Action of the human rights of women and the girl child as 'an inalienable, integral and indivisible part of universal human rights' and that states should 'prohibit and eliminate' any 'harmful aspect of certain traditional, customary or modern practices that violates the rights of women'.[57]

III. WOMEN, PEACE, AND SECURITY

A second strand of relevant international activity relates to women in times of conflict, whether during or after hostilities. This concern goes back at least to the Women's International Congress in 1915.[58] CEDAW General Recommendation no. 19 on violence against women, adopted in 1992, had noted that 'wars, armed conflicts and the occupation of territories often lead to increased prostitution, trafficking in women and sexual assault of women, ... requir[ing] specific protective and punitive measures', but otherwise had not addressed the applicability of the Convention to situations of armed conflict.[59] In 1995 at the Beijing Conference this issue became one of the Critical Areas of Concern and states and international bodies were called upon to '[i]ncrease the participation of women in conflict resolution at decision-making levels and protect women living in situations of armed and other conflicts or under foreign occupation'.[60]

---

[56] See, e.g., *Ms AT v. Hungary*, CEDAW Committee Comm. No. 2/2003, 26 January 2005; *Vertido v. The Philippines*, CEDAW Committee Comm. No. 18/2008, 16 July 2010; *RPB v. The Philippines*, CEDAW Committee Comm. No. 34/2011, 21 February 2014; *Angela González Carreño v. Spain*, CEDAW Committee Comm. No. 47/2012, 16 July 2014.
[57] Beijing Declaration and Platform for Action (n. 26) paras 213, 216, 224.
[58] Freya Baetens, 'International Congress of Women (1915)' in Rüdiger Wolfrum (ed.), *Max Planck Encyclopedia of Public International Law* (Oxford University Press 2010) 455.
[59] This was clarified in CEDAW Committee General Recommendation no. 30, 'Women in conflict prevention, conflict and post-conflict situations' CEDAW/C/GC/30, especially para. 9 (hereafter CEDAW Committee General Recommendation no. 30).
[60] Beijing Declaration and Platform for Action (n. 26), Strategic Objective E.1.

The levels of widespread and systematic sexual violence against women in the conflicts arising out of the break-up of the former Yugoslavia (1992–95) had highlighted the issue, as did the sexual violence that was integral to the genocide in Rwanda in 1994. The failure to take account of the Beijing Platform's recommendation with respect to the participation of women in peace processes in the negotiations at Dayton in 1995 spurred further attention to women and armed conflict. This time women's groups directed their activism towards the UN body responsible for the maintenance of international peace and security—the Security Council—rather than the human rights system, thereby targeting the most powerful mainstream institution within the UN. The adoption of Security Council Resolution 1325[61] in October 2000 launched what has become known as the 'Women, Peace and Security' (WPS) agenda, and, since that time, the Council has become an important forum for the development of normative standards with respect to women in armed conflict.

Resolution 1325 drew attention, first, to women's participation in peace processes and, second, to the inclusion of a 'gender perspective'[62] 'in all efforts for the maintenance and promotion of peace and security'.[63] The first aspect urged greater participation and representation of women in all stages of conflict prevention, management, and resolution. The second defined a gender perspective as taking account of the 'special needs of women and girls' in post-conflict processes and state-building. The Resolution also called for compliance with existing international humanitarian and human rights law and for the protection of women and girls 'from gender-based violence, particularly rape and other forms of sexual abuse' and an end to impunity by prosecuting genocide, war crimes, and crimes against humanity, including sexual violence.

Security Council Resolution 1325 was the first time that the Council had formally considered an issue relating specifically to women, and it set a new standard for the Security Council, UN member states and the United Nations system as a whole.[64] It has been followed by seven further resolutions,[65] which have inconsistently elaborated the terms of Resolution 1325.[66] Taken together, the eight resolutions formulate the four themes or 'pillars' of WPS: women's participation and representation in the resolution of conflict, in pertinent decision-making, in peace operations and in key positions; protection of women from

---

[61] SC Res. 1325, S/RES/1325 (31 October 2000) (hereafter SC Res. 1325).
[62] Ibid, preamble para. 8.
[63] Ibid, preamble para. 5.
[64] Natalie Hudson, *Gender, Human Security and the United Nations: Security Language as a Political Framework for Women* (Routledge 2009) 44.
[65] SC Res. 1820, S/RES/1820 (19 June 2008) (hereafter SC Res. 1820); SC Res. 1888, S/RES/1888 (30 September 2009) (hereafter SC Res. 1888); SC Res. 1889, S/RES/1889 (5 October 2009); SC Res. 1960, S/RES/1960 (16 December 2010); SC Res. 2106, S/RES/2106 (24 June 2013) (hereafter SC Res. 2106); SC Res. 2122, S/RES/2122 (18 October 2013) (hereafter SC Res. 2122); SC Res. 2242, S/RES/2242 (13 October 2015) (hereafter SC Res. 2242).
[66] See Paul Kirby and Laura Shepherd, 'Reintroducing Women, Peace and Security' (2016) 92 *International Affairs* 249.

conflict-related violence, especially sexual violence; prevention of sexual and gender-based violence in armed conflict and, although somewhat more ambiguously, of conflict itself; and relief and recovery. Responding to incidents of sexual exploitation by peacekeepers, the Security Council has also instituted a 'zero tolerance' policy of sexual exploitation and abuse in all UN peacekeeping operations.[67] Despite the claim that the WPS agenda is a human rights project,[68] the WPS resolutions make minimal use of human rights concepts. For example, Resolution 2122 (2013) categorizes medical, legal, psychosocial, and livelihood matters in the language of 'services', rather than as women's entitlements to economic and social rights.

The Security Council uses the notion of gender in an indiscriminate manner in the WPS agenda. For instance, in Resolution 1325 alone we find the terms 'gender perspective', 'gender component', 'gender-sensitive training', 'gender-based violence', 'gender considerations', 'gender dimensions of peace processes', and 'gender mainstreaming'. Unlike the CEDAW Committee,[69] the Security Council offers no explanation of the idea of gender but apparently equates 'gender' with women. Indeed, men are only mentioned in Resolution 1325 in the context of disarmament where 'all those involved' were encouraged 'to consider the different needs of female and male ex-combatants'. Men are implicitly portrayed as perpetrators of sexual violence, or as protecting women against other men's commission of such crimes. In later resolutions men appear 'as partners in promoting women's participation in the prevention and resolution of armed conflict',[70] but in only two resolutions is the phenomenon of sexual violence against men and boys recognized.[71] The Council here displays no understanding of the relational aspect of gender[72] or indeed of any theory of gender.[73]

---

[67] 'Letter Dated 24 March 2005 from the Secretary-General to the President of the General Assembly' A/59/710 (24 March 2005). The policy of zero tolerance was reaffirmed in SC Res. 1820 (n. 65); SC Res. 1888 (n. 65); SC Res. 1960, S/RES/1960 (16 December 2010); SC Res. 2106 (n. 65); SC Res. 2242 (n. 65); SC Res. 2272, S/RES/1325 (11 March 2016).

[68] 'It must not be forgotten that resolution 1325 was conceived of and lobbied for as a human rights resolution that would promote the rights of women in conflict situations', see United Nations Entity for Gender Equality and the Empowerment of Women (UN Women), *Preventing Conflict, Transforming Justice, Securing the Peace: A Global Study on the Implementation of Security Council Resolution 1325* (UN Women 2015) 15 <http://wps.unwomen.org/pdf/en/GlobalStudy_EN_Web.pdf> accessed 31 January 2019 (hereafter UN Women, *Global Study*).

[69] CEDAW Committee General Recommendation no. 28 (n. 22) para. 5.

[70] SC Res. 2242 (n. 65) preamble.

[71] SC Res. 2106 (n. 65) preamble: 'Noting with concern that sexual violence in armed conflict and post-conflict situations disproportionately affects women and girls, ... while also affecting men and boys'.

[72] The CEDAW Committee has explained this relational aspect: 'The term "gender" refers to socially constructed identities, attributes and roles for women and men and society's social and cultural meaning for these biological differences resulting in hierarchical relationships between women and men and in the distribution of power and rights favouring men and disadvantaging women', see CEDAW Committee General Recommendation no. 28 (n. 22) para. 5.

[73] Joan Scott, 'Gender: A Useful Category of Historical Analysis' (1986) 91 American Historical Review 1053.

The WPS resolutions have prompted considerable institutional activity, including training programmes and a plethora of policies, action plans, and guidelines.[74] Many UN member states have adopted national action plans on the implementation of resolution 1325.[75] In addition, the CEDAW Committee has asserted the continued application of the Convention in armed conflict[76] and that the Security Council's WPS agenda must be read and implemented in the framework of the CEDAW and its Optional Protocol.[77] The Security Council references the Convention throughout the WPS resolution but does not engage with its provisions.[78]

Within the practice of the Security Council, the WPS agenda remains compartmentalized and on the margins of the Council' work. While Resolution 2242 (2015) expressed the Council's intention to incorporate WPS more systematically in its work and its decision 'to integrate women, peace and security concerns' in its country-specific situations,[79] this has yet to materialize. More generally, the promise of the WPS agenda is not matched by political will for implementation. In 2015 a Global Study on Resolution 1325 stated that '[t]hough there is a great deal of rhetoric supporting women, peace and security, funding for programmes and processes remains abysmally low across all areas of the agenda'.[80]

The WPS agenda is also limited in its conceptual scope. First, many of the WPS resolutions present the major harm for women caught up in conflict as sexual violence. Concentration on women as victims of crimes of sexual violence obscures the many other ways in which women experience armed conflict, such as the disappearance of male family members, displacement, and the destruction of property and food sources for women who are the primary carers within family and community. While some language refers to the 'full range of threats and human rights violations and abuses'[81] that women face in armed conflict, it does not provide any detail of the locations, manifestations, and consequences of such abuses. This contrasts with the human rights approach of the CEDAW Committee in its General Recommendation no. 30. The focus on sexual violence also assumes that women are innately vulnerable,[82] rather than—as is recognized by General Recommendation no. 30—made vulnerable

---

[74] UN Security Council, 'Women and Peace and Security: Report of the Secretary-General' S/2010/498 (28 September 2010) para. 122.

[75] As of November 2018 there were seventy-nine national action plans, see PeaceWomen, 'Member States' (November 2018) <http://www.peacewomen.org/member-states> accessed 31 January 2019.

[76] CEDAW Committee General Recommendation no. 30 (n. 59) para. 26.

[77] For a comparison between the Security Council WPS agenda and CEDAW Committee General Recommendation no. 30, see Hilary Charlesworth and Christine Chinkin, 'An Alien's Review of Women and Armed Conflict' in Dale Stephens and Paul Babie (eds), *Imagining Law: Essays in Conversation with Judith Gardam* (University of Adelaide Press 2016) 171.

[78] The United States has been a leading proponent of the WPS agenda but is not a party to the Convention.

[79] SC Res. 2242 (n. 65) para. 5.

[80] UN Women, *Global Study* (n. 68) 14.

[81] See, e.g., SC Res. 2122 (n. 65).

[82] See, e.g., SC Res. 2122 (n. 65) preamble, paras 6 and 7.

by circumstances such as economic hardship and structural disadvantage. The assumption of vulnerability is exacerbated by references to the omnibus category of 'women-and-children'.

Emphasis on sexual violence against women also obscures men's experience of such violence in conflict. This is an aspect of the role that gender plays in violence during conflict, which depends on particular constructions of femininity and masculinity.[83] There is comparatively little research and information on sexual and gender-based violence against men and boys, a gap that has been emphasized in recent discussions of conflict-related violence.[84]

Other manifestations of women's assumed victimhood include that women can never freely consent to sexual relationships with particular categories of people in periods of conflict and post-conflict. The projection of women as vulnerable rather than as active agents is illustrated in the UN Secretary-General's policy of 'zero tolerance' towards sexual relationships between UN peacekeepers and local people in conflict situations.[85] Dianne Otto has argued that this policy gives insufficient attention to 'the grinding poverty or the poorly resourced charity-based models of aid that produce economies of survival sex', diverting attention from the politics of social justice in order to 'save the UN's humanitarianism from scandal. It makes the survival of the "victims" it claims to protect even more precarious'.[86]

A second limit of the WPS agenda is its instrumentalization of women. The agenda urges increased participation and representation of women in policy and decision-making in all phases of armed conflict, redressing to some extent the image of women solely as victims. It offers no rationale but appears to be based on the pervasive view that women are simply 'good at peace'.[87] UN documentation now points to evidence of the greater durability of peace agreements when women have been involved in their negotiation.[88] Women's participation is thus not promoted as an issue of equality, but rather as in the service of international peace

---

[83] Sandesh Sivakumaran, 'Sexual Violence against Men in Armed Conflict' (2007) 18 European Journal of International Law 253; Chloe Lewis, 'Systematic Silencing: Addressing Sexual Violence against Men and Boys in Armed Conflict and its Aftermath' in Gina Heathcote and Dianne Otto (eds), *Rethinking Peacekeeping, Gender Equality and Collective Security* (Palgrave 2014) 203.

[84] See, e.g., the UK Preventing Sexual Violence Initiative: G8 United Kingdom 2013, 'Declaration on Preventing Sexual Violence in Conflict' (UK Foreign and Commonwealth Office, 11 April 2013) <https://www.gov.uk/government/uploads/system/uploads/attachment_data/file/185008/G8_PSVI_Declaration_-_FINAL.pdf> accessed 31 January 2019. Then UN Special Representative for Sexual Violence in Conflict (Zainab Hawa Bangura) also called for better information on sexual violence against boys and men, see, e.g., the Annual Report for 2012 of the Secretary-General, 'Sexual Violence in Conflict' A/67/792-S/2013/149 (14 March 2013) para. 10.

[85] UN Secretariat, 'Special Measures for Protection from Sexual Exploitation and Sexual Abuse' ST/SGB/2003/13 (9 October 2003).

[86] Dianne Otto, 'Making Sense of Zero Tolerance Policies in Peacekeeping Sexual Economies' in Vanessa E Munro and Carl F Stychin (eds), *Sexuality and the Law: Feminist Engagements* (GlassHouse Press 2007) 259.

[87] Hilary Charlesworth, 'Are Women Peaceful? Reflections on the Role of Women in Peace-Building' (2008) 16 Feminist Legal Studies 347.

[88] UN Women, *Global Study* (n. 68) 41–4.

and security.[89] Further, the WPS agenda addresses conflict and immediate post-conflict periods, but does not look beyond this. For example, it does not engage with the evidence that women frequently lose the foothold in the public sphere that they have acquired during times of conflict once a level of stability returns.

Third, the promise of security contained in the rubric of 'women, peace, and security' is limited by the Security Council's traditional understanding of security which centres on state security rather than human security. The Global Study and Security Council WPS Resolutions 2242 (2015) and 2467 (2019) acknowledge contemporary security challenges, especially those of violent extremism and terrorism. For most women, however, these are not their major security concerns, which remain situations such as poverty, violence, and displacement.

A fourth, and related, limit is the co-option of the WPS agenda into the Security Council's security agenda, in particular its linkage with the 'Countering Violent Extremism' agenda. This is made explicit in Resolution 2242, which calls for:

> the greater integration by Member States and the United Nations of their agendas on women, peace and security, counter-terrorism and countering-violent extremism which can be conducive to terrorism, requests the Counter-Terrorism Committee (CTC) and the Counter-Terrorism Committee Executive Directorate (CTED) to integrate gender as a cross-cutting issue throughout the activities within their respective mandates, including within country specific assessments and reports, recommendations made to Member States, facilitating technical assistance to Member States, and briefings to the Council, encourages the CTC and CTED to hold further consultations with women and women's organizations to help inform their work, and further encourages the Counter-Terrorism Implementation Task Force (CTITF) to take the same approach in activities within its mandate.

While this integration gives WPS greater political prominence, the price for this is potential submersion of the WPS agenda when state security interests are deemed to be at stake.[90]

The political nature of the WPS agenda thus constrains its scope conceptually. Although women have gained access to what appears as the heartland of

---

[89] See, e.g., the Concept Note prepared by Italy and the United Kingdom for a UN Security Council Open Arria Meeting on Women, Peace and Security and Mediation: Permanent Mission of Italy to the UN and United Kingdom Mission to the UN, 'United Nations Security Council Open Arria Meeting on Women, Peace and Security and Mediation "Increasing the Participation of Women in Global Conflict Prevention and Mediation: Towards the Creation of a Mediterranean Women Mediators Network": Concept Note' (27 March 2017) <http://www.peacewomen.org/sites/default/files/March 27 Arria Meeting WPS and Mediation - Concept Note.pdf> accessed 31 January 2019; see also Report of the Secretary-General, 'Special Measures for Protection from Sexual Exploitation and Abuse: A New Approach' A/71/818 (28 February 2017) para. 24.
[90] See Dianne Otto, 'The Exile of Inclusion: Reflections on Gender Issues in International Law over the Last Decade' (2009) 10 Melbourne Journal of International Law 11.

international institutional power, they have been quickly relegated to its margins: the inclusion of women is justified either as furthering some other objective of the Council, or on the basis of women's 'special needs'. Indeed, the WPS agenda has bestowed considerable legitimacy on the Security Council by offering a veneer of attention to the human rights of half the world's population. The Security Council pays little attention however to the diversity of women: they are either victims, handmaidens of peace, or potential participants in UN peace operations. Women have thus been brought into the Security Council on the institution's terms, which do not offer any consideration of what might constitute security for women. For instance, the WPS resolutions do not address structural inequalities or drivers of violence such as the arms trade[91] or, more generally, militarism. The WPS resolutions accept military action as the ultimate protection for women in conflict and indeed promote the inclusion of greater numbers of women in UN military and police contingents.[92]

IV. CONCLUSION

In this chapter we have described the diversification of international regimes for the protection of women's human rights and the shuttling between various margins and mainstreams. There appears to be an unruly array of agendas for women's rights, implicating many different types of legal standards, instruments, and institutions. Specialist regimes promote focused attention to women's lives, but allow the mainstream to proceed undisturbed: human rights remain men's rights and women's rights become issues of development[93] or 'special cases' in light of women's 'special needs'. When women's human rights are mainstreamed, as in the WPS agenda, they quickly lose their bite. This can occur through their focus on only fragments of women's lives and experiences, or by being co-opted into serving other political agendas, or simply by being ignored or overlooked. Despite all the activity, there is little attention given to the structural causes of human rights abuses against women. The movement between the areas of human rights and WPS shows that the locations of both margins and mainstream are fluid, changing, and

---

[91] SC Res. 2106 (n. 65) and SC Res. 2122 (n. 65) make preambular reference to the Arms Trade Treaty (adopted 3 June 2013, entered into force 24 December 2014) Article 7(4), which relates to exporting states taking into account the risk of arms being used to facilitate gender-based violence. SC Res. 2122 (n. 65) also noted the contribution the treaty can make to reducing conflict-related violence. The treaty addresses illegal arms trading but does not curtail legal trading.
[92] See, e.g., SC Res. 2122 (n. 65) para. 9.
[93] This is exemplified through the inclusion of gender equality as goal number five of the Sustainable Development Goals, see United Nations, 'Sustainable Development Goal 5: Achieve Gender Equality and Empower All Women and Girls' <http://www.un.org/sustainabledevelopment/gender-equality/> accessed 31 January 2019.

contingent. Indeed, there are locations at which margins and mainstream meet, merge, and separate again.

The oscillation between the margins and the mainstream is echoed in debates in the feminist international legal literature about whether feminist scholars should aim for the margins or the centre of the discipline. The margin is often understood as the place we want to leave behind as we head for the centre, the mainstream, where, it is assumed, power resides and all the action takes place. However, the periphery also has its pleasures and virtues. It can be an attractive vantage point, offering a sense of adventure, of originality, of solidarity with the (often vaguely defined) oppressed against those with power.

Feminist scholarship pays attention to the locations of power within a society. Power is often dispersed and is not always concentrated in a centre. Patriarchal power exists at the level of the state, but it also shapes local communities and family relationships. Power is thus best understood as a network, operating in complex and inconsistent ways.[94] For this reason, although international women's groups have long campaigned for enhanced legal regulation,[95] one might conclude that international law will always be an imperfect tool to unravel patriarchal power and will be most effective when it is woven with other forms of regulation and influence.

Bibliography

Baetens F, 'International Congress of Women (1915)' in Wolfrum R (ed.), *Max Planck Encyclopedia of Public International Law* (Oxford University Press 2010) 455

Charlesworth H, 'Are Women Peaceful? Reflections on the Role of Women in Peace-Building' (2008) 16 Feminist Legal Studies 347

Charlesworth H and Chinkin C, 'The New United Nations "Gender Architecture": A Room with a View?' (2013) 17 Max Planck Yearbook of United Nations Law 1

Charlesworth H and Chinkin C, 'An Alien's Review of Women and Armed Conflict' in Stephens S and Babie P (eds), *Imagining Law: Essays in Conversation with Judith Gardam* (University of Adelaide Press 2016) 171

Chinkin C, 'Gender and Economic, Social, and Cultural Rights' in Riedel E, Giacca G, and Golay C (eds), *Economic, Social and Cultural Rights in International Law: Contemporary Issues and Challenges* (Oxford University Press 2014) 134

Connors J, 'Article 28: Reservations' in Freeman MA, Chinkin C, and Rudolf B (eds), *The UN Convention on the Elimination of All Forms of Discrimination against Women: A Commentary* (Oxford University Press 2012) 565

Edwards A, 'Displacement, Statelessness and Questions of Gender Equality and the Convention on the Elimination of All Forms of Discrimination against Women' (2009)

---

[94] Sneja Gunew, 'Feminist Knowledge: Critique and Construct' in Sneja Gunew (ed.), *Feminist Knowledge: Critique and Construct* (Routledge 1990) 13, 23.

[95] An example is the current campaign for a global treaty on violence against women. See Report of the Special Rapporteur on violence against women, its causes and consequences (Rashida Manjoo), 'Twenty years of developments within the United Nations and a reflection on the continuing challenges' A/HRC/26/38 (1 April 2014) para. 69.

United Nations High Commissioner for Refugees Background Paper 2009/02 <https://www2.ohchr.org/english/bodies/cedaw/docs/unhcr_cedaw_background_paper4.pdf> accessed 31 January 2019

Fraser A, 'Becoming Human: The Origins and Development of Women's Human Rights' (1999) 21 Human Rights Quarterly 853

Gallagher A, 'Ending the Marginalization: Strategies for Incorporating Women into the United Nations Human Rights System' (1997) 19 Human Rights Quarterly 283

Ghodsee K, 'Revisiting the United Nations Decade for Women: Brief Reflections on Feminism, Capitalism and Cold War Politics in the Early Years of the International Women's Movement' (2010) 33 Women's Studies International Forum 3

Gunew S, 'Feminist Knowledge: Critique and Construct' in Gunew S (ed.), *Feminist Knowledge: Critique and Construct* (Routledge 1990) 13

Hudson N, *Gender, Human Security and the United Nations: Security Language as a Political Framework for Women* (Routledge 2009)

Kirby P and Shepherd L, 'Reintroducing Women, Peace and Security' (2016) 92 International Affairs 249

Kouvo S, 'The United Nations and Gender Mainstreaming: Limits and Possibilities' in Buss D and Manji A (eds), *International Law: Modern Feminist Approaches* (Hart Publishing 2005) 237

Lewis C, 'Systematic Silencing: Addressing Sexual Violence against Men and Boys in Armed Conflict and its Aftermath' in Heathcote G and Otto D (eds), *Rethinking Peacekeeping, Gender Equality and Collective Security* (Palgrave 2014) 203

Otto D, 'Lesbians? Not in My Country. Sexual Orientation at the Beijing World Conference on Women' (1995) 20 Alternative Law Journal 288

Otto D, 'Making Sense of Zero Tolerance Policies in Peacekeeping Sexual Economies' in Munro VE and Stychin CF (eds), *Sexuality and the Law: Feminist Engagements* (GlassHouse Press 2007) 259

Otto D, 'The Exile of Inclusion: Reflections on Gender Issues in International Law over the Last Decade' (2009) 10 Melbourne Journal of International Law 11

Pietilä H, *The Unfinished Story of Women and the United Nations* (United Nations Non-Governmental Liaison Service 2007)

Scott J, 'Gender: A Useful Category of Historical Analysis' (1986) 91 American Historical Review 1053

Sivakumaran S, 'Sexual Violence against Men in Armed Conflict' (2007) 18 European Journal of International Law 253

Stoeckl K, *The Russian Orthodox Church and Human Rights* (Routledge 2014)

14
Women's Rights are Human Rights
A Response to Hilary Charlesworth and Christine Chinkin from a Chinese Perspective

Bai Guimei

I. INTRODUCTION

Eve n before the Vienna Declaration and Platform for Action was adopted in 1993, feminist international law scholars, human rights non-governmental organizations (NGOs) and advocates have been struggling for the recognition and implementation of the maxim 'Women's rights are human rights' at the international and domestic level. It is a struggle to bring the marginalized issue of women's rights to the mainstream of human rights. It is in fact the continuation of the women's movement which started over a century ago. At that time, the goal was that women were not regarded as property anymore but as human beings, not anymore as objects but as subjects of rights. Today, we are fighting for changing the issue of women's rights to one of human rights, that is, we are striving for a move from the margins to the mainstream. The rationale is very simple: women are human, thus women's rights should not be marginalized as a special issue but should be part of the mainstream of human rights. It is a long march. Unfortunately, we are at times lingering in-between and moving from one extreme to the another. Why is this so? Why is this task so difficult that it takes generations or maybe our lifetime to fight for it? One reason are the conflicting approaches. Specialists and generalists have different ideas about which approach is better for the protection of women's rights. Ultimately, as Professors Charlesworth and Chinkin discuss in their chapter, the reasons are complex. The primary cause, as they see it, is 'the structural bases of women's disadvantage'. However, the breeding ground for women's disadvantageous structural bases is not the same in different societies. They can be political, religious, cultural, or something entirely different. Therefore, as stated in the conclusion to this chapter, the solutions cannot and must not be the same. As Professors Charlesworth and Chinkin note: '[I]nternational law will always be an imperfect tool to unravel patriarchal power and will be most effective when it is woven with other forms of regulation and influence.'[1] Actually no tool will be perfect when it is used without auxiliary means. This commentary note focuses on three points: the margin and mainstream discourse, the specialist and generalist approaches, and the family value debate.

II. THE MARGIN AND MAINSTREAM DISCOURSE

What are the margin and the mainstream? Models of a patriarchal or a matriarchal society cannot give us any references since our goal is not to return to a matrilineal society (as in China before 2000 BC) but ideally achieve an equal one, where men and women have substantially equal rights and where the maxims are 'women's rights are human rights' and vice versa 'men's rights are human rights'. The ideal 'panarchical' or 'polyarchical' society we are now struggling for is the one where there is no distinction between the margin and the mainstream or, to put it in terms of gender, where the distinction between men and women is meaningless. It will, however, take a long time to reach this goal and we will undoubtedly feel hopeless at times.

Coming back from the utopian ideal to the real society, no one will deny that our society has margins and mainstreams and that patriarchal power is still generally occupying the mainstream. It took a long time for women to become not the objects but the subjects of rights. Women had not been even in the discourse of margin and mainstream until the international human rights movement made great strides in the United Nations (UN), marked by the coming into force of the core human rights conventions in the mid-1970s. The feminist movements proposed the now famous slogan that 'women's rights are human rights' and fought to bring the marginalized women's 'issue' to the human rights mainstream.

This slogan was generally welcomed and recognized in the human rights field. China is, however, a special case. The concept of human rights remains politically sensitive. Here, tellingly the rights of women are (still) better protected under the banner 'women's rights' than they would be under the banner of 'human rights'. Put another way, feminist activities, either academic or practical, are 'safer' being labelled as a women's issue than as human rights. Ultimately, because human rights are no more likely to be in the mainstream than women's rights in China, the slogan that women's rights are human rights cannot be popular. Thus Chinese women's rights remain outside the margin and mainstream discourse of human rights, and this might be to their advantage.

---

[1] Hilary Charlesworth and Christine Chinkin, 'Between the Margins and the Mainstream: The Case of Women's Rights' in Bardo Fassbender and Knut Traisbach (eds), *The Limits of Human Rights* (Oxford University Press 2019) 205, 220.

III. THE SPECIALIST AND GENERALIST APPROACHES

In the first place, the discourses about margin and mainstream on the one hand and specialist and generalist on the other are not the same. The former addresses broadly the location and role of gender in society; the latter addresses different approaches, institutions, and regimes for the protection of women's rights. Nevertheless, the two are interrelated. For example, specialist institutions can be criticized for marginalizing women's rights; and generalist institutions do not always want to be equated with the mainstream. While the two discourses have the same goal, namely, to protect women's rights, the particular goals and methods of the participants in the discourses differ. For example, some 'specialists' support affirmative action in order to realize substantive equality, others do not; some generalists focus on mainstream activities or neutral concepts, but not all do. However, because the different discourses share the same goal, they should not stand in conflict with each other but should instead complement each other. They should exist side by side and play a shared role, as exemplified by the co-operation between the specialized Committee on the Elimination of Discrimination Against Women (CEDAW) and more general UN human rights bodies, such as the Human Rights Committee, the Committee on Economic, Social and Cultural Rights, or the UN Human Rights Council. Other special institutions for women are as important as CEDAW, such as UN Women, the Special Rapporteur on violence against women, its causes and consequences, and the Working Group on the issue of discrimination against women in law and in practice. These special institutions for women should not be regarded as 'marginal' because they are operating *in the centre* of the UN, even if their members are mostly women. CEDAW, the convention they try to implement, is one of the core human rights conventions. In short, the relation between specialist–generalist or margin–mainstream approaches can be complementary to each other and specialized institutions are not, at least regarding their purposes, automatically marginalized.

IV. THE FAMILY VALUES DEBATE

The resistance of conservative movements against women's equality has never stopped. In China, even traffic jam problems have been blamed on women's equal opportunity to work. The logic is as follows: If women went back to the family and took care of children, the traffic problem would be easily resolved since the number of employees commuting to work would be reduced to almost half. Also children would not have to go to day care which means parents would not have to take them to and from kindergartens.[2] In 2011, a member of the Chinese People's Political Consultative Conference (CPPCC) advanced a proposal that women should leave paid employment and go back to the family.[3] Similar proposals have been made by other members of CPPCC in the past decades.[4] Since China started the process of changing from a system of state planning to a market economy in the 1980s, the number of these kind of debates has quadrupled.[5] It is not entirely clear whether recent debates in China are also related to the UN family value debate but in her proposal, Zhang Xiaomei did blame gender equality and the lack of femininity, motherhood, and female literacy. She regarded these as constituting a serious new social problem and related them to a fear of men, an increase in homosexuality, shortage of child care, insufficient children's education, an increasing rate of juvenile delinquency, lack of geriatric care, a continuous increase in the divorce rate, and a serious imbalance of social structure etc. She said all these problems were closely related to the increasing lack of feminine sensibility and family values as well as the absence of family care.[6] Was that by coincidence a positive response to the UN family values debate? It should come as a surprise that China was in favour of the resolution promoted by Russia. In fact, several Chinese human rights and constitutional law scholars, philosophers, and historians have addressed the relation between human rights and traditional values and the question of whether there exists a human rights concept in Chinese traditional values.[7] However, most of these scholars consider that the notion of human rights does not stand in absolute conflict with Chinese traditional thinking whilst also asserting that those decadent feudalistic ideas are serious obstacles to the realization of human rights. The UN family values debate

---

[2] For this reason some complain, e.g., that female doctoral candidates are wasting public resources because they are supposed to marry and raise children according to Chinese traditional thinking.

[3] The draft proposal was published on her blog: Zhang Xiaomei, 'Women's Proposal: Encouraging Some Women to Return to the Family is the Basic Guarantee of China's Happiness' (Personal Blog, 8 March 2011) <http://blog.sina.com.cn/s/blog_47768d4101017xsd.html> accessed 31 January 2019 (hereafter Zhang, 'Women's Proposal').

[4] For example, another CPPCC member suggested a sabbatical from employment for all mothers, which meant that female employees would stay home after giving birth to a child. Once the child went to kindergarten or school, the mother would be allowed to go back to work.

[5] The first debate took place at the end of 1980s on working or staying home; the second debate happened in the mid-1990s and was about reducing the rate of female employment in order to solve the unemployment problem; the third debate was triggered by a proposal made by Wang Xiancai, a member of the CPPCC, in 2001 on women taking employment breaks; the fourth debate was in 2011 when Zhang Xiaomei, a member of the CPPCC, published her proposal on her blog that some middle class female employees should leave paid employment and return to the home.

[6] She argued that some women should return to the home in order to increase the overall happiness index of the family and society as a whole, see Zhang, 'Women's Proposal' (n. 3).

[7] See, e.g., Xia Yong, *The Origin of the Human Rights Idea* (2nd edn, China University of Political Science and Law Press 2001); Liang Tao (ed.), *Virtues and Rights: On Confucianism and Human Rights from Cross-Cultural Perspectives* (China Social Sciences Press 2016); Deng Xiaojun, 'Confucianism and Taoism: Stand by the Side of Human Rights—The Consistency between Confucianism, Taoism and Human Rights' (12 November 2016) <http://www.sohu.com/a/118787374_523132> accessed 31 January 2019 (all titles translated from the Chinese original).

is running in the same spirit as the debates in China triggered by economic reforms or proposals on women returning to the home.[8] These are all based on stereotypes about the social role of women and men and about their respective roles within 'the family'. Therefore, the problem is not that the UN Human Rights Council emphasizes family or traditional values but persisting stereotypes about gender roles. The problem remains the private–public dichotomy, the attachment of women to the family, and 'the structural bases of women's disadvantage'. The ultimate strategy to solve this problem is to implement Article 5 of CEDAW. I will return to this point later.

V. WOMEN IN ARMED CONFLICTS: THE SECURITY COUNCIL RESOLUTION 1325

It is not surprising that human rights language is hardly used in Security Council Resolution 1325 (hereafter the Resolution) and that 'gender' basically equates to women. The Resolution contains little human rights language because, first, it is based foremost on international humanitarian law (IHL) and not on human rights law. Secondly, only when the issue of human rights is closely related to peace and security can it be part of the agenda of the Security Council. The word gender is equated with women because gender equality is commonly associated with issues of discrimination against women. In armed conflict, women and children are protected by others (mostly men) not vice versa. Interestingly, in the Chinese version of the Resolution the formulation 男女平等 (Nánnǚ Píngděng) is used for gender equality, meaning equality between men and women.[9] Thus, in the Chinese version of the Resolution the actual Chinese word for gender 社会性别 (Shèhuì Xìngbié) cannot be found.

Professors Charlesworth's and Chinkin's trenchant critiques of the UN WPS agenda relate to the following four points: first, its focus on sexual violence against women rather than other consequences of armed conflicts, such as disappearance of family members or destruction of family property; second, its instrumentalization of women; third, its traditional focus on UN member state security rather than human security; fourth, its potential submersion when state security interests are

---

[8] See a proposal of Yuan Ailing, a female university professor from South China Normal University, published by *China Youth Daily*. She suggested that maternity leave should be extended from six months to one year because ideally, women should bring up their children themselves. At the same time she recommended that more nurseries for children aged between birth and three should be established and regulated by the state (most Chinese kindergartens are open only to children of three years and upwards). See Lin Jie, 'Yuan Ailing, Professor of the South China Normal University College of Education: "It is recommended that women have a one-year maternity leave"' China Youth Daily online (Beijing, 24 August 2018) <http://zqb.cyol.com/html/2018-08/24/nw.D110000zgqnb_20180824_2-08.htm> accessed 31 January 2019.

[9] In Chinese, the word gender is translated to 社会性别 (Shèhuì Xìngbié) which means 'social sex'. It is not known why Shèhuì Xìngbié is not used in the Chinese version of the Resolution.

at stake. I think these critiques are very much to the point. All the limits of women's human rights are ultimately grounded upon prejudices, practices, and stereotyped roles of women and men which Article 5 CEDAW aims to eliminate.

VI. ARTICLE 5 OF CEDAW AND ITS IMPLEMENTATION

The importance of Article 5 of CEDAW cannot be overemphasized. However, as Simone Cusack indicated, this powerful legal framework for addressing gender stereotyping has been left largely unexplored.[10] The obligations it imposes on states parties are abstract and vague. The key stipulations are not defined, such as 'social and cultural patterns of conduct', 'stereotypes', 'inferiority', 'superiority', etc. It is difficult to alter or eliminate them. The toughest task is of course to change people's stereotyped thinking about the roles of both women and men in the family and society. The family values debate at the UN is a stark reminder that the most important task is to change decision-makers' mistaken gender stereotypes. If decision-makers believe, like the drafters of the Russian proposal for the family values resolution, that the movement for women's equality is the cause of multiple social problems, it remains unlikely that these state parties of CEDAW will implement Article 5. The same applies to the members of the CPPCC and their proposals to return mothers to the home and family. A fundamental task, indeed one that is crucial for generations to come, is to change people's minds, particularly the minds of male and female decision-makers, as well as educators working in schools. However, there are too many wrongful stereotypes, as Simone Cusack calls them, to eliminate simultaneously. Expressions like 'men go and women stay', 'good wives and good mothers', or 'assisting the husband and bringing up children' exemplify these stereotypes which tie women to the family. These stereotypes should be addressed first because they are the deeper causes of almost all discrimination against women. In China, the common standard for evaluating a successful woman remains the ability 'to present with graceful manners in the living room along with culinary skills in the kitchen'.

This is why Article 5(b) of CEDAW stipulates that family education should include 'a proper understanding of maternity as a social function and the recognition of the common responsibility of men and women in the upbringing and development of their children'. The problem is how to achieve this. Article 5 leaves to the state parties the choice of what measures to take to modify or eliminate those wrongful stereotypes. I agree that legislative and administrative measures are

---

[10] See Simone Cusack, 'The CEDAW as a Legal Framework for Transnational Discourses on Gender Stereotyping' in Anne Hellum and Henriette Sinding Aasen (eds), *Women's Human Rights: CEDAW in International, Regional and National Law* (Cambridge University Press 2013) 124, 125.

crucial and should be taken immediately. Yet measures in other fields are just as important, such as those in education and in mass media.

VII. CONCLUDING REMARKS

Stereotypes about women and their role in the family and society are hard to change. Especially if they are held by political decision-makers or if they are institutionalized, stereotypes tend to persist. It is thus crucial for we feminists to promote the implementation of Article 5 CEDAW both internationally and domestically. Internationally, UN institutions such as UN Women, UNESCO, UNICEF, and the UN Human Rights Council are important fora. At the national level, governments, national human rights institutions, the workplace, schools, but also civil society composed of individual women and men, are central to achieving change. It is a difficult and ongoing task which requires us to be passionate, persistent, and patient. We must not give up our goal—which is not to take over patriarchal power at all levels, and certainly not a return to a matrilineal society—but rather, to build an equal community without wrongful stereotypes about either women or men.

Bibliography

Charlesworth H and Chinkin C, 'Between the Margins and the Mainstream: The Case of Women's Rights' in Fassbender B and Traisbach K (eds), *The Limits of Human Rights* (Oxford University Press 2019) 205

Cusack S, 'The CEDAW as a Legal Framework for Transnational Discourses on Gender Stereotyping' in Hellum A and Sinding Aasen H (eds), *Women's Human Rights: CEDAW in International, Regional and National Law* (Cambridge University Press 2013) 124

Deng X, 'Confucianism and Taoism: Stand by the Side of Human Rights—The Consistency between Confucianism, Taoism and Human Rights' (12 November 2016) <http://www.sohu.com/a/118787374_523132> accessed 31 January 2019

Liang T (ed.), *Virtues and Rights: On Confucianism and Human Rights from Cross-Cultural Perspectives* (China Social Sciences Press 2016)

Lin J, 'Yuan Ailing, Professor of the South China Normal University College of Education: "It is recommended that women have a one-year maternity leave"' China Youth Daily online (Beijing, 24 August 2018) <http://zqb.cyol.com/html/2018-08/24/nw.D110000zgqnb_20180824_2-08.htm> accessed 31 January 2019

Xia Y, *The Origin of the Human Rights Idea* (2nd edn, China University of Political Science and Law Press 2001)

Zhang X, 'Women's Proposal: Encouraging Some Women to Return to the Family is the Basic Guarantee of China's Happiness' (Personal Blog, 8 March 2011) <http://blog.sina.com.cn/s/blog_47768d4101017xsd.html> accessed 31 January 2019

15
Women's Progress and Women's Human Rights*

Martha C. Nussbaum**

Now let's be clear, this problem is bigger than football. There has been, appropriately so, intense and widespread outrage following the release of the video showing what happened inside the elevator at the casino. But wouldn't it be productive if this collective outrage, as my colleagues have said, could be channeled to truly hear and address the long-suffering cries for help by so many women? And as they said, do something about it? Like an on-going education of men about what healthy, respectful manhood is all about.

Consider this: According to domestic violence experts, more than three women per day lose their lives at the hands of their partners. That means that since the night of February 15th in Atlantic City [when the elevator incident occurred] more than 600 women have died.

James Brown, CBS Sports, Thursday, 11 September 2014[1]

---

* Martha C. Nussbaum, 'Women's Progress and Women's Human Rights' (2016) 38 Human Rights Quarterly 589–622 © 2016 Johns Hopkins University Press. Reprinted with permission of Johns Hopkins University Press. References to internet sources have been updated where possible. Since the composition of this article in 2014, Professor Nussbaum has developed and revised her views in her book *The Cosmopolitan Tradition: A Noble but Flawed Ideal* (The Belknap Press of Harvard University Press 2019).

** I am grateful to Adam Chilton, Saul Levmore, and Eric Posner for valuable comments on an earlier draft, and to Nethanel Lipshitz for excellent research assistance. This article was prepared for a conference at the University of Chicago Law School in October 2014. Many participants also gave me valuable comments.

[1] Will Brinson, 'CBS Sports' James Brown delivers anti-domestic violence message' (*CBS Sports*, 11 September 2014) <https://www.cbssports.com/nfl/news/cbs-sports-james-brown-delivers-anti-domestic-violence-message/> accessed 31 January 2019.

Martha C. Nussbaum, *'Women's Progress and Women's Human Rights'*. Reprinted as Chapter 15 in *The Limits of Human Rights* First Edition. Edited by Bardo Fassbender and Knut Traisbach. © Johns Hopkins University Press 2016. Reprinted with permission of Johns Hopkins University Press by Oxford University Press 2019. DOI: 10.1093/oso/9780198824756.003.0017

I. WOMEN'S PROGRESS: WHAT DOES INTERNATIONAL LAW HAVE TO DO WITH IT?

Women are making progress.[2] In 1893, New Zealand became the first nation to offer women the right to vote.[3] In 2015, every nation of the world allowed women the right to vote, with Saudi Arabia being the last to join as of December 2015.[4] In 1900, there was no female member in any national parliament. In 2013, according to the World Bank, the proportion of seats held by women is 21.77 percent, rapidly up from 12.74 percent in 1990. In educational enrollment and attainment, although some nations still show substantial gaps, women have basically closed the gap worldwide, coming up to parity with men in primary and secondary enrollment, and surpassing men in tertiary enrollment.[5] Women's labor force participation is also advancing, although it still lags behind men worldwide: 50.6 percent as contrasted with 76.7 percent for males.[6] Although aging women and single female heads of households still exhibit a dramatically higher-than-average rate of poverty, women are on average slowly rising economically, so that their share of national poverty is around 50 percent in Europe, Latin America, and Africa.[7]

In the very basic areas of life and health, we also see dramatic improvement. Women's life expectancy at birth has climbed from fifty-four years in 1950 to seventy-two years in 2015, about the same increase that we see for men.[8] Women now outlive men in virtually every country. Maternal and infant mortality are

---

[2] I am indebted to an exhaustive compilation of data by Nethanel Lipshitz, on file with author, which amalgamates data from the World Bank, the Human Development Reports, the UN World Women's Report, and numerous other sources. I simply pick a few examples here.

[3] 'New Zealand Women and the Vote' (*New Zealand History*, 20 December 2018) <http://www.nzhistory.net.nz/politics/womens-suffrage> accessed 31 January 2019. One should note, however, that women in the territory of Utah got the right to vote in 1870, until it was taken away from them by Congress in 1887—a history that complicates facile assumptions about Mormon 'patriarchy'. Beverly Beeton, *Women Vote in the West: The Woman Suffrage Movement, 1869–1896* (Garland 1986).

[4] 'Saudi Arabia's women vote in election for first time' (*BBC*, 12 December 2015) <http://www.bbc.com/news/world-middle-east-35075702> accessed 31 January 2019.

[5] 'Proportion of seats held by women in national parliaments (%)' (*The World Bank Data*, 2016) <https://data.worldbank.org/indicator/SG.GEN.PARL.ZS?end=2016&start=1990> accessed 31 January 2019. The US is lower than the world average, with 18.5 percent of total seats in House and Senate held by women. The UN Women's and Inter-Parliamentary Union' Report for 2016, 'Women in national parliaments', gives 10 percent for lower or single houses of parliament in 1995, the year of the Beijing Platform for Action, and 17 percent by 2009 <http://archive.ipu.org/wmn-e/world-arc.htm> accessed 31 January 2019.

[6] 'Ratio of female to male labor force participation rate (%)' (*The World Bank Data*, 2016) <https://data.worldbank.org/indicator/sl.tlf.cact.fm.zs?end=2016&start=1990> accessed 31 January 2019. This does not count unsalaried domestic or care labor, a big issue, on which further below. Some nations have a much larger participation gap: in the Arab States, for example, the female rate is 24.7 percent, the male rate 73.2 percent. South Asia also has a very large gap.

[7] UN Department of Economic and Social Affairs, 'The World's Women 2010: Trends and Statistics (2010)' ST/ESA/STAT/SER.K/19.

[8] Ibid, 12.

declining, though there are still severe problems. Women appear to enjoy nutritional status in childhood similar to that of males. We see few disparities in immunizations or rate of communicable diseases. Even HIV affects women and men equally. A lot of this progress comes from development and affluence. But women's relative status has improved even in many nations that are still lagging behind in overall economic development.

One area in which progress lags is contraception. In developed countries, around 70 percent of women ages fifteen to forty-nine who are sexually active practice some form of contraception.[9] That rate is far lower in developing countries, and is only 28 percent in Africa.[10]

The most recalcitrant issue that women appear to still be facing is sexual violence. According to the 2014 Human Development Report, about one third of the world's women will experience sexual or other physical violence in their lifetime, usually from an intimate partner. Reliable data in this area is extremely hard to come by, but it is clear that the problem is not endemic to poorer nations, and that the rate in the US is appallingly high. The National Intimate Partner and Sexual Violence Survey, published in 2010 by the Centers for Disease Control and Prevention, gives a graphic and depressing picture of women's lives in the US.[11] To mention just the first few sentences of this report:

> On average, 20 people per minute are victims of physical violence by an intimate partner in the United States. Over the course of a year, that equals more than 10 million women and men. Those numbers only tell part of the story—nearly 2 million women are raped in a year and over 7 million women and men are victims of stalking in a year.[12]

Even on these issues, however, once highly controversial, or (worse) neglected as the way family life just is, there is an emerging international consensus that violence against women ought to be taken more seriously. Rape, domestic violence, and sexual harassment still occur with depressing regularity, but they are now publicly deplored differently than in the past. What was once 'daily life', is now 'big news'. When Boko Haram kidnaps young women, an event that has occurred for centuries without protest, it is now the object of widespread international protest. The former Prime Minister of Italy, Enrico Letta, shined a spotlight on the frequency of domestic violence, stalking, and killings motivated by male jealousy,

---

[9] Jacqueline E Darroch and Susheela Singh, *Trends in Contraceptive Need and Use in Developing Countries in 2003, 2008, and 2012: An Analysis of National Surveys* (Guttmacher Institute 2013) 10.
[10] Ibid, 13.
[11] Centers for Disease Control and Prevention, *The National Intimate Partner and Sexual Violence Survey* (CDC 2010) (hereafter CDC, *National Intimate Partner and Sexual Violence Survey*).
[12] Ibid.

saying that Italy is 'at war against femicide'[13]—thus placing these crimes in a category comparable to that of genocide, as feminists have long since urged.[14] He followed this up with new tough laws.

Even in one of those still quite primitive and patriarchal nations, the United States, there is movement.[15] For years, rape on college campuses, fueled by alcohol abuse and the toxic atmosphere created by big-time college sports, has gone virtually unreported, as complainants are routinely dissuaded from pursuing their complaints. Now, the President of the United States[16] has directed his attention to this issue, launching a campaign against campus sexual assault and even publishing a list of fifty-five especially problematic institutions, on which, I am sorry to say, the University of Chicago figures.[17] And lately, wonder of wonders, the most all-American institution of all, the National Football League, is writhing in distress after a wave of domestic violence issues involving prominent players: Ray Rice is gone, a mere unsigned free agent. Greg Hardy is gone, another unsigned free agent. Jonathan Dwyer is gone, another unsigned free agent.[18]

Of course these are not new events: it is the climate of their reception—from fans, politicians, twelve sports journalists, and, perhaps most important, the league's corporate sponsors[19]—that has undergone a virtual revolution. When you listen

---

[13] Simone Lalli, 'Italy's "War on Femicide": An Unsuitable Approach to Reduce Violence Against Women' (*Armed Violence Reduction Monitor*, 10 April 2014) <http://www.avrmonitor.org/blog/entry/is-italy-s-war-on-femicide-an-unsuitable-approach-to-reduce-violence-against-women> accessed 31 January 2019 (hereafter Lalli, 'Italy's "War on Femicide"').

[14] On both of these cases, and on the feminist argument about genocide, see below.

[15] I put it this way because, after the notorious gang rape in India, numerous Americans took a superior stance, calling India a 'patriarchal' nation, and a group of feminists at Harvard Law School published a report announcing that they had formed a task force to advise 'India and other developing nations' on the problems of sexual violence that 'their' people face. See Nivedita Menon, 'Harvard to the Rescue!' (kafila, 16 February 2013) <https://kafila.online/2013/02/16/harvard-to-the-rescue/> accessed 31 January 2019 (written by a prominent member of India's very old and well-developed feminist movement). 'It's been a long hard haul,' wrote Menon, 'so it's a great relief that the Harvard Law School has stepped in to take this burden off our shoulders.' Ibid. Charity should begin at home. In India female university students are comparatively safe (no campus sports, most students live at home), and domestic violence has not been a hallmark of big-time sports role models such as cricketers and tennis players.

[16] Really, the Vice-President, who has long been an extremely energetic voice for women's issues, and was the main proponent of the Violence Against Women Act.

[17] I have not been able to get an account of the reasons for our inclusion, but the general sort of reason is sluggish handling of complaints.

[18] See John Schuppe, 'Still Playing: 12 NFL Players Have Domestic Violence Arrests' (*NBC News*, 17 September 2014) <http://www.nbcnews.com/storyline/nfl-controversy/ still-playing-12-nfl-players-have-domestic-violence-arrests-n204831> accessed 31 January 2019. The one accused person who emerges with honor is NFL receiver Brandon Marshall, who did have a string of domestic violence arrests, one leading to a battery conviction in 2008, but who has sought help for 'borderline personality disorder' and has become a national spokesperson for mental illness issues. See Avery Stone, 'Brandon Marshall opens up about mental illness in new PSA' (*USA Today*, 21 January 2015) <https://ftw.usatoday.com/2015/01/brandon-marshall-opens-up-about-mental-illness-in-new-psa> accessed 31 January 2019. Since that time he has had no further violence issues, see ibid.

[19] See 'Anheuser-Busch Says 'not yet satisfied' with the way NFL has handled recent incidents' (*CNBC*, 16 September 2014) <http://www.cnbc.com/2014/09/16/anheuser-busch-says-not-yet-satisfied-with-the-way-nfl-has-handled-recent-incidents.html> accessed 31 January 2019 (Radisson,

to 'The Score' (a typical sports talk station in Chicago) these days, it is quite astonishing: you might almost be at a 1980s feminist consciousness raising session run by Andrea Dworkin. Even beer has joined the women's movement. On Tuesday 16 September, NFL corporate sponsor and beer brewing company, Anheuser Busch, stated: 'We are disappointed and increasingly concerned by the recent incidents that have overshadowed this NFL season. We are not yet satisfied with the league's handling of behaviors that so clearly go against our own company culture and moral code.'[20] Wow; either staggering hypocrisy or revolutionary change. And in a sense, even hypocrisy would itself be a revolutionary change, reflecting deference to new social norms (see Section III below).

So what is happening to render these changes, and what has caused it? Does international human rights law have anything to do with the worldwide changes we are seeing?[21]

The international women's movement has been very successful. Although international human rights law is only a small aspect of the women's movement, it has enabled the movement to grow and prosper. While human rights law lags well behind the women's movement in some crucial ways, it nonetheless helps initiatives to network across national boundaries and to develop a sense of common purpose, a common language, a common set of demands. Together these initiatives create a sense that progress is being made, which is very important for a movement, especially an international movement, and for members who feel isolated or relatively powerless. In a few cases, moreover, CEDAW has had a real, if limited, legal significance when implemented by friendly jurists.

The following analysis suggests that the influence of international human rights law ought to be assessed, often at least, in this broader way, looking at the role of documents in political and social movements. I begin with a question about the usefulness of law in general in this area. I then argue that the widespread expression of a set of new equality norms is already a type of improvement, even if those norms are often flouted. I then turn to the history of CEDAW within the larger context of the international women's movement.

Is the women's movement unique? In one way, it surely is. Women are one-half the world's population, and yet they have until recently been grossly underserved by laws and institutions. One might hypothesize that what women primarily need is solidarity, and a sense of common purpose. Given those things, how could so many people fail to make at least some progress?[22] Other international causes lack

---

Nike, and Target all quickly dropped sponsorship of Peterson, and Anheuser Busch made perhaps the most influential move of all).

[20] Ibid.
[21] The US has not ratified CEDAW—along with Iran, Somalia, Sudan, South Sudan, Palau, and Tonga.
[22] Consider the title of the book by the great women's activist, Ela R Bhatt, *We Are Poor but So Many: The Story of Self-Employed Women in India* (Oxford University Press 2006).

these numbers. But some, for example the disability rights movement and the children's rights movement, may share some features of this case: dispersed people, with common problems, need international documents as a focal point for networking and transnational organizing. These parallels deserve investigation.

II. DOES LAW DETER CRIMES AGAINST WOMEN?

Some human rights norms apply to the behavior of states as states: they must set up a human rights commission, etc. But CEDAW is primarily, though not solely, concerned with crimes committed by individuals and groups in society, matters typically covered under the criminal and civil law. It concerns itself with states only to the extent that in some cases it urges the formulation of suitable laws in the areas of most concern to women, where those laws do not currently exist. So it would seem that before asking whether international human rights law does any good in this area, we really need to ask whether law does any good. That is, does the existence of laws against sex discrimination, sexual harassment, rape, domestic violence, and a variety of crimes against women effectively deter crime? This question is rarely posed and there is a reason for the silence: the question suffers from a vexing baseline problem. We rarely have a situation where laws suddenly come into existence after a complete absence of law. Far more often, there are gradual changes in the nature and reach of the law (for example the changing definition of rape so as not to require physical resistance by the woman, and the inclusion of marital rape as rape), and changing attitudes to law enforcement (as police and courts begin to take domestic violence more seriously, for example, and to treat rape victims better). So the question, 'What good does law do?' is both too deracinated (lacking a baseline) and too vague (not distinguishing between law on paper and the energetic enforcement of law). Underreporting of course makes the problem much worse.

In the area of women's human rights, then, we should get clear about the more general question of law's deterrent impact, and we have great difficulty studying that. In some areas of life, we have the intuitive feeling that law has virtually no deterrent effect: a paradigm case is underage drinking, where everyone knows that law does not deter the problem, and, if anything, by preventing adult supervision, makes the problem worse. Where crimes against women are concerned, some of them fall into this class. Thus, with marital rape and domestic violence, both often precipitated by alcohol abuse, we have the intuition, based on anecdotal evidence and the more solid evidence of the sheer frequency of these crimes, that law itself has very little deterrent effect.[23] Underreporting makes a respectable before-after comparison impossible, even in those cases where there is a clear 'before', as with

---

[23] See CDC, *National Intimate Partner and Sexual Violence Survey* (n. 11).

states that did not criminalize marital rape, and then decided to do so. But one certainly has the intuitive feeling that the behavior of the NFL (for example), and, perhaps more important, of its corporate sponsors has more influence, where the deterrence of domestic and intimate partner violence is concerned, than the existence of laws against it. The illegality of his actions did not deter Ray Rice; his suspension by the NFL may possibly deter others.

In the case of sexual harassment, by contrast, we have the intuitive sense that law, by making a clear statement about the badness of this behavior, defining it clearly, and attaching serious sanctions to it, has caused a great decrease in inappropriate activity. Awareness and social norms seem to have made a huge difference, although both laws and workplace codes play a role. The behavior in question used to be regarded as just fine, even admirable (being a manly man), and thus men who wanted to behave well would engage in it. Now it is regarded as not fine, and legal change is at least a part of that story. Well-intentioned men, certainly the majority in any workplace, will avoid it, and many less well-intentioned men will be deterred by sanctions. Intuition and experience tell us this, and yet precise quantification is doomed by the fact that virtually no reporting of the ex ante situation exists, except anecdotally.[24]

A related issue is that of variation in enforcement. We would all agree that laws that exist on paper but are never enforced have virtually no deterrent effect. Thus laws against fornication and adultery are useless today, even though many are still on the books, and they do not even have an expressive purpose, since most people assume they are still on the books only because nobody has bothered to repeal them. Laws against sodomy, though rarely enforced, were enforced so punitively and in such a hostile manner. When they were enforced the thought that one's life could be ruined surely led at least to more concealment if not to less homosexual activity. With laws against date rape and domestic violence, two of the most serious issues for women, the variation in type and aggressiveness of enforcement is so large, both between jurisdictions and over time, that even within the United States we have no clear way of asking about law's deterrent impact. The behavior of law enforcement so severely deters reporting that we just do not know. We know that college campuses have a lot of rape despite the existence of law, and that the military has a virtual epidemic of rape despite the existence of law; in both cases problems of enforcement are the key issue, not problems in the law itself. Indeed the proposed remedy is typically that these crimes be reported to duly constituted legal authorities, rather than to those who have an obvious interest in cover-up. So it would be harsh to say 'laws against rape are useless' because of these cases, when we can easily envisage changes in reporting and enforcement that would make deterrence more effective.

---

[24] See Catharine A MacKinnon, *Sexual Harassment of Working Women: A Case of Sex Discrimination* (Yale University Press 1979).

If there is no clear understanding of law's deterrent effect, *a fortiori* there can be little clear understanding of the deterrent effect of transnational norms, that is, of the extra deterrent impact of adding a transnational norm to domestic laws. And if there is no deterrent impact without effective enforcement, and if, as is the case for women's human rights, international human rights laws rely entirely on local and national enforcement, it seems obvious that they cannot be effective wherever enforcement is ineffective.

Still, let us do what we can. I first make a point about public recognition as an achievement in itself. Then I turn back into history to summarize the reasons why it was so difficult to get women's concerns recognized in international human rights law, and why CEDAW was a struggle: its very existence represents a culmination of decades of human rights work by transnational women's human rights activism. CEDAW is thus more effect than cause, and the real force is the transnational women's movement, which certainly did not view CEDAW as the end of its activities, but began immediately to push beyond it. I then turn to some areas in which, from the point of view of women's concerns, international human rights law still has serious defects that CEDAW has not corrected. Finally, I ask what good CEDAW may have done.

III. 'ALREADY A FORM OF IMPROVEMENT IN ITSELF'

The first thing that we must say about the existence of CEDAW and related international human rights laws that affirm women's equality and condemn gender-based discrimination is that their very existence is somewhat astonishing. For centuries and in all nations, women's inequality in social and political life had been regarded as so natural, so much a part of the way things are, that any questioning of the gender hierarchy was met with derision, even amid other equality struggles. We are all familiar with the condescension with which women's demands for equality were greeted even by American abolitionists, who forbade Elizabeth Cady Stanton to attend the meeting at which the full equality of black men was ringingly affirmed. (William Lloyd Garrison was an honorable exception to this hypocrisy.) We know the scorn with which John Stuart Mill was greeted when he introduced the first bill for women's suffrage in Parliament in 1867. One could go on and on. So even if CEDAW were to turn out to be utterly useless, a mere set of words on paper, the sheer fact that the nations of the world could agree on such words, and ratify them, even if at times in bad faith and hypocritically, is a breathtaking triumph, which changes the world. It means that henceforth, though the very same behavior might continue to occur unchanged, its meaning has been altered by an international consensus: now it is named as bad behavior, whereas before it was just 'nature'. The fact that the naming is recent is important: it expresses a current normative consensus.

A similar point was made by Immanuel Kant, near the end of his life, about the French Revolution, which changed the meaning of feudalism in the eyes of the watching world:

> We are here concerned only with the attitude of the onlookers as it reveals itself in public while the drama of great political changes is taking place: for they openly express universal yet disinterested sympathy for one set of protagonists against their adversaries, even at the risk that their partiality could be of great disadvantage to themselves. ... And this does not merely allow us to hope for human improvement; it is already a form of improvement in itself. ... The revolution which we have seen taking place in our own times in a nation of gifted people may succeed, or it may fail. It may be so filled with misery and atrocities that no right-thinking man would ever decide to make the same experiment again at such a price, even if he could hope to carry it out successfully at the second attempt. But I maintain that this revolution has aroused in the hearts and desires of all spectators who are not themselves caught up in it a sympathy which borders almost on enthusiasm, although the very utterance of this sympathy was fraught with danger.[25]

Kant, we should bear in mind, was not a supporter of the French Revolution, believing, as he did, that there was no right of revolution, even against an utterly unjust authority. His point is, rather, that widespread enthusiasm for the revolution is already a repudiation of feudal ideas of the naturalness of hierarchy, whether the Revolution succeeds or fails. Henceforth, human inequality is named as unjust, not founded in some natural fittingness of things.[26]

Feudalism and gender hierarchy are similar phenomena: in both cases, a hierarchy was established by force and long custom, but people came to believe it innate, unalterable, and founded in the way things must be and ought to be. Even though the physical differences between lords and serfs were caused by nutrition and health, people believed that there were basically two races of people, different innately; and in the case of gender, they believed this all the more firmly. As Mill points out in *The Subjection of Women*, people who loved to think of themselves as liberal democrats and who, in (male) political life insisted on the strictest equality, would just assume without even thinking about it that there is a nature-based inequality of ability, power, and competence between male and female that sufficiently grounds the permanent 'subjection' of females to males. His title, of course,

---

[25] Immanuel Kant, 'The Contest of Faculties' in Hans Reiss (ed), *Kant: Political Writings* (2nd edn, Cambridge University Press 1991) 176, 182–83.
[26] Ibid.

is deliberate: it is a reminder that Britain, while apparently repudiating feudalism, nourished a form of feudal hierarchy right in the bosom of the family, where all young people grow up and learn their norms.[27]

International women's rights documents change the picture, just by existing and commanding public assent, even if lots of it is insincere. Now when bad behavior occurs, it will not be coded as unremarkable and natural. The baseline of public expression has changed. This widespread acceptance of a new baseline is, as Kant said, already a form of improvement in itself. And this is so even should behavior not change at all in any nation of the world. Indeed, it is so even should most men harbor in their hearts great doubt and even resentment concerning the equality to which they pay lip service. Lip service, in short, is not nothing. What people ratify is not necessarily what they intend to live by, but it is what they think it prudent to own to publicly, and that, in turn, is a sign that women's concerns have won international recognition.

Think about sexual harassment. In the old days the behavior that is now called 'sexual harassment' was commonly and publicly spoken of as a type of virile sport, as 'seduction', 'flirtation', 'eroticism'. Now, even though many men probably long for a return to those days, they almost always pay lip service to the new norms and the new language, because they are ashamed not to. Thus, when a prominent person is convicted of sexual harassment, occasionally male colleagues rise to his defense— but then, when more facts (of a sort that would have been regarded as utterly banal thirty years ago) are revealed, they back off and make apologetic noises.[28] Is that not improvement? Of course this widespread shame does usually lead to widespread changes in behavior. But the bare statement that the behavior in question is a form of sex discrimination and is wrong is itself improvement.

Let us return to the NFL. Even if henceforth exactly as many women get beaten up by football players (who might just learn to cover their beatings more effectively, as Detroit Lions star Reggie Bush has urged in the case of child beatings),[29] the sheer fact that the discourse has changed is an astonishing improvement. That is a case of the larger point this article makes about women's equality.

---

[27] John Stuart Mill, 'The Subjection of Women' in Stefan Collini (ed), *J.S. Mill: On Liberty and other writings* (Cambridge University Press 1989) 117.

[28] I am thinking about the case of philosopher Colin McGinn and the hasty retreat of his early male defenders. Jennifer Schuessler, 'A Star Philosopher Falls, and a Debate Over Sexism Is Set Off' *The New York Times* (New York City, 2 August 2013) <https://www.nytimes.com/2013/08/03/arts/colin-mcginn-philosopher-to-leave-his-post.html> accessed 31 January 2019.

[29] Josh Katzowitz, 'Reggie Bush says he'll discipline his daughter "harshly"' (*CBS Sports*, 16 September 2014) <https://www.cbssports.com/nfl/news/reggie-bush-says-hell-discipline-his-daughter-harshly/> accessed 31 January 2019. 'I have a 1-year-old daughter, and I discipline her,' Bush said on CBS. 'I definitely will try to—will obviously not leave bruises or anything like that on her. But I definitely will discipline her harshly depending on what the situation is', ibid.

IV. CEDAW AS A VICTORY AND MIDPOINT

For many years, international human rights law was basically deaf to women's urgent concerns. Despite the prominent role women such as Eleanor Roosevelt, Hansa Mehta,[30] and Vijaya Lakshmi Pandit[31] played in the earlier phases of international human rights law, men dominated the UN and other international organizations for many years. Indeed, it was only the watchful eye of Mehta that changed 'All men' in the draft UN Charter to 'All human beings', and 'should act like brothers', to 'should act ... in a spirit of brotherhood'.[32] Not surprisingly, given male dominance in the institution, human rights laws were consistently formulated in terms of the situation and problems of males.[33] In other words, the imagined subject was a citizen and salaried worker who was threatened, above all, by the illegitimate use of state coercion. Issues of concern to men were seen as general human concerns. Issues of urgent concern to women—such as domestic violence, sexual harassment, and gender-based discrimination—were seen as specialized and peripheral, not the concerns of humanity in general.[34]

Greatly contributing to this marginalization was the traditional distinction between the public sphere and the private sphere—the former being seen as the place where law has a role to play, and the latter being seen as a space insulated from law. (Although this distinction is sometimes blamed on Western liberal political philosophy, and although it is certainly found there, it is found, as well, in other traditions, independently of Western philosophical or cultural influence.)[35] A large proportion of women in the world over work in the home and spend most of their time there. Even if they also work outside the home and exercise the rights and

---

[30] An Indian activist and author, she was India's delegate to the UN Human Rights Commission in 1947–1948 and became its vice-chairman in 1950.
[31] A sister of Jawaharlal Nehru, she was India's first female cabinet minister; she headed its UN delegation from 1946 to 1968, and in 1953 became the first female President of the UN General Assembly.
[32] Devaki Jain, *Women, Development, and the UN: A Sixty-Year Quest for Equality and Justice* (Indiana University Press 2005) 20.
[33] For good critiques of this history, see Charlotte Bunch, 'Transforming Human Rights from a Feminist Perspective' in Julie Stone Peters and Andrea Wolper (eds), *Women's Rights, Human Rights: International Feminist Perspectives* (Routledge 1994) 11 (hereafter Bunch, 'Transforming Human Rights'); Elisabeth Friedman, 'Women's Human Rights: The Emergence of a Movement' in ibid, 18; Hilary Charlesworth, 'Human Rights as Men's Rights' in ibid, 103 (hereafter Charlesworth, 'Human Rights as Men's Rights'); Allida Black, 'Are Women "Human"? The UN and the Struggle to Recognize Women's Rights as Human Rights' in Akira Iriye, Petra Goedde, and William I Hitchcock (eds), *The Human Rights Revolution: An International History* (Oxford University Press 2012) 133 (hereafter Black, 'Are Women "Human"?').
[34] See Charlesworth, 'Human Rights as Men's Rights' (n. 33) 105.
[35] See Martha C Nussbaum, 'Sex Equality, Liberty, and Privacy: A Comparative Approach to the Feminist Critique' in Zoya Hasan, Eswaran Sridharan, and Ramaswamy Sudarshan (eds), *India's Living Constitution: Ideas, Practices, Controversies* (Anthem Press 2005) 242 (hereafter Nussbaum, 'Sex Equality, Liberty, and Privacy'). A shortened version published under the title Martha C Nussbaum, 'What's Privacy Got to Do With It? A Comparative Approach to the Feminist Critique' in Sibyl A Schwarzenbach and Patricia Smith (eds), *Women and the United States Constitution: History, Interpretation, and Practice* (Columbia University Press 2003) 153.

duties of citizenship, what happens to them in the home is of enormous importance for whether they are able to function effectively in these other spheres.[36]

The story that leads to CEDAW's adoption by the UN in 1979 begins, in fact, with Eleanor Roosevelt in 1945, when she became the first chair of the United Nations Human Rights Commission. She had a lot on her agenda, prominently including the cause of economic and social rights; but women's rights were always among her central concerns. Although she has been much criticized for her opposition to a separate commission for women's human rights, the criticism is probably unfair: she believed that women must assume power within the single organization, and that to give them a separate commission of their own would lead to denigration and marginalization of their concerns.[37] Until her resignation from the UN in 1953, she continued to champion women's rights and a strong organizational role for women in the UN.

The early years of human rights law saw little progress on women's rights, beyond a narrow list of traditional causes, such as equal political and civil rights. The adoption of the Covenant on Economic and Social Rights in 1966 expanded the scope of the United Nations concerns, but still failed to address the critique described above, which was made with increasing vehemence as the women's movement began to assume international prominence in the 1970s.

Networking across national boundaries, women finally began to achieve a presence and prominence that enabled them to exert pressure on the UN. The year of 1975 saw the first UN Conference on Women in Mexico City, attended by four thousand women, which succeeded in getting the UN to declare 1975 as International Women's Year and 1975–85 as the United Nations Decade for Women.[38] It also achieved the creation of UNIFEM, the UN fund dedicated to advancing women's rights, and drafted CEDAW, which was presented at the second international women's conference in Copenhagen in 1980. The official presentation was preceded by CEDAW's adoption by the UN General Assembly in 1979.

Still, CEDAW was more idea than reality until a new wave of activism pushed the UN to focus energetically on women's demands. This activism was evidently spurred on by the passage of CEDAW, since numbers of involved women jumped immediately. The Third World Conference on Women in Nairobi in 1985, attended by 15,000 participants, made progress over the two earlier meetings in getting women to work together across lines of race and region. They drew up the Nairobi Forward-Looking Strategies, which emphasized three points.[39] First, eliminating

---

[36] See Charlesworth, 'Human Rights as Men's Rights' (n. 33) 106, 108; Bunch, 'Transforming Human Rights' (n. 33) 14.
[37] See Black, 'Are Women "Human"?' (n. 33) 134–41.
[38] UN Women, 'The Four Global Womens' Conferences 1975—1995: Historical Perspective' (*UN Department of Public Information*, 20 May 2000) <https://www.un.org/womenwatch/daw/followup/session/presskit/hist.htm> accessed 31 January 2019 (hereafter UN Women, 'The Four Global Womens' Conferences 1975—1995').
[39] Black, 'Are Women "Human"?' (n. 33) 147.

discrimination against women does not mean simply achieving facial neutrality; it requires assessing the social factors that contribute to sex discrimination, and addressing these causes. (This is already emphasized in CEDAW's Article 5.) Second, violence against women, whether customary or used as a weapon of war, threatens world peace. (This whole area is left entirely vague in CEDAW, and must be read as an instance of forbidden sex discrimination.) Third, governments need to establish mechanisms to monitor women's progress. (CEDAW established a committee and a reporting procedure, see below, but it was only with the Optional Protocol in 2000 that there was an institutional mechanism for individuals to access this committee.) This document, and the international publicity and energy involved in the meeting itself, drew attention to CEDAW's goals as urgent concerns for governments, and pushed CEDAW interpretation itself toward a more energetic focus on violence.

Influenced by Nairobi, participants in the 1993 Vienna Human Rights Conference emphasized women's issues, including rape in wartime, since the Bosnian conflict had made this issue prominent. The Declaration and Program of Action addressed women's rights and domestic violence in detail, and specifically linked women's rights to human rights, saying: 'The human rights of women and of the girl-child are an inalienable, integral and indivisible part of universal human rights.'[40]

The next dramatic step occurred at the Fourth World Conference on Women, held in 1995 in Beijing, attended by 47,000 women and men.[41] Notice the dramatic jump in numbers: galvanized by previous successes (and CEDAW, with all its flaws, was certainly a prominent element in the sense of accomplishment), women poured into the movement and became even more assertive. The Beijing Declaration and Platform for Action involved intense controversy. The Vatican objected to the mention of abortion rights and contraception.[42] Many in the United States objected to sending an American delegation to communist China. Nonetheless, that delegation, headed by Hillary Clinton, made a very strong statement against genital mutilation, trafficking, and domestic violence, and even insisted on women's right to family planning concluding with the now well-known words: 'If there is one message that echoes forth from this conference, let it be that human rights are women's rights and women's rights are human rights, once and for all.'[43] Although the Beijing Declaration is an aspirational document with no legal status, it did push the UN to include women's concerns prominently in the Millennium Development Goals. The third Goal directs member nations to take measurable steps to 'promote

---

[40] Ibid, 149.
[41] UN Women, 'The Four Global Womens' Conferences 1975—1995' (n. 38).
[42] 'Beijing Meeting Affirms Sexual Rights of Women' *Los Angeles Times* (Los Angeles, 16 September 1995) <http://articles.latimes.com/1995-09-16/news/mn-46385_1_sexual-rights> accessed 31 January 2019.
[43] Black, 'Are Women "Human"?' (n. 33) 150.

gender equality and empower women'.[44] The UN Foundation made women and population one of its four investment priorities. And Beijing also led to a series of interpretations of CEDAW by the CEDAW Committee that filled in some of the most egregious gaps in that law. Meanwhile, as we'll see, a group of Asian jurists signed their own Beijing Declaration, which emphasized the duty of the judiciary as custodians and enforcers of human rights.

Today, the progress continues, and the women's movement has widened, becoming mainstream through institutional power, both in the UN and in member nations, in something like the way Eleanor Roosevelt originally wished. A large proportion of the world's nations have had female heads of state. Even a nation as patriarchal as the United States might possibly join Germany, France, India, Great Britain, Bangladesh, Pakistan, Poland, Australia, New Zealand, and so many others. Partly as a result of this 'politics of presence', thirty women's issues are now foregrounded both in the UN and in many if not most member nations.

Obviously CEDAW did not accomplish this. CEDAW was an expression and an interim success of a developing movement. It encapsulated and consolidated the successes of that movement to date, and it also rallied the troops for further efforts, rather in the manner of Henry V giving the St. Crispian's Day speech. Still, it is worth taking a closer look to see what it is and what it could plausibly be said to have accomplished.

V. CEDAW, THE CEDAW COMMITTEE, THE PROTOCOL, THE RECOMMENDATIONS

CEDAW's first sentence is an interesting falsehood: for it states that the United Nations 'reaffirms' not only 'faith in fundamental human rights', but also in 'the equal rights of men and women'.[45] Of course the UN had never fully or consistently affirmed this equality, so it really could not reaffirm it. The lie is like the lie at the opening of the University of Chicago, whose founders refused to celebrate an 'opening' day, on the grounds that they wanted the university to seem to have existed since time immemorial.[46] It is a cheerful and reassuring sort of lie: for it treats women's equality not as some faddish will-o'-the-wisp, which might disappear tomorrow, but as something that had been there all along, implicit in the charter of the UN and (in the next sentence) in the Universal Declaration of Human Rights. The pretense of 'reaffirming' thus roots the equality claim more deeply than an

---

[44] United Nations Millennium Declaration, GA Res 55/2 (6 September 2000) (hereafter UN Millennium Declaration).
[45] Convention on the Elimination of All Forms of Discrimination against Women (adopted 18 December 1979, entered into force 3 September 1981) 1249 UNTS 13 (hereafter CEDAW Convention).
[46] See Martha C Nussbaum, *Political Emotions: Why Love Matters for Justice* (Belknap Press 2013) ch 11, 378.

announcement of a new change of heart could have done. (Similarly, Abraham Lincoln's Gettysburg Address roots racial equality in the nation's Founding in a manner that is somewhat duplicitous, but resonant nonetheless.)

After a lot of uplifting rhetoric, CEDAW gives a definition of 'discrimination' and then announces that parties will condemn sex discrimination and agree to adopt appropriate legal measures to combat it, as well as special temporary measures to accelerate women's progress. Subsequent Articles oppose trafficking, support women's full political equality, give women equal rights in the nationality of their children (see below), and discuss at some length women's equal rights in education, employment, health care, and economic life (loans, credit, etc.). There is significant emphasis on the role of cultural traditions in creating an unpromising situation for women, and state signatories are committed to attempting to transform these by combating gender stereotypes. An interesting article (14) discusses the special problems faced by rural women and urges some sensible strategies for their empowerment and health. The more controversial move inside the family domain is made very abstractly in Article 16, to be further discussed below, which grants women equal rights with men in marital and family life, including marital choice, adoption and guardianship, and choice of a name.

The real teeth of CEDAW, if any, come in Part V, where Article 17 establishes a Committee on the Elimination of Discrimination Against Women, specifying its membership and the selection process. The Committee is supposed to receive reports from state parties and to monitor compliance. At least one report must be submitted every four years, and the Committee is to convene annually. State parties agree to draw up legislation implementing the goals of CEDAW, and to report on their progress. (A process of ratifying with reservation is then described.)

So what is the upshot? First, the reporting process has no real teeth: countries who don't submit their reports on time are not sanctioned, and the Committee has no formal mechanism to check whether the reports are true although they may informally receive information from NGOs. Only states can access the Committee, so there is no procedure for complaint if states are not doing their job.

This problem was in part fixed by the Optional Protocol, added to CEDAW in 2000, but ratified by many fewer countries than the original convention. The Protocol allows individuals or groups to approach the Committee directly with complaints of various types. As we shall see below, however, the Committee is rather deferential to national courts, and it's hard to see how it could be otherwise, since it lacks authority and enforcement power. The Protocol has only 106 state parties and fourteen signatories.[47] CEDAW has 189 state parties and two signatories.

---

[47] Optional Protocol to the Convention on the Elimination of All Forms of Discrimination against Women (adopted 10 December 1999, entered into force 22 December 2000) 2131 UNTS 83 <https://treaties.un.org/Pages/ViewDetails.aspx?src=TREATY&mtdsg_no=IV-8-b&chapter=4&lang=en> accessed 31 January 2019.

Another addition to CEDAW has been made by the Committee itself, which has adopted many Recommendations, expanding on and further interpreting some articles of the treaty.[48] As we shall see, a lot of the work introducing some of the really urgent material about sexual assault in the family has been done in this way. And some of these led to the acceptance by the UN, in 1994, of a declaration opposing violence toward women.

Finally, in 1993 a Special Rapporteur on Violence Against Women was appointed by the UN. This office is not paid, and the person who holds it has to try to raise funds to support her work. Energetic holders of this office do try to travel around and make persuasive visits to countries that have problems, but it principally relies upon shining the international spotlight upon violations.

Has all this done any good? First we must face the prior question whether the document itself, and related documents, are good.

VI. THE LIMITS OF INTERNATIONAL HUMAN RIGHTS LAW FOR WOMEN'S HUMAN RIGHTS

Despite CEDAW and the grudgingly accepted Protocol, international human rights law still suffers from some serious defects, where women's human rights are concerned, over and above difficulties of implementation. Basically, these defects are the same old thing: the home, and violence in the home, are insulated from legal critique.

The first point that feminist critics have made, both before CEDAW and after, is that numerous aspects of international human rights law define the crimes in question with an eye to a person's public and political vulnerability, ignoring the existence of similar crimes in the daily world of the home. As Catharine MacKinnon has effectively argued, the definition of torture ignores the use of violence to control and intimidate women in the home.[49] When torture occurs 'in homes in Nebraska ... rather than prison cells in Chile', the system treats it as not the same sort of thing at all.[50] If one should try to reply that political torture is different from crimes against individuals, she has a reply ready: 'Why isn't this political? ... The fact that you may know your assailant does not mean that your membership in a group chosen for violation is irrelevant to your abuse. It is still systematic and group-based. It ... is defined by the distribution of power in society.'[51]

---

[48] See General Recommendations made by the Committee on the Elimination of Discrimination Against Women <https://www.ohchr.org/EN/HRBodies/CEDAW/Pages/Recommendations.aspx> accessed 31 January 2019 (hereafter CEDAW Committee General Recommendations).
[49] See Catharine A MacKinnon, *Are Women Human?: And Other International Dialogues* (Harvard University Press 2006).
[50] Ibid, 21.
[51] Ibid, 22.

A similar point can be made about genocide. Genocide, as defined by the UN Convention on Genocide, is either killing or inflicting serious bodily or mental harm on members of a group, with intent to destroy that group, either entirely or in part. The groups mentioned are 'national, ethnical, racial, or religious' groups: so in that sense violence against women clearly doesn't qualify. On other grounds, however, one could well argue that a great part of violence against women does involve exactly similar infliction of 'serious harm' on women because they are women, and its aim can well be said to be to destroy 'in part'—for 'destroy', if mental harm is sufficient for genocide, must mean not 'kill', but 'remove from the ranks of the fully human'—and this happens to women all the time. Examining a wide range of cases in which rape occurs in the context of a recognized genocide (including both the Holocaust and the Bosnian conflict), MacKinnon argues that these rapes are not sui generis. Similar violations take place all the time. 'In this light, what rape does in genocide is what it does the rest of the time: ruins identity, marks who you are as less, as damaged, hence devastates a community, the glue of group.'[52] It is convenient not to notice a genocide this dispersed, this multinational, this perpetual. MacKinnon summons the international community to notice, and to grapple with the question of how to dignify violence against women as an atrocity worthy of the name. 'If women were seen to be a group, capable of destruction as such, the term genocide would be apt for violence against women as well. But that is a big if.'[53]

Terrorism, she argues, is another concept that needs to be rethought with women's lives in view. In confronting the reality of terrorism after 9/11, the international community had to find ways to conceptualize and condemn a new sort of organized violence, which didn't fit previous definitions of war. It did so—but, again, it didn't notice the implications of the new concepts for the lives of women. Terrorism is unlike war, in that the perpetrators are non-state actors, and they are not combatants in a declared war. 'Common elements include premeditation rather than spontaneity, ideological and political rather than criminal motive, civilian targets (sometimes termed 'innocents'), and subnational group agents. What about violence against women fails to qualify?'[54] A lot of this violence, including gang rapes, much stalking and sexual harassment, and most trafficking, is planned. Its victims are 'innocents'—aren't they? And surely the status of women in relation to men is 'political'—isn't it? And, once again, the motives of men are not just those of the isolated criminal 'sicko'; they are often quite fully ideological, expressing a view that women are there for men's use and control. What the precise consequences of the recognition of these similarities should be for law are left general. One thing is very clear: states that make a big deal of saying that they will do thus and so to states that 'harbor terrorists', fail to have the slightest interest in the fact

---

[52] Ibid, 230.
[53] Ibid, 265.
[54] Ibid, 264.

that a given state might condone the non-enforcement of laws against violence against women—are hypocritical.

CEDAW certainly makes progress on this basic issue, in the sense that it turns attention to the home and insists repeatedly that women have equal rights in the home, and equal rights with regard to marital choice, education, nationality of children, and other 'private' matters. It also insists on stamping out trafficking in women. Still, it does not explicitly address violence against women or sexual coercion in the home. These issues, however, are repeatedly foregrounded in the Optional Recommendations of the CEDAW Committee, as interpretations of CEDAW.[55] Thus a 1989 recommendation states that violence within the family or workplace is banned under CEDAW as a form of sex discrimination, and charges state parties to report their attempts to eradicate it. A 1990 recommendation states that 'female circumcision'[56] is illegal under CEDAW and charges states to report on attempts to eradicate it and to give appropriate support to women's groups combatting it. A lengthy 1992 recommendation further defines violence against women, firmly linking it to the text of several Articles of CEDAW, and insisting on the importance of this issue for the right to life, the right to health, and the right to the equal protection of the laws. The Recommendation makes it clear that CEDAW applies not just to states, but to private actors, and it goes on to further define trafficking, sexual harassment, etc. (See the discussion of *Vishaka* below.)

Thus, CEDAW itself is weak and vague, although the Committee's Recommendations are far better, linking the vague language to concrete duties. But even insofar as CEDAW is effective, it has so far been impotent to alter the rest of the international law system, which continues to ignore many aspects of women's predicament. At any rate, the women's movement did not ignore these issues, as the subsequent international women's congresses showed: issues of sexual terror, domestic abuse, and genital mutilation have routinely been front and center in those meetings. Since this article treats CEDAW as a part of an international political movement, the right conclusion to draw is, it seems, that it is vague but not hopeless in this area, a midpoint rather than an endpoint, and that subsequent political developments in the movement have encouraged the tough interpretations by the CEDAW Committee that make vagueness concrete, many of which have been ratified by domestic legislatures.

A related and notorious defect of CEDAW is its utter silence about artificial contraception and abortion rights. It is well known that the Roman Catholic Church, together with some conservative religious authorities in other religions, made specific language on these points impossible. Access to reliable contraception

---

[55] CEDAW Committee General Recommendations (n. 48).
[56] I keep this term in scare quotes, because its very presence is a sign of compromise. There had been already, and continues to be, much criticism of the term, as creating an inapposite parallel between male and female 'circumcision'. Most feminists prefer 'female genital mutilation', so the presence of the more conservative term is interesting.

is surely of the greatest importance to women's equality. The issue is mentioned in CEDAW, but in an evasive way. In Article 16, subsection (e), women are accorded 'The same rights to decide freely and responsibly on the number and spacing of their children and to have access to the information, education, and means to enable them to exercise those rights.' The same as men, that is. This surely stops well short of guaranteeing access to legal artificial contraception, since a nation could totally ban contraception for both women and men equally without running afoul of this section. Or, more likely, it could decide that what is permissible is education in 'natural' methods of contraception, such as the so-called 'rhythm method', but continue to ban all artificial contraception. It's obvious that conservative religious leaders could be happy with this section.

Abortion rights are simply not mentioned at all, even vaguely, despite the fact that many feminists believe these rights to be crucial to women's full autonomy and equality. In this case, unlike that of violence, the subsequent recommendations of the Committee are also quite vague. In 1994, a recommendation concerning the interpretation of Article 16 opposes forced pregnancy, forced sterilization, and forced abortion, but where contraception is concerned, says only this: 'There is general agreement that where there are freely available appropriate measures for the voluntary regulation of fertility, the health, development and well-being of all members of the family improves.'[57] The words 'artificial contraception' are notably absent.

Was there any purpose of the vague language of Article 16? Would it not have been better to leave this out? The women's movement could reasonably regard this article as a placeholder for their urgent concerns. Had these concerns not been mentioned at all, it would seem that the movement had capitulated to external pressures and agreed simply to remove them from consideration. As it is, the document makes it evident that control over family planning is an important issue for women's full equality. It has expressive content, even if it is too vague to lead to legal implementation. In terms of the further development of the international women's movement, it is an important statement: we may have encountered an obstacle, but we are here to stay and are not backing down.

A third area of neglect in CEDAW is its utter failure to address issues of sexual orientation. Sexual orientation has been a topic of longstanding controversy within the international women's movement. Some women believe that the pursuit of full gender equality requires solidarity with gays and lesbians who are seeking equal respect. They argue that the two causes are connected, because both causes call traditional patriarchal arrangements into question and suggest non-traditional modes of household organization. They claim that the resistance to equal respect for gays and lesbians is inspired at least in part by a desire to shore up traditional patriarchal

---

[57] CEDAW Committee General Recommendations (n. 48).

control of women. Other feminists argue that the two causes are distinct, and that one should not undermine support for gender equality by linking it to a religiously and, often, politically much more unpopular cause. Some make this point strategically, but many feminists in the global context believe that homosexuality is immoral.[58] Recently, feminist opposition to same-sex relations has softened considerably, but there is still the strategic issue to consider. Should a feminist in India, where sodomy is still a felony, taint her cause by this alliance?

Of course in the context of CEDAW the strategic point was huge. The embrace of same-sex relationships would have alienated many if not most of the nations who ratified the treaty, and it is certainly plausible to hold that the price was worth paying. But then, one should acknowledge that a price was paid, and possibly a type of coherence and integrity lost.

A quite different defect of the current international law regime, CEDAW included, is its failure to take a stand on the economic valuation of domestic and care work in the home as work. It is notorious that national income accounts do not count this type of labor as productive labor.[59] The result is a devaluation of women's contribution to economic life. This devaluation has many consequences. To give just one example, when damage claims are made after a wrongful death, the economic contribution of the 'non-working' spouse, usually female, is counted as zero.[60] Feminist economists have made many proposals for how to assign a monetary value to domestic work, and this seems to be an urgent issue in order to give women (and other domestic workers who do not earn a salary) full respect as people and workers. Even the very mainstream 'Sarkozy Commission' report on the measurement of welfare devotes attention to this problem.[61] But CEDAW sidesteps it, even in Article 16, dealing with equality in marriage and the family. Given that a large proportion of the world's women are occupied with domestic labor and child and relative care, whether or not they also earn a wage outside the home, this omission is huge.

CEDAW's failure to regard women as making a productive contribution impacts directly the other things that CEDAW does attend to. Bargaining approaches to the family hold that the 'perceived contribution' of each party to the household's welfare directly affects their bargaining position, hence their ability to stand up to domestic abuse and neglect.[62] If women are perceived as having a valuable asset

---

[58] I have been asked, by women who are in the field risking their bodily safety for gender equality, 'Why is there so much sexual perversion in the US?'.

[59] See generally Nancy Folbre, *The Invisible Heart: Economics and Family Values* (New Press 2001).

[60] Ibid.

[61] Report by the Commission on the Measurement of Economic Performance and Social Progress (14 September 2009) 174–75 <https://www.insee.fr/en/statistiques/fichier/2662494/stiglitz-rapport-anglais.pdf> accessed 31 January 2019. The commission was chaired by Joseph E Stiglitz, Amartya Sen, and Jean-Paul Fitoussi, and included feminist economists Bina Agarwal and Nancy Folbre as members.

[62] See Amartya Sen, 'Gender and Cooperative Conflicts' in Irene Tinker (ed), *Persistent Inequalities: Women and World Development* (Oxford University Press 1990) 123; Bina Agarwal, '"Bargaining" and Gender Relations: Within and beyond the Household' (1997) 3 Feminist Economics 1 (hereafter Agarwal, '"Bargaining" and Gender Relations').

that they can take away from the marriage—whether this asset is land, or personal property, or, as in this case, labor power—this increases their bargaining power within it.

International norms and laws are certainly not the only source of social perceptions, but they are one source.[63] To the extent that women's economic contribution is neglected in international human rights laws and norms, it is a missed opportunity to begin shifting social perceptions. Indeed it is likely that more progress on issues such as domestic abuse and women's treatment within the home will be accomplished by shifting women's economic position than by direct intervention in the home, which is always met with resistance. So CEDAW, by failing to foreground this extremely important issue, appeared to deprive women of a major weapon toward full equality.

However, in the light of the emphasis on this issue in the Nairobi Forward-Looking Strategies for the Advancement of Women, a 1991 Recommendation of the CEDAW Committee states that Article 11 of CEDAW (equality in employment) should be interpreted so as to require monetization of women's domestic work and regular measurement and quantification of that work. States are urged to support research in this area and to take appropriate steps to include women's unpaid work in GNP. This emphasis is welcome, even if unenforceable.

The gross defects of international law identified by feminist critics remain. CEDAW's Recommendations address them, but not in a way that has led to change in the other highly influential documents, which continue to pick and choose which crimes are really serious in a manner that reflects male concerns and devalues women. In light of this failure, one might even wonder whether CEDAW has not done exactly what Eleanor Roosevelt feared, giving women a separate marginal treaty that absorbs their energies and serves to keep their concerns on the periphery. One could look at this far more optimistically, since it does seem that CEDAW has slowly been having influence on such mainstream documents as the Millennium Development Goals.[64] But the question must be pressed.

VII. CEDAW'S MODEST CONTRIBUTIONS

Apart from the large contribution CEDAW makes by virtue of its sheer existence and publicity, what can it be said to have accomplished?

First, the very process of its formation brought women from all nations together to confer and formulate a single statement of goals that could not be impugned as a 'Western imposition' and that had very strong transnational democratic credentials. Just to have brought people together to talk, lobby, and decide what they want

---

[63] See Agarwal, '"Bargaining" and Gender Relations' (n. 62).
[64] UN Millennium Declaration (n. 44).

to shoot for is a huge achievement in today's world, and especially huge for women, who are frequently isolated, since they usually live with men rather than with one another. Indeed we might say that the CEDAW process created a common living space for women, a kind of 'facilitating environment' for future work on shared goals. International organizations such as the ILO are typically male-dominated; NGOs are typically local and in need of connection to others, rather than performing a connecting function themselves. So the CEDAW process, very much including the meetings leading up to it and the work that has followed and continues, has made things better for women in one quite important way, facilitating coordination and communication, and providing a template that can serve as reference point for future work.

We could also say that CEDAW solves the Eleanor Roosevelt problem by both bringing women together and building solidarity, while at the same time not marginalizing them, by making their concerns those of all women and men in all nations.

Second, the very existence of a document ratified by most of the nations of the world nudges politicians and judges by giving them a language to use, particularly in combination with persuasive visits by the Special Rapporteur, or, more likely, pressure from domestic interest groups. Thus, for example, the statement by Prime Minister Enrico Letta that Italy has a problem of 'femicide', followed a UN report in 2012 that found that 30 percent of Italian women had suffered from domestic abuse, and also followed informal discussions with the Special Rapporteur.[65] Letta alluded to the language of the protocol in introducing Law 119, which establishes severe penalties for violence against women, especially intimate partner violence and stalking. Even here things are not perfect, since the law has been criticized by some feminists and organizations for emphasizing punishment ex post rather than education and prevention.

Still, particularly given the short tenure of recent prime ministers in Italy, it is welcome that a durable document such as CEDAW has outlived Letta's fall, and one hopes progress will continue. In nations where international law is viewed with great suspicion by the electorate, such as the United States, CEDAW (not even ratified anyway) does no good, though probably it does no harm either. But when one observes leaders all around the world denouncing the kidnappings by Boko Haram, and harshly criticizing Nigerian leader Goodluck Jonathan for not doing more to combat the terrorists and find the girls, one observes a subtle tilt in the balance, since Jonathan's behavior would have been utterly unremarkable fifty years ago. It is plausible to think that the existence of international documents is among the factors explaining that tilt, although the mobilization of public opinion that preceded the documents is surely even more important.

---

[65] Lalli, 'Italy's "War on Femicide"' (n. 13).

Finally, there are cases in which national courts have enforced the provisions of international human rights law in cases involving women. This article examines only three. There are many others in which the litigants lose in domestic courts and then bring their cases to the CEDAW committee, sometimes winning there, but with unclear consequences for enforcement. This discussion focuses, therefore, on cases in which domestic courts used the treaty to uphold litigants' claims and thus human rights law has clearly defined consequences.[66]

1. *Vishaka v. State of Rajasthan*[67] was brought by petition to the Supreme Court of India in 1997[68] by a group of women's groups and NGOs, on the occasion of an alleged brutal gang rape of a social worker in a village in Rajasthan. (This case was the subject of a separate criminal action, and it played no further role in the petition.) The petitioners argue that they and other working women are unsafe and unprotected from harassment in the workplace because of the failure of both employers and the legal system to address this problem. They argue that the sexual harassment of women in the workplace violates the fundamental constitutional rights of both gender equality and 'life and liberty' (under Articles 14, 15, and 21 of the Constitution). It is also argued that these violations entailed violations of rights to 'practice any occupation, trade, or business' guaranteed under Article 19.

In arguing their case, the petitioners made repeated reference to CEDAW, which has been ratified by India, arguing that the definitions of gender equality in this document 'must be read into these provisions to enlarge the meaning and content

---

[66] For additional cases discussed on the CEDAW Protocol website, concerning appeals by plaintiffs to the CEDAW Committee under the Protocol, see generally the website by Simone Cusack, 'Optional Protocol to CEDAW' <http://opcedaw.wordpress.com> accessed 31 January 2019. Plaintiffs do not often succeed in showing that domestic courts have violated CEDAW; the standards of review seems rather deferential, ibid. It is unclear from the document what occurs next, procedurally, following the issuance of a decision that is favorable to the plaintiff. *Elisabeth de Blok et al v. The Netherlands*, CEDAW Committee Comm no 36/2012, 17 February 2014, concerning the denial of maternity benefits to some self-employed female workers, plaintiff wins; *R.P.B. v. The Philippines*, CEDAW Committee Comm no 34/2011, 21 February 2014, concerning gender stereotyping in a rape case, plaintiff wins; *N v. The Netherlands*, CEDAW Committee Comm no 39/2012, 17 February 2014, an asylum case, plaintiff loses; *M.S. v. The Philippines*, CEDAW Committee Comm no 30/2011, 16 July 2014, a sexual harassment case, plaintiff loses; *M.E.N. v. Denmark*, CEDAW Committee Comm no 35/2011, 26 July 2013, an asylum case, plaintiff loses; *M.N.N. v. Denmark*, CEDAW Committee Comm no 33/2011, 15 July 2013, an asylum case, plaintiff loses; *M.S. v. Denmark*, CEDAW Committee Comm no 40/2012, 22 July 2013, an asylum case, plaintiff loses; *Maïmouna Sankhé v. Spain*, CEDAW Committee Comm no 29/2011, 11 October 2013, right to work case, plaintiff loses; *M.K.D.A.-A. v. Denmark*, CEDAW Committee Comm no 44/2012, 18 October 2013, child custody case, plaintiff loses.

[67] *Vishaka v. State of Rajasthan* [1997] 6 SCC 241 (hereafter *Vishaka v. State of Rajasthan*). I first analyzed this case in Martha C Nussbaum, 'The Modesty of Mrs. Bajaj: India's Problematic Route to Sexual Harassment Law' in Catharine A MacKinnon and Reva B Siegel (eds), *Directions in Sexual Harassment Law* (Yale University Press 2004) 633. My general line was to contrast the Vishaka route to sexual harassment, which focused on equality notions and on CEDAW, to the approach pursued in another case, using an archaic British criminal statute that makes it a crime to 'outrage the modesty of a woman'.

[68] Art 32 of India's Constitution provides for this procedure in cases involving violations of Fundamental Rights. Naturally, the Court can hear only a small fraction of the cases with regard to which they are approached by petition. The provision thus gives the Court great latitude to intervene in issues they select as important.

thereof, to promote the object of the constitutional guarantee'.[69] They argue that this way of understanding the binding force of CEDAW is entailed by Article 51(c) of the Constitution, which holds that 'The State shall endeavour to ... foster respect for international law and treaty obligations in the dealings of organised people with one another'.[70] Thus it was argued that the account of rights of women in the workplace described in CEDAW was binding on India through its ratification of the treaty.[71] (Notice, however, that Article 51 is in the nonbinding aspirational section of the Constitution, called Directive Principles of State Policy, not in the section defining Fundamental Rights.)

The Court accepted the petitioners' argument, holding that indeed the meaning of the relevant articles of the Indian Constitution was what the petitioners said it was. (One striking example: the right to life means 'life with dignity', and the nation has the responsibility of enforcing such 'safety and dignity through suitable legislation'.[72] This interpretation of 'right to life' was not new with this case, but had been introduced in several earlier cases.)[73] Furthermore, the relevant Constitutional provisions should, as the petitioners say, henceforth be read in the expanded manner suggested by petitioners: 'In the absence of domestic law occupying the field, to formulate effective measures to check the evil of sexual harassment of working women at all work places, the contents of international Conventions and norms are significant for the purpose of interpretation [of the relevant Articles of the Indian Constitution].'[74]

They turn to two international sources: CEDAW and the Beijing Statement of Principles of the Independence of the Judiciary in the Lawasia Region,[75] signed in Beijing in August 1995 by a distinguished group of Asian jurists (and amended

---

[69] *Vishaka v. State of Rajasthan* (n. 67).
[70] Ibid.
[71] For discussion of the case and its implications, see Adirupa Sengupta, 'Supreme Court Moves to Check Sexual Harassment' *India Abroad* (New York City, 22 August 1997); Rasheeda Bhagat, 'Checking Sexual Harassment: A Long Overdue Measure' *The Hindu Business Line* (Chennai, 2 September 1997); 'Editorial: A Welcome Recognition' *The Hindu* (Chennai, 7 September 1997); Laxmi Murthy, 'Sexual Harassment: Who Will Slay the Dragon?' *The Hindu* (Chennai, 15 September 1997); 'India: Harassment of Women: Complaint Cell Sought in Work Places' *The Hindu* (Chennai, 3 December 1997). More recently, see Avani Sood, 'Legal Efforts for Social Reform through the Indian Supreme Court' (2010) 51 Harvard International Law Journal 63; Avani Mehta Sood, 'Redressing Women's Rights Violations through the Judiciary' (2009) 1 Jindal Global Law Review 137.
[72] *Vishaka v. State of Rajasthan* (n. 67).
[73] See *Francis Coralie Mullin v. Administrator, Union Territory of Delhi* [1981] AIR 746, female prisoner was denied the right to see her family and her lawyer; the Court held that the 'right to life' involved a right to 'such functions ad activities as constitute the bare minimum expression of the human self' and then linked this idea to that of human dignity. See *Olga Tellis v. Bombay Municipal Corporation* [1986] AIR 180, concerning the eviction of pavement dwellers, the Court held: '"Life" means something more than mere animal existence. It [includes] the right to livelihood because no person can live without the means of living'.
[74] *Vishaka v. State of Rajasthan* (n. 67).
[75] See 6th Conference of the Chief Justices of Asia and the Pacific, 'Beijing Statement of Principles of the Independence of the Judiciary in the LAWASIA Region' (adopted 19 August 1995) <https://www.lawasia.asn.au/sites/default/files/2018-05/Beijing-Statement-19Aug1995.pdf> accessed 31 January 2019.

in Manila in 1997). The latter document gives the judiciary the job 'to ensure that all persons are able to live securely under the Rule of Law' and 'to promote, within the proper limits of the judicial function, the observance and the attainment of human rights'.[76] No mention is made of any adoption by the domestic legislature, but the sitting Justice of the Supreme Court of India was among the signatories, as were the Chief Justices of most Asian nations and Australia and New Zealand. They understand the document to give them broad authority to protect women's human rights.[77]

They then turn to CEDAW, quoting Article 11, which defines women's equal rights in employment. This Article in fact makes no mention of sexual harassment, but they then note that the CEDAW Committee has subsequently interpreted the general language of the Article to prohibit sexual harassment. They quote a recommendation regarding Article 11 that was adopted by the CEDAW Committee in 1992:

17. Equality in employment can be seriously impaired when women are subjected to gender-specific violence, such as sexual harassment in the workplace.

18. Sexual harassment includes such unwelcome sexually determined behaviour as physical contact and advances, sexually coloured remarks, showing pornography and sexual demand, whether by words or actions. Such conduct can be humiliating and may constitute a health and safety problem; it is discriminatory when the woman has reasonable grounds to believe that her objection would disadvantage her in connection with her employment, including recruitment or promotion, or when it creates a hostile working environment.[78]

The Court then gets to work. It issues an admirably clear and comprehensive set of guidelines, subsequently known as the '*Vishaka* guidelines', fleshing out the general remarks in the CEDAW committee's recommendations. They define sexual harassment in terms of unwelcomeness and potential job disadvantage and/or humiliation, closely following the language of the CEDAW Committee. Both quid-pro-quo and hostile environment harassment are described as sex discrimination. The Court then goes on to outline preventive measures to be taken by employers. These include notification of the prohibition of all forms of harassment, establishment of a complaint mechanism, and appropriately set internal penalties. Internal complaint committees must be headed by a woman and at least half of their members must be women. In an especially interesting and creative step, the Court said that in order to prevent undue influence from higher levels in the business in question, complaint committees must involve a third party, usually an NGO. Finally,

---

[76] Ibid.
[77] Ibid.
[78] *Vishaka v. State of Rajasthan* (n. 67).

the Court concludes that 'The Central/State Governments are requested to consider adopting suitable measures including legislation to ensure that the guidelines laid down by this order are also observed by the employers in private sector'.[79]

At this point, however, the Court came up against legal reality. Court-made law in this area has limited reach and enforceability. The directives are said to be 'binding and enforceable in law' until suitable legislation is enacted.[80] But what did this mean in 1997? For government employers, it really did mean something. An employer who failed to follow the directives and to set up appropriate procedures could henceforth be held in contempt of court. For large private employers covered by the Industrial Employment (Standing Orders) Act of 1946, the Directives also had some force, in that the Court instructed the Government to amend standing orders under the Industrial Disputes Act so that the Guidelines became applicable to private employers. The Standing Orders, however, apply only to workers and staff, not to executives. Nor would male-dominated trade unions be likely to support the amendment process. The only value of the Directives in the private sector would have been to increase awareness of sexual harassment as a problem. However, over 90 percent of India's workers are not covered by this labor legislation at all, and an even higher percentage of women.[81] The Directives would have had no impact on these workers, until the Legislature creates new legislation. Even the Court anticipated that such legislation (which it instructs Parliament to construct) would take 'considerable time'.

In a nation in which Christian women won the right to divorce on grounds of cruelty only in 2001, because the groundwork (negotiating with clergy, then approaching Parliament, then working with its Law Committee, and finally proposing and passing legislation) took so many years, one might well have wondered, in 1997, how long that 'considerable time' might be.

We now have a precise answer: sixteen years! On 22 April 2013, the Parliamentary Gazette announced the passage of the Sexual Harassment of Women at Workplace (Prevention, Prohibition and Redressal) Act, 2013, which does all the things the Supreme Court had requested, placing particular emphasis on the CEDAW-mandated Internal Complaint Committees, which it replicates in exact detail. The law is extremely closely modeled on *Vishaka*, hence, in part, on the Recommendations of the CEDAW Committee, so we can say that CEDAW had a major effect, though several steps removed. Of course we have no way of knowing whether that law will be enforced, and early signs are not altogether promising.[82]

---

[79] Ibid.
[80] Ibid.
[81] Swati Saxena, 'India needs to rethink proposed changes to labour laws: Here's why' *The Indian Express* (Noida, 8 December 2015) <http://indianexpress.com/article/blogs/labour-law-modi-government-economy-intuc-conference-labour-law-modi-government-economy-intuc-conference/> accessed 31 January 2019.
[82] See Shilpa Phadnis and Sujit John, 'Sexual harassment at workplace law gets tepid response' *The Times of India* (Mumbai, 1 May 2014) <https://timesofindia.indiatimes.com/business/india-business/

But that is just back to the original problem about whether law in general makes a difference. At least we may conclude that CEDAW, and especially the CEDAW Committee, made a difference to the law—when a domestic legislature had already ratified the pertinent documents.

2. *Dow v. Attorney-General*.[83] Unity Dow is a citizen and resident of Botswana. In 1984 she married Peter Nathan Dow, a longtime resident of Botswana, but a citizen of the United States.[84] The couple have three children, one born before their marriage and two born after it. According to the 1984 Citizenship Act, the first child is a citizen of Botswana, because the nationality of an illegitimate child follows that of the mother; but the other two children are not citizens of Botswana, because in the case of births in wedlock, citizenship follows the father.[85] This meant that both husband and children were vulnerable to expulsion should the father's residency permit not be renewed, and that, should the father leave Botswana voluntarily, the children could stay only if granted residency permits. Dow, a lawyer, went to court to challenge the constitutionality of the nationality law, citing equality provisions in Botswana's Constitution. The Attorney General argued that she lacked standing, since she had suffered no personal injury, and contested her constitutional claim.

Justice Martin Horwitz ruled in her favor in a far-reaching opinion.[86] With regard to the standing issue he rebuts the Attorney General's argument, showing the implications for a mother who is vulnerable to being separated from her children, and who could thus be forced to follow her husband out of the country, even should she prefer to remain. He then argues that the Citizenship Act is discriminatory and denies women fundamental rights and freedoms; it is thus null and void, given that the Constitution forbids discriminatory laws.

The Attorney General, however, contends that the Constitution's failure to allude explicitly to discrimination as forbidden (it just says 'discrimination') shows us that Botswana wishes to leave open the possibility of discrimination based upon sex. Horwitz replies: 'It is difficult if not impossible to accept Mr Kirby's argument that Botswana is a discriminatory society and that the word sex was left out of the Section because Botswana believes that there should be discrimination based on sex.'[87] It is at this point that international law becomes relevant.

Sexual-harassment-at-work/articleshow/34450315.cms> accessed 31 January 2019, which describes resistance or stonewalling by many private employers.

---

[83] *Dow v. Attorney-General* [1991] BLR 233 (HC) <http://www.elaws.gov.bw/desplaylrpage.php?id=2616&dsp=2> accessed 31 January 2019 (hereafter *Dow v. Attorney-General*).

[84] Dow came to Botswana as a Peace Corps volunteer in 1977 and has described his experiences in an interview with Ross Szabo, 'Has Peace Corps Become Posh Corps? Comparing Volunteers Then and Now' (*Huffington Post*, 30 August 2011) <http://www.huffingtonpost.com/ross-szabo/peace-corps-posh-corps_b_887566.html> accessed 31 January 2019.

[85] Citizenship (Amended) Act 1984, Parliament of Botswana.

[86] Botswana, like South Africa, has a significant Jewish community that has played a major role in legal and judicial matters. For a detailed description, see Rabbi Moshe Silberhaft, *The Travelling Rabbi: My African Tribe* (Jacana Media 2012) 188–97.

[87] *Dow v. Attorney-General* (n. 83).

Although Botswana did not ratify CEDAW until 1996, Judge Horwitz cited to both the O.A.U. Convention on Non-Discrimination and the UN Declaration on the Elimination of Discrimination Against Women[88] as interpretative tools to finding that Botswana did not intend to permit sex discrimination as urged by the government. The Court of Appeals affirmed this decision. Nevertheless the government refused to implement the decision until the president decided to head up the delegation to the 1995 Beijing Conference on Women. The Dow Case was well-known internationally and it was decided that it would be prudent to comply with the decision rather than risk being embarrassed at the important international gathering.

Unity Dow has gone on to become the first female justice of the nation's High Court, as well as a prolific and well-regarded novelist. She has resigned from the Court and is now a member of Parliament and the Minister of Education. She has received numerous honorary degrees and other awards.

3. *The Chairman, Railway Board & Ors v. Mrs Chandrima Das.*[89] Turning briefly from CEDAW, there is a remarkably interesting case involving women's human rights, albeit argued from the Universal Declaration of Human Rights rather than CEDAW. It is important to begin by laying out the facts.

Hanuffa Khatoon, an elected official of the Bangladesh Union Board, arrived at Howrah Station in Calcutta on the afternoon February 26, 1998, planning to catch the Jodhpur Express that night. Because her sleeping car reservation had not yet been confirmed, she contacted the Train Ticket Examiner, who asked her to wait in the Ladies Waiting Room. At around 5 PM, two railway officials came to confirm her sleeping berth; they also offered to show her to the station's restaurant, where she could get dinner before the departure. Ms Khatoon followed a station-boy to the restaurant and ordered some food, but immediately began to vomit. She returned to the Ladies Waiting Room, quite ill. The railway officials then offered to take her to the official Station hotel managed by the Railways Board. She insisted on checking their credentials first, but when the official on duty at the Ladies Waiting Room told her that their credentials were in order, she agreed to go. In the hotel room she was brutally gang raped for several hours by a group of four station employees. Finally she escaped and returned to the platform, bleeding and in a state of shock. There she found another railway official who pretended to assist her. He said he would take her to his wife, who would take care of her until she could get another train in the morning. At the wife's alleged residence, she was brutally gang

---

[88] Declaration on the Elimination of Discrimination against Women, GA Res 2263 (XXII) (7 November 1967).

[89] *The Chairman, Railway Board & Ors v. Mrs Chandrima Das* [2000] AIR 988 (hereafter *The Chairman, Railway Board & Ors v. Mrs Chandrima Das*). I discussed this case earlier in Martha C Nussbaum, 'Sex, Laws, and Inequality: What India Can Teach the United States' [2002] Daedalus 95, available at <https://www.amacad.org/publication/sex-laws-inequality-indias-experience> accessed 31 January 2019. Mrs Chandrima Das is Ms Khatoon's lawyer. (Presumably she is named in the case because of Ms Khatoon's foreign nationality.)

raped again, and two of the employees tried to suffocate her. Hearing her cries, the landlord called the police, who finally rescued her.

Two years later, in a landmark judgment, Ms Khatoon won a large damage award from the Railway Board in a case in which the Supreme Court of India declared rape to be a violation of the fundamental right to life with human dignity, under both the Indian Constitution and the Universal Declaration of Human Rights. 'Rape', wrote the Court:

> is a crime not only against the person of a woman, it is a crime against the entire society. It destroys the entire psychology of a woman and pushes her into deep emotional crisis. Rape is therefore the most hated crime. It is a crime against basic human rights and is violative of the victim's most cherished right, namely, right to life which includes right to live with human dignity.[90]

Rape had been an issue on the agenda of the Indian women's movement for some time before that judgment. Thus we should not suppose that the recent reforms in rape law occasioned by the high-profile gang rape in 2013, and concrete legal proposals made in the subsequent Verma Commission report, were new phenomena. They simply continued a pattern of legal activism, against the background of an inefficient criminal justice system.

One concern had long been the use of rape as a weapon against women crusading for political change.[91]

Another problem was custodial rape. The 1972 case of Mathura, a sixteen-year-old tribal woman (and a dalit), who was raped by two policemen within a police compound (where she had gone to register a complaint against her brother), energized the feminist and legal community.[92] The lower court acquitted the policemen in 1974, on the grounds that Mathura had eloped with her boyfriend and hence was 'habituated to sexual intercourse'; they reasoned that she thus could not be raped.[93] The High Court overturned the decision, holding that mere passive surrender under threat cannot be counted as consent to intercourse. The Supreme Court, however, reinstated the lower court decision in 1979, stating 'Because she was used to sex, she might have incited the cops (they were drunk on duty) to have intercourse with her'.[94] This judgment triggered widespread public protest and publicity; rape and rape law were discussed widely and openly, in effect for the

---

[90] Ibid.
[91] One salient example was the gang rape of Bhanwari Devi in 1993, a precipitating factor in the Vishaka case. While doing political work she was gang-raped by a group of higher-caste men, and the police refused to record her complaint until it was too late to perform the necessary medical examination.
[92] *Tuka Ram and Anr v. State of Maharashtra* [1979] AIR 185 <https://indiankanoon.org/doc/1092711> accessed 31 January 2019.
[93] Ibid.
[94] Ibid.

first time. Four Delhi University law professors, including well-known academics Upendra Baxi and Lotika Sarkar, wrote a petition to the Supreme Court calling for a rehearing of the case. The petition, unfortunately, was dismissed. It did, however, energize the women's movement and the academic community to demand legal change. More important, a Law Commission was set up by the government to consider changes in rape law, leading to the Criminal Law (Second Amendment) Act of 1983.[95] One significant result was a shift in the burden of proof in custodial rape cases, and a set of mandatory minimum sentences for rape. Other feminist demands, such as the demand that a woman's prior sexual history should not be deemed relevant evidence, were not included in the version of the new legislation that was passed in 1982. But provisions to shield the identity of victims were included.

In general, delays in the criminal justice system often create a lapse of ten years between rape and court date, making it very difficult for women to pursue their cases, even when they want to. Often they don't want to, because assumptions about the woman's behavior and dress continue to influence the resolution of rape trials. Defendants can usually win a continuance on the flimsiest of pretexts, and their strategy typically is to delay and delay until the woman gives up the prosecution. Roop Rekha Verma, a leading women's activist and professor of philosophy and women's studies at University of Lucknow (now Emerita) urged a former student to pursue her rape complaint and accompanied her to court whenever the case surfaced—until, after five years, the woman had remarried and just did not want to hear about her rape any longer.

Hanuffa Khatoon's case unrolled, then, against a background of intense concern and activism, in which the Supreme Court had at first played a somewhat obtuse role—but had shifted, in *Vishaka*, to a more engaged and progressive posture, responding sympathetically to women's interest groups and invoking international law to help them. (Since the Indian Supreme Court hears cases in three-judge panels, one cannot be sure that there is a shift, as opposed to a different set of individuals.) The railway case showed this progressive internationalist tendency continuing.

It is clear that the Court could have reached the same result without mentioning international agreements. They make this abundantly clear, saying that rape is both a 'crime against basic human rights' and a violation of the right to life with dignity guaranteed under Article 21. The Justices argue, moreover, that the fundamental right to life with dignity under Article 21 belongs not only to citizens of India, but to all 'persons' (like the Bangladeshi visitor Ms Khatoon) within the territory of India. So they do not need international law to get to their conclusion protecting a foreign visitor. Still, the Court draws attention to the fact that their judgment has a

---

[95] The Criminal Law (Second Amendment) Act 1983, Indian Penal Code.

twofold source: the fundamental rights guaranteed in the Universal Declaration of Human Rights, and the Indian Constitution.

Then, in a most interesting discussion, the Courts point out that the two sources are actually one: the Fundamental Rights in the Indian Constitution were closely modeled on the list of rights in the Universal Declaration of Human Rights. They mention particularly the Declaration's emphasis on equal human dignity (Article 1); the right to life, liberty, and security of person (Article 3); the prohibition of 'cruel, inhuman or degrading treatment' (Article 5); the guarantee of non-discrimination and the equal protection of the laws (Article 7); and the prohibition of arbitrary detention (Article 9). They argue that the purpose of the section on Fundamental Rights in the Indian Constitution was to enact the Universal Declaration and 'to safeguard the basic human rights from the vicissitudes of political controversy'.[96] This being so, the meaning of the word 'life' in the Indian Constitution can be further interpreted with reference to the Declaration. They note that earlier Supreme Court decisions have already given 'life' a broad construction, including the idea of life with human dignity.[97]

Since gang rape is obviously inconsistent with human dignity, and the rape was committed by Government employees, the judgment of the Kolkata High Court awarding Ms Khatoon damages from the Railways Board is upheld.

The Court says, then, that all the human rights jurisprudence in the history of the Republic derives, ultimately, from the Universal Declaration; so they make a much bolder claim for the legal significance of international law than one might have imagined possible. How plausible is their claim? The specific claim about rape is very shaky, since the Universal Declaration never mentioned rape, and indeed the resistance to any discussion of rape even in CEDAW was what made the issue wait for the Optional Protocol years later. The framers of the Universal Declaration spoke of dignity at a very high level of generality, and, while it is not implausible to apply their ideas to the case of rape, it is surely a further step, not clearly entailed by anything in the document. The Court did invoke the 1993 UN General Assembly Declaration on the Elimination of Violence Against Women.[98] As for the Indian Constitution: it is clear that at the time of the constitutional framing the attitude of Parliament to women's demands was quite negative. It was the general resistance to any sort of sex equality claim that led B. R. Ambedkar, the primary architect of the Constitution, to resign as Nehru's Law Minister in 1951. He said (*apropos* of a failed piece of legislation reforming Hindu personal law), 'To leave untouched the inequality between class and class, between sex and sex, and to go on passing legislation relating to economic problems is to make a farce of our Constitution and

---

[96] *The Chairman, Railway Board & Ors v. Mrs Chandrima Das* (n. 89) 11.
[97] Ibid.
[98] Declaration on the Elimination of Violence against Women, GA Res 48/104 (20 December 1993) <http://www.un.org/documents/ga/res/48/a48r104.htm> accessed 31 January 2019.

to build a palace on a dung heap'.[99] Of course he is stating that he himself sees the Constitution as an equality-promoting document, but he acknowledges that a majority of those who ratified it do not see it that way.

As for the claim about the Constitution: it is quite implausible to suggest that Ambedkar, a legal giant who had consulted all sorts of legal materials on the way to framing the Constitution, was simply trying to implement the Universal Declaration. That was one of his sources, but he also (being educated in the US) devoted much attention to the US Constitution, pondered its achievements and its defects, and wrote copiously about the need for a conception of rights that could not be used to preclude affirmative action, as was not the case with the US document. He also consulted extensively with Felix Frankfurter about the issue of substantive due process, ultimately opting (as Frankfurter urged) to avoid it in favor of procedural due process.[100] So he was no mechanical cribber from any particular source. The Court simply neglects Ambedkar's independence and creativity as a legal thinker. (Indeed, in light of their history of caste-based prejudice, as in Mathura's case, there is something ugly about the idea that the ideas most Indians impute to the great dalit lawyer are really the creation of Eleanor Roosevelt and her elite friends.)

To summarize: *Vishaka* is a reasonably convincing case of the influence of international human rights law on domestic courts and, ultimately, the legislature. The influence of the Recommendations is substantial: they supplied a clear account of sexual harassment that was the basis for the Court's detailed recommendations. In *Unity Dow*, international sources are again significant in the constitutional argument, though probably unnecessary. Justice Horwitz would have reached the same result without it, interpreting Botswana's Constitution, though his opinion might have been more vulnerable to criticism, and possibly to subsequent reversal. The railways case is extremely ambitious in its claims for international human rights law, but less convincing. The Court appears to be engaging in rhetorical hand-waving more than in serious legal and historical analysis.

On the whole, these cases show that international human rights law gives judges and legislators a tool-kit to use, but they have to want to use it. And they have to have nations that respect them and take their initiatives seriously (one reason why *Vishaka* lays such emphasis on the Beijing document concerning the independence of the Judiciary). An independent judiciary is clearly an important element in these cases. Another unifying feature is that both nations have common law traditions of jurisprudence, combined with a written account of fundamental rights, a combination that appears to encourage independent judges to implement rights creatively.

---

[99] BR Ambedkar, Nehru's Law Minister, Resignation Speech (1951).
[100] For the history of this, see Nussbaum, 'Sex Equality, Liberty, and Privacy' (n. 35).

To conclude: in the larger struggle for women's equality, movements and interest groups play a huge role, international law a small one. But international law plays a reasonably substantial role in the formation of movements and interest groups, giving women dispersed in many different nations a unity of purpose and a sense of accomplishment, and providing a clear, if imperfect, focal point for further organizational efforts.

Bibliography

'Anheuser-Busch Says "not yet satisfied" with the way NFL has handled recent incidents' (*CNBC*, 16 September 2014) <http://www.cnbc.com/2014/09/16/anheuser-busch-says-not-yet-satisfied-with-the-way-nfl-has-handled-recent-incidents.html> accessed 31 January 2019

'Beijing Meeting Affirms Sexual Rights of Women' *Los Angeles Times* (Los Angeles, 16 September 1995) <http://articles.latimes.com/1995-09-16/news/mn-46385_1_sexual-rights> accessed 31 January 2019

'Editorial: A Welcome Recognition' *The Hindu* (Chennai, 7 September 1997)

'India: Harassment of Women: Complaint Cell Sought in Work Places' *The Hindu* (Chennai, 3 December 1997)

'New Zealand Women and the Vote' (*New Zealand History*, 20 December 2018) <http://www.nzhistory.net.nz/politics/womens-suffrage> accessed 31 January 2019

'Saudi Arabia's women vote in election for first time' (*BBC*, 12 December 2015) <http://www.bbc.com/news/world-middle-east-35075702> accessed 31 January 2019

Agarwal B, ' "Bargaining" and Gender Relations: Within and beyond the Household' (1997) 3 Feminist Economics 1

Beeton B, *Women Vote in the West: The Woman Suffrage Movement, 1869–1896* (Garland 1986)

Bhagat R, 'Checking Sexual Harassment: A Long Overdue Measure' *The Hindu Business Line* (Chennai, 2 September 1997)

Bhatt ER, *We Are Poor but So Many: The Story of Self-Employed Women in India* (Oxford University Press 2006)

Black A, 'Are Women "Human"? The UN and the Struggle to Recognize Women's Rights as Human Rights' in Iriye A, Goedde P, and Hitchcock WI (eds), *The Human Rights Revolution: An International History* (Oxford University Press 2012) 133

Brinson W, 'CBS Sports' James Brown delivers anti-domestic violence message' (*CBS Sports*, 11 September 2014) <https://www.cbssports.com/nfl/news/cbs-sports-james-brown-delivers-anti-domestic-violence-message/> accessed 31 January 2019

Bunch C, 'Transforming Human Rights from a Feminist Perspective' in Stone Peters J and Wolper A (eds), *Women's Rights, Human Rights: International Feminist Perspectives* (Routledge 1994) 11

Charlesworth H, 'Human Rights as Men's Rights' in Stone Peters J and Wolper A (eds), *Women's Rights, Human Rights: International Feminist Perspectives* (Routledge 1994) 103

Craven Nussbaum M, 'Sex, Laws, and Inequality: What India Can Teach the United States' [2002] Daedalus 95, available at <https://www.amacad.org/publication/sex-laws-inequality-indias-experience> accessed 31 January 2019

Craven Nussbaum M, 'The Modesty of Mrs. Bajaj: India's Problematic Route to Sexual Harassment Law' in MacKinnon CA and Siegel RB (eds), *Directions in Sexual Harassment Law* (Yale University Press 2004) 633

Craven Nussbaum M, 'What's Privacy Got to Do With It? A Comparative Approach to the Feminist Critique' in Schwarzenbach SA and Smith P (eds), *Women and the United States Constitution: History, Interpretation, and Practice* (Columbia University Press 2003) 153

Craven Nussbaum M, 'Sex Equality, Liberty, and Privacy: A Comparative Approach to the Feminist Critique' in Hasan Z, Sridharan E, and Sudarshan R (eds), *India's Living Constitution: Ideas, Practices, Controversies* (Anthem Press 2005) 242

Craven Nussbaum M, *Political Emotions: Why Love Matters for Justice* (Belknap Press 2013)

Darroch JE and Singh S, *Trends in Contraceptive Need and Use in Developing Countries in 2003, 2008, and 2012: An Analysis of National Surveys* (Guttmacher Institute 2013)

Folbre N, *The Invisible Heart: Economics and Family Values* (New Press 2001)

Friedman E, 'Women's Human Rights: The Emergence of a Movement' in Stone Peters J and Wolper A (eds), *Women's Rights, Human Rights: International Feminist Perspectives* (Routledge 1994) 18

Jain D, *Women, Development, and the UN: A Sixty-Year Quest for Equality and Justice* (Indiana University Press 2005)

Kant I, 'The Contest of Faculties' in Reiss H (ed.), *Kant: Political Writings* (2nd edn, Cambridge University Press 1991) 176

Katzowitz J, 'Reggie Bush says he'll discipline his daughter "harshly"' (*CBS Sports*, 16 September 2014) <https://www.cbssports.com/nfl/news/reggie-bush-says-hell-discipline-his-daughter-harshly/> accessed 31 January 2019

Lalli S, 'Italy's "War on Femicide": An Unsuitable Approach to Reduce Violence Against Women' (*Armed Violence Reduction Monitor*, 10 April 2014) <http://www.avrmonitor.org/blog/entry/is-italy-s-war-on-femicide-an-unsuitable-approach-to-reduce-violence-against-women> accessed 31 January 2019

MacKinnon CA, *Sexual Harassment of Working Women: A Case of Sex Discrimination* (Yale University Press 1979)

MacKinnon CA, *Are Women Human?: And Other International Dialogues* (Harvard University Press 2006)

Menon N, 'Harvard to the Rescue!' (*kafila*, 16 February 2013) <https://kafila.online/2013/02/16/harvard-to-the-rescue/> accessed 31 January 2019

Mill JS, 'The Subjection of Women' in Collini S (ed), *J.S. Mill: On Liberty and other writings* (Cambridge University Press 1989) 117

Murthy L, 'Sexual Harassment: Who Will Slay the Dragon?' *The Hindu* (Chennai, 15 September 1997)

Phadnis S and John S, 'Sexual harassment at workplace law gets tepid response' *The Times of India* (Mumbai, 1 May 2014) <https://timesofindia.indiatimes.com/business/india-business/Sexual-harassment-at-work/articleshow/34450315.cms> accessed 31 January 2019

Saxena S, 'India needs to rethink proposed changes to labour laws: Here's why' *The Indian Express* (Noida, 8 December 2015) <http://indianexpress.com/article/blogs/labour-law-modi-government-economy-intuc-conference-labour-law-modi-government-economy-intuc-conference/> accessed 31 January 2019

Schuessler J, 'A Star Philosopher Falls, and a Debate Over Sexism Is Set Off' *The New York Times* (New York City, 2 August 2013) <https://www.nytimes.com/2013/08/03/arts/colin-mcginn-philosopher-to-leave-his-post.html> accessed 31 January 2019

Schuppe J, 'Still Playing: 12 NFL Players Have Domestic Violence Arrests' (*NBC News*, 17 September 2014) <http://www.nbcnews.com/storyline/nfl-controversy/still-playing-12-nfl-players-have-domestic-violence-arrests-n204831> accessed 31 January 2019

Sen A, 'Gender and Cooperative Conflicts' in Tinker I (ed), *Persistent Inequalities: Women and World Development* (Oxford University Press 1990) 123

Sengupta A, 'Supreme Court Moves to Check Sexual Harassment' *India Abroad* (New York City, 22 August 1997)

Silberhaft M, *The Travelling Rabbi: My African Tribe* (Jacana Media 2012)

Sood A, 'Redressing Women's Rights Violations through the Judiciary' (2009) 1 Jindal Global Law Review 137

Sood A, 'Legal Efforts for Social Reform through the Indian Supreme Court' (2010) 51 Harvard International Law Journal 63

Stone A, 'Brandon Marshall opens up about mental illness in new PSA' (*USA Today*, 21 January 2015) <https://ftw.usatoday.com/2015/01/brandon-marshall-opens-up-about-mental-illness-in-new-psa> accessed 31 January 2019

Szabo R, 'Has Peace Corps Become Posh Corps? Comparing Volunteers Then and Now' (*Huffington Post*, 30 August 2011) <http://www.huffingtonpost.com/ross-szabo/peace-corps-posh-corps_b_887566.html> accessed 31 January 2019

UN Women, 'The Four Global Womens' Conferences 1975—1995: Historical Perspective' (UN Department of Public Information, 20 May 2000) <https://www.un.org/womenwatch/daw/followup/session/presskit/hist.htm> accessed 31 January 2019

16
The Limits of Law
A Response to Martha C. Nussbaum

Fareda Banda

Reading Professor Nussbaum's chapter brought to mind an end of year report for a student who had initially shown much promise, but had later disappointed her teacher. The 'student' is CEDAW, an acronym that is often used interchangeably to mean both the United Nations Convention on the Elimination of all Forms of Discrimination against Women of 1979 and also the twenty-three member Committee of independent experts that oversees that Convention. Professor Nussbaum suggests that CEDAW has failed to have the transformative effect on women's lives that was anticipated at its adoption. Her paper does not blame the student for her failure to live up to expectation, but rather considers the conditions that have led to the result. These include the fact that the foundations of CEDAW are themselves poor, either ignoring or failing to give sufficient weight to issues that directly impact women such as violence and the need for reproductive rights including the right to terminate pregnancies. Like many before her, Professor Nussbaum acknowledges that passing laws or adopting human rights instruments is not a guarantee that those rights will be respected or indeed enforced. Her analyses call to mind the earlier work of Antony Allott whose book on the *Limits of Law* identify many of the same blockages to the effective enjoyment of rights.[1] These include a lack of political will to honour pledges made in international fora, the resistance to change by those who feel they have much to lose, and the general difficulty of changing social attitudes.[2]

Framing CEDAW as part of a social movement, Professor Nussbaum shows that there has been what she calls modest progress, but concludes that much remains to be done. This in turn leads her to question the efficacy of CEDAW and international law in the struggle for women's equality.[3] She concludes that there is a

---

[1] Antony Allott, *The Limits of Law* (Butterworths 1980). Nussbaum engages with some of these issues in her earlier work. Martha C Nussbaum, *Sex and Social Justice* (Oxford University Press 1999) (hereafter Nussbaum, *Sex and Social Justice*). See also Amy Shupikai Tsanga, *Taking Law to the People: Gender, Law Reform, and Community Legal Education in Zimbabwe* (Weaver Press 1996).

[2] See also Kwame A Appiah, *The Honor Code: How Moral Revolutions Happen* (WW Norton & Co 2010).

[3] There have been many studies on this including: Sally Engle Merry, *Human Rights and Gender Violence: Translating International Law into Local Justice* (University of Chicago Press 2006) (hereafter Merry, *Human Rights and Gender Violence*); Thomas Risse, Stephen C Ropp, and Kathryn Sikkink

Fareda Banda, *The Limits of Law: A Response to Martha C. Nussbaum*. In: *The Limits of Human Rights*. Edited by: Bardo Fassbender and Knut Traisbach, Oxford University Press 2019. © The Several Contributors.
DOI: 10.1093/oso/9780198824756.003.0018

symbiotic relationship in which: 'international law plays a reasonably substantial role in the formation of movements and interest groups, giving women dispersed in many different nations a unity of purpose and a sense of accomplishment, and providing a clear, if imperfect, focal point for further organizational efforts'.[4]

One needs to understand Professor Nussbaum's assessment of CEDAW as one of an impatient teacher who sees the potential of her student and who wishes to see faster progress. In her earlier work *Sex and Social Justice* she noted: 'The focus on women is justified, it seems to me, by the urgency of the problems facing women in today's world and by the sorry record of our dealings with (and evasions of) these problems.'[5]

I would like to take on the role of Professor Nussbaum's teaching assistant. While echoing her frustration about the slow rate of change, I would tell her that our student has made a great deal of normative progress in three of the key areas identified in Professor Nussbaum's chapter: intersectionality, reproductive rights, and violence against women. I would also highlight how much CEDAW has impacted positively on the work of other committees and in the development of human rights standards globally.

I. ON SEEING THE UNSEEN: CEDAW AND INTERSECTIONALITY

Professor Nussbaum criticizes CEDAW's failure to address the rights of LGBTQI+ individuals. It is indeed true that the Convention is poor on intersectionality. One could argue that the 'CEDAW woman' is assumed to be heterosexual, able-bodied, married (or likely to marry), and to have, or want, children. Yes, the silence, or omission of LGBTIQ+ people, is regrettable, but to say that they should have been included in 1979 is to be anachronistic. The idea that LGBTIQ+ people are both human and have rights, is still, sadly, a subject of debate and, in some regions, remains contentious. While the legal recognition of LGBTIQ+ rights has come in leaps and bounds in the past twenty years, they were not on national, let alone international radar during the drafting process of CEDAW which was adopted in 1979. This was the 'decriminalization of homosexuality' phase in Western society. It was a moot point in the rest of the world, with many states either holding onto

---

(eds), *The Persistent Power of Human Rights: From Commitment to Compliance* (Cambridge University Press 2013).

[4] Martha C Nussbaum, 'Women's Progress and Women's Human Rights' in Bardo Fassbender and Knut Traisbach (eds), *The Limits of Human Rights* (Oxford University Press 2019) 231, 263 (hereafter Nussbaum, 'Women's Progress'); Margaret E Keck and Kathryn Sikkink, *Activists Beyond Borders: Advocacy Networks in International Politics* (Cornell University Press 1998); see also Janet Halley, *Split Decisions: How and Why to Take a Break from Feminism* (Princeton University Press 2006).
[5] Nussbaum, *Sex and Social Justice* (n. 1) 9.

prohibitive colonial legacy laws or simply ignoring or not acknowledging the presence of sexual minorities. This human rights phase was not focused on the granting of legal personhood to this group. The Netherlands became the first country to give legal recognition to same sex relationships in 1985.

While it is true that there has not been sisterhood or consensus within the feminist movement(s) about the place of LGBTIQ+, it is important to acknowledge that, in its General Recommendations and dialogue with states parties, the CEDAW Committee has now started to address LGBTIQ+ issues.[6] However, it is telling that it takes a cautious approach to LGBTIQ+ (as it does to abortion) noting, in General Recommendation 29, that where same sex relationships are recognized, then the state 'should ensure the protection of the economic rights of women within those relationships'.[7] The Committee does not demand recognition, but merely asks for protection where recognition is given. Other Committees, notably the Committee on the Rights of Persons with Disabilities, are more progressive.[8] A comparative history of treaty bodies shows that rights evolve over time until we are left to wonder what the problem was that led to the prejudice in the first place.[9] I acknowledge that it is outrageous for society to tell one group to 'wait its turn in the human rights queue'.

There is a conversation to be had about the reasons for rendering invisible so many groups, but it is important to acknowledge that in treaty drafting, it may be that focusing on the bigger prize of acknowledgement of the whole, is all that may be feasible, in temporal and political terms. Perhaps the focus should not be on the listing of categories of people, but rather on the efficacy of the law in protecting their interests. Nevertheless, it is worth noting and celebrating that the direction of human rights travel is for greater respect and recognition of the rights LGBTIQ+ individuals.[10]

---

[6] UN Committee on the Elimination of Discrimination against Women (hereafter CEDAW Committee) General Recommendation no. 28, 'Core obligations of States parties (art 2)' CEDAW/C/GC/28, para. 18 (hereafter CEDAW Committee General Recommendation no. 28); CEDAW Committee Concluding Observations on Uganda (5 November 2010) CEDAW/C/UGA/CO/7 paras 43 and 44; CEDAW Committee Concluding Observations on the Russian Federation (16 August 2010) CEDAW/C/USR/CO/7 paras 40 and 41.

[7] CEDAW Committee General Recommendation no. 29, 'Economic consequences of marriage, family relations and their dissolution (art 16)' CEDAW/C/GC/29 para. 24; see also the 'abortion provision' in CEDAW Committee General Recommendation no. 24, 'Women and Health (art 12)' A/54/38/Rev.1 ch I, para. 11, but see also para. 14 (hereafter CEDAW Committee General Recommendation no. 24).

[8] CPRD Committee General Comment no. 3, 'Woman and Girls with Disabilities' CRPD/C/GC/3.

[9] *Atala Riffo and Daughters v. Chile*, IACtHR Series C no. 239, 24 February 2012.

[10] See UN Secretary-General in a video message to an Oslo conference on Human Rights on Sexual Orientation and Gender Identity (15 April 2013) <http://www.un.org/press/en/2013/sgsm14944.doc.htm> accessed 31 January 2019; HR Council Res., 'Human Rights, Sexual Orientation and Gender Identity' A/HRC/27/L.27/Rev.1 (24 September 2014); African Commission on Human and Peoples' Rights (hereafter ACommHPR) Res., 'Protection against Violence and other Human Rights Violations against Persons on the basis of their real or imputed Sexual Orientation or Gender Identity' 55th session/2014/Res. 275; also noteworthy is the appointment of an Independent Expert on Sexual Orientation in June 2016 by HR Council Res., 'Protection against Violence and Discrimination Based on Sexual Orientation and Gender Identity' A/HRC/32/L.2/Rev.1 (30 June 2016); see also CEDAW

As Professor Nussbaum acknowledges, the CEDAW Committee has sought to plug its intersectional normative gaps by way of General Recommendations; so that the rights of persons with disabilities, migrant women, older women, rural, and asylum-seeking women have been added.[11] CEDAW can also be seen to be making an effort to incorporate intersectional analyses in its decision-making under the Optional Protocol to the Convention. Worthy of note are cases such AS *v. Hungary* which identified the violation of a Roma woman's right to receive information in a language that she understood before being sterilized and *Jallow v. Bulgaria* which identified racism as a factor in the denial of access to justice to an abused migrant woman.[12] Similarly the Optional Protocol Article 8 Inquiry undertaken by the Committee in Canada identified prejudice, stereotyping and the state's general failure to protect indigenous women from violence and murder as directly linked to their status as indigenous women, more often than not, also poor.[13]

II. REPRODUCTIVE RIGHTS

Abortion is a tricky issue nationally and internationally. There is no consensus on the issue.[14] Professor Nussbaum's criticisms of the limits of the liberal model of equality in CEDAW are well articulated. The 'family planning' provisions talk about men and women having 'the same rights'.[15] She argues that a state could ban contraception for both men and women, ignoring the fact that women bear the

Committee General Recommendation no. 35, 'Gender-based violence against women, updating General Recommendation no 19' CEDAW/C/GC/35 para. 12 (hereafter CEDAW Committee General Recommendation no. 35).

[11] CEDAW Committee General Recommendation no. 18, 'Disabled Women' A/46/38; CEDAW Committee General Recommendation no. 26, 'Women Migrant Workers' CEDAW/C/2009/WP.1/R; CEDAW Committee General Recommendation no. 27, 'Older women and protection of their human rights' CEDAW/C/GC/27; CEDAW Committee General Recommendation no. 32, 'The gender-related dimensions of refugee status, asylum, nationality and statelessness of women' CEDAW/C/GC/32; CEDAW Committee General Recommendation no. 34, 'The Rights of Rural Women' CEDAW/C/GC/34.

[12] *AS v. Hungary*, CEDAW Committee Comm. No. 4/2004, 14 August 2006; *Jallow v. Bulgaria*, CEDAW Committee Comm. No. 32/2011, 23 July 2012; *RPB v. The Philippines*, CEDAW Committee Comm. No. 34/2011, 21 February 2014; *Pimenthel v. Brazil*, CEDAW Committee Comm. No. 17/2008, 25 July 2011.

[13] CEDAW Committee Report of the inquiry concerning Canada of the Committee on the Elimination of Discrimination against Women under article 8 of the Optional Protocol to the Convention on the Elimination of All Forms of Discrimination against Women (CEDAW Inquiry) CEDAW/C/OP.8/CAN/1; see also *Kell v. Canada*, CEDAW Committee Comm. No. 19/2008, 28 February 2012.

[14] Jonathan Todres and Louise N Howe, 'What the Convention on the Child Says (and Doesn't Say) about Abortion and Family Planning' in Jonathan Todres, Mark E Wojcik, and Cris R Revaz (eds), *The U.N. Convention on the Rights of the Child: An Analysis of Treaty Provisions and Implications of U.S. Ratification* (Transnational Publishers 2006) 163.

[15] See Articles 12(1), 14(2)(b), 16(1)(1)(e) CEDAW.

disproportionate reproductive burden. There is also no guarantee of the right to access artificial contraception.[16] It is for this reason that the African Protocol on Women's Rights of 2003, the only regional convention on women's rights, focuses on *women's* reproductive rights including the right to control their own fertility, to decide when and whether to have children, and also to choose any method of contraception.[17] It makes no reference to a male comparator. Equally, it provides for the rights of women to access abortion in certain limited circumstances, a global first.[18]

In its interaction with states, the CEDAW Committee has not remained silent on abortion. In its General Recommendation 24 the Committee noted that the failure to provide services needed only by women, constituted discrimination against them. It called on states to ensure that, where legal, staff were available to carry out terminations.[19] In its revised General Recommendation, No. 35, on Violence, the Committee asked states to repeal discriminatory laws including those criminalizing abortion.[20] In the Optional Protocol case of *LC v. Peru* the author alleged multiple breaches of the Convention including Article 1 on discrimination, 2 on state obligations, 5 on stereotyping, and 12 and 16(1)(e) on health care and family planning, read with CEDAW General Recommendation no. 24.[21] A thirteen-year-old girl who had fallen pregnant as a result of sustained sexual abuse tried to commit suicide by jumping out of a window. Her back operation was postponed when it was discovered that she was pregnant. The girl and her mother requested an abortion, which procedure (therapeutic abortion) was recognized in the Peruvian Penal Code. They were denied. She eventually miscarried and was left paralysed. The CEDAW Committee found that Peru had indeed fallen short of its obligations to provide adequate care and that its failure to provide her with a health service that was available and accessible constituted a breach of LC's rights. The Committee recommended that Peru review its laws to prevent a recurrence of the problem and also that the state should 'establish

---

[16] Nussbaum, 'Women's Progress' (n. 4) 248.
[17] Protocol to the African Charter on Human and Peoples' Rights on the Rights of Women in Africa (adopted 11 July 2003, entered into force 25 November 2005) AHG/Res.240 (XXXI) (hereafter Protocol to the African Charter on Rights of Women) Article 14(1)(a–c).
[18] Ibid, Article 14(2)(i). The first two General Comments on the Protocol to the African Charter on Rights of Women (n. 17) relate to Article 14 on sexual and reproductive rights, see ACommHPR General Comment no. 1, 'Article 14(1)(d) and (e)' and General Comment no. 2, 'Article 14.1(a), (b), (c) and (f) and Article 14.2(a) and (c)'. Charles Ngwena, Eunice Brookman-Amissah, and Patty Skuster, 'Human Rights Advances in Women's Reproductive Health in Africa' (2015) 129 International Journal of Gynecology & Obstetrics 184.
[19] CEDAW Committee General Recommendation no. 24 (n. 7) para. 11; this is also the approach taken in Committee on the Rights of Child (CRC) General Comment No. 4, 'Adolescent Health and Development' CRC/GC/2003/4, para. 24.
[20] CEDAW Committee General Recommendation no. 35 (n. 10) para. 29(c)(i). In the same paragraph, the Committee also calls for the repeal of laws criminalizing people on the basis of their sexual orientation or gender identity.
[21] *LC v. Peru*, CEDAW Committee Comm. No. 22/2009, 17 October 2011, para. 1.

a mechanism for effective access to therapeutic abortion under conditions that protect women's physical and mental health'.[22]

Meanwhile, in February 2018, the Committee released its findings on a confidential inquiry into the failure of the United Kingdom to ensure that women in Northern Ireland had the same access to reproductive rights services, including abortion, as women in the other UK countries.[23] CEDAW's commitment to reproductive rights can also be seen in its findings in an inquiry which condemned the refusal to provide contraception by the state government of Manila in the in Philippines.[24] The Committee found that even in a devolved system of decision-making, the central government remained responsible for ensuring that Convention provisions were adhered to nationally. The Committee further noted the link between lack of provision of contraception and high maternal mortality and unsafe abortion.[25] The Committee's findings buttressed the lobbying of local feminists and contributed to the promulgation of a law permitting contraceptive use in defiance of the vehement opposition of the Catholic Church.

The reach and influence of CEDAW can also be seen in national jurisdictions such as Nepal where the Supreme Court noted that the state had a duty to ensure that abortion, which had been legalized in 2002, was available to poor women.[26] The Supreme Court also dismissed a case which challenged the abortion law on grounds of discrimination against men because they could not block a termination, thus impinging on Article 16(1)(e) CEDAW which allows men and women an equal say in decision-making with respect to deciding on the number and spacing of children.[27]

As with LGBTIQ+, the tide is starting to turn on the issue of abortion. Referencing CEDAW General Recommendation no. 24 on health, is the 2016 General Comment on health and reproductive rights of the Committee on Economic, Social and Cultural Rights (CESCR) which calls for a recognition of the different reproductive

---

[22] Ibid, para. 12(b)(i). In paras 2.15, 5.5, and 5.6 reference was also made to the UN Human Rights Committee decision on abortion in *KL v. Peru*, HR Committee (ICCPR) Communication no. 1153/2003, 24 October 2005 and the ECtHR decision in *Tysiac v. Poland*, App. No. 5410/03, 20 March 2007. The UN Human Rights Committee held that by failing to provide legal abortion services, the state had violated KL's rights to basic dignity, health, and to be free from degrading and inhuman treatment. The state was ordered to pay compensation.

[23] CEDAW Committee Report, 'Inquiry concerning the United Kingdom of Great Britain and Northern Ireland under article 8 of the Optional Protocol to the Convention on the Elimination of All Forms of Discrimination against Women' CEDAW/C/OP.8/GBR/1 (6 March 2018).

[24] CEDAW Committee Summary, 'Inquiry concerning the Philippines under article 8 of the Optional Protocol to the Convention on the Elimination of All Forms of Discrimination against Women' CEDAW/C/OP.8PHL/1 (22 April 2015).

[25] Ibid, para. 47.

[26] *Lakshmi Dhikta v. Government of Nepal*, Writ no. 0757, 2067 (2002) (SC). See Melissa Upreti, 'Toward Transformative Equality in Nepal: The *Lakshmi Dhikta* Decision' in Rebecca J Cook, Joanna N Erdman, and Bernard M Dickens (eds), *Abortion Law in Transnational Perspective: Cases and Controversies* (University of Pennsylvania Press 2014) 279 (hereafter Upreti, 'Toward Transformative Equality in Nepal').

[27] *Achyut Kharel v. Government of Nepal*, Writ no. 3352, 2061 (2008) (SC); see also Upreti, 'Toward Transformative Equality in Nepal' (n. 26) 288–91.

needs of men and women and asks states to make alternative provision for delivery of services in the event of a provider citing conscientious objections. It addresses the impact of unsafe abortions and calls for decriminalization.[28] The CESCR General Comment goes further and condemns states that use their foreign aid to prohibit the giving of information on reproductive services including abortion.[29]

The next section addresses Professor Nussbaum's assertion: 'But even insofar as CEDAW is effective, it has so far been impotent to alter the rest of the international law system, which continues to ignore many aspects of women's predicament.'[30] In fairness, she does go on to note that there have been congresses which have addressed issues such as violence against women, before observing that 'CEDAW ... is vague but not hopeless in this area, a midpoint rather than an endpoint ... '.[31] I would like to argue that, as already shown, CEDAW has played an important role in raising the profile of women's rights and experiences globally. It has impacted the work of other UN and regional treaty bodies forcing them to address a key criticism made by feminist international lawyers; that of the rendering invisible women's experiences in both the framing and interpretation of human rights law. An example is the decision of the African Commission on Human and People's Rights in *Egyptian Personal Rights Project and Interights v. Egypt.* [32] The Commission referenced CEDAW in its assertion that the principles of non-discrimination and equality were universal. This is particularly important in light of Egypt's reservations to both CEDAW and the African Commission provisions requiring equality.[33]

---

[28] Committee on Economic, Social and Cultural Rights (ICESCR) General Comment no. 22, 'The Right to Sexual and Reproductive Health (art 12)' E/C.12/GC/22, paras 13, 14, 18, 21, 28, 34, 41, and 49(e).

[29] Ibid, para. 52.

[30] Nussbaum, 'Women's Progress' (n. 4) 248.

[31] Ibid.

[32] *Egyptian Personal Rights Project and Others v. Interights*, ACommHPR Comm. No. 323/06 [2011] paras 87–90 (hereafter *Egyptian Personal Rights Project and Others v. Interights*). CEDAW is also frequently cited by African women challenging unfair inheritance laws, see, e.g., *ES and SC (Represented by the Women's Legal Aid Centre and the International Women's Human Rights Clinic) v. Tanzania*, CEDAW Committee Comm. No. 48/2012, 2 March 2015; *Law and Advocacy for Women in Uganda v. Attorney General of Uganda* [2007] UGCC 1; regarding discriminatory grounds for divorce in Uganda, see *Uganda Association of Women Lawyers and 5 others v. The Attorney General* [2004] UGCC 1; regarding child marriage in Zimbabwe, see *Mudzuru and Tspodozi v. Minister of Justice, Legal & Parliamentary Affairs and 2 others*, App. No. 79/14, Judgment no. CCZ 12/2015; regarding discrimination in registering property in Swaziland, see *The Attorney-General v. Mary-Joyce Doo Aphane*, [2010] SZSC 32. CEDAW has also positively impacted constitutional law-making in Kenya in 2010 and in Zimbabwe in 2013.

[33] Amongst other reservations, Egypt has made reservations to Article 16 CEDAW on equal rights of men and women to property in marriage, to Article 18(3) African Charter on Non-Discrimination and Equality, and Article 21(2) African Charter on the Rights and Welfare of the Child on child marriage; see Statement by the Institute for Human Rights and Development in Africa and the Cairo Institute for Human Rights Studies on the Reservations made by Egypt to the African Charter on Human and Peoples' Rights <http://www.ihrda.org/2011/04/3033/> accessed 31 January 2019; for CEDAW reservations, see <http://www.un.org/womenwatch/daw/cedaw/reservations-country.htm> accessed 31 January 2019; see also the advisory opinion of the Inter-American Court of Human Rights in *Juridical Condition and Rights of the Undocumented Migrants*, OC-18/03, 17 September 2003, [2003] Ser. A no. 18, paras 82–110.

III. BEYOND CEDAW

Professor Nussbaum is right to say that, as originally drafted, CEDAW showed poverty of ambition. However, in CEDAW General Recommendation no. 28 on State Obligations, the Committee noted: 'The spirit of the Convention covers other rights that are not explicitly mentioned in the Convention, but that have an impact on the achievement of equality of women with men, which impact represents a form of discrimination against women.'[34]

CEDAW has had a huge impact in many areas not least violence against women. CEDAW General Recommendation no. 19 on violence has, as Professor Nussbaum notes, led to the adoption of the UN Declaration on the Elimination of Violence against Women in 1993 (DEVAW) which in turn influenced the drafting and adoption of the Inter-American Convention on the Prevention and Eradication of Violence against Women (Belém Do Pará).[35] Inter-American case law has shown that Belém do Pará has been used to tackle inaction by states on issues pertaining to systematic violence against women as well as reproductive rights abuses including the failure to provide abortion services.[36] Some of these decisions have in turn led to changes in domestic law so that following the *da Penha* case, Brazil put in place a law on domestic violence, the Maria da Penha law.[37]

The first inquiry brought to CEDAW into the abduction, rape, and murder of women in and around Ciudad Juárez, Mexico and the state's failure to investigate was mirrored in the *Cotton Field* case before the Inter-American Court of Human Rights (IACtHR).[38] Similar findings were made about the failure of the Mexican State to exercise due diligence to prevent, investigate, prosecute, and punish the perpetrators. The Mexican government accepted the findings and promulgated the General Law of Access for Women to a Life Free from Violence (GLAWLFV) designed to address the failings found in the case. It is worth noting that a similar pattern was followed in the inquiry by the CEDAW Committee into extremely high levels of violence against aboriginal women and girls in Canada. The IACtHR launched its own inquiry which yielded similar findings to the Committee's. The

---

[34] CEDAW Committee General Recommendation no. 28 (n. 6) para. 7.
[35] Declaration on the Elimination of Violence against Women, A/RES/48/104 (20 December 1993); Inter-American Convention on the Prevention, Punishment and Eradication of Violence against Women (adopted 9 June 1994, entered into force 5 March 1995) 33 ILM 1534.
[36] *Ramírez Jacinto v. Mexico* (Friendly Settlement), Petition no. 161-02, 9 March 2007, Report no. 21/07 (also citing Article 12 CEDAW on health); *Maria da Penha v. Brazil*, Case no. 12.051, 16 April 2001, Report no. 54/01.
[37] See 'Maria da Penha Law: A Name that Changed Society' (*UN Women*, 30 August 2011) <http://www.unwomen.org/en/news/stories/2011/8/maria-da-penha-law-a-name-that-changed-society> accessed 31 January 2019.
[38] CEDAW Committee, 'Report on Mexico produced by the Committee on the Elimination of Discrimination against Women under article 8 of the Optional Protocol to the Convention, and reply from the Government of Mexico' CEDAW/C/2005/OP.8/MEXICO (27 January 2005); *Gonzalez, Monreal and Monarrez ('Cotton Field') v. Mexico*, Series C no. 205, 16 November 2009, para. 116 where the IACtHR referenced the CEDAW Committee's Mexico Inquiry.

domestic impact was that in 2016 the Canadian government set up an independent inquiry to look into the high numbers of disappearances and murders of indigenous women and girls and to consider reasons for state failure to act.[39]

The African Protocol on Women's Rights and the Council of Europe Protocol on the Elimination of Violence against Women are two instruments that have also benefitted enormously from critiques of CEDAW (i.e. what is missing) and also CEDAW jurisprudence. Both have provisions on all the controversial areas identified by Professor Nussbaum, for example, female genital mutilation, as well as comprehensive guidelines for states to follow to prevent and address violence.[40] In the *Personal Rights v. Egypt* case discussed above, the African Commission used both CEDAW and the provisions of the African Protocol on Women's Rights to assert that gender-based violence constituted discrimination against women and to hold Egypt responsible for the violations that had occurred to the four complainants who had been arrested and ill-treated by the police while in custody.[41] All these initiatives point to the dynamism of human rights.

The cases and documents highlight a point made by Professor Nussbaum about the impact of civil society, including the women's movement in the advancement of women's rights. The *Cotton Field* case shows that there were at least sixteen amicus briefs from international non-governmental organizations (NGOs) as well as university human rights clinics and a law firm. It is noteworthy that there was jurisdictional spread—they did not all come from the Americas, meaning that this regional issue was framed more broadly as one of global concern. The interconnectedness of peoples and human rights norms is also captured in the Southern African Development Community (SADC) Protocol on Gender and Development of 2008, which lists as one of its objectives the harmonization of the implementation of the various regional and international human rights instruments ratified by SADC states, starting the list with CEDAW.[42]

This harmonization project can also be seen in the jurisprudence of other UN treaty bodies. Recognizing that the girl child sits at the intersection of child and adulthood, the two committees under CEDAW and the CRC drafted a joint general recommendation/comment on traditional practices.[43] The Committee on

---

[39] Government of Canada, National Inquiry into Missing and Murdered Indigenous Women and Girls <http://www.aadnc-aandc.gc.ca/eng/1448633299414/1448633350146> accessed 31 January 2019.

[40] Protocol to the African Charter on Rights of Women (n. 17); Council of Europe Convention on Preventing and Combating Violence against Women and Domestic Violence (adopted 11 May 2011, entered into force 1 August 2014) CETS no. 210.

[41] *Egyptian Personal Rights Project and Others v. Interights* (n. 32) paras 87–90; see also the decision by the ECOWAS Community Court in *Dorothy Chioma Njemanze & 3 Ors v. Federal Republic of Nigeria*, Suit no. ECW/CCJ/APP/17/14, 12 October 2017.

[42] SADC Protocol on Gender and Development (adopted 17 August 2008, entered into force 22 February 2013) preamble <http://www.sadc.int/files/8713/5292/8364/Protocol_on_Gender_and_Development_2008.pdf> accessed 31 January 2019; see also Protocol to the African Charter on Rights of Women (n. 17) preamble; CEDAW Committee General Recommendation no. 28 (n. 6).

[43] Joint CEDAW Committee General Recommendation no. 31/ Committee on the Rights of the Child (CRC) General Comment no. 18, 'Harmful Practices', CEDAW/C/GC/31-CRC/C/GC/18.

Economic Social and Cultural Rights consulted with the CEDAW Committee and women's rights advocates in drafting its General Comment no. 16 on equality between men and women.[44] The CESCR General Comment no. 20 on non-discrimination and the Human Rights Committee General Comment no. 28 on equality between men and women both benefitted from and highlight the impact that CEDAW jurisprudence.[45] The adoption by these two human rights committees of the CEDAW perspective is particularly important not least because there are 'refusenik' states such as Sudan and the United States which have refused to ratify CEDAW. Their recalcitrance no longer matters because most of the objectives of CEDAW are captured in CCPR General Comment no. 28 on equality between men and women.

By working with other UN agencies such as the office of the UN High Commissioner for Refugees (UNHCR) and the Food and Agricultural Organisation (FAO) to draft its General Recommendations on women seeking asylum and also rural women respectively, CEDAW has been immeasurably enriched by the practical insights of agencies on the ground. They in turn have also benefitted from their interactions with CEDAW by having their conceptual framing and legal obligations brought into sharper focus.[46] More recently, CEDAW has been used as the template in the drafting and setting of targets for goal five on gender equality of the Sustainable Development Goals.[47] This global reach of the Convention should not be underestimated.

IV. ON THE CHALLENGE OF MEASURING PROGRESS

Professor Nussbaum is rightly concerned about what is known in some regions as 'domestication of human rights norms'. As already noted, there is a great deal of evidence to show that there has been greater use of CEDAW by local lawyers and, more importantly, judicial uptake of the Convention's principles in many jurisdictions.

Nevertheless, one has to acknowledge that Professor Nussbaum is right to highlight the difficulty of measuring progress and change. Attitudinal change, the focus

---

[44] Committee on Economic, Social and Cultural Rights (ICESCR) General Comment no. 16, 'The equal right of men and women to the enjoyment of all economic, social and cultural rights (art 3)' E/C.12/2005/4; 'Montréal Principles on Women's Economic, Social and Cultural Rights' (2004) 26 Human Rights Quarterly 760.

[45] Committee on Economic, Social and Cultural Rights (ICESCR) General Comment no. 20, 'Non-discrimination in economic, social and cultural rights (art 2(2))' E/C.12/GC/20; HR Committee (ICCPR) General Comment no. 28, 'The equality of rights between men and women (art 3)' CCPR/C/21/Rev.1/Add.10.

[46] This is in keeping with Article 22 CEDAW.

[47] The Sustainable Development Goals are contained in the 2030 Agenda for Sustainable Development, GA Res. A/RES/70/1 (21 October 2015).

of CEDAW's transformative equality approach, is hard to capture.[48] Equally difficult is compelling state compliance. This is not unique to CEDAW. The limits of CEDAW are the general limits of human rights dependence on state co-operation and a lack of direct enforceability.[49]

Meanwhile the use of indicators has recently come under scrutiny and been found wanting, especially when measuring gender-based violence.[50] The evidence that is available, which includes Sally Engle Merry's work investigating how civil society (acting nationally and transnationally) has used CEDAW to lobby domestically, shows that Nussbaum is right to highlight the importance of social movements in pushing states towards implementation of rights obligations they entered into.[51] Noteworthy here is also Moyn who argues that it is not clear that international human rights can necessarily be credited with change at the domestic level, not least because 'it is obvious that social mobilisation can do just fine—and achieve great things—without international law'. He further notes that domestic groups, sometimes acting in alliance with compatriots in other countries 'have done more good in the world so far than those operating under the colour of the additional authority provided by human rights treaty ratification'.[52]

There remains much to celebrate and the glass is definitely more than half full. Kathryn Sikkink challenges the current fashion for denigrating human rights. In her 2017 book *Evidence for Hope*, she bemoans the 'rise of economic inequality' but identifies the improvement in 'gender equality' as well as the rights of sexual minorities and those with disabilities.[53] She argues that treaties such as CEDAW provide the legal back-up for claims made by citizens and NGOs.

---

[48] Rikki Holtmaat, 'Article 5' in Marsha A Freeman, Christine Chinkin, and Beate Rudolf (eds), *The UN Convention on the Elimination of All Forms of Discrimination against Women: A Commentary* (Oxford University Press 2012) 141; Rebecca J Cook and Simone Cusack, *Gender Stereotyping: Transnational Legal Perspectives* (University of Pennsylvania Press 2009).

[49] HR Council, 'Report of the Working Group on the issue of discrimination against women in law and in practice' A/HRC/35/29 (19 April 2017).

[50] Kevin E Davis, Angelina Fisher, Benedict Kingsbury, and Sally Engle Merry (eds), *Governance by Indicators: Global Power through Quantification and Rankings* (Oxford University Press 2012).

[51] Merry, *Human Rights and Gender Violence* (n. 3).

[52] Samuel Moyn, 'Do Human Rights Treaties Make Enough of a Difference?' in Conor Gearty and Costas Douzinas (eds), *The Cambridge Companion to Human Rights Law* (Cambridge University Press 2012) 329, 343; Moyn's critique is of the work of Beth A Simmons, *Mobilizing for Human Rights: International Law in Domestic Politics* (Cambridge University Press 2009).

[53] Kathryn Sikkink, *Evidence for Hope: Making Human Rights Work in the 21st Century* (Princeton University Press 2017) 141; on progress on women's rights see ibid, 9–10 and 151–2; at 152 she cites academic research showing that 'CEDAW has been one of the most effective human rights treaties to date'.

V. CONCLUSION

While true that CEDAW as drafted is a thin version and vision of women's rights, the Committee has not allowed itself to be constrained by its drafting.[54] As the human rights corpus has grown, so too has CEDAW's framing of the problems. It has worked with other agencies. Its influence can be seen in the lobbying work of civil society, in interactions with governments in national and international forums. Moreover, its widespread citation in domestic case law points to its growing legitimacy and persuasive power. Of all the international human rights instruments, CEDAW, more than any other, has demonstrated its efficacy.

Bibliography

Allott A, *The Limits of Law* (Butterworths 1980)
Appiah KA, *The Honor Code: How Moral Revolutions Happen* (WW Norton & Co 2010)
Cook RJ and Cusack S, *Gender Stereotyping: Transnational Legal Perspectives* (University of Pennsylvania Press 2009)
Craven Nussbaum M, *Sex and Social Justice* (Oxford University Press 1999)
Craven Nussbaum M, 'Women's Progress and Women's Human Rights' in Fassbender B and Traisbach K (eds), *The Limits of Human Rights* (Oxford University Press 2019) 231
Davis KE, Fisher A, Kingsbury B, and Merry SE (eds), *Governance by Indicators: Global Power through Quantification and Rankings* (Oxford University Press 2012)
Halley J, *Split Decisions: How and Why to Take a Break from Feminism* (Princeton University Press 2006)
Holtmaat R, 'Article 5' in Freeman MA, Chinkin C, and Rudolf B (eds), *The UN Convention on the Elimination of All Forms of Discrimination against Women: A Commentary* (Oxford University Press 2012) 141
Keck ME and Sikkink K, *Activists Beyond Borders: Advocacy Networks in International Politics* (Cornell University Press 1998)
Merry SE, *Human Rights and Gender Violence: Translating International Law into Local Justice* (University of Chicago Press 2006)
Moyn S, 'Do Human Rights Treaties Make Enough of a Difference?' in Gearty C and Douzinas C (eds), *The Cambridge Companion to Human Rights Law* (Cambridge University Press 2012) 329
Ngwena C, Brookman-Amissah E, and Skuster P, 'Human Rights Advances in Women's Reproductive Health in Africa' (2015) 129 International Journal of Gynecology & Obstetrics 184
Risse T, Ropp SC, and Sikkink K (eds), *The Persistent Power of Human Rights: From Commitment to Compliance* (Cambridge University Press 2013)
Shupikai Tsanga A, *Taking Law to the People: Gender, Law Reform, and Community Legal Education in Zimbabwe* (Weaver Press 1996)

---

[54] See CEDAW Committee General Recommendation no. 25, 'Temporary special measures (art 4(1))' CEDAW/C/GC/25 para. 3, where the Committee describes the Convention as a 'dynamic instrument'.

Sikkink K, *Evidence for Hope: Making Human Rights Work in the 21st Century* (Princeton University Press 2017)

Simmons BA, *Mobilizing for Human Rights: International Law in Domestic Politics* (Cambridge University Press 2009)

Todres J and Howe LN, 'What the Convention on the Child Says (and Doesn't Say) about Abortion and Family Planning' in Todres J, Wojcik ME, and Revaz CR (eds), *The U.N. Convention on the Rights of the Child: An Analysis of Treaty Provisions and Implications of U.S. Ratification* (Transnational Publishers 2006) 163

Upreti M, 'Toward Transformative Equality in Nepal: The Lakshmi Dhikta Decision' in Cook RJ, Erdman JN, and Dickens BM (eds), *Abortion Law in Transnational Perspective: Cases and Controversies* (University of Pennsylvania Press 2014) 279

PART IV
LIMITS OF PRAGMATISM, LIMITS OF COMPROMISE: THE CASE OF ARMED CONFLICT

17
The Limits of the Laws of War

Frédéric Mégret

Every normative project contains the limits that are the secret to its dynamism. It is by not doing certain things that a project can positively engage in others. This is certainly true of the humanitarian tradition, a tradition very much fixated on what it is not and should not be about in order to be what it is and ought to be. At the same time, every limitation of this kind involves normative choices and hierarchies of priorities. It foregrounds a certain principle of action in the world at the expense of others. This renders every project susceptible to the critique that it is not doing more to deal with what it has excluded or to at least offset its specialization. It is important to note that a normative project can be quite candid about such limitations, seeing them as very deliberate, even as it exposes itself to such criticisms.

It is also worth noting the irony that the laws of war are in a sense all about *limiting* war. As one author puts it, for example, '[t]he objective of international humanitarian law is to *limit* the suffering caused by warfare and to alleviate its effects'.[1] Or, to take a foundational Hague law statement, 'the right of parties to an armed conflict to choose methods or means of warfare is not *unlimited*'. In that sense, the essence of the project is already about limiting what is imagined as being unlimited were it not for law's intervention. It may be that this view is simplistic: in limiting, the laws of war also *constitute* war as a specific form of violence that they also enable. In that sense, any project's limits can also be the source of its resilience.

At any rate, these limits, the limitations brought by law to war, are not what will be understood as the 'limits' of the humanitarian tradition; rather this chapter will be interested in 'the limits of limiting', where limits are understood as shortcomings rather than just conditions of possibility of the project. The humanitarian tradition is a very distinctive reformist project, steeped in a certain mindset that has evolved but that exhibits certain fundamental traits over time. This chapter seeks to portray it in its richness even as it emphasizes its limitations. The chapter distinguishes between what it describes as contingent and inherent limits. Contingent limits are limits that are seen as limits that do not define the tradition but merely constitute so many obstacles that it may encounter in the world (section I). Inherent limits point to some deeper limitation of the project anchored in its very existence, that is

---

[1] Hans-Peter Gasser, *International Humanitarian Law: An Introduction* (Haupt Publishers 1993) (emphasis added).

Frédéric Mégret, *The Limits of the Laws of War*. In: *The Limits of Human Rights*. Edited by: Bardo Fassbender and Knut Traisbach, Oxford University Press 2019. © The Several Contributors.
DOI: 10.1093/oso/9780198824756.003.0019

to say limits that arise within the humanitarian tradition itself (section II). The argument is that the contingent limitations, which are the ones that are most emphasized by the tradition itself, tend to be overemphasized at the expense of inherent limitations that far more durably constrain the enterprise.

I. CONTINGENT LIMITS

Contingent limitations are understood here as limitations that depend on elements that may well characterize the law at any one time but that do not fundamentally define it. Such limitations may be significant and focus much of the attention of the project but they can also be minimized and even temporarily overcome. Not only is the tradition quite aware of them but it has generally been quite devoted to dealing with them. In fact, the existence of contingent limits is inevitable and in some ways constantly produced by the interaction between the law and the worlds.

A. Lag behind the Reality of War

One of the chronic limitations of the humanitarian tradition is the tendency of war to evolve constantly beyond what it had previously been understood as being. If war is the laws of war's object then it has proved a remarkably evolving and at times elusive one. War moved from relatively predictable battlefield encounters, to trench warfare, to total war, to internecine conflicts. Whilst its targets may once have been predominantly combatants, they have increasingly become civilians. This has led to a sense that the laws of war are constantly running after developments, and often late by a war. Hardly a decade passes that does not bemoan the tendency of the laws of war to have fallen behind the times.[2] This has been particularly the case in a post 9/11 world wherein complex 'extra-territorial non-international armed conflicts' at times seem to create insoluble puzzles for lawyers.[3] The laws of war can thus appear to be engaged in a sort of race against time to prevent types of atrocities that have not been named yet. In the process, their fundamental blueprint for regulation may come under question.[4]

Nonetheless, this is not a limitation that the humanitarian tradition has particularly failed to respond to. Much of the dynamics of the laws of war has related to the effort to update the project. The key to the dynamism of the laws of war has

---

[2] See, e.g., Stephen E White, 'Brave New World: Neurowarfare and the Limits of International Humanitarian Law' (2008) 41 Cornell International Law Journal 177.

[3] Glenn M Sulmasy, 'The Law of Armed Conflict in the Global War on Terror: International Lawyers Fighting the Last War' (2005) 19 Notre Dame Journal of Law, Ethics & Public Policy 309.

[4] Frédéric Mégret, 'War and the Vanishing Battlefield' (2011) 9 Loyola University Chicago International Law Review 131.

historically been the adoption of more and more instruments devoted to filling some of the gaps that the latest conflict had rendered visible. States have shown themselves relatively willing to help nudge the laws of war forward. The resulting overall corpus is impressive and particularly rich. Moreover, the nature of the tradition is that it does consist in a series of principles that can be gradually spelled out to take into account the changing nature of war. In some cases, the laws of war have even anticipated technological developments that had not fully been realized.[5] The International Committee of the Red Cross (ICRC) has a particularly proactive attitude towards detecting emerging humanitarian issues. For example, projects exist to regulate cyber-warfare, killer robots, and even deal with the question of enhancements to soldiers.

At any rate, nor should the absolute need for change be overemphasized. At times, calls for a fundamental overhaul based on radically changed circumstances have been precocious and involved an insufficiently worked out theory of change. This means that little more is required in some circumstances than for the laws of war to simply stand their ground. It is also in the nature of the law that it cannot merely be anticipatory. In order to get traction from states and interest from civil society, the laws of war as a pragmatic enterprise must deal with known problems. Although some instruments have arrived too late, they have also often filled gaps for the future once they have arrived.

B. Lack of Enforcement

One key and frequently deplored limitation of the laws of war consist in its lack of enforcement. This has of course often been decried as one of the limitations of international law generally. There have historically been few forums where violations of the laws of war could be litigated. Compared to victims of human rights violations, victims of war crimes were not traditionally understood to have a right to remedy. However, there does seem to be a specificity to the laws of war as the precarious attempt to impose regulation in the most violent of environments, in a context of intense political passions and in the absence of strong mediating actors.

One may wonder, however, whether lack of enforcement as a complaint is not overinflated. It seems to rely on an Austinian investment in the threat of force as a measure of law's legality that we have reason to be sceptical of for international law generally. True, lack of enforcement when it comes to the laws of war may be not only particularly widespread but also particularly problematic given the gravity of the violations involved. Nonetheless, it seems that the question of *compliance* should be more important than the question of enforcement, and that the latter

---

[5] Burrus M Carnahan and Marjorie Robertson, 'The Protocol on "Blinding Laser Weapons": A New Direction for International Humanitarian Law' (1996) 90 American Journal of International Law 484.

cannot simply be equated with the former. In that respect, although it would certainly be hazardous to say, paraphrasing Lou Henkin, that most states respect most of the laws of war most of the time, it is also quite clear that there can be and probably is a degree of compliance with the laws of war despite minimal enforcement.

Traditionally, theorists of international humanitarian law have emphasized a range of ways in which the laws of war may be implemented short of enforcement. These include first and foremost reciprocity, whose role in war can be particularly efficient. Reciprocity helps explain why states adopt forms of restraint in war that seem to hamstring them: they constantly calculate the extent to which not submitting themselves to certain norms may lead other states to do the same. It is true that the laws of war have increasingly excluded what was once viewed as one of the most effective forms of implementation, namely reprisals, but these had always been of dubious effectivity, not to mention of course problematic from a rights perspective. Moreover, a range of sui generis means of compliance have been developed relatively effectively by international humanitarian lawyers. For example the ICRC has long offered a form of discreet humanitarian mediation that is often considered to be more effective than strident and public denunciations of violations. Since human rights non-governmental organizations (NGOs) have become more committed to the implementation of international humanitarian law, they have added their own voice.

At any rate, if that complaint about significant limitations in terms of enforcement was ever true, it has certainly been tempered by the progresses of enforcement, notably in the form of war crimes tribunals. Since the creation of the International Criminal Tribunal for the former Yugoslavia (ICTY) and the International Criminal Tribunal for Rwanda (ICTR) as well as the International Criminal Court (ICC), many prominent figures have been prosecuted for war crimes. Their trials, in addition, are only the emerged part of the iceberg of increasingly frequent trials by domestic or hybrid courts. To the search for individual accountability should be added the occasional interstate adjudication. For example humanitarian issues featured prominently as early as the *Nicaragua v. US* case, as well as in the advisory opinions on nuclear weapons and the wall in the occupied territories. Occasionally, reparations have been paid by states or individuals for violations of the laws of war. Finally, even if the laws of war remain lacking in terms of enforcement, there is no reason to believe that they are more so than any other norm of international law.

C. The Interstate Character of the Regulation of War

A significant limit of the regulation of war is its embeddedness in the interstate matrix of international law specifically. Do the laws of war really express a humanitarian ambition or is that ambition significantly curtailed by the law's sovereign trappings? The suspicion is that states are not only interested in humanizing war but more generally favouring a particular sovereign vision of legitimate violence. This is of course not untrue. The system is limited by the fact that it is predicated on a high degree of State voluntarism. The laws of war, at least in their modern configuration, could not exist without state support. Treaties only exist because of state ratification, custom because of state practice, and 'general principles' are those practised by states. The laws of war also express a distinct sovereign sensitivity that is, for example, quite fixated on the idea of military necessity as not merely a limitative but also fundamentally permissive device.

This is, however, again something that needs to be relativized. Sovereignty is not necessarily the opposite of humanitarianism as much as the other side of the same coin. The two have often historically gone hand in hand, as states modernized and increasingly sought to uphold certain basic values in war. The ICRC is an organization which has had considerable state support, for example. The laws of war can probably never hope to entirely transcend this interstate character. In many ways, it is an inevitable byproduct of the investment in international law. Moreover, state embeddedness is not incompatible with a capacity to move beyond addressing only states. As a result of the increasing criminalization of breaches of the laws of war, individuals are considered to be directly liable under international law for the war crimes they commit, to the point that they are generally held to be under an obligation to disobey orders or risk criminal liability. The 'Geneva Call' initiative which seeks to elicit support for humanitarian instruments directly from non-state actors is a case in point.[6]

At any rate, the entire arc of the history of the law of armed conflict can be seen as an evolution from an emphasis on the necessities of war to one in which the protection of non-combatants takes centre stage. From the outset the laws of war expressed more than mere sovereign fiat. The initiative for them often came from outside the core circles of sovereign power. The principle of 'humanity' arguably always provided a counterpoint to the principle of necessity. Moreover, the laws of war have undergone a gradual process of 'humanization'.[7] This extends not only to caring increasingly about civilians but also refers more generally to the influence of human rights on the structure of international humanitarian law. It is not as if international humanitarian law has become synonymous with human rights, but the law of armed conflict reflects an increasingly less harsh concept of what is acceptable in war.

---

[6] See Geneva Call, 'Mission' <https://www.genevacall.org/who-we-are/> accessed 31 January 2019.
[7] Theodor Meron, 'The Humanization of Humanitarian Law' (2000) 94 The American Journal of International Law 239.

II. INHERENT LIMITS

Inherent limits are limitations that are largely embedded into the law and thus much harder to escape. One might describe them as constitutive limitations: limitations that make the humanitarian tradition possible but at the same time constrain what it can become. Such limits may at times be almost too obvious to be noticed, even though their effect is manifest in certain failures of the humanitarian project. This section highlights three major limits inherent in the humanitarian tradition, those of legalism (A), compromise (B), and pragmatism (C).

A. The Limits of Legalism

One inherent limitation of the humanitarian project is its early investment in positive international law, at the expense of various traditions that had preceded it such as chivalrous restraint or Just War thinking. For much of its history, the humanitarian project (or what loosely preceded it) had not taken a distinctly legal form, at least as understood today. A great deal of anachronism is involved in seeing early natural law thinking about the 'jus' of war as directly foreshadowing the project that began to emerge in the second half of the nineteenth century. In fact, the very founding idea of the contemporary humanitarian tradition is not the humanitarian intuition (an intuition that had arguably existed for centuries, if not longer) but an intuition about the need to merge that earlier idea with the rising trust in international law as a mode of regulation. This is very clear early on, for example, in Henry Dunant's idea that what was needed was the '[a]doption by all civilized nations of an international and sacred principle which would be assured and placed on record by a convention to be concluded between governments'. The rise of the humanitarian sensitivity in international law is impossible to distinguish, as it happens, from the rise of international legal positivism and the role of a 'civilizing' avant guarde.[8]

As part of that embrace of the international legal form, several assumptions stand out. First, the law is a promise of a greater deal of determinacy. Second, the laws of war are to be anchored not in speculation about natural law or divine will but the reality of international society, as incarnated by states. Third, the law is to be irrevocably binding. It is not clear that the humanitarian tradition has been served well by these assumptions, and it may be that legalization promised too much. The binding character of the law is perhaps its most endurable and at least conceptually undeniable appeal. But it is unclear that the laws of war are more determinate than the natural law thinking they have displaced and, in fact,

---

[8] Martti Koskenniemi, *The Gentle Civilizer of Nations: The Rise and Fall of International Law, 1870–1960* (Cambridge University Press 2002).

much reasoning in the laws of war often ends up taking the appearance of sophisticated moral casuistry as principles such as 'necessity', 'humanity', or 'proportionality' seem to beg the questions they are meant to answer. As to the foundation of the laws of war in the social reality of the international system, it remains very equivocal, given the porous nature of such concepts as 'humanity', 'civilization', or 'international society'.

But even if the law delivered on all these things, the investment in the law would arguably still create some serious limitations. In particular, it would still exclude all traditions that are henceforth not reducible to this legal formula, in ways that may impoverish our understanding of how restraint in war is actually brought about. In this context, efforts to reexplore the potential of certain traditions in upholding restraint in war, such as chivalry,[9] are welcome, but remain limited and academic in nature. Initiatives to vernacularize the laws of war remain problematically dependent on the law: the vernacular always seems to be there to convey the law, rather than being treated as a normative language in its own right. The range of cultural, religious, or philosophical reasons why any army would respect limitations in war has not been fully mapped out; nor is there a clear understanding of how non-positive or non-state-based normative systems might co-exist with the dominant apparatus of sovereign regulation.

Another reason for investing in international law is the possibility of expanding a certain regulatory model principally born, in its contemporary version, in Europe to the rest of the world. In that respect, the laws of war have certainly served as a vehicle to expand a certain understanding of 'proper warfare' to the globe, although this may be a mixed blessing.[10] The belief in the universalism of the laws of war, however, remains somewhat problematic and the fact that the Geneva Conventions have been extremely widely ratified does not guarantee against cultural scepticism towards them.[11] Finally, it remains unclear that if and when the laws of war are respected they are respected as a result of the laws of war. Correlation (the existence of laws and the existence of compliance with them) is not the same thing as causation, and the laws of war might be complied with for other reasons, or at least not the reasons that the investment into the law would lead one to believe.

---

[9] Theodor Meron, *Bloody Constraint: War and Chivalry in Shakespeare* (Oxford University Press 1998).

[10] Frédéric Mégret, 'From "Savages" to "Unlawful Combatants": A Postcolonial Look at International Humanitarian Law's "Other"' in Anne Orford (ed.), *International Law and its Others* (Cambridge University Press 2006).

[11] Frédéric Mégret, 'The Universality of the Geneva Conventions' in Andrew Clapham, Paola Gaeta, and Marco Sassòli (eds), *The 1949 Geneva Conventions: A Commentary* (Oxford University Press 2015).

B. The Limits of Compromise

The laws of war remain fundamentally limited in their humanitarian aspiration because in order to have any traction they must remain relatively close to the reality of war whilst simultaneously not being overcome by that reality. The result is a constant compromise that is at times promising, yet at others, insipid and weak. The laws of war certainly prohibit some conduct but they also do so as part of a complex quid pro quo which leads them to fundamentally license other conduct.[12] The regulative dimension of the laws of war may turn out to be less important than their constitutive dimension. In effect, the laws of war constantly operate a compromise between the 'apology' of 'necessity' and the 'utopia' of 'humanity'[13] which leaves very little space for anything but reform at the margins of something that is fundamentally tolerated.[14]

To begin with, the humanitarian tradition is born from a fundamental faith in the possibility of there being something such as law in war; that something, moreover, is not to be mistaken with a fundamental licence for ruthlessness. Contra early apostles of *Kriegsraison* and its echoes in later wars, humanitarians insisted that the laws of war were an essential element of the civilized character of the international community. If the laws of war merely instructed armies to do that which they already do, presumably for some other reason, they would be 'respected' scrupulously but for reasons that had little to do with the law, and made a mockery of the law's reformist ambitions.

Yet the laws of war also become too detached from the reality of war at the risk of irrelevance or failure. The laws of war have long been faulted for being utopian, based on naïve sentimentalism, disconnected from the reality of war. Historically, attempts to outlaw weapons which states, for whatever reason, had no interest in regulating have failed. For example, the effort to outlaw aerial bombing in the 1920s went nowhere. In fact, the condition of regulating war must be a fundamental acceptance of its reality. One can only hope to regulate what one recognizes. The *jus in bello* cannot become another way of outlawing war or destroy itself in the process. Hence the laws of war's tendency to constantly 'skim the surface'.

This is clear in a range of areas. For example, there is no doubt that the killing of civilians is abhorrent and should be avoided at all costs. At the same time, a prohibition on *any* civilian casualties, however accidental, would raise the threshold of humanitarianism so high as to make it virtually impossible to conduct war legally.

---

[12] Frédéric Mégret, 'Thinking About What International Humanitarian Lawyers "Do": An Examination of the Laws of War as a Field of Professional Practice' in Wouter Werner, Marieke de Hoon, and Alexis Galán (eds), *The Law of International Lawyers: Reading Martti Koskenniemi* (Cambridge University Press 2017) 265.

[13] Martti Koskenniemi, *From Apology to Utopia: The Structure of International Legal Argument* (Cambridge University Press 2005).

[14] Chris af Jochnick and Roger Normand, 'The Legitimation of Violence: A Critical History of the Laws of War' (1994) 35 Harvard International Law Journal 49.

As a result, the laws of war seek to 'save what can be saved' by at least prohibiting the direct targeting of civilians, but simultaneously allowing for a measure of collateral harm to civilians under certain apparently strict conditions. In some ways this safeguards a deontological core, but it also introduces a huge systemic indeterminacy at the heart of the law that is rife with violence.

Methods of combat (such as bombings), for example, are prohibited if they cause collateral harm that is disproportionate to the military advantage sought. But how much advantage to harm does it take? And is the law not measuring things that are fundamentally incommensurable? Predictably, the law is rather quiet on how these weighing exercises are to be carried out. The impossibility of outlawing harm to civilians altogether means significant harm to civilians collaterally is the price to pay for outlawing direct harm. In practice of course it is not clear that great humanitarian strides have been accomplished in the process: although something is undeniably safeguarded by prohibiting direct harm, this may be more than offset by harm of the collateral sort. This is especially the case in situations where sophisticated militaries incorporate the law's constraint to such a point that its permissive potential becomes at least as important as its regulative and limitative capacity.[15]

Beyond the difficulties of protecting civilians, one of the greatest limitations of regulation in war is the protection of combatants. Aside from the fact that combatants-who-are-no-longer-combatants (the wounded, those who surrender) benefit from a range of protections, combatants do enjoy certain humanitarian benefits in the course of hostilities. These include the prohibition on superfluous injury or unnecessary suffering, on certain weapons that are associated with such effects, and the prohibition of certain methods of combat (e.g. ordering 'no quarter'). This still leaves considerable potential for the killing of combatants which is indeed protected under the laws of war in the sense that combatants can never be prosecuted merely for having killed other combatants. Recent efforts at conceptualizing some further humanitarian restraint in relation to combatants have been resisted quite strongly and cannot avoid that fundamental reality.[16]

In the end, the suspicion may be that, as a result of the humanitarianism's very reformist limitations, the laws of war do not only regulate but end up *constituting* a particular acceptable form of warfare. The cliché of Henry Dunant *arriving* on the battlefield as humanitarianism and law *arrive* to war as benign and civilizing influences risks neglecting the extent to which law's regulation has always been intrinsic to war. Insights from the theory of rules, notably as they pertain to language or games, may be useful. All rules are both limitative *and* permissive. For instance, the rules of grammar do not simply limit me in whatever language, they also quite

---

[15] David Kennedy, *Of War and Law* (Princeton University Press 2006).
[16] Gabriella Blum, 'The Dispensable Lives of Soldiers' (2010) 2 Journal of Legal Analysis 115; Ryan Goodman, 'The Power to Kill or Capture Enemy Combatants' (2013) 24 European Journal of International Law 819.

literally make it possible for one to express oneself in that language (the same could be said of the rules of chess, which do not merely hinder what would otherwise be a free—but clearly non-sensical—game of chess). The laws of war in this respect limit what can be done, but the process also licenses certain behaviour. As a result, having outlined an 'ideal' war, they may make it harder to challenge it. The limitations of the humanitarian compromise may explain why part of international humanitarian law is now so tempted to move towards an approach much more inspired by human rights.

C. The Limits of Pragmatism

The laws of war's relationship to the very idea of war and its legality has long been fraught. In the Just War tradition, the *ad bellum* and *in bello* conditions of the legitimacy of waging war were never entirely separated. To wage a war justly, one needed to do so both for good cause and in a just way, among others. The formalization of the laws of war as such has led to the radical separation of the regulation of the waging of war from the broader conceptual apparatus concerned with its fundamental legality. This is often credited to humanitarianism's overriding pragmatism: given the persistence of war, the difficulty of assessing who is on the right and legal side of any given conflict, and the likelihood that both will claim that they are, there is a space for a pragmatic humanitarian regulation that sets a baseline of behaviour in conflict. Although it is generally claimed that this distinction really only emerged in a *jus contra bellum* era after the Second World War, it is quite clear that it already created tensions at the time of the emergence of the *jus in bello*. For example, the joint award of the first Nobel Peace Prize to Henry Dunant and Frédéric Passy, a well-know pacifist of the time, gave rise to a controversy in which pacifists criticized the award of a peace prize to a group whose vocation was the humanization of war.[17]

A well-known tenet of the laws of war tradition became that their operation depends, in fact, on the radical separation between the *jus in bello* and the *jus ad bellum*.[18] This was reinforced after the Second World War despite or because of the fact that war had henceforth been clearly recognized as illegal. Aside from the odd challenge to the separation notably in the 1970s as a result of struggles of national liberation, it has become one of the fundamental pillars of the *jus in bello*. From a humanitarian perspective of course it makes sense that certain limitations

---

[17] André Durand, 'Le premier Prix Nobel de La Paix (1901): Candidatures d'Henry Dunant, de Gustave Moynier et du Comité international de la Croix-Rouge' (2001) 83 International Review of the Red Cross 275.

[18] Jenny Martinez and Antoine Bouvier, 'Assessing the Relationship between *Jus in Bello* and *Jus Ad Bellum*: An "Orthodox" View' (2006) 100 Proceedings of the Annual Meeting (American Society of International Law) 109.

should apply to both sides, namely the aggressor and the self-defending state. The fact that one is waging a just/legal war does not make attacks that are gratuitous or that harm non-combatants any more fathomable. The distinction needs to be maintained in the face of attacks of this sort, which have long threatened the operation of the laws of war.

More troublesome, however, is the idea that, in a *jus contra bellum* era, the acts of *both* sides are privileged so that killing by aggressor combatants is just as legal as killing by the self-defending state's combatants. This aspect of the conventional understanding of the laws of war has been intensely criticized by some contemporary just war theorists,[19] although most end up deferring to the laws of war on prudential grounds. From a legal point of view, one of the concrete effects may be the at least objective undermining of the prohibition against war, and an effective 'humanitarian laundering' of what may be, in some cases at least, deliberate participation in an unlawful war.[20] Some human rights scholars have noted that the idea that human rights should defer to the *lex specialis* of the laws of war gives up a little too easily on the human right interest in making sure that the 'right to peace' is respected.[21] It is to be noted that the laws of war aspire to regulate non-international armed conflicts, despite neither side—but certainly not armed groups—being particularly privileged. In other words, an asymmetrical view of the regulation of armed conflict, one where both sides have the same humanitarian obligations but not the same privileges is not just theoretically but also practically conceivable.[22]

Nonetheless, the equality of belligerents remains a cardinal principle to this day, perhaps as a result of the inability to better distinguish between obligations and privileges in the laws of war. The idea that war may be illegal but that the killing of combatants within one is always legal reinforces the particular exorbitant status of war in international law. It means that one can 'legally participate in an illegal war', in ways that would be inconceivable when it comes to genocide or crimes against humanity and that reinforce the ethical exceptionalism of war. In that respect, the tradition of the laws of war is also part of the reification of war and its unchallengeability as a form of violence. This is arguably even more the case in non-international armed conflicts where there is no legal 'ad bellum' dimension and where regulation is entirely left, at best, to humanitarianism and human rights.

Even though international humanitarian lawyers may claim to be pacifist, therefore, they are pacifist in a very different, world-wary way than most pacifists have

---

[19] Jeff McMahan, *Killing in War* (Oxford University Press 2009).
[20] Frédéric Mégret, 'What Is the Specific Evil of Aggression?' in Claus Kreß and Stefan Barriga (eds), *The Crime of Aggression: A Commentary* (Cambridge University Press 2016) 1398.
[21] William A Schabas, '*Lex Specialis*? Belt and Suspenders? The Parallel Operation of Human Rights Law and the Law of Armed Conflict, and the Conundrum of Jus Ad Bellum' (2007) 40 Israel Law Review 592.
[22] Frédéric Mégret, 'Response to Claus Kreß: Leveraging the Privilege of Belligerency in Non-International Armed Conflict Towards Respect for the Jus in Bello' (2014) 96 International Review of the Red Cross 16.

historically been pacifists. The claim that respect for certain minimum humanitarian standards can help pave the way to peace in war for example,[23] whilst undeniably correct, is not the same thing as the claim that wars of aggression should be absolutely prohibited, and that no privilege of the combatant should attach to those knowingly participating in an unlawful war. In fact, the laws of war at times seem more in line with a tradition that has been sceptical of the very possibility of the *jus contra bellum*.

III. CONCLUSION

The laws of war exist in a space of contingent limitations that can be contingently overcome and inherent ones that are merely reproduced by any effort (if there is any such effort) to transcend them. The project remains remarkably mired in some of the assumptions that were present at its genesis in the mid-nineteenth century. This has conferred on it a remarkable resilience but it is also what makes it irrelevant in many contexts and may explain why, despite the accumulation of instruments, it is unclear whether the laws of war can, in the long run, be described as a success or a self-fulfilling prophecy of endless violence.

Bibliography

Blum G, 'The Dispensable Lives of Soldiers' (2010) 2 Journal of Legal Analysis 115
Carnahan BM and Robertson M, 'The Protocol on "Blinding Laser Weapons": A New Direction for International Humanitarian Law' (1996) 90 American Journal of International Law 484
Durand A, 'Le premier Prix Nobel de La Paix (1901): Candidatures d'Henry Dunant, de Gustave Moynier et du Comité international de la Croix-Rouge' (2001) 83 International Review of the Red Cross 275
Gasser HP, *International Humanitarian Law: An Introduction* (Haupt Publishers 1993)
Goodman R, 'The Power to Kill or Capture Enemy Combatants' (2013) 24 European Journal of International Law 819
af Jochnick C and Normand R, 'The Legitimation of Violence: A Critical History of the Laws of War' (1994) 35 Harvard International Law Journal 49
Kennedy D, *Of War and Law* (Princeton University Press 2006)
Koskenniemi M, *The Gentle Civilizer of Nations: The Rise and Fall of International Law, 1870–1960* (Cambridge University Press 2002)
Koskenniemi M, *From Apology to Utopia: The Structure of International Legal Argument* (Cambridge University Press 2005)

---

[23] Michel Veuthey, 'International Humanitarian Law and the Restoration and Maintenance of Peace' (1998) 7 African Security Review 26.

Martinez J and Bouvier A, 'Assessing the Relationship between Jus in Bello and Jus Ad Bellum: An "Orthodox" View' (2006) 100 Proceedings of the Annual Meeting (American Society of International Law) 109

McMahan J, *Killing in War* (Oxford University Press 2009)

Mégret F, 'From "Savages" to "Unlawful Combatants": A Postcolonial Look at International Humanitarian Law's "Other"' in Orford A (ed.), *International Law and its Others* (Cambridge University Press 2006)

Mégret F, 'War and the Vanishing Battlefield' (2011) 9 Loyola University Chicago International Law Review 131

Mégret F, 'Response to Claus Kreß: Leveraging the Privilege of Belligerency in Non-International Armed Conflict Towards Respect for the Jus in Bello' (2014) 96 International Review of the Red Cross 16

Mégret F, 'The Universality of the Geneva Conventions' in Clapham A, Gaeta P, and Sassòli M (eds), *The 1949 Geneva Conventions: A Commentary* (Oxford University Press 2015)

Mégret F, 'What Is the Specific Evil of Aggression?' in Kreß C and Barriga S (eds), *The Crime of Aggression: A Commentary* (Cambridge University Press 2016) 1398

Mégret F, 'Thinking About What International Humanitarian Lawyers "Do": An Examination of the Laws of War as a Field of Professional Practice' in Werner W, de Hoon M, and Galán A (eds), *The Law of International Lawyers: Reading Martti Koskenniemi* (Cambridge University Press 2017) 265

Meron T, *Bloody Constraint: War and Chivalry in Shakespeare* (Oxford University Press 1998)

Meron T, 'The Humanization of Humanitarian Law' (2000) 94 The American Journal of International Law 239

Schabas WA, '*Lex Specialis*? Belt and Suspenders? The Parallel Operation of Human Rights Law and the Law of Armed Conflict, and the Conundrum of Jus Ad Bellum' (2007) 40 Israel Law Review 592

Sulmasy GM, 'The Law of Armed Conflict in the Global War on Terror: International Lawyers Fighting the Last War' (2005) 19 Notre Dame Journal of Law, Ethics & Public Policy 309

Veuthey M, 'International Humanitarian Law and the Restoration and Maintenance of Peace' (1998) 7 African Security Review 26

White SE, 'Brave New World: Neurowarfare and the Limits of International Humanitarian Law' (2008) 41 Cornell International Law Journal 177

18
The Banality of Humanity (as an Absolute)
A Response to Frédéric Mégret

Knut Traisbach

'Whoever invokes humanity, wants to cheat.' So goes the famous adage of Carl Schmitt. He objected to a false universalism that obscures hegemonic interests. For Schmitt it was impossible to eschew the political by invoking the universal. What else should substitute for this universalizing language, and what kind of politics is expressed through this universalizing language are, of course, important questions to ask in this context. An additional problem with this type of statement is that one can replace the word 'humanity' with almost anything else: truth, universality, justice, ethics, politics, international law, human rights, but also evil, hegemony, or particularism—it would all fit in this sentence and would hold some truth. How illuminating is it then to think in terms of 'whoever invokes ... wants to cheat' or, as the title of this comment suggests, 'the banality of ... '? I argue in this comment that these formulations point us less to tensions between the universal and the particular (or the hegemonic and the inclusive), but to the problem of absolutes in political and legal discourses.

In his thought-provoking essay on the limits of the humanitarian tradition, Professor Frédéric Mégret seems to avoid absolutes. Neither does he overly praise humanitarian law, nor does he proclaim its failure. He describes different limits of the humanitarian tradition and different functions of these limits. He identifies limitations to what international humanitarian law (IHL) has achieved and can achieve, but also explains how limits may enable and legitimize a particular form of warfare and its legal regulation.

The first section of his essay deals with contingent limits which he defines as limits that characterize but do not fundamentally define the law of armed conflicts because they can be contingently overcome. Professor Mégret discusses the need for adaptation to the evolving nature of war, the difficulties of enforcement, and the complex ways in which IHL navigates between multiple interests of state and non-state actors. He acknowledges these contingent limits but simultaneously relativizes them considerably for a more balanced assessment. This is comforting because the limits he discusses—related to changing realities, compliance, and state voluntarism—resonate equally in human rights law and public international law.

Knut Traisbach, *The Banality of Humanity (as an Absolute): A Response to Frédéric Mégret*. In: *The Limits of Human Rights*. Edited by: Bardo Fassbender and Knut Traisbach, Oxford University Press 2019.
© The Several Contributors.
DOI: 10.1093/oso/9780198824756.003.0020

Also in the latter two normative settings these limits are not absolute and have contingently changed: limits can be moved (think of 'humanization'), their function can be altered (think of 'relativized' sovereignty), and new actors can enter the field and move towards the centre (think of international institutions and non-state actors).

In the more challenging second section, Frédéric Mégret goes on to discuss inherent limits that he defines as constitutive, for they 'make the humanitarian tradition possible but at the same time constrain what it can become'.[1] He identifies IHL and humanitarianism throughout as a 'project', a 'mindset', or a 'tradition', and it is in this context that his critical legal thinking becomes most evident. I agree with a great deal of his analysis and will try to expand his logic of inquiry a bit further beyond the observation that IHL oscillates between the 'apology of necessity' and the 'utopia of humanity', or between resilience and irrelevance.[2] These absolutes remain the inherent limits in Mégret's own analysis.

I. THE LIMITS OF LAW

In his discussion of the inherent limits of IHL Frédéric Mégret highlights that expressing the humanitarian 'sensitivity' through law relates to a particular positivistic tradition which always remains under the suspicion of reflecting (also) partisan and civilizing interests of mainly European pedigree. The international codification of IHL might in the end promise too much and consequently impoverish our understanding of how war is or could be constrained by 'non-positive or non-State-based normative systems'.

It is certainly true that law does not 'solve' dilemmas of partisanship and dominance. The legal regulation of war provides the desired determinacy only ostensibly. Through legalization the same contentious issues are often just expressed in a different vernacular.[3] The legal prohibition of war is an apt example. International lawyers hardly argue anymore in terms of 'just war' but instead they exchange legal arguments about whether the conditions for self-defence are met, they argue about the immanency of attacks, or about the applicability of humanitarian rules to a 'global war on terror'. The legal prohibition of torture, as another example, means that lawyers cannot (and should not) justify torture anymore, instead they argue now about whether certain 'techniques' qualify as torture or not. The legal prohibition has displaced the discussion; it has not solved the dilemma. In no instance

---

[1] Frédéric Mégret, 'The Limits of the Laws of War' in Bardo Fassbender and Knut Traisbach (eds), *The Limits of Human Rights* (Oxford University Press 2019) 283, 288 (hereafter Mégret, 'The Limits of the Laws of War').

[2] Ibid, 290 and 294.

[3] Knut Traisbach, 'International Law' in Stephen McGlinchey (ed.), *International Relations* (E-International Relations 2017) 57, 68–9.

does the legal regulation mean that law provides easy answers due to its alleged determinacy, concreteness, and binding effect. Law hardly promises more than a 'common' language and techniques administered by experts who are trained in the required practice but cannot shun politics and biases. It would thus be interesting, as Professor Mégret suggests, to map out more fully the cultural, religious, or philosophical reasons beyond law that can motivate respect for limitations of war. We would then also need to ask whether any of these alternatives could avoid promising 'too much', shun partisan purposes, or refrain from referring to porous and morally overburdened concepts such as 'humanity'.

Professor Mégret identifies as a second inherent limit the need for a constant compromise between the reality of war and staying true to the humanitarian ideal. He speaks in this context of IHL's fate to 'skim the surface' and a huge systemic indeterminacy that becomes evident, for example, in appeals to a proportionality as a balancing act that law itself cannot determine unequivocally. The fact that IHL permits certain bellicose acts during armed conflicts despite the general prohibition of war also testifies to the compromising nature of IHL. IHL 'licenses' and 'constitutes' a particular acceptable form of warfare which makes it, Mégret argues, more difficult to otherwise challenge war. Even more, it makes the parties to an armed conflict more acceptable, too. IHL's pragmatic neutrality requires that it does not privilege or discriminate against any party even if one of them has illegally started the conflict or knowingly participates in an unlawful war.

It is difficult to disagree with the brighter and darker sides of humanitarian law that Professor Mégret describes. However, I feel that his focus on oscillations between 'opposite' interests overemphasizes absolutes at either end of the oscillation. This in turn results in the identification of particular limits and conclusions that reinforce this oscillation rather than challenge it. All of his conclusions regarding the inherent limits—the questionable promise of legalism, the compromising nature, the humanitarian laundering and the reification of war—ultimately reflect a thinking about humanitarian law that is bound by opposing absolutes. In the following section, I exemplify this proposition with reference to Hannah Arendt and her thoughts on 'humanity' which in a particular instantiation is one of IHL's 'porous' guiding principles.

II. INHERENT LIMITS

In his essay, Professor Mégret shows us both end points of the oscillation: reality and ideal; determinacy and porosity; limiting the excessive and constituting the permissive. There is the side of realism, state voluntarism, necessity, hegemony, licensed behaviour, mainstream, and sovereign privilege. And there is the side of adaptation, compliance, socialization, normative restraint, and pragmatism.

'[H]ow much reality must be retained even in a world become inhuman if humanity is not to be reduced to an empty phrase or a phantom'? This is a question that Hannah Arendt once asked in her address on accepting the Lessing Prize.[4] We could ask the same question about humanitarian law and also about human rights law and 'humanized' international law.

Hannah Arendt's question related to her thinking about humanity in dark times and in a wider sense about evil and the human condition. What I would like to show in this comment is how Arendt conceived of different conceptions of humanity. She criticized notions of humanity based on absolutes and passivity. She favoured instead a conception that emphasized relations, the enablement of politically relevant action, and responsibility.

A first conception of humanity Arendt locates in the philosophical roots of Enlightenment and in particular in Rousseau.[5] It is the humanity of the pariah in dark times which she connects to a shrunken interspace between humans. The space 'in-between'[6] humans disappears because persecuted humans and enslaved groups are forced to withdraw from the public realm and move, in Arendt's image, closer together towards an interior realm. A wordlessness and unreality of human relationships prevails.

The humanitarianism of brotherhood between the pariahs results from a withdrawal from the world, and it finds its counterpart in feelings of compassion and solidarity of those who do not belong among the pariahs. For Arendt, this conception of humanity is based on ideas of a common human nature but it is not about actively speaking and acting in a common world. The common world, the politically relevant space between humans, is lost.[7] The empathy of others can derive from a common rationality or a common sentimentality, but these 'psychological substitutes' are, according to Arendt, temporary and fleeting.[8] Even more, this state of humanity, where the common world is lost and meaningful action is impossible, is 'in political terms ... absolutely irrelevant'.[9] The withdrawal from the world is not voluntary, for not all others feel compassion. Those who withdraw are forced to do so because others regard them as less than human and deny them an equal status of humanity.[10] This is why Arendt considered the insistence on one's humanity, like

---

[4] Hannah Arendt, 'On Humanity in Dark Times: Thoughts about Lessing' in Hannah Arendt (ed.), *Men in Dark Times* (Harcourt Brace & Co 1995) 3, 22 (hereafter Arendt, 'Humanity in Dark Times').

[5] Ibid, 14.

[6] Jeremy Waldron, 'The Constitutional Politics of Hannah Arendt' in Jeremy Waldron (ed.), *Political Theory* (Harvard University Press 2016) 290, 294 (hereafter Waldron, 'The Constitutional Politics of Hannah Arendt').

[7] Arendt, 'Humanity in Dark Times' (n. 4) 12 and 16.

[8] Ibid, 16: 'The humanity of the insulted and inured has never yet survived the hour of liberation by so much as a minute'.

[9] Ibid, 16–17 and 22.

[10] See Richard Rorty, 'Human Rights, Rationality, and Sentimentality' in Stephen Shute and Susan Hurley (eds), *On Human Rights: The Oxford Amnesty Lectures 1993* (Basic Books 1993) 111.

in Lessing's *Nathan the Wise*, 'as nothing but a grotesque and dangerous evasion of reality'.[11]

Another notion of humanity is noticeable in Arendt's thinking about 'crimes against humanity'. This new crime was for her a crime '"against the human status," or against the very nature of mankind'.[12] But humanity in this context did not refer to an abstract global conscience or an imagined human family. Arendt spoke here rather of a crime against human plurality and diversity as fundamental characteristics of the human condition.[13] A crime like genocide broke a different order and violated a different community because it attacked the very plurality of humankind.[14]

I believe that these two notions of humanity—characterized by humaneness, kinship, solidarity, plurality, community, and representation—are the conceptions that resonate most in humanitarian law and that also shine through Professor Mégret's analysis of the nature of IHL and its inherent limits. There is the notion of humanity as a guiding humanitarian principle that intends to preserve the human status and aims at reducing unnecessary suffering in the exceptional state of armed conflict.[15] There is also a notion of humanity that stands closer to natural law thinking, moral casuistry, and functions as a guiding, humanizing, even rule-inducing but ultimately equivocal and porous principle.[16] These notions of humanity are countered by state voluntarism, sovereign prerogative, and the realities of war.

---

[11] Arendt, 'Humanity in Dark Times' (n. 4) 18 and 23; to which Amos Elon added: 'In the real, as against the mythical, world, insisting that one was first and foremost a *Mensch* was never enough to ensure respect for one's human rights. To be a *Mensch* was a private, not a political, quality. In the real world, it was only as political creatures that minorities were able to demand and, if they were lucky, win acceptance of diversity and eventually gain equality, too. Politically, when they insisted that they were nothing but *Menschen*, they were, in Arendt's words, already lost', see Amos Elon, *The Pity of It All: A Portrait of the German-Jewish Epoch 1743–1933* (Picador 2002) 64 (emphasis in the original).

[12] Hannah Arendt, *Eichmann in Jerusalem: A Report on the Banality of Evil* (Penguin 1994) 268 (hereafter Arendt, *Eichmann in Jerusalem*).

[13] Ibid, 268–9; Seyla Benhabib, 'International Law and Human Plurality in the Shadow of Totalitarianism' in Seyla Benhabib (ed.), *Politics in Dark Times: Encounters with Hannah Arendt* (Cambridge University Press 2010) 219, 222, 224 and 239–42 (hereafter Benhabib (ed.), *Politics in Dark Times*); see also Richard J Bernstein, *Radical Evil: A Philosophical Interrogation* (Polity 2002) 212.

[14] Arendt, *Eichmann in Jerusalem* (n. 11) 272 and 276.

[15] Mégret, 'The Limits of the Laws of War' (n. 1) 287.

[16] Ibid, 288; for the particular tendency to regard 'humanity' as a guiding principle in IHL and general international law, see, e.g., Hugo Slim, 'Sharing a Universal Ethic: The Principle of Humanity in War' (1998) 2 The International Journal of Human Rights 28; René-Jean Dupuy, *Dialectiques du droit internationale. Souveraineté des Etats, Communauté Internationale et Droits de l'Humanité* (A Pedone 1999); Catherine Le Bris, *L'humanité saisie par le droit international public* (Éditions LGDJ 2012); Ruti G Teitel, *Humanity's Law* (Oxford University Press 2011); Anne Peters, 'Humanity as the A and Ω of Sovereignty' (2009) 20 European Journal of International Law 513; Luigi D A Corrias and Geoffrey M Gordon, 'Judging in the Name of Humanity: International Criminal Tribunals and the Representation of a Global Public' (2015) 13 Journal of International Criminal Justice 97; for an excellent overview, see Matthew Zagor, 'Elemtary Considerations of Humanity' in Karine Bannelier, Theodore Christakis, and Sarah Heathcote (eds), *The ICJ and the Evolution of International Law: The Enduring Impact of the Corfu Channel Case* (Routledge 2012) 264.

There is, however, a further notion of humanity in Arendt's thought, one that she aligns with Lessing and antiquity. This conception of humanity is not based on an egalitarian common human nature or a communal feeling of solidarity and compassion. Rather this conception of humanity stands, so Arendt, closer to friendship which means that it implies a deliberate openness towards others but also that it is deliberately selective and open to compromise.[17] Arendt emphasizes that this notion of humanity preserves a reference to the world (instead of withdrawing from it and requiring the compassion and protection of others) and *enables* politically relevant action. It materializes through *active* participation in the world and through political demands.[18] It is a deliberate and deliberative conception of humanity and arguably the most political. Arendt mistrusts an understanding of humanity that passively relies on commonness, solidarity, compassion, and a community in which humans supposedly become brothers and sisters. As I read her, the more meaningful conception of humanity acknowledges that acting politically relevant involves taking sides. It means active understanding, judging, and acting, but eschews 'a definite world view' and a single perspective.[19] It is about actively seeking and preserving political relevance, autonomy, and responsibility.

It is this last conception of humanity that somehow does not fit in Professor Mégret's analysis of IHL, and I believe it does not fit because there is no place in the oscillation for such a compromising, affirmative, participatory, and non-ideal conception of humanity. If we conceive of IHL and its limits in terms of an oscillation between inherent conflicting absolutes, then by definition there has to be the 'apology of necessity' and also the 'utopia of humanity'. For a less absolute conception of humanity there is no space left.

I read Arendt also as a warning against absolutes and their effects on political and legal thinking, because absolutes draw our focus towards oppositions and oscillations between them.[20] The space 'in-between' the absolutes becomes passive because it is impossible to escape the inherent limits. Here the 'in-between' is not physical but normative and conceptual.[21] Absolutes, in Arendt's thought, end all discourse because they run counter to the essential relativity of relations.[22] They impose a definite world view but are often exclusionary and sectarian. Thus, when we describe IHL and its limits in terms of inherent opposing interests, we

---

[17] Arendt, 'Humanity in Dark Times' (n. 4) 12.
[18] Ibid, 24–7.
[19] Ibid, 7–8.
[20] Richard J Bernstein, 'Are Arendt's Reflections on Evil Still Relevant?' in Benhabib (ed.), *Politics in Dark Times* (n. 13) 293, 294–96.
[21] Waldron, 'The Constitutional Politics of Hannah Arendt' (n. 6) 294.
[22] Arendt, 'Humanity in Dark Times' (n. 4) 27, where she writes: '[T]he inhumanity of Kant's moral philosophy is undeniable. And this is so because the categorical imperative is postulated as absolute and in its absoluteness introduces into the interhuman realm—which by its nature consists of relationships—something that runs counter to its fundamental relativity', see also 30–1.

are inevitably drawn to think of the compromising nature of IHL in terms of a failure, unfulfilled promise, and latent irrelevance in light of either one of the absolute ends.

Our own thinking becomes limited. Once we have identified opposing interests and the dynamic between them, we follow the assumption that the limits are inherent, systemic, inescapable, and can merely be reproduced. Thus we speak of 'the' tradition and 'the' project, or assume that there is 'one' college of humanitarians. It is the focus on absolutes that reduces the plurality. This in turn blinds us to the recognition that these opposing absolutes themselves are not just there (inherent) but that they, too, are socially constructed, historically contingent, depend on context, and, especially, that they change over time. For example, we commonly speak of the International Committee of the Red Cross (ICRC) and think of Geneva and The Hague, but beyond the different emblem there might exist other histories, other limits, and other compromises in the Red Crescent Movement and in Islamic legal thought of how to conduct hostilities. Are they just part of the same oscillation and the same opposing forces?

In other words, I believe that by thinking about limits in terms of inescapable and reproducing opposing absolutes we limit and condition ourselves to imagine that there are either no alternatives, or that they are 'somewhere out there' instead of 'in the middle' where the compromise and dilemma is. If we focus on the oscillation, always peering hard at the absolute at either side, we are drawn to a binary iconolatry that overstates the absolutes and reduces the politically and legally more relevant 'in-between'.

III. CONCLUSIONS

Absolutes distort our vision. If we focus too much on opposing absolutes, always there but never really achieved, we risk—to use another (unfortunate) Arendtian notion—banalizing our thinking. When we assess the limits of IHL—or of human rights for that matter—in terms of oppositional aspirations, I fear we may miss the spaces 'in-between' these absolutes, the Arendtian *Zwischen*, where there is plurality but also partisanship and therefore relevant *activity*. It is not the absolute that enables relevant action but the compromise. This is especially true for international humanitarian law. Humanity as vocation (countering 'necessity') and humanity as cliché ('sophisticated moral casuistry') are but two aspects of the same presence. Limits tie things together as efficiently as they keep them apart. What matters most is whether the space between limits, between interests, and between aspirations is enabling or impeding. The greatest challenge that Frédéric Mégret poses is perhaps how to avoid inherent limits of our own thinking about the limits of humanitarian law. The most important compromise of IHL is to preserve a relevance for law in an otherwise lawless situation. The most important compromise that we need to make is to conceive of limits in a way that enables debate, judgement, and active choice of which side to take.

Bibliography

Arendt H, 'On Humanity in Dark Times: Thoughts about Lessing' in Arendt H (ed.), *Men in Dark Times* (first published 1955, Harcourt Brace & Co 1995) 3

Arendt H, *Eichmann in Jerusalem: A Report on the Banality of Evil* (first published 1963, Penguin 1994) 268

Benhabib S, 'International Law and Human Plurality in the Shadow of Totalitarianism' in Benhabib S (ed.), *Politics in Dark Times: Encounters with Hannah Arendt* (Cambridge University Press 2010) 219

Bernstein RJ, *Radical Evil: A Philosophical Interrogation* (Polity 2002)

Bernstein RJ, 'Are Arendt's Reflections on Evil Still Relevant?' in Benhabib S (ed.), *Politics in Dark Times: Encounters with Hannah Arendt* (Cambridge University Press 2010) 293

Corrias LDA and Gordon GM, 'Judging in the Name of Humanity: International Criminal Tribunals and the Representation of a Global Public' (2015) 13 Journal of International Criminal Justice 97

Dupuy R-J, *Dialectiques du droit internationale. Souveraineté des Etats, Communauté Internationale et Droits de l'Humanité* (A Pedone 1999)

Elon A, *The Pity of It All: A Portrait of the German-Jewish Epoch 1743–1933* (Picador 2002)

Le Bris C, *L'humanité saisie par le droit international public* (Éditions LGDJ 2012)

Mégret F, 'The Limits of the Laws of War' in Fassbender B and Traisbach K (eds), *The Limits of Human Rights* (Oxford University Press 2019) 283

Peters A, 'Humanity as the A and Ω of Sovereignty' (2009) 20 European Journal of International Law 513

Rorty R, 'Human Rights, Rationality, and Sentimentality' in Shute S and Hurley S (eds), *On Human Rights: The Oxford Amnesty Lectures 1993* (Basic Books 1993) 111

Slim H, 'Sharing a Universal Ethic: The Principle of Humanity in War' (1998) 2 The International Journal of Human Rights 28

Teitel RG, *Humanity's Law* (Oxford University Press 2011)

Traisbach K, 'International Law' in McGlinchey S (ed.), *International Relations* (E-International Relations 2017) 57

Waldron J, 'The Constitutional Politics of Hannah Arendt' in Waldron J (ed.), *Political Theory* (Harvard University Press 2016) 290

Zagor M, 'Elemtary Considerations of Humanity' in Bannelier K, Christakis T, and Heathcote S (eds), *The ICJ and the Evolution of International Law: The Enduring Impact of the* Corfu Channel *Case* (Routledge 2012) 264

19
The Limits of Human Rights in Times of Armed Conflict and Other Situations of Armed Violence

Andrew Clapham

I. INTRODUCTION

Human rights law has been encroaching on the battlefield. A series of high profile cases and campaigns have tested both the limits of what courts consider the applicability of human rights law and the patience of those on the receiving end of these complaints. Human rights and human rights lawyers are accused of making it impossible to fight wars and terrorism. Of course human rights law contains within itself mechanisms such as the regime for derogations and a number of limitations that could allow adaptation to exceptional circumstances. But the current tension goes beyond any underestimation of the various ways in which human rights can actually be limited. In order to understand the contemporary challenges faced by human rights law we need to break down the different contexts in which human rights are being tested to their limits. The chapter is divided into two sections: II. Human Rights in Armed Conflict, and III. Human Rights in Other Situations of Armed Violence. The reason is simple. In the first context we need to consider the effect of international humanitarian law, in the second context we do not.

II. Human Rights in Armed Conflict

A. A Limited Role for Human Rights in Targeting Decisions?

In times of armed conflict it was often assumed that targeting questions are simply governed by the law of armed conflict, and that human rights law is either inapplicable or displaced. The matter became more nuanced in the wake of the jurisprudence of the International Court of Justice (ICJ) which affirmed the continuing application of human rights law in times of armed conflict, and introduced the idea that the scope of a human rights norm might find its limits defined by another branch of international law relating, say, to prohibited weapons or international humanitarian law.[1] In part this is because multiple human rights treaties speak of a prohibition of an 'arbitrary' deprivation of life, and in turn it follows that arbitrariness must encompass illegality, including illegality under international humanitarian law. The controversy starts when one starts to define the limits of arbitrariness merely as compliance with the law of armed conflict. Is there anything left of the human right to life if a life has been extinguished in an armed conflict without a violation of the laws of war?

Two particular controversies are worth highlighting. First, the European Court of Human Rights (ECtHR) has held that the procedural aspects of the right to life continue to apply in times of armed conflict. In this way it follows that there can be an obligation to conduct an inquiry into a killing, even if the circumstances may mean the state is compelled to use 'less effective measures of investigation ... the obligation under Article 2 to safeguard life entails that, even in difficult security conditions, all reasonable steps must be taken to ensure that an effective, independent investigation is conducted into alleged breaches of the right to life.'[2]

In his book on *The Law of Targeting*, Boothby suggests this is a problem: 'To argue for the full application of the right to life, including the investigative obligations, during a high intensity and potentially protracted armed conflict makes little sense and is unlikely to have been the Court's intention.'[3] Schmitt has reasonably asserted that under international humanitarian law the requirement 'to investigate and prosecute war crimes attaches in both international and non-international armed conflict',[4] but he is also circumspect about the exigencies of this aspect of human rights law during hostilities: 'human rights measures deemed appropriate in the relative stability of peacetime, such as the duty to conduct autopsies, involve family members, or maintain strict chains of custody, would generally be ill-suited to the realities of conducting an investigation in the midst of combat or its immediate aftermath.'[5]

Nevertheless the procedural obligations connected to the right to life in armed conflict are still being clarified even beyond the jurisdiction of the ECtHR. The UN's Human Rights Committee, which is responsible for monitoring implementation of the International Covenant on Civil and Political Rights (ICCPR), has drafted a new General Comment on the Right to Life, the text of which includes the following passage:

> States parties should, in general, disclose the criteria for attacking with lethal force individuals or objects whose targeting is expected to result in deprivation

---

[1] Legality of the Threat or Use of Nuclear Weapons (Advisory Opinion) [1996] ICJ Rep 226, para. 25; Legal Consequences of the Construction of a Wall in Occupied Palestinian Territory (Advisory Opinion) [2004] ICJ Rep 136, para. 106; and Case concerning Armed Activities on the Territory of the Congo *(Democratic Republic of the Congo v. Uganda)* (Judgment) [2005] ICJ Rep 168, para. 216.
[2] *Al-Skeini v. United Kingdom*, App. No. 55721/07, 7 July 2011, para. 164.
[3] William H Boothby, *The Law of Targeting* (Oxford University Press 2012) 525.
[4] Michael N Schmitt, 'Investigating Violations of International Law in Armed Conflict' (2011) 31 Harvard National Security Journal 31, 48 (hereafter Schmitt, 'Investigating Violations').
[5] Schmitt, 'Investigating Violations' (n. 4) 55.

of life, including the legal basis for specific attacks, the process of identification of military targets and combatants or persons taking a direct part in hostilities, the circumstances in which relevant means and methods of warfare have been used, and whether less harmful alternatives were considered.[6]

This passage also introduces the second controversy. Human rights law is concerned with all lives and not just those of civilians and those *hors de combat*. While the killing of members of the armed forces from the other side in times of armed conflict may not necessarily be a violation of international humanitarian law, could it represent a violation of their human rights? Say in a situation where there were less lethal alternatives to achieve the same military objective? Or where the action was illegal under another branch of international law, say because it was part of an aggression or was a disproportionate use of force in self-defence? If non-arbitrariness requires legality, then the human right to life is not limited merely by compliance with international humanitarian law, but also requires compliance with the law on the use of force, and perhaps even the rules on non-intervention.[7]

The limits of this argument are only just starting to be tested. In the legal scholarship we find authors such as Schabas[8] and Mégret[9] suggesting that aggression should be considered as part of the evaluation of whether the human right to life of certain civilians and combatants has been violated. In contemporary moral philosophy, questions are being asked about the moral equivalence of soldiers (from

---

[6] HR Committee (ICCPR) General Comment no. 36, 'Article 6: Right to Life' CCPR/C/GC/36, para. 64 (footnote omitted).

[7] See, e.g., the important statement by the ICJ: 'There can be no doubt that, as a general rule, a particular act may be perfectly lawful under one body of legal rules and unlawful under another. Thus it cannot be excluded in principle that an act carried out during an armed conflict and lawful under international humanitarian law can at the same time constitute a violation by the State in question of some other international obligation incumbent upon it.' Application of the Convention on the Prevention and Punishment of the Crime of Genocide (*Croatia v. Serbia*) (Merits) (Judgment), [2015] ICJ Rep 3, para. 474. See also the General Comment No. 3 (2015) on the Right to Life (Article 4) in the African Charter on Human and Peoples' Rights. The article reads: 'Human beings are inviolable. Every human being shall be entitled to respect for his life and the integrity of his person. No one may be arbitrarily deprived of this right.' The General Comment (para. 12) states: 'A deprivation of life is arbitrary if it is impermissible under international law, or under more protective domestic law provisions. Arbitrariness should be interpreted with reference to considerations such as appropriateness, justice, predictability, reasonableness, necessity and proportionality.' And (para. 13): 'The right to life continues to apply during armed conflict. During the conduct of hostilities, the right to life needs to be interpreted with reference to the rules of international humanitarian law.' See also with regard to arbitrary detention the suggestion that a violation of the rules on non-interference would render a detention arbitrary. International Committee of the Red Cross, Harvard Law School Program on International Law and Armed Conflict, and Stockton Center for the Study of International Law at U.S. Naval War College, 'The Future of U.S. Detention under International Law: Workshop Report' (2017) 93 International Law Studies 272 (hereafter ICRC et al., 'The Future of U.S. Detention under International Law').

[8] William A Schabas, '*Lex Specialis*? Belt and Suspenders? The Parallel Operation of Human Rights Law and the Law of Armed Conflict, and the Conundrum of *Jus ad Bellum*' (2007) 40 Israel Law Review 592.

[9] Frédéric Mégret, 'What is the Specific Evil of Aggression?' in Claus Kreß and Stefan Barriga (eds), *The Crime of Aggression: A Commentary*, vol. 2 (Cambridge University Press 2016) 1398, 1436.

the aggressive side with those engaging in legitimate self-defence).[10] While from within the sphere of the law of armed conflict arguments are being made that the laws of war need to move beyond the idea that killing is simply a question of status, and start to take seriously the principles that suggest that the lives of soldiers, fighters, even terrorists may not be taken based on status determinations alone.[11] Nevertheless, several authors have cast doubt on the appropriateness of applying human rights law as an extra layer, when there is a status-based targeted killing which would seem to satisfy the principles of international humanitarian law. It has been suggested that such an extension of human rights standards not only takes us to the 'logical limits' of human rights in armed conflict, but is also 'operationally debilitating',[12] even endangering individual members of the armed forces 'by producing an inevitable hesitancy to employ deadly force'.[13] In particular it is sometimes said that such an application of human rights law would create an inequality in a non-international armed conflict, as human rights law would only attach to the state party.[14] More generally it is said that arguing for the simultaneous application of human rights and humanitarian law 'may have contributed to the blurring of the line between war and not-war'.[15]

There is surprisingly little case law on these outer limits of human rights protection. The ECtHR has reasonably preferred to stress the state's obligations with regard to planning and investigations, rather than consider an actual killing a violation of the substantive right to life. In a way this reflects the wider scope of human rights law over international humanitarian law, when it comes to targeting the latter stresses the information about possible civilian damage available to the reasonable commander and combatant, while human rights law demands from the state a range of actions to be taken at various stages and designed to protect all life unless the circumstances justify its extinction. And, as pithily explained by Garraway, from the perspective of the human rights victim the attack requires a

---

[10] See Jeff McMahan, *Killing in War* (Oxford University Press 2009); David Rodin, 'The Moral Inequality of Soldiers: Why jus in bello Asymmetry is Half Right' in David Rodin and Henry Shue (eds), *Just and Unjust Warriors: The Moral and Legal Status of Soldiers* (Oxford University Press 2008) 44.

[11] See Gabriella Blum, 'The Dispensable Lives of Soldiers' (2010) 2 Journal of Legal Analysis 69; Ryan Goodman, 'The Power to Kill or Capture Enemy Combatants' (2013) 24 European Journal of International Law 819; Report of the Special Rapporteur on extrajudicial, summary or arbitrary executions (Christof Heyns), 'Armed Drones and the Right to Life' A/68/382 (13 September 2013) (hereafter Heyns, 'Armed Drones and the Right to Life').

[12] Geoffrey Corn, 'Mixing Apples and Hand Grenades: The Logical Limit of Applying Human Rights Norms to Armed Conflict' (2010) 1 Journal of International Humanitarian Legal Studies 52, 83.

[13] Ibid, 89–90.

[14] Jann K Kleffner, 'Section IX of the ICRC Interpretive Guidance on Direct Participation in Hostilities: The End of *Jus in Bello* Proportionality as We Know It?' (2012) 45 Israel Law Review 35, 49–50.

[15] Naz K Modirzadeh, 'Folk International Law: 9/11 Lawyering and the Transformation of the Law of Armed Conflict to Human Rights Policy and Human Rights Law to War Governance' in Jens David Ohlin (ed.), *Theoretical Boundaries of Armed Conflict and Human Rights* (Cambridge University Press 2016) 192, 225 (hereafter Ohlin (ed.), *Theoretical Boundaries*).

human rights justification and not simply a reference to the absence of a specific prohibition in another branch of law:

> Human rights law looks at the situation through the eyes of the victim. If there is a loss of life or damage to property, it must be justified under the strict requirements of the law. Whereas international humanitarian law accepts that in war lives will be lost but seeks to minimize the loss of innocent lives, human rights law starts from the premise that any loss of life must be justified to a high standard. The onus is on the attacker and the loss of life itself creates a prima facie case.[16]

One judicial decision does stand out in this area. The Israeli Supreme Court considered that in the context of 'preventative strikes which cause the death of terrorists', targeting decisions have to be not only compliant with international humanitarian law (it was presumed that there was an armed conflict between Israel and various armed groups) but also satisfy a proportionality requirement derived from human rights law:

> [A] civilian taking a direct part in hostilities cannot be attacked at such time as he is doing so, if a less harmful means can be employed. In our domestic law, that rule is called for by the principle of proportionality. Indeed, among the military means, one must choose the means whose harm to the human rights of the harmed person is smallest. Thus, if a terrorist taking a direct part in hostilities can be arrested, interrogated, and tried, those are the means which should be employed.[17]

Of course this national court may have been applying national human rights law,[18] but the lesson for those searching for the limits of enforceable human rights law is clear. Human rights are not limited to compliance with international humanitarian law when it comes to this sort of targeted killing.

The latest thinking on these issues of the relationship between human rights law and the laws of war suggests that we admit that there are no obvious limits between

---

[16] Charles Garraway, 'The Law Applies, But Which Law? A Consumer Guide to the Laws of War' in Matthew Evangelista and Henry Shue (eds), *The American Way of Bombing: Changing Ethical and Legal Norms, from Flying Fortresses to Drones* (Cornell University Press 2014) 87, 101.

[17] *Public Committee against Torture et al v. Government of Israel et al*, 13 December 2006, para. 40.

[18] Although the judgment draws on international human rights law and goes on to quote approvingly a paragraph from the ECtHR judgment in *McCann v. United Kingdom*, App. No. 18984/91, 27 September 1995. A pertinent example of the ECtHR's proportionality test in the context of planning bombardments can be found in *Isayeva (Zara Adamovna) v. Russia*, App. No. 57950, para. 181, and *Isayeva (Medka Chuchuyevna) et al v. Russia*, App. No. 57947/00, paras 196–9, both judgments of 24 February 2005; this proportionality test (albeit here applied to the planning) is said to be different from the test usually applied in international humanitarian law, see Kenneth Watkin, *Fighting at the Legal Boundaries: Controlling the Use of Force in Contemporary Conflict* (Oxford University Press 2016) 554 (hereafter Watkin, *Fighting at the Legal Boundaries*), but in fact the ECtHR was considering the failure to prevent disproportionate injury to civilians. A real divergence would emerge should the Court consider

the scope of human rights law and international humanitarian law. In fact there can be overlaps and even simultaneous application, nevertheless there will be situations where the intermingling is hard to disentangle. A violent demonstration may contain armed fighters; a checkpoint in occupied territory may come under fire; house to house searches could be part of a battle. An International Committee of the Red Cross (ICRC) introductory book highlights how choosing the hostilities paradigm over the law enforcement paradigm will open up more space for greater lethal violence under international law.[19] So we have to admit that in practice a choice will be made by the armed forces whether to apply a law enforcement paradigm or a hostilities model; nevertheless the better solution is to also admit that the two branches of law work in combination with one being used to interpret the limits of the other.[20]

B. A Limited Role for Human Rights in Challenging Internship and Detention?

The other area where human rights have been seen as having limited application in times of armed conflict is detention. While issues of the internment of prisoners of war and civilians in occupied territory have been generally seen as better dealt with under international humanitarian law,[21] the issue of the human rights of detainees in non-international armed conflicts has given rise to considerable disagreement.[22]

the proportionality or necessity of an attack involving loss of life which involved no civilians or civilian objects.

---

[19] 'In practice, it may be difficult to determine which situations are governed by which paradigm. For example, a state engaged in a non-international armed conflict will regard armed opposition fighters not only as legitimate military targets under IHL but also as criminals under domestic law. Thus, the armed forces of that state using force against those fighters may be considered as simultaneously conducting hostilities and maintaining law and order. Difficult situations may also arise when civil unrest coincides with combat operations, or when persons engaged in combat intermingle with civilian rioters or demonstrators. The choice of the applicable paradigm may have significant legal and humanitarian consequences, given that the conduct of hostilities paradigm is generally more permissive than the law enforcement paradigm, most notably in terms of the deliberate use of lethal force and of incidental harm to the civilian population.' Nils Melzer and Etienne Kuster, *International Humanitarian Law: A Comprehensive Introduction* (International Committee of the Red Cross 2016) 30.

[20] 'Under the "active hostilities" framework both the law of armed conflict and international human rights law are applicable. However, the law of armed conflict provides the primary framework.' Daragh Murray (ed.), *Practitioners' Guide to Human Rights Law in Armed Conflict* (Oxford University Press 2016) 90. 'Under the "security operations" framework both the law of armed conflict and international human rights law are applicable. However, international human rights law provides the primary framework, and the law of armed conflict must be interpreted in the context of international human rights law.' Ibid, 91.

[21] Yuval Shany 'A Human Rights Perspective to Global Battlefield Detention: Time to Reconsider Indefinite Detention' (2017) 93 International Law Studies 102, 118–20 (hereafter Shany, 'A Human Rights Perspective').

[22] Lawrence Hill-Cawthorne, *Detention in Non-International Armed Conflict* (Oxford University Press 2016); Claire Landais and Léa Bass, 'Reconciling the Rules of International Humanitarian Law with the Rules of European Human Rights Law' (2015) 97 International Review of the Red Cross 1295.

Again it has been argued that it is simply not practicable to apply human rights guarantees to those captured on the battlefield or interned for imperative reasons of security.[23] Leaving aside the issue of derogations, the approach has been to consider that human rights continue to apply, but they will be modified to take account of the situation. The absence of detailed treaty provisions under international humanitarian law means that the emerging norms in this area suggest an expansion of human rights law rather than its limitation through international humanitarian law. McCosker, an ICRC legal adviser writing in her personal capacity, suggests that where international humanitarian law (IHL) applies, 'then ambiguities or gaps in particular IHL norms could be interpreted by reference to relevant norms formed within international human rights law'.[24] The UN Human Rights Committee explained in its General Comment on liberty and security of the person that '[i]f, under the most exceptional circumstances, a present, direct and imperative threat is invoked to justify the detention of persons considered to present such a threat, the burden of proof lies on states parties to show that the individual poses such a threat and that it cannot be addressed by alternative measures, and that burden increases with the length of the detention'.[25]

Other human rights bodies have gone even further. The UN Working Group on Arbitrary Detention does not see limits to the application of human rights even with regard to situations of armed conflict. Its Guiding Principle 4 (finalized in 2015) states that '[t]he right to bring proceedings before a court to challenge the arbitrariness and lawfulness of detention and to obtain without delay appropriate and accessible remedies is not derogable under international law'. And it demands that this right not be restricted 'even in times of war, armed conflict or public emergency'.[26] Furthermore '[p]risoners of war should be entitled to bring proceedings before a court to challenge the arbitrariness and lawfulness of the deprivation of liberty and to receive without delay appropriate and accessible remedies where the detainee [inter alia]: (a) challenges his or her status as a prisoner of war'.[27]

We might end this section with three conclusions. First, the human right for detainees to bring proceedings would seem to supplement the specific rights contained in international humanitarian law and is apparently not limited by them.

---

[23] Sean Aughey and Aurel Sari, 'Targeting and Detention in Non-International Armed Conflict: Serdar Mohammed and the Limits of Human Rights Convergence' (2015) 91 International Law Studies 60.
[24] Sarah McCosker, 'The Limitations of Legal Reasoning: Negotiating the Relationships between International Humanitarian Law and Human Rights Law in Detention Situations' in Gregory Rose and Bruce Oswald (eds), *Detention of Non-State Actors Engaged in Hostilities* (Brill 2016) 23, 44.
[25] HR Committee (ICCPR) General Comment no. 35, 'Article 9: Liberty and security of person' CCPR/C/GC/35, para. 15, discussed in Andrew Clapham, 'The Complex Relationship between the 1949 Geneva Conventions and International Human Rights Law' in Andrew Clapham, Paola Gaeta, and Marco Sassòli (eds), *The 1949 Geneva Conventions: A Commentary* (Oxford University Press 2015) 701, 721. See further Shany 'A Human Rights Perspective' (n. 21) 118–24 and 130–1.
[26] Report of the Working Group on Arbitrary Detention, 'United Nations Basic Principles and Guidelines on the right of anyone deprived of their liberty to bring proceedings before a court' WGAD/CRP.1/2015 (4 May 2015) paras 22 and 23.
[27] Ibid, para. 48.

Secondly, because detainees' human rights are not displaced by international humanitarian law, but are rather to be interpreted in the light of this law, the specific human rights of detainees that are absent in international humanitarian law may continue. The following issues have been highlighted: family contact, solitary confinement, access to open air, exercise, and searches of cells and prisoners.[28] Thirdly, the permission to intern derived from international humanitarian law is no longer seen as limiting the human right not be subjected to indefinite detention.[29]

III. Human Rights In Other Situations of Armed Violence

A. Human Rights Law for Those Subjected to Targeted Killings by Drones

Outside the context of armed conflict, the issue of targeted killing by drones poses a different set of questions. Rules relating to direct participation in hostilities and assumptions about combatant status disappear. Recent official explanations from key law officers of the United Kingdom and the United States regarding the legal framework for such drone targeting have failed to use the language of human rights.[30] It is as if we are approaching the limits of how far human rights are considered appropriate considerations at all. One assumption is perhaps that an extraterritorial drone attack entails a victim who falls outside the jurisdiction and therefore outside the scope of human rights protection. Although such an approach has been effectively challenged in the doctrine,[31] states will continue to want to confine their human rights treaty obligations to situations where they are in effective control on the ground. Whether or not the ECtHR or other fora choose to limit their own jurisdiction over human rights issues in this way,[32] we are faced with some pretty big questions about the limits of human rights. Are one's human rights limited to being

---

[28] ICRC et al., 'The Future of U.S. Detention under International Law' (n. 7) 285.
[29] Shany 'A Human Rights Perspective' (n. 21) 130.
[30] See Jeremy Wright, 'The Modern Law of Self-defence: Attorney General's Speech at International Institute for Strategic Studies', 11 January 2017, <https://www.gov.uk/government/uploads/system/uploads/attachment_data/file/583171/170111_Imminence_Speech_.pdf> accessed 31 January 2019 (hereafter Wright, 'The Modern Law of Self-defence'); Brian Egan, 'International Law, Legal Diplomacy, and the Counter-ISIL Campaign: Some Observations' (2016) 92 International Law Studies 235 (hereafter Egan, 'International Law').
[31] Marko Milanovic, *Extraterritorial Application of Human Rights Treaties: Law Principles, Policy* (Oxford University Press 2011); Marko Milanovic, 'Extraterritorial Derogations from Human Rights Treaties in Armed Conflict' in Nehal Bhuta (ed.), *The Frontiers of Human Rights: Extraterritoriality and Its Challenges* (Oxford University Press 2016) 55.
[32] See the invitation from the Court of Appeal to the ECtHR in *Al-Saadoon et al v. Secretary of State for Defence* [2016] EWCA Civ 811, paras 58ff, and the conclusion by Jones LJ for the Court that, in order to establish a principle of extraterritorial jurisdiction under Article 1 of the European Convention on Human Rights (ECHR), there should 'be an element of control of the individual prior to the use of lethal force' para. 69.

enjoyed only when one is in the threatening state's territory or under its effective control on the ground? Can a state simply check its human rights obligations at the frontier, like some sort of 'left luggage', and take off unencumbered by the obligations that it would have had had it stayed at home?

The idea of human rights is that individuals enjoy these rights due to their individual dignity and worth. If this is limited by the idea that the right to life is not applicable when you are targeted by foreign armed forces it does not seem to be much of a human right after all. It would seem that, whatever the exact scope of the jurisdiction of the international human rights courts, the customary international law of human rights must protect the right to life from all-comers in all places.[33] International human rights law is not a variant of constitutional law where rights are territorially granted to citizens as part of a social contract. The UN Special Rapporteur has referred to 'the status of the right to life as a general principle of international law and a customary norm. This means that, irrespective of the applicability of treaty provisions recognizing the right to life, states are bound to ensure the realization of the right to life when they use force, whether inside or outside their borders.'[34]

But the language and logic of human rights are apparently having limited effect in this context. The US Presidential Policy Directive of 2013 on 'procedures for approving direct action against terrorist targets located outside the United States and areas of active hostilities', and the UK Attorney General's speech on 'the legal basis for British military strikes against terror targets overseas'[35] omit references to human rights.[36] In part, as already mentioned, this is perhaps explained by the continuing idea that human rights law does not apply abroad in such circumstances. But in part this is probably also explained by the assumption that, when such weapons are used, it will be enough to invoke continuing adherence to international humanitarian law. But as countless reports have attempted to show, international human rights law applies to these actions, and the test is that '[l]ethal force under human rights law is legal if it is strictly and directly necessary to save life.'[37] This idea of direct necessity has, however, seemingly been overtaken or overshadowed by explanations about the right to self-defence and a focus on alternative understandings of the significance of an 'imminent' attack put forward in the abovementioned speeches of the US and UK legal officers. The contours of this proclaimed right to self-defence have become known in some circles as the 'naked self-defence' model. (Readers are warned that googling this term can lead

---

[33] Kevin Jon Heller, 'The Use and Abuse of Analogy in IHL' in Ohlin (ed.), *Theoretical Boundaries* (n. 15) 232, 247.
[34] Heyns, 'Armed Drones and the Right to Life' (n. 11) 9.
[35] Wright, 'The Modern Law of Self-defence' (n. 30).
[36] Similarly Egan, 'International Law' (n. 30).
[37] Report of the Special Rapporteur on extrajudicial, summary or arbitrary executions (Philip Alston), 'Study on Targeted Killings' A/HRC/14/24/Add. 6 (28 May 2010) 11; Avery Plaw, Matthew S Fricker, and Carlos R Colon, *The Drone Debate: A Primer on the U.S. Use of Unmanned Aircraft Outside Conventional Battlefields* (Rowman and Littlefield 2016) 215 et seq.

to surprising images on the screen.) A clear explanation of how this model was developed in isolation from human rights law can be found in the new book by Watkin.[38] For present purposes we can suggest that the term 'naked self-defence' implies that such use of force need be, neither clothed with compatibility with the laws of war, nor with human rights law. Pejic has submitted that: 'under current international law, the right to self-defence is a concept of the *jus ad bellum* and not a stand-alone legal regime governing how force may be used'.[39]

Watkin considers that human rights law (or the law enforcement paradigm) may still have a role to play in this context, even if this may be primarily for policy reasons. Hessbrueger goes much further, and, using sources from human rights law, has mounted a strong rebuttal of the idea that 'naked self-defence', even if in compliance with Article 51 of the UN Charter, can operate in ways that override the human right to life. He concludes that 'Article 51 cannot provide a justification for deliberately depriving someone of his right to life'.[40] It would seem that here the limits of human rights law are being severely tested.

B. Human Rights for Those under the Control of Armed Groups

The last context we might examine concerns whether human rights are limited by their supposed inability to create obligations for armed groups. While it is increasingly accepted that armed groups have international obligations under international humanitarian law, the issue arises as to the human rights obligations of these groups, especially in the period before or after the armed conflict, but also with regard to how a group treats its own members or others not-connected to the conflict. For some there is a traditional approach that conceives human rights as merely constituting limits to *state* powers. But this seems to have given way to what the late Sir Nigel Rodley has admittedly called the 'modified traditional view'.[41] In his words this is 'the at least theoretical acceptance that if another entity—a non-state actor (NSA)—exercises "effective power" analogous to that of the state, then such an entity should logically be seen as capable of being obliged to respect the human rights of those subject to that power'.[42]

What then are the limits to human rights in this context? In practice the issue arises that the entity may not be in an analogous position to the state, or rather

---

[38] Watkin, *Fighting at the Legal Boundaries* (n. 18) 311–22.
[39] Jelena Pejic, 'Extraterritorial Targeting by Means of Armed Drones: Some Legal Implications' (2015) 96 International Review of the Red Cross 67, 75.
[40] Jan Arno Hessbruegge, *Human Rights and Personal Self-Defense in International Law* (Oxford University Press 2016) 233.
[41] Sir Nigel Rodley, 'Non-State Actors and Human Rights' in Scott Sheeran and Sir Nigel Rodley (eds), *The Routledge Handbook of International Human Rights Law* (Routledge 2013) 523.
[42] Ibid.

that states and commentators would prefer not to see the non-state actor as a state-like actor. What to do about the so-called Islamic State? Or Al Qaeda? Or a drug-trafficking gang? Or a criminal organization? As the lines between organized rebels and criminal opportunists become blurred, how limited should the application of human rights law become? Again, from the perspective of the victim, limiting human rights to those who are at the mercy of analogous state entities is of little interest. Detention, torture, or sexual abuse, feel more or less the same whether the captor is the state, an analogous entity, or something which could never be compared to a state. The dignity and worth of the individual are just as threatened. But there must be limits. Does the obligation to provide education, health care, and water surely belong exclusively to states? Perhaps not; recent scholarship is building the theoretical foundations which would expand the apparent limits to the application of human rights law to these armed non-state actors and adapt the obligations to fit the context of various armed groups.[43] While there is still room to question the routes by which international law is said to attach to such groups,[44] the United Nations and various non-governmental organizations (NGOs) have been forced to hold these groups accountable to relevant human rights standards.[45]

Even as we admit that human rights obligations have adapted to circumscribe the legality of the behaviour of certain armed groups, are there not limits to this application of human rights law to this expanded list of human rights duty-bearers? In closing, let us consider one particularly knotty conundrum. We know that armed groups keep people in detention, perhaps with a view to some future exchange of detainees, or perhaps as a disciplinary measure for their own members, or as part of the public order measures necessary to their operations or 'governance'. No state really accepts that armed groups are entitled to detain or try anyone. As we try to adapt fair trial principles to these situations we inevitably find that such an exercise risks somehow being seen as legitimizing the group. Moreover in designing or counselling minimum standards one has to adapt to the fact that some fundamental principles may not be so easily adapted. Consider a future manual for a small, relatively ill-equipped rebel group in its early formation having to develop the principles related to: an independent judiciary, the assistance of counsel of one's choice, legal aid, the right to appeal conviction, double jeopardy, and restrictions

---

[43] See Daragh Murray, *Human Rights Obligations of Non-State Armed Groups* (Hart Publishing 2016); Katharine Fortin, 'The Application of Human Rights Law to Everyday Civilian Life under Rebel Control' (2016) 63 Netherlands International Law Review 161; Tilman Rodenhäuser, 'International Legal Obligations of Armed Opposition Groups in Syria' (2015) 2 International Review of Law 1 <http://www.qscience.com/doi/pdf/10.5339/irl.2015.2> accessed 31 January 2019.

[44] Marco Sassòli, 'Two Fascinating Questions: Are All Subjects of a Legal Order Bound by the Same Customary Law and Can Armed Groups Exist in the Absence of Armed Conflict? Book Discussion' (*EJIL: Talk!*, 4 November 2016).

[45] Annyssa Bellal, *Human Rights Obligations of Armed Non-State Actors: An Exploration of the Practice of the UN Human Rights Council* (Geneva Academy of International Humanitarian Law and Human Rights 2016).

on the death penalty.[46] At this point an overenthusiastic application of the full panoply of human rights obligations applicable to states may be not only impracticable but also counterproductive. There are limits.

Bibliography

Aughey S and Sari A, 'Targeting and Detention in Non-International Armed Conflict: Serdar Mohammed and the Limits of Human Rights Convergence' (2015) 91 International Law Studies 60

Bellal A, *Human Rights Obligations of Armed Non-State Actors: An Exploration of the Practice of the UN Human Rights Council* (Geneva Academy of International Humanitarian Law and Human Rights 2016)

Blum G, 'The Dispensable Lives of Soldiers' (2010) 2 Journal of Legal Analysis 69

Boothby WH, *The Law of Targeting* (Oxford University Press 2012)

Clapham A, 'The Complex Relationship between the 1949 Geneva Conventions and International Human Rights Law' in Clapham A, Gaeta P, and Sassòli M (eds), *The 1949 Geneva Conventions: A Commentary* (Oxford University Press 2015)

Clapham A, 'Detention by Armed Groups under International Law' (2017) 93 International Law Studies 1

Corn G, 'Mixing Apples and Hand Grenades: The Logical Limit of Applying Human Rights Norms to Armed Conflict' (2010) 1 Journal of International Humanitarian Legal Studies 52

Egan B, 'International Law, Legal Diplomacy, and the Counter-ISIL Campaign: Some Observations' (2016) 92 International Law Studies 235

Fortin K, 'The Application of Human Rights Law to Everyday Civilian Life under Rebel Control' (2016) 63 Netherlands International Law Review 161

Garraway C, 'The Law Applies, But Which Law? A Consumer Guide to the Laws of War' in Evangelista M and Shue H (eds), *The American Way of Bombing: Changing Ethical and Legal Norms, from Flying Fortresses to Drones* (Cornell University Press 2014) 87

Goodman R, 'The Power to Kill or Capture Enemy Combatants' (2013) 24 European Journal of International Law 819

Heller KJ, 'The Use and Abuse of Analogy in IHL' in Ohlin JD (ed.), *Theoretical Boundaries of Armed Conflict and Human Rights* (Cambridge University Press 2016) 232

Hessbruegge JA, *Human Rights and Personal Self-Defense in International Law* (Oxford University Press 2017)

Hill-Cawthorne L, *Detention in Non-International Armed Conflict* (Oxford University Press 2016)

International Committee of the Red Cross, Harvard Law School Program on International Law and Armed Conflict, and Stockton Center for the Study of International Law at U.S. Naval War College, 'The Future of U.S. Detention under International Law: Workshop Report' (2017) 93 International Law Studies 272

Kleffner JK, 'Section IX of the ICRC Interpretive Guidance on Direct Participation in Hostilities: The End of *Jus in Bello* Proportionality as We Know It?' (2012) 45 Israel Law Review 35

---

[46] Andrew Clapham, 'Detention by Armed Groups under International Law' (2017) 93 International Law Studies 1.

Landais C and Bass L, 'Reconciling the Rules of International Humanitarian Law with the Rules of European Human Rights Law' (2015) 97 International Review of the Red Cross 1295

McCosker S, 'The Limitations of Legal Reasoning: Negotiating the Relationships between International Humanitarian Law and Human Rights Law in Detention Situations' in Rose G and Oswald B (eds), *Detention of Non-State Actors Engaged in Hostilities* (Brill 2016) 23

McMahan J, *Killing in War* (Oxford University Press 2009)

Mégret F, 'What is the Specific Evil of Aggression?' in Kreß C and Barriga S (eds), *The Crime of Aggression: A Commentary*, vol. 2 (Cambridge University Press 2016) 1398

Melzer N and Kuster E, *International Humanitarian Law: A Comprehensive Introduction* (International Committee of the Red Cross 2016)

Milanovic M, *Extraterritorial Application of Human Rights Treaties: Law Principles, Policy* (Oxford University Press 2011)

Milanovic M, 'Extraterritorial Derogations from Human Rights Treaties in Armed Conflict' in Bhuta N (ed.), *The Frontiers of Human Rights: Extraterritoriality and Its Challenges* (Oxford University Press 2016) 55

Modirzadeh NK, 'Folk International Law: 9/11 Lawyering and the Transformation of the Law of Armed Conflict to Human Rights Policy and Human Rights Law to War Governance' in Ohlin JD (ed.), *Theoretical Boundaries of Armed Conflict and Human Rights* (Cambridge University Press 2016) 192

Murray D, *Human Rights Obligations of Non-State Armed Groups* (Hart Publishing 2016)

Murray D, (ed.), *Practitioners' Guide to Human Rights Law in Armed Conflict* (Oxford University Press 2016)

Pejic J, 'Extraterritorial Targeting by Means of Armed Drones: Some Legal Implications' (2015) 96 International Review of the Red Cross 67

Plaw A, Fricker MS, and Colon CR, *The Drone Debate: A Primer on the U.S. Use of Unmanned Aircraft Outside Conventional Battlefields* (Rowman and Littlefield 2016)

Rodenhäuser T, 'International Legal Obligations of Armed Opposition Groups in Syria' (2015) 2 International Review of Law 1

Rodin D, 'The Moral Inequality of Soldiers: Why jus in bello Asymmetry is Half Right' in Rodin D and Shue H (eds), *Just and Unjust Warriors: The Moral and Legal Status of Soldiers* (Oxford University Press 2008) 44

Rodley N, 'Non-State Actors and Human Rights' in Sheeran S and Rodley N (eds), *The Routledge Handbook of International Human Rights Law* (Routledge 2013) 523

Sassòli M, 'Two Fascinating Questions: Are All Subjects of a Legal Order Bound by the Same Customary Law and Can Armed Groups Exist in the Absence of Armed Conflict? Book Discussion' (*EJIL: Talk!*, 4 November 2016)

Schabas WA, '*Lex Specialis?* Belt and Suspenders? The Parallel Operation of Human Rights Law and the Law of Armed Conflict, and the Conundrum of *Jus ad Bellum*' (2007) 40 Israel Law Review 592

Schmitt MN, 'Investigating Violations of International Law in Armed Conflict' (2011) 31 Harvard National Security Journal 31

Shany Y, 'A Human Rights Perspective to Global Battlefield Detention: Time to Reconsider Indefinite Detention' (2017) 93 International Law Studies 102

Watkin K, *Fighting at the Legal Boundaries: Controlling the Use of Force in Contemporary Conflict* (Oxford University Press 2016)

Wright J, 'The Modern Law of Self-Defence: Attorney General's Speech at International Institute for Strategic Studies', 11 January 2017, <https://www.gov.uk/government/uploads/system/uploads/attachment_data/file/583171/170111_Imminence_Speech_.pdf> accessed 31 January 2019

20
The End of the War/Peace Limit on the Application of International Human Rights Law
A Response to Andrew Clapham

Yuval Shany

In 'The Limits of Human Rights in Times of Armed Conflict and Other Situations of Armed Violence', Andrew Clapham explains how the dynamics of international human rights law (IHRL), which give effect to foundational principles such as universality and the non-derogability of core humanitarian norms, have extended the limits of IHRL in recent decades. This process of normative expansion leads, inter alia, to the application of IHRL to conflict situations, and to an increased overlap between IHRL and other branches of international law governing conflict situations—*jus in bello*, and perhaps also, *jus ad bellum*. As Clapham notes these developments are not problem-free; rather they raise concerns about complications created by the erosion of old limits and by uncertainties as to what, if any, new limits can and should be introduced to IHRL.

One set of concerns discussed by Clapham involves the *disruptive* effect of the application of IHRL on the substantive regulation of situations of conflict by bodies of law that do not share many of IHRL normative assumptions. Another set of concerns relates to the need for functional limits on the powers of IHRL monitoring bodies such as the European Court of Human Rights (ECtHR) and the UN Human Rights Committee (UN HRC), who are not well-equipped to deal with the massive humanitarian implications of large-scale military conflicts. These institutional concerns may explain some of the inconsistencies and hesitations that characterize the relevant case law of the aforementioned IHRL-monitoring bodies. Finally, the debate about the limits of IHRL is informed by concerns of a political backlash against IHRL norms and institutions. Such a backlash may affect not only how states and other political actors react to 'excesses' in the application of IHRL; they might also weaken the application of IHRL within the traditional limits of its operation.

This comment discusses these three sets of concerns, which are also touched upon by Clapham explicitly or implicitly. It also offers a number of critical

Yuval Shany, *The End of the War/Peace Limit on the Application of International Human Rights Law: A Response to Andrew Clapham*. In: *The Limits of Human Rights*. Edited by: Bardo Fassbender and Knut Traisbach, Oxford University Press 2019. © The Several Contributors.
DOI: 10.1093/oso/9780198824756.003.0022

observations on how IHRL has developed so far in relation to situations of armed conflict and how IHRL monitoring bodies should apply IHRL in such situations.

I. SUBSTANTIVE EXPANSION

The ICJ *Nuclear Weapons* advisory opinion, pronouncing that the International Covenant on Civil and Political Rights (ICCPR) continues to apply in times of armed conflict but that it should be interpreted in light of the more specific provisions of IHL, has set the stage for the process of substantive expansion of IHRL due to two inter-related elements of the opinion: First, the opinion rejected the notion that there are doctrinal limits to IHRL that would prevent it from applying in times of conflict, discarding the relevance of the classic laws of war/ laws of peace dichotomy, which regarded the legal regulation of the conduct of hostilities as a self-contained regime governed exclusively by IHL.[1] Indeed, the existence of derogation clauses in instruments such as the European Convention on Human Rights (ECHR) and the ICCPR modifying their application in times of war or other serious emergencies[2] render the reading implausible that such instruments require the blanket exclusion of IHRL from situations of armed conflict.

Second, the normative convergence methodology embraced by the Court, according to which the term 'arbitrary deprivation of life', found in Article 6 of the ICCPR, allowed for the introduction of substantive norms of IHL into Article 6, rendered IHL norms on targeting and weapons the legal yardstick for the determination whether or not Article 6 was violated. Arguably, the same logic applies to other international law yardsticks of legality, which regulate activities intended for or resulting in the deprivation of life in times of conflict, including *jus ad bellum*.[3] Furthermore, other provisions of IHRL relevant to the regulation of conflict, such as the prohibition of arbitrary deprivation of liberty, may be similarly implicated and informed by the laws of armed conflict and other relevant international law norms.[4]

Post-1996 International Court of Justice (ICJ) decisions have clarified that IHRL complements the laws of armed conflict and that issues not regulated by IHL

---

[1] Legality of the Threat or Use of Nuclear Weapons (Advisory Opinion) [1996] ICJ Rep 226, 240.
[2] European Convention for the Protection of Human Rights and Fundamental Freedoms (adopted 4 November 1950, entered into force 3 September 1953) ETS 5, Article 15 (hereafter ECHR); International Covenant on Civil and Political Rights (adopted 16 December 1966, entered into force 23 March 1976) 999 UNTS 171, Article 4 (hereafter ICCPR).
[3] See, e.g., HR Committee (ICCPR) General Comment no. 36, 'Article 6: Right to Life' CCPR/C/GC/36, para. 70 (hereafter HR Committee (ICCPR) General Comment no. 36).
[4] See, e.g., HR Committee (ICCPR) General Comment no. 35, 'Article 9: Liberty and Security of Person' CCPR/C/GC/35, para. 64 (hereafter HR Committee (ICCPR) General Comment no. 35).

continue to be regulated by IHRL in conflict situations.[5] As Clapham notes, IHRL monitoring bodies have put much emphasis in this regard on developing 'second order' norms relating to the duty to investigate violations of the international norms applicable to armed conflicts (focusing on investigating violations of IHRL norms, whose contents may be informed by IHL norms). Furthermore, once the traditional war/peace limit has been breached, the contents of IHRL itself has undergone changes in order to adjust it to the special circumstances that may present themselves during armed conflict situations and to minimize the disruptive effect of its application. For example, in *Hassan v. UK*, the ECtHR held that grounds for detention recognized under IHL should be read into the list of exceptions to the prohibition against deprivation of liberty found in Article 5 of the ECHR, effectively amending thereby the text of the Convention.[6] In the same vein, the UN HRC accepted that, under very exceptional circumstances, preventive security-detention would not be considered arbitrary in nature, accepting thereby a new freedom-security equilibrium for the 'global war on terror' era with a permanent and enhanced terrorism threat.[7] The mixed paradigm introduced by the Supreme Court of Israel in the 'targeted killing' case[8] and the famous ICRC Principle IX of the Interpretative Guidance on Direct Participation in Hostilities[9] are other illustrations of an attempt to address the disruptive effect of co-application of IHL and IHRL.

One important explanation for the increased propensity of IHRL-monitoring bodies and scholars to opt for an expanded application of IHRL beyond traditional limits, is the growing erosion of the boundaries between war and peace, which underlay the traditional distinction between IHRL and the laws of armed conflict.[10] Whereas in the past armed conflicts tended to be of a rather short duration and represented a clear break from pre-existing and post-war peaceful relations between states or warring factions within a state, the post-9/11 'global war on terror', the rise of religion-driven home-grown terrorism, prolonged civil wars in failed states, and open-ended situations of belligerent occupation produced a reality in which certain levels of political violence and military action are perpetuated and transformed into the 'new normal' in international relations. In such circumstances, the application of IHL is at times contested; at other times, such as those involving isolated drone strikes outside the theatre of hostilities, new legal frameworks containing few if any safeguards or restraining principles regulating the use

---

[5] See Legal Consequences of the Construction of a Wall in the Occupied Palestinian Territory (Advisory Opinion) [2004] ICJ Rep 136, 178; Armed Activities on the Territory of the Congo (*Democratic Republic of the Congo v. Uganda*) (Judgment) [2005] ICJ Rep 168, 242–3.

[6] *Hassan v. UK*, App. No. 29750/09, 16 September 2014.

[7] HR Committee (ICCPR) General Comment no. 35 (n. 4), para. 15.

[8] HCJ 769/02, *Public Committee against Torture in Israel v. Israel*, ILDC 597 (IL 2006).

[9] International Committee of the Red Cross (ICRC), Interpretive Guidance on the Notion of Direct Participation in Hostilities under International Humanitarian Law, Principle IX (2009).

[10] For a discussion, see David Luban, 'Human Rights Thinking and the Laws of War' in Jens David Ohlin (ed.), *Theoretical Boundaries of Armed Conflict and Human Rights* (Cambridge University Press 2016) 45, 63 (hereafter Ohlin (ed.), *Theoretical Boundaries*).

of lethal force have being advocated. Moreover, in many contemporary conflict situations questions are raised relating to the suitability of IHL to deal with problems unanticipated at the time in which key IHL instruments were drafted, such as prolonged or transformative belligerent occupation, cross-border spill-over of internal conflicts, and cyber-attacks. Addressing such questions often invites the consideration of IHRL as a default legal framework offering minimal protection to all potential victims affected by the exercise of state power. It is the combination of the doctrinal breakthrough undertaken by the ICJ and IHRL-monitoring bodies, which enables the management of the 'disruption' caused by IHRL to IHL, and the emergence of a 'liminal space' between war and peace[11] that drive the process of erosion of the traditional war/peace limits for the application of IHRL.

If the old substantive limits no longer make sense, what new limits on the scope of application of IHLR are in place (assuming that limits on IHRL can and should be introduced)? Clapham discusses in his contribution two important sets of limits, which are found in the practice of IHRL-monitoring bodies, questioning in both cases their logic and legal significance. First, he addresses the notion of jurisdiction found in various human rights treaties, requiring a degree of control over territory or individuals by the state in question.[12] Clapham is right, I believe, in criticizing attempts to exclude for lack of jurisdiction extraterritorial military operations, such as the targeting of suspected terrorists by drones, for example, from the scope of application of IHRL instruments. Still, I have doubt about his claim that customary international law can provide a fix to the problem caused by treaty language that makes jurisdiction a prerequisite for application of IHRL protection.

First, the assertion that customary IHRL lacks a jurisdictional requirement for triggering state obligations appears questionable since there is little to suggest that state practice is compatible with an even broader notion of state obligations under IHRL than what is found in IHRL treaties, especially when we consider the practice of state parties to IHRL treaties that oppose the broad application of the jurisdictional provisions found thereunder. Neither does it seem plausible that the *opinio juris* of states has gone beyond the jurisdictional limits articulated in the IHRL instruments. IHRL has developed as an attempt to implement human rights values through the existing state system and the notion of jurisdiction serves in this system as an important link between state power and state responsibility and as a principle of division of labour between sovereign states. It is unlikely that states that explicitly introduced such a condition into their IHRL treaties have

---

[11] Jens David Ohlin, 'Acting as a Sovereign versus Acting as a Belligerent' in Ohlin (ed.), *Theoretical Boundaries* (n. 10) 118, 142.

[12] Article 1 of the ECHR; Article 2(1) of the ICCPR; *Al Skeini v. UK*, App. No. 55721/07, 7 July 2011, paras 131–40; HR Committee (ICCPR) General Comment no. 31, 'The Nature of the General Legal Obligation Imposed on States Parties to the Covenant' CCPR/C/21/Rev.1/Add.13, para. 10 (hereafter HR Committee (ICCPR) General Comment no. 31).

implicitly waived it in their subsequent practice. Second, even if Clapham is right and states do owe a broader duty to foreign individuals under customary international law, I fear that without entrusting IHRL-monitoring bodies operating under the relevant IHRL treaties (that contain the jurisdictional requirement) with the power to enforce the said norm, the actual protection afforded to foreigners under such a broader construction of state obligations would likely remain illusory.

It thus seems difficult to me, and perhaps undesirable, to ignore jurisdiction as a limit on the scope of state obligations under IHRL. Still, as Clapham suggests, existing attempts to construe jurisdiction as denoting physical control do not adequately capture the extent to which state power is deliberately projected outside state territory, and how such power effectively brings foreign nationals under state control. Already in its General Comment no. 31 (2004), the UN HRC construed jurisdiction as covering 'anyone within the power or effective control of that State Party, even if not situated within the territory of the State Party'.[13] In its General Comment no. 36 on the right to life, the Committee further expressed the view that individuals whose right to life is impacted by Statestate acts or omission in a 'direct and reasonably foreseeable' manner would be protected by Article 6 of the Covenant, thus falling within the jurisdiction of the state parties, wherever they are situated in the world.[14] In the same vein, the Inter-American Court of Human Rights in its recent advisory opinion on the Environment and the Right to Life regarded a causal relationship between territorial conduct over which a state exercises effective control and significant extra-territorial harm as meeting the jurisdictional requirements of the American Convention on Human Rights.[15] The upshot is that international treaty law on IHRL's jurisdiction requirement can be construed, and is increasingly construed, as to govern all deliberate measures taken in or outside armed conflict, which directly impact the human rights of individuals in a significant and foreseeable measure. Under this construction, jurisdiction serves as a rather weak limit on the scope of application of IHRL.

Another doctrinal limit on the applicability of IHRL to situations of armed conflict identified by Clapham is the fact that IHRL treaties only bind states. By contrast, international law governing the activities of armed groups and international organizations is, at best, unsettled. This legal situation not only results in significant protection gaps for many victims of abuse by non-state actors, but also leads to significant differences between the scope of legal obligations imposed on parties

---

[13] HR Committee (ICCPR) General Comment no. 31 (n. 12) para. 10.
[14] HR Committee (ICCPR) General Comment no. 36 (n. 3) para. 22.
[15] Inter-American Court of Human Rights, Advisory Opinion OC-23/17, 15 November 2017 (State Obligations in Relation to the Environment in the Framework of the Protection and Guarantee of the Rights to Life and to Personal Integrity—Interpretation and Scope of Articles 4.1 and 5.1, in relation to Articles 1.1 and 2 of the American Convention on Human Rights), paras 101–3 (in Spanish).

to armed conflicts. This, in turn, dis-incentivizes states to accept the application of IHRL in conflict situations—a move that further exacerbates the normative gap between the parties' scope of obligations.[16]

While there is much to be said in favour of requiring entities exercising state-like powers to abide by legal standards analogous to those applicable to states, this appears at this point to represent *lex ferenda*; and, even then, Clapham is correct in cautioning us against an automatic extension of all IHRL standards to actors who almost inevitably have more limited capacities than those enjoyed by states. Still, recent moves in IHRL bodies to condemn human rights abuses by non-state actors such as ISIS,[17] on the one hand, and UN Peacekeepers,[18] on the other hand, may suggest that customary international law is gradually building up in this area. This, in turn, may mean that statehood no longer poses a limit to the applicability of IHRL to conflict and non-conflict situations.

II. INSTITUTIONAL CONCERNS

I believe Clapham is right in doubting whether the values that underlie IHRL—individual dignity and equal worth of all persons—support the introduction of substantive limits on the scope of application of IHRL as a whole (as opposed to the specific limits attendant under IHRL to the application of specific rights in specific circumstances). The question of limits on the power of institutions monitoring the application of IHRL is different, however. Here, concerns about legal authority and legitimacy, practical capacity and effectiveness, and the need for a division of labour between different legal institutions may justify the imposition of limits on the jurisdiction of IHRL-monitoring bodies and to impose conditions on the admissibility of cases brought before them.

For example, the ECtHR only monitors the compliance with the ECHR of state parties to the Convention, excluding from its scope of review third states, non-state parties, and international organizations (including international organizations comprising state parties to the ECHR).[19] This inevitably entails the exclusion of numerous military operations from the purview of the ECtHR. The ECHR also bars the ECtHR from hearing certain cases which were submitted to it in delay,

---

[16] It should be noted, however, that non-state actors typically remain bound by provisions of domestic law, which often authorize the application of military force by the government and outlaw such application by other political entities.

[17] See, e.g., Report of the Independent International Commission of Inquiry on the Syrian Arab Republic, 'Rule of Terror: Living under ISIS in Syria' A/HRC/27/CRP.3 (19 November 2014).

[18] See, e.g., Report of an Independent Review on Sexual Exploitation and Abuse by International Peacekeeping Forces in the Central African Republic, 'Taking Action on Sexual Exploitation and Abuse by Peacekeepers' (17 December 2015) <http://www.un.org/News/dh/infocus/centafricrepub/Independent-Review-Report.pdf> accessed 31 January 2019.

[19] See, e.g., *Behrami v. France*, App. No. 71412/01, 2 May 2007.

have been addressed by other monitoring bodies, or are trivial in nature.[20] It is within this context, that some limits on the exercise of monitoring of the application of IHRL to conflict situations can be envisioned. For example, situations effectively monitored by other mechanisms (such as claims commissions) or fully addressed by a post-war settlement may be excluded from the ECtHR.

A difficult question that arises in this connection is whether IHRL-monitoring bodies should weigh institutional considerations when construing the substantive rights in their constitutive instruments. For example, the UN HRC provided in its General Comment no. 36 on the right to life that: 'States parties engaged in acts of aggression as defined in international law, resulting in deprivation of life, violate ipso facto article 6 of the Covenant.... States parties that fail to take all reasonable measures to settle their international disputes by peaceful means might fall short of complying with their positive obligation to ensure the right to life.'[21] This language follows the logic of the *Nuclear Weapons* advisory opinion—that is, that a violation of international law which results in deprivation of life is arbitrary in nature. Still, this legal construction is susceptible to allegations that it might open up the 'floodgates' and generate very large numbers of potential new right holders (including, soldiers in the service of a lawfully self-defending state) who may wish to vindicate their rights before the Committee. It might also require the UN HRC to consider questions of *jus ad bellum* (e.g. who is the aggressor in a given armed conflict), arguably going beyond the core expertise of its members and resulting in an unhealthy level of politicization of its proceedings. Note, however, that arguments about opening up the 'floodgates' were also raised in connection with the adoption of the Optional Protocol to the International Covenant on Economic, Social and Cultural Rights establishing the right of individual petitions for victims of violations of the Covenant.[22] So far, only a trickle of petitions has been submitted.

In any event, I believe that institutional concerns should be addressed through structural and procedural limits on the operation of IHRL-monitoring bodies, such as rules on standing, evidence, *de minimis* thresholds,[23] and the like. By contrast, limits on the contents of human rights norms should derive from a substantive theory of human rights, the experience of victims of abuse of power by public authority, and the overarching legal framework in which IHRL operates, but not from institutional constraints such as lack of resources or the political sensitivities of any particular treaty constituency.

---

[20] Article 35 of the ECHR.
[21] HR Committee (ICCPR) General Comment no. 36 (n. 3) para. 70.
[22] See, e.g., Michael J Dennis and David P Stewart, 'Justiciability of Economic, Social and Cultural Rights: Should There be an International Complaints Mechanism to Adjudicate the Right to Food, Water, Housing and Health?' (2004) 98 American Journal of International Law 462, 507.
[23] See Optional Protocol to the International Covenant on Economic, Social and Cultural Rights (adopted 10 December 2008, entered into force 5 May 2013) A/RES/63/117, Article 4.

III. FEAR OF BACKLASH

The final consideration providing a backdrop to the discussion of the substantive extension of IHRL to conflict situations and to the institutional capacity of IHRL-monitoring bodies to review these conflict situations, is the fear of a political backlash that may ensue as a result of the erosion of limits to the application of IHRL. Indeed, the 'disruptive' effect of IHRL on IHL means that at times states would be held to higher legal standards when conducting hostilities, and the expansion of institutional monitoring is likely to result in a higher degree of scrutiny. Such an enhanced level of legal accountability and the narrower 'operational space' under international law is not going to be popular with states involved in armed conflicts, especially in conflicts of an asymmetric nature where application of IHRL is likely to increase the normative gap between the parties. As indicated above, it is questionable whether under existing law IHRL applies to a non-state party to the conflict, and the actual compliance of such parties with applicable IHL is often very partial.

The possibility that the legal, political, and operational consequences of the application of IHRL in armed conflict situations might result in a backlash against IHRL norms and institutions is not a hypothetical one. The particular sensitivities of applying IHRL to overseas military operations have already led the UK Prime Minister to threaten a departure from the ECHR[24] and appear to be at the bottom of the opposition of the United States and other states to the interpretation of Article 2(1) of the ICCPR as applying the Covenant extra-territorially.[25]

Nevertheless, although I am of the view that IHRL-monitoring bodies need to consider the actual capacity of states to comply with their decisions—that is, seek to avoid normative overreach—such a consideration must take, as a normative matter, a backseat to the legally binding canons of interpretation under the Vienna Convention on the Law of Treaties, which prioritizes the ordinary language in its context and in light of the object and purpose of the treaty in question.[26] Subsequent state practice or agreements, including practice or agreements relating to the application of IHRL to conflict situations, should only be taken into account as a secondary source of interpretation under this legal scheme.

This does not mean, however, that state positions and anticipated reactions should be regarded as irrelevant by IHRL-monitoring bodies. For example, they may adjust the parties' evidentiary burdens and the scope of positive obligations to the circumstances prevailing in conflict situations (including the conduct of

---

[24] See, e.g., Peter Walker and Owen Bowcott, 'Plan for UK military to opt out of European convention on human rights' *The Guardian* (London, 4 October 2016).
[25] See, e.g., Aldo S Zilli, 'Approaching the Extraterritoriality Debate: The Human Rights Committee, the U.S. and the ICCPR' (2011) 9 Santa Clara Journal of International Law 399, 412–13.
[26] Vienna Convention on the Law of Treaties (adopted 23 May 1969, entered into force 27 January 1980) 1155 UNTS 331, Article 31.

investigations into alleged violations of IHRL). They may also accord some degree of deference to the work of IHL applying bodies, such as court martials, and afford victims remedies which acknowledge the complicated terrain in which IHRL needs to be implemented. In other words, savvy exercise of monitoring powers rather than refusal to exercise such powers is the proper response to fears of a political backlash against the removal of limits from the scope of application of IHRL.

Bibliography

Dennis MJ and Stewart DP, 'Justiciability of Economic, Social and Cultural Rights: Should There be an International Complaints Mechanism to Adjudicate the Right to Food, Water, Housing and Health?' (2004) 98 American Journal of International Law 462

Luban D, 'Human Rights Thinking and the Laws of War' in Ohlin JD (ed.), *Theoretical Boundaries of Armed Conflict and Human Rights* (Cambridge University Press 2016) 45

Ohlin JD, 'Acting as a Sovereign versus Acting as a Belligerent' in Ohlin JD (ed.), *Theoretical Boundaries of Armed Conflict and Human Rights* (Cambridge University Press 2016) 118

Walker P and Bowcott O, 'Plan for UK military to opt out of European convention on human rights' *The Guardian* (London, 4 October 2016)

Zilli AS, 'Approaching the Extraterritoriality Debate: The Human Rights Committee, the U.S. and the ICCPR' (2011) 9 Santa Clara Journal of International Law 399

PART V
LIMITS OF PROSPECTS, LIMITS OF MEANS: AN OUTLOOK

21
The Limits of Human Rights in a Moving World—Elements of a Dynamic Approach*

Mireille Delmas-Marty

I. INTRODUCTION: LIMITS, CROSSING LIMITS, AND REFUSING ANY LIMIT

The idea that all human beings belong to the same world community, which inspires both the humanist and the universalist ideal of human rights, has a long history. We can find traces of this thought already in Confucius, Greco-Roman authors, and in Christian thought. But its legal corroboration has taken centuries and still remains unfinished. The famous Habeas Corpus Act of 1679 confined humanism to English law. Earlier, Grotius' treatise 'On the Law of War and Peace' (1625) had reserved universalism to international law. Building on his work, scholars of the natural law tradition proposed the first rationalist and humanist version of international law that was adopted by European powers. Yet Emer de Vattel's 'The Law of Nations' (original title: *Le Droit des gens ou Principes de la loi naturelle, appliqués à la conduite et aux affaires des Nations et des Souverains*), published in 1758, must be understood in the Latin sense of a right of 'peoples' (*gentes*) and not of individuals. The actual birth of rights 'of man and of the citizen' that the Declaration of 1789 has established stems from Enlightenment philosophers.

What is Enlightenment? In December 1784, a Berlin-based journal published Immanuel Kant's answer to this question. According to the philosopher, Enlightenment is 'man's emergence from his self-incurred immaturity'.[1] Adding that '[f]or enlightenment of this kind, all that is needed is *freedom*', he immediately posed the question of the limits to freedom: 'But which sort of restriction prevents enlightenment, and which, instead of hindering it, can actually promote it?'[2]

---

* Dr Camila Perruso has kindly helped the editors with the review of our translation from French into English of Professor Delmas-Marty's contribution.
[1] Immanuel Kant, 'An Answer to the Question: "What is Enlightenment?"' in Hans Reiss (ed.), *Kant: Political Writings* (2nd edn, Cambridge University Press 1991) 54–60, 54 (emphasis in the quoted translation omitted) (hereafter Reiss (ed.), *Kant: Political Writings*).
[2] Ibid, 55 (emphasis in the quoted translation).

Mireille Delmas-Marty, *The Limits of Human Rights in a Moving World—Elements of a Dynamic Approach*. In: *The Limits of Human Rights*. Edited by: Bardo Fassbender and Knut Traisbach, Oxford University Press 2019. © The Several Contributors.
DOI: 10.1093/oso/9780198824756.003.0023

Two centuries later, Michel Foucault tried to answer the same question.[3] Using the definition of Kant, the French philosopher proposed to transform the Kantian question (of knowing which limits knowledge shall not cross) into a practical criticism of which crossings are possible. Accordingly, we could rephrase the question: Does the emergence from immaturity ultimately mean to free oneself from any limit?

The question of limits, of crossing limits, and even of the refusal of any limit lies at the heart of the notion of human rights—so much so that the editors of the present volume have chosen to dedicate a collective work to this question, stating that the limits do not necessarily imply 'weaknesses or gaps' but a call to clarify 'what "limits of human rights" are and what these limits can "mean"'.[4]

The limits shift as human rights evolve. Already in 1789, 'the rights of man and of the citizen' had implicit political limits reflecting an unequal society that excluded women and reserved the right to vote for 'active citizens' after 1791. On the other hand, there were few explicit legal limits. Liberty 'consists in the power to do anything that does not harm others', and the limits of human rights 'can only be determined by law' (Article 4 of the Declaration of the Rights of Man and Citizen). Inequalities have been slowly challenged and limits have been established against the omnipotence of the law. This shows that human rights are neither a static concept nor a Western dogma but a transformative process. To paraphrase a formula of the European Court of Human Rights (ECtHR), they are 'a living instrument, which must be interpreted in the light of present-day conditions'.[5]

Conditions of life have indeed profoundly changed. Humanism did not prevent the rise of nationalism, and universalism adopted imperialistic traits. It required the indignation over 'barbarous acts which have outraged the conscience of mankind'[6] committed by nations that regarded themselves as 'civilized' to finally enshrine human rights in a 'universal' declaration in 1948. But they were no longer a static and absolute truth to which one adhered without debate. Of course, the 'Peoples of the United Nations' still proclaimed 'their faith in fundamental human rights'.[7] But the 'inalienable and sacred' rights of 1789 became 'fundamental' rights, and reason, mentioned on purpose in Article 1 of the Universal Declaration, evoked more imagination than revelation. Reason led to the consolidation of

---

[3] Michel Foucault, 'Qu'est-ce que les Lumières?' in Michel Foucault, *Dits et écrits (1954–1988), vol. IV: 1980–1988* (Gallimard 1994) 562 et seq.

[4] See Bardo Fassbender and Knut Traisbach, 'Introduction: A Ride on the Human Rights Bus' in Bardo Fassbender and Knut Traisbach (eds), *The Limits of Human Rights* (Oxford University Press 2019) 1.

[5] *Loizidou v. Turkey*, App. No. 15318/89, 18 December 1996, para. 71.

[6] Universal Declaration of Human Rights, GA Res. 217 A(III) (10 December 1948) [1948–49] UN Yearbook 535–7, preamble, para. 2.

[7] Charter of the United Nations (adopted 26 June 1945, entered into force 24 October 1945) 892 UNTS 119, preamble, para. 3, to which reference is made in the Universal Declaration of Human Rights, preamble, para. 5.

the 'declaration' by a whole series of 'conventions' (including the International Covenants of 1966) which specify the content and limits of human rights.

Today, we witness a return of nationalism and imperialism. From the United States to Europe, in particular in France, we (re)discover that these dynamics can be reversed and that human rights can regress as 'societies of fear' develop. By limiting freedoms in the name of a right to security, which appears to have become the prime, if not the only, human right, these societies seem willing to legitimate a seemingly triumphant 'reason of state' (*raison d'État*). It is an alleged triumph only because the promise to regain a fully autonomous and independent sovereignty is contradicted by the growing interdependencies that accompany globalization.

By becoming part of positive law, human rights reveal not only internal[8] but also external contradictions between, on the one hand, the underlying humanist and universalist ideal and, on the other hand, the pragmatism that governs the world.

The first contradiction is illustrated, for example, by the humanitarian disaster of refugees: states open their borders to goods and capital, but close them to human beings fleeing wars or misery. The economic reason which, in the name of free competition, can weaken the universalism of social rights will not be specially developed here. Actually, human rights are a weak defence against security concerns that cause states to erect walls and other barriers because of a dubious mix of concerns about migration and terrorism. Hence, we need to ask whether the *raison d'État* (reason of state) imposes limits that can be reconciled with the humanist and universalist ideal of human rights.

The second contradiction arises when the anthropocentric humanism of the Enlightenment—which lies at the heart of human rights—is juxtaposed with a humanism of interdependence that takes into account also future generations and living nonhumans. The conservation of the ecosystem, for example, calls for a precautionary principle that limits the rights of present generations in the name of an 'ecological reason' whose anticipatory reach may be infinite.

Finally, the rise of technological innovations, accelerated by the so-called 'post-human' or 'trans-human' movements, raises a third question: Do human rights limit 'technoscientific reason', or does the latter contrarily render all limits obsolete?

I will address the question of limits in light of this threefold dynamic that challenges the ideal of human rights: first, 'reason of state' and the limits which accompany it; secondly, 'ecological' or 'planetary reason' and the need for anticipation of risks in order to protect the safety of the planet and the ecosystem; thirdly, a 'technoscientific reason' which has become the prime reason for refusing all limits.

---

[8] See Mireille Delmas-Marty, 'Les faiblesses de l'universalisme juridique ou l'incomplétude des idées' in Mireille Delmas-Marty, *Le Relatif et l'Universel. Les Forces imaginantes du droit*, vol. 1 (Seuil 2004) 53 et seq.

II. THE LIMITS OF 'REASON OF STATE' IN LIGHT OF THE HUMANIST AND UNIVERSALIST IDEAL OF HUMAN RIGHTS

We can split the question of limits in two parts: We may regard human rights as limits to national interests (human rights *or raison d'État*); or we can conceive these two as mutual limits that are part of the same standard (human rights *and raison d'État*).

A. Human Rights *or* Raison d'État

In 1789, the human rights system remained an ideal without any real legal impact. Kant's *Project for Perpetual Peace* (1795–96) was hence not based on human rights but on practical reason that already evoked the process of globalization. According to Kant, the right not to be treated as an enemy in the country where one arrives (the principle of 'universal hospitality') results from the spherical shape of the earth which obliges us to tolerate each other because we cannot scatter infinitely. It is the insight that we live in a finite world (a globe) from where the philosopher deduces his cosmopolitan vision: 'The peoples of the earth have thus entered in varying degrees into a universal community, and it has developed to the point where a violation of rights in *one* part of the world is felt *everywhere*. The idea of a cosmopolitan right is therefore not fantastic and overstrained; it is a necessary complement to the unwritten code of political and international right, transforming it into a universal right of humanity'.[9] Even if nature separates nations, '[o]n the other hand, nature also unites nations which the concept of cosmopolitan rights would not have protected from violence and war'.[10] Kant's confidence in the spirit of commerce which he believed 'cannot exist side by side with war' seemed to open the way to a 'reason of state' which recognizes only those limits which nature requires 'by the actual mechanism of human inclinations'.[11]

In the nineteenth century, many jurists openly defended the colonizations, invoking even the humanist ideal in the name of a so-called 'civilizing mission' in which many of them sincerely believed. By moving from human nature to 'civilized' nature, or from human reason to 'civilized consciousness' they tried to justify the wave of European colonial expansion that was developing. After

---

[9] Immanuel Kant, 'Perpetual Peace: A Philosophical Sketch' in Reiss, *Kant: Political Writings* (n. 1) 93, 107–8 (emphasis in the quoted translation) (hereafter Kant, 'Perpetual Peace'); Peter Kemp, *Citizen of the World: The Cosmopolitan Ideal for the Twenty-First Century* (Humanity Books 2010); see also Mireille Delmas-Marty, 'Vers une communauté mondiale de valeurs?' (2012) 2 Eco-ethica 21 and the other contributions on cosmopolitanism and plurality in the same issue.

[10] Kant, 'Perpetual Peace' (n. 9) 114.

[11] Ibid.

all, trade sat well with imperialism and slavery. It succeeded less in pacifying peoples than in generating a spirit of competition that brought about or revived economic wars.

It is no coincidence that the revival of the universalist movement began in Asia that was quasi-colonized by Western powers. The Chinese scholar Kang Youwei, exiled to Japan for attempting to reform the Chinese Empire, wrote the *Da Tong Shu* (1884–85), the 'Book of Great Unity', inspired by the theory of the three ages of humanity in Chinese classics (Great Disorder, Upward Peace, and Great Peace). Far from the individualistic humanism of human rights, he imagined in great detail the organization of a world government based on a Confucian model tinged with Buddhism. Yet the upheavals towards the end of the Chinese Empire had him forfeit the publication of his project.

In Europe, lawyers such as the French scholar Raymond Saleilles built on the new discipline of comparative law and suggested a 'common law with variable content' (1901) which was, however, different to usual comparative studies both regarding its object and its methodology. This formula, inspired by the 'natural law with variable content' of the German legal philosopher Rudolf Stammler,[12] foreshadowed a future human rights law. But the path was long and winding because at that time this new kind of common law—supposed to be worldwide—was still limited to a 'civilized humanity'.

It was only after the First World War that the hope of a 'Truly Common Law'[13] was revived in international law with the creation of the International Labour Organisation (ILO) and the League of Nations. Thus, the French scholar Georges Scelle, convinced that the concepts of inter-national law or of an interstate law were outdated, proposed (in 1932!) to describe and analyse the relations between members of politically distinct communities in terms of an 'organic solidarity' overarched by an 'international community', understood primarily as a community of individuals and not as one of peoples.[14]

But in the climate of disillusionment of the late 1930s, this genuinely humanist and universalist movement proved powerless to counter the rise of nationalism: 'A man's home is his castle', proclaimed the Nazi leaders to make it clear that national sovereignty is absolute and 'Staatsräson' without limit. We know to what horrendous practices of dehumanization this doctrine led the world.

Only after the Second World War did the interactions between international and domestic law really develop on the regional and international level towards a 'common law with variable content'—a common standard that concerned the whole of humanity by linking human rights and 'reason of state'.

---

[12] Rudolf Stammler, *The Theory of Justice* (Isaak Husik transl, The Lawbook Exchange 2000) 515.
[13] Mireille Delmas-Marty, *Towards a Truly Common Law: Europe as a Laboratory for Legal Pluralism* (Cambridge University Press 2002).
[14] Georges Scelle, *Précis de droit des gens*, vol. 1 (Sirey 1932).

B. Human Rights *and* Raison d'État: Towards a Common Standard

Perhaps we can understand the scope of the notion common 'standard' better today because the legal systems set up at the regional, and sometimes global, level steer towards harmonization. That is to say, they are prone to reduce differences but not to dissolve them completely. This shared pluralistic law is politically more acceptable than a unified law, but its flexibility makes it also more complex legally.

Things became more complex after 1948 with the development of limits that are explicitly permissible. The limits which law imposes on human rights must have a legitimate aim: 'In the exercise of his rights and freedoms, everyone shall be subject only to such limitations as are determined by law solely for the purpose of securing due recognition and respect for the rights and freedoms of others and of meeting the just requirements of morality, public order and the general welfare in a democratic society' (Article 29(2) of the Universal Declaration of Human Rights (UDHR)).

Morality, public order, and general welfare belong to the many components of the 'reason of state'. Hence we can recognize the contour of a standard that may be called 'common' because it reconciles, despite its variable content, human rights *with* 'reason of state'. Some regional systems for the protection of human rights, such as the European Convention on Human Rights (ECHR) (1950), facilitate this reconciliation. The ECtHR distinguishes, for example, between three types of limits. The strongest limit are derogations that result in a temporary suspension of the guarantee of a particular right by a state party (Article 15 of the ECHR specifies the exceptional circumstances). Hence the debate in France on the successive prolongations of the state of emergency proclaimed in November 2015 and finally abolished in November 2017. It should also be recalled that the derogation clause specifies 'non-derogable' rights which entail, inter alia, the rights fundamental to the equal dignity of all human beings, such as the prohibition of torture, inhuman or degrading treatment or punishment, or the prohibition of slavery. It is on this legal basis that the ECtHR has prohibited such derogations, even in the context of terrorism. Secondly, there are legal exceptions which are explicitly mentioned but subject to conditions specified by the Convention. Only specific exceptional circumstances permit these exceptions (see, e.g., Article 2 on the right to life, or Article 5 on rights to liberty and security). Thirdly, restrictions are possible that are 'necessary in a democratic society' (see paragraph 2 of Articles 8 to 11 of the Convention, in particular the right to respect for private life and freedom of expression) which authorize interferences by the state under the condition that it observes the principles of legality and proportionality and pursues a legitimate aim. In applying this standard, the Court has granted national authorities a 'margin of appreciation' with regard to the measure taken and the pursued aim (public order, morals, economic well-being, etc.).

These limits make it in a way possible to 'reason about the "reason of state"', that is to say not to abandon it, but to frame it legally in accordance with the rule of law. Through its flexibility, in particular when a 'national margin' is granted, this approach makes it possible to reconcile the humanist ideal and its universal vocation with diverse national particularities. But the 'national margin' is not recognized outside the European Convention, and the notion of non-derogable right, which is included in the International Covenant on Civil and Political Rights (ICCPR) (see Article 4(2)), is not controlled by a judge at the global level. We hence come back to a binary choice between the universalist ideal of human rights and the sovereign particularism of 'reason of state'. Thus, in the face of the threat of global terrorism, the United States has started to legitimize inhuman and degrading treatment or even torture in the name of security.

Nevertheless, by allowing the emergence of a common but variable standard, the game of limits seems preferable to a unified world law: instead of *opposing* the humanist ideal of human rights to the 'sovereigntism' of the 'reason of state', we *compose* a flexible model with a variable set-up and multiple velocities. We have a variable set-up because the implementation of the limits requires at times a balancing logic which favours the principle of proportionality through a reciprocal limitation of human rights and the 'reason of state'—for example, when the ECtHR authorizes interceptions of communications for security reasons in the name of the fight against terrorism. On the contrary, it may follow the logic of legal prohibitions when the Court opposes acts of torture with the absolute limits of 'non-derogable' rights even in the event of terrorist acts or other threats to the survival of the nation.

We also have multiple velocities imposed by globalization, which, for example, accelerates the regulation of trade and investment according to a quasi-global model, while at the same time promoting a slow integration of human rights into domestic law, as evidenced by the slow establishment of international criminal courts. These differences in velocities of multiple normative orders can have disastrous consequences for the weakest members of society such as migrants. To put the different normative logics in order and synchronize the velocities would imply a reorganization of the limits of human rights. Yet the return of sovereignty announces a nationalism marked by a retreat of human rights in the name of 'reason of state'.

The old principle of sovereignty, which is so present in the legal culture of peoples, remains enshrined in the Charter of the United Nations and continues to be the foundation of a great deal of international law and national practices. Not only the 'great powers' (the United States, China, Russia, etc.) invoke it, but it is also present in the general trend towards security which is characterized by the establishment of 'societies of fear' in response to momentary threats, as mentioned in the introduction.

Coincidently, at the very moment when human rights should return to the centre of debate as a means to limit the 'reason of state', a broader 'reason of the planet' emerges and blurs the picture of global governance. It requires us to overcome the limits of time in the name of the security of the planet and of the ecosystem of which humanity is a part.

III. THE 'REASON OF PLANET' AND RISK ANTICIPATION AS OVERCOMING THE LIMITS OF TIME

The globalization of risks is the example chosen by Jürgen Habermas to celebrate the bicentenary of Kant's perpetual peace: '[T]hose of us who do not doubt the capacity of the international system to learn have to place our hopes in the fact that they very globalization of these dangers has already objectively brought the world together into an involuntary community of shared risks.'[15] We need to move now from an 'involuntary' community to a voluntary community, especially in the face of ecological risks that have already materialized, but even more often are still uncertain. Thus, legal expressions such as 'precautionary principle', 'sustainable development', or 'future generations' limit human rights—but not in the name of 'reason of state', rather because of a 'reason of Planet' which imposes a duty of crossing the limits of time, that is to anticipate measures before irreversible damage occurs.

Beyond the prevention of proven risks, the precautionary principle addresses uncertain but potentially serious or irreversible risks. The principle results from the duty to anticipate. We could say that we need to cross the limits that until now have connected but also separated human rights and 'raison d'État'. Today, there can be no doubt that the effects of certain human decisions affect the survival of humanity and the balance of the biosphere. We need to protect the safety of the state to ensure the safety of the planet. A reason that could be called 'planetary' would sometimes require action before the event takes place; it necessitates a process of anticipation. This principle of 'precaution/anticipation' can be regarded as an extension of human rights to future generations, but it is perceived by the present populations as a limit to their rights.

A. 'Reason of Planet' as a Limit of Human Rights: The Precautionary Principle

By (trans)forming nature, human beings have (de)formed nature in the literal sense. Water, for example, is a rare resource. The French Conseil d'État issued

---

[15] Jürgen Habermas, 'Kant's Idea of Perpetual Peace, with the Benefit of Two Hundred Years' of Hindsight' in James Bohman and Matthias Lutz-Bachmann (eds), *Perpetual Peace: Essays of Kant's Cosmopolitan Ideal* (MIT Press 1997) 113, 133–4.

this warning in a report already in 2010: 'At the beginning of the 21st century, we face new concerns about global warming and its consequences for the sufficient availability and quality of water and for risks related to more intense floods or droughts.'[16] We are also beginning to fear the depletion of natural resources. Agriculture will have to face a population that will reach nine billion people by 2050, and global warming threatens the equilibrium of the biosphere. Even China, one of the first major countries to ratify the Paris Climate Agreement, now recognizes the need to reconcile environmental protection and the right to economic development.[17]

Economists believed they found the solution with the concept of 'sustainable development' (United Nations Development Program, UNDP 1987) because it postulated a synergy between economic and environmental law. Ecologists gathered at the Earth Summit in Rio de Janeiro in 1992 and introduced 'future generations' into the legal field, notably in the context of climate change (United Nations Framework Convention on Climate Change 1992 and the Kyoto Protocol of 1997). But the former Chair of the World Commission on Sustainable Development, Gro Harlem Brundtland, pointed to continuing difficulties in UNDP's Human Development Report for 2007/2008: 'Sustainability ... is about finding a balance between people and planet—a balance that addresses the great challenges of poverty today, while protecting the interests of future generations'.[18] When we want to care about the future, we cannot forget the present, nor can we erase the weight of the past. Globalization multiplied ecological imbalances before it could equalize economic opportunities. How can we expect countries that have never or hardly experienced growth to accept measures that limit growth?

In the context of climate change, the stalled debate on the implementation of the Kyoto Protocol (from Copenhagen in 2009 to Rio + 20 in 2012) showed the need for a mixed model of pluralist universalism (or ordering pluralism) which embraces both 'reason of Planet' with a universal vocation and 'reason of state' on the national level. This will ultimately be the meaning given to the principle of 'shared but differentiated' responsibilities in the Paris Climate Agreement (adopted in 2015 and entered into force in 2016).

But how far into the future should or can we anticipate? The dream of living in a predictable world could lead to even more intrusive warning and control mechanisms and ultimately result in an unlimited responsibility that ignores humans' finite nature. This would be a senseless vision, writes Paul Ricoeur, because our cognitive abilities are insufficient to control 'the gap between the intended

---

[16] Études et documents du Conseil d'État, L'eau et son droit (EDCE no. 61), 2010, 8, <http://www.conseil-etat.fr/Media/CDE/Francais/eau_droit_rapport> accessed 31 January 2019.

[17] Jean-François Huchet, *La crise environnementale en Chine* (Presses Sciences Po 2016).

[18] United Nations Development Programme, Human Development Report 2007/2008, 'Fighting Climate Change: Human Solidarity in a Divided World' 59 <http://hdr.undp.org/sites/default/files/reports/268/hdr_20072008_en_complete.pdf> accessed 31 January 2019.

effects and the number of innumerable consequences of our actions'.[19] To hold us fully accountable would paralyse any action, especially because the gap between the global dimension of risk and the national dimension of political decision-making powers is considerable. As the joke goes: 'Carbon cycles do not respect political cycles'. But does this mean that we need to impose unlimited liability on decision-makers?

If anticipation limits human rights according to the severity of the risk, we must nevertheless recognize that in many areas, notably in the context of climate change, a 'zero risk' does not exist. Risks form part of human life. It is therefore necessary to replace the concept of 'zero risk' with that of 'acceptable risk' and to determine an acceptability threshold according to a logic of degree (a fuzzy logic). In short, we must also limit the limits.

B. From Zero Risk to Acceptable Risk: Limiting Limits

The difficulty is that there are no uniform criteria for evaluating risks. The notion of seriousness is based on scientific criteria such as the probability of the risk, the reliability of the evidence, the frequency and the geographical or temporal extent (reversibility) of the risk. On the other hand, the notion of acceptability rests on more subjective social, economic, and even cultural criteria. We face therefore, on the one hand, the difficulty of balancing between the security of the planet and the rights of the present generation and, on the other hand, the complexity of political decision-making. The decision-maker will have to take into account both the scientific criteria determining the seriousness of the risk and the social, economic, political, and cultural context that varies locally.

In the case of genetically modified organisms (GMOs), for example, the decision to authorize or prohibit them may take into account not only the objective seriousness of environmental or health risks but also political criteria such as the risk of servitude of farmers due to the power of enterprises supplying seeds for the duration of a term of a patent; or social criteria such as the cultural importance of organic agriculture invoked by Austria against GMOs; or even religious criteria such as the Christian conception of life brought in by Poland. The Court of Justice of the European Union (CJEU) does not exclude the use of such criteria in the assessment of the acceptable risk, but verifies its reasonableness and seriousness. The World Trade Organization (WTO) Appellate Body appears to accept that the particular national context can be invoked independently of scientific criteria.

---

[19] Paul Ricœur, 'Le concept de responsabilité, essai d'analyse sémantique' [1994] Esprit no. 206, 28, 47.

Similarly, in the context of climate change, the legal debate has expanded beyond science to include criteria particular to the national context which are explicitly admitted by the 2015 Paris Agreement. Examples include the historical context, such as the 'ecological debt' in industrialized countries; the economic context such as the level of development; or the geographical context such as the degree of vulnerability of certain countries.

By distinguishing between criteria of seriousness and acceptability of risks (some of them universal and others context-dependent), the 'reason of Planet' avoids the imposition of an unlimited responsibility on political decision-makers and scientists in the name of a duty to anticipate. This leads me to my last point: When we apply the logic of progress, a 'reason of Technology and Science' may lead to the refusal of any limit, and therefore of all responsibility.

IV. DOES 'TECHNO-SCIENTIFIC REASON' LEAD TO THE REFUSAL OF ANY LIMIT?

New technologies, be they information technologies or biotechnologies, are ambivalent. They entail both the hope of freeing us from the constraints of nature and the fear of new modes of enslavement. But in the name of what principle do the rights of man privilege either hope or fear?

A. The Ambivalence of New Technologies

The speed of innovations enhances the ambivalence of new technologies, be they information technologies or biotechnologies. As soon as a certain speed is reached, the steering of world affairs is in danger of going into autopilot. There are already signs of a profound and radical transformation marked by the emergence of a new co-operative model that could be called 'knitted'. This model replaces the common organizational networks in tree or star form with horizontal structures in which co-operation occurs without prior determination. Examples are so-called 'smart' cities or 'smart' objects. The co-operation is inherent in the feedback of the system itself. In these smart networks, objectives are no longer defined by human will, but result, so to speak, automatically from the interactions between human systems and machines.

Similarly, biotechnology sets out to improve the capacities and creativity of every human being by exalting individual freedom, but in practice it can facilitate the commodification and/or commercialization of the body (e.g. by allowing a selling and buying of organs, or a renting of the uterus) which weakens the principle of equal dignity. Another example is biological formatting (e.g. through the selection of embryos) which reduces the margin of indetermination so much that there is a risk of diluting the individual in the species.

We know that assisted reproductive technology was developed to meet the demand of infertile couples. Scientific advances have led to the first 'test tube babies' (generated in the laboratory by in vitro fertilization followed by the transfer of the embryo into a female body). The method makes it possible to select embryos through preimplantation diagnosis; and it enables 'surrogacy' which has become a 'baby business' in some countries such as India and Ukraine. The fabrication of humans has thus begun to be commonplace without anybody having really wished for it. This raises the question about the limits to actions affecting the human being, whether it concerns the access of same-sex couples to assisted reproductive technology, or practices that combine biotechnology with information and communication technologies, such as cyber-reproduction or autonomous robots.

And so humanity, which at the end of a biological evolution over millions of years seemed eternal, begins to appear as a humanity 'in transition'. The trans-humanist movement regards itself already as a precursor to overcoming humanity in its present state which it regards as imperfect or even as failed. At the very moment that law begins to become universal, trans-humanists claim to demonstrate the uselessness of any normative, moral, religious, or legal norm. Concentrated on embodiment in the biological sense, trans-humanism is disinterested in humanization in the ethical sense: technologies will prevent any medical dysfunction and improve the human species just like the bovine species was improved.

So should we allow or prohibit this type of technology? If we return to the spirit of the Enlightenment for a moment, emerging from one's self-incurred immaturity undoubtedly neither requires us to blindly obey nature nor to totally free us from it, but it does require that we rethink the limits of the technoscientific innovation in terms of human rights, perhaps by posing again the question of the non-derogability which is closely linked to the right to equal dignity of all human beings. This right, which can never be waived, even in exceptional circumstances, has been enshrined in the European and American human rights conventions and the ICCPR in order to prohibit torture, slavery and inhuman or degrading treatment. Also Article 7 of the ICCPR, as an indirect result from the trials of Nazi physicians by the Military Tribunal in Nuremberg, prohibits the subjecting of a person to medical or scientific experimentation without her or his free consent. The provision does not directly address innovation but the lack of consent. By outlining the contours of an irreducible human core, human rights could draw a dividing line between different types of innovation.

B. The Contours of the 'Irreducible Human Core'

At the intersection of 'non-derogable' rights and their corollary of crimes to which statutory limitations are not applicable (i.e. genocide, war crimes, crimes against humanity), international law has implicitly sketched the outlines of what might be called 'the irreducible human core' according to two principles: the principle of *singularity* which forbids reducing a human being to the group of which he or she forms part, and the principle of *equal membership in the human community* which states that beyond the social (local, national, or regional) context the global community is at the same time a biological fact (a sole species) and a cultural reality (the preamble of the UDHR speaks of all members of the 'human family').

By enabling new methods for the extension and production of human life, technological innovations have revived the debate, possibly suggesting the emergence of a new principle. This principle could be called the *'indeterminacy'* principle which informed already the draft resolution on human cloning initiated by Germany and France in 2001, which then led to the United Nations Declaration on Human Cloning of 2005.[20]

Indeed, indeterminacy seems to be necessary for the survival of the species because it encourages creativity and adaptability, while at the same time nourishing a sense of freedom which constitutes human beings as such in their human dignity. Such a principle, situated at the intersection of biological evolution (incarnation) and cultural evolution (humanization), would allow human rights to impose limits on dehumanizing practices. First, it would restrict security measures that transform criminal justice into a predictive justice by transposing without any hesitation the precautionary principle from the context of animals and dangerous products to allegedly dangerous human beings. But it would also limit technological innovations, such as reproductive cloning, pre-implantation eugenics, genetic manipulation, or neurological treatments that inhibit any feeling of alterity. These would be limited as long as they precondition human behaviour.

V. CONCLUSION

In these times of doubt, one (re)discovers that history is discontinuous and humanization is reversible. Even in a democracy, dehumanization is never far away. Human rights, through their limits, are on a global level our best means to contribute to a humanistic imagination of the world that many of us hope will preserve its human face.

In times of globalization, human rights seem more than ever necessary for the emergence of a 'common legal standard' and perhaps a 'truly common law'. The well-regulated game of limits would allow this common law to be made more flexible through a variable content that adapts better to the diversity of the real world. This, instead of weakening human rights, could transform them into a living instrument at the service of the humanization of our species. In short, this could be

---

[20] United Nations Declaration on Human Cloning, GA Res. 59/280 (8 March 2005).

a way to establish, if not the 'perpetual peace' of Kant or the 'Great Peace' of Kang Youwei, at least a 'peace in the making' which could be conceived as a work in progress for a world in process.

Unless we abandon the dream of the two Ks and admit, following Foucault's question and the logic of the trans-humanist movements, that leaving one's immaturity might lead to one's leaving the state of humanity. For when it comes to improving human capacities, it would be legitimate not to obey nature, law, or ethics, and whatever is possible should also be permissible. In a famous painting by Goya the sleep of reason produces monsters. It remains to be seen whether the invocation of a practical reason left to itself by the disappearance of any boundary will produce other monsters, post-human ones that have renounced any limit for the hope to overcome human finitude. We will know, perhaps before the end of the century, if the 'great acceleration' leads to a 'great collapse' or to a 'vast decoupling' which would announce the metamorphosis of our species.

Bibliography

Delmas-Marty M, *Towards a Truly Common Law: Europe as a Laboratory for Legal Pluralism* (Cambridge University Press 2002)

Delmas-Marty M, 'Les faiblesses de l'universalisme juridique ou l'incomplétude des idées' in Delmas-Marty M, *Le Relatif et l'Universel. Les Forces imaginantes du droit*, vol. 1 (Seuil 2004) 53

Delmas-Marty M, 'Vers une communauté mondiale de valeurs?' (2012) 2 Eco-ethica 21

Fassbender B and Traisbach K, 'Introduction: A Ride on the Human Rights Bus' in Fassbender B and Traisbach K (eds), *The Limits of Human Rights* (Oxford University Press 2019) 1

Foucault M, 'Qu'est-ce que les Lumières?' in Michel Foucault, *Dits et écrits (1954–1988), vol. IV: 1980–1988* (Gallimard 1994) 562

Habermas J, 'Kant's Idea of Perpetual Peace, with the Benefit of Two Hundred Years' of Hindsight' in Bohman J and Lutz-Bachmann M (eds), *Perpetual Peace: Essays of Kant's Cosmopolitan Ideal* (MIT Press 1997) 113

Huchet JF, *La crise environnementale en Chine* (Presses Sciences Po 2016)

Kant I, 'An Answer to the Question: "What is Enlightenment?"' in Reiss H (ed.), *Kant: Political Writings* (2nd edn, Cambridge University Press 1991) 54

Kant I, 'Perpetual Peace: A Philosophical Sketch' in Reiss H (ed.), *Kant: Political Writings* (2nd edn, Cambridge University Press 1991) 93

Kemp P, *Citizen of the World: The Cosmopolitan Ideal for the Twenty-First Century* (Humanity Books 2010)

Ricœur P, 'Le concept de responsabilité, essai d'analyse sémantique' [1994] Esprit no. 206, 28

Scelle G, *Précis de droit des gens*, vol. 1 (Sirey 1932)

Stammler R, *The Theory of Justice* (Isaak Husik trans., The Lawbook Exchange 2000)

22
Where are the Limits of Human Rights? Four Schools, Four Complementary Visions
A Response to Mireille Delmas-Marty

Marie-Bénédicte Dembour

It is an honour to respond to this contribution, the more so since Professor Delmas-Marty's scholarship has towered over my own development ever since I was an early career researcher. When I was asked in my first academic job to teach human rights to undergraduate students enrolled in a variety of interdisciplinary programmes, I knew little about human rights as an academic discipline. My training in law and social anthropology would enable me to remain one or two steps ahead of my students, my doctoral supervisor reassured me. Reading Delmas-Marty greatly helped this necessarily fast learning curve. It was refreshing and invigorating to come across a lawyer who could think of law as fuzzy.[1] It was reassuring to have a senior colleague intensely alert to the dangers of *raison d'État* for human rights.[2] More than anything else, I appreciated Delmas-Marty's acute awareness of the world's pluralism and her injunction to take its measure and then seek to put it in order (*'l'ordonner'*). Her repeated calls for harnessing creative forces (*'forces imaginantes'*) in order to address the world's accelerating dynamics and, most recently, contrary winds[3] are music to my ears. These hallmarks of her scholarship remain visible in her contribution to the present volume.

In this contribution, Delmas-Marty discusses the limits of human rights in relation to state security and *raison d'État* (section I), the challenges ecological dysfunctions entail for the planet (section II), and human nature's future in the face of robotic developments (section III). Observing that instead of human rights limiting the reassertion of sovereignty, *raison d'État* appears to be limiting human rights logic and practice, section I calls for *raison d'État* to be limited in such a

---

[1] Mireille Delmas-Marty, *Le flou du droit* (Presses universitaires de France 1986).
[2] Mireille Delmas-Marty, *Raisonner la raison d'état: Vers une Europe des droits de l'homme* (Presses universitaires de France 1989).
[3] Mireille Delmas-Marty, *Aux quatre vents du monde: Petit guide de navigation sur l'océan de la mondialisation* (Seuil 2016).

Marie-Bénédicte Dembour, *Where are the Limits of Human Rights? Four Schools, Four Complementary Visions: A Response to Mireille Delmas-Marty*. In: *The Limits of Human Rights*. Edited by: Bardo Fassbender and Knut Traisbach, Oxford University Press. 2019 © The Several Contributors.
DOI: 10.1093/oso/9780198824756.003.0024

way that it can be reconciled with human rights. Section II operates a similar argument by reference to human rights and 'reason of planet'. The risks engendered by climate change are to be scientifically evaluated, but the acceptation of counteracting measures depends on social factors, so that the declaration of an anticipatory duty referencing the human rights of future generations must be judicially mitigated. Section III relates to techno-scientific reason. It asks whether robotic innovations might end up transforming human nature beyond recognition which, if it happened, would mean that human rights had not managed to put effective limits to the dehumanizing process triggered by these innovations. In sum, for Delmas-Marty, human rights would ideally limit the excesses of state security policies, help formulating an effective response to climate change, and keep in check technological follies.

The contribution is thought-provoking and wide-ranging. Nonetheless, at first I found it difficult to see how its three sections interconnected. In retrospect I can see that this difficulty arose because I would not instinctively have approached the limits-of-human-rights theme at the core of this volume as Delmas-Marty does. In short, she sees human rights as *limiting*, whilst I see them as *limited*.

To elaborate, my instinct is not to share Delmas-Marty's optimism, or at least high hopes, that human rights could successfully perform the limiting, positive role she assigns them. I approach the field from the other end of the stick, so to speak, and tend to think of human rights as inherently limited. For example, my book, *Who Believes in Human Rights?* discusses how important and persistent critiques of human rights—by realists, utilitarian thinkers, Marxists, feminists, and cultural relativists—find faults not only with the practice but also with the very concept of human rights, which celebrates the individual to the neglect of social values such as solidarity, and which sustains power relationships without seeming to be aware of this.[4] In a different vein, the central message of my most recent monograph, *When Humans Become Migrants*,[5] could be said to be that human rights fail, in crucial respects. In the system of the European Court of Human Rights (ECtHR), the central argument of this book goes, migrants are too often considered as subjects to the sovereignty of the state before being considered as human beings endowed with human rights; instead of being the core principle, human rights become an exception to the state sovereignty principle.

What strikes me, then, is that despite our common interests in trying to think about diversity and communality in an increasingly global world, Delmas-Marty and I start from different perspectives. This explains why I did not immediately

---

[4] Marie-Bénédicte Dembour, *Who Believes in Human Rights? Reflections on the European Convention* (Cambridge University Press 2006) (hereafter Dembour, *Who Believes in Human Rights?*).
[5] Marie-Bénédicte Dembour, *When Humans Become Migrants: Study of the European Court of Human Rights with an Inter-American Counterpoint* (Oxford University Press 2015).

grasp the interconnections of the thoughts her contribution offers. My eureka moment in this respect emerged as I was revisiting my four-school human rights model for a keynote lecture I was invited to present. It suddenly dawned on me that Delmas-Marty fitted best the category of what my model calls a 'natural scholar', whilst I remained at heart a 'discourse scholar' (despite being attracted by the four schools). Delmas-Marty is very much aware of the problems the world faces, and she looks at them right in the eye. Her contribution discusses the essential problems—essential because if not addressed adequately, they knell the end of the world as we know it. And she nourishes the (almost desperate) hope that human rights will be able *to limit* the various excesses these problems represent. By contrast, to me, human rights always have been, and thus not surprisingly continue to be, an *inherently limited* tool. In my view, it would be short-sighted to expect human rights to be able to cure the ills of the world; solutions need to be found beyond them.

A detour through my four-school model will make it possible to spell out our different perspectives more clearly, and why we require both of them, as well as another two. The discussion offered here will make two additions to the presentation I made of my model in *Human Rights Quarterly* (HRQ) in 2010.[6] On the one hand I will discuss how the different schools approach the theme of the limits of human rights. On the other hand I will examine how they view the history of human rights. In the HRQ article, I had cited work by, respectively, four philosophers, four lawyers, four political theorists, and four anthropologists, which each time occupied the four quarters of my model, thus showing that no academic discipline can be associated with one particular school. Here I shall similarly demonstrate that historians can be found in the whole field of human rights, as represented by my four schools.

I. THE FOUR-SCHOOL HUMAN RIGHTS MODEL

My model proposes that people approach human rights in different ways. It identifies four broad schools of thought, as follows: the natural school approaches human rights as *a given*; the deliberative school as *agreed upon*; the protest school as *fought for*; and the discourse (or double-talk) school as *talked about*. These schools are meant to act as ideal-types rather than to encapsulate single-track thought patterns; they represent broad orientations, shared not only by scholars but also by non-academic lay people.

---

[6] Marie-Bénédicte Dembour, 'What Are Human Rights? Four Schools of Thought' (2010) 32 Human Rights Quarterly 1 (hereafter Dembour, 'What Are Human Rights?'). See also ch. 8 of my book *Who Believes in Human Rights?* (n. 4).

The natural school embraces the most common and well-known definition of human rights: that which identifies human rights as those rights one possesses simply by being a human being. This school has traditionally represented the human rights orthodoxy. It conceives of human rights as entitlements which are based on 'nature', a short-cut that can stand for God, the Universe, reason, or another transcendental source. Natural scholars (who can be lay people) believe that human rights exist independently of social recognition. Their preference is nonetheless for human rights to be recognized, especially in human rights law. For them, human rights derive simply from being human. They are thus linked to the very essence of humankind, and this is why they consider them to be natural rights, that is, inalienable and universal.[7]

In a world where differences of opinion regarding the foundations of morality abound, the human rights orthodoxy has moved away from the natural school to the deliberative school. This school conceives of human rights as political values that liberal societies *choose* to adopt. Deliberative scholars see human rights as originating in social agreement and consisting in good principles of governance (rather than entitlements). Contrary to natural scholars, deliberative scholars do not believe that human rights exist beyond human rights law. They nonetheless tend to hold law, especially constitutional law, in high esteem for its ability to entrench the human rights principles that are agreed upon. The efforts of the adherents of this school are geared at identifying, agreeing, and consolidating these principles, which can only *become* universal if every government around the globe commits to them.[8]

Protest scholars have yet another take on human rights. For them, human rights are the voice of the suffering, and their prime function is to articulate rightful claims by the poor, the unprivileged, the oppressed, the forgotten. Protest scholars look at human rights as the outcome of struggles which have been animated by the moral imperative to challenge the status quo. Thus, they too seek to have human rights enacted in law. However, they are mindful of the risk that human rights law will be hijacked by the powerful as soon as it is enacted. For them, the human rights ethic is a tall, infinite order: once 'my' human rights are secured, I must ensure that the rights of my neighbour are secured, and then the rights of the neighbour of my neighbour, and so on and so forth.[9]

---

[7] As illustrations of the natural school, my article 'What Are Human Rights?' (n. 6) provides quotations from the philosopher Alan Gewirth, the political scientist Jack Donnelly, the lawyer Michael Perry, and the anthropologist Mark Goodale.

[8] As illustrations of the deliberative school, my article 'What Are Human Rights?' (n. 6) provides quotations from the philosopher Jürgen Habermas, the political scientist Michael Ignatieff, the lawyer Tom Campbell, and the anthropologist Sally Engle Merry.

[9] As illustrations of the protest school, my article 'What Are Human Rights?' (n. 6) provides quotations from the philosopher Jacques Derrida, the political theorist Neil Stammers, the lawyer Upendra Baxi, and the anthropologist June Nash.

The discourse (or double-talk) school stands out from the others in that it does not believe in human rights. Discourse scholars observe that human beings have lived through millennia without referring to human rights. In the perspective of this school, human rights exist only insofar as they are talked about—a historically recent phenomenon. In addition, this school points out that human rights have been and continue to be an imperialist tool which too often serves to mask injustice, inequality, oppression. Discourse scholars may accept that human rights has become a powerful language in which to articulate political claims in today's world, making it instrumentally useful to resort to this language. However, their hope is that projects of emancipation superior to human rights could be imagined and put into practice.[10]

The four schools are placed along two axes (see Figure 22.1). The vertical axis represents the nature of the origin of human rights from man-made at the bottom to transcendental at the top. The horizontal axis refers to the holding of a highly individualistic conception of the public good at its start to a decisively collective one at its end. These axes appear in the model as broken lines so as to stress that the four quarters of the constituted field should not be regarded as clearly separated entities but as ideal-types. Indeed, all kinds of various combinations as to how human rights are thought of are encountered in practice. Most people make pronouncements about human rights which would justify locating them in more than one school—possibly the four of them.

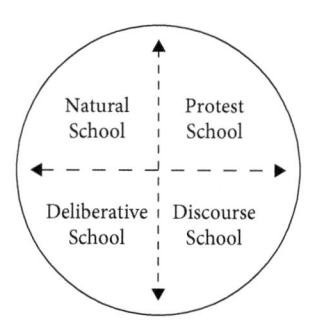

Figure 22.1 The human rights field.

---

[10] As illustrations of the discourse school, my article 'What Are Human Rights?' (n. 6) provides quotations from the philosopher Alasdair MacIntyre, the political theorist Wendy Brown, the lawyer Makau Mutua, and the anthropologist Shannon Speed.

II. THE LIMITS OF HUMAN RIGHTS ACCORDING TO THE FOUR SCHOOLS: INHERENT DEFECTS, LIMITED RESULTS, SPECIFIC DOMAIN, UNFORTUNATE 'MISHAPS'

The four schools are inclined to approach the theme of the limits of human rights—central to this volume—in very different ways, as will now be discussed. The discourse school being most acutely aware of the limits of human rights, I shall start the section with this school. I shall then discuss the other schools in the reverse order from that in which they were presented in the above section.

Awareness of the limits of human rights is precisely the hallmark of the discourse school, which keeps observing that human rights fail to deliver their promises. The central tenet of this school could be said to be that human rights are unfit to accomplish their purported job. This school accordingly never ceases to highlight that the ascent of human rights in the post-1945 era has not contributed to instil more humanity, equality, and liberty in the world—a trajectory explained by discourse scholars by reference to human rights' individualism, collusion with imperialism and/or dependence on capitalism. To discourse scholars, the limits of human rights are their *inherent defects*. The summary I have given above of my monographs locates me squarely in this school (somewhat to my chagrin, as I find the insights of the other three schools important and worthy of consideration). The protest school shares some of the discourse school's misgivings towards human rights, in that protest scholars fear the hijacking of human rights law by the elite. Moreover, they accept that human rights is a task that always needs to be re-started, almost like in the Sisyphus myth. Once an obstacle has been overcome and a victory won, another struggle raises its head which demands to be fought. However, by contrast to the more sceptical discourse scholars, protest scholars believe in the idea of human rights. To them, human rights are always worth fighting for—with passion, with consistency, with determination. If human rights are limited, it is partly because their ethical demands are infinite. Human rights victories only ever bring *limited results*, which constantly require to be renewed.

The deliberative school approaches human rights as a matter for reasonable agreement, to be reached within the context of political institutions. This does not prevent deliberative scholars from committing to human rights. However, they stress that human rights cannot be a response to every moral, social, and human problem. To them, the aim of human rights is to provide guidance for political action, and to do this only—which of course is already a lot. In their view, the other schools are therefore misguided in expecting human rights to govern other aspects of human life. Deliberative scholars tend to think about the limits of human rights by reference to their conception of human rights' proper and *exclusive domain* as the *political sphere*.

As we have seen, the natural school conceives of human rights as existing beyond social recognition, in perfect form. This explains that natural scholars are the most upbeat about human rights. Having said this, they are aware that the transposition of the idea of human rights in human rights law and/or practice can be problematic. Whilst natural scholars do not see the gaps between theory and practice as something that affects the human rights core, which remains beyond critique, they recognize that errors of transposition from the idea to the real world can arise, in which case these errors need to be corrected. To them, human rights are not inherently limited, but they can become limited because of what could be called '*mishaps*'.

Such mishaps are precisely what Delmas-Marty's contribution warns against. She is worried that *raison d'État* could be allowed to supplant human rights, future generations could be prevented from enjoying life on earth, and robotic developments could dehumanize our world. In the face of these dangers, what Delmas-Marty wishes is for human rights to fulfil a *limiting* role. This is an approach that leaves the concept of human rights as it were intact, which corresponds in my model to a natural school inclination.

This classification is indirectly confirmed by the fact that Delmas-Marty does not fit better in any other school, even if some of her pronouncements reflect the views of the other three schools. For example, the ambition to 'compose a flexible model with a variable set-up and multiple velocities' rather than simply '*opposing* the humanist ideal of human rights to the "sovereigntism" of the "reason of State"'[11] can be associated with the deliberative school; the attachment to the precautionary principle and the need to protect the rights of future generations can be related to the protest school's injunction to protect the rights of others—who could be here conceptualized as one's 'future neighbours'; the distrust of techno-scientific reason and the perception that it could be transformed into imperialist tools hints at the discourse school.[12] Despite this, the human rights interventions Delmas-Marty calls for are probably too broad for the deliberative school, her hopes of success too unmitigated for the protest school, and her general argument not critical enough for the discourse school. Her most natural affiliation is the natural school. Were this needed, confirmation of this affiliation can be found in the uses she makes of history, as the next section will explain.

---

[11] See Mireille Delmas-Marty, 'The Limits of Human Rights in a Moving World—Elements of a Dynamic Approach' in Bardo Fassbender and Knut Traisbach (eds), *The Limits of Human Rights* (Oxford University Press 2019) 331, 337.

[12] I thank Knut Traisbach for having thought through these various possible affiliations.

III. THE HISTORY OF HUMAN RIGHTS AS VIEWED BY THE DIFFERENT SCHOOLS

The meeting at which I was asked to present my four-school model which proved crucial in clarifying to me why I was not immediately able to grasp Delmas-Marty's contribution, was mostly attended by historians.[13] This prompted me to want to add a history element to the criteria which my previous publications had highlighted as schools' key identifiers (namely their respective conceptions regarding human rights' nature, source, possible universality, and regard for human rights law). What this exercise made me realize is that the four schools approach the history of human rights in different ways.

For natural scholars, human rights have no history; they have always been there and they will always be there, for as long as humanity exists.[14] Deliberative scholars, who regard human rights as operating in the political sphere, are attracted by a political if not institutional history of human rights.[15] As for protest scholars, they look at the history of human rights as a 'plus ça change' manifestation: the suffering, the protests, and the struggles keep coming back in different forms, however much they express a recurrent condition.[16] Finally, discourse scholars seek to denounce the entanglements of human rights with oppression, including imperialism and the colonial past.

Samuel Moyn is probably the most famous human rights historian of a discourse school persuasion. His main thesis is that human rights came to dominate the political scene only in the 1970s and only because other utopias such as revolutionary communism and nationalism had collapsed. He has no qualms about explaining in *The Last Utopia: Human Rights in History*[17] that human rights' impact on the world is on the terrain of idealism rather than being material, that their continual interplay with power is neither innocent nor innocuous, and that human rights might soon be superseded by another utopia. He also does not mince his words in attacking other histories of human rights. To quote:

> Historians of human rights approach their subject, in spite of its novelty, the way church historians once approached theirs. They regard the basic cause ... as a saving truth, discovered rather than made in history. If a historical phenomenon can be made to seem like an anticipation of human rights, it is interpreted

---

[13] Conference on 'Calendar Propaganda' of Human Rights, organized by Monika Baar at the University of Leiden on 14–16 June 2017.

[14] See, e.g., the first pages of Micheline Ishay, *The History of Human Rights: From Ancient Times to the Globalization Era* (University of California Press 2008) (hereafter Ishay, *The History of Human Rights*).

[15] See, e.g., Steven LB Jensen, *The Making of International Human Rights: The 1960s, Decolonization, and the Reconstruction of Global Values* (Cambridge University Press 2016).

[16] See, e.g., Christopher Roberts, *The Contentious History of the International Bill of Rights* (Cambridge University Press 2015).

[17] Samuel Moyn, *The Last Utopia: Human Rights in History* (Harvard University Press 2010).

as leading to them... Meanwhile, the heroes who are viewed as advancing human rights... are generally treated with uncritical wonderment... And the organizations that finally appear to institutionalize human rights are treated like the early church: a fledging but hopefully universal, community of believers struggling for good in a vale of tears.[18]

It seems to me that Moyn's words do not address all histories of human rights but, rather, those conducted from a natural school orientation, which tend not to be written by academically trained historians.

A good example of this type of work is *The History of Human Rights: From Ancient Times to the Globalization Era*, by International Relations scholar Micheline Ishay.[19] The book opens with a chapter that contains a multitude of references to ancient religious scriptures, such as the Indian Vedas, Babylonian, Hebraic, Chinese, Hellenistic, Roman, early Christian and classical Islamic texts. Unfortunately, these forty-five pages are, so a reviewer tells us, 'packed with inaccurate scholarship and shoddy citations'.[20] One might wonder why Ishay would choose to enter a terrain which can only leave her out of her depth. The answer, one assumes, is that she feels that executing this historical move helps her to assert the universality of human rights in which she believes.

In my opinion, Delmas-Marty—also not a historian—falls into the same trap when she starts her contribution in this volume by referring to Confucius, Greco-Latin authors, and early Christian thought. Moyn's critique of uncritical wonderment is arguably apposite, as my margin annotations at the first reading of her text indicate. 'Nothing about the colonial subjects or the poor', I wrote next to her fifth paragraph, about the 1789 French Declaration. I was irritated by her lack of precision regarding the proclamation of the Universal Declaration of Human Rights (UDHR)—by the UN in 1948 when many states were not yet independent. Another serious omission in my view, this time regarding the European Convention on Human Rights (ECHR), was that she did not mention Article 63 of the ECHR, which, as a whole chapter of my book *When Humans Become Migrants* explains, ensured that colonial subjects were left out of the Convention's reach. The reader can imagine what else I wrote in the margin of Delmas-Marty's contribution. Of course, my remarks, inspired by a discourse scholar orientation, are as predictable as Delmas-Marty's silences are.

---

[18] Ibid, 5–6.
[19] Ishay, *The History of Human Rights* (n. 14).
[20] Aakash Singh, 'Review—The History of Human Rights' (2008) 12 Metapsychology Online Reviews <http://metapsychology.mentalhelp.net/poc/view_doc.php?type=book&id=4594&cn=458> accessed 31 January 2019. See also David Penna, who remarks that Ishay's would-be universalist method leaves out any possible contribution by Africans, David Penna, 'Review of Ishay, Micheline R., *The History of Human Rights*' (*H-Net Reviews*, December 2004) <http://www.h-net.org/reviews/showrev.php?id=10029> accessed 31 January 2019.

IV. CONCLUSION

Once I understood this, I smiled. I was then also able to re-read Delmas-Marty's text, skipping whatever I had originally found misguided and now seeing the connections between the different parts of her insightful contribution. Clearly, what had happened was that my instinctive approach to the theme of the limits of human rights—as the need to denounce the inherent defects of human rights—had made it impossible for me to appreciate her key message. As soon as I understood where Delmas-Marty sat in my model and, thus, why she was saying what she was saying, I was instantly able to grasp what she was getting at. I would summarize it as follows: we must both hope for human rights to do their limiting job and worry that, if we do not harness all creative forces to this goal, the values represented by human rights will be engulfed and defeated in a world which risks denaturalizing a sound understanding of what politics should be about (section I of the contribution); planet earth as we have known it for the greatest part of history (section II); and even what it is to be human (section III). I can relate to these fears, and so I expect will most human rights scholars. This is another way of saying that we need the four schools to make sense of the promises and limits of human rights. Being clear about our respective assumptions should hopefully help us to have necessary 'trans-school' conversations.

Bibliography

Delmas-Marty M, *Le flou du droit* (Presses universitaires de France 1986)

Delmas-Marty M, *Raisonner la raison d'État: Vers une Europe des droits de l'homme* (Presses universitaires de France 1989)

Delmas-Marty M, *Aux quatre vents du monde: Petit guide de navigation sur l'océan de la mondialisation* (Seuil 2016)

Delmas-Marty M, 'The Limits of Human Rights in a Moving World—Elements of a Dynamic Approach' in Fassbender B and Traisbach K (eds), *The Limits of Human Rights* (Oxford University Press 2019) 331

Dembour MB, *Who Believes in Human Rights? Reflections on the European Convention* (Cambridge University Press 2006)

Dembour MB, 'What Are Human Rights? Four Schools of Thought' (2010) 32 Human Rights Quarterly 1

Dembour MB, *When Humans Become Migrants: Study of the European Court of Human Rights with an Inter-American Counterpoint* (Oxford University Press 2015)

Ishay M, *The History of Human Rights: From Ancient Times to the Globalization Era* (University of California Press 2008)

Jensen SLB, *The Making of International Human Rights: The 1960s, Decolonization, and the Reconstruction of Global Values* (Cambridge University Press 2016)

Moyn S, *The Last Utopia: Human Rights in History* (Harvard University Press 2010)

Penna D, 'Review of Ishay, Micheline R., *The History of Human Rights*' (*H-Net Reviews*, December 2004) <http://www.h-net.org/reviews/showrev.php?id=10029> accessed 31 January 2019

Roberts C, *The Contentious History of the International Bill of Rights* (Cambridge University Press 2015)

Singh A, 'Review—The History of Human Rights' (2008) 12 Metapsychology Online Reviews <http://metapsychology.mentalhelp.net/poc/view_doc.php?type=book&id=4594&cn=458> accessed 31 January 2019

23
Strategizing for Human Rights: From Ideals to Practice*

Douglas A. Johnson and Kathryn Sikkink

Human rights are the result of hard fought political and social struggles in the past and in the current moment.[1] Those who equate human rights discourse or law as the expression of interests of powerful states misunderstand this crucial aspect of human rights history. The movement for the international protection of human rights was far more diverse than the United States and Western Europe, including many states and activists from the Global South.[2] The value of human rights norms and law has often been for the weak, both citizens and states, aspiring to justice and fairness in the systems in which they are embedded.

Since struggle is at the core of human rights work, the strategies and tactics that human rights organizations and movements use are the essential tools of the field. We argue that some important 'limits of human rights' are not in human rights norms or law themselves, but in the imagination and the tactics of many human rights organizations and movements. In particular, human rights organizations have often been too wedded to a small handful of tactics, especially 'naming and shaming' that may not be effective in all contexts or on all issues. Organizations and movements display inflexibility or even inertia in adopting new tactics. To confront these limits, human rights activists need to be more strategic and outcome oriented.[3] The introduction to this volume and other recent work speaks of

---

* The title of this chapter comes from the name of a course that Douglas A Johnson teaches annually at the Harvard Kennedy School. He wishes to thank his students for their contributions to his thinking about these topics.

[1] Bardo Fassbender and Knut Traisbach, 'Introduction: A Ride on the Human Rights Bus' in Bardo Fassbender and Knut Traisbach (eds), *The Limits of Human Rights* (Oxford University Press 2019) 1, 4. The argument that human rights progress has been the result of long struggles, often led by oppressed people, is one of the main themes of Kathryn Sikkink's book *Evidence for Hope: Making Human Rights Work in the 21st Century* (Princeton University Press 2017) (hereafter Sikkink, *Evidence for Hope*).

[2] See, e.g., Sikkink, *Evidence for Hope* (n. 2) chs 3 and 4, and Steven LB Jensen, *The Making of International Human Rights: The 1960s, Decolonization, and the Reconstruction of Global Values* (Cambridge University Press 2016) (hereafter Jensen, *The Making of International Human Rights*).

[3] This chapter grew out of our own collaboration and also a series of conversations with colleagues on building a community of practice for teaching human rights, funded in part by the Open Society Foundation. We particularly wish to recognize the contributions of the following colleagues: Karina Ansolabehere, Elazar Barkan, Jacqueline Bhabha, Charlie Clements, Anne Denes, Barbara Frey, César Rodríguez Garavito, Tyler Giannini, Katrin Kinzelbach, Gerald Knaus, Miloon Kothari, Emily Martinez, Nancy Pearson, Michael H Posner, Kristof Zoltan Varga, and Frans Viljoen. In particular, we

---

Douglas A. Johnson and Kathryn Sikkink, *Strategizing for Human Rights: From Ideals to Practice*. In: *The Limits of Human Rights*. Edited by: Bardo Fassbender and Knut Traisbach, Oxford University Press 2019. © The Several Contributors.
DOI: 10.1093/oso/9780198824756.003.0025

'pathologies' of human rights. We think the word pathology is too strong. Such limits are not inherent and human rights activists are able to change and innovate. All over the world, human rights groups are innovating, as seen, for example, in the now hundreds of tactics documented in the New Tactics in Human Rights Project.[4] We will focus on limits, not pathologies. One key explanation for the inflexibility or tactical inertia of human rights organizations is that historically, human rights work has been dominated by lawyers and so when they imagine what can and should be done, they always turn first to law, without asking whether a legal approach is going to be the most effective to address the human rights problem at hand. Human rights organizations have a professional bias towards fact-finding, the creation of more human rights law and the enforcement of such law through courts. In some cases, such as mass atrocity prevention, such a legal approach is appropriate and effective but it is not in others, for example, such as addressing female genital cutting.[5] The excessively legal focus of human rights may not need to be 'limited or cured' but it does need to be diversified, and the tactics of the movement adjusted more to the nature of the human rights problem to be addressed. In the cases of social movements, tactical inertia may be the result of a misreading of some of the iconic struggles of the past. People remember Gandhi's Salt March, or Martin Luther King's March on Birmingham or Washington, without paying attention to the years of training and other tactics that preceded and followed them. As a result, activists tend to overuse the tactic of large demonstrations. While large demonstrations can provide energy and display power, excessive use of demonstrations can lead to burn out and smaller numbers. In more repressive regimes, excessive emphasis on large demonstrations can frighten potential supporters and deprive new movements of crucial leadership when leaders get imprisoned.

While using human rights law or large demonstrations are essential tactics for human rights struggles, more diverse and creative approaches are needed to have more effective outcomes. In particular, human rights advocates can think more strategically about the nature of the human rights problems they hope to address and the appropriate clusters of tactics to achieve positive outcomes on those issues.

---

draw here on a summary of the discussion of a meeting held in the Carr Center for Human Rights in October 2014, with these participants.

[4] See the site <http://www.newtactics.org> sponsored by the Center for Victims of Torture <http://www.cvt.org> accessed 31 January 2019.

[5] On the effectiveness of human rights prosecutions as tactics, see Kathryn Sikkink, *The Justice Cascade: How Human Rights Prosecutions Are Changing World Politics* (WW Norton & Co 2011). On why such tactics do not work for female genital cutting, see Gerry Mackie, 'Ending Footbinding and Infibulation: A Convention Account' (1996) 61 American Sociological Review 999.

I. CONTEXT AND BACKGROUND

A more strategic and outcome oriented human rights practice is particularly urgent in the new political context where human rights are under attack, both from the highest levels of the US government, as well as from authoritarian regimes and movements around the world. If one looks towards Russia and China, for example, and the 1.7 billion people that encompass their populations, we are not looking at human rights outliers but at governments promoting new norms. As a result of what one author has called 'the Dictator's Learning Curve', many authoritarian regimes have become much more savvy about countering the manoeuvres of democracy promotion campaigns and human rights movements.[6] Repressive regimes have learned how to silence and harass human rights workers ever more effectively, often using the very tools of law and courts.[7] Dictatorial or 'electoral authoritarian' regimes are challenging human rights even within the institutions once considered bastions of human rights ideals, such as the Council of Europe.[8] Since electoral authoritarian regimes are more legitimate because their leaders were elected, this creates new kinds of challenges for human rights organizations operating there.

Alarmed by the successful use of non-violent campaigns in the Ukraine, Serbia, Egypt, Tunisia, and elsewhere, these regimes have studied the nature of their successes and moved with new tactics to repress them. Because the targets of human rights advocacy learn and change, repeated use of the same tactics, such as information politics and naming and shaming, allows those targets to adapt to counter previously effective tactics. One can imagine the power of the first letter-writing campaign from Amnesty International because the tactic was so surprising. But after fifty years, most states have learned to bureaucratize a response and protect themselves from this tactic. Amnesty International has invested resources into developing its repertoire of tactics now well beyond its trademark action, seeking tactics that effectively pressure its targets by engaging its constituency.

There is no 'one size fits all' tactic for human rights today, if there ever was one. Different tactics are effective against different targets, and different tactics appeal to different constituencies.[9] As a result, human rights organizations need to tailor their strategies and tactics to their targets, finding those that will have the fullest

---

[6] William J Dobson, *The Dictator's Learning Curve: Inside the Global Battle for Democracy* (Anchor Books 2013).

[7] Kendra Dupuy, James Ron, and Aseem Prakash, 'Foreign Aid to Local NGOs: Good Intentions, Bad Policy' (openDemocracy, 15 November 2012) <http://www.opendemocracy.net/kendra-dupuy-james-ron-aseem-prakash/foreign-aid-to-local-ngos-good-intentions-bad-policy> accessed 31 January 2019.

[8] See, e.g., Gerald Knaus, 'Europe and Azerbaijan: The End of Shame' (2015) 26 Journal of Democracy 5.

[9] Parts of this section draw on Douglas A Johnson, 'The Need for New Tactics' in The New Tactics in Human Rights Project (ed.), *New Tactics in Human Rights: A Resource for Practitioners* (Center for Victims of Torture 2004) 12 <https://www.newtactics.org/sites/default/files/resources/entire-book-EN6.pdf> accessed 31 January 2019.

possible impact in their setting. When tactics fail to affect targets in desired ways, groups must learn to innovate new and more effective tactics.

II. WHAT DOES IT MEAN TO STRATEGIZE?

In order to begin to talk about a more strategic approach to human rights, we first need to define what we mean by strategy and tactics. Strategy is the science or art of combining and employing the methods of action into a coherent plan to direct large-scale operations. There is nothing mysterious about strategy, though it is often difficult to think strategically. Strategy is not a single decision, but rather a confluence of decisions: the selection of key objectives and appropriate targets, an understanding of needed constituencies and resources and decisions on which tactics to use and when. Three critical elements of strategy are targets, tactics, and timing. So, for example, in the international baby milk campaign, the Nestlé Corporation was selected as the target both because of its marketing practices and dominant size; a consumer boycott was the main tactic; timing for the American effort was auspicious, because Nestlé had announced the intention of doubling its sales in the United States within five years. As Sun Tzu advised on the shaping of offensive strategy, 'what is of supreme importance in war is to attack the enemy's strategy'.[10] Building an economic boycott in the heart of Nestlé's planned growth area magnified the impact of the campaign, an example where selection of the target is accentuated by knowing and disrupting its plans (good timing). When we talk about 'strategizing', we mean undertaking the intentional process of selecting objectives and targets, deciding what tactics you will use to affect your target(s), asking how timing will affect your process and targeting, and whether you can you imagine stages in your campaign. Thus, 'Strategy is intentional—a pathway that we shape by making a series of choices about how to use resources in the present to achieve goals in the future'.[11]

III. IS THERE A DOWNSIDE TO A MORE STRATEGIC AND OUTCOME ORIENTED HUMAN RIGHTS PRACTICE?

Some human rights activists and human rights organizations are sceptical about discussing strategy and tactics. These are terms very much associated with military

---

[10] Sun Tzu, *The Art of War* (Samuel B Griffith ed., Oxford University Press 1963) 77 (hereafter Sun Tzu, *The Art of War*).
[11] Marshall Ganz, *Why David Sometimes Wins* (Oxford University Press 2009) 8 (hereafter Ganz, *Why David Sometimes Wins*).

action, as we see in Sun Tzu's quote above. Because the militaries in repressive regimes were often the adversaries of human rights work, it seems suspect to adopt their way of thinking about action. Human rights organizations are devoted to non-violent action, so using insights from a military mindset where violence is always a key tactic may seem counterintuitive.

Another sometimes heard objection to this more strategic and outcome oriented approach to human rights is that it might be too calculating, using cost/benefit analysis, or even become consequentialist in ways that might undermine the very ethical basis of human rights. So, for example, in a recent *Foreign Affairs* article, Douglas Johnson, Alberto Mora, and Averell Schmidt document the strategic costs of the Bush torture and rendition policy to US long-term interests, arguing that the policy hurt America because other institutions and countries believed in and enforced international human rights law.[12]

Some worry that the normative dimension of human rights might get lost when human rights become more strategic, including a cost-benefit analysis of effectiveness.[13] We want to be clear here that *being strategic does not imply giving up one's normative commitments*. Indeed every exercise in strategic planning starts with clarifying the values, mission, and goals of the organization. This allows any human rights organization to clarify its normative goals and connect them to its practice. Rather than neglecting normative commitments, working more strategically allows organizations to actually be clearer about their values and goals and adopt tactics that are more likely to produce positive results.

Likewise, human rights advocates don't only need to think about the effectiveness of their own tactics, but also be prepared to debate the assumptions of efficacy of their adversaries. Former Vice-President Dick Cheney justified torture 'because it works' to gain intelligence needed to protect American lives. It is possible both to sustain a normative commitment against torture, and to contest the simple minded and unsupported assertions about the effectiveness of torture. If we only insist that torture is normatively wrong, but fail to contest Cheney's assertion that useful intelligence was obtained by torture, we cede the field of thinking about consequences to the self-interested. The US Senate Intelligence Committee Report on the CIA torture programme completely undermined Cheney's assertion that torture worked. The decision to use torture was a tactical decision, and it ignored the broader strategic goals of the US government. Cheney should have been asking what else would result from a torture policy. Loss of soft power, diminishment of US moral authority, easier recruitment for terrorist organizations, resistance from allies, legal accountability, and other damage also came from the torture policy.

---

[12] Douglas A Johnson, Alberto Mora, and Averell Schmidt, 'The Strategic Costs of Torture: How "Enhanced Interrogation" Hurt America' (2016) 95 Foreign Affairs 121.
[13] We are indebted to Knut Traisbach for raising this question.

The Bush administration policy of torture shows how enchantment with a tactic can lead to unstrategic thinking.

IV. HOW TO STRATEGIZE FOR A MORE EFFECTIVE AND OUTCOME ORIENTED HUMAN RIGHTS PRACTICE

More than two thousand years ago, Sun Tzu taught 'Know the enemy, know yourself; your victory will never be endangered. Know the ground, know the weather; your victory will then be total'.[14] To those who suggest that an organization 'adopt this strategy' as though it were a prepackaged action plan, we answer that strategies are unique. The decisions emerge from understanding the adversary (its goals, strategy, strengths, and weaknesses), understanding ourselves (our allies, our strengths and limits), and understanding the terrain (where your struggle will be fought). The combination of these elements will always be unique, never generic. Of greatest importance, however, is the realization that we do have adversaries who think and act, often to great effect. Human rights organizations face smart, powerful adversaries with substantial resources, who often reap substantial rewards from committing human rights violations. Repressive leaders use human rights violations to retain power and accumulate wealth. It is essential to try to understand these adversaries and the contexts (terrain) where they operate, in order to work effectively to constrain them. The adversary's tactics are a key component to its strategy and knowledge of such tactics aids us in counteracting them. What we can accomplish, including which tactics we know and which we can successfully implement, will affect the formation of our strategy.

A broad tactical repertoire is therefore a critical component of strategic thinking. A tactic is a specific action that one takes within a strategy and a way to organize our resources to effect change in the world. A tactic may be as small as an activity (writing a report), or as large as establishing an institution (setting up a national human rights commission, which in turn will determine its set of tactics). Tactics will manifest themselves differently depending on the size, capability, and resources of the organization. Tactics embody how one goes about making change, while a strategy involves decisions on which tactics to use, which targets deserve focus and which resources can be employed. Our knowledge of tactics also shapes the strategy we choose. Tactical thinking is essential to strategic thinking and thus to an effective struggle for human rights.

In the past thirty years 'strategic planning' has become the norm in non-governmental organizations (NGOs). Curiously, the notion of tactics has not

---

[14] Sun Tzu, *The Art of War* (n. 10) 129.

accompanied the development of strategic planning and still remains, for many, a pejorative term. We commonly say something or someone is 'tactical' rather than 'strategic', meaning subject to limited, short-term thinking rather than long-term, core thinking. For some, tactics imply manoeuvring for short-term gain or position, perhaps in an unethical manner. So why are we using the word 'tactic' rather than another word such as approach, methodology, or technique? Leaders who have had more experience in shaping the strategy of an organization realize that the more they understand about tactics, the more flexibility they have to set new strategic directions. We are not arguing, then, that tactical thinking or training supersedes strategic thinking, but rather that tactical development enriches strategic thinking. Thus, we use 'tactic' because of its integral relationship to the concept of 'strategy'. Strategy defines what is important to do, tactics embody how to do it. The relationship between 'the what' and 'the how' is an important one in understanding—and demystifying—the concepts of strategy and tactics. Tactics are one of the key building blocks of strategy.

To illustrate these arguments, it may be useful to discuss some of the novel tactical principles from the Serbian movement to remove Milosevic, *Otpor*. Otpor realized that multiple and varied tactics should be used to create surprise and keep the adversary off balance. They believed that something should happen every day to attract media attention and to engage activists, and that tactics involving humour were particularly valued for their power to diminish fear. Following the teaching of non-violent theorist Gene Sharp, Otpor believed that too much emphasis should not be placed only on large demonstrations, what Sharp called a tactic of concentration, but attention should be paid to tactics of dispersion, that is, small actions that were safer, allowing activists to gain experience, training, and confidence, while dispersing the resources of the police and security forces. Finally, they believed that their tactics should 'leave no one behind', that is, they had to have careful planning in advance of actions to minimize the possibilities of arrest, but once activists were arrested, the organization also needed to use tactics to pressure for rapid, safe release. So, for example, activists in Serbia trying to secure the release of their colleagues who had been detained found that it was more effective to hold an outdoor rock concert outside the gates of the jail focused on getting the prisoners released, than to write letters or do a press release. They backed this up with a phone tree of retired people who had the time to call the police station to ask 'about that nice young boy' who was arrested. The concert diminished fear of both the police and the activists, and kept the activists there until the prisoner was released to a hero's welcome, ready to act another day.[15]

---

[15] Olena Nikolayenko, 'Origins of the Movement's Strategy: The Case of the Serbian Youth Movement Otpor' (2013) 34 International Political Science Review 140. This section is also informed by co-teaching courses on non-violence with Srđa Popović and Slobodan Djinovic, two of youth leaders of the Otpor movement.

It is on tactical decisions that Otpor leaders used cost-benefit analysis to force themselves to consider the expected impact of a tactic versus the resources required to carry it out. Large demonstrations, for example, are risky; an invitation to the adversary to concentrate the police and security forces into one area, the possibility of violence from provocateurs or under-trained activists, even the numbers of people who might show up are all risk factors. A campaign of dispersal tactics first provides training and discipline, group cohesion, and even an improved ability to project numbers when it is believed that a major public demonstration is needed to push the campaign along. Should human rights organizations have the capacity to make these calculations or shy away from them as tainted? The ability to foresee probable outcomes of action, both those of the adversary and one's own is a critical aspect of strategic thinking.

These principles illustrate a variety of crucial insights on tactics. Tactics are training systems for engaging participants and allies in the organization's work. Some tactics may be short-term (such as a march), some longer-term (such as a boycott). But all of them require planning, co-ordination, and direction. They can create opportunities for many citizens to be involved, to learn, and to become more committed to the work of the organization or campaign. Involvement on a tactical level is an excellent training ground for younger or newer staff and volunteers. Diverse tactics are also useful because they appeal to different constituencies. Some people find picketing in front of a torturer's home a very frightening tactic; others find letter writing too removed from where the change is needed. We can debate who is right or we can recognize that people respond differently to a tactic based on their notions of causation, their tolerance for risk, the time they have available, or their way of processing information. If the human rights community responds by offering only one or two tactics to engage the public, we will appeal only to the narrow constituency to whom those tactics make sense. Filing a legal case, for example, is notoriously difficult to use with wide sectors of the population: legal cases are long-term efforts carried out by a small group of legal professionals. Such legal cases are important, but we also need to employ other tactics that give more people the chance to be participants rather than observers. In cultures that have experienced repression, people have learned to withdraw from public life. To engage constituencies in cultures such as these we need to offer tactics that appeal to different risk tolerances and different views of social change.

Good strategy and effective campaigns have a number of key components. They need to have clear, focused, measureable goals, be capable of building strategic alliances across sectors, and then strategizing across sectors to use respective strengths. Effective campaigns make careful choices of terrain and show moral courage.

Marshall Ganz asserts that organizations should pay attention to the 'strategic capacity' of both the adversary and one's own organization, which he defines as 1) the depth of its motivation; 2) the breadth of its salient knowledge; and 3) the robustness of its reflective practice (Heuristic processes).[16] Each of these factors can be increased through leadership teams with diverse backgrounds and skills, such as different tactical repertoires, that augment flexibility. Ganz analyses why the United Farmworkers succeeded when the Teamsters Union failed to organize California farmworkers. The added motivation came from farmworkers themselves being engaged in the leadership, incorporating a more diverse set of leaders into its decision-making, and a commitment to learn from both failures and victories as outcomes of action to influence future action. As Sun Tzu pointed out, the first of the five fundamental factors in conflict is moral influence, 'that which causes the people to be in harmony with their leaders, so that they will accompany them'.[17] Ganz advises that these are not the prerogative of one super human leader, but skills and capacities that can be sought out, recruited, and learned.

A. Using Tools and Exercises for Strategic Training

In our teaching and training, we use tools and exercises to help our students and human rights advocates to answer these questions and plan more strategically. In response to the directive 'Know Your Adversary', for example, groups need to clarify who exactly is the adversary, and whether the adversary chosen is the correct one. In campaigns against torture, for example, human rights advocates have tended to focus on pressuring national governments to prohibit torture. This makes sense in the case of a top down State-sponsored policy of torture. But in some cases, torture may fester in a particular jail or police precinct because of leadership there, not orders from above. In those cases, more targeted actions on the individuals actually responsible for torture will be more effective. To help activists identify these individuals, we use a tool, 'tactical mapping' (see Figure 23.1 for an example), developed by the New Tactics for Human Rights Project at the Center for Victims of Torture.[18] Tactical mapping asks participants to create a diagram of the relationships and institutions that surround, receive benefit from, and sustain a specific human-rights abuse. The emphasis is on relationships between people and institutions (rather than on concepts or 'causes' of human-rights violations). When this diagram is sketched out, it provides not just a map of adversaries, but also a map of the micro-terrain of the human rights struggle. It helps actors to select appropriate targets for intervention and consider possible tactics to influence issues of concern. Thus, using the map helps activists to plan and monitor how a tactic might function and which relationships it should influence to effectively intervene. Because multiple groups can use the diagram to map their

---

[16] Ganz, *Why David Sometimes Wins* (n. 11) 10.
[17] Sun Tzu, *The Art of War* (n. 10) 64.
[18] See <http://www.newtactics.org/> accessed 31 January 2019.

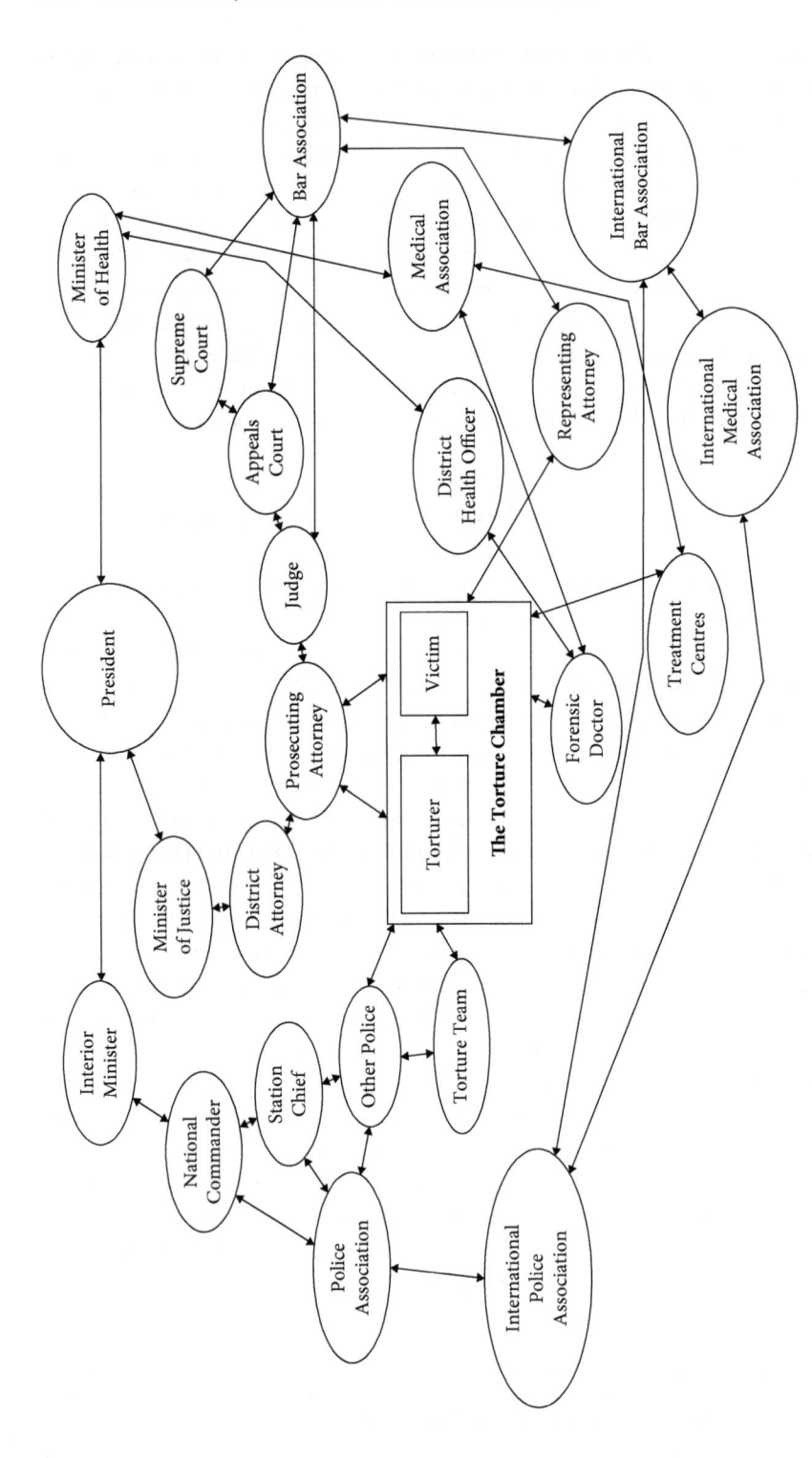

Figure 23.1 An example of a quickly sketched tactical map on torture
Source: Created by Douglas A Johnson

respective targets and interventions, the tactical map becomes a co-ordinating tool that creates a more comprehensive strategy than is possible when groups act independently.[19]

Such a tactical map can help organizations select targets, one essential aspect of strategy. The tactical map will help them consider the multiple levels of actors in the system, not only the people at the top. A map can also be useful to create a diagram of the causal chain (leading to torture, for example), to challenge activists to consider alternative targets and to fully understand what they expect to happen when the tactic is applied to the selected target(s). Finally, it allows them to explore whether the tactic is likely to have impact throughout its causal chain or if it will lose force and efficacy as it travels across many layers (as in an action that targets a national president). Other take-aways from a tactical mapping exercise can include the knowledge that the systems we seek to change are complex and mutually reinforcing. It can dispel the tendency to treat the terrain as if it were simple. A map can also illustrate how change can be created, but create awareness that pressure must come from multiple sources in a sustained manner. As such, it becomes clear that no one organization can affect the depth and breadth of change needed. Comprehensive, multi-faceted strategy require allies and a willingness to develop deep collaborations. Finally, a tactical map may suggest to activists that different tactics will be needed to affect different parts of the system. Above all, a map should encourage activists to be creative and think about what action they want from the target. Will the tactic you select give you the action you want?

One of the most crucial skills needed in the human rights community is the ability to build and sustain more effective coalitions. But perceived funding imperatives and the 'top-down' approach often favoured by major international human rights NGOs make it difficult for human rights organizations to collaborate with one another. There needs to be more collaboration and more horizontal organizational structures. Collaboration is a skill as well as a framework, but human rights activists may have little or no formal training on building collaboration, either within countries or across borders.

There is an exercise developed in the 1960s called the 'Spectrum of Allies' that can be a very useful tool for helping human rights advocates think about how to build collaboration. Often activists have a simple idea of struggle that places 'us' at one end and the adversary on the other. The 'Spectrum of Allies' exercise encourages more complex thinking about adversaries and possibilities for collaboration. Along that spectrum are our natural allies, as well as the adversaries'

---

[19] This sections draws on material from Douglas A Johnson and Nancy Pearson, 'Tactical Mapping: How Non-profits Can Identify Levers for Change' (The Nonprofit Quarterly, 20 August 2009) <https://nonprofitquarterly.org/2009/08/20/tactical-mapping-how-nonprofits-can-identify-the-levers-of-change/> accessed 31 January 2019. We thank Nancy Pearson for her permission to use some co-authored material here.

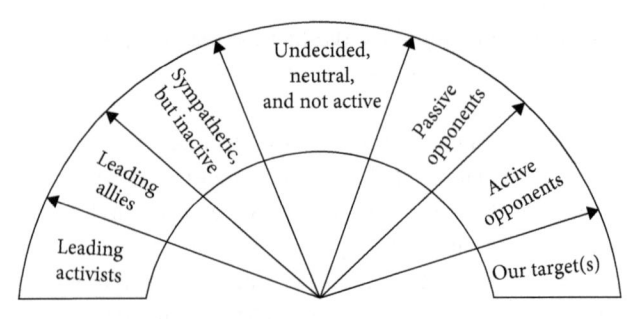

Figure 23.2 Spectrum of Allies
Source: Concept from Oppenheimer & Lakey

active allies. There are people and groups who tend to support one side or the other, but who remain passive. And in nearly all cases, there is the largest group of all, the neutral, inactive middle. The 'Spectrum of Allies'[20] starts with a very simple visual (see Figure 23.2), and asks advocates to think through the groups that fall into each of the categories on the spectrum, what must be done to gather more allies, and to strip allies from the opponent. Over the years, others have recommended particular approaches (do nothing to stimulate the passive opponents to action) and some specific tactics to move all groups counter-clockwise.[21] Even meeting with very experienced human rights advocates trying to strategize about how to protect rights under the Trump administration, we found that reminding them about the 'Spectrum of Allies' stimulated more creative thinking. As Chenoweth and Stephan have shown, one strong advantage that non-violent campaigns have over violent resistance is the ability to attract larger numbers to their support.[22] Those numbers are in the middle, among the undecided and neutral sectors, to which all successful campaigns must appeal. Another advantage non-violence has is the ability to neutralize the passive opponents, shifting them at least to the undecided sector where some can be reached to become sympathetic to the campaign. The 'Spectrum of Allies' creates the challenge to target each sector, realizing that each will require a different set of tactics to effectively engage them.

---

[20] Martin Oppenheimer and George Lakey, *A Manual for Direct Action: Strategy and Tactics for Civil Rights and All Other Nonviolent Protest Movements* (Quadrangle Books 1965).

[21] See, e.g., <http://beautifultrouble.org/principle/shift-the-spectrum-of-allies/> accessed 31 January 2019.

[22] Erica Chenoweth and Maria J Stephan, *Why Civil Resistance Works: The Strategic Logic of Nonviolent Conflict* (Columbia University Press 2012) 30 (hereafter Chenoweth and Stephan, *Why Civil Resistance Works*).

B. Using Historical and Social Science Research for Training

Social science literature can also be used in training to help human rights advocates to know themselves, know the adversary, and know the terrain. We often think that the academic world is completely divorced from the world of human rights practice. But as we have learned in our lifetime of work together as a practitioner and a human rights scholar, there is much that scholars can learn from activists, and much that activists can learn from scholars. This often takes some translation, to make the concerns and the language of each group transparent and relevant to the other. In this section, we will focus on how different types of academic work can be incorporated into training advocates for a more strategic and outcome oriented human rights practice.

First, some historical and social science research can help address erroneous perceptions activists may hold that affects their planning or morale. So, for example, historical research on the diverse origins of human rights in the Global South, mentioned above, could be useful for helping Southern-based activists respond to those who argue (including many authoritarian leaders) that human rights are a form of cultural imperialism.[23] In the same vein, some authors and activists argue that human rights ideas don't work as mobilizing tools in the Global South because people there believe that human rights institutions and NGOs are at the service of the great powers, and the United States in particular. Such a belief could dramatically affect strategic choices activists make. In this case, we have a rare opportunity to bring survey data to bear on this topic. James Ron and David Crow conducted surveys of 9,380 respondents in six countries in four world

---

[23] See, e.g., Roland Burke, *Decolonization and the Evolution of International Human Rights* (University of Pennsylvania Press 2010); Jensen, *The Making of International Human Rights* (n. 2); Mary Ann Glendon, 'The Forgotten Crucible: The Latin American Influence on the Universal Human Rights Idea' (2003) 16 Harvard Human Rights Journal 27; Greg Grandin, 'The Liberal Traditions in the Americas: Rights, Sovereignty, and the Origins of Liberal Multilateralism' (2012) 117 The American Historical Review 68; Greg Grandin, 'Human Rights and Empire's Embrace' in Jeffrey N Wasserstrom (ed.), *Human Rights and Revolutions* (2nd edn, Rowman & Littlefield 2007); Johannes Morsink, *The Universal Declaration of Human Rights: Origins, Drafting, and Intent* (University of Pennsylvania Press 1999); Susan Waltz, 'Universalizing Human Rights: The Role of Small States in the Construction of the Universal Declaration of Human Rights' (2001) 23 Human Rights Quarterly 44; Liliana Obregón, 'The Colluding Worlds of the Lawyer, the Scholar and the Policymaker: A View of International Law from Latin America' (2005) 23 Wisconsin International Law Journal 145; Arnulf Becker Lorca, *Mestizo International Law: A Global Intellectual History 1842–1933* (Cambridge University Press 2014); Paolo Carozza, 'From Conquest to Constitutions: Retrieving a Latin American Tradition of the Idea of Human Rights' (2003) 25 Human Rights Quarterly 281; Jan Herman Burgers, 'The Road to San Francisco: The Revival of the Human Rights Idea in the Twentieth Century' (1992) 14 Human Rights Quarterly 447; Rainer Huhle, 'Latinoamérica: Continente de la paz y los derechos humanos' (Nürnberger Menschenrechtszentrum, December 2007) 1 <https://d-nb.info/991186621/34> accessed 31 January 2019; Rainer Huhle, 'América Latina y la fundamentación del sistema internacional de protección de los derechos humanos después de la Segunda Guerra Mundial' (2008) 4 Memoria: Revista sobre cultura, democracia y derechos humanos 33; Patrick William Kelly, 'On the Poverty and Possibility of Human Rights in Latin American History' (2014) 5 Humanity: An International Journal of Human Rights, Humanitarianism, and Development 435.

regions: Colombia, Ecuador, India, Mexico, Morocco, and Nigeria. They asked people about their attitudes towards the US government, human rights, and local and international human rights organizations. There was some interesting variation by country but, overall, Ron and Crow find that people in these six countries in four different regions of the developing world have 'pretty good' levels of trust in their local human rights organizations, clearly closer to the most trusted institutions in their countries than the least trusted. Such trust is not limited to one group of people, such as those with higher incomes or greater transnational connection. Rather, people with different levels of education, income, and geographic locations (urban and rural) have trust in human rights organizations, and those who report they have had contact with these human rights organizations are more likely to trust them. Finally, local human rights organizations are not perceived as handmaidens of powerful countries, and awareness that they receive foreign funding does not diminish trust in most countries.[24] This suggests that human rights organizations continue to have appeal in these countries and could be used as a mobilizing tool in campaigns.

Second, in order to strategize to be more effective, human rights organizations have to be able to agree on whether or not they are leading to positive change. Yet there are critical gaps in terms of conceptualizing, evaluating, and measuring what constitutes effective human rights practice and progress. The key question here is 'Are we actually contributing to meaningful change "on the ground" and how do we better measure these impacts?' Sometimes we encounter an 'information paradox' where activists, by creating new issues and producing new information, can sometimes give the impression that practices are getting worse, when in reality we just know more and care more about them.[25] Pessimism about human rights progress is widespread. Whether on the news, or in the academy, or when one talks to a member of the general public, the standard view is that all types of human rights practices are getting worse in the world rather than better. Some academics critique human rights law, institutions, and movements for this perceived lack of progress.[26] Such pessimism can have an impact on the wellbeing of human rights activists. A recent survey of 346 individuals currently or previously working in the field of human rights found that this work is associated with elevated levels of depression and Post-Traumatic Stress Disorder (PTSD), especially among those who

---

[24] James Ron and David Crow, 'Who Trusts Local Human Rights Organizations? Evidence from Three World Regions' (2015) 37 Human Rights Quarterly 188. See also James Ron, Shannon Golden, David Crow, and Archana Pandya, *Taking Root: Human Rights and Public Opinion in the Global South* (Oxford University Press 2017).

[25] For more on the information paradox, see Ann Marie Clark and Kathryn Sikkink, 'Information Effects and Human Rights Data: Is the Good News about Increased Human Rights Information Bad News for Human Rights Measures?' (2013) 35 Human Rights Quarterly 539.

[26] Stephen Hopgood, *The Endtimes of Human Rights* (Cornell University Press 2013); Eric A Posner, *The Twilight of Human Rights Law* (Oxford University Press 2014); Mark J Osiel, 'The Demise of International Criminal Law' (Humanity Journal, 10 June 2014 <http://humanityjournal.org/blog/the-demise-of-international-criminal-law/> accessed 31 January 2019.

have negative self-appraisals about the effectiveness of their efforts.[27] This suggests that one of the most difficult parts about being a human rights activist is the doubt about whether you are contributing to positive change.

This is a management and leadership responsibility too often ignored in human rights organizations. Saul Alinsky counselled that even small victories were vital to maintain the morale and engagement of activists.[28]

Using primarily empirical comparisons with careful use of human rights data can generate persuasive evidence for the effectiveness of human rights law and activism. The human rights situation in the world is characterized by some areas of retrogression and worsening, such as the current situations in Syria, Egypt, Mexico, and the United States, but also by other areas of increasing awareness and improvements, such as current developments in gender equality, rights of sexual minorities, and rights of people with disabilities. Although human rights change takes a long time and its progress ebbs and flows, we do not see wholesale abandonment of human rights ideas or loss of confidence in the institutions designed to advance and protect these rights. Unless scholars and activists are able to distinguish areas of improvement from areas of worsening, we cannot take the next step to evaluate what works. In order to be more strategic, it is also useful to train human rights activists in the use of methods and techniques to evaluate their work more effectively.[29]

Third, social science research can help illuminate causal relationships that may be useful to human rights activists, including the conditions under which human rights work is likely to be effective. In her 2010 book, *Mobilizing for Human Rights*, Beth Simmons specifies the conditions under which human rights law is most likely to be effective.[30] She shows that international human rights law has the most impact in transitional countries where domestic human rights activists have both the motivation and the opportunity to mobilize to pressure for change. Such research can help activists choose targets and tactics more effectively. Keck and Sikkink's book, *Activists beyond Borders: Advocacy Networks in International Politics* makes a series of arguments about the conditions under which transnational networks are more likely to be effective.[31] They group these conditions in categories including 'Network characteristics' that corresponds to 'knowing yourself', and 'Target characteristics' that correspond to 'knowing your adversary',

---

[27] Amy Joscelyne, Sarah Knuckey, Margaret L Satterthwaite, Richard A Bryant, Meng Li, Meng Qian, and Adam D Brown, 'Mental Health Functioning in the Human Rights Field: Findings from an International Internet-Based Survey' (2015) 10 PLoS ONE no 12, <http://journals.plos.org/plosone/article?id=10.1371/journal.pone.0145188> accessed 31 January 2019.
[28] Recalled by one of the authors from training with Alinsky in 1969 at the Industrial Areas Foundation, Chicago.
[29] These two paragraphs draw on material from Sikkink, *Evidence for Hope* (n. 1).
[30] Beth A Simmons, *Mobilizing for Human Rights: International Law in Domestic Politics* (Cambridge University Press 2009).
[31] Margaret E Keck and Kathryn Sikkink, *Activists beyond Borders: Advocacy Networks in International Politics* (Cornell University Press 1998).

and 'Issue characteristics' which constitute one part of the terrain. Thinking about these characteristics might help activists choose targets. For example, campaigns against targets that are morally or materially vulnerable (or both) are likely to be more effective than campaigns against targets that are less vulnerable. In the case of the Nestlé Boycott, for example, Nestlé was more vulnerable to a consumer boycott than other infant formula producers because it had a wide variety of common consumer products, clearly identified as Nestlé products. Likewise social science literature can be useful in helping choose tactics. For example, Erica Chenoweth and Maria Stephan's findings that non-violent movements are more effective than violent movements for change, can be useful reading for any human rights movement as it considers the advantages of incorporating citizen mobilization into its strategic objectives.[32] Chenoweth and Stephan stress that non-violent movements are more effective exactly because they can attract a wider variety of allies. Building alliances and coalitions, thus, is not just another tactic for groups, but a key to their effectiveness.

V. CONCLUSIONS

We hope that this chapter has made it clear that we need to find new ways of working together—and new ways of working—in order to create effective strategies of change. In the new global context, we believe that no single methodology or approach to human rights will work. Although 'naming and shaming' has become the most common and most scrutinized tactic among many human rights actors, it is not and should not be the only or even the main tactic used. NGOs are aware of the need for innovation and are developing programmes, such as the 'New Tactics in Human Rights Project', that research novel tactics used around the world in human rights work and then encourage activists to write up descriptions or workbooks on their methods and to train other activists. Keeping this in mind, perhaps human rights activists should rely less on naming and shaming and large demonstrations, and more on what we might call 'effectiveness politics'—identifying techniques and campaigns that have been effective to discern how best to improve human rights. The human rights movement should move from a certain inflexibility and inertia to more diverse, innovative, and creative strategies and tactics to keep human rights struggles fresh and unexpected, to build larger constituencies, and keep adversaries off balance.

---

[32] Chenoweth and Stephan, *Why Civil Resistance Works* (n. 22).

Bibliography

Becker Lorca A, *Mestizo International Law: A Global Intellectual History 1842–1933* (Cambridge University Press 2014)

Burgers JH, 'The Road to San Francisco: The Revival of the Human Rights Idea in the Twentieth Century' (1992) 14 Human Rights Quarterly 447

Burke R, *Decolonization and the Evolution of International Human Rights* (University of Pennsylvania Press 2010)

Carozza P, 'From Conquest to Constitutions: Retrieving a Latin American Tradition of the Idea of Human Rights' (2003) 25 Human Rights Quarterly 281

Chenoweth E and Stephan MJ, *Why Civil Resistance Works: The Strategic Logic of Nonviolent Conflict* (Columbia University Press 2012)

Clark AM and Sikkink K, 'Information Effects and Human Rights Data: Is the Good News about Increased Human Rights Information Bad News for Human Rights Measures?' (2013) 35 Human Rights Quarterly 539

Dobson WJ, *The Dictator's Learning Curve: Inside the Global Battle for Democracy* (Anchor Books 2013)

Dupuy K, Ron J, and Prakash A, 'Foreign Aid to Local NGOs: Good Intentions, Bad Policy' (openDemocracy, 15 November 2012) <http://www.opendemocracy.net/kendra-dupuy-james-ron-aseem-prakash/foreign-aid-to-local-ngos-good-intentions-bad-policy> accessed 31 January 2019

Fassbender B and Traisbach K, 'Introduction: A Ride on the Human Rights Bus' in Fassbender B and Traisbach K (eds), *The Limits of Human Rights* (Oxford University Press 2019) 1

Ganz M, *Why David Sometimes Wins* (Oxford University Press 2009)

Glendon MA, 'The Forgotten Crucible: The Latin American Influence on the Universal Human Rights Idea' (2003) 16 Harvard Human Rights Journal 27

Grandin G, 'Human Rights and Empire's Embrace' in Wasserstrom JN (ed.), *Human Rights and Revolutions* (2nd edn., Rowman & Littlefield 2007)

Grandin G, 'The Liberal Traditions in the Americas: Rights, Sovereignty, and the Origins of Liberal Multilateralism' (2012) 117 The American Historical Review 68

Hopgood S, *The Endtimes of Human Rights* (Cornell University Press 2013)

Huhle R, 'Latinoamérica: Continente de la paz y los derechos humanos' (Nürnberger Menschenrechtszentrum, December 2007) 1 <https://d-nb.info/991186621/34> accessed 31 January 2019

Huhle R, 'América Latina y la fundamentación del sistema internacional de protección de los derechos humanos después de la Segunda Guerra Mundial' (2008) 4 Memoria: Revista sobre cultura, democracia y derechos humanos 33

Jensen SLB, *The Making of International Human Rights: The 1960s, Decolonization, and the Reconstruction of Global Values* (Cambridge University Press 2016)

Johnson DA, 'The Need for New Tactics' in The New Tactics in Human Rights Project (ed.), *New Tactics in Human Rights: A Resource for Practitioners* (Center for Victims of Torture 2004) 12 <https://www.newtactics.org/sites/default/files/resources/entire-book-EN6.pdf> accessed 31 January 2019

Johnson DA and Pearson N, 'Tactical Mapping: How Non-profits Can Identify Levers for Change' (The Nonprofit Quarterly, 20 August 2009) <https://nonprofitquarterly.org/2009/08/20/tactical-mapping-how-nonprofits-can-identify-the-levers-of-change/> accessed 31 January 2019

Johnson DA, Mora A, and Schmidt A, 'The Strategic Costs of Torture: How "Enhanced Interrogation" Hurt America' (2016) 95 Foreign Affairs 121

Joscelyne A, Knuckey S, Satterthwaite ML, Bryant RA, Meng L, Meng Q, and Brown AD, 'Mental Health Functioning in the Human Rights Field: Findings from an International Internet-Based Survey' (2015) 10 PLoS ONE no 12, <http://journals.plos.org/plosone/article?id=10.1371/journal.pone.0145188> accessed 31 January 2019

Keck ME and Sikkink K, *Activists beyond Borders: Advocacy Networks in International Politics* (Cornell University Press 1998)

Kelly PW, 'On the Poverty and Possibility of Human Rights in Latin American History' (2014) 5 Humanity: An International Journal of Human Rights, Humanitarianism, and Development 435

Knaus G, 'Europe and Azerbaijan: The End of Shame' (2015) 26 Journal of Democracy 5

Mackie G, 'Ending Footbinding and Infibulation: A Convention Account' (1996) 61 American Sociological Review 999

Morsink J, *The Universal Declaration of Human Rights: Origins, Drafting, and Intent* (University of Pennsylvania Press 1999)

Nikolayenko O, 'Origins of the Movement's Strategy: The Case of the Serbian Youth Movement Otpor' (2013) 34 International Political Science Review 140

Obregón L, 'The Colluding Worlds of the Lawyer, the Scholar and the Policymaker: A View of International Law from Latin America' (2005) 23 Wisconsin International Law Journal 145

Oppenheimer M and Lakey G, *A Manual for Direct Action: Strategy and Tactics for Civil Rights and All Other Nonviolent Protest Movements* (Quadrangle Books 1965)

Osiel MJ, 'The Demise of International Criminal Law' (Humanity Journal, 10 June 2014 <http://humanityjournal.org/blog/the-demise-of-international-criminal-law/> accessed 31 January 2019

Posner EA, *The Twilight of Human Rights Law* (Oxford University Press 2014)

Ron J and Crow D, 'Who Trusts Local Human Rights Organizations? Evidence from Three World Regions' (2015) 37 Human Rights Quarterly 188

Ron J, Golden S, Crow D, and Pandya A, *Taking Root: Human Rights and Public Opinion in the Global South* (Oxford University Press 2017)

Sikkink K, *The Justice Cascade: How Human Rights Prosecutions Are Changing World Politics* (WW Norton & Co 2011)

Sikkink K, *Evidence for Hope: Making Human Rights Work in the 21st Century* (Princeton University Press 2017)

Simmons BA, *Mobilizing for Human Rights: International Law in Domestic Politics* (Cambridge University Press 2009)

Sun Tzu, *The Art of War* (Samuel B Griffith ed., Oxford University Press 1963)

Waltz S, 'Universalizing Human Rights: The Role of Small States in the Construction of the Universal Declaration of Human Rights' (2001) 23 Human Rights Quarterly 44

24
Historical Strategies for Human Rights
A Response to Douglas A. Johnson and Kathryn Sikkink

Micheline Ishay

In 'Strategizing Human Rights: From Ideals to Practice', Douglas Johnson and Kathryn Sikkink address a topic not sufficiently discussed elsewhere: the importance of relevant strategies for human rights progress.[1] They argue that 'human rights organizations have often been too wedded to a small handful of tactics, especially "naming and shaming" and large demonstrations, that may not be effective in all contexts or on all issues'. Particularly since repressive governments have learned to counter such approaches, Johnson and Sikkink rightly argue that the human rights community needs to show greater flexibility to make further inroads in politics. Refuting the split between theory and practice, the authors call for the exploration of broad strategies before identifying the tactics needed to advance a given human rights agenda.

Drawing from Sun Tzu's *The Art of War*,[2] the authors suggest devising strategies for human rights by 'understanding the adversary (its goals, strategy, strengths, and weaknesses), understanding ourselves (our allies, our strengths and limits), and understanding the terrain (where your struggle will be fought)'. In practice, it seems that these categories of understanding intertwine. For instance, when illustrating what it means to 'know your adversary', the authors present a tactical map on torture that 'provides not just a map of adversaries, but also a map of the micro-terrain of the human rights struggle'.

It is incontestable that human rights activists need a proper understanding of their enemy's social terrain, as different contexts shape distinctive strategic operations. Johnson and Sikkink identify helpful tools of analysis, but a list of items in the toolbox of a practitioner, if not employed with a proper understanding of the social and historical context, can also produce negative results. The following remarks develop some of their suggested points and question their proposed tactics and strategies.

---

[1] Douglas A Johnson and Kathryn Sikkink, 'Strategizing for Human Rights: From Ideals to Practice' in Bardo Fassbender and Knut Traisbach (eds), *The Limits of Human Rights* (Oxford University Press 2019) 357.
[2] Sun Tzu, *The Art of War* (Samuel B Griffith ed., Oxford University Press 1963).

Micheline Ishay, *Historical Strategies for Human Rights: A Response to Douglas A. Johnson and Kathryn Sikkink.* In: *The Limits of Human Rights.* Edited by: Bardo Fassbender and Knut Traisbach, Oxford University Press 2019. © The Several Contributors.
DOI: 10.1093/oso/9780198824756.003.0026

I. MAPPING THE TERRAIN OF HUMAN RIGHTS

Mapping the terrain to recognize friends and enemies of human rights, as exemplified by Johnson's diagram on torture, is certainly a powerful way to create an understanding of networks and inform strategic thinking. But one would expect different criteria for operations depending upon social contexts. For instance, the expected tactics for change in Western countries, where the economy is advanced and institutions are more developed and anchored in civil societies, calls for what Antonio Gramsci calls a 'war of position', or a 'war of tactics'.[3] A war of position slowly strengthens the social foundation of a State, creating alternative institutions and intellectual resources within an existing society. In less developed or backward economies, where civil society is gelatinous (or fragmented) and serves as an extension of the State apparatus, the terrain is more propitious for revolutionary change. In these contexts, revolutionary movements (e.g. the Bolsheviks) can move swiftly, unobstructed by civil institutions, and overthrow a regime. In the wake of the Bolshevik revolution, Gramsci identified tactics that would not work in more developed and more liberal societies, particularly: a 'war of maneuver' (which he also calls a 'war of movement'). Marx was well aware of differences in tactics when he argued in his 1872 Amsterdam address that in the United States, the Netherlands, and England, countries already endowed with a parliamentary system, the terrain was not auspicious to violent revolution but to reform.[4]

II. SUSTAINING THE CAPACITY FOR CHANGE

The authors are right to point out that both social movements and human rights organizations need to understand their capacity and resources if they are to sustain successful change. This approach should be adopted regardless of the scope of their goals. Here again, Johnson's and Sikkink's insights would be further textured if they took into account an organization's evolving capacity over different stages of a campaign. For instance, the 'March for our Lives' movement, calling for arms control in light of school shootings in the United States, clearly galvanized young people in the spring of 2018. At the time of writing, however, it remains unclear whether this movement will have sufficient funding and organizational capacity to continue to pressure politicians beyond the next election. In other words, to gain longevity, this movement will need to win a war of tactics deployed in successive stages of its operations. In a different setting, during the Egyptian uprising of

---

[3] Quintin Hoare and Geoffrey Nowell-Smith (eds), *Selections from the Prison Notebooks of Antonio Gramsci* (International Publishers 2014).

[4] Karl Marx, 'On the Possibility of a Non-violent Revolution (*On the Hague Congress*, 1872)' in Micheline R Ishay (ed.), *The Human Rights Reader* (2nd edn, Routledge Press 2007) 232 (hereafter Ishay (ed.), *The Human Rights Reader*).

2011, human rights organizations were able to mobilize people and overthrow the Mubarak region in a period of eighteen days through a 'war of maneuver'. But they were unable to consolidate their power once the leader was toppled, and they could not manage the country's social and economic grievances once the new Egyptian president, Mohamed Morsi, came to power. With little foreign funding, and alienated from the army, the post-revolutionary government was not able to survive the June 2014 military coup. In short, the forces and strategies that lead to uprisings may be quite different from those needed to consolidate a post-revolutionary government, let alone those required for a transition from a consolidated government to one shaped by human rights aspirations.

III. MASS DISPERSAL VERSUS MASS CONCENTRATION

Drawing lessons from the Serbian resistance movement, Otpor, that pushed President Slobodan Milosevic out of office, the authors argue that the activists' cost-benefit analysis regarded large demonstrations as overly risky. Clearly, dispersal strategies are more effective in such contexts, as they dilute the concentration of security forces and spread them in different areas. In a war of tactics, Otpor was indeed able to decentralize its operation, taking the culture of resistance against the regime to the countryside. The Egyptian revolutionary Ahmed Maher learned a great deal from these tactics. Johnson and Sikkink would likely agree that, in other settings, the cost-benefit analysis would yield a different result. In democracies, even illiberal ones, mass demonstrations offer important shocks to the political system without fear of military interference. The women's march of 2017 is one of many such cases. Such tactics are less auspicious in repressive regimes which use brutal force to disperse marching crowds. Here the distinction between different types of *social* terrains should be kept in mind.

IV. THE IMPORTANCE OF A 'SPECTRUM OF ALLIES'

The authors illustrate the skill of collaboration by describing an exercise called the 'Spectrum of Allies'. Arranging people and groups into categories across a broad spectrum from affinity to antagonism, they suggest that human rights advocates learn 'to target each sector, realizing that each will require a different set of tactics to effectively engage them'. This is a realistic strategy, though one can anticipate opposition from purists, who, fearing to corrupt their agenda, would be unprepared to compromise with prospective middle of the road constituents. A movement, however, can be ideologically coherent without being ideologically pure, cultivating consensus without abandoning core principles. The example of Occupy Wall Street, which withered away because of its anarchical decentralization, illustrates the importance of such coherence to the acquisition of hegemonic power. Gramsci associated hegemony with what he also called a 'historical bloc', a type of political alliance that reduces internal contradictions. This bloc is a conscious social force that must not only have influence within civil society and the economy, but also needs to persuade and offer argument and initiative; it builds universal consensus. As such, it will succeed in catalyzing and developing a robust and sustainable political network and organization. As such moral norms and ideologies are a significant part of the strategic toolkit.

V. HUMAN RIGHTS IDEOLOGY AND STRATEGIC THINKING

The authors concede that human rights norms remain essential to tactics and strategic analyses. They seem to overlook, however, that human rights themselves can serve as means and as ends. Even for Niccolò Machiavelli, morality (or rather moralizing action) was an instrument of power for the leader. As a means, human rights lifts the morale of those who experience setbacks; it motivates those who feel they have nothing to lose but their chains; it reduces despair during tough times by elevating hopes for better ones. As ends, human rights should prioritize the most legitimate claims, determining where tactics, resources, and time should be allocated. There are countless forms of social grievances—blacks, women, Latinos in the United States; Sunnis, Shias, Copts, Jews in the Middle East. Whose rights should come first? Competing narratives over which groups are most afflicted risk splitting the human rights movement. Human rights practitioners need to conduct a sort of triage before taking action. Thus, the dialectic conversation between human rights norms and effective instruments cannot be separated. Further, a key question for all practitioners of human rights is at what cost certain tactics can be used. Georges Danton, calling for the restoration of the Declaration of the Rights of Man and of the Citizen during the Reign of the Terror, was condemned to death by the Committee of Public Safety for supporting the middle class. In his view, the revolution had gone too far, becoming like the god Saturn, who ate his own children alive. When are tactics for change no longer acceptable, especially if they override their desired ends? This question leads to another question that preoccupies the authors, namely the use of non-violence.

VI. ARE NON-VIOLENCE TACTICS MORE LIKELY TO LEAD TO SUCCESSFUL STRATEGIES?

Citing Erica Chenoweth and Maria Stephan, Johnson and Sikkink seem to agree that non-violent tactics are generally more beneficial for human rights strategies.

The philosophical underpinning of this position is not new, as Danton, Immanuel Kant, John Dewey, Karl Kautsky, Mahatma Gandhi, and Martin Luther King, Jr., to name a few, were committed to the view that non-violence is always more commendable than waging violent protest or revolution. During the Bolshevik revolution, the orthodox-Marxist Karl Kautsky condemned the use of terror and the dictatorship of the proletariat, favouring instead parliamentary democracy as the means towards achieving socialism; both were 'means and ends'.[5] Advancing a similar view, Gandhi explained: 'There is an inviolable connection between the ends as the seeds and the tree ... '. Hence, he continues, 'experience convinces me that permanent good can never be the outcome of truth and violence'.[6]

What the authors fail to entertain is the possibility that force and violence in certain circumstances might be a necessary tactic to defend or promote human rights. After all, there is compelling evidence that some violent revolutions had long-term beneficial effects. 'Can the violence of the slave against the master', Trotsky asked during the Bolshevik revolution, 'be equated with the violence of the master against the slave?'[7] These words were not left on deaf ears when Frantz Fanon, in his famous 'Wretched of the Earth', decried more than a century of colonial brutality to explain the inevitability of violence during the anti-colonial struggle.[8] If violence begets violence, as critics would have it, does that leave passive resistance as the only defence against physical brutality? For Trotsky, the means could be justified only by its end, but the end must be justified as well, so the question remains as to whether the means employed *really* leads to the liberation of humanity. With that question firmly in mind, when confronting genocide or large-scale massacres, might violent force also be part of the human rights toolkit, to be employed as a last resort, with proportionality and discrimination, by proper authority?

Furthermore, the argument that non-violent campaigns are more likely to be successful is historically unconvincing. For instance, the Arab uprisings of 2011 began as non-violent social protests, yet most resulted in violent military crackdowns or still unresolved civil wars. Earlier revolutionary contagions, such as the 1848 revolutions, the 1968 Prague Spring, and the 1970s Latin American uprisings, had similar results. Most revolutions begin non-violently; for instance, prior to the 1789 revolution, the French called for reforms in the States-General (*États généraux*), and in 1917 the Russians called for political reforms in the Duma, but passive protests were met with violent crackdown and later, after short-term success, by counter-revolutionary regimes. It did not help that Syrian rebels used

---

[5] Karl Kautksy, 'On Political Reform and Socialism (*The Dictatorship of the Proletariat*, 1918)' in Ishay (ed.), *The Human Rights Reader* (n. 4) 240.

[6] Mahatma Gandhi, 'Means and Ends, 1909–1947' in Ishay (ed.), *The Human Rights Reader* (n. 4) 318.

[7] Leon Trotsky, *Their Morals and Ours* (Pathfinder Press 1973) 38.

[8] Frantz Fanon, *The Wretched of the Earth* (Constance Farrington trans., Grove Press 1963). Originally published in French as *Les Damnés de la Terre* (Éditions François Maspero 1961).

non-violent means against a repressive government. Assad was indifferent to their passive resistance and their cause, responding with torture, barrel bombs, and chemical weapons against his own people, fortified by an endless supply of armaments from Russia and Iran. Here again, the question of foresight, or what Machiavelli called *virtù* (prudence and courage) in the face of *fortuna* (unforeseen circumstances) is the dilemma that all human rights practitioners have to face. One could plausibly argue that an early use of outside force might have stopped the Syrian bloodshed and the nightmarish hell that Syrians continue to experience.

Just as non-violent tactics can easily deteriorate into violence, the opposite is equally true. For example, one can analyse the overthrow of Milosevic in terms of the effective tactical campaign of the Serbian political opposition. It is worth pointing out that Milosevic had been secured in power until NATO's violent air campaign, 'Operation Noble Anvil', to reverse ethnic cleansing in Kosovo. Serbs rallied in nationalist support of Milosevic when the campaign began, including the non-violent occupation of bridges to prevent their being bombed. In the end, the bridges were bombed when unoccupied, as were factories and military installations. Ultimately, thousands of civilian deaths and the collapse of the Serbian economy contributed both to the Serb population's disillusionment with Milosevic and the sense that it was safe—thanks to strong NATO backing—to organize the non-violent strategy and tactics that led to Milosevic's arrest and trial for war crimes. In this respect, force created an auspicious terrain for a non-violent coup de grace to the Serbian regime.

Finally, the question as to what tactics need to be used for what ends (strategic or normative) is a very important one, but it cannot be addressed apart from an understanding of the post-revolutionary socio-economic opportunity that may bring relief to those who have been in distress. The Velvet Revolution of 1989 was more successful than other contagious uprisings because Soviet leaders had lost the will (or the wish) to intervene, leading ultimately to the political and economic integration of many Eastern European countries into the European Union. Beyond the tactics and strategy of the revolution itself, structural economic improvement is necessary for sustained social transformations.

VII. WHEN CAN WE DECLARE 'SUCCESS'?

Behind all these discussions is a more fundamental question: What is a successful strategy? Here the authors need to be clearer. Johnson and Sikkink call for human rights activists to be trained in the methods and techniques of assessment in order to evaluate their work more effectively. Such an approach is obviously helpful, especially where goals are incremental and the effects of one's action can be isolated. It should be cautioned, however, that the simpler the goal, the more facile the measurement, and, at least potentially, the higher the rate of one's alleged success in the short term. The data are happy, but not necessarily the people. But at what point in time, particularly for more ambitious campaigns, is a strategy considered successful? Did the toppling of Ben Ali constitute human rights progress in Tunisia? What of the difficulties experienced by post-revolutionary Tunisia in securing stability, economic prosperity, and democracy? Perhaps essential to such broad campaigns is an understanding that history progresses in a non-linear way, with inevitable reversals. In this respect, Johnson and Sikkink correctly recognize that 'human rights change takes a long time and its progress ebbs and flows'.

VIII. CONCLUSION

Human rights is in crisis, revealing its limits. Johnson and Sikkink rightly deplore the widespread pessimism about human rights in the media, academia, and the general public. 'The standard view', they write, 'is that all types of human rights practices are getting worse in the world rather than better'. There is clearly a sense of defeatism, which the authors strongly challenge. But how should the normative discourse be improved? How can human rights address major challenges such as widespread populism and nationalism? Defending the significance of human rights is critical in a world going in reverse.

Where should we start? The answer must draw on both tested ideas and practical experience. With a deep understanding of conflicting human rights traditions, activists need to become more adept at recognizing the existence of possibilities in the midst of contradictions. The authors provide a good start in this direction: they recommend developing a wide variety of strategies, employed according to the demands of each situation, drawing from the tools of historical and social science research. To further their efforts, more historically informed analysis would shed light on contemporary human rights challenges. It is illuminating how great human rights leaders, while upholding similar values, debated tactics and strategies in the context of revolutionary processes or major campaigns, of which we now know the outcome. These sources of strategic know-how, vetted by our study of history, are essential for moving beyond the current limits of human rights.

Bibliography

Fanon F, *The Wretched of the Earth* (Constance Farrington trans., Grove Press 1963)
Hoare Q and Nowell-Smith G (eds), *Selections from the Prison Notebooks of Antonio Gramsci* (International Publishers 2014)
Johnson DA and Sikkink K, 'Strategizing for Human Rights: From Ideals to Practice' in Fassbender B and Traisbach K (eds), *The Limits of Human Rights* (Oxford University Press 2019) 357

Kautksy K, 'On Political Reform and Socialism (*The Dictatorship of the Proletariat*, 1918)' in Ishay MR (ed.), *The Human Rights Reader* (2nd edn, Routledge Press 2007) 240

Mahatma Gandhi, 'Means and Ends, 1909–1947' in Ishay MR (ed.), *The Human Rights Reader* (2nd edn, Routledge Press 2007) 318

Marx K, 'On the Possibility of a Non-violent Revolution (*On the Hague Congress*, 1872)' in Ishay MR (ed.), *The Human Rights Reader* (2nd edn, Routledge Press 2007) 232

Sun Tzu, *The Art of War* (Samuel B Griffith ed., Oxford University Press 1963)

Trotsky L, *Their Morals and Ours* (Pathfinder Press 1973)

Index

Note: *For the benefit of digital users, indexed terms that span two pages (e.g., 52–53) may, on occasion, appear on only one of those pages.*

Adams, John (1735–1826) 48–49, 56–57, 59–60
advocacy 3–4, 25–26, 35–36, 78, 85–86, 128–30, 141–42, 177–82, 188–90, 195–96, 198, 199–200, 357–58, *see also* civil and political rights; economic, social, and cultural rights; social movement; strategies
African Charter on Human and Peoples' Rights, Protocol on the Rights of Women in Africa (Maputo Protocol) 209–10, 270–71, 275
African Commission on Human and Peoples' Rights 141–42, 273, 275
Ambedkar, Bhimrao Ramji (1891–1956) 261–62
Arendt, Hannah (1906–1975) 11, 79, 299–304
　absolutes 302–3
　humanity 299–303
armed conflict, *see* international humanitarian law
autonomy, *see* individual

Barère, Bertrand (1755–1841) 52
Brexit 76, 77–78, 109–11

Calhoun, Craig (1952–) 76–77
capability approach 191–92
Cicero, Marcus Tullius (106BC–43BC) 89, 102–3
citizenship 25–26, 27, 31, 45–48, 49–50, 69, 75, 84–85, 241–42
　exclusionary effect, 48–52, 75, 82, 332
　link to nation State 49–50, 69, 75, 81–82, 260–61, 313
　status 74–75, 84, 257–58
civil and political rights 27, 34–35, 73, 178
　International Covenant, *see* International Covenant on Civil and Political Rights
　relation to economic, social, and cultural rights 29–30, 140, 176–83, 186–88, 190–95
　see also rights
civil society 4–5, 67, 78, 98, 100, 137, 139, 142, 229, 275, 277, 285, 363–65, 376, 377–78, *see also* non-governmental organisation (NGO); social movement
climate, *see* environment
Cloots, Anacharsis (1755–94) 51

colonialism 75–76, 84–85, 131–33, 196, 206–7, 268–69, 334–35, 352, 353, 379, *see also* self-determination
Committee on the Elimination of Discrimination against Women (CEDAW):
　functions 207–9, 225, 245
　General Recommendations 207–8, 213, 215–17, 246, 248, 269, 271–72, 274, 275–76
　compliance 23, 24–29, 70, 81–82
　measuring 142, 177–78, 198, 276–77
　monitoring 31, 32, 141, 150–51, 159–60, 190–91, 207–8, 245, 319
　see also economic, social, and cultural rights: realisation; rights: realisation; strategies; women's rights: realisation
constitution 29, 35–36, 48, 89–90, 100, 101–6, 163, 187, 192–93, 225–27, 313, 348
　crisis 45–48, 109–12, 113, 126
　India 253–57, 258–62
　progressive realisation 104–5
　supranational 2–3
　see also populism; state of emergency
Constitutional Court of Colombia 32–33, 198
Constitutional Court of South Africa 30–31
Convention on the Elimination of All Forms of Discrimination against Women (CEDAW) 28–29, 225
　common language 251–52, 275–76
　efficacy 238–63, 273–77
　equality 210, 244–45
　normative consensus 206–7, 238–39
　normative development 205–8, 242–43
　Optional Protocol 207, 245
　see also Committee on the Elimination of Discrimination against Women; women's rights
corporations 71, 73, 139, 143–44, 147, 360
cosmopolitanism 70–71, 74, 76, 334, 337, *see also* solidarity
courts:
　dialogue 141, 154
　enforcement of economic, social, and cultural rights 30–34, 159–60, 182, 192–93, 198
　enforcement of women's rights 253–62

courts: (*cont.*)
  policy choices 31, 33–34, 182, 187–88
  regional 141–42, 150–51, 190–91, 209–10, 336
  see also Constitutional Court of Colombia; Constitutional Court of South Africa; European Court of Human Rights; Inter-American Court of Human Rights; International Court of Justice; International Criminal Court; rule of law; welfare
culture:
  changeable nature 43
  learning 43–48
  relativism 28–29

Das, Chandrima, *see* Khatoon, Hanuffa
Declaration of Independence, United States of America 39, 45, 83
  drafting history 42, 56–63
  see also Adams, John; Declaration of the Rights of Man and Citizen; Franklin, Benjamin; Jefferson, Thomas; self-evidence; Sullivan, James
Declaration of the Rights of Man and Citizen, France 39, 40, 41, 42, 49–50, 69, 83–84, 332, 353, *see also* Declaration of Independence; self-evidence
Declaration Toward a Global Ethic 67
democracy:
  elections 34
  political parties 31–32, 33–34, 78
  requirements 34–35, 78
  separation of powers 31, 34, 187–88
  see also rule of law
Devi, Bhanwari (1952–), *see* Vishaka platform of action
discrimination, *see* equality; women's rights
Dow, Unity (1959–) 257–58
drones, *see* international humanitarian law: targeted killing

economic, social, and cultural rights:
  economic development 183, 339
  economic resources (national budgets) 176, 177–78, 179–80, 194
  enforcement, *see* economic, social, and cultural rights: realisation
  International Covenant, *see* International Covenant on Economic, Social and Cultural Rights
  nature of obligation 176–77, 190–95
  realisation 23, 29–30, 32, 176–78, 180–82, 186–88, 192–93
  relation to civil and political rights, *see* civil and political rights
  see also advocacy; courts; rights; welfare

emergency, *see* state of emergency
empathy 52, 300–1
environment 26, 323, 338–41, *see also* precautionary principle
equality:
  autonomy 48–49
  gender, *see* Committee on the Elimination of Discrimination against Women; Convention on the Elimination of All Forms of Discrimination against Women; women's rights
  imagined 43, 75
  standard of comparison 210
  see also inequality
European Convention for the Protection of Human Rights and Fundamental Freedoms (ECHR) 23–24, 76, 110–11, 115, 320, 336–37, 353
European Court of Human Rights (ECtHR) 72–73, 112–16, 149, 160–61, 306, 308–9, 320–21, 324–25, 336, 337, 346
extraterritorial application of human rights 72–73, 312–13, 322

Feinberg, Joel (1926–2004) 6–7
Four-School Human Rights Model
  deliberative 348, 350–51, 352
  discourse 349, 350, 352–53
  natural 348, 351, 352, 353
  protest 348, 350, 352
Franklin, Benjamin (1706–90) 42, 56–57, 60

Global Ethic Project (*Projekt Weltethos*), *see* Declaration Toward a Global Ethic
Grivel, Guillaume (1735–1810) 42

hegemony 128–30, 137, 138, 140, 141, *see also* universalism
Hobbes, Thomas (1588-1679):
  political morality 100–1
  public authority 96–97
  self-preservation as human right 99–100
  social contract 96–97
  theory of punishment 99
  see also rule of law; sovereignty; state of emergency; Williams, Bernard
Hopgood, Stephen (1965–) 129
human security 218
humanisation 2, 299–300, *see also* international humanitarian law: relation to human rights
humanitarian intervention 70, *see also* Responsibility to Protect
humanity
  human core 342–43

legal principle 2–3, 175–76, 287, 288–89, 298–99
meanings 297, 300–2, 335
see also Arendt, Hannah; humanitarian law
Hume, David (1711–76) 42

idealism 28–29, 35, 71, 82–83, 159, 331, 333, 334, 352
individual:
 autonomy 48–49, 52
 personhood 43
 rights bearer 24, 121
inequality:
 economic 32, 196–97
 gender, *see* Committee on the Elimination of Discrimination against Women; Convention on the Elimination of All Forms of Discrimination against Women; women's rights
 States 75–76, 81
 see also economic, social, and cultural rights; welfare
institutions:
 expertise 3–4, 157, 159–60
 functions 70, 152–53, 155, 163
 funding 147–49, 152–53
 individual actors within 168–71
 interests 148, 154, 156, 157, 158–59
 internal structure 168
 structural bias 155–62, 357–58
 types 141–42, 150–53, 168–69
 see also United Nations; United Nations: Special Rapporteur
institutionalisation 150–57, 167–68
Inter-American Convention on the Prevention, Punishment and Eradication of Violence against Women (Convention of Belem do Para) 274
Inter-American Court of Human Rights (I-ACtHR) 274–75, 323
intergovernmental organisation, *see* institutions; United Nations
International Committee of the Red Cross (ICRC) 284–85, 286, 303, 320–21
international community 2–3, 128, 247–48, 290, 335, *see also* solidarity; sovereignty; State
International Court of Justice (ICJ) 159, 167–68, 305–6, 320–21
International Covenant on Civil and Political Rights (ICCPR) 23, 24, 27–28, 34, 131–32, 306, 320, 337, 342
International Covenant on Economic, Social, and Cultural Rights (ICESCR) 23, 27, 131–32, 325, *see also* economic, social, and cultural rights

International Criminal Court (ICC) 66, 70, 128–29, 286
international criminal tribunals 128–29, 150–51, 161, 286, 337
international humanitarian law:
 armed groups 314–16, 323–24
 categories of persons 307
 codification 288–89
 compliance 285–86, 305–6, 307, 309
 compromising nature 286–87, 290–92, 302–4
 constitutive effect 290–92, 293
 customary law 313, 322–23
 detention 310–12, 320–21
 drones, *see* international humanitarian law: targeted killing
 enforcement 285–86, 324–25
 indeterminacy 288–89, 290–91, 298–99
 monitoring, *see* international humanitarian law: enforcement
 nature of conflicts 284–85, 321–22
 politics 286–87, 302, 326–27
 pragmatism 285, 292, 302–4, 326–27
 reality of war, *see* international humanitarian law: nature of conflicts
 relation to human rights 287, 305, 309–10, 312–16, 320–27
 right to life 305–7, 320, 323, 325
 targeted killing 305–10, 312–14
 war/peace distinction 321–22
international organisation, *see* institutions; United Nations
International Red Cross and Red Crescent Movement, *see* International Committee of the Red Cross
intersectionality, *see* women's rights: gender notion; women's rights: sexual orientation

Jefferson, Thomas (1743–1826) 7, 40, 42, 56–65, 66
Judt, Tony (1948–2010) 4, 5
jus cogens 70, 336
justice:
 global 69, 75, 78, 79, 81–82
 social 77–78, 86, 189, 195–97
 see also welfare

Kant, Immanuel (1724–1804) 239, 331–32, 334, 338
Khatoon, Hanuffa 258–59
Küng, Hans (1928–), *see* Declaration Toward a Global Ethic

Lee, Richard Henry (1732–94) 56–57, 60–61
legitimacy 2–3, 40–41, 95, 100–1, 122–23, 125, 126, 133–34, *see also* state of emergency

LGBTQI+ 172, 209, 268-69, *see also* women's rights: gender notion; women's rights: sexual orientation
Livingston, Robert R. (1746-1813) 56-57
localism 82-83, 85-87, 198-99, 289
Locke, John (1632-1704) 41-42, 55-56, 58, 83, 89-90, 98

Madison, James (1751-1836) 61
Mason, George (1725-92) 57, 58
Mehta, Hansa (1897-1995) 241
morality 18, 35-36, 70, 74, 93, 95, 100, 114-15, 121, 131, 159-60, 288-89, 307-8, 336, 348, 377-78
Moyn, Samuel (1972-) 130-31, 132-33, 196-98, 199-200, 277, 352-53

nationalism 76-77, 78, 332-33, *see also* populism
new technologies 341-42
non-governmental organisation (NGO) 26, 70, 78, 141-42, 149, 151-52
North Atlantic Treaty Organization (NATO) 161-62

peremptory norm, see *jus cogens*
Podemos (Spanish political party) 78, 85-86
populism 77-78, 142-43
power 2-3, 122-25, 139-40
  Protean 124-25, 127-28
  see also realism
precautionary principle 338-41

Rabaut Saint-Étienne, Jean-Paul (1743-93) 45-48
realism in international relations 121-23, 137-40, 149, *see also* power
Reid, Thomas (1710-96) 42
relativism 90, 94, *see also* culture; morality; religion
religion 41, 60, 62, 114-16, 207-8, 248-49
responsibility 75-76
Responsibility to Protect 2, 70, 71-72, 128, 129, *see also* humanitarian intervention
rights:
  connection to nation State and representative government 40, 71-79, 82-83, 126, 332-33, 335, 337
  critique 128-31, 195-98, 288-89, 290-92, 352
  effectiveness 24, 378
  enforcement, *see* rights: realisation
  equality of 41, 127
  globalization of 69, 70, 72-73, 75
  natural 40-41, 45, 57, 58, 81, 83, 348
  nature of obligation 24-29, 79, 138, 176-80
  pluralism 86-87, 138, 141-42
  politics 76, 82, 130, 195-96
  proliferation 3-4, 35-36
  realisation 27, 71-72, 159-60
  religious and secular 41, 42, 62-63, *see also* religion
  revolution 121-22
  terminology 43-48, 58, 126-27, 224
  universal, *see* universalism
  women, *see* women's rights
  see also autonomy; civil and political rights; compliance; democracy; economic, social, and cultural rights; individual; *jus cogens*; legitimacy; self-evidence
Robespierre, Maximilien (1758-94) 45-48
Roosevelt, Eleanor (1884-1962) 66-67, 241, 242, 244, 251, 252, 262, 276
Rousseau, Jean-Jacques (1712-78) 45, 66-67, 83-84, 300
rule of law 2, 72, 89-90, 109-17, 337
  institutions 101
  legality 92, 102, 105-6, 116-17
  see also courts; institutions; state of emergency

sanction 25-26, 70, 159, 194
Schmitt, Carl (1888-1985) 89-90, 93, 94-95, 101-2, 103, 104-5, 297
self-determination 74-75, 84-85, 131-33, 142-43, *see also* colonialism
self-evidence 4
  exclusions 48-52, 63-65
  meaning 40-41, 61-63, 65-66
  origin 39-42, 56-63
  see also Declaration of Independence; Declaration of the Rights of Man and Citizen; Hume, David; Locke, John; Reid, Thomas
Sen, Amartya (1933-) 191-92
Sherman, Roger (1721-93) 56-57
slave trade 64
social movement 6, 128, 198-99, 235, 263, 275, 277, 357-58, 359, 363-64, 376-77
solidarity 2-3, 67, 75-77, 220, 235-36, 249-50, 252, 300-1, 302, 304, 335, 346
sovereignty:
  popular 39, 75, 81-82
  State 2, 24, 74-75, 81, 89, 122-23, 287, 337-38
  see also realism; State
State:
  central role in international affairs 69, 79
  European ideal-type 72
  Head of 72-73
  material and moral resources 72-74, 114-15
  national interest 122-23
  reason of (*raison d'État*) 89, 92, 101-4, 149, 333, 334-38, 339, 351
  security 23-24, 48, 72-73, 112, 113, 193, 214, 337-38, 343

see also citizenship; democracy; nationalism; sovereignty
state of emergency:
  flight from reason 110–14
  jural community 91, 96, 102–3
  justification 91, 98, 103, 111–16
  prerogative 72–73, 89–90
  safety of the people 89, 90
  see also Cicero, Marcus Tullius; rule of law; State security; Williams, Bernard
strategies 24–25, 26, 71, 79
  alliances 364, 367, 377–78
  analysis 359–60, 363–64, 369–71, 378
  effectiveness 361–62, 371–72, 377, 380–81
  ideology 378
  innovation 131–32, 198–99, 360
  litigation 72, 76
  long-term 376–77
  mapping 365–68, 376
  non-violence 358, 371–72, 378–80
  tactics 362–63, 364, 380
  training 365–67, 369
  see also advocacy; social movement
Straumann, Benjamin (1974–) 102–4
Sullivan, James (1744–1808) 48–49

tactics, *see* strategies
targeted killings, *see* international humanitarian law: targeted killing
technological innovations, *see* new technologies
Third World Approaches to International Law (TWAIL) 196, 206–7, 209, 242–43, 369–70
traditions, *see* culture
treaty:
  bodies 25, 150–51, 225
  scope 23
  violations of 24, 25–29

United Nations (UN):
  Charter 70
  Commission on the Status of Women 205–6
  Educational, Scientific and Cultural Organization (UNESCO) survey 85
  human rights bodies 150–51, 306
  Human Rights Council 151, 171–73, 210–11, 212, 225–27, 323, 325
  Peacekeepers 157–59
  Special Rapporteur 168–71, 199, 209, 212, 225, 246, 252, 313
  see also institutions; treaty: bodies
Universal Declaration of Human Rights (UDHR) 27, 66–67, 70, 81–82, 128, 175, 185–86, 244–45, 258–59, 260–62, 332–33, 336, 353

universalism:
  divisional 49–52
  link to nationalism 331–33
  rights 24, 40, 66–67, 84, 86–87, 121, 132, 176, 336–38
  see also hegemony; Hume, David; Locke, John; rights: pluralism; Rousseau, Jean-Jacques; Voltaire
use of force 72–73, 307, 313–14

vernacularism, *see* localism
violation:
  response to 24–29
  systemic 26
  time frame of response to 27
  see also rights: nature of obligation; treaty
Virginia Bill of Rights 57
Virginia Declaration of Rights 57–58
Vishaka platform of action 253–57
Voltaire (François-Marie Arouet) (1694–1778) 40–42

welfare 31–32, 33, 175, 191–92, 196–97, 200, 250, 336, *see also* inequality
Williams, Bernard (1929–2003) 91–96, 155
  Basic Legitimation Demand 93, 104
  see also Hobbes, Thomas; rule of law; state of emergency
women's rights:
  conflict, *see* women's rights: violence; Women, Peace and Security Agenda
  Declaration on the Elimination of Violence against Women (DEVAW) 209, 261–62, 274
  deterrent effect of law 237–38
  education 228–29, 232
  efficacy 219–20, 236–38, 240, 262, 273–76
  enforcement, *see* women's rights: realisation
  family 211–13, 225–27
  gender notion 215, 217, 224
  health 232–33
  historic development 205–10, 241–44
  mainstream/margin 208–9, 219–20, 224, 251
  movement 235, 263, 275, 277
  peace processes 214–15
  poverty 232
  progress 276–77
  public/private sphere 212–13, 217–18, 241–42, 246
  realisation 228–29, 236–38, 251–63
  reproductive rights 248–49, 270–73, 342
  sexual harassment and violence 233–34, 237, 240, 247, 253–57, 259–62

women's rights: (*cont.*)
   sexual orientation 249–50, 268–70
   social and cultural patterns of conduct 206–8, 213, 228
   terminology 224
   traditional values 210–11, 213, 225–27
   violence 207–8, 209, 247–48, *see also* Women, Peace and Security Agenda
   United Nations Security Council, *see* Women, Peace and Security Agenda
   workplace 232, 250–51
   see also African Charter on Human and Peoples' Rights Protocol on the Rights of Women in Africa (Maputo Protocol); Committee on the Elimination of Discrimination against Women; Convention on the Elimination of All Forms of Discrimination against Women; courts; equality; Inter-American Convention on the Prevention, Punishment and Eradication of Violence against Women; social movement; United Nations: Special Rapporteur; Women, Peace and Security Agenda

Women, Peace and Security Agenda 214–19, 227